A SOCIOLOGY OF LANGUAGE

Joyce O. Hertzler ❦ UNIVERSITY OF NEBRASKA

A SOCIOLOGY

OF LANGUAGE

RANDOM HOUSE NEW YORK

SECOND PRINTING

© *Copyright, 1965, by Random House, Inc.*

All rights reserved under International and Pan-American Copyright
Conventions. Published in New York by Random House, Inc. and
simultaneously in Toronto, Canada, by Random House of Canada Limited.
Library of Congress Catalog Card Number: 65-17444
Manufactured in the United States of America by
The Haddon Craftsmen, Inc., Scranton, Pa.

Acknowledgments

Great appreciation is expressed to Charles H. Page for his painstaking critical reading of the manuscript. He has given me new seminal insights and perspectives, and has made innumerable suggestions regarding the scientific reliability of statements, style, precision of meanings, and desirable deletions and additions.

I am also indebted to Professor David W. Crabb of Princeton University who read the manuscript and gave valuable criticism, revealed informational errors and gaps, and suggested new features. Neither Professor Page nor Professor Crabb is responsible for any of the uses or abuses of their valued contributions.

In this, as in many other enterprises, I am deeply obligated to my wife for her never-failing encouragement, her constructive criticism, and her secretarial assistance.

JOYCE O. HERTZLER

Contents

Introduction

   1. *The Social Interest in Language*   3
   2. *The Special Sociologies and the Sociology of Language*   5
   3. *Special Orientations of the Present Study*   9
   4. *Major Distinctions in Linguistics*   10
   5. *The Recent and Contemporary Linguistic Schools*   13
   6. *The Symbol-System: The Nature and Place of Analysis*   16

I   The Centrality of Language in Human Existence   19

II   The Basic Concepts Involved in a Sociology of Language: A Paradigmatic Treatment

   1. *The Environments of Man*   23
   2. *Experience*   25
   3. *Meaning*   25
   4. *Communication and Action*   26
   5. *Conceptualization*   27
   6. *The Symbol-System: The Nature and Place of Language*   28
   7. *The Language Community*   32
   8. *The Context of the Physical, Cultural and Social Situation*   34

III   The Major General Functions of Language

1. *Words as Fundamental Components of Language
   as Instrument*   38
2. *The Identification (Naming) Function*   39
3. *The Categorization (Classification) Function*   40
4. *Language as the Means of Perception*   41
5. *Language as the Means of Thinking*   42
6. *Language as the Corpus of Our Facts*   44
7. *Language in Creative Activity*   47
8. *Language, and Man as Technologist*   48
9. *Language as a Record and as Human Memory*   49
10. *Language as the Means of Transmitting Knowl-
    edge Across Space and Time*   50
11. *Language as the Agency for Conceptualizing and
    Adjusting to Space and Time*   53
12. *Language as the Medium for Man's Grasp of the
    Abstract and the Supernatural*   55

IV   Language as a Social Phenomenon and Social Agency

1. *Language as a Human Social Emergent*   58
2. *Language as the Instrument, Basic Form and Product of Social Behavior*   59
3. *Language as the Primary Social and Societal Instrumentality*   62

V   Language as a Social Institution

1. *The General Place and Nature of Social Institutions* 69
2. *Language Viewed as a Social Institution*   71
3. *Peculiarities of Language as an Institution*   74
4. *The Institutional Features of Language: Its Systemic Organization*   75
5. *Standard Language*   92
6. *Language: The Basic Institution*   94

VI   Language as Sociocultural Index, Record and Determinant

1. *The Cultural System and Language*   100
2. *Language as Sociocultural Index*   102

3. *Language as the Record of the Sociocultural History of Its Speakers.* 106
4. *Names as Culture Recordings* 109
5. *The Linguistic System as Partial Determinant of the Perceptual–Conceptual Processes of the Language Community* 116

VII Sociocultural Change and Changing Language

1. *The Necessity of Change of Standard Language* 140
2. *The Main Types of Language Change* 142
3. *The Sociocultural Factors in Linguistic Change* 149
4. *The Tempo of Linguistic Change* 176

VIII The Uniformation and Extension of Language: Historical, Contemporary

1. *Introduction* 179
2. *The Sociological Principles Relating to the Acceptance of New Cultural Features* 182
3. *The Factors in Uniformation Within the Language Community* 185
4. *The Spreading of Some Languages and the Development of Linguistic "Empires"* 196
5. *Language for "One World"* 206

IX Language as a Centripetal Factor in Human Societies

1. *Language the Social Unifier* 227
2. *Social Assimilation and Language* 231
3. *Language and Nationality, Nationalism and Nation* 233

X Language as a Centrifugal Factor in Human Societies

1. *The Multiplicity of Languages and Difficulties of Communication* 248
2. *The Interplay of the Different Kinds of Isolation, Language Diversity and Social Separation* 249
3. *Some Social and Social-Psychological Separative or Antagonistic Effects of Language* 255

4. *The Deliberate Use of Language for Separative Pur-*
poses   257
5. *Language and Political Divergence and Conflict*   258
6. *America's Linguistic Provincialism*   260

XI   **The Language of Social Control and the Social Control
of Language**

1. *The Sociology of Social Control*   264
2. *The General Significance of Language in Social
Control*   266
3. *The Magical Power of Words*   268
4. *The Special Control Significance of Names*   270
5. *The Social Efforts to Control Certain Categories of
Words*   274
6. *Language in Dynamic Social Action*   280
7. *The Kit of Verbal Control Tools*   289

XII **Social Differentiation and Linguistic Specialization in the
Language Community: I. Theoretical Orientation; the
Dialects**

1. *The Place and Nature of the "Special" Languages*   300
2. *Mainly a Characteristic of Complex Societies: Historical Trends*   302
3. *The Major Types of Special Languages*   302
4. *The Language Forms at the Different Levels of
Usage*   304
5. *The Horizontally Differentiated Special Languages*   308

XIII **Social Differentiation and Linguistic Specialization in the
Language Community: II. The Special Group and Technical Languages**

1. *The Vertically Differentiated Special Languages*   317
2. *The Biosocial Categories and Groups*   318
3. *The Speech Differentiations of Ethnic Groups
Within a Community*   322

4. *The Language Specialisms of Groups Stressing Concealment or Secrecy of Action* 324

5. *The Special Technical and Organizational Languages of the Major Institutional Areas* 329

6. *Some Distinguishing Features of the Special Languages in Different Institutional Systems* 338

XIV Social Differentiation and Linguistic Specialization in the Language Community: III. The Languages of the Social Classes

1. *The Correlation of Social and Linguistic Stratification* 365

2. *The Kinds of Distinctions Among the Strata in the Use of Language* 368

3. *Language as Reflector of Social Stratification* 372

4. *Language as an Agent in Maintaining Social Distance and Social Position* 377

5. *Language and Social Mobility* 380

6. *A Resumé of the Sociocultural Significance of the Special Languages* 382

XV Language and the Individual

1. *Language in the Personal and Social Life of the Individual* 391

2. *The Part of Language in the Orientation and Range of the Individual in Time* 401

3. *Language as a Means of the Freedom and the Enslavement of the Individual* 401

4. *The Effects of Lack of Language or Impairment of Language Facility Upon the Socialization of the Individual* 402

5. *Language as the Index and Revealer of the Individual* 406

XVI Plural Lingualism in the Modern World

1. *Intra-Community Plural Lingualism: Nature and Extent* 416

2. *Significant Sociocultural Variables and Facts Regarding the Plural Lingual Community*   418
3. *The Plural Lingual Individual*   427
4. *The International Plural Lingualism of the Year 2000*   432

XVII   The Sociology of Writing

1. *The Place of Writing in Language*   441
2. *What Writing Does*   442
3. *The Recency of Writing and the Restrictedness of Literacy*   445
4. *The Main Historical Forms of Writing*   447
5. *Writing as an Earmark of Civilization*   454
6. *Sociocultural Aspects of Writing*   459
7. *A Note on Modern Storage and Retrieval of Information*   469

XVIII   Mass Communication, Language and Modern Society

1. *The Relation of Mass Communication to the Present Study*   473
2. *The Development of the Technical Media*   476
3. *The Setting: Mass Society*   477
4. *What the Mass Media Do to and for Language*   478
5. *Crucial Sociological Features of Mass Communication*   481
6. *The General Social Functions Performed by Mass Communication*   487
7. *Some Social and Social-Psychological Effects*   489
8. *The Significance of the Audience in Mass Communication*   496
9. *The Mass Media and Social Control*   498
10. *Social Control of the Messages*   505
11. *Mass Communication and International Relations*   506

Bibliography   515

Index   549

A SOCIOLOGY OF LANGUAGE

Introduction

1. The Social Interest in Language

The proverbs of the primitives and the admonitions and some of the philosophical discourse of the ancients reveal some awareness of the significance of language in human affairs. These were particularly concerned with speech of the individual that would not cause social complications with or among others. In the *Teaching of Amen-em-apt* (2212–2182 B.C.) from ancient Egypt, we note:

> The word that is uttered by man with malicious intent is swifter to hurt than the wind that precedes the storm. . . . He gives utterance to strings of words. . . . He loads the boat with the discourse of iniquity, he makes himself the ferryman of him that catches men in a net of words. . . . His lips are date-syrup; his tongue is a deadly dagger.

Gautama the Buddha (in the early fifth century B.C.), in his famous address at the deer park Isapatama, near Benares, shortly after the Enlightenment, proclaimed for all men as the third of his "Noble Eightfold Path": "Right speech: kindly, open, truthful." In his "The Small, Middle, and Great Moralities," addressed mainly to monks, the following (among others) characterized the behavior of the good—the model —man:

> Abandoning falsehood, he speaks the truth, is truthful, faithful, trustworthy, and breaks not his word to people.
>
> Abandoning slander, he does not tell what he has heard in one place to cause dissension elsewhere.
>
> Abandoning harsh language, his speech is blameless, pleasant to the ear, reaching the heart, urbane, and attractive to the multitude.

Abandoning frivolous language, he speaks duly in accordance with the doctrine and discipline, and his speech is such as to be remembered, elegant, clear, and to the point.[1]

With the fourth century B.C., especially among the Greeks, there begins to be something in the way of specialized study of the nature of language as such, and of some of the problems of its source and elements, its grammatical rules and changes, and so on—a study primarily engaged in by philosophers, although other types of scholars became interested in increasing numbers. Seemingly, however, there was no great consciousness of its crucial and universal importance until men became cognizant of the multiplicity and the great diversity of languages. This came in the sixteenth century with the Age of Discovery and the closely related Renaissance, when explorers, conquerors, traders, slavers, adventurers, missionaries, and peripatetic scholars established extended facilities for interpeople contact, traffic, and communication in general, and began to note the strategic and indispensable part played by language in all forms of human interaction. Some of the discoverers assembled and made public different kinds of linguistic materials from all over the world. The invention of printing at this time also extended the use and range of language in almost every area of social life, and invited the comparative study of languages.

Since the end of the eighteenth century, language has come to be copiously and comprehensively studied by the philosophers, the linguists and philologists, the semanticists, and the literary critics. Particularly noteworthy is the fact that we have at this time the beginning of the modern science of linguistics, with its systematic study by appropriate methodologies of speech sounds and their combination, of the development and the comparison of languages, and especially of the structure and operation of language, as imbedded in its constituent elements, maintained by its systematizing principles, and governed by its codes.

While most of the linguistic studies of the modern era have made only occasional or incidental reference to language in its social context, several have made rather penetrating examinations. They have sought a human and sociocultural orientation for, and an explanation of, this aspect of human life, especially in terms of its social and societal relationships, implications, functions, and effects. The term "social linguistics" has sometimes been used to designate such study.

Among the social scientists, the chief contributors to language study have been the anthropologists and psychologists. The anthropologists have been concerned with language as a cardinal aspect of culture, language origins and development, the analysis of primitive languages and the reciprocal relationships of these languages with primitive mental and social life, as well as with the circumstances and effects, linguistic and sociocultural, of some of the known instances of their interrelationship. The general, social, educational, and abnormal psychologists have been concerned with the stages of speech development in human beings, especially the speech development of children, the relationships of speech and abnormal psychological states, the strategic significance of language in personality development and in the socialization of the individual, and its relationship to the processes of thought. Some of the political scientists and historians have been interested in language as related to national origins and ethnic boundaries, the relation between language and nationalism, and the analysis of language as used in propaganda and other aspects of political manipulation and control. Recently, groups involved in mass communication have been paying considerable attention to certain aspects of language, as affected by their media, their messages, and their audiences.

There has been increasing reference to language in the sociological literature in the last three decades—in some of the textbooks on introductory sociology and social control, several monographs, and occasional articles. The treatment in books has usually been in connection with the examination of social interaction and communication. These analyses differ widely in approach, content, and purpose. With a few notable recent exceptions, they are more or less superficial, unsystematic, or confined only to certain limited or special aspects of language in society. In the main, they have merely skirted the edges of a sociology of language. They have not envisioned the full dimensions of the sociological study that is possible with the materials now available. These treatments by sociologists, however, do indicate a growing awareness of the sociological importance of the subject, as well as of the types of contribution that sociologists can make.

2. *The Special Sociologies and the Sociology of Language*

This book presents a "sociology" of language. During the last half century, sociologists have been developing an array of special disciplines, the "sociologies" of significant and pertinent orders of human experience and endeavor, such as innovation, knowledge, values, the family, law, government and politics, the military, religion, the occupations (especially the professions), medicine, art, science and technology, education, and industry. The "sociological" approach to knowledge or values or science or art or law or religion does something that the "philosophical" or any similar approach does not and cannot do. These specialties have grown out of the study both of society as a whole and of the particular, largely institutionalized, blocs of sociocultural phenomena. They are concerned with the relations between given categories of social phenomena and other existential factors in the society or culture. A given special sociology provides a minute or close-up view, so to speak, and an intensive treatment of a particular area of sociological concern; it does not give the overview of society sought in the principles of sociology. Human societies display these unique and inimitable features of distinctively human experience, contrivance and conceptualization. The intensive study of these is a reflection of the fact that sociology is taking its rightful and indispensable place in the analysis of man's actions in his world.

The "sociology" of a sociocultural phenomenon has two aspects, which are in continual and unavoidable interplay and interdependence with each other. There is, first, *the significance of the particular order or system of phenomena as a causal, contributory, or otherwise effective factor in society.* More specifically, this aspect is concerned with: (1) the place and operational significance of the order of phenomena in human society; (2) the influence exerted by it, and the effects created by it, upon the societal structures, functions, processes, and relations; (3) the human uses of it. The second aspect is the converse of the first, being concerned with the *effect of the given society or culture area and epoch upon the particular order of phenomena.* More particularly, this deals with the human and sociocultural factors which determine the nature and operation of the order of phenomena in human society, especially in particular groups, societies, and cultures. In brief, the special sociologies are concerned with the reciprocal relations of society and its notable operational features; each is at once the cause and effect of the other.

The sociology of language is still in its rudimentary stage of development. It has lagged behind the sociologies of knowledge and science, which are so dependent upon language. We are still *moving toward* a systematic, comprehensive sociology of language.[2] Much of the pertinent available material must be gleaned from non-sociological sources, for example, from the works of social linguists, historians of language, philosophers of language, folklorists, and especially anthropologists. At the same time, being concerned with the reciprocal relations between language and society, the sociology of language must take into consideration the work of those other disciplines that are concerned directly or tangentially with language. No area of study is utterly self-contained. Unavoidably, therefore, the sociology of language must pay considerable attention to linguistics, with its body of knowledge regarding the structure and techniques of language as such, including the differentiations revealed by the comparative study of languages; the philosophy of language, with its attention to language as the organ or medium for comprehending reality, and the closely related field of semantics, with its attention to the problem of meaning; the relation between language and the peculiar environments and cultural history of a people, and the consequent *Weltanschauung,* as analyzed by anthropologists; the relation between language and man, the psychic entity in a social setting, as studied by psychologists and social psychologists and students of psychopathology; the relation between language and the subject matter of certain other special sociologies obviously involved with it, especially the sociologies of knowledge, science, and literature. But these will have significance only in so far as they provide information pertinent to our main objective—that is, conducting a study of language in its multiple social contexts, more particularly a study of language structure, function, and process in relation to societal structure, function, and process. The subject matters of the successive chapters of this book will indicate these manifold ramifications, even as thus limited.

The most superficial examination of language in the affairs of men shows that sociology has abundant reasons for examining it in its sociocultural context. It has crucial significance in the operation of human society. As a sociologist, we do not intend to give an extensive anatomical and physiological treatment of man's physical speech mechanisms, to discuss at length hypotheses regarding the origins and early development of language, or to examine the technical details of the different, though interrelated, types of formal language structure or symbolism or semantics or communication theory and technical organization. These will be noted only to the extent that they throw light upon language in the social and societal scheme of things. The physiological, philosophical, psychological, philosophical, and technological concerns with language are of profound importance, as is attested by a most extensive literature. We are concentrating upon another strategically significant aspect when we examine language from the social-scientific—especially the sociological—point of view. Language study is, in a high degree, a social science. In fact, many facets of language can be appropriately and revealingly treated only by sociologists. It is therefore surprising that they have paid so little attention to it.

This work does *not* represent primary research by the author in the area of the sociology of language. Furthermore, many of the items of information and some of the points of view here presented are already known to various categories of specialists, although usually in their particular subject-matter contexts. Our purpose is to survey and summarize the available materials, and to present a systematic synthesis from the sociological point of view. Because of facts that will be noted at considerable length—namely, that language is a social emergent, a social invention, and a major indispensable social instrumentality; that it has multiple general human functions and an impressive array of specifically social functions; that it has a close relationship to the differential aspects of social structure; that it has determinable sociocultural effects; and finally that it is utilized for innumerable social purposes —the science of society *must* treat language with the profoundest respect.

One specific feature of the present study is the fact that it is a sociological interpretation of the indicated reciprocal relationships, and that its analyses and interpretations are cast in terms of major sociological concepts, such as social interaction and communication; groups, communities and regions; institutions and institutionalization; social integration and social change; uniformation and consolidation; social isolation and separation; social differentiation and stratification; social space, distance and mobility; social specialization, cross-fertilization, and cultural exchange; social influence and power, social control, dominance and submission; majorities versus minorities; ethnicity, and ethnic variation; group identity and identification; ecology and demography; enculturation and socialization.[3]

Such established sociological evidence as exists will be marshaled, but there is a marked paucity of it. This work, in the main, is an extensive study, an overview of the recognized aspects and the potentialities of a sociology of language. The seeming "knowns" are presented as generalizations; these, in turn, should be viewed as hypotheses— that is, as tentative explanations of the phenomenon in question. Scientific investigative studies of a further exploratory or of a confirmatory or critical nature spread out fanwise from almost every generalization made. The field cries for both extensive and intensive research and analysis.

The English language will be the main linguistic frame within which the study will operate; most of the illustrations will be taken from it. Most of the readers of this study will be speakers and readers of English; it is desirable that their own language experience be utilized, and it is important that they see the principles of the sociology of language as these emerge from and apply to their language. Occasional comparisons with other languages will be made. Almost all the principles to be noted will have a high degree of universality. (Incidentally, the study will represent a distillation of a vast amount of material.)

It might be considered poor business for a sociologist to seem to be poaching upon linguistic territory. The writer is not, and makes no pretense of being, an accomplished student of formal linguistics. This may result in some flaws, or "slips" of a factual nature. The reader, however, should also be aware of the fact that this is not a book on linguistics as such, but on certain aspects of language that a social scientist is in a position to tackle. No subject can afford to avoid, ignore, demean, or spurn new or different orientations and perspectives, a new type of assemblage of factors involved in the situations with which it is concerned, or new facts regarding relations and effects.

3. *Special Orientations of the Present Study*

Some aspects of language and some types of sociologically significant factors and effects may be examined in two or even more chapters. This is not repetition. Each chapter stands as an analytical assignment in itself. The reader is presented with a relevant sociological concept and types of sociologically significant facts. Each time the concept or fact appears it will be in conformity with the theoretical context and the analytical purpose of the particular chapter; one or more new features of it will be presented. The later analysis often rests upon the earlier one. In order to help the reader see both the different significations and the relationship of these features, frequent cross references have been inserted.

Sociologically sophisticated readers will note that some aspects of language are treated which are not strictly of sociological significance, thus producing what seems to be a more-than-sociology coverage. This extension into contiguous areas of interest is inevitable in any special sociology. The special segment of culture being examined is never simple or single-faceted; its various features are intertwined, and each feature is functionally related to the others. Thus, for example, in the adequate treatment of the sociology of knowledge it is unavoidable— in fact essential—that philosophical, psychological, including psychoanalytic, and even ecological, as well as the social factors be considered.

A similar situation prevails in the sociological study of language: individual psychological, natural physical, social-psychological, technological, or even metaphysical factors must be considered, as well as those of a contemporary standard sociological and linguistic nature. These extra-sociological aspects of language situations appear in almost every chapter in some degree; they stand out especially in Chapter III, in the latter part of Chapter VI, in Chapters VII and VIII, in the first part of Chapter XI, and in Chapters XIII, XV, and XVIII.

Stress is placed upon the international, interpeople, and intercultural characteristics and uses of language, and upon both related social problems and social advantages. Wider perspective is a new and essential emphasis in the social sciences and the humanities—indeed, in every field of scientific and cultural interest. Chapters particularly concerned with these world aspects and implications are Chapters VI, VII, VIII, IX, X, XVI, and XVIII.

4. *Major Distinctions in Linguistics*

As has been indicated, this is not a study in scientific linguistics as blocked out by the contemporary linguistic specialists, particularly those from university language or anthropology departments. However, the study directly involves and is dependent upon linguistics for the standard terminology regarding the different aspects of language, for theories regarding language as system, for facts emerging from the study of the major structural–functional divisions of language, and for some of the findings from the different branches of linguistic study. We must occasionally make reference to such items. Furthermore, many of the readers of this book will have something in the way of a sociological, but not a formal linguistic, orientation. It is desirable, therefore, to present, with a minimum of detail, some of the most pertinent features of linguistics.

While the great Genevan linguist, Ferdinand de Saussure (1857–1914), is mentioned less and less by contemporary linguists, he can be regarded as one of the main architects of the linguistic science of Western society, for he gave it much of its tone, some of its main emphases, directions, distinctions and terminology. Some of these are now the common property of linguistics, even though they are used without the Saussurian label.[4]

a / The distinction between language and speech. This is a crucial distinction in linguistic study, and comes from de Saussure. He classified the terms as follows:

$$\text{Langage} \begin{cases} \text{Langue} \\ \text{Parole} \end{cases}$$

Langage was the abstract term, covering *all* aspects of human linguistic communicative activity. It was divided into: (1) *langue,* that is, each and every system of sound symbols used in communication, and independent of the volition of individual speakers, and (2) *parole,* the individual act of will and intelligence. These three terms have, in English usage, merged into two: *language* and *speech.*

Language is a social product of the human faculty of speech. Fundamentally, it is the *system* of rules and principles of construction, classification, and combination of the standard linguistic elements. Socially, it is the essential passively accumulated, culturally inherited, and institutionalized instrument created through time by the language community to enable its members effectively to use their faculty of speech for their communicative purposes. As de Saussure put it: "It (language) exists only by virtue of a sort of contract signed by the members of a community." In general, language is the culturally established code —the "rules of the game"—governing all linguistic communication, both vocal forms and their written substitutes or surrogates. As Entwistle has noted, it is by means of the linguistic system, which exists wherever we find language, that *ego* and *tu* are able to understand each other. *Speech,* on the other hand, is the act of individuals as they convey their messages to others (or themselves) by speech-utterances. It is mainly the behavioral manifestation of the speakers, as they use the sounds in conformity with the coded dictates of the language system to express their thoughts. In their speaking, however, they inevitably show some degree of individual uniqueness—physiological, physical (acoustic), and psychic or social personality eccentricities.

The two very different linguistic "facts"—*the social code,* as against *the individual act*—however, cannot be separated. The peculiar faculty of articulating words is exercised only with the help of the systemic instrument created by the collectivity and provided for its use. Language gives continuity, unity, uniformity, codification, and organization to speech. Obversely, changes of the language system come only through speaking. The speakers, as they speak, and as they are constituted socially, ethnically, culturally, generation after generation, bring about innovations in the way of new forms, substitutes, new usages, etc., which they inaugurated. It is in speaking that the germ of all change is found; each change is launched by a certain number of individual speakers. As Entwistle has noted, "Nothing exists in language which has not previously existed in speech." The new speech forms, repeated many times, and accepted by the community, become a fact of language; if they are *not* adopted by the community, they do not become part of the language.[5]

b / Synchronic and diachronic linguistics. De Saussure posited the two main, but interdependent, substantive and analytical branches of linguistics as *synchronic* and *diachronic*—a categorization practically universal in present-day linguistics. They involve two closely related sets of axes: (1) *internal–external,* and (2) *static–historical* study of language.

With respect to the *internal–external dichotomy,*[6] synchronic linguistics is *internal* linguistics. As such, it studies languages as autonomous systems, without reference to anything except other linguistic systems. A language is a system of signs that has "its own arrangement of elements." As de Saussure points out later, this internal synchronic study is the description and explanation of what he calls the "language-state," and of the operational relations of these elements, including their own principles of change within the system. Internal linguistics is "pure" linguistics.

Diachronic linguistics is concerned with the *external* aspects of a language. It deals with what is outside the organism or system of language, yet affects it, such as "the relations that link the history of a language and the history of a race or civilization"; "the relations between language and political history"; "the relations between language and all sorts of institutions"; and "finally, everything that relates to the geographical spreading of languages and dialect splitting."

The *static–historical axis* divides linguistic study on the basis of "the factor of time." From this analytical point of view, the subject matter of linguistics can be aligned along two subaxes: (1) the *axis of simultaneities,* involving "the relations of coexisting things . . . from which the intervention of time is excluded," and (2) the *axis of successions,* "upon which are located all the things on the first axis *together with their changes.*" On this basis, synchronic linguistics is also *static* linguistics—a distinction quite compatible with its internal characteristics; diachronic linguistics is concerned with the "evolutionary"—the term preferred by de Saussure to "historical"—study of language. More specifically, synchronic linguistics is concerned with "the logical and psychological relations that bind together coexisting terms and form a system in the collective mind of speakers," everything that relates to "the constituents of any language-state" at any given time. In this connection, synchronic linguistics is also called descriptive linguistics, in that it particularly stresses the characteristics of language systems at given points in their histories.

Diachronic linguistics is concerned with the "evolutionary phase," "the stream of language," with the divergences in time and the relations between successive terms that are substituted for each other within the system in time.[7] This branch of language study, describing changes in language systems over periods of time, is today usually referred to as historical and comparative linguistics. In sum then, synchronic linguistics is concerned with internal–static study, diachronic linguistics with external–developmental examination.

c / Geographical linguistics. The third major part of linguistics, according to de Saussure and contemporary linguists, is entitled *geographical linguistics*. It might also be called "the geographic diversity of languages." It is concerned with the spatial relations of linguistic phenomena, especially those linguistic differences that appear as one passes from one country to another or even from one region to another. This branch, of course, involves both descriptive (synchronic) and historical (diachronic) considerations.

5. *The Recent and Contemporary Linguistic Schools*

As we have noted, interest in language and concern about its nature and uses go back to ancient times. For centuries, men have been in process of developing a scientific linguistics.[8] The viewpoints and emphases, methodologies and interpretations of the various "authorities" and "schools" of linguistic investigation and theorizing have differed greatly, as one might expect. A brief indication of the major characteristics of the more influential among the recent and contemporary "schools" is desirable. The thought of these schools indicates some of the distinctive content of contemporary linguistics, its tone and direction. There is some tendency to identify the schools by the locale of their origin and early development.

The key member of the Genevan school is Ferdinand de Saussure, some of whose basic contributions have been referred to above. He was the first to develop a structural and functional conception of language—that is to say, that language is a self-contained system, whose interdependent parts function and acquire value through their relationship to the whole. He paid special attention to phonology, and particularly to phonemes in the "spoken chain" of language. The present members of the Geneva school are sometimes referred to as the modern Saussurians.

The so-called French school, made up of such writers as Antoine Meillet, Joseph Vendryes, Charles Bally, Maurice Grammont, and A. Sommerfelt, consists in large measure of students and followers of de Saussure. Different ones have continued the phonetic study; most have devoted themselves to social, historical, comparative, and structural–functional studies.

Another seminal contributor, strongly influenced by de Saussure, is Nikolai S. Troubetzkoy (1890–1938), professor of philosophy at the University of Moscow until 1922, when he assumed the chair of Slavic philosophy at the University of Vienna, where he remained for the fertile last sixteen years of his relatively short life. In his *Grundzüge der Phonologie* (1939), later issued in French as *Principes de phonologie* (Paris: J. Contineau, 1949), he broke away from comparative linguistics and, like de Saussure, took the position of "phonemicism," which conceives of a language as a structure or system, composed elementally of phonemes complexly integrated into combinations and sequences of linguistic forms. His old friend Roman Jakobson, of Charles University in Prague, accepted his thought and developed it further in his own book *On the Identification of Phonemic Entities* (Copenhagen: Travaux du Cercle Linguistique de Copenhagen, 1949). At Prague, Jakobson founded the Prague Linguistic Circle, which became the organizational nucleus of the "Prague (or "European") School," which, in turn, has made Troubetzkoy's book its Bible. The school was more specifically denominated as the "phonemic" school of linguistics, also as "structuralist–functionalist," because its members were devoted to defining and isolating the phoneme, to developing the concept of language as a self-consistent structural whole, and to establishing the structuralist approach to the description of grammatical phenomena.

Copenhagen was the locale of a great linguist of recent times, and a contemporary "school" carries its name. Otto Jespersen (1860–1943), who was connected with the University of Copenhagen from 1893 on, made several classic contributions. His *Language, Its Nature, Development and Origin* (1922) not only dealt with general linguistics, but was rich in historical and comparative examples of many different linguistic phenomena. His interest in the general relationship between logic and grammar is demonstrated in *The Philosophy of Grammar* (1924) and *The Logic of Grammar* (1924). In *Mankind, Nation, and the Individual* (1925), he deals with linguistic standards, unity and uniformation, and differentiation, while *Growth and Structure of the English Language* (1905) is his classic study of our language. In general, he contended that languages tended to evolve into more regular, logical, coherent, and efficient patterns.

The present day "Copenhagen School" has as its central figure Louis Hjelmslev; its basic text is his *Concerning the Foundations of Linguistic Theory* (1943).[9] He made up the term *glossematics* to describe his highly abstract theory of language. He and his fellows have sought to develop a system of "linguistic algebra." This exclusively formal system of postulates is to be so complex and comprehensive that all conceivable languages may fit into the framework through the discovery and the establishment of those features that are common to all languages, and which may therefore be considered characteristic of language as such.

Soviet Russia and Eastern Europe have a special brand of Marxist "materialist" linguistics. Russian linguistics, after the establishment of the Soviet regime, was dominated by the theories of N. Y. Marr (1864–1934); his theories were, in fact, for a while declared "official." He developed the "Japhetic Theory," according to which the pre-Indo-European languages of Europe were all related to each other and spoken by a single race or racial group. He also concluded that "language and thought are dialectically united" and that "language [is] a superstructure which is acted upon by the base through historically developing consciousness." In 1950, however, Stalin himself insisted that Marr had "introduced into linguistics an erroneous, un-Marxist formula of language as a superstructure." "The base is the economic structure of society . . . the superstructure comprises the political, legal, religious, artistic and philosophical views of society and their corresponding political, legal and other institutions. Language cannot be a superstructure, because it does not change as the base changes, for after all, the Russian language had not changed essentially after the Russian Revolution." Hence the theories of Marr had to be rejected.[10] The "newer" schools, both at home and among their adherents elsewhere, pay much attention to the method of dialectical materialism as applied to language and to the relation of language to social class.[11]

American linguistics has no dominating "school," although it has been much influenced by the European "schools." Probably its first notable personage was William Dwight Whitney of Yale College, whose books, *Language and the Study of Language* (1867) and *The Life and Growth of Language* (1874), constituted what are to this day good introductions to linguistics. However, European-trained Franz Boas of Columbia University set the stage for the development of modern linguistic science in America; in connection with his studies of American Indian languages, he presented the problems of descriptive linguistics. Perhaps the two most important American linguists to date have been Edward Sapir (1884–1939) and Leonard Bloomfield (1887–1949), each of whom wrote a book entitled *Language*, published respectively in 1921 and 1933, although Bloomfield had published an *Introduction to the Study of Language* in 1914. Sapir not only produced a general work with a concern for technical linguistic problems, but also carried on the study of a wide variety of languages, especially American Indian. Bloomfield devoted himself rigorously to the theoretical framework of linguistics.[12]

A variety of theoretical and methodological emphases and trends are found in recent American linguistics.[13] There are those primarily concerned with historical linguistics (e.g., Louis H. Gray: *Foundations of Language,* 1939); the comparative linguists and ethnologists (most of them interested in the American Indian languages); a sizable body of followers of the phonemic school (Charles F. Hockett, Bernard Black, George L. Trager, E. A. Nida); some independents; metalinguistics, with its roots in some of Sapir's thought, but its main substance in the voluminous writings of Benjamin L. Whorf; the linguistic geographers, of whom Hans Kurath is probably the most distinguished; the physiological phoneticists, particularly Kenneth L. Pike; the structuralists, who apply to a greater or lesser degree the methods and procedures of mathematical, or mathematical-engineering, analysis to linguistic analyses, especially George Zipf, Charles C. Fries, Zellig S. Harris, and Martin Joos, and a few other somewhat special emphases. The primary stress in recent decades has been on synchronic linguistics, particularly on phonology and descriptive–structuralist, algebralike linguistics, and much less on historical, etymological, and semantic analyses.[14]

6. *The Major Areas of Contemporary Linguistic Analysis*

The actual examination of language as system or institution, in terms of the analysis of its different categories of interdependent structural–functional components and levels of operation, is the basic reason for the existence of linguistics as a science. The major divisions of linguistic analysis, as envisaged by the experts at this time, are (without elaboration or details):

a. *Phonetics:* the systematic study of the vocal sounds used in language systems.

b. *Phonemics:* concerned with the classification of the basic units of sounds of language called phonemes.

c. *Morphology:* the study of the structure of words; more particularly, the identification and arrangements in words of morphemes (the smallest units of language structure, embodying grammatical (correct) usage or lexical (dictionary) meanings, and, in turn, composed of phonemes; the recording of the ways in which the morphemes of a language are constituted from the phonemes, and the study of the "parts of speech" (the form-classes of morphemes or words).

d. *Syntax:* closely related to morphology; concerned with the manner in which sentences are constructed from the different form-classes of words.

e. *Lexicography:* the inventorying for dictionary purposes of the words of a language: their morphemic composition, their history (etymology), their grammatical features, their pronunciation, and their meanings or equivalences.[15]

These major departments of linguistic study, in turn reflecting major structural–functional linguistic categories, will be dealt with more extensively in the discussion of "The Institutional Features of Language: Its Systemic Organization."[16] However, they will also, in a manner appropriate to the objectives of this particular study, be dealt with somewhat selectively and with some adaptations and supplementation.

N O T E S

1 For other admonitions regarding the use of language in relations with others, from ancient Egypt, Babylonia, Persia, India and the Hebrews, see Joyce O. Hertzler, *The Social Thought of the Ancient Civilizations* (New York: McGraw-Hill, 1936; reprinted New York: Russell & Russell, 1961), pp. 60–61, 103, 109–111, 149–150, 154–155, 189–193, 196–197, 328, 332, 369–370.

2 The most comprehensive and systematic treatment to date, known to the present writer, is by one of France's greatest linguists of the last four decades, Marcel Cohen, in his *Pour une sociologie du langage* (Paris: Albin Michel, 1956).

3 Some of our terminology and many of our categorizations and allocations of subject matter, while appropriate to our sociological analytical stance, will not

conform to the terminology or categorization of the linguists (insofar as there is agreement among them).

4 Cf. Ferdinand de Saussure, *Cours de linguistique générale* (first edition in 1916). Compiled from notes taken by his students, and edited by Charles Bally and Albert Sèchehaye, in collaboration with Albert Reidlinger. Published in English as *Course in General Linguistics,* trans. Wade Baskin (New York: Philosophical Library, 1959). All references to de Saussure in the ensuing pages will be to this English translation. See also Rulon S. Wells, "De Saussure's System of Linguistics," *Word,* 3 (1947), 1–31; or the same in Martin Joos (ed.), *Readings in Linguistics: The Development of Descriptive Linguistics in America Since 1925* (New York: American Council of Learned Societies, 1958), pp. 1–18.

5 This analysis has been taken from de Saussure, pp. 9–15, 98, and William J. Entwistle, *Aspects of Language* (London: Faber & Faber, 1953), pp. 73–75. See also Cohen, pp. 85–86, 89–90, 124–129, 229, and John P. Hughes, *The Science of Language* (New York: Random House, 1963), pp. 22–23, 239.

6 Discussed by de Saussure, pp. 20–23.

7 *Ibid.,* pp. 79–100, 101, 140.

8 For concise and illuminating treatments of the history of language study, both prescientific and scientific, see John B. Carroll, *The Study of Language: A Survey of Linguistics and Related Disciplines in America* (Cambridge: Harvard University Press, 1953), pp. 15–23; Hughes, pp. 34–74; and Mario Pei, *Voices of Man: The Meaning and Function of Language* (New York: Harper & Row, 1962), pp. 1–18.

9 The title of the English translation is *Prolegomena to a Theory of Language,* trans. Francis J. Whitfield (Baltimore: Waverly Press, Indiana University Publications in Anthropology and Linguistics, Memoir 7, 1953).

10 For Stalin's own efforts to set things straight, see his *Marxism and Linguistics* (New York: International Publishers, 1951).

11 For a more extended treatment of Soviet linguistics see Carroll, pp. 235–236, from which most of the above has been obtained, and Herbert Rubenstein, "Recent Conflict in Soviet Linguistics," *Language,* 27 (1951), 281–287.

12 He established many of the basic concepts and generally used linguistic terminology in his classic "A Set of Postulates for the Science of Language," *Language* 2 (1926), 153–164; also in Joos (ed.), pp. 26–31.

13 This is not intended to be a directory of prominent American linguists.

14 Cf. Einar Haugen, "Directions in Modern Linguistics," *Language,* 27 (1951), 211–222. See also Joos (ed.), pp. 357–363.

15 For one of the most concise, clearcut, inclusive, and generally acceptable outlines of the analytical areas and levels of linguistics, and the one from which the above has been largely derived, see Carroll, pp. 23–29.

16 Chap. V, Sect. 4.

I ❧ The Centrality of Language in Human Existence

The origin of language is hidden in a remote, dim and irrecoverable antiquity. There is every reason, however, for believing that language developed concomitantly with the earliest human society. At any rate, we find fully developed languages as far back as historical study enables us to penetrate the human past. We find also that all human beings everywhere, of whom we have any archaeological, traditional, or documentary records, regardless of their level of cultural development, have had their languages, sometimes quite complex ones.[1]

It has also been pointed out that, according to all indications, there were far more languages spoken in the early part of human history than there are at present; each of the little scattered and strictly local groups seems to have had its own language. In brief, language was probably one of man's first cultural inventions, and it has functioned universally as a fundamental instrumentality.

Nevertheless, in spite of its antiquity and universality, most of us are unaware of the importance of language in everything we do, throughout time and wherever we are. We are born into a language atmosphere or milieu; during every moment of our lives, waking and dreaming, from birth to death, we are literally bathed in a sea of words.[2] Ordinarily, we are so unconscious of the place of language that we overlook its central significance in our every endeavor, whether this be in our individual psychic life or in our social behavior. Human existence is welded to language.

As we will note in greater detail later, without language man cannot perceive in an accurate and specific manner, or think, or conceptualize, or exercise his creative potentialities and capacities. Language is the paramount, all-inclusive medium of communication in human societies. Without it, our communication with others is limited in range, being confined to what can be indicated by gestures—hence, no possibility of precise messages. Without it, there can be no statement or preservation of the effects of experience, and no transmission of it to our fellows in time and space. Language is the primary condition and factor of human interaction. Without it, association and participation with our fellows could not rise above the level of instinct; there could not be culture or cultural adaptation to the fundamental exigencies of social life, or the bonding which establishes a human community or society. Language is fundamental to all social processes, and to the persistence and maintenance of all social structures; it is involved in almost every act of social behavior. It is the one institution that every human being must master in order to function in any of the other institutionalized areas of social life.

Conversely, as we will also develop later, the active language of a people is a primary outgrowth of their life, and centers about things and occurrences that are essential to them. Hence it reflects every phase and aspect of their life, represents all the known realities of life and tremendously influences every facet of life; in fact, it determines in considerable part what we are aware of, what we believe, how we pattern our thought and how we act.

Attention should be called to another aspect of language which is insufficiently stressed and only dimly realized—namely, its significance as the keystone of human achievement and as the essence of humanness. The list of man's more apparent unique accomplishments as compared with all other creatures is awe-inspiring:

> The discovery of the uses of fire
> The domestication of plants and animals
> The development of the capacity to innovate: discovery and invention
> The making of complex tools and the specialization of skills in their manipulation
> The socially devised division of labor in carrying on tasks requiring two or more persons
> The harnessing of natural forces and the productive manipulation of materials: the physical technologies
> The conceptualization of continuity as history
> The capacity for abstraction in general

The deliberate contrivance of all manner of devices and techniques
   for the organization of social systems—the social technologies
The conceptualization of the supernatural

Above all these is the contriving by man of the means to conceive,
to receive from and transmit to others, and to record human knowledge
—that is, what has significance for him as *Homo sapiens*. This achievement is language; and all of his other distinctions rest fundamentally on
it. This is another way of saying that language is not only the key creation of man—his greatest single accomplishment—but also perhaps his
most distinctive and exclusive individual and cultural attribute.

There is an unbridgeable gap, or at any rate a thus far missing link,
between animal communication and man's communication by means
of language. As Suzanne Langer puts it, language is ". . . that great
systematic symbolism . . . that sets men apart from their zoological
brethren. The line between animals and men is, I think, precisely the
language line."[3]

Wilhelm von Humboldt, nearly a century and a half ago, thinking
along the same line, stated: "Man is man by virtue of language."[4]
Lotz remarks that, "Truly language marks the birth of man"[5] and Lee
refers to language as "the unique ingredient in man."[6] It is a typically
and solely human *modus operandi*. The crucial correlate of language is
man's reasoning ability, and the unmistakable sign of the presence of
reason is language.[7]

Where language does not exist, there remains little that is human.
One need only try to conceive of a human group trying to get along without language, to realize what it means to us. A baby, for example,
is unable to behave at the human level until it acquires language. There
are also the rather well-known consequences of lack or impairment of
language among isolated and feral children, the blind–deaf, and the
aphasiacs (persons with a loss or disturbance of language responses),
the "persons without words."[8]

The almost total bafflement and helplessness of an otherwise adult
and normal individual in a foreign community where the gestures and
other symbolic signs, as well as the spoken and written language, are so
different from his own that he does not understand them is further
evidence of the language's operational importance. It is the primordial
kit of tools, which enables men to act like human beings. As Révész
has succinctly put it: "Man made language, and language fashioned man
and made him human."[9]

N O T E S

1 "No race of mankind, however lowly, is known which does not possess the power of speech. Nay, more—the linguistic attainment may be subtle, complex, flexible, and eloquent, even though the cultural level be primitive in the extreme. It is indeed difficult to identify among the races of man anything which can be justly termed 'primitive tongue.' " (Dr. Macdonald Critchley, in an address at the University of Chicago, celebrating the centenary of the publication of Darwin's *Origin of Species;* reported in *Saturday Review,* Dec. 12, 1959, p. 50.)

2 S. I. Hayakawa uses the phrase, "swimming in words," *Language in Thought and Action* (New York: Harcourt, Brace, 1949), p. 18.

3 Suzanne K. Langer, "Philosophy: The Growing Center," in Lynn White, Jr. (ed.), *Frontiers of Knowledge* (New York: Harper & Brothers, 1956), pp. 257–286.

4 Wilhelm von Humboldt, *Über die Verschiedenheit des menschlichen Sprachbaues und ihren Einfluss auf die geistige Entwicklung des Menschengeschlechts,* appeared in complete form in 1836–39 (Berlin: Verlag von S. Calvary, 1876).

5 John Lotz, "Linguistics," in White (ed.), pp. 207–231.

6 Irving J. Lee, *Language Habits in Human Affairs* (New York: Harper & Brothers, 1941), p. 31. See also Geza Révész, *The Origins and Prehistory of Language* (New York: Philosophical Library, 1956), pp. 1–7.

7 "Speech is the best show man puts on. It is *his* own 'act' on the stage of evolution, in which he comes before the cosmic backdrop and really 'does his stuff.' " (Benjamin L. Whorf, *Language, Thought, and Reality,* John B. Carroll (ed.) (Cambridge, Mass.: The Technology Press, 1956; and New York: John Wiley & Sons, 1956), p. 249.)

8 Cf. Alfred R. Lindesmith and Anselm L. Strauss, *Social Psychology,* revised edition (New York: Holt, Rinehart and Winston, 1956), pp. 131–158.

9 Révész, p. 210.

II ❧ The Basic Concepts Involved in a Sociology of Language: A Paradigmatic Treatment

Sociology's concern with language rests upon its pivotal place in the social scheme of things, particularly upon the fact that it is at once a fundamental emergent from, and a basic instrument and primary determinant of, societal life. An understanding of the sociology of language can best be provided by indicating the theoretical elements involved as ingredients in such an analysis. This can be most economically presented in the form of a paradigm or analytical model. Such a device is a means of (a) systematically stating and developing the minimally essential concepts involved, (b) indicating their logical sequence, and (c) revealing their reciprocal relationships.[1] The elements here discussed will provide us with a set of working conceptual tools for our entire study. All of the items presented will be referred to later, and several of them will be treated at considerable length, either directly or indirectly, because they are concerned with fundamental aspects of language as a phenomenon of central sociological significance.

1. The Environments of Man

Man lives in the universe. He has contacts with this universe in the form of two major sets of environments. First, there is the *physical environment,* reaching out into the infinities of space. This affects him through its *cosmic features,* such as the influences of the sun and the moon and the other planetary systems that affect diurnal, seasonal and climatic cycles, and the other great rhythms. It is especially influential through its terrestrial forms and forces. These consist particularly of such *general physical factors* as space itself, gravity, altitude, oxygen supply, and barometric pressure; *geographic factors,* which may be subdivided into *physiographic elements* (terrain)—topographic or relief or land-form features, such as plains, deserts, mountains, bodies of water—gravity and altitude; *climatic and meteorological* features: seasons and weather, and such factors as wind, moisture and aridity, heat and cold; *inorganic natural resources,* including the minerals and metals and the sources of physical power; and, finally, the *organic natural world,* which takes in all forms of plant and animal life.

Second, and equally important for him as a human being is the *social–cultural environment,* which consists of his fellow human beings, past and present, in communication and association with each other, and their cultural achievements. This environment consists minimally of the various forms and levels of societal structure or combinations of interacting persons, and of the social processes or identifiable typed patterns of social action and interaction in which people engage, in conducting social functions as the constituent populations of the structures. Part of the social environment—in fact a major feature of it—is the cultural environment, which consists of all that man has wrought in the way of physical and social, technological and conceptual instrumentalities and procedures, by means of which he has produced his current physical, social, and intellectual relationship to the universe.

This culturally constructed environment may be thought of more specifically in terms of its subforms. There are: (1) the *physicosocial* environment, consisting of the technological modifications of the physical environment, and taking such forms as tools, weapons, ornaments, machines, transportation systems—in fact, all manner of equipment, apparatus and other physical goods available for human use; (2) the *biosocial environment*—the technological modifications of the biological environment—domesticated plants, domestic animals for food, power, and fibers, and medicines; (3) the *psychosocial environment,* consisting of the socially established uniformities of *inner* behavior that occur in collective units and are perceived as customs, folkways, conventions, traditions, beliefs, mores, and so on. Especially important are: (4) the great *institutionalized control environments*—economic, political, educational, esthetic—which govern the behavior of men at all times and in every major department of social life. A particularly significant part of institutionalized social–cultural environment is "in men's heads," and is not scientifically determinable—namely, the *supernatural environment*. This is an illimitable realm of belief and imagination, extending beyond the known physical and social universe, and one that almost all men, past and present, have been preoccupied with, often more so than with the tangible environments. It involves the mysterious but presumably supremely potent domain of extraordinary and extra-human power and process. This environment is as "real" in its human effect as are the physical and the more concrete social environments.

Man cannot avoid any of these environments. All that he *is* and *becomes* is in great measure due to them; all that he *does* is some sort of adjustment to, or utilization or transformation of them.

2. *Experience*

Human beings, as they live in, have contact with, react to these various environments, have an awareness, a "registering of consciousness" with regard to the attributes and the consequences (to themselves) of these environments. They become cognizant of things and events, situations and conditions, of themselves as entities, their own actions and relations, their relationships with each other and with the universe and its mysteries. These awarenesses come to them by way of the senses, enter their minds, and are registered as patterns in their brains. The impressions or registerings that we call experience are, for human beings, the primordial *source* of all their *knowable* reality. Their experiences interplay continually with all their actions and reactions.

3. *Meaning*

All that is experienced has affect and effect. When man experiences, he has more than sensation and the correlative reflexive and instinctive responses. Experiences produce mental responses; they arouse interest. Men have recall, imaginings and reflections about their manifold experiences; they estimate and interpret them. They compare the properties and qualities (for themselves) of classes of things, events, processes, situations, and relations—the "referents," as we technically designate them. Finally, in this connection, men come to conclusions about their experiences: they assign meanings, more or less specific significances, to them. This assigning of meaning is a *necessary* human activity: without it, no experience has existence or reality. Thus these meanings or "abstractions," at various levels of complexity, become man's working realities. Men could not function in their environments without them. All knowledge is experience that has specific meaning. But it should be noted that the assigning of significance or meaning is also a distinctively *human* act: meaning is thus primarily a property of human behavior, and only secondarily a property of objects or of events or situations. Furthermore, as John Dewey pointed out, meaning is based on consensus; that is, the devising of meaning is a joint act of human beings.[2] In fact, to be significant, meanings must be shared. "Any individual, as a group member, and any continuing group can conduct necessary actions only on the basis of meanings that are not subjective, not private (and hence perhaps eccentric), but *social and universal* within the group."[3]

4. *Communication and Action*

While experiencing is a personal phenomenon, individuals do not do their experiencing as isolates. Each individual's experiencing influences that of others with whom he is in contact. These interactions, in fact, produce among those associated a specific experiential complex. As noted above, the meanings that individuals attach to their experiences have no significance as purely individual possessions; they have been developed jointly and are in large measure commonly held and commonly interpreted. This means that men unconsciously and consciously reveal experiences to others, share with others—exchange the meanings of their experiences. This they do by communication, that is, by the transmission of a "message" from originator ("sender") to destination or audience ("receiver").[4] Each combination of interacting individuals has its "communication net" and a continuous "flow" within the net. The members must have this in order to adjust themselves to each other and to their various environments.

Communication is not an end in itself. It is, in fact, the elemental social process—the social technique upon which all social processes depend. Its elemental significance rests upon the fact that without it there can be no semantic transfer. This is of crucial importance in that meaning alone is communicable and communicated; the rest, as will be noted, is "instrument" and "conditioner." Moreover, communication is necessary in order to establish all social ties, to conduct action with or against others. Without it—and in sufficient quantity, quality and range—there can be no interstimulation and reciprocal response, no establishment of common meaningful conceptualizations, no informative, instructional, provocative, invitational, or directive action, no invention, no recording, accumulation, and transmission of knowledge, no social organization, no planning and reorganization.

While some communication is incidental or accidental, for the most part it is intentional and purposive, directed toward specific objectives and ends.

5. Conceptualization

To retain the essence of experiences, to understand and interpret their meanings, to refer to them, communicate them, and act upon them, requires that their meanings be conceptualized: they must be given *cognitive form*. Discrete fragments of things, qualities, events, of relations between things and actions—the ingredients, traits, or operational characteristics of things or events, obtained through perception—in order to be "knowable," must be intentionally integrated, in conformity with a definite plan or "rule," into an empirical concept. What we know about "facts" is a matter of concepts. The concept is, in effect, an ordered "mental image," an "imaginative synthesis," or a "convenient capsule of thought," which converts what would otherwise be a chaos of experience into explicitly identified and categorized form. All human experience is presented in terms of a conceptual scheme. Thus the concepts which specifically express these meanings are not private affairs. To have durable significance and daily utility for their holders as members of groups, and to be communicable between senders and receivers, they must be depersonalized, generalized, and standardized. Thus the concepts held by a body of communicants are the products of cooperative and critical abstraction, of logical construction and generalization. That is how common working statements of meaning are achieved.

While animals also communicate, they probably communicate only intentions and direct emotional excitements. Man communicates not only what he has sensed and instinctively desired, but also what he has concluded or imagined about the meanings of things and events.

6. *The Symbol-system: The Nature and Place of Language*

The conceptualizations of experience that men convey to each other, and by means of which they deal with the universe and each other—in fact, all expressions beyond those very general, simple and automatic communications provided by instinctive and reflex noises and gestures —are not and cannot be models or resemblances of what they refer to; they are represented instead by *symbols*. All human societies have their symbol-systems.

a / The symbol-system in general. Symbols must be distinguished as a special kind of *sign*. Like many other creatures, man uses signs. Signs in general, as the name implies, call attention to *sign*ificances: they relate to what has been perceived; they point to, indicate, or denote something other than themselves. As used by human beings, a sign is a common *referent* between the user and the subject with whom communication is sought. It functions as a carrier of meaning, as a cue or stimulus to action. A distinction can be made between "natural" and "conventional" signs.[5] A natural sign is a thing, movement, sound or any other stimulus, —always tied in with a concrete situation in an immediate space-time framework—that influences some subject or leads to action (a dog barking; a man giving his wife the "high sign" to leave at a dinner party; water dripping from a tree as an indication that it has rained).

A symbol is a conventional sign. It is a culturally identifiable, culturally selected or contrived, and generally recognizable means—in the form of any kind of object or movement or mark—whereby meanings prevailing among human beings are presented, represented, and transmitted, and a more or less uniform response is produced. The importance of a symbol does not lie in its intrinsic properties; the symbol stands for, refers to, indicates *something else.* It is a representation of conceptualized things, actions, occurrences, qualities, or relationships —a surrogate or substitute, not the object or happening itself. Furthermore, the symbol is not the total reality of what it stands for, but only that portion of it that it designates. The symbol involves conceptual behavior as it transmits "understanding" and "meaning." There is nothing *in the nature of* any of the signs (things, movements, events) used as symbols that gives them the meanings they carry; these meanings we human beings bestow upon them by agreement or convention. Thus, the word "rain" is a symbolic sound to convey the idea of rain or rain-ing; a book on astronomy, consisting of a hundred thousand man-made words as symbols, is not the heavenly bodies, distances, and movements which actually make up the stellar universe; "beauty" is a symbol for a meaning found in human experience, and the sound of it or the mark for it is nothing in itself.

Man is the only creature with symbol-forming power. This is one of the powers that distinguish him as man, and upon it rest many of his other uniquely human powers. Not only does he have the *capacity* for making symbols; he needs to create them, in order to cope humanly with his infinitely diverse and complex experience. Thus, with his unique physiological, psychological, and cultural aptitudes, he has invented a *system of symbols*. This system provides the common, quick, and economical conventionalized means of defining or referring to the classes of everything that he perceives, feels, surmises, imagines, knows, and wishes to know or to do. Mankind operates on the principle that unclarified complex realities can be replaced or represented by these simple and ordered devices, which can be manipulated with incomparably greater facility than the primary things or situations or occurrences or even abstractions themselves. Moreover, the symbols make possible, within the group using them, a "universe of discourse." Their significance, their sole *raison d'être,* depends upon their use as media of exchange of knowledge, wishes, desires, and expressional urges. As we shall explain at greater length below, they are the instrumentalities whereby men codify experience, or create a "map" of the territory of experience.[6] Their utility depends upon the fact that all group members are conditioned to react more or less uniformly to them. Without symbols men could not either recall or record their knowledge, nor could they communicate in space and time. Symbols are also the means of orienting one person to another, thus functioning as the "directing pivots" of social action.

b / The language system. Almost everything that man produces is symbolical. Science, art, morality, rituals, myths, religion and law, for example, are symbolical; they are complexes of symbols that specify particular groupings or patterns and emphases of experiences, and carry bodies of distinctively human meanings. But *the key and basic symbolism of man is language.* All the other symbol systems can be *interpreted* only by means of language. It is the instrument by means of which every designation, every interpretation, every conceptualization, and almost every communication of experience is ultimately accomplished. What is not expressed in language is not experienced and has no meaning;

it is "beyond" the people. By means of language, the content and meaning of experience become conscious and are made explicit—thinkaboutable and talk-aboutable—and hence socially usable.

A language is a culturally constructed and socially established system —that is, a body of self-consistent and rule-governed interrelated parts —of standardized and conventionalized—that is, generally accepted as required—symbols, which have a specific and arbitrarily determined meaning and common usage for purposes of socially meaningful expression, and for communication in the given society (or, technically, in the given "language community," next to be examined). This symbol system usually consists of certain more or less conventionalized signals and gestures, but especially of orderly (differentiated and combined) spoken sounds and, very late in human history, of written (graphic) characters.

Language is first and foremost a system of communication by means of fixed and arbitrary spoken or written symbols. *Speech* itself consists of physically and physiologically possible vocal sounds, which have been converted into defined, articulated, controlled, and limited sound symbols, such as can be clearly differentiated from one another by the ear. These standardized vocal sounds and sequences of sounds develop into what are conventionally known as *words*.[7] Our English language, for example, consists of about a half-million of them. The separate sounds of any language have been phonetically ordered, and the words have been morphologically, syntactically, and lexically organized, and semantically established.[8] As the result of this organization, the vocal sounds in their various combinations and orders of utterance are mutually intelligible to all normal members of the group or groups speaking them.

Each of the words is endowed with a specific meaning by the human beings using the language system, and serves its communicative function by virtue of this intellectually assigned meaning. Thus the "organs of speech" are not the real seat of language as symbolic communication; it is in man's brain.[9]

Fundamentally, the spoken *word*, or its equivalent or functioning counterpart in the languages that do not have "words," is the only all-inclusive and basic medium of communication. There are, of course, other forms of conveying messages interpersonally, which express ideas, emotions, intents, or directives: laughter, sobbing and panting; gestures, facial expressions and postures; mechanical signals; dancing, drawing, music and pantomime; especially, writing. But these *other* signs, signals, expressions, and marks, and all other symbolic systems relate to words, imply words, are translations, substitutes, adjuncts, or supplements of words; they simply serve as media for representing or enhancing and extending the range and potency of ordered words in space and time. Bereft of their relation to, and interpretation in terms of, language they would be meaningless.[10] Thus, for example, among us the raucous guffaw means "You're a fool!!"; the wave of an arm by an acquaintance means "Hello"; the green light at the intersection means "Go!"; the nod and wink means "Come on," the beckoning gesture means "Come!"; the Civil Defense siren means "Be on the alert!"

When a people have reached the stage of literacy in their language development, they have *writing* or written language; that is, words or auditory symbols are translated into the form of physical objects, pictures or pictograms, lines, alphabet, or other standardized, conventionalized, visible figures or marks, such as the "ideographies" of mathematics, symbolic logic and many branches of science. These, in various combinations, make possible the recording and perpetuation of meanings and their transmission across space and time. But speech always precedes writing. In societies like our own, communication by language is further facilitated and extended by mechanical means of transmitting either speech or writing, such as postal service, printing in its multiple uses, telegraph, telephone and teletype, radio, photography, motion pictures, and television. These are sometimes referred to as secondary symbolic systems.

Certain distinguishing aspects of language should be specially stressed. First, it is *man's invented tool*.[11] Of all the tools that he has ever devised and used, it is the most characteristic, spectacular and basic, and has almost infinite further productive and creative possibilities. It should be noted that some other creatures have tools. Some of the higher apes not only use rudimentary tools, but do some simple inventing and even making of them. Man alone creates, establishes, institutionalizes and uses language. Only man has the tremendous range in the kind and quality of communication across space and time that language makes possible. Man as the "word-using" animal is in a highly distinctive tool-using category. What is epochal is not *Homo fabricans* (tool-maker) but *Homo loquens* (speaker or verbalizer).

A second aspect of language, alluded to above, is the fact that it is much more than mere human vocal noises. It is a distinctive verbal ("word") system. Almost all other creatures that have contact with their fellows—insects, birds, fishes, mammals—communicate with them. Some of them make communicative noises, in some instances of considerable range and variety—such as the chirps and songs of birds, the calls and warning cries of some animals, the "signal dances" of the bees—but these are all "natural" noises, repeated over and over again in unchanged form, expressing an instinctive or reflexive animal urge, and conveying a limited and momentary message. The human vocal mechanism ("noise-box") is capable of issuing an enormous range and variety of sounds with vast possibilities of the combination and sequence of tone qualities, pitch, relationship, volume, and so on. But these human vocal noises that constitute the elements of a given speech or "tongue" are always culturally selected noises, uttered in specific standardized and established combinations and patterns. Animal vocal communication (for example, between cows or hens) is mere *vocalizing*; human vocal communication is *verbalizing* or verbal formulation, that is, *making and using words*. It is always a specifically and arbitrarily combined, definitely conventionalized, and generally required and used *system* of vocal noises. As the result of their systemic organization, the sounds in their combinations and orders of utterance are mutually intelligible to normal speakers of the language. The almost infinite array and number of possible verbal symbols among men makes possible a vast number of meanings in the interpretation of experience. The verbal repertoire can be associated with concrete objects, spatial relationships of objects, abstractions, conditions and situations, events and processes, and qualities. In fact, the given language makes it possible for its users to state almost everything they are aware of, imagine or wish to do.

A third signal aspect of language has to do with its primary role in human life. All the means of meaningful mediation between the individual and himself, and between an individual and one or more other persons, ultimately resolve themselves into verbalizations. As such an agency, language enables the individual to be articulate about himself, to express himself, to be meaningful to himself. It is also the means of bringing one person into an effective relationship with another or others in a community situation. The speaker (sender) speaks to the listener (receiver) a message about something of significance to one or both. The process is one of *semantic transfer*. Language thus serves all the purposes of human activity; it functions as the means of expression for the personality and as the basic means of communication, and hence of operation, in all social relations.

7. The Language Community

Experience is social; meaning is a matter of consensus; communication is always a social event, and the language which the communicators employ is a social product, emerging from and used by a given body of people. The people who express themselves, who interact and to some extent cohere by means of a given language system, comprise a community of lesser or greater extent and compactness, and of some degree of cultural uniformity. "Communication" and "community" have a common root; this reflects the indispensable reciprocal relationship of the two: each is the counterpart of the other. The people of a community have a common experiential, conceptual, and societal life, and hence must have relatively uniform speech ways. We refer technically to this communing combination of the users of a given standard language as a language community.

Language is always both a form and an expression of community life. It arises, develops, exists and possesses meaning *only* within a speech community. It depends for its existence upon a speaking population. In the speech community, intimate and continuous contact among the members produces a common usage of linguistic forms and shared speech habits. Each language community has uniform words, word-forms, pronunciations, grammatical constructions and connotations, attached to or conveyed by words and word combinations. The speech community makes language the self-perpetuating system that it is. Language is "communally organic."[12]

It is within the language community that we have the greater "universe of discourse." The people born in it speak the language as their "mother tongue." It has mutual intelligibility among them. They must speak it with its familiar and approved words, and with their familiar and approved meanings, if they are to make themselves understood. All more or less permanent in-migrants must learn it and use it. Language is language—the medium of mutually comprehensible expression and of inter-person and inter-group communication—only among colinguals.

While the boundaries of most speech communities cannot be sharply drawn, there is nevertheless a recognizable line of separation and difference, or more accurately, a "broad band frontier"; for each is in various significant respects a unique organization by virtue of its particular language system as the medium for expressing its particular historical and contemporary experiences and meanings. Most people are not bilingual or polyglot, though the number of these is probably increasing.

A given language community may vary in extent from a small, localized group of several dozen or several hundred members, through larger regional areas, to language "empires" involving groups in several continents. It is not necessarily a geographic area. There may be a considerable range of ethnicity of the people involved, and in the institutions of the larger language community. It may or may not be a political entity; it may include all or part of several political units. Thus the "English" speech community includes England, the United States, English Canada, New Zealand, Australia, and much of South Africa; the "French" community includes France, French Switzerland, French Canada, and parts of Africa, Central America, and islands of the South Pacific. Each speech community has a center (or centers) and leading groups which influence, even dominate, the words and speech forms used. The leading groups set the *standard* language, both in its colloquial and written form. The radiated speech forms have influence and are accepted because they have great utility or prestige, marked vogue or "cultural correctness."

Complete speech uniformity does not prevail, especially in the larger language communities, nor will all the members of a speech community possess *all* of the linguistic items which properly belong to the language. Different segments of the population have special items of interest and concern in their "map" of experience, and different determinants of and needs for expression. There are usually local or regional (geographical) sublanguages, known as dialects; there are "special" languages among different functional groups, such as criminal argots, the technical terminologies of different occupations, the "marginal" or "mixed" forms of certain somewhat culturally specialized groups, such as "Pennsylvania Dutch" and "Brooklynese," the differences of speech among diverse educational, cultural, and class levels of the population. These dialects and special languages, however, while not necessarily reciprocally comprehensible in their entirety, are all etymologically related to the standard language, and consist mainly of special variations of pronunciation, special additions, or the bestowing of special refinements of meaning upon terms.

8. *The Context of the Physical, Cultural and Social Situation*

Languages are both determined by and determinative of the reactions of the users to the physical, cultural and social environmental conditions and situations in which the languages play a part. They are especially *socially* determined and *socially* determinative. Every language community is coterminous with or part or all of a given group, or even contiguous with part or all of a society. Every society has its own special characteristics; its language has a pragmatic character and fundamentally utilitarian functions, both of a general cultural and specifically societal nature (to be discussed in some detail in separate chapters below).

The content, form, and uses of the language of each community mirror its physical setting, what its members are aware of and concerned about, and what their vicissitudes and successes with it have been, including especially the level of technological development achieved. In fact, the language carries the definitions of *all* situations; it is the dissecting agent by which the structures, functions, processes, relations and factors of the general and particular world are laid bare. By means of it, all environments are objectified, and all the actions of the group or society are carried on. Not only is language the institutionalized medium whereby the activities of all other institutions, each with its special patterns and techniques of behavior, are conducted; the complexity and richness of these institutions are of necessity paralleled by a corresponding diversity and quality of language. Each institutional system has its own special vocabulary and forms. The language reveals a host of social situations and processes—especially societal cohesion and separation; assimilation and ethnic diversity and conflict; social and cultural stratification; all sorts of demographic, occupational, and other cultural specializations; social power and social control; kinds and levels of cultural development, as well as cultural history and texture; all historical contacts, including those by migration, invasion, and conquest; the social values, preoccupations, standards, and objectives; the size, complexity, and forms of social organization. Thus, the language reflects situational imperatives and happenings, and every feature of the community's mental climate—its culture and its societal organization and operation. In short, the language of the group or community is an index of most of its characteristics.

Conversely, the very form, extent and complexity of the conceptual, cultural and social structures and the functions these perform vary with and are affected by the established and current language system. The language structure (vocabulary, grammar, semantics) as it stands at any given time operates as a ready-made metaphysical framework, by means of which we do all our perceiving and conceptualizing. Thus, the language of the member of the given language community is his means of interpreting reality; it shapes his comprehension of his environment and supplies the definitions and categories of all that he experiences; it determines the nature and extent of his working concepts and beliefs along various lines, including causality, components of entities and qualities; it provides him with perspectives of time and space and his conceptions of numbers and dimensions; it is the elemental medium of all of his creativity and contrivance in the way of abstractions, techniques and material constructs.

The defects, distortions and inadequacies of language, or the inadequate command of language, retard cultural development and the acquisition of culture, and impair societal organization and operation. Furthermore, language and society must change in parallel fashion. New societal needs and new cultural experiences make it necessary to enlarge the resources of the language by the borrowing or actual invention of new vocabulary, formulae and phrases, the extension of meaning of some terms, and the rendering of greater specificity of meaning to others.

Thus the language system and the metaphysical and sociocultural texture and context of a society or even a group cannot be separated. Each reflects the other; each is operationally related to the other; each is both cause and effect of the other.[13]

N O T E S

1 Robert K. Merton, *Social Theory and Social Structure,* 2nd ed. (Glencoe, Ill.: Free Press, 1957), pp. 16–20, 55.

2 John Dewey, *Experience and Nature* (New York: Open Court, 1925), p. 179.

3 Cf. George H. Mead, *Mind, Self and Society: From the Standpoint of the Social Behaviorist* (Chicago: University of Chicago Press, 1934), pp. xx–xxi, 75, 90.

4 For a model of the elements of a typical communication situation, see John B. Carroll, *The Study of Language: A Survey of Linguistics and Related Disciplines in America* (Cambridge: Harvard University Press, 1953), pp. 88–93.

5 Alfred R. Lindesmith and Anselm L. Strauss, *Social Psychology,* revised edition (New York: Holt, Rinehart and Winston, 1956), pp. 53–58.

6 "A theoretically perfect Symbol would, in all its ramifications, reveal the underlying pattern of experience." (Kenneth Burke, *Counter-Statement* (New York: Harcourt, Brace, 1931), p. 200.)

7 As we shall see in Chap. V, some languages do not have what the structural linguists define as "words." The Indo-European languages, to which ours belongs, do have words as basic sounds or combinations of sounds serving as thought-carriers. All languages, however, have *unit* or separately uttered thought-carriers, some of them carrying complex messages, that correspond to our words in their communicative functioning. These are what appear when dictionaries are constructed for, and when English words are translated into,

"wordless" languages. Words are the ultimate morphological objective and product, the items that are syntactically manipulated and arranged.

8 These organizational features will be briefly examined in Chap. V.

9 Cf. Leslie A. White, "The Origin and Nature of Speech," in M. H. Fried (ed.), *Readings in Anthropology* (New York: Crowell, 1959), Vol. I, pp. 155–162.

10 The social significance of words in language will be examined more extensively in Chap. III, Sect. 1, and Chap. XI, Sects. 1–3.

11 A tool may be thought of as a natural or contrived device used to extend the always limited physiological and instinctive capacities of the users.

12 Arthur S. Diamond, *The History and Origin of Language* (New York: Philosophical Library, 1959), p. 14.

13 This brief discussion of situational contexts is, in effect, a cataloguing of the major treatments of the remainder of this study.

III ❧ The Major General Functions of Language

Language as the primary and key instrumentality of humankind has many functions. Most of the general population is quite unaware of these; language for them is part of the "givens," like light and air. Moreover, some of language's important functions are barely recognized by many linguists and social scientists. And yet these functions are strategic and indispensable; human existence depends upon them.

Our main concern, as noted, is with the sociological aspects of language—language as both cause and effect of social situations and actions. This would seem to focus attention exclusively upon social functions. However, it is important in this study also to have some knowledge of the more general functions of language because these are fundamentally related to most cultural, social-psychological and societal functions. Without such knowledge we lack orientation for the study of many of the sociologically important features, functions and dysfunctions of language.

A concise but fairly complete inventory follows, in the form of the sequential and logical stages of language as a fundamental functional factor in human society.

1. Words as the Fundamental Components of Language as Instrument

The nature of words, and of their place in the structure and operation of language, is essential to an understanding of the general as well as the special social functions of language in human life, for words are its fundamental components. The magical and sacred powers of the word—the verb, *Logos*—have been recognized ever since the inception of civilization.[1] Even more significant in the everyday affairs of men are the pragmatic and mundane uses and effects of words.

Words are constructed by man; each word is a deed, stands for a deed, and makes a deed existential. Viewed operationally and concretely, words are the significant units of connected speech; they are also the smallest units of verbal behavior and the smallest vehicles of meaning.[2] All words have something behind them; they stand for something. As practical devices, they are at any given time the rather definite number of means by which reality, as experienced by man in its myriad, diverse and kaleidoscopic details and characteristics, is perceived, articulated, labeled and transmitted. They are the media—literally—of reactions to, evaluations of, orientations toward life facts. By means of them, man "comes to terms with his world"; they give him the feeling that he does not have "terrifying isolation in the universe," "separation from that cosmic collectivity of which he is a legitimate and indispensable part."[3]

Reality, to be sure, is infinitely complex. At the same time, there cannot be an uncountable number of words to portray it, since the memory and skill of the human users are limited. By means of a limited number of words, this complex reality is reduced to a system of orders, ranks, and classes that can be managed.

Words are abbreviated contrivances, products of group living, residues of specific past acts, devised for all these purposes as the members of the group have worked out their schemes of intercommunication and of adjustment to both their tangible and imagined environments. They have been invented and continually perfected through use. Each word is a sort of generalization, which selects and labels a feature, or class of features, from among the welter of irrelevant features. Each *type* of word has its own special function, as a "chiseled and refined" indicator of the different aspects of reality. By means of words properly organized, men are able to identify, objectify, describe, standardize, classify, and universalize all their different types of experience.[4]

We now take up these and other general functions of language in some detail.

2. *The Identification (Naming) Function*

Labeling or naming, as we have noted, is one of the fundamental functions of language. To name is to affix a verbal label and establish a verbal usage; that is to say, it is a process by which some experienced object, quality, act, person, or event, is identified, so that it may be subsequently recovered and referred to in communication with self and others. The first step in knowledge is always to give a *name*. Names are our means of representing and presenting all that *is* for us; they bring what is experienced *by us* into effective existence *for us*. That which is named is not unknown to us anymore; we can use it and manipulate it in our human conduct. The name furnishes us with a handle by means of which we can group the essentials of any situation.[5] We *must* have names for everything that we are aware of.

The function of language as a means of *group* identification is important from the sociological point of view. He who speaks a language can be located socially as to the group or groups to which he belongs. By means of it, others can tell some of his characteristics, whether he is a friend or foe, whether he is an "in-group" or "out-group" person.

Closely related to the identifying function of language is the *denotative* function, which is concerned with marking out, designating or signifying, and the *indicative* function, which directs attention to or points out that which has been experienced.

3. *The Categorization (Classification) Function*

The very act of identification involves classification. Every language is a basic device for categorizing experience—that is, for locating precisely given kinds of entities, conditions, events, qualities among the infinite variety of them; separating them from each other, sorting them, and placing them within a given compartment of knowledge, so that they can be distinctively differentiated, comprehended, and utilized. A language may, in fact, be thought of as a language community's system of introducing and maintaining order in its complex of experience, by codification and classification of its "realities" of existence. Each language, of course, does this in its own specific way; each picks out only certain among the possible comparisons and contrasts that are to be found in the universe, and symbolizes them.

Through the various kinds of words, but especially by means of nouns, verbs, adjectives, and adverbs, language presents types of unities, or the classes and subclasses of what the particular groups and the continuities of its speakers have noted. The users can conceive of some experience, which is concerned with the things or events, being represented in nouns; other experience, involving the action or oc-currence, indicated by verbs; other again, implying qualities, or specially identifying characteristics of things or occurrences, presented through adjectives and adverbs. Every language thus provides facility for selec-tion and discrimination among different kinds of experience. Any par-ticular object that is referred to, for example, is a representative of the named class or subclass, as distinguished from other classes or sub-classes. We can distinguish "cow" from "horse," and different varieties of cows from others, on the basis of such attributes as size, color, disposi-tion, action, and purpose. Thus, in our vocabulary we have a kind of framework for locating types of experience—a ready-made system of classification, which we inherit from our ancestors. This categoriza-tion enables us to view the world as relatively stable, predictable and orderly. The words of language, functioning as categories of experi-enced reality, not only facilitate more precise analysis, but also aid in the comparison of one portion of experiential data with other portions. This might be referred to as "cross-classification."

As will be noted later in some detail, each language has its own distinctive linguistic habits, and hence its specific identifications and categorizings of experience.

4. *Language as the Means of Perception*

Our given language, through the habits of identification and categori-zation which it develops in us, determines what we, the speakers, perceive in our environment—that is, what we notice, what we are conscious of, what is important to us, what can be ignored. We can perceive the ob-jects, events, conditions of being and relationship of our experience only through types of knowns, as particularly represented by nouns, verbs and adjectives. These symbols *alert us* to what is for us "real," to what has existence and distinction of kind and detail among "things" and "actions," "states" and "qualities." These words function as spectacles for us, as we look out upon our world, and also as molds of and frame-works for comprehension (as we shall note later in greater detail). As Walter Lippmann put it in his aphorism: "First we look, then we name, and only then do we see." Without this language function, our world—concrete and abstract, non-human and human—would be "a big, boom-ing, buzzing confusion," to use William James's phrase. In this respect, language may be likened to a sieve: it admits the examples of what have come to be parts of reality for us, and excludes what have not. Language thus is our cultural instrument for the conquest and the construction of what is reality for us. New words learned, as attention-callers, mobilize us to direct our attention to previously latent features of the physical or social intellectual landscape.

An often overlooked function of language as agent of perception is the fact that it is also the *basis of my awareness of myself as a being,* as well as of *being in general.* I can realize my existence only in terms of words, come to terms with myself, arrive at judgments and decisions regarding myself, by "talking" to myself.

✦5. *Language as the Means of Thinking*

We have already taken note of language as the essential element in conceptualization, in step five of the paradigm presenting the components of the social phenomenon of language in Chapter II. It was brought out there that, in order for us to retain the essence of experiences, and adequately to present their nature and meanings, so as, in turn, to communicate them and act upon them, these attributes and meanings must be conceptualized—that is, explicitly stated in verbal form, and verbally or otherwise symbolically defined and described. Conceptualization consists of putting into verbal form what has been identified and located vis-à-vis other things, in order that it may be more comprehensively known. In fact, "a conception is fixed and held only when it has been embodied in a symbol."[6] Language, of course, with its vocabulary and its grammatical and semantic organization, provides the tool and technique of conceptualization. Without it, we could not develop even the simplest mental pictures.

We are here especially concerned with the function of language in thinking—the major dynamic mental activity in conceptualization—which is man's fundamental procedure first in *Verstehen,* and then in all his paraphernalia of ideas—his reflection, evaluation, imagination and creation.

Man operates within an *ideational framework*—that is, a body of ideas of interpretations and analyses, which he has developed, and by means of which his observations of the universe and all that it contains, as well as his reactions to it, become meaningful. He can be said to live in a world of ideas. But it is within and by means of the *linguistic framework* that the ideationally established world exists and operates. Language is the means and mode of man's whole mental existence.

Language, as such, is man's primary vehicle for thinking. Brains think with words. It is not mere verbal play to say that we cannot think without speaking, or speak without thinking. Most men suffer acute mental discomfort until the urge to express an idea, to define, to reason, to interpret has been formulated in words or in formulae, diagrams, equations or other symbolic devices which involve words. Without properly ordered specific words, thought is vague and misty, seen dimly through the depth of "feeling" and "intuition." "The only way to pin down a thought before it can slip away . . . is to jump on it with both verbal feet, to pin it down with language."[7]

In this same connection, it has been pointed out that, when unconscious mind emerges into consciousness, it begins to symbolize in terms of language.[8] There is direct point to the oft-quoted remark that Plato puts into the mouth of Socrates: "When the mind is thinking, it is talking to itself." In fact, if we stop to take note of what we are doing when we are "thinking," we shall find that actually we are engaged in a form of imaginary conversation. Speaking broadly, our active minds have their being in *perpetual conversation.*

Grammar is of significance in thinking. Through the use of the various kinds of words, the logical and creative aspects of the mind are able to express kinds and orders and relationships of meaning. Thinking is never more precise, complex or extensive than the language of the thinker.

In general, words grammatically organized are the ultimate symbols and incarnation of ideas. By means of them, we can formulate almost all the ideas—all the statements and propositions about the nature of things, conditions, actions, surmises, ends—that we have. Bertrand Russell summarizes this aspect of language when he says: "Language serves not only to express thoughts, but to make possible thoughts which could not exist without it."[9] Similarly, Cassirer says: "All theoretical cognition takes its departure from a world already preformed by language; the scientist, the historian, even the philosopher, lives with his objects only as language presents them to him."[10]

The significance of language in the *communication* of "thought" is further brought out by Cherry:

> The writer or speaker does not communicate his *thoughts* to us; he communicates a representation for carrying out this function, under the severe discipline of using the only material he has, sound and gesture. Speech is like a painting, a representation made out of given materials—sound or paint. The function of speech is to stimulate and set up thoughts in us having correspondence with the maker's desires. But he has not transmitted a copy of his thoughts, a photograph, but only a stream of speech—a substitute made from the unpromising material of sound.[11]

Related to the thinking function is the declarative function—that is, language used to state the effects of the environment—physical, social, supernatural—upon individuals. This use of language ranges from everyday conversation (for example, declarations about the weather) to the highest levels of aesthetic, religious, and other abstract philosophical communication. Particularly significant is the fact that, through the declarative function, language has the effect of establishing a *community of thought*.

Finally, language is not only the guide to perception, as noted above, it is also the guide to the thought of its speakers. Deeply grooved linguistic habits make it impossible for us to escape from the influence that the range and structure and form of language exert upon our thinking. The very forms of thought are couched in language terms. This fact is evidenced in differences in the kind and range of the thinking of people who have language differences, because of their membership in different language communities, or because of different levels of literacy and education within a language community, or other divergences of cultural sophistication. New experience also, in order to be conceptualized and hence communicable, must be fitted to the most appropriate word or words of the language. Thus, in the process, it tends to become colored by the meanings already attached to the language elements utilized. At the same time, it should also be noted that language is almost always an imperfect model or garment for thought. We can express only those portions, kinds and attributes of our potential thoughts that our linguistic medium permits. Furthermore, thinking can never be more precise than the language it uses.

The subject matter of the last four sections could be summarized by saying that, in verbalizing reality, we identify and designate the entities of all sorts that we are aware of, their attributes and properties, and the relations and connections between them, thus taking them out of the realm of the hidden or the implicit. We assign these designated items to restricted and classified areas of experience and, in this verbalization, develop and establish our understanding of what we have experienced— *what is actuality for us.*

6. *Language as the Corpus of Our Facts*

The examination of the role of language in the identification and categorization of experience, and in perception and thinking, provides us with a foundation for the understanding of the relationship between language and those products of experience that we call "facts." Facts are the fundamental elements with which human beings think, evaluate, make their decisions, and act. They are the conceptions of those parts of reality that men have discovered (become aware of) and designated (named), categorized (typed and distinguished from other phenomena) and defined (described as to characteristic nature and attributes). A "fact" is thus not the discovered thing or event itself. It is a human construct, an achievement, a thing made. The word stems from the Latin "facere," meaning "to make" or "to do." A fact is something which has been extracted out of a vast, complex, and interwoven reality—some bit of the heretofore unknown.[12] The phenomena themselves—the "existences," the "realities"—have been pre-existent, probably for a long time, but they had not come into the experience of men. They had not been caught and arbitrarily labeled and described. A fact is thus an artificial representation of reality, a sort of "portrait" or "model" of some part of it. There are doubtless millions of phenomena of every imaginable kind that we are not aware of, which we have not corralled and branded; there are doubtless an infinity of them that we will never experience. Nevertheless, we operate with a vast multiplicity and variety of facts. There are *substantive* facts (for example, physical, historical, psychological, social, and so on), *causal* facts, *relational* facts, and *effect* facts. They all are the means whereby we, the experiencing subjects, "come to terms" with our world.

The point of significance for our study, however, is that reality as evidenced is not something visible, tangible or in any sensuous way perceptible. Its framework is something intellectual, capable of being apprehended only through symbols. Our empirical observations of the phenomena making up reality are symbolically presented in vocal and written words and in other verbal symbols. Hence language, especially written language, makes what would otherwise seem to be transitory and indefinite, permanent and precise.

Effective reality is, for us, essentially a language-made affair: we catch it and encircle it comprehensively by means of words. Words not only stand proxy for the things and acts experienced; they are the vehicles that carry all of our constructed meanings regarding things and acts. By means of them we achieve a working relationship with actuality. More specifically, *the world of facts exists for us only in the world of words* which describe the existences. We realize the existence of a certain thing as "house," a certain process as "burning," a certain attribute as "white." By language, we mold and embody the notions of thinghood, causality, number, quality, motion, occurrence, and effect. Language thus not only contributes to the formation, and participates in the constitution, of a fact; it *is*, in a real sense, *the corpus of our facts*.

Furthermore, our words, expressing all of our different kinds of facts, are an accumulation of knowledge; they make up all that we now "know" about our life and our world. Similarly *new* words, or words used in a new sense—with us, for example, "atom," "outer space," "mach"—represent elemental items in the additions to our store of knowledge. Learning a new language adds many new items of conceptualized experience to one's store of working facts.

An accurate analysis of language as our body of facts is the expression "map."[13] A map is an artificed representation of one or more aspects of the area which is the object of concern. It represents only what we know, and usually only one or more types of items of relevance in connection with the immediate presentational purpose—cities, comparative altitudes, topographical features, highways, location of particular resources, mean temperatures, variations in rainfall, and so on. A map does not and cannot give every aspect, but we can get an enormous number and variety of facts on it. The language of a people is the most complete "map" of all that they have factualized. Its words represent, locate and, in some measure, explain their available and known life-facts.

A final aspect of language as the body of facts is that it functions as *a storehouse of experience*. The vocabulary is a sort of "intellectual checking account," a "word-hoard." For different individuals the word-hoard varies in size and variety and depth, and hence also in usability. It is always an important factor in the range and quality of the thinking and acting of individuals. For the speakers of the language as a whole, it becomes, as a body of established facts, a means of avoiding the arduous repetition of experiences: it functions as an economical substitute or *surrogate*. It enables men to condition their responses to symbolic stimuli, or words which have come to mean certain behavior, and thus to reproduce this behavior of others indefinitely. Therefore, with the use of language, it is no longer necessary to see behavior performed before we can repeat it. Instead, we can respond to the words which stand for any given behavior, and reproduce any behavior for which we have words.

7. *Language in Creative Activity*

Language, as the means of conceptualizing—especially as the means of thinking, and as the medium for expressing and storing facts and the relation of facts (in some instances formally presented as "principles")—also plays a crucial and indispensable role in all human creative activity. All creativity, whether it be that which produces a new physical tool, or a technique for manipulating the physical world, or a new abstraction —a new belief, ideology, or utopia, a new conception of goodness, rightness, beauty, or other new value—requires imagination. Imagination is, mainly, the formation of new mental images of entities or situations or occurrences, these images being, in turn, mental syntheses of concepts taken from the store of factualized experiences.

Invention is perhaps the most important specific process involving imagination. It consists of actively and experimentally combining or synthesizing, and applying, in a new, unusual and meaningful form, known and available culture elements—objects, ideas, or ways—previously discovered or devised by others. The particular invention is the product of an act of contrivance, which consists of carrying into effect an imagined, heretofore non-conceived combination of things or ideas, the product being a new instrument or technique, concrete or abstract, for manipulating or interpreting what is of concern to men.

Creativity is essentially a type of thinking—high-level thinking— and thinking, as noted, takes place by means of words. The imaginative act puts into specific words a heretofore unthought idea or an anticipation of some heretofore unthought of thing or happening or other creative possibility. Language provides the creative person with all of the facts to combine through creation, and all of the conceptualizations, in the form of principles and techniques, for the purpose of combining the facts; it enables him to utilize the collective experience, in the form of knowledge, and the past collective imagination of the entire group of language users. In the end, this creativity is a new combining and ordering and manipulating of verbalization—a manipulation that may be quite impossible with the things or conditions that the verbal symbols stand for. The "castles in the air" that we build, some of which top the hills of history, are made of words.

The language symbols, being themselves partly imaginative, lend themselves to, and even encourage, all sorts of imaginative combinations. Creative thinking, in fact, may include creating new word symbols as a means of indicating and stating new potentialities and constructions. Man constantly re-forms his ideas so as to meet new or newly imagined needs by re-forming his words. He also has the means, by exercising imagination and creativity, to prepare for situations that he has not yet experienced—possibilities, probabilities, desirabilities—and thus to gain some control over the future.

8. *Language, and Man as Technologist*

Man as a creative being is also man the technologist—that is, the contriver (as well as user) of technics (tools, implements, machines) and techniques (skilled procedures or operations in using the tools). Technics and techniques are of three kinds: (1) mechanical, operating in the physical realm; (2) symbolic, involving ideas, traditions, philosophies, and sciences; and (3) organizational, used and applied by groups in institutionalized ways.

By means of their technologies, men are able to comprehend the nature of the universe, work in conformity with it, predict some of its occurrences, invent and otherwise deliberately and consciously innovate upon it—in short, increasingly to manipulate some of its features in a planned and organized manner in the pursuit of human ends.

Here, too, language is the essential preliminary and the continuously sustaining instrumentality. The creative contrivance and organization of tools and procedures—thinking and inventing—presupposes language, as just noted above. In fact, the development of the symbols themselves and the symbol system is perhaps the earliest form of technology, and the foundation of all other technologies.

> Man became a skilled tool-maker and tool-user because he was a word-maker and word-user. And he did not greatly improve his tools until he had advanced sufficiently in constructing language, that is, in the technology of making symbols.[14]

Man can construct tools and devise procedures to serve a given end only if he has the linguistic means for surveying and visualizing the task at hand, and then engaging in the mental processes involved in the creation (invention) of the appropriate means. Furthermore, the continuous maintenance and the extension in scope and efficiency of the technological system depend upon the continuous development of the thought system, which, in turn, depends upon the development of the linguistic system, both in the store and the forms of usage of its symbols, especially its words. Finally, language gives man a high degree of control of reality—a fundamental objective of the technological system. Words are the means for manipulating reality by creating descriptions and categorizations of the different experienced portions of it, and by inventing both the ends and the technologies.

↲ 9. *Language as a Record and as Human Memory*

We have noted that men are unique among the creatures of the earth in being able specifically to identify, categorize and conceptualize their infinite array of experiences, and to establish them as facts and principles; to think, create and innovate continuously, and to extend their technologies into the ever-expanding areas of experience and factualized reality. They also have the unique ability of recording this accumulating body of knowledge about what they have wrought, thus keeping it from being lost or distorted. Language is the main and always the ultimate medium through which this process of recording takes place. All human records appear in some linguistic form, spoken or written. Even those records that are non-linguistic in the ordinary sense of the term—archaeological findings, rituals, and artistic, architectural, and musical products—must be translated into language to be fully understood.

Among preliterates, the recording takes place through effective oral-linguistic vehicles, since they do not have writing and archives. The wisdom must be couched in forms that can be orally transmitted without loss of meaning or content. Hence they must be relatively concise, attention-catching, and trenchant, even pungent in statement. The outstanding forms are known collectively as folklore—the wisdom-store of the folk—and consist of myths, sayings, legends, maxims, fables, apothegms, proverbs, rhymes, riddles, medical formulae, genealogies, standardized prayers, standardized speeches for certain occasions, tales of all sorts, songs and ballads, decalogues and other concisely stated rules, maintained and retained by finger-counting and by verbal rituals utilizing mnemonic aids. Similar linguistic devices are also used for the recording and transmitting of wisdom among illiterates. Preliterates have also, of course, depicted and stored some of their wisdom in a pictorial manner—for example, by using drawings and carvings and physical objects carrying conventional meanings—but these "meanings" must still be translated into words.

When writing develops among a people, its wisdom is recorded in written form. Even though many of the preliterate societies had remarkable oral devices for containing and retaining their wisdom, they had a limited, and doubtless, in many areas of experience, a distorted "group memory." Only a written language provides the conditions and the means for both a relatively *exact* and an *extended* recording of a people's diversified knowledge. With the birth of writing, facts and ideas in every area of human interest and concern can be set forth in infinite detail, in precisely stated and relatively enduring form, and in a way which ensures a fairly uniform interpretation of meaning by all readers. Without it, abstract thinking can hardly be recorded; there can be no very definite theology or cosmology; there can be no science in the modern sense, for science requires a written record of its highly esoteric, exact, and complex knowledge, and the procedures of observation and testing whereby the knowledge is validated.

Language as the record of human experience through time also functions as the basis for individual and group (race) memory. Memory is the recalling or reliving of previous experience in conceptualized, hence specifically verbalized, form. If human beings could not utilize words and phrases, their recall would be similar to that of the lesser creatures—namely, no more than impressions set off by previously experienced types of situations, each with its particular related stimuli. Language is a means of both individual and group memory. With writing, obviously, we are able in large measure to remove the limitations of individual memory, and build up an extensive, accurately couched, and durable memory, either group or society-wide. Oral folk recordings, literature of all sorts, art, institutions, and even physical structures are the main embodiment of this memory. Today the universities are the chief perpetuating agencies; the libraries, the major depositories.

10. *Language as the Means of Transmitting Knowledge Across Space and Time*

The fact that language is the memory agent implies that it is also the major vehicle whereby we transmit—that is, impart or send and receive—our factualized experience (all sorts of knowledge, in the form

of definitions, concepts, descriptions, interpretations, as well as techniques, taboos, rules and principles) to others across space and time;
that is, to accomplish the transmission of these from one individual, one
area, one generation, one era, one cultural group to another. Thus, by
means of language, man can range mentally through space and time.
What is more, language has been the means by which the skills and
wisdom of the race, as these have emerged in different areas and eras,
could be compared, factually and logically tested and, finally, widely
utilized.

Some of man's transmission across space has been by imitation, but
he can fully transmit in that way only overt behavior or his grasp of
the external nature of things. Inner behavior induced by imitation comes
through by imprecise suggestion or implication. The transmission of
conceptualizations—thoughts, definitions, abstractions, instructions,
plans—requires language. Furthermore, before there was writing or
other means of physical or graphic notation, the transmission and exchange of information required the actual face-to-face contact of
senders and receivers, either directly or through intermediaries. After
men have achieved writing, and especially after they have attained the
present great array of technological devices and techniques for the
transmission of sound and writing, there is a vast extension of the
spatial range of communication.

Language is also the major instrument by which the cultural forms,
the humanly contrived and established items of experience of a society—
in fact, of the civilizations—are transmitted from one point in time to
another. This time-binding and time-bridging function of language is
worthy of special attention. Other animals can live only in the present:
because they lack language, their behavior is limited to instinct plus
what they have in the way of learning, as acquired through direct observation and imitation and by trial and error. Such learning can never
accumulate socially; it remains static from one generation to the next.
Through the recording function of language, however, man is able to live
simultaneously in the past, present, and future. Human beings utilize
knowledge and respond to activities dating back thousands of years. We
have already noted the forms through which vocal language has been
used to record the accumulated wisdom of the past. When culture materials can be transmitted by writing, we can utilize the knowledge embodied in "dead languages." With the aid of "Rosetta Stones," we can
plumb the wisdom and life of men long since gone.[15]

What is more, with language man can manipulate and in some measure control what happens to him in time. Not only can he participate

vicariously in the experiences and learning of his predecessors, he can work over and enlarge upon what he has received. In fact, each individual and each generation, as heir to the gathered wealth of an immeasurable past, does not have to recapitulate the cultural career of mankind to date, but can begin by standing on the shoulders of the present in the development of knowledge and of the different varieties of technological achievement. Each generation can not only project its accumulated knowledge and instruments and techniques into the future, but can also predict occurrences and draw plans, policies, programs and specifications for future action. In brief, by means of language, men can recall and educe from the past, communicate in and live in and through the present, and project into and make ready for the future.

Through its transmission across space and time, knowledge can be shared and accumulated by many people, both among contemporaries and across the generations. In being shared with others, it can become a social—potentially even a universal—rather than an individual possession. This means that human beings live in a great stream of shared knowledge, most of which they have inherited from previous generations of many peoples and cultures. Furthermore, while given individuals and peoples participate in the "stream" for a time, they come and go; by means of language and languages, however, the stream of knowledge goes on.

It should be noted that there are also possibilities for distinct disadvantages in the generalizations couched in the symbolisms of language. Bredemeier and Stephenson among others have pointed out that the ability to abstract certain properties from situations and symbolize them may *prevent* the solution of problems, as well as aid in solving them. This is due to the fact that, since symbols canalize perception and response, they may also act as "blinders," focusing attention only on some aspect of things or events, and not on others. Furthermore, errors too may be embalmed in language forms, and each generation may learn the errors as well as the achievements of the previous generations. The language symbols can also give "the feeling of certainty and comprehension, when such feeling is entirely inappropriate." This is because we get the feeling of comprehension by applying a symbol for something we know (or think we know) to something we do *not* know. This is because the feeling of comprehension comes from the feeling evoked by the symbol, and not from the "something" that is unknown. It is referred to as a sort of "verbal forgery."[16]

11. *Language as the Agency for Conceptualizing and Adjusting to Space and Time*

The function of language in transmitting knowledge across time and space points to another one of its boons. It enables men to overcome the limited time-and-space perspectives of the subhuman creatures. It is, in fact, man's means of mentally breaking through the space-time barrier. The possession of language has actually made it possible for human beings to "invent" space and time and the mental space-time world of conscious reason.

Space and time are both infinite. They cannot be "physical," and they cannot be empirically experienced. Nor are they "innate ideas." Both are *produced in* our minds; they are imaginative or creative constructions —"interpretative frames"—whereby we interpret those intangible aspects of nature that we "innerly sense" and must cope with in our every action. In brief, "space" and "time" are for us conceptualizations. But it is by means of our "kit of language" that both, in all their infinity, intangibility and abstractness become conceivable to us and capable of being discussed by us; that is how we are enabled to adjust to them.

The strategic place of language in the expression of "space" and "time" is brought out in the fact that both are very differently conceived, and enter into the life and thought of the speakers of different language communities in different ways, by virtue of the peculiar linguistic forms and structures through which they are expressed.

With respect to "space," different languages have very different means of expressing *extent,* and a different ability to provide *qualifications* of space. For example, the lack of adverbs on the one hand (or an abundance, on the other) is elemental in indicating the range of *shadings* of extent. The working concepts of "time," as they involve *duration, succession,* and *flow,* also differ as the result of differences in the languages. There are, for example, notable variations in the uses of tenses. We have the minute temporal distinctions which we recognize as "present," "present perfect," "past," "past perfect," "past future," "future," "future perfect," and "past future perfect." Some have only basic language forms, which indicate "past" and "present" and "future." We are able to indicate precisely "yesterday" and "tomorrow," while some languages permit only "now" and "not now." We can think of time in terms of its "continuity"; that is impossible in some other languages.

In general, the conceptualization of the nature and extent of phenomena, and of their location in both space and time takes place through linguistic devices. The preciseness or vagueness of these concepts depends upon the preciseness or abundance or lack of the linguistic devices—nouns, adverbs, adjectives, prefixes, suffixes, negatives—used to express them. Thus the language we speak is the basic factor in the way in which we *interpret* the world of spatial and temporal conditions and relations.

Language also enters into man's *use of and adjustment to* "space" and "time." In order for men to live with and in limitless *space,* several means of designating it are necessary. There must be markers, boundaries, units of measurement, directions, and distinction of areas. All of these must be conceptualized by means of symbols—which, in the last analysis, means that they must be verbalized. Also, all adjustment to space—all conformity to ends, and all use of instruments, procedures, directives, plans, policies, and programs—rests upon language. Finally, language makes it possible for men to control space, to use it, maintain contacts in it, and conduct all manner of enterprises across it.

Language has played an important part in enabling man to cope with the fourth dimension—*time,* the basic consideration in all becoming. Man lives in time, and all that he does takes place in time. However, while time is infinite, men endure in it for only an infinitesimal fraction of an instant. To attain some degree of adjustment to it and control over it, they must construct and maintain time systems which make possible the reckoning and measuring of time, and they must establish points of reference ("time-markers"), and means of locating and relating significant events of all kinds in the endless flow of time. But all of this is done by means of symbols, which are ultimately resolvable into language forms.[17]

Man has made striking gains as the result of the time-binding made possible by language. He is not only able to transmit experience in time beyond the life span of any individual, group, generation, society, or culture; he is also able to inhabit simultaneously the past (through legend, traditions, and formal records), the present and the future (by means of declared ideals, projections, anticipations, plans and programs). In fact, by his use of language, man can in some measure even control future events.

The great humane effect of language as the agency for the transmission of culture—especially knowledge and technology—across space and time, and hence as space-binder and time-binder, is that all men (potentially, if not actually) are in interaction with each other, either negatively or positively. Furthermore, every one can establish an association with his fellow men, one or many, near or far, dead, living or unborn.

12. *Language as the Medium for Man's Grasp of the Abstract and the Supernatural*

Related to the conceptualizing of space and time is the fact that, in general, it is by means of language that man develops all manner of abstractions, and becomes able to extend the horizon of his universe beyond the peripheries of nature's concrete physical laws—beyond the world of physically visible and tangible things and processes—and to reason about the subtler realities and the transcendent aspects of life. By means of conceptualization, he is able to develop and live in the abstract world of intellectual experience—the world of ethical, aesthetic, evaluational, teleological, spiritual, and supernatural considerations. For example, "goodness" as an ethical aspect, or "beauty" as an aesthetic characteristic, are not inherent in the event or the object; they are nonexistent, except in so far as we "perceive" and "conceive" them in terms of words. With language, we can wrestle with such perplexing questions as "truth" and "error," "right" and "wrong," "existential" and "transcendental." Words can stand for such abstractions as electricity, force, justice, time, space, future, deity—ideas which cannot possibly be represented by any visual picture. With language, we can reason about conduct and build a body of moral principles; we can discuss "causation" and possible "effect"; we can engage in the highly abstract handling of pure ideas that we find in mathematics; we can reason about the superhuman, the nature of deity, the hereafter and the eternal, and we can develop religious tenets and beliefs; we can develop and consider purposes and remote goals, and can imaginatively contrive programs and plans for their future achievement—all this, quite apart from any actual events.

It is only by means of language that the realms of the spirit have any definite and organized *being* at all; similarly, language is the basis of man's spiritual development. In fact, there is some validity to the contention that not only is spiritual development conditioned by language, but the scope of spiritual development rests in considerable part upon the scope and diversity of the vocabulary and the richness of the forms of linguistic construction, which in turn affect the range and diversity of the possible abstractions.

N O T E S

1 On this phase of language, see Chap. XI, Sect. 3. It should be pointed out that the definition of language as "a system of *words* and rules for combining words" is not entirely sound. For languages have been discovered and studied which manage quite well to get along without the kind of structural element to which our term "word" could apply. Most of the American Indian languages, for example, do not have words as "parts of speech," for every "word" is or can be a sentence. Cf. John P. Hughes, *The Science of Language* (New York: Random House, 1962), pp. 76, 78, 110. Our linguistic tradition and practice, as well as our historical and contemporary societal life generally, is that of the Indo-European languages, spoken today by more than one-third of the world's people; in these languages, the word is the first level of structure, and the sentences are built out of words and word groups.

2 The minimum complete communication is a sentence.

3 Cf. Ruth N. Anshen, in Anshen (ed.), *Language: An Inquiry into Its Meaning and Function* (New York: Harper & Brothers, 1957), p. 349.

4 The classes of words and their organization will be discussed in Chap. V, "Language as a Social Institution." On the place and function of words in general see: Otto Jespersen, *Mankind, Nation and Individual* (London: Allen & Unwin, 1946), 166–185; Bronislaw Malinowski, *Coral Gardens and Their Magic* (New York: American Book, 1935), Vol. II, pp. 52–62; Mario Pei, *The Story of English* (Philadelphia: J. B. Lippincott, 1952), pp. 234–244; Stephen Ullman, *Words and Their Use* (New York: Philosophical Library, 1951); Ernest Weekley, *The Romance of Words* (New York: Dover Publications, 1961).

5 Note the following: "A name is a tool for cutting a little slice out of the flux of experience and fixing it in attention." (Charles H. Cooley, Robert C. Angell and Llewelyn J. Carr, *Introductory Sociology* (New York: Scribner's, 1933), p. 41.) "The attachment of a name to various objects is like sticking a similar label on them. They are picked out from the bewildering chaos of the external world and grouped together." (Leonard R. Palmer, *An Introduction to Modern Linguistics* (London: Macmillan, 1936), p. 173. The social and societal significance of names will be dealt with in later chapters.)

6 Ernst Cassirer, *Language and Myth* (New York: Dover Publications, 1946), p. ix.

7 Colin Cherry, *On Human Communication: A Review, A Survey, and A Criticism* (New York: John Wiley, with Technological Press of M. I. T., 1957), pp. 76–77. Max Müller in his famous *Three Lectures* on "The Identity of Language and Thought" in 1887 presented his dictum: "No thoughts without words." At that time, it aroused much controversy; now it is quite generally accepted.

8 Morris M. Lewis, *Language in Society* (London: Thomas Nelson & Sons, 1947), p. 92.

9 Bertrand Russell, *Human Knowledge: Its Scope and Limits* (New York: Simon & Schuster, 1943), p. 60.

10 Cassirer, p. 28.

11 Cassirer, pp. 71–72.
12 When we, in our everyday experience, find something which has been heretofore unknown to us specifically designated, classified and conceptualized, we often say: "Why, that's a *fact,* isn't it!"
13 The use of the term "map" in this connection was developed by Korzybski, and thus has doubtless been suggested to others. Alfred Korzybski, *Science and Sanity* (New York: International Non-Aristotelian Publishing Company, 1948), p. 48. See also Irving J. Lee, *Language Habits in Human Affairs* (New York: Harper & Brothers, 1941), pp. xxiii, 15–25.
14 Charles Singer, *Technology and History* (London: Oxford University Press, 1952), pp. 8–9. See also C. Singer, E. J. Holmyard, and A. R. Hall, *A History of Technology* (Oxford: Clarendon Press, 1954), p. 18.
15 The sociocultural importance of "dead languages" will be dealt with in Chap. VI, Sect. 3.
16 Harry C. Bredemeier and Richard M. Stephenson, *The Analysis of Social Systems* (New York: Holt, Rinehart & Winston, 1962), pp. 7–8.
17 For Emile Durkheim's famous discussion of the "categories" of "space" and "time" (as well as other fundamental categories of knowledge) as products of collective elaboration and experience, see his *The Elementary Forms of Religious Life,* trans. Joseph W. Swain (New York: Macmillan, 1915), pp. 10–19, 436–442. On the relation of language to space and time see William H. Werkmeister, *A Philosophy of Science* (New York: Harper & Brothers, 1940), pp. 49–76, 126–129, 524; Joyce O. Hertzler, *Society in Action* (New York: The Dryden Press, 1954), pp. 44–48. On time, see Wilbert E. Moore, *Man, Time, and Society* (New York: John Wiley, 1963), pp. 3–68.

IV ❧ Language as a Social Phenomenon and Social Agency

Social linguists and philosophers of language, as well as social scientists, have concluded that language is "social" in its origin, nature, development, and function. Vendryes has referred to it as "the social fact par excellence."[1] The treatment in Chapter II of the basic concepts involved in language has also pointed in its every component and in its logical development to language as fundamentally a social phenomenon. Some of the more general social aspects will be briefly examined in the present chapter.

1. *Language as a Human Social Emergent*

Language has its biological and physical aspects, which involve, especially, the human speech organs, and its physical (especially acoustical) aspects, which involve the physical conditions that affect the traveling of sound waves until they reach the ear of the hearer. But the words and phrases into which the sounds are formed, the meanings attached to them, and the concepts developed by means of them are not automatic consequences of the fact that men are physical organisms, else all human beings everywhere would spontaneously talk as much alike as they walk alike, and a humanity-wide universality of words and meanings and concepts would prevail. Actually, as we shall note throughout this study, how each community or society talks and writes depends upon the *socially* established, standardized, and acquired sounds and marks. Moreover, while the physics of sound is certainly involved, men everywhere as technologists have mightily transformed the physical conditions, forces, and processes that affect the use and transmission of both human verbal sounds and mechanical sounds for communicative purposes. Thus, language is both *superorganic and superphysical.*

No particular natural language is something given or suddenly created intact. It is a purely historical heritage of the community: the continually emerging handiwork of many people through time, developed by means of a set of complicated social and cultural processes. As Kroeber has said: "The total aggregation of words, forms of grammar, and meanings which constitute any language are the cumulative and joint product of millions of individuals for many centuries past."[2]

No individual user of language is likely to have invented or constructed by himself more than a very few words or phrases in the language. The language that individuals speak and write comes to them ready-made, from myriad predecessors, from their immediate elders and peer groups, and from other fellow communicants of their language community. And the meanings of the words are socially achieved and assigned. Language is thus likewise *superindividual;* it is something enormously bigger and more significant than the speech of any individual man.[3] "Nobody made it; everybody made it."[4]

Finally, as will be noted at considerable length at different points in this study, language is itself a gradual product of social invention, variation, selection, borrowing, unconscious and conscious modification. It is the transmission of the whole societal and cultural history of the people (or peoples) who have spoken it, and is intelligible only in the light of this long, complex and locally varied history. Each language is a unique social-action pattern, and reveals a parallel unique social and cultural world. Language is a supreme example of Durkheim's "social representations."[5]

2. Language as the Instrument, Basic Form and Product of Social Behavior

Not only does language and its resultant forms of human activity, especially thought, furnish or constitute the atmosphere of social behavior; it is also the basic form, the indispensable primary instrument, and the signal product of social activity.

First, language is the primary instrument for communication; *as such, it is always social in its nature.* A linguistic transaction is never entirely an individual act; it is a matter of give-and-take, of influence back and forth between the people who use it. The transaction consists of three fundamental elements: at least one sender (speaker or writer), at least one receiver (listener, correspondent, audience), and the message, which is something the sender wishes to make known to the receiver. Related to this is the fact that the fundamental use of speech—for long, the primary aspect of language and the commonest use of speech through the ages—is a blend of the desire on the part of one human being to make himself understood by someone else, and the request for some kind of response, usually in the form of some kind of action, addressed by one person to another.[6] In the great majority of instances, the message involves something that is of mutual or reciprocal interest or concern, as between the interacting sender and receiver. Thus, a language has no separate existence: it is a functioning of certain *interacting* human beings; it is *shared behavior,* and a genuinely shared sociocultural phenomenon. In the same sense, all linguistic behavior is essentially social reciprocity. Furthermore, the language responses themselves are the result of association—of social stimulation and social response on the part of the members of the language community.

Second, as implied in the paradigm of Chapter II, *every language has its basis in the common experiences of its historical and contemporary users.* The language provides the generally accepted and more or less uniform identification, statement, classification, and interpretation of these experiences. It is the primary instrument in coping with them. The ability to assess, to reason about, and to transmit to posterity their successes and failures of comprehension and adjustment is a major factor in the existence of the members of the continuing group.

Third, the standard symbolic forms, vocal and written, that constitute a language, *are the result of long social usage.* A social usage, as Radcliffe-Brown has pointed out, can exist in reality *only* in a social system, since it is a set of *relations of interdependence.* Thus speech usages exist in reality and function properly only in so far as they prevail in an adequately organized social system.[7] "Correct" speech, whether in the general language of the language community or in the "special" languages of its subgroups, is established and maintained by the respective members. Thus each linguistic group has made its own language, and the language owes its form and development to their usage.[8]

The relation between a language and a people who speak it is so close that the two can scarcely be thought of apart. It could not have come into existence if human groups had not used it continuously in the past. This does not apply only or necessarily to the group in which it originated, but also to all groups that took it over as the result of contact, whether the contact was peaceful or hostile, and whether the acquisition was incidental, deliberate, or forced. A language lives and develops only so long as there are people who speak it, and use it as their native tongue. It is a collective construct and instrument.[9]

Fourth, a language is not only a matter of common usage, but *the prevailing usages are the result of common, although not necessarily conscious or formal, accord.* In its particular existent forms, a language has become agreed upon, endorsed, and accepted as required by the members of the community, as they have used it. The reasons for this are rather obvious. A language cannot exist with any degree of permanence, if it has only one speaker, or only a one-man interpretation of its symbols. Neither the word nor the meaning given it has an independent and self-sufficient existence. A word is a symbol, and the meaning of any symbol is assigned to it by the particular group or community using it. Thus the assemblage of linguistic symbols—language—cannot function normally unless the whole assemblage of its users use its symbols alike. The sounds become language when two or more—usually many —have given similar interpretations to the sounds. The standardization or conventionalization of meanings is thus a *result of consensus;* language is community-determined.

Sounds and meanings may differ widely in different languages. Three different languages may have very different words for the same object; for example, *tree, Baum, arbre.* Two languages may have very similar sounds, but with very different meanings and uses: for example, *pour* (French) and *poor* (English). But, in each language community, the specific meanings attached to specific sounds are identical and a matter of common property, not so readily accessible to the consciousness of speakers of *other* languages. In brief, words as social products can have meanings and directly suggest things and events *only* in their given society. At the same time, the conventional *meanings of the words* are social facts.

Finally, language has to be a collectively held and uniformly used instrument. Only thus can there be similar and mutually comprehensible and usable perceptions, definitions, classifications, and generalizations for all the individual members and separate groups of the community.

3. *Language as the Primary Social and Societal Instrumentality*

Not only does language come into existence as the result of stern social necessity; it is the basic and indispensable instrumentality in all social and societal life. Without language, there can be only the most limited communication; without communication, there can be no common human life or social action.[10] To be sure, sharing a common language does not guarantee participation in the community life of a given society. This is brought out in the distinction between a language community (discussed in the paradigm) and a societal system. A language community consists of a collectivity of people who speak a common language, and among whom a great amount of communication and a high degree of mutual intelligibility usually prevail. A societal system is an organized group, usually including a large number of people, which covers an extensive common area, and effectively operates as a distinctive and independent structural–functional entity. It is obvious that a language community and a societal system are not necessarily identical: as noted above, a language community may extend beyond the given societal system in which a common language is spoken; it may, in fact, extend over several societal systems (as in the case of the English language). However, every societal system must be a language community; that is, it must have a single language system as the instrument of all social participation within its area of functioning. Furthermore, any communication beyond that accomplished by means of reflexive and instinctive signs and gestures requires social organization—especially, as we shall see, in the form of regularized contacts and relationships. Conversely, the language system is the means by which the members of any social system refer to, interpret, justify, record and help maintain that social system. Moreover, all societal organization—that is, society as a structured and functioning mechanism—rests on language as the key agent of its composition, operation and maintenance. Says Warner: "It (language) is indispensable to the persistence of a social system and is inextricably interwoven with the structure of which it is a part."[11] Thus, just as language is a social emergent, a primary social product, and impossible without a social system, so a social system is impossible without language.[12] A society is a web of conduct and the actors composing it are bound together by various interchanges and reciprocal adjustments which individuals and groups make to one another. Language is the major device for such give and take.[13]

In similar vein, when we as members of a human society are without the right words (whether we lost them, or never made them, or never otherwise acquired them), or are for some reason unable to use them (because of ignorance, laziness, or physical or mental handicaps), we are not only communicatively but also socially paralyzed.

The main purpose of this study is to examine in detail the more important aspects of the interplay between language systems and social systems. At the moment, we wish merely to give the reader a most general orientation, so that he can have some notion of the place of the different special features in the whole picture and their relationship to each other.

The influence of any social system can extend only as far as its members have effective channels of communication. Thus language as the chief form of communication, in addition to its crucial significance in the structure and functioning of all social systems, is also a fundamental factor in determining the size of social groups, the range and character of the relations between the members, and the quantity, variety and quality of information available to them. There is also a definite relation between language, the size and kind of social structure and the pattern of social structure—that is, how people talk to each other under different relational conditions, for example, in small versus large groups, informal versus formal groups and so on. It is also significant that the larger the social unit, the more essential are mutually intelligible means of communication over the entire socially organized area.

Attention should also be called to the fact that, while all communication implies community of living, most communication for common living takes linguistic form; further, while effective communication is necessary for the proper functioning and maintenance of simple societies, it is even more crucial for the existence and survival of complex ones. This is what Lewis calls "The Linguistic Revolution," that is, "the increasing intervention of language in group life."[14] So much more communication is now necessary among so many more people, in ever more complex, and, of necessity, more highly organized relationships. These relationships involve very large numbers of people, and the messages and information have become of more and more universal significance. In modern society, language is ever more intimately interwoven into every form of group behavior.

Here are, very briefly, some of the more important general aspects of the relationship of language and social organization. Without communication, most human groups could not exist. If human beings are to live together—to function adequately as members of groups—

and to be organized into groups, there needs to be *consensus*: that is, men must have a body of common information regarding the essentials of individual and joint existence, but beyond that a certain community of interests and solidarity of beliefs, and a certain amount of understanding, agreement and shared knowledge as to common values and purposes and ends. This bridging of interhuman and intergroup space would be impossible without communication media which are comprehensible to, and used by, the great majority of the members. Even slightly or momentarily organized social structures must have a "communication network" that is coordinate and coextensive with the "group network."

Language is the medium through which human cooperation is brought about. It is the indispensable link in all concerted human action. By means of it, the diverse contributory activities of the people involved are coordinated and correlated with each other. In each joint action, there are certain essential ingredients, all of which rest upon language that is adequate to the various special subfunctions. There must be description and specification of what things are involved and what actions are to be engaged in. Goals and plans must be clearly formulated and transmitted to the personnel. Tactics and strategy must be discussed. The common procedures and techniques, the ways of using all instruments, must be formulated, stated openly and widely, and commonly understood. This involves also the transmission of procedural traditions, of knowledge of successful usages and utilizations, and of information on the nature and formation of skills. The specific actions required of all the specialized participants must be described and prescribed; rules and regulations must be formulated and announced and their enforcement supervised; instructions and directives or commands must be given; in more extensive and more formally organized cooperative undertakings, correspondence must be conducted, reports must be made and records kept. Not a single interest of any kind in this over-all joint undertaking can be represented without language.

Although language is not a *guarantee* of cooperation, it is an *essential* condition. Cooperation in the local community, as well as in the world as a whole, is perpetually being thwarted by limitations of language, by its variations within the community, and by the great number of and great differences among languages. Conversely, the richer and wider, the more complicated and intricate is the cooperation in the major functional areas of social life—economic, political, scientific, technological, but also philosophical, artistic, and religious—the greater is the need for diversified and accurate language.

With the establishment of written language and of the modern mechanical extensions of speech and writing, there can be complex, enduring and highly integrated organizations, or bodies of cooperating individuals and groups, extending far beyond the range of person-to-person contacts. Notable example would include not only such secondary forms of organization as states and nations, which conduct political action over wide areas, but also extensive associations which carry on economic production and exchange, religious activity, scientific and technological activity, and sports and other forms of recreation.

Language is the principal means of establishing rapport between members of a group, and the main instrument for maintaining that cohesiveness and solidarity of groups, upon which their durability and the free and effective cooperation of their members depends. As Park put it tersely, "People who speak the same language find it convenient to live together."[15]

Social solidarity is almost synonymous with *linguistic* solidarity. Language serves more effectively than any other social element to hold individuals together in social relationships. Identity of language almost automatically creates a definite bond of understanding and sympathy among people.

Language is also significant as a cohesive factor, in that it reflects and records a group's common historical experiences and transmits its traditions. Everywhere, also, language functions as the badge or *symbol* of the group; it is the major and obvious indicator of the group's identity and unity. By means of language, the "out-groups" are marked off from the "in-groups."

Often, when the integrity of a people is threatened—as when they are on the defensive against cultural, especially political, inroads—they become conscious of their language as one of their most distinctive characteristics. It comes to be a cherished thing, to be preserved at great cost, if necessary. Throughout history, ethnic and national groups have maintained their identity and cohesion by rigidly adhering to their common language. On the other hand, the spread of the majority language has always been one of the major elements in the assimilation of minorities, or of strangers, for that matter. Conversely, diversity of tongues has always been a serious barrier to cohesion and solidarity, as is evidenced in the relations not only of national and ethnic groups, but also of special groups and categories within a given society, with their different dialects, the sharp divergences among the languages of different social strata, the special languages (or sublanguages) of the different institutional systems and the different occupations and professions.

Language and society change reciprocally. Among the important sociocultural factors are demographic changes; changes in the organization and social institutions of the society, especially those induced by changes in the different technologies, the influence of innovative persons and "schools" and of social movements, and the appearance of new systems of ideas; finally, the manifold changes that come through contacts with other cultures, peoples and languages—as for example, through migration, exploration, travel, war and conquest, invasion and colonization.

Language is a great agency in socialization. The continuous instruction, indoctrination and training of the young and the newcomers to a society, as well as the constant reorientation of the entire population, which is essential to the society, obviously cannot be accomplished without language. The learning of words as part of the "apprenticeship to language" is a process of socializing the individual, making him a part of the conscious world inhabited by others who use the same language.

Related to the preceding social-organizational functions of language, and in a sense summarizing them, is its function in social control—that is, its role in regulating, directing, adjusting and organizing the social conduct of individuals and groups in the interest of effective societal operation. Social control is impossible without a linguistic system. This becomes apparent when we note some of the detailed essentials in the social-control process. The right kind of language is basic: (1) in understanding the prohibitions and requirements of behavior, (2) in presenting rules and directives, (3) in articulating public opinion behind these sanctions, and (4) in conducting the formal and informal agencies for administering and enforcing the sanctions. There is also a broader social-control aspect of language. Since language is the means by which people think and express their emotions and sentiments, control of the language, both oral and written, and its mechanical extensions, especially those involved in mass communication, implies control in some measure of *what* and *how* the people using the language feel and act. It is possible to control or at least to direct their interests and preoccupations, and to suggest the forms of responsive conduct. The efforts range from those engaged in during ordinary everyday conversation and address, through those of special pleaders, advertisers and propagandists, to the rulers of totalitarian countries.

One should not lose sight of the correlation between linguistic and societal stratification. The versions of the language used respectively by the different social strata have distinctive features. Equally significant is the part language plays as a reflector of social stratification, and as an agency in the maintenance of social distance and social position.

N O T E S

1 Joseph Vendryes, *Language: A Linguistic Introduction to History* (London: Kegan Paul, Trench, Trübner & Co., 1925), p. xiv.

2 Alfred L. Kroeber, *Anthropology* (New York: Harcourt, Brace & Co., 1948), p. 255.

3 "Superorganic" and "superindividual," as here used, are the terms used by Kroeber, pp. 222–223, 255. Note also the following statement: "Language is neither root nor trunk, but flower and fruit of social life. It is therefore in a sense super-social." Karl Vossler, *The Spirit of Language in Civilization* (London: Routledge & Kegan Paul, 1951), p. 187.

4 William G. Sumner and Albert G. Keller, *The Science of Society* (New Haven: Yale University Press, 1927), Vol. I, p. 161.

5 Émile Durkheim, *Rules of Sociological Method* (Glencoe, Ill.: Free Press, 1938), pp. 2, 14, 82.

6 When a person talks to himself, argues with himself, reasons or thinks by himself, he acts as if he were conversing as one person to another.

7 Alfred R. Radcliffe-Brown, *A Natural Science of Society* (Glencoe, Ill.: Free Press, 1957), p. 57.

8 Note the trenchant statement of the fact that men's usage makes language by Walt Whitman in 1885: "Language is not an abstraction of the learned or of the dictionary-makers, but is something arising out of the work, needs, ties, joys, affections, tastes, of long generations of humanity, and has its bases broad and low, close to the ground." From "Slang in America," in *The Complete Poetry and Prose of Walt Whitman,* with Introduction by Malcolm Cowley (New York: Pellegrini & Cudahy, 1948), Vol. II, pp. 420–424.

9 The recluse may, of course, talk only to himself, but he does it with a language developed and used by and learned from others.

10 Cf. Talcott Parsons, "Language as a Groundwork of Culture," in T. Parsons, E. Shils, K. D. Naegle and J. R. Pitts, (eds.), *Theories of Society: Foundations of Modern Sociological Theory* (New York: The Free Press of Glencoe, Inc., 1961), Vol. II, pp. 971–976 (976).

11 W. Lloyd Warner, *American Life: Dream and Reality* (Chicago: University of Chicago Press, 1953), p. 153.

12 Cf. Talcott Parsons, *The Social System* (Glencoe, Ill.: Free Press, 1957), p. 34. In a recent article on "Evolutionary Universals in Society," *American Sociological Review,* 29 (June, 1964), 339–357 (340–342), Parsons has analyzed "evolutionary universals" in the social world. By these he means the organizational developments "hit upon" in human societies that initially provide them with major adaptive advantages over societies not developing them— "an integrated set of evolutionary principles at even the earliest human level." The four features are religion, technology, social organization through kinship, and communication with language. "No known society has existed without *all* four in relatively definite relations to each other. In fact, their presence constitutes the very minimum that may be said to mark a society as truly human." Religion embodies the "main *cultural patterns* that regulate the social, psychological and organic levels of the total system of action" (p. 342). "Technology clearly is the primary focus of the organization of the adaptive relations of the human system to its physical *environment.*" Kinship, which seems to be the evolutionary origin of *social organization,* is "the social extension of the individual *organism's* basic articulation to the species through bisexual repro-

duction." Finally, "cultural and symbolic communications are integral to the human level of individual *personality* organization"; "social relations among personalities, to be distinctively human, must be mediated by linguistic communication" (p. 342). Of the language "pattern" of orientation, Parsons further states: ". . . since a cultural system—never any more an individual matter than a genetic pattern—is shared among a plurality of individuals, mechanisms of *communication* must exist to mediate this sharing. The fundamental evolutionary universal here is language: no concrete group lacks it" (p. 341).

13 "The first and prime instrumentality for the exchange of anything between human beings is language." Sumner and Keller, p. 60.
14 Morris M. Lewis, *Language and Society* (London: Thomas Nelson & Sons, 1947), pp. 94–111 (96).
15 Robert E. Park, *The Immigrant Press and Its Control* (New York: Harper & Brothers, 1922), p. 51.

V ❦ Language as a Social Institution

1. The General Place and Nature of Social Institutions

Any society as a "going concern"—that is, as a fairly effective systematized scheme of social life—consists of a master network of social institutions. These are the great clusters of established, accepted and implemented ways of behaving socially. They are the basic working parts of the social organization of the society, the basis of its orderly operation, maintenance and regulation. The major structural–functional departments of social life—communicative, scientific–technological, familial, economic, political, educational, religious, esthetic, health, recreational, welfare—are each an institutionalized sector. They encompass every important field of human relationships and activities. The level of the effectiveness of a society's operation—in the last analysis, its perpetuation and survival—depends upon the adequacy in number and kind, as well as in quality and coordination, of performance of the institutions constituting the over-all system.

The social scientists have discovered that the readiest and most comprehensive, as well as most revealing and accurate, way to envisage the salient features of the social organization of any society under examination is to understand its major institutions and the relations between them. They supply a distinguishing "profile" to a given society, and provide the key elements for the comparative analysis of different societies.

The ubiquity, persistence, and universality of social institutions in every known society—primitive, ancient, medieval, and contemporary —point to certain conditions and situations among mankind which make them imperative. The behavior of individuals and groups in the different departments of social life cannot be haphazard, eccentric, and uncertain; it must be patterned and structured, expectable and predictable—in short, "institutionalized." When social behavior is institutionalized, the people of the society are capable of functioning together systematically and effectively. In fact, the ultimate objective of all social institutions is the establishment and maintenance of the rules and practices essential to human existence.

An institution is a complex structural–functional agency, comprising both intangible and tangible constituents. It consists, *first,* of a *body of norms or rules,* both of positive and prohibitive intent, governing the correct behavior of the actors. *Second, these behavioral directives and expectations are expressed concretely as roles,* or patterned forms of action, in the different types of social positions, relations and situations. *Third, the role performances, as set by the rules, are sanctioned*—that is, behavior according to the rules is approved and rewarded in various ways, while behavior in violation of the rules is frowned upon and penalized. *Fourth,* the actors are aided in performing correctly by *a combination of conformity-producing social usages and procedures, implementing social organizations, symbolic materials and, in most instances, physical equipment.*

A particular institution which has been conceptualized by most of the population of the society is a "model." It sets up ideal–typical goals as to what is "legitimately expected," and is an ideal–typical means of coping with typical situations and relations. The actual performance, as in the case of anything existential, is at some variance with the model. The institution is also a "system" in itself at any given time, quite apart from its particular, momentary members, or participants or beneficiaries. The individuals performing according to its requirements come and go; they may die and be forgotten. The rules and regulations, the conventions and traditions and the associational forms may change. But the institution, as a complex entity of established expectations, requirements, procedures and sociocultural features, with durable social structurings and persistent functions to perform—that goes on.

While each major institutional system has to take care of its own particular area of human–social life, all institutions perform certain general types of function. Thus (1) institutions function as *the operative bases of the social order.* Most of the activities essential to the operation of a society are presided over and conducted by means of institutions. There is much point to the statement that very few of the actively functioning institutions of a given community or society could be withdrawn or eradicated without impairing the operation of the community or society. (2) The institutions are the particular societal mechanisms whereby *all of the major and imperative forms of regulation are conducted.* It is by means of most of the major categories of institutions that societies forestall such behavior of individuals and groups as is likely to impair social order and operation, and also assure themselves that there will be a sufficiency of positive socialized and societally necessary behavior. The controls that institutions exercise by means of their norms and roles and sanctions operate both internally and externally; they are omnipresent, universal and enforced. (3) Institutions also serve not only as regulators but also as *conditioners and socializers of human beings and as motivators, guides and directors of the behavior of individuals.* The institutions surround an individual like an atmosphere and influence him all his life, shaping his values and cultivating in him unconscious habits of conformity and functional proficiency (and sometimes inefficiency or "trained incapacity"). They embody the standard expectations of what is essential as behavior in most of the major departments of life, and act as an impetus to appropriate action. Related to this is the fact that institutions *tell the individual how to act;* they provide the avenue along which individuals can safely adjust themselves to other individuals and to the groups to which they belong. (4) Institutions function as *the carriers of the society's culture.* In them are found most of the outstanding creative cultural elements that the centuries, with their inexorable testing and selective processes, have permitted to endure and develop. (5) Finally, social institutions function as *preserving and conserving agencies in social life.* They express and protect the values and most of the other precious gains of human and social experience and, since their function is to establish and maintain order, they are, of necessity, conservative in their outlook and effect. Furthermore, as group habits, they cause change to take place gradually, and without seriously disturbing men's ways of life.

2. *Language Viewed as a Social Institution*

Language is here treated as a human institution. In this respect, it is viewed from a distinctly sociological perspective. This is a social-scientific way of noting its standardized, organized structural and operational features, as it serves as a basic and universal agency in every community and society.

Language is an institution, and institutions are sociocultural systems. "System" refers to some orderly combination or arrangement of parts into a whole which, in turn, is more than a conjunction, aggregate, or chance assembly of parts, more than a mere sum of the parts. Although the parts are identifiable, and although they may be semi-autonomous, they are coherent, coexistent, interdependent or complementary, interacting and consistent with each other, mutually and reciprocally variable; they constitute a whole and produce an over-all unity of function. The plural parts or elements are usually more or less differentiated, even heterogeneous; they are structured—that is, they jointly constitute a configuration or patterned relationship of functionally interacting components. As long as the system exists, there is a relative equilibrium of elements internally and externally with other systems. Systems have relative constancy, identity, and stability of existence, as well as orderliness and regularity of operation. Systemic organization makes possible the repetition and prediction of the same events or actions.[1]

Language as a social system (as contrasted, for example, with a natural astronomical or physiochemical organism or assembly) is a constructed, even though not planned, human institution. It is learned by the members of the community, firmly established in their communicative behavior, and involved in most of their other social behavior. It is voluntarily, not instinctively, engaged in as a form of action.

In order to be able to perform both its general and its specific social functions, language *must* be institutionalized. It *must* have a high degree of regularity, unity, and stability of form and procedure. Its signs and symbols, singly and in combination, must be so uniform and universal that they are generally comprehensible and reproducible in sufficiently similar forms in all parts of the language community, among all segments of its population, tomorrow as well as today. The symbols must have approximately the same signification and meaning for the members in all the types of situation to which they relate. Finally, all the language components must be used in approximately the same ways—that is, they must have stable configurations, articulations and relationships. To be sure, no language can remain entirely constant; at the same time, its forms, meanings and usages cannot be erratic, haphazard or ephemeral. Only through institutionally established language can large numbers of users, spread over great areas of the earth, convey fairly precise meanings to each other as they transmit a great variety of messages, adjust to each other, and carry on all other kinds of reciprocal and joint activities.

Thus *every* language is a durable, highly organized system, resolvable into common types of structural and functional components. The forms and organization which it takes, and the processes whereby it carries on its functions, have developed across space and time, through internal variation, addition, selection, reorganization, and the modifications that develop out of its transmission from generation to generation and its contacts with other cultures and languages. Thus every language, as a functional agent, is unavoidably complex and intricate. But, as the more or less efficient and adequate instrument that it is, it is also highly regularized and systematic; it has, in fact, the systematization and established character of all durable and efficient institutions.[2]

Thus, a language is not a merely accidental collection of elements and processes. Just as in a family system, in which every person has his place as father or mother, as child or grandchild, as aunt or uncle with the correlated standard responsibilities and roles, so in a language community every person, as he engages in language behavior, must observe the standard form, function and relationships of every linguistic element. If he fails to do this, he fails to communicate and thereby ceases to be a part of the social going concern. The systematization of language is what gives it consistency, coherence, continuity and general comprehensibility among its users. It makes possible a *universe of discourse.*

Language as an institutional system is first and foremost a systematic complex of well-elaborated principles, norms and rules, tacitly and largely unconsciously accepted and conformed to by all the users of the language. These principles, norms and rules have to be complied with at every level and in every structural–functional division and subdivision of language, wherever thought is to be expressed, communicated or understood. Second, as people perform according to the guidelines set by the rules, they employ sets of usages and procedures which also make language a set of relations of interdependence that amounts to a system of behavioral control. The specific acts of speech of the participants in a speech exchange consist of certain standardized sets of behavior. In fact, the function of linguistic rules, like the rules of other institutions, is to develop appropriate language behavior—behavior which has become habitual. Thus, fundamentally, a language is "a body of speech usages" conducted "in terms of a set of rules."[3] In sum, each language has its essential, regularized and conventionally used rules or codes, its accepted and required structural forms or modes of combining its elements, its modes and instruments of performance, and its widely accepted meanings. As Keller puts it, dramatically, "The great wonder, when one comes to realize it, is that language, built up premeditatively by millions of unthinking and casual users, shows a regularity and orderliness . . . comparable to the regularity of the solar system."[4] The variations and "specialties" of usage by families, cliques, social classes, occupational groups, regions and educational levels within the language community cannot depart too widely from the "standard," or their speech becomes so eccentric as to be useless. To speak or write a language "correctly" is to do so according to its codes; learning a language involves learning the related linguistic codes.

In brief, the language institution of a people comprises a more or less consistent, coherent, coded and patterned set of elements. These are standardized in forms, usages and meanings. The fact that each language has its own identifying *standard features* makes possible both the classification and the comparison of languages.

3. *Peculiarities of Language as an Institution*

While language shows most of the common features of institutions, it also has several peculiarities. First, in spite of its social importance and its indispensability in the life of individuals and in the functioning of groups, small and large, *its users* (the speakers and writers of the language community) *are largely unconscious of it as a factor in regulating their lives*. In this respect language as an institution is unlike, for example, those omnipresent political, administrative and judicial arrangements that more or less forcibly impose their authority and sanctions; it is unlike the continual awareness on the part of the believers in a religious system of the necessity of abiding by its dictates, or unlike the much stressed requirements of the code of sex regulation, along with the widespread consciousness and policing involved. Of course, when a language is imposed upon a people by conquerors, or in some other situation involving obligatory acceptance, then there is consciousness of it, not however as a regulatory social institution, but as a tool of oppression or a badge of subservience. This is usually a temporary matter, for if the enforced use of the language persists, it is likely that succeeding generations will have become assimilated to it and unconscious and passive users of it.[5]

Second, as de Saussure pointed out, language as an institution has a *higher degree of immutability than most other institutions*. Like almost all institutions, it is the product of historical forces; like some other institutions, it resists arbitrary modification. In each institutional area, there is a different proportion between fixed tradition and the free action of the members of the society in acting institutionally. But, for several reasons, language in the main is more fixed and less free than other institutional systems. Reflection does not enter into its active use. As just noted, the speakers are largely unconscious of the rules and other requirements of their language; if aware, they do not know how to modify them. Furthermore, as a system dominated by arbitrary and (to the average person) abstract codes, language lacks the necessary bases for discussion. In a society like ours, there is much more or less rational criticism, much private and public discussion and controversy about the rules and usages and reasonableness of many institutions, for example, sexual and marital, economic, political, health, educational. There is almost no criticism of language as an institution, except among the numerically negligible specialized linguists. This situation is due in part to the complexity of the language system, a complexity which can be grasped only through reflection. The great masses who use the language daily are ignorant of its complexity and, even for those somewhat informed, the complexity discourages innovation, except in regard to vocabulary. There is, in fact, a collective inertia toward innovation.[6]

Finally, while language too is a product of human experience, it is distinctive in that *it is the organized way of registering, communicating and recording human experience itself,* while other institutions are organized ways that have developed out of experience, for conducting the different types of regulatory and maintenance operations.

4. *The Institutional Features of Language: Its Systemic Organization*

We are here presenting in barest outline the elemental and basic features of language as an institutionalized social system operating effectively for human communicative purposes.[7] Such a minimal elementary knowledge of the nature and operation of the language system as will be provided is essential to the treatment and understanding of the sociological perspectives, facts, and principles relating to language.[8]

In this examination, we are not interested in *what* is communicated, but primarily in the *vehicle* of communication: the complex structural instrument as it is composed and ordered or patterned, as its parts are functionally interrelated, as its main message-carriers have meaning and as it is societally implemented and maintained, particularly in civilized societies. We are mainly concerned with what has been previously referred to as "internal," "static," or "synchronic" linguistics in contrast to "external," "historical," or "diachronic" linguistics.[9]

The major categories of basic *elements* of language are, as far as we know, well-nigh universal.[10] The language families and the separate languages within the families differ, of course, as far as details are concerned. There is not, however, complete agreement as to the major *divisions of study*. Vendryes presents, as headings of the three relevant parts of his book, sounds, grammar and vocabulary; Entwistle also distinguishes "the three different elements of language: sounds, grammar and vocabulary," though he also stresses "stylistics."[11] Carroll, as noted in the Introduction, has a more extensive list of the "branches of linguistics" as a sort of synthesis of the recent dominant points of view, but it resolves itself fundamentally into an analysis of vocal sounds, of the study of morphology, of syntax, and of lexicography.[12] In his recent book, Pei mentions "four divisions of language, phonology (or sounds), morphology (or grammatical forms), syntax (or word arrangement) and vocabulary (or words)."[13] The traditional approach regarding the "parts of speech," according to Hughes, "assumes that the phenomena comprising any language can be classified in one or another of four categories, according as they concern: (1) the sound-units making up the syllable; (2) the structural units making up the words; (3) the syntactic units (words or word groups) making up the simple, compound or complex sentences, and (4) the inventory of words in use in the language." The traditional names for these categories, which he follows in his book, are Phonology, Morphology, Syntax, and Lexicon (or Dictionary). He notes that the first three are often treated together in one book called *the grammar,* and the last in a separate book called *the dictionary.*[14]

We should keep in mind the fact, however, that these divisions or levels of analysis, whatever they might be most logically, are merely means arbitrarily established by professional language students for clarity of treatment of the makeup and of the understanding of the operation of language as a whole. As de Saussure and Vendryes have pointed out, any distinction drawn between sounds, grammatical forms and words, or any other categorization of apparent elements, is an artificial distinction. Different as the types of elements may seem, as Vendryes puts it, "they are intimately connected, and have no separate existence. They melt into the unity which is language itself." Similarly, de Saussure asserts that "Forms and function are interdependent and it is difficult, if not impossible, to separate them." With respect to the conventionally accepted major divisions of grammar—morphology and syntax—he notes, "Linguistically, morphology has no real, autonomous object. It cannot form a discipline distinct from syntax," and he adds

". . . it is not logical to exclude lexicology from grammar." "Morphology, syntax, and lexicology interpenetrate because every synchronic fact is identical."[15]

There is a hierarchy of interdependences: the human vocal sounds selected for the given language are significant only when they are combined into speech forms that convey meanings; these forms and arrangements are of no significance in message conveyance until they are organized as phrases and sentences; the phrase and sentence structures must have words of different functional classes. As Carroll has pointed out, there is also a hierarchy of units developing from the smallest sound units (the phonemes) into morphemes, from morphemes to phrase types and words, from words to the larger units of clause and sentence patterns which draw on the entire dictionary and make possible involved statements.[16]

From the point of view of language as a system, it should be kept in mind that the conditions of the functioning of language manifest themselves in the establishment of certain equilibria in the phonetic, grammatical and lexical materials that maintain the language state at any given time. At the same time, and of particular sociological significance, is the fact that linguistic phenomena—grammatical and lexical—realize themselves in the framework of social events.[17]

a / The organization of the unit sounds. Language in its concrete, observable aspect is human speech, and *the vocal sounds produced by human beings are the basic material of the systematic oral articulation called speech.*[18] These sounds in themselves, however, do not constitute speech or language. By themselves they are physical phenomena—merely "noises," without human relevance or cultural existence. Nevertheless, the utilization of *some* of them in some organized form or manner by human beings in their patterned schemes of utterance makes their examination a fundamental step in linguistic study.[19]

Every language employs only a small proportion of the thousands of distinguishable sounds that man is physiologically and physically capable of making with his vocal apparatus. Furthermore, the sound signals used in any given language are not a haphazard array or a blur of vocal noises. To become effective elements of the language system, the sounds must themselves be systematized. Those that are to be used as the signal elements must first be selected, in a limited number, and then, in effect, agreed upon by the members of the speech community. They are thus usually peculiar to that language or language family. These selected sounds are then combined conventionally and organized into various patterns, ranging from simple to complex, to which are arbitrarily assigned a variety of expressional and communicative functions and meanings. In their different organized and meaningful forms—such as morphemes, words, clauses, phrases, sentences and sequences of sentences—they come under the regulatory jurisdiction of language in the sense of language as coded utterance.

The production of sounds rests first on certain anatomical and physiological factors involving human speech facility. For his phonetic apparatus, man has his lips, oral cavity, tongue, teeth and the uvula of his mouth; his nasal chamber; his facial muscles, the vocal chords and muscles of his throat; and his diaphragm. As he breathes in and breathes out air past his lips, past the teeth and tongue, into the throat, past the vocal chords, through the nasal passages, he creates vibrations of the air in the form of articulate sounds differing in kind and intensity. These sounds can be recorded and measured today, thus permitting experimentation, with the aid of modern instruments and techniques, such as tapes, phonograph records, stroboscopes, and oscillographs.

The particular sound features agreed upon as significant in any given language—the ones that give it its own phonetic distinctiveness as compared with another language—are limited in number; in fact, they are surprisingly few. This is because a very large number would be impossible to remember and too cumbersome to be of service. They can be noted as distinctive acoustic elements recurring in recognizable and relatively constant shapes in any successive utterance in the language. The speakers of the language of a given speech community have learned how to produce and recognize them in their current speech. Speakers of any language may first become aware of them as distinctive features of their own language when they listen to a strange language being spoken.[20]

The sounds of speech are broken up into segments distinguishable from each other. The minimal sound feature or sound unit which carries distinctiveness (but not meaning), and into which any given flow of speech in a given language can be analyzed, is called a *phoneme*. The phoneme has been referred to as "the linguistic atom."[21] It is a closely coherent group or bundle of sounds consisting of one or (sometimes) more frequent *phones* or *chief sound members* (also called *segmental phonemes*), together with other related phones or *allophones,* which are the *variants* or the variable members of the phoneme (also called *supra-segmental phonemes*). The phones or segmental phonemes are produced in particular places in the mouth, and the variants, allophones, or supra-segmental phonemes, take shape near this position.[22] While the number of possible phonemes is almost infinite, the number of phonemes actually employed in the different languages of the world varies from approximately fifteen to fifty, each language having its own phonemic pattern.[23] English, for example, has 44 or 45, a high number, while French and German have 35 or 36.

Phonemes are usually divided into consonants and vowels; some, however, lie midway between consonants and vowels. Some languages have heavy consonant clusters—that is, sequences of several contiguous clusters. Others tend to have no consonant clusters but rather an alternation of consonants and vowels.[24]

In English there are 33 minimal segmental phonemes, including 9 vowels, 21 consonants, and 3 semivowels (*h, w,* and *y*). In the normal enunciation of our speech, there is also a set of 12 suprasegmental phonemes, consisting of 4 levels of *pitch* or *tone,* 4 degrees of *stress* or *accent of loudness,* and 4 lengths of *pause* or *juncture* between the phonemes and their combinations, in the form of morphemes, word linkages, and sentences.[25] "Thus," states Warfel, "there are 45 phonemes in English. All that can be said in the language results from combinations of these 45 phonemes, just as all that can be written can be transliterated into 26 alphabetic letters, a unit of space, and 12 punctuation marks, a total of 39."[26]

The phonemes in any given language are closely allied to each other. They constitute a coherent and closely knit system, remarkable for its simplicity, in which all the parts fit together. This means that a language is not simply made up of phonemes, but is a *system of phonemes.* Each language has a phonemic system peculiar to itself, which has its own regularity and continuity.[27] As the result of this basic phonemic system, the speakers of the language of a given speech community use the same array of phonemes; hence, each such speaker is at least partly identifiable by his set of sounds and the timbre of his voice. Thus, when a foreign speaker reproduces the phonemes of our language sufficiently well to be understood, and yet does not enunciate certain finer distinctive features (for example, in English, the distinction between the phonemes *p* and *b*) as well as the habitual users, we say that he speaks with a "foreign accent."

In the organization of the total linguistic system, the system of phonemic production does two very important things: (1) it provides the kit of select speech sounds which are combined into the vocabulary units and the ordered and patterned arrangements of the language; (2) with its patterned arrangements of pitch, stress, pause or time, and juncture, it gives the language its intonational pattern.

Given the kit of basic sounds for the given language, its essence, as the comprehensive and precise instrument of communication, is the body of its principles and rules—its "constitution and bylaws," its reigning statutes and ordinances, its corpus of "laws"—whereby it constructs its meaningful arrangements of the standard sounds, and combines these meaning units as partial and complete utterances. This area of language study is known as grammar; as usually conceived, grammar encompasses the entire patterning of language. The purpose of the codification and standardization imposed by grammar is to give language its basic structuring, without which it could not operate as an over-all medium of communication. Without the codes governing its constructions and processes, we could neither contrive (encode) messages as conceivers and senders, nor convey messages of current comprehension in the community nor, finally, could we take apart and interpret (decode) messages as receivers.

With this grammatical structuring, however, the patterning of utterance is so clear and complete that one can diagram it in terms of its types of constituent words, phrases and clauses, and the relationship of these to each other. What is more, by fitting the various forms into the pattern established by the rules governing the different types of relationships, one can say things never heard before and never rehearsed, and yet be perfectly understood by all those who know the rules.[28]

While the grammars of the different languages furnish the same or similar answers to the same or similar needs, each language has its grammar, and linguists agree that there is no universal grammar. Each language has its own scheme, its peculiar patterns and regularities, which are evidenced concretely by what its users do with it. Furthermore, there is nothing fixed or final about the grammar of any given language; while it cannot tolerate massive changes in a short time and still serve its purpose, it is changing continually, as may be seen by periodical comparisons.

In the following discussion, we shall note the major related subdivisions of language analysis, the grammatical constructions and procedures that are *morphological,* and those that are *syntactic.*

b / The morphological organization. The selected and established distinctive perceptual vocal sounds of a given language—its particular system of phonemes—are *organized into meaning-carrying units.* The study of this area of linguistics is called morphology. Its function in language study corresponds to that branch of biology which treats of the form and structure of living organisms; the term is also employed in connection with the formation of geological structures. In the case of linguistic structural analysis, the basic morphological units are morphemes and words.

[1] *Morphemes.* Morphemes are composed of phonemes. A morpheme is analyzable into one or a small number of phonemes; it cannot be resolved into smaller units of structure which embody grammatical or lexical meaning (for example, the *boy-* and *-ish* in *boyish*), and it has no likeness in sound or meaning to any other language form.[29] The crucial point is that the morpheme is the current significant or meaningful element or unit of language.[30] Where one phoneme functions as a morpheme, it may be either a consonant or a vowel; where several phonemes function as such, it is a sequence of phonemes. It may be a word or part of a word—that is, several morphemes may be arranged as a word. Singly or in different combinations in different grammatical contexts, morphemes enable us to express any lexical or semantic meaning.[31]

[2] *Words.* Morphemes are the structural units out of which words are formed. But words are *not linguistic units.* Words are the autonomous, arbitrarily constructed and established, *conventional segments of utterance or discourse,* the smallest units of thought and sense vocally expressible.[32] Every utterance can be divided into successive meaningful portions, and each such portion may be called a word. A word results from the association of a meaning that has been fixed and accepted by convention—it functions as a *counter of thought*—with a given complex of sounds. There are languages that do not have the kind of linguistic structure to which our term "word" applies, either for completeness of form or for precision of meaning.[33] However, the greater proportion of the world's languages, and the majority of the languages most familiar to us, do have words. The Indo-European languages, of which ours is one, have words, as do the somewhat related Semitic and Ural-Altaic languages, and the present speakers of these languages constitute approximately three fourths of the world's population. For them, the existence and usage of words is of the utmost importance.[34]

A fundamental aspect of the arrangement of morphemes into words has to do with the *free* and *bound* forms (to use the terminology established by Bloomfield).[35] A *free* form of morpheme can occur by itself as a single word; thus *man, book, book* of the word *book-s, book-* and *-mark* of the word *bookmark,* are words consisting of a free form of morpheme. A morpheme of *bound* form cannot occur independently as a word, but only within a word, as part of a word; it has meaning only as attached to the free form. Thus *-s* in *books, -ing* in *writing, -er* in *writer, -ly* in *manly, -ed* in *played, -al* in *personal* are all bound morphemes, significant only in so far as they are bound to the free morphemes of the respective words. Very many words are combinations of free and bound morphemic forms.

[3] *Construction of words.* The morphological processes whereby morphemes are combined to form words are of significance in the understanding of the structuring of words and their place in a linguistic system. These processes differ even among the languages of a given language family. We are mainly concerned with our language, an Indo-European language which is an inflecting (or flexional) language. It is to be distinguished from the "wordless" (polysynthetic or incorporating) languages mentioned above. It is also different in word structure from the other types of languages with words—namely, the analytical or isolating languages, such as Chinese—where every syllable is a word and, conversely, all words are monosyllabic; or the agglutinative languages, such as the Ural-Altaic family, in some respects akin to the polysynthetic languages, in which the constituent morphemes are relatively distinct and constant, marked off from each other and independent of each other in the chain of speech.

Each language that has words has its own manner of word construction. The morphemes that make up a word are never placed by chance, but according to definite patterns. In the pattern, however, there is always the *root* or free form, plus (in most classes of words) the bound forms that give it its distinctive significance.

While our language, like others, has its standard patterns of word structure, the linguists differ somewhat as to the major categories of word-construction processes, and also as to what they include in a given category.[36] For our language, there seem to be two main categories of patterns of words, the *compounds* and the *derived* words, although some scholars attempt to draw a distinction between the processes of derivation and inflection, and to set up a third category to cover the inflectional process.

Compound words are the product of the composition process, which produces compound words by the juxtaposition of free morphemic elements. The two or more elements combined can (and generally do) occur as independent words. Thus, for example, we may have words compounded of two or more nouns (*animal-trainer, bookcase, hearthstone, doghouse*), or of an adjective and a noun (*hothouse, blackbird*), or of other combinations; in fact, there are almost limitless possibilities. Compounding is one of the chief means a language has of increasing its stock of words.

Derived words are made up of *free* morphemes, the message-carriers, and the remaining morphemes, all of which are *bound* forms. The one category, produced by affixation, attaches affixes—prefixes, infixes, and suffixes—all of them bound forms, to the root form or base. *Pre-*

fixes are placed *before* the root: *be-* in *beyond, in-* in *inflate, over-* in *overdrive. Infixes* are placed *within* the base: *-n* in *sta-n-d. Suffixes* are placed *after* the base or already existing word: *-ness* in *goodness, -er* in *harder, -er* in *driver, -ic* in *atomic.*

By derivation, a single basic stem may be extended to form a family of related words—a family of words with a common basic sense, each word having some nuance of meaning. By the use of affixes we may get, for example, using *cycle* as the base: *bi-cycle, cyclical, en-cyclic-al,* or, with *stable* as a base, such a family as *unstable, stability, instability, stabilize, stably.*

Another category of derived words, overlapping with those produced by affixes, is obtained by adding inflectional endings to the stem or root. These endings are intended to give the word a specific role in a grammatical pattern and to fit it in with the other words in that pattern. The words thus formed express additional information or some significant modification of basic information, particularly such as to mark distinctions which depend upon the different form-classes of words and the different languages, of case, gender, number, tense, person, mood, and voice. Thus, for nouns, for example, *-s* is added to *book* to indicate the plural, while *-ess* in *actress* and *-ine* in *heroine* indicate feminine gender.[37]

c / The syntactical organization. In the languages familiar to us, words, whatever their structural forms, are the first level of meaning-carriers. They must be built up first, before they can become aids in communication. But they cannot be uttered or written in helter-skelter fashion, or combined at random, if they are to convey a message. They have communicative significance only in their linguistic context—that is, in their relationships and positions with respect to each other, as expressional forms within the whole utterance. Thus every language has a system of ordering and systematically arranging its different functional types or classes of words into more or less complete and patterned structures—notably phrases, clauses, and sentences—which have meanings as wholes. This system of structuring is known as *syntax.* The essence of syntactical usage—that is, syntax in its operational aspect—is to speak or write "correct" or "standard" language. This correct usage is achieved by conforming to the basic principles and rules of composition, sometimes referred to as the "traffic rules of language." Syntax is literally "taking together": words properly "taken together" are significant; they are means of expressing complete concepts. The meaning of the whole is determined by the plan and functional unity of the parts. Sequences of words which violate the rules—for example, *jealousy monkey live*—lead to misunderstanding and, in many instances, to utterly meaningless utterances. As Hughes notes, every linguistic utterance has a structure; certain principles determine which words may occur in it, and the forms and order in which they may occur. Each word has a function in the structure, which it would not fulfill if it were differently placed.[38]

[1] *The sentence.* The definite structure of an utterance is always one pattern of words, or a combination (sequence) of a few basic patterns, of words. This structure has been traditionally called the "sentence." It has been stated that the *true unit of speech* is "neither the individual sound nor the individual word, but the sentence."[39] It may consist of a single word or a group of words; in either case, it expresses a complete concept and a unitary idea. The standard fractional or incomplete utterances have generally known meanings. While they usually stand for sentences, they have omitted one or more words of what would be the fully stated concept. For example, "Good morning" stands for "I wish you a good morning"; "No Parking" means "No parking here" (or "on this side," or "at this place"). Some imperatives (commands), such as "Run!" "Down!" "Go!" "Come!" and ejaculations ("Hi!" or most of the expletives) stand for sentences. Some questions and expressions of negation, as well as other complete concepts, may be stated in one or a few words ("How?" or "How come?" "No!"). Usually, however, sentences consist of two or more words.

[2] *The basic structural word classes.* Words are not all alike. They do not have the same functions in the formation of concepts or the transmission of meanings, and they do, according to their functional type, have different positions with respect to each other in the structure of the sentence. All words are formally categorized into word classes, or to use the conventional term, "parts of speech."[40] With them, men have flexible instruments for communicating facts and knowledge, opinions and feelings, as well as for furnishing stimuli and expressing responses. However, the number and description of the parts of speech vary with the semantic scope and the grammatical forms and usages of the given language; the parts they play as elements of the sentence of the particular language also vary. For English, the more "conventional" grammarians usually give eight (nine, if articles are included) "parts of speech." The four main and constantly recurring forms are nouns, verbs, adjectives and adverbs. These have a distinctive and indispensable function to perform in the building of the sentence, and complement each other in coordinated speech.

The *naming,* or indicative words, consist mainly of nouns and their substitutes, pronouns. *Nouns* are names—names of specific items, such as objects, persons, other creatures, places, events, relations, conditions, situations, actions and patterns of activities, abstractions in the form of ideas, personal states, and such abstract elements as qualities (a good) and processes (a tremor, an awakening). The naming step probably came first in the making of language. It is estimated that at least eighty-five per cent of the base-forming vocabulary of every language comprises nouns.[41] To nouns are added the distinction of showing case (in English, for example, the possessive case: John's) and number (singular, or one; plural, or more than one). *Verbs* are indicators of action, process, occurrence, mode, state of being, these being attributed to the concrete and abstract entities; they "put the noun into action." To verbs are added distinctions of tense (the concepts of past, present, or future action); of number (of *he* or one, or of *they* or several, acting); of person (masculine, feminine, or neuter acting); of mood (indicative or definitely occurring, subjunctive or possible of occurrence, imperative or ordered to occur, and infinitive or generalized). The noun *and* verb make possible the basic statement-sentence pattern. When we have a combination of these two word-classes, we are able to express outward facts and conditions, inward feelings and thoughts.

Adjectives are the qualifiers of nouns. They present some specific attribute, quality, qualification, or other distinctive feature of the objects, occurrences, situations, and conditions (*good, bad, hot, cold, white, black*). *Adverbs* are the modifiers of verbs and adjectives, indicating the manner (tempo, intensity, location, etc.) in which the action takes place (*now, here, there, soon*) or in which the quality is conceived (*greatly, slowly, calmly*).[42]

The other "parts of speech" revolve about these four; they are supplemental technical tools, which serve as economizers or facilitators, or are used to add refinement or emphasis to meaning. *Pronouns* are substitutes for nouns, differentiated further as *personal* (substitutes for names of persons already mentioned or known or forming the subject of inquiry, such as *I, he, you*); *demonstrative* (*this, that*); *indefinite* (*another, any, both, none, some*); *interrogative* (*who, which, whose*); and *possessive* (*his, our, their*). *Articles* are limiters or individualizers of nouns (definite pronouns: *the, this;* indefinite: *a, an*). *Prepositions* indicate a variety of relations among nouns, or between nouns and other classes (the owner *of* the house, to sail *from* the harbor). *Conjunctions* connect clauses or coordinate words in the same clause (*and, but, or, than, if, when*). *Interjections* are ejaculatory or exclamatory terms (*Ah! Alas! Bah!*) standing outside ordinary sentences.

[3] *Sentence organization.* A sentence is like a tool of several parts;

each part has a functional relation to the other parts. The sentence is the expression of the speaker's or writer's intentions within the frame of the given circumstances. It consists essentially of two parts, the *subject* or theme, and the *predicate* or statement concerning the theme.[43] It may consist of a single word, as noted above; in that case, the same word contains the two components. Usually, however, it consists of a group of words.

Both the older and more conventional, and the newer "structuralist" analyses of English sentences stress the peculiar *organizational* aspects of the different kinds of sentences. It should be recalled that *all* languages have standard syntactical arrangements of their elements, but that those of each language are peculiar to it. Such facts simply underscore the institutionalized nature of language.

In the older, more conventional grammars, two different kinds of the classification of sentences have prevailed, each stressing a different kind of meaning content. The first classification, which stresses logical structure, distinguishes: (1) the *simple* sentence, which expresses a single independent thought—only one predication—and consists of only one independent clause; (2) the multiple or *compound* sentence, which consists of two or more independent propositions, presented in the form of two or more connected and coordinated clauses; (3) the *complex* sentence, consisting of two or more unified thoughts, one of which is the main or principal thought and has dependent on it one or more subordinate thoughts, the whole taking the form of one principal proposition and one or more subordinate propositions. In the case of the compound and complex sentences, the sense of any coordinate or subordinate clause is incomplete by itself: the meaning of these clauses depends for completeness on the statement of the main clause; their function is to supply special conceptual additions or qualifiers to the main clause. The second classification, which stresses the communicative content of the sentence, distinguishes among sentences as: (1) *declarative,* making a factual statement; (2) *interrogative,* asking a question; (3) *imperative,* making a request or command; (4) *exclamatory,* an utterance expressive of strong emotion, or giving expression to a command or desire.

The so-called "structuralists" in American linguistics have concluded, on the basis of a study of thousands of free utterances, that it is possible to establish the basic sentence-patterns of the English language—that is, the patterns to which all actual utterances can be reduced, and in terms of which any possible sentence can be analyzed. They do not name the form classes of words, but refer to them in terms of their identifying characteristics as they function in the utterance (sentence). While they do not ignore the differences among classes of words from the point of view of the kind of logical or semantic functions that the words are intended to perform, the structuralists are primarily concerned with the particular appropriate "positions" to which they are assigned in the different basic patterns of sentences. Charles C. Fries's work,[44] while by no means a model of the structuralist point of view is, nevertheless, more or less representative; at any rate, it was the first book-length attempt to treat the English sentence on the basis of structuralist principles. According to Fries, linguistic utterance, like other forms of human behavior, is a matter of stimulus and response. Hence, in the study of language as a functioning tool of human society, attention can be given to: "1. The speech sounds in correlation with the situations which usually call them forth, or, 2. The speech sounds in correlation with the responses which they usually elicit."[45] The older, more conventional procedure was to follow the first line of study. Now, however, it is possible to observe directly the responses that particular language forms elicit in a speech community. He states that, on the basis of such observation, "We can proceed on the assumption that if a particular response *regularly* occurs after a speech form or a language pattern, then this pattern or form 'means' this response. The regularity with which the response follows the utterance of the language pattern becomes the basis for the kind of prediction of a following response that makes the functioning of the language possible."[46] At least two kinds of meaning of words must be sharply distinguished within the total meaning of the utterance: the *lexical meanings,* "the meanings of the separate words as the dictionary would record them," and the *structural meanings,* that is, what the words mean with respect to the kinds of actions—what, by whom, when, what kind or form of action. No utterance is intelligible without both lexical meanings and structural meanings. But it is the devices that signal structural meanings that constitute the grammar of a language.[47]

Fries posits three main categories of communicative utterances: I. Utterances regularly eliciting "oral" responses only: A. *Greetings.* B. *Calls.* C. *Questions* (all three are later referred to as "questions"). II. Utterances regularly eliciting "action" responses: *requests* or *commands* (both later referred to as "requests"). III. Utterances regularly eliciting conventional signals of attention to continuous discourse: *statements.*[48] To describe the distinctive contrasts of pattern that mark the structures of these various kinds of sentences, he presents four classes of major "parts of speech" (I, II, III, IV), which he does not name but which correspond roughly, though not exactly, to nouns, verbs, adjectives and adverbs, and fifteen categories ("Groups" A to O) of "function words," which include among them the conventionally known prepositions, conjunctions, interjections, some pronouns and auxiliary verbs. These Class I-IV "parts of speech" and Group A-O "function words" have their distinctive patterns of word order and intonation in the three major types of sentences. By way of further utterance analysis, he deals with the "structural meanings" of "subjects" and "objects," with "modifiers," and with "sequence" and "included" sentences, in relation to the words of the four major classes. In general, the structure of a language is a matter of the selection of the part-of-speech units and of their form and positional arrangement. These units are words— words acting, according to form and function, as the content of the recurrent structural frames.

d / Lexical or vocabulary organization. A final strategic set of factors in any given linguistic system is its vocabulary or lexicon—that is, the standard list or inventory of its words. Functionally, the lexical and syntactical elements of the system intersect or even blend. The "traffic rules" of language by themselves can do nothing and, as we previously mentioned, a jumble of words is meaningless. The vocabulary puts the codal elements to work, and the message transmitted by them results from the employment of vocabulary. It is the words of the vocabulary that the structural principles fit together to convey some of the infinite array of meanings made possible by the language. Finally, as implied above and as will be further demonstrated below, the meaning and communicative efficacy of each word in its particular utterance context arises from its connection with, and its specific quality or denotation in relation to, the other words in the utterance.

The systematic nature of the words used by a given language community is revealed in their unabridged dictionary—that is, their alphabetically arranged list of words. Here will be found precise and succinct information about the "standard" pronunciations of words, their definitions or their accepted, current, limited, similar and opposite meanings, their usage as different word classes, their morphology, and their etymology or origins and historical derivations.

No two languages ever have exactly the same vocabulary; hence, many of the words of one language are not translatable into the words of another language with complete accuracy. Each language, as noted, has its physical–environmental, its historical–cultural, and its contemporary societal contexts. These factors give the meanings of its words certain characteristic peculiarities. They also affect the size of its dictionary. The English unabridged dictionary is huge, having in excess of a half-million words. This is not because English is a superior language, but because English speakers, among other things, have a long and complex cultural heritage into which much has been blended as the result of contacts with many peoples of many eras and areas. It can also be traced to the fact that our recent and present societal system is characterized by a high level of scientific, technological, and economic developments and the multiple cultural effects of these developments, by a great array of philosophical and political interests, and hence by a vast number of specialized fields of attention. This has required the production of vast numbers of "thought-counters." Every language has to have a sufficient number and variety of words to express all of the meanings of the people who use it.

It is desirable that given words have an established and limited meaning; otherwise the users could achieve no agreement as to what the words represent or the meanings of utterances in which they are made. Nevertheless, particular words can have multiple meanings—that is, different meanings in different contexts. The ability of words to possess different meanings, which correspond to their different uses, and to maintain themselves in the language with these various meanings is referred to as *polesemy*. Thus, for example, the English word *teeth* may refer to (1) those of our mouth (dentures), (2) cogs of a gear-wheel, (3) the cutting projections of a saw, (4) the points of a comb, (5) the prongs of a rake, (6) the tynes of a harrow, or (7) the marginal lobes of a leaf.[49] Similarly, the French word *bureau* may mean (1) a kind of material or fabric, (2) a piece of furniture covered with this fabric, (3) occupations carried on in a room, (4) the persons engaged in these occupations, and finally, (5) the group of persons directing an organization.[50] The English word *bear* may be a noun naming an animal, or a verb meaning "to carry" or "to give birth to" or "to endure."

Because of the conventional nature of words, their number and variety are continually changing. Changing circumstances result in the obsolescence and disappearance of some words, and also require the creation of whole new terminologies, as will be shown in Chapter XIII. As we have more and more to speak about, we must have more and more words to speak with. Time and circumstances also cause the creation of new meanings for existent words. Changing social life favors transformations in vocabularies, for it multiplies the causal factors which act upon words. As Vendryes states, "there is no field in which the causes for the transformation of phenomena are more complex, numerous or varied."[51]

e / The logical and semantic organization. Language in use involves more than the different functional forms and combinations of sound-units grammatically organized into utterances. Its basic function is expression of thought, and this, even in the speech of socially simpler and nonliterate peoples, involves something in the way of specific and determinate analyses and syntheses of what has been experienced. Nowhere is linguistic expression a mere copy of an object, event, relation, or situation. Every morpheme, word, phrase or sentence is a vehicle or link in a process of interpretation of the experience. Every language thus unavoidably has a tangential philosophical, more specifically, *a logical aspect,* if it is to serve its fundamental communicative purposes. This involves, first, the relationship of linguistic forms to facts. The user of the language must be concerned with validity, the extent to which his statements conform to reality, or else he is prating untruth, gibberish, or nonsense. This means that he must abide by at least the elementary (but more or less established and current) tests of truth prevailing in the given language community. More specifically, he must use the functional categories of language accurately, especially nouns, verbs, adjectives, and adverbs—the most accurate names, types of occurrences, qualities, qualifications, and other identifying characteristics.

Secondly, meaningful linguistic expression requires that the thought be sequentially developed and amplified phrase by phrase and, where it is more complex and extended, sentence by sentence and paragraph by paragraph. This does not mean that the refined and precise principles of the syllogism must necessarily be applied. It does mean, however, that the more or less common principles (or canons) of reasoning of the community must be observed—particularly in the development of ideas step by step, so that each succeeding step presents an extension, or greater detail, or further qualification as compared with the preceding one, and the whole process produces a complete and coherent (although possibly somewhat intricate) conceptual whole.

The over-all objective in logical organization is to establish firmly the accuracy and reasonableness of what one intends to indicate, interpret or transmit. This implies a close relationship between the logical system and the syntax of the language: the more precise the logic to be developed—that is, the more valid and accurate the thought processes—the more accurate and systematized the syntax must be.

Closely related to the logical system is the *semantic* or meaning system. Its part in the operation and purpose of the linguistic system is a vital one. To be sure, many American descriptive (structuralist) linguists are opposed to the inclusion of semantics in the analysis of language, preferring to deal with the latter solely on the basis of mechanical structure and function. However, among some structuralists it is recognized that the meanings of linguistic forms need to be considered in the building up of the structural analyses. When language is viewed purely as a mechanism, then an understanding of it can very well rest solely on form and function; but when a language is thought of (as it must be) as the major socially instrumentalized means of human communication, then its relationship to meaning becomes undeniable and indissoluble. For, from this angle, the *purpose* of language must be faced, and that purpose is absolute—namely, the transfer of meaning from one human mind to another. Leonard Bloomfield, held by many to be the founder of contemporary American linguistics, indicated that the chief business of language is to communicate meanings of various kinds, and that the linguistic student must constantly deal with meanings. "To put it briefly, in human speech different sounds have different meanings. To study this co-ordination of certain sounds with certain meanings is to study language."[52]

Words, taken singly and in combination, and the other signs used for communicative purposes, have reference to various somethings which are said to "have meaning." Conversely, if the phonetic, morphological, syntactical, and lexical structures and processes of the linguistic system do not serve to carry meaning from mind to mind, they are "sounding brass and tinkling cymbal."[53] *Pari passu,* these linguistic devices must carry *established and relatively durable meanings,* or they are useless among the speakers. These meanings are arbitrarily attached to the respective language-forms.

Every established group, every community has its body of meanings (of common and communal understandings), which are more or less systematized. This meaning system is embodied in the language system as the conveyor and depository of meanings. In fact, as will be noted in some detail later, an established language is intrinsically a more or less self-contained meaning system, inextricably correlated with its grammatical system and implemented by it, and yet something apart, which produces its own kind of determining and ordering. This meaning system not only embodies and summarizes all the meanings already arrived at; it also has its own particular forms of abstraction, its own conceptions, categorizations, and interpretations of kinds and qualities of things and occurrences, of motion, action, and causation, of space, time, relationship. The meaning system also indicates what has *much* meaning, what has *general* meaning, what has *specific, highly specialized and highly distinctive* meaning. To the outsider it indicates what is *without* meaning in the language community, either because there are no "guides" in the language for perception (no names, definitions, or categories along a particular line), or because there is ignorance of the existence of the thing or situation.

Conventional meanings are, of course, concretely conveyed through syntactical combinations and logical organization of words, phrases, sentences and combinations of sentences.

f / The personnel and associational components. Language, like other institutionalized ways of life, has its own personnel and, in societies like our own, its organizations and associations of special personnel. There is, of course, the whole community of speakers of the particular language; they are mainly its passive recipients and more or less unconscious performers of its organized behavior. The special functionaries of each language are of central institutional significance. These are the instructors and indoctrinators of the language—both the *informal* ones, such as parents, older siblings, playmates, and other associates, and the *formal* instructors, such as the teachers in the educational system. There are also the guardians of language—the grammarians, academicians, also often the teachers, who try to preserve its "correctness" or "purity."

Then there are the associations for the formation, inculcation, preservation, improvement, extension, or other implementation of language, such as those that consist of teaching and research professionals (for example, The American Modern Language Association and its various more specialized subdivisions); associations of nationalists or religionists, who promote a given language as a symbol of nationality, or as a means of preserving a religious organization; associations for the development and promotion of universal languages; organizations of men who more or less unconsciously develop a pragmatic "special" language, such as the special terminologies and formulae of the different sciences and technologies.

These various functionaries and organizations, like those of other institutions, have their necessary material and mechanical equipment, and institutional procedures of the sort indicated above, which are the characteristic aspects of the operation of institutions.

5. Standard Language

The terms "standard" or "correct" language have been used several times so far. They are employed by the linguists to refer to the linguistic product prevailing in a given language community at a given time, as the result of institutionalization processes. Certain aspects, developmental factors and social considerations require brief explication.

While no language performance of individuals or groups is absolutely uniform,[54] the community must have—and, if its social interactions are effective and satisfactory to the actors, it does have—a *model* by which to operate. Conversely, there must be some limitation of the number of variations or types of a given language. "Standard English," like any standard language, is a matter of approximate uniformity of vocabulary, regularity of syntax, similarity of pronunciation and uniformity of meaning of terms used. Without this uniformly patterned speech, there would be too much confusion, too many "gaps" in communication between the population elements.

The so-called "standard" is not necessarily a superior sort of speech technically—that is, from the point of view of communicative efficacy; it is "standard" by virtue of social establishment and social valuation. It is the language that is looked upon as good and right. Any considerable departure from its accepted features is uncouth language. The principle of sanction that prevails in connection with most institutionalized behavior usually applies here. The use of "correct" language is rewarded, while those who misuse it or use it incorrectly are looked down upon and often penalized in other ways.

The standard features and requirements are specifically set forth in the grammars, the dictionaries and the textbooks used to instruct neophytes and foreigners in the language. The standard forms are particularly demonstrated in the language used in the schools and colleges, in the churches, by publicists, in the public press, in public gatherings, in the activities of administrative organizations, by radio and television announcers and commentators, and in all discourse that officially concerns the whole community, as takes place in law courts and legislative assemblies.

Nevertheless, within the standard language there are minor differences as between speakers of different cities and regions, or of different social classes, differences based on level and kind of education and upon occupational division, differences in the way of slang and certain argots and lingoes, to mention only the more common ones.[55] Standard language does not exclude or override any of the variants. It simply serves as the general medium of discourse over the entire language community. None of these variants, however, can diverge too widely from the standard, or their speakers lose their ability to communicate satisfactorily with their fellows. Historically, as now, once a unified language has been established, there is a tendency for the somewhat variant forms (notably dialects) to give way to the standard language, even a tendency to discourage or to repress the use of some—although, as will be noted, there are conspicuous exceptions in the case of certain contemporary "special" languages.

Operationally, a standard language, regardless of its origins and the multiple elements that have contributed to its development in time, is a matter of established *usage* and general belief regarding correctness, and not a matter of a statute or of anyone's decree. It may have developed out of a dialect (as it almost invariably has) and, in the course of its career, absorbed much slang, many colloquialisms and items from other dialects, special languages, and even foreign languages. It may have added many new words and phrases, modified the meaning of old ones, and changed some of the hitherto accepted modes of expression. Usage may even have consecrated original errors and given them correct linguistic currency. But if these are used constantly by a sufficient number of users, they are woven into the institutional requirements and regarded as standard.

To be sure, certain types of individuals and certain population segments—authors, orators, great leaders and lawmakers, the people of the court, the universities, the educated classes, and to some extent "language authorities"—are more influential and determinative in establishing what is correct language than are other social elements. Much of language becomes "right" if it is advocated by or is sufficiently used by the "right people."[56]

6. *Language: The Basic Institution*

All the institutional systems in the different areas of social life overlap; they are functionally interrelated, interacting, competitive–cooperative, and hence, inter-supportive and interdependent in various ways and degrees. Furthermore, some functions of some institutions can be shifted to other institutions; for example, many educational functions are shifted from family to school, and many family functions to economic, political, religious or recreational institutions. Language too has many interdependencies with other institutions, and some other institutions *assist* it in conducting some of its functions; for example, the family and school are important agents in the child's learning to speak and write the native language, and the mass communications media transmit messages across space and time. However, language is not merely interrelated and interdependent with some of the other institutions; it is the primal and fundamental system among all of the coded and ordered systems of interpersonal and intergroup behavior. This primacy is patently revealed in many ways.

In the first place, institutions are complicated mechanisms; their development and continued organization and operation rest upon many different linguistic facilities. Institutions can exist only among that animal species that possesses language behavior ability. *Language can be said to be the prerequisite for all of institutional development.* Until language had evolved to a considerable degree, the ideas and beliefs necessary for the origin and growth of institutions could not have come into existence. All of that accumulation of knowledge by which man has been able to devise, continue and change the great variety of his material and nonmaterial institutions has rested upon language. Language is the technique—the key technique—that stands behind all other techniques, including, in the present instance, the techniques whereby social order, social regulation and social maintenance are conducted.

Not only has language served as the indispensable preliminary to the formation of almost all other institutions; out of it grew writing, literature, much of education, and all of the derived communicative institutions.

Second, *language is the indispensable factor in the operation of the institutions in every functional area of life:* in religion, the family, all economic activity, in all forms of political activity, in education, science and technology, in art, especially literature, and in welfare. Concretely, it is essential to the definition of order in each institutionalized area of societal life; to the presentation of factual knowledge, values, ideas and beliefs regarding the behavioral area; to the statement of the institutions' codes, and the explication of role requirements; to the delineation of the behavioral compulsives, permissives and prohibitions under the codes, and the presentation of rewards for conformity to the codes and penalties for their violation; to the process of indoctrinating the members of the society with the rationale and values of the institutions, and carrying into effect the institutional procedures and techniques; to providing instruction, practice, training and discipline in the ways and means of the institution, and in the conduct of special institutional occasions. In general, the effectiveness of any other institutional system depends upon the effectiveness of the system of communication within the society. It is also known that the more extensive, complicated, and intricate becomes the operation of any of the institutional areas of social life, the greater is its need for diversified, quick, and accurate language.[57]

Third, the *instituted language of a people is the indispensable instrument whereby the lore and principles of all the other institutions are transmitted across time (from past to present to future and from generation to generation), among contemporaries (from adults to the young and from natives to newcomers), and across space (from group to group, from geographical section to section).* It is also the means whereby institutional successes and failures are recorded and made available for others elsewhere who live under the particular institution, and for later generations.

Finally, *language is the basic instrumental factor in the reorganization of institutions:* in the recording and spreading of the facts regarding the malfunctioning of the particular institution and the presentation of the crisis situation; in discussion and criticism, and the development of terminology to describe the situation; in the articulation of the reorganizational plan, and the presentation of the rationale of the plan and of resources for carrying the plan into effect; in the propagandizing of the plan, and in developing the consensus for change; in the organization of the social movement to promote and conduct the undertaking.

N O T E S

1 On "System and Systems," see J. O. Hertzler, *American Social Institutions: A Sociological Analysis* (Boston: Allyn & Bacon, Inc., 1961), pp. 3–17 and bibliography, p. 29.

2 Jean-Jacques Rousseau, in his *Essai sur l'origine des langues,* refers to speech as "the first social institution." Henri Berr says: "Language is truly social . . . a creation of society, an institution inherent in society," in his Foreword to Joseph Vendryes's *Language: A Linguistic Introduction to History* (London: Kegan Paul, Trench, Trubner & Co., 1925), p. xiv. Note also: "Languages are, in many ways, as much institutions as a country's religion or its law is an institution." (Eric Partridge, *The World of Words* (London: George Routledge & Sons, 1938), p. 4.)

3 Cf. Alfred R. Radcliffe-Brown: *A Natural Science of Society* (Glencoe, Ill.: Free Press, 1957), p. 107.

4 Albert G. Keller: *Social Evolution* (rev. ed.) (New York: Macmillan Co., 1931), p. 156.

5 These points have been suggested in part by Marcel Cohen: *Pour une sociologie du langage* (Paris: Albin Michel, 1956), pp. 81–82.

6 Cf. Ferdinand de Saussure: *Course in General Linguistics,* trans. Wade Baskin (New York: Philosophical Library, 1959), pp. 71–78.

7 The treatment is not to be construed as even an attempt to present an abbreviated overview of the major analytical areas of contemporary formal linguistics. For such a study, see the bibliography for this chapter.

8 As suggested, for example, in the table of contents of the present book, or of Marcel Cohen, pp. 391–396.

9 This knowledge will come in large part from the formal linguistic scientists. This material, however, like that now coming from any other growing analytical field, is by no means entirely uniform and consistent. There is sometimes a sharp difference of opinion as to some of the essential systemic features of language, and what the proper content areas and fields of linguistic methodology are. This disagreement is brought out in Einar Haugen's address as president of the Linguistic Society, "Directions in Modern Linguistics," *Language* 27 (1951), pp. 211–222. The non-specialist is especially confused by the occasional lack of uniformity in terminology; he must sometimes translate the terms employed by one authority for a given linguistic item into those of another—and, he suspects, with some loss in exactitude of meaning. We seek to avoid becoming involved in contending claims of different recent and contemporary "schools," and we are also trying to arrive at a working consensus of the somewhat diverse definitions and interpretations of those authorities, supposedly of much the same theoretical position, and to present the more or less generally accepted views regarding the areas of linguistic analysis and the basic subject matter of the areas. Some aspects of language as a complete, institutionalized, communicative system will be discussed, aspects which formal structural linguists do not include within their purview. This is due to the fact that the sociologist sees as essential aspects of the total system not only purely linguistic features, but also a considerable number of inseparable social psychological, logical and semantic elements.

10 Cf. Vendryes, p. 234.

11 Vendryes, *ibid.;* William J. Entwistle, *Aspects of Language* (London: Faber & Faber, 1953).

12 John B. Carroll, *The Study of Language* (Cambridge: Harvard University Press, 1953), pp. 23–29.

13 Mario Pei, *Voices of Man: The Meaning and Function of Language* (New York: Harper & Row, 1962), p. 91.

14 John P. Hughes, *The Science of Language: An Introduction to Linguistics* (New York: Random House, Inc., 1962), pp. 147–148.

15 De Saussure, pp. 134–137; Vendryes, pp. 233–234.

16 Carroll, pp. 93–94.

17 Cf. Cohen, p. 37.

18 Says Leonard Bloomfield: "The description of language . . . begins with phonology"—that is, the science describing human sounds. (*Language* (New York: Henry Holt & Co., 1933), p. 38.) Phonology is viewed by the linguists as being a part of external linguistics, and at a level of analysis, therefore, below that of synchronic linguistics. One structuralist refers to it as "pre-linguistics." It is subordinate to the code of word construction, the code governing grammatical forms and the primary code of sentence-making. It is also outside of time, in so far as the human articulatory mechanism does not change.

19 Charles C. Fries, Introduction to Kenneth L. Pike, *Phonemics: A Technique for Reducing Languages to Writing* (Ann Arbor: University of Michigan Press, 1947). See also Charles F. Hockett, *A Course in Modern Linguistics* (New York: Macmillan Co., 1958), pp. 15–144.

20 Bloomfield, pp. 79–80.

21 Martin Joos, "Description of Language Design," in Joos (ed.), *Readings in Linguistics* (New York: American Council of Learned Societies, 1958), pp. 349–356 (352). Hughes uses the term in the title of his Chapter XIV.

22 Simeon Potter, *Modern Linguistics* (London: Andre Deutsch, Ltd., 1957), pp. 39–40; Harry R. Warfel, *Language: A Science of Human Behavior* (Cleveland: Howard Allen, Inc., 1962), pp. 55–57; Entwistle, pp. 97–113. See also the Introduction by Charles C. Fries to Pike, *op. cit.*

23 Vendryes, p. 34; Potter, p. 40.

24 Pike, p. 60.

25 Warfel, pp. 40, 57.

26 *Ibid.*, p. 57.

27 The contents of this paragraph have been taken almost verbatim from Vendryes, p. 34.

28 Hockett, p. 148.

29 The term *form* is widely used in linguistics. A form is a vocal or phonetic feature or unit, common to the same (or partly the same) human utterances or acts of speech; it is an aggregation of phonemes and has a meaning. It may be a morpheme, a syllable, a word, a phrase or a sentence; in fact, "every utterance is made up wholly of forms." Bloomfield, "A Set of Postulates for the Science of Language," in Joos, p. 27; Bloomfield, *Language*, p. 138.

30 Joos speaks of morphemes as "meaningful" molecules, subassemblies which roughly correspond to the customary subdivisions or categorizations of the real world. (*Op. cit.*, pp. 349–356 (350).)

31 A by-product of recent linguistic analysis has been the burgeoning of what Entwistle has referred to as the *-eme* family of terms relating to the structure of a given language. Not only are there phonemes and morphemes, but also *chronemes* (relating to *length of sound units*), *tonemes* (pitch), *stronemes* (stress), *tagmemes* (relating to *grouping,* and consisting of the smallest meaningful units of grammatical form), *taxemes* (the simplest element of grammatical arrangement, corresponding to the phoneme as the smallest unit of form), *lexemes* (grammatical forms relating to word-formation), *semantemes* (the portions of words conveying meanings), *sememes* (the meaning of morphemes), and *episemes* (the meanings of tagmemes). Entwistle, pp. 79–80; Bloomfield, p. 166. Different ones among these have significance respectively in pronunciation, or in word construction or syntactic construction.

32 In an utterance, a word is the smallest significant unit arrived at for some particular language, as the most conveniently structured entity to separate by spaces; it constitutes one of the units of the language, which may be uttered by itself. (Pike, p. 89.) For other definitions see Michael Girsdansky, *The Adventure of Language* (Englewood Cliffs, N. J.: Prentice-Hall, 1963), pp. 76–77.

33 These are the languages classified as *polysynthetic.* The American Indian languages, including Eskimo, fall into this category. They do not have word classes or parts of speech. What for us appears as a "word," in these languages is or can be a sentence.

34 Entwistle points out that this is evidenced in the special language studies that are concerned with words: *etymology,* which deals with the origin, development, and status of words; *morphology,* which is concerned with the construction and parts of words; *syntax,* the arrangement of words in the sentence; *lexicography,* the history of the meanings of words, and of their arrangement into most convenient sequences; *semantics,* which is concerned, among other things, with the meaning of words. He also notes that phonetic transcriptions are divided into words, and that geographical linguistics is primarily grounded on words, entering words on its linguistic maps in dialect studies, even where sounds and phrases are the chief concern, because these latter vary according to the words that compose them. (*Op. cit.*, p. 226.)

35 "A Set of Postulates for the Science of Language," p. 27, or *Language,* p. 160. See also Bernard Black and George L. Trager, *Outline of Linguistic Analysis* (Baltimore: Linguistic Society of America, 1942), p. 54.

36 Cf. Potter, pp. 78–103; Hockett, pp. 209–213, 240–245; Hughes, pp. 194–205.

37 On the relation between word construction and social contact and social change, see Chap. VII, Sect. 2.

38 *Op. cit.*, p. 157.

39 Louis H. Gray, *Foundations of Language* (New York: The Macmillan Co., 1939), pp. 224–225. Potter also says that "the sentence is the chief unit of speech." (*Op. cit.*, p. 104.)

40 The parts of speech, or form-classes of words, are often discussed under morphology. A good case can be made for their inclusion in either analytical

category, which shows both that the boundary lines between morphology and syntax are not sharp and clear, and that the two are very closely related in the study of linguistic structure. The parts of speech are occasionally called the "elements of the sentence."

41 Warfel, p. 49.

42 For a strict structuralist's description of these four major classes of words, see Fries, pp. 76–86.

43 These terms, it should be noted, are logical and not linguistic distinctions.

44 *The Structure of English* (New York: Harcourt, Brace & Co., 1952).

45 *Ibid.,* p. 35.

46 *Ibid.,* p. 36.

47 *Ibid.,* pp. 55–56.

48 *Ibid.,* p. 53.

49 This illustration from Potter, p. 147.

50 Illustration from Vendryes, p. 198. For further illustrations and social implications of this situation, see Chap. X, Sect. 2, p. 249.

51 *Ibid.,* p. 193. As noted above, Entwistle mentions "stylistics" as a branch of linguistic study. It has received special attention in Western Europe, especially for the German and French languages, and extensive bibliographies exist. With us, style in language is mainly the concern of aesthetics in literature. The European proponents of stylistics posit a "characterology" of language. This is evidenced in the peculiar intellectual quality, and the special affective and emotive creative uses of the common resources of the language, within the limits of its conventional phonological, morphological, syntactical, and lexical constitution. Particularly significant are the tendencies to avoid the purely automatic or mechanical, and to seek special effects through the use of standard forms in special contexts, the affective use of different parts of speech, of idiom, formulas, metaphor, abstraction or concretion, fancy, and so on. (Cf. Entwistle, pp. 265–283.) In general, also, each language as an institutional system differs from any other language in "character" as well as in codal and structural forms, as do the other institutions of peoples.

52 Bloomfield, *Language,* p. 27. See also Postulate II,6 of "A Set of Postulates, etc."

53 "Speech-sounds without regard to their meanings are abstractions." Bloomfield, *Language,* p. 139.

54 Nor are its rules and principles observed and followed with 100 per cent perfection of accomplishment, any more than are those of any other institution.

55 The variations in standard language led Bloomfield to refer to five main types of standard language in a complex speech community: (1) Literary standard (as in literature); (2) Colloquial standard (as in everyday usage); (3) Provincial standard (regional dialects); (4) Substandard (as in the various special languages); (5) Local dialects (as of part of a city: "Brooklynese"). (Bloomfield, *Language,* p. 52.) Gray (p. 28) also mentions (1) Literary standard; (2) Colloquial standard; (3) Substandard; and (4) Regional standard.

56 The factors involved in the development and establishment of standard language will be examined in greater detail in Chap. VIII below, on "The Uniformation and Extension of Languages: Historical, Contemporary."

57 Other aspects of the functional interrelationship of language with other institutions will be examined in some detail in Chap. VII, Sects. 2, 3; Chap. VIII, Sect. 3; Chap. XIII, Sects. 5–6.

VI ❧ Language as Sociocultural Index, Record and Determinant

1. *The Cultural System and Language*

The cultural system of a society affects the ways in which the other basic operative systems function among men—that is, the natural environment (physical and biological), the demographic structure and the concrete societal structural–functional forms (groups, ecological organization, the stratified arrangements of human populations). It also provides the distinctively man-made media whereby all the social systems function as they do. Unlike any other species, man has always been distinguished by the fact that he is the culture-producing, culture-maintaining, culture-transmitting, and culture-perpetuating creature. Culture is man's peculiar handiwork.

Culture rests upon the special abilities of men. They have the powers of discovery and invention, contrivance and constructiveness, appropriation and manipulation, imagination and interpretation. By culture we mean what man has himself created, unconsciously and consciously, in making himself at home in the world: the modifications of nature that he has brought about in the way of the manipulation and utilization of nature's processes, and of contrived material objects (artifacts); the modifiers of nature that he has devised in the form of all sorts of tools, prescriptions, appliances, machines and other instruments; the behavior patterns (habits, skills, techniques, arts, essential social routines, usages and ceremonies) that he has developed; the whole vast array of his institutional systems; the distinctive non-material elements of his life—his knowledge, ideas, beliefs, rules, values, expectations, the vehicles and systems of his meanings, purposes and ends. These elements embody the long experiences of man—his successes in living in his physical, mental, social, and spiritual world. *In toto,* as the cultural system, they furnish the design and the ways and means of life of the people and the era. Culture thus is the store of shared social experience.

Culture is also a *continuum,* a stream of material and non-material products and events, that flows freely—and usually unconsciously—down through time from one generation to another.

The culture system and the over-all social system are so much intertwined in nearly all social action that we frequently use the term "sociocultural" in referring to the structural condition or form of action. *Language* is the means of making all human achievement possible, the *sine qua non* of culture. Without it, the discoveries and inventions of man could not have been retained and communicated. Especially important is the fact that language itself, in a very real sense, more comprehensively embodies and reveals the entire human sociocultural heritage, in all its past and present aspects, than does any other block or sector of institutions, because there must be communication, internal and interpersonal, by means of words and phrases, in order to express *every* concern and interest, conceive *every* experience and conduct *every* operation—individual, institutional, conceptual—in *every* department of human life. In other words, the sphere of action of a given language embraces *all* spheres of the users' activities; in its spoken and written form, it *depicts* what its speakers, however widely separated in time and space, have experienced and wrought. A sociocultural "going concern" is thus in the last analysis a verbal complex. A further fact is that the durability of this going concern and its language, its crucial medium of continuity, are reciprocally related: to be meaningfully connected, the generations must have a common language; the language, to persist, must be transmitted—taught and learned—from generation to generation. Both factors greatly influence each other in this reciprocity. On the strength of these functional characteristics of language, it is able to serve several outstanding sociocultural functions. It is the *index,* or even *inventory,* of the sociocultural life of a language community at a given time, a concise, accurate and highly revealing *record* of its ramified sociocultural history. Since each language is an established "going" medium, yet at the same time the product of a long development under its own unique complex of conditions, through which its users perceive and interpret their world, it is a partial *determinant* of the perceptual–conceptual processes and the *Weltanschauung* of the members of the language community. It is a determinant of how and what they experience and comprehend. We shall now briefly examine these aspects.

2. *Language as Sociocultural Index*

An up-to-date unabridged dictionary, with its listing and definitions of all the standard words and all of the functional varieties of words, serves as a great window, offering a wide perspective of the entire life of the people whose language it depicts.[1] For while a dictionary is "a book about words," the words indicate all manner of things: events, viewpoints, imaginings, and interpretations. The dictionary provides this picture of life in an even more comprehensive manner than a report of the census bureau of a modern advanced nation. The very existence of the dictionary itself indicates a high level of cultural development, which includes wide literacy, widespread concern about the accuracy of words and phrases used to name all sorts of both experienced and imagined things and events involved in daily life, and the awareness of an almost infinite number of details of a highly complex sociocultural life that must be clearly defined and distinguished from each other.

In general, the language of a people at any given time provides an almost complete "index," both in the sense of being an indicator of contents or a symbolic guide, and as a gauge or measuring-rod of almost every facet of their culture.[2] It is the first of these that concerns us especially. Ethnologists have long recognized that language presents a practically exhaustive listing and classification of the concerns about, and the objects and events in the universe of, primitive speakers.[3] Hunting and collecting people have detailed lists of animals and plant names, and they name the topographic features of their environment with care and precision. The terms used by all primitive people while engaged in their daily activities indicate what they eat and drink and wear, the work they do, what they construct, the things and activities they enjoy, the beliefs and superstitions they hold. In the realm of social organization, the kinship terminology, for example, affords abundant materials for the interpretation of the kinship-system—the relations between spouses and between siblings, the different categories of kin, forms of address, taboos and incest regulations. Status systems are reflected in vocabulary, for example, in salutations, and in certain partially grammatical features of language, such as the system of pronouns. Furthermore, among primitives, the enumeration systems, sex attitudes and sex relations, the numerous diverse and involved taboos, the forms of magic and many other related topics can be studied in the language forms.

In a complex civilization like our own, the vocabulary (and, in many instances, the grammatical forms) provide indices of the multitudinous aspects of our material life (buildings, food, apparel, tools and appliances), of our occupations, our sports and games, our technology, our vast number and variety of social relations, our typical social processes and procedures, our social institutions (familial, religious, economic, political, legal, educational, welfare, aesthetic), our conceptions of time and space and of temporal and spatial relationships, our behavioral standards and sanctions, our values, our bodies of purposes and ends, our interpretations of the nature of, and of our relations with, the intangible and supernatural. Our language not only indicates the universal features of life, which we share with all other peoples, but also reflects the peculiar and inimitable characteristics of our own sociocultural existence.

The language gives some evidence of the demographic and societal structuring of the speakers. For example, an analysis of proper names enables one to draw cogent inferences regarding the ethnic composition of the population. Terms for status distinctions, status incumbents, and status roles (for example, *sire, lord, upper, middle,* or *lower class, peasant*) throw light on the stratification system.

In general, the language is a reflector of the given peoples' cultural level, particularly with regard to the structure of their knowledge and the degree and diversity of their technological development. The language of primitives, for example, includes conceptions of mystical happenstance or the animistic transformation of reality (things, events and actions), and evidences of a subjective and anthropomorphic perspective, as against the more or less objective, scientific, cause-and-effect analysis of the advanced peoples, with its requirements of logical schemata involving a high degree of abstraction, adequacy and precision of terminology, conceptualization and definition, specificity of taxonomy and clarity of generalization, appropriately facilitated by adequate symbols (for example, mathematical symbols) and essential refinements of vocabulary, grammar and semantics.

The different categories of language reflect the interests, predilections and major preoccupations, as well as the emphases, usages and utilities of a given people. For example, in the language of the Angles and Saxons, there were many words relating to war and to the admiration they held for prowess in fighting and for personal bravery. To illustrate this point, there is the almost classic example, used about a quarter of a century ago, of Arabic with some 6000 words referring to *camel*— color, bodily structure, sex, age, movement, condition, equipment, and so on—but (at that time) the single word *tomobile,* covering all makes and models of cars, trucks, buses, and tractors.[4] The natives of the Sahara have 200 words for the *date,* their staff of life, and twenty different ways of describing the shape of sand dunes.[5] In English we have only one word for *snow,* but the Eskimo has dozens of words for different characteristics of snow. With us there is a profusion and ever-expanding body of words relating to large-scale government, to organization and administration, to commerce, to science and technology. For example, because of the importance of automobiles in our culture, we not only have hundreds of words for automobile parts, processes, sales, and so forth, but have also developed such special terms as "hot-rods," "sports cars," "stock cars," "convertibles," and "jalopies" or "heaps."

When words and phrases are dropped from a language (for example, many of the "camel" words have disappeared from Arabic in recent decades), this is because the conditions they referred to and the related interests have disappeared; conversely, as among us, when new words are coined or added—for example, the almost bewildering array of words relating to electronics, new drugs and biologicals, atomic fission, space missiles, "Cold War" international relations, and psychopathology —it is because new conditions exist and are being met. The development of technology in our culture is accompanied by the development of language terms and forms to meet the need for new kinds of calculation and counting, for abstraction and the systematization and precise statement of complex ideas, for the organization of techniques and instruments, and for specific directives and instructions. It might also be noted that the body of these terms reflects the level, extent and diversity of our technological organization.

The language shows the way in which people conceptualize and react to abstruse elements of space and time (see especially Chapter III, Section II). As reflected in their linguistic space and time references, there are marked differences, as between cultures, in space and time categories and distinctions, and in the fixation of space and time relations, chiefly because of the great range of spatial and temporal awareness. For example, many primitives have limited spatial awareness; there is no possibility, in dealing with them, of referring to objects 282 million light-years away, or of calculating speed in the traversing of outer space. Many have little or no conception of time as a flow and unity, but conceive it only in its individual and momentary phases; they therefore do not need precise time-markers or time-measurers. Time is not "money" for them; nor do they live "by the watch."[6]

The language also reflects the "number system" of a people, which, in turn, involves their comprehension of amounts and degrees of "plurality" in conformance with their needs and desires with respect to "countable" objects, and their developed schemes of numbering. For example, Central Australian tribes were unable to count beyond *four* and *five*, and had no need to; the Chuckchee counted by hand and foot digits, and in terms of these (*ten* means *two hands, twenty* means *one man*), while we must keep account of a national debt, of distances in outer space, and other "astronomies" and "geometries."

Several other aspects of language, closely related to its function as sociocultural index, should be mentioned. One is the fact that it acts quite accurately as a sociocultural "marker"—a guide in indicating the boundaries or the extent of a culture, even of a culture group.[7] For example, French-Canadian language and French-Canadian culture are inextricably correlated; each indicates the presence and the extent of the other. Carroll notes that linguistic facts are often far more reliable than other cultural markers, such as the tools used by a culture, or its style of architecture. Tools and architecture are often cross-cultural and interchangeable. The language of a culture, however, in its vocabulary and grammatical forms and usages, for reasons already indicated, is its most characteristic and most specifically revealing cultural feature. The members of a culture are usually aware, consciously or unconsciously, of language as a cultural indicator. The American regards one who speaks Spanish as his mother tongue as being identified with certain cultural features; the Northerner, upon hearing someone speak with a "Southern" accent, designates him as belonging to a particular American subculture; substandard speech, especially with respect to grammar and pronunciation, usually indicates that the speaker belongs to a poorly educated social class or population segment. Ethnic groups may be distinguished for several generations by their continued use of the mother tongue, and often by accent in the use of the newly acquired language. Bossard's work, to be examined later, indicates that even families reveal their special features in their speech peculiarities—peculiarities of vocabulary, accent, idiom and syntax.

Another significant aspect has been presented in a recent study by Samora and Deane. They point out that language usage in a culture-contact situation is an excellent measure of acculturation, and therefore provides a reliable index of acculturation. For the language as used not only reveals visible patterns of behavior, but also meanings and implications, attitudes, and other psychological dimensions. Important aspects of language usage as a measure of acculturation are: the facility with which the new language is used; whether or not the subtleties of the language are understood; the language used by preference; the language best understood without conscious effort; and the degree to which idiom is appropriately used.[8]

A final aspect of language as culture index is that it reflects the essence of the culture of which it is both part and symbol so specifically that another language cannot serve as an adequate substitute. Many words and phrases of a language can be understood only by explaining them in their particular cultural setting. Similarly, many aspects of another culture cannot be expressed in a particular language because it does not have the words to do so.[9]

3. Language as the Record of the Sociocultural History of Its Speakers

We have pointed out that language is a social emergent, a product of social usage, a cultural index of the language community as it is at the moment. We have also indicated that language is the major agency for transmitting the social heritage, and thus the most important means whereby the community maintains historical continuity. In turn, the ongoing community is essential to make the specific language complex a self-perpetuating system. These two interrelated facts point to a third, of special significance—namely, that the language, as it develops, and as its developments are exemplified in its vocabulary, active and passive, and in its dialects and "special" languages, functions as a sensitive, concise, explicit and comprehensive reflector, recorder, biography-carrier, preserver, storehouse, catalog, inventory, or depository, as it is variously put, of the entire sociocultural history of its associated speakers through time.[10] For whatever men do, whatever happens to them, has an influence on and is reflected in and preserved by their language as a product of the past. It is, in fact, a documentation of the ever-changing life, generation by generation, era by era, of *all* the language communities that have used it, or parts of it, in the past, and all contacting societies that, wittingly or unwittingly, have contributed to it. In this connection, it has been appropriately referred to as a "diary of our ancestors," "the biography of nations," "the mirror of civilization," and "the reservoir of civilization." By means of it, we are, in truth, "heirs of all the ages."

Man's life in the past is revealed by various ways of recording evidence: incidental archaeological evidence such as is found in artifacts and other physically preserved culture indicators, such as buildings and monuments; orally transmitted evidence, especially folklore materials mentioned in the preceding section, and all sorts of written materials—some of it specifically intended as description and record—beginning among some peoples about 6000 years ago. Language, however, reflects what actually occurred in the past much more comprehensively and copiously than do the incidental carriers, and the formally and professionally written histories. These are all partial and selective; the formal histories often have particular axes to grind in what they portray of the past and how they portray it, and are thus colored by the class, professional, or other viewpoints of the writers.

Language, as has been shown above, as an indispensable communicative agency, functions in every department of life; its sphere of action embraces *all* the other spheres of man's activity. Hence, it records whether intentionally or not almost every phase of life in the past.[11]

In this respect, the dictionary is more than a spelling book or a guide to pronunciation, more even than an index of the sociocultural life of the community at the time of its compilation. It is a "storehouse," a "public treasury," an inexhaustible set of archives, containing a wealth of historical information crystallized in the language as it has developed. In the etymology or "genealogy" or "pedigree" of the words listed, there is evidence of almost every kind of physical, social, intellectual and spiritual experience of its people in the past.

This outstanding feature of language even enables us to determine much of the life of vanished peoples and cultures. The so-called "dead languages"—for example, Greek and Latin—give us a vast amount of detailed information about features, once common and flourishing, of the civilizations they represented. They can be thought of as "dead," only in the sense that archives are dead. They are not dynamic, but descriptive and instructive; we may have, in these languages, a record of past greatness. Says Baugh, "Sometimes the cultural importance of a race or nation has at some former time been so great that their language remains important among cultivated people long after it has ceased to represent political, commercial, and other greatness."[12]

Gray mentions that it is frequently possible through language to determine the views and ideas and ways of people living "before history began to be recorded." In fact, "Not infrequently linguistic investigation is the sole means of determining the earlier history of a (vanished) people." He (others later copied him) uses the archaeological analogy. He states, with special reference to language as a record of spiritual and mental development: "It is scarcely an exaggeration to say that the study of language . . . is to a knowledge of the spiritual and mental development of man what archaeology is to that of his material evolution, or embryology is to that of his physical evolution. Just as a palaeontologist reconstructs the extinct beasts and birds, fishes and reptiles, which roamed the earth in pre-historic periods, . . . and just as the geologist can determine the earlier configuration of the world from evidence which to the untrained mind is meaningless, so the linguist can trace . . . the history of man's long and toilsome development in thought. He is the mental archaeologist. . . ."[13]

More specifically, however, the language of a people records their life cycle or, at any rate, the sequences of their existence to date. It shows how they coped with and continually adjusted themselves to their environments; what they acquired through the contacts they have had with other peoples and cultures, as the result of migration, invasions and conquests, missionization, and trade; what they discovered, invented, learned from others; the knowledge they built up and what they discarded (as reflected, in part, in their linguistic archaisms); their denotations of every known category of concrete objects: the ways in which they named people, artifacts, and places; the forms and revisions of their great adjustive mechanisms—that is, their economic, familial, political, religious, scientific, educational, status and aesthetic institutions; their sports and pastimes; their beliefs, prejudices, superstitions, fears, and erroneous views; their attitudes and values, ideas, philosophies, and ideologies; the development of their technology, and consequently the changes, accepted or induced, in the whole physical and social organization of their life.

It should be noted, however, in all candor, that the history revealed by language is not always easy to read. We have to be cautious about drawing historical references from historical sources alone. For a given language is a vast—and to the uninitiated a confusing—mixture of elements from various sources. In the course of time, and because of social changes, decisive linguistic items of a historical character may have been lost. Strange things may happen to the meanings of words (as will be noted below); for example, a family, at least one of whose ancestors was once a weaver and which, according to prevailing practice, came to be named *Weaver,* is now headed by a man who is an attorney. Nevertheless, the language does reflect the confusing sources of change and the changes as well.[14]

Several specific types of language as record may be noted. The language of *a region* is a source of information about it: it reflects, for example, (1) through present day dialect isoglosses, certain territorial boundaries of earlier days; (2) through the rise and spread of certain words or pronunciations, the social forces and intellectual currents of a given period. It also (3) presents the objects of material culture in great detail, as well as many regional variations. Our own American language includes many "provincialisms" that picture aspects of our earlier social life. These are exemplified in phrases relating to farm life ("fly off the handle"), hunting and gunmanship ("make the fur fly"), warfare ("put on the war paint"), pioneering ("to make tracks," "to blaze a trail").[15] Some European scholars have utilized lexical data to trace the local effect of specific cultural movements. Theodore Frings, for example, has given us studies on Roman influence in ancient Germany and on the itinerary of the Reformation in Germany in its early stages.[16] Social movements may be recorded through changes wrought in the language. The French Revolution, for example, is reflected in such linguistic developments as the introduction of new words ("citizen"), the resort to familiar forms of address, and the renaming of the days of the week, aimed especially at the abolition of Sundays and holy days. Hughes has pointed out that the migrations of the Indo-European peoples from about 2000 B.C. are known to us from linguistic, not historical, evidence—namely, the spread of the Indo-European languages. He indicates the many different directions of the migrations and the accompanying language deposits.[17]

Some of the more universal aspects of the relationship between changing society and its changing language, particularly the major types of language change and the important social and cultural events and circumstances that are correlated with linguistic changes, will be examined in the next chapter. Further instances of language as index and record will also be presented in connection with other phases of the present study.

4. *Names as Culture Recordings*

The identification function of names was briefly examined in Chap. III, Sect. 2 above. The significance of the names of persons and groups with respect to the social power they give, their role as social classifiers and as social status indicators, and the effects of change of name will be treated in Chap. XIV, Sect. 2 below.

Places, things, persons, families and all sorts of discoveries and inventions are named as they are for many different reasons. Some of these reasons will be presented in the discussions to follow. Consonant with the special theme of this chapter, however, our intention at this point is briefly to examine some of the ways in which names and changes of names indicate and record cultural origins, social situations prevailing at given times, changing conditions (especially changing folkways, customs and institutions), epochal political or economic occurrences, and outstanding cultural values, preoccupations and interests, at different points of time and place in the past. The examination of these different kinds of names will epitomize the major principles presented thus far in this chapter, and provide factual illustrations.

It is also worthy of note that, in many instances, the names of places, things and persons are durable records of the past, often outliving the entities that they indicated. In the case of place-names, ancient designations for localities have often persisted with great tenacity, surviving invasions and conquests, stupendous economic and technological shifts, and other accidents and incidents of time.

a / Place-names. One can derive a great deal of the history of an area from its place names, for many of them indicate the way in which the factors and features of the natural environment impressed its settlers, and reflect especially the past values and beliefs, the ethnic makeup, the cultural backgrounds and social interests of its settlers and later inhabitants, as well as signaling social events during its history.

Early natural factors that impressed the first settlers and led to their use as the basis for place-names were mountains or other striking physiographic or physical features (Mountain View, Breeze Creek, Buena Vista, Fir Top Mountain, Fresh Water Lagoon); at-site resources, in many instances later exhausted or despoiled (Agate Creek, Gold Bluffs, Gold Hill, Box Springs Canyon); notable animals and plants, some long since disappeared (Eagle Peak, Goose Lake, Wolf Point, Antelope Creek, Elk Flats, Ouzel Basin, Sunflower Valley).

Other place-names indicate the use of the site. For example, the names ending in the Anglo-Saxon *-burg, -burgh, -borough* (Hamburg, Edinburgh, Pittsburgh), which means "fortified town," were originally designations for fortresses or for places of refuge for the surrounding countryside. Similarly, the *-chester, -caster, -cester* endings are Latin (*castrum* = "encampment" or "fort"). Former economic use is often indicated ("Street of the Silversmiths," "Market Street," "Mill Creek"). The early use of sites is sometimes reflected in the present name. Telegraph Hill in San Francisco, for example, originally was used to semaphore the arrival of ships coming through the Golden Gate, to the inhabitants of the town. Gas Point in California is where old prospectors gathered to "gas and spin yarns." There are hundreds of place-names like "Scaffold Meadows," "Smuggler's Cove," "Battle Mountain," and "Battle Creek." Harpers Ferry was once a ferry terminal.

Places of origin of early settlers, or places abroad of great repute, have been important elements in American place-names. We have a whole series of "New's"—New York, New Jersey, New Orleans, New Hampshire, New London, New Bedford, New Richmond—reflecting the early origins, and possibly the nostalgia for the ancestral place, of at least some of the founding fathers. Also reflective of the origin of early settlers, or of their sharp interest in the foreign places, are Dublin, Amherst, Richmond, Paris, Oxford, Cambridge, Berlin, Manchester, Moscow, Dresden, Norwich, Maidstone, Bath. Places of classical antiquity have had high prestige in our American culture heritage, and are reflected in such place-names as Troy, Ithaca, Syracuse, Utica, Thebes, Carthage, Athens, Rome, Memphis, Cairo.

Many of the names of our cities and towns reveal our historical interest in important personages: royalty and nobility, great warriors, statesmen, explorers, outstanding pioneers and settlers, local benefactors. We have at least one and in some instances several dozen places named Baltimore, Elizabeth, Raleigh, Franklin, Madison, Lincoln (there are 26 Lincolns in the United States), Washington, Pittsburgh or Pittsfield, Jefferson, Monroe, Harrison. Frequently, the community revealed its conception of greatness by its choice of the name of the "type of hero"; it has also felt that, in doing so, it was honoring itself. Like many other peoples, we have sought to honor our great men by naming streets and highways after them.

The American Indian background in our history is copiously demonstrated. There are towns named after Indian chiefs, such as Pontiac and Tecumseh. The names of Indian tribes appear in such cities and places as Mohawk, Allegheny, Natchez, Cherokee, Walla Walla, Kalamazoo, Sioux City, Sioux Falls, Mackinac, Ponca City. The following states have names derived from Indian terms: Arkansas, Massachusetts, Connecticut, Minnesota, Mississippi, Missouri, Nebraska, Florida, the Dakotas, Oklahoma, Iowa, Ohio and Wyoming. Lincoln, Nebraska has almost a dozen streets named after the important Indian tribes of the region.

The familiarity of the frontiersmen with the Bible is reflected in the many places with Biblical names: Bethel, Jordan, Canaan, Bethlehem, Gilead, Goshen, Hebron, Mt. Carmel, Zion, Moab, Eden. The strong interest in the Christian Church, and the fact that many of the founders of American places were staunch Catholics, shows up in the places named after Catholic saints: San Francisco, San Gabriel, San Pedro, Santa Clara, Santa Catalina (Catherine), Saint Augustine, St. Petersburg, St. Louis. The names of towns derived from the Book of Mormon (for example, Moroni, Nephi, Lehi) reveals the fact that Utah was largely settled originally by Latter-day Saints.

Persons who were important in the early history of an area, as soldiers, engineers, naturalists, geologists, are indicated in the names they have given to places: Agnew Lake, Muir Woods, Donner Pass, Lake McConaughy.

A significant aspect of place-names is the fact that changes in them recorded changes in the "political weather" of the place or region. With the British conquest of Manhattan Island and its environs in 1664, Nieuw Amsterdam became New York. In Russia since the Revolution of 1917, there has been a notable changing of names of places, as the political administration and the social ideology have changed. A conspicuous instance is St. Petersburg, which became successively Petrograd and then Leningrad. With the shift to "moderation" under Khrushchev, especially regarding the Soviet international program, there was a widespread abandonment of "Stalin" as a place-name or as a component of place-names.

b / Thing names. The names of things, in some instances quite unexpectedly, reveal places of origin or early appearances of things, or their discoverers or inventors or persons in other ways connected with the object.

The names of some things are derived from and identified with the name of the country, region or town in which an industry carried on their production: *damask* from Damascus, *muslin* from Mosul on the Euphrates, *cambric* from Cambrai, *gin* from Geneva, *sherry* from Jerez in Spain, *frankfurter* from Frankfurt, *hamburger* from Hamburg. The names of certain varieties of dogs register their place of origin: *Newfoundland* came from the island of Newfoundland; *Pomeranian* from Pomerania; *Pekingese* from the city of Peking; *Airedale* from the valley or "dale" of Aire in Yorkshire, England.

The names of other things record the inventor: the *sandwich* is named after the Earl of Sandwich, who could not take time for regular meals away from the gambling table, and had a slice of meat between two slices of bread brought to him as he gambled; *daguerrotype* is from Daguerre, its inventor, *macadam* from McAdam or Macadam, who contrived that type of road surfacing, *marconigram* from Guglielmo Marconi, the inventor of wireless telegraphy; *pralines* are named after Marshall du Plessis-Praslim of France, whose cook first produced them in the seventeenth century; the *guillotine* was named for Dr. Guillotin, French physician, by its inventor, Dr. Antoine Louis. In English we have an array of names for electrical units that record and celebrate their physicist inventors: *ampère* from André Marie Ampère, the Frenchman; *watt* from the Scottish James Watt; *volt* and *voltage* from Allesandro Volta, the Italian; *ohm* from the German, Dr. G. S. Ohm; *farad* from Sir Michael Faraday, the Englishman; and the *galvanometer* from the Italian physicist, Luigi Galvani. Some verbs indicate important or notorious actions of certain persons: for example, *boycott* after Captain Charles Boycott, a notable early victim in Ireland of that type of action; *gerrymander,* after Governor Elbridge Gerry of Massachusetts, during whose term of office (and with whose connivance) such an arbitrary piece of redistricting was effected; *pasteurize,* from Louis Pasteur, the great French chemist and bacteriologist.

Some of the more recently discovered flowers are named after their discoverers, or in honor of some distinguished individuals; thus, the *dahlia* is named after Andreas Dahl, Swedish botanist; the *camellia* after the Jesuit, Josef Kamal; the *lobelia* after the Flemish botanist, Matthias de Lobal; *zinnia* after the German medical doctor, J. G. Zinn; and the *magnolia* after the Frenchman, Pierre Magnol.

Several of the Anglo-American days of the week indicate our early devotion to the ancient Teutonic gods and goddesses. Thus *Tuesday* is Tew's day, the day named after the Teutonic god of war; *Wednesday* is the day of the god Woden; *Thursday* is the day of Thor, god of thunder; *Friday* belongs to Frig, wife of Woden; *Saturday* is Saturn's day, indicating the Roman influence.

The emergence of astronomy among peoples whose minds were dominated by mythology is reflected in the large number of mythological names given to stellar systems and units, and to other astronomical phenomena.

c / Personal and family names. The names of persons, both given and family names, in greater or less degree record certain types of facts, historical or contemporary. *Personal names,* in general, if traced back in time and culture, provide valuable leads as to personal qualities and characteristics, traditional folklore (which has a bearing upon or suggests possible "identification tags"), the religious beliefs of the users, forms of endearment (and obloquy), and special nationality interests.[18] Some widely used personal or first names among us record certain significant interests of our culture. Most outstanding of all is the manner in which first names show the weight of the Christian Church heritage and the prestige of Biblical personages and saints of the Church. While some of them are not so widely used as a century ago, some first names of Biblical origin for males still occasionally found are: Adam, Abraham, Isaac, Jacob, Noah, Ezekiel, David, Daniel, and Job from the Old Testament, and Joseph, Matthew, Mark, Luke, John, Peter, Andrew, James, Stephen, Timothy and Thomas from the New Testament. Biblical female names of common use are Eva, Deborah, Rachel, Ruth, Naomi, Mary, Martha. Some names are due to great Church emphasis (for example, "Mary," in the Roman Catholic division), or to the fact that that person was particularly favored by, or especially endeared himself to Christians (for example, the disciple John); they have had and still have very wide currency. It is reported that in the United States alone there are over *six million Marys and four million Johns*.[19] "John," particularly in the form of Jean, Johann, Giovanni, Evan, Yves, and Ivan is a highly-favored name in the languages of many other Christian peoples. Among Spanish-speaking Christians, there is a wide use of "Jesus" as a first name, though this use is frowned upon by English-speaking Americans. Rather common first names from saints are Anthony, Bernard, Gregory, Nicholas, Augustine (August, Austin), and Vincent.

Other first names, popular for some time partly, at least, because they were the names of great heroes, include William (William the Conqueror) and Frederick or Fred (Frederick the Great).

Most of the *family names* have roots that go back to antiquity; in the course of time they have undergone many modifications. English surnames have been derived mainly in one of four ways: (1) from the personal name of some person, usually a sire or ancestor (the patronymics such as *Peterson,* son of Peter, or *Williamson,* son of William, or *Babson,* Barbara's son; (2) from a locality of some key ancestor (Hill, Wells, Rivers, Banks, Wood, Green, Ford, Field, Meadows, Moore (moor), Lee (lea), or Hastings, Lincoln, London, Berlin, Frankfurter, Schweitzer, Rosenfeld, Lilienthal, Churchill, Haywood, Underwood; (3) from the trade or office of some ancestor (Cook, Weaver, Barber, Smith, Taylor, Clothier, or Reeves, Constable, Marshall, Major (overseer), Beadle, Bailey (bailiff), Ward (guard); (4) from some outstanding physical or personality (especially moral) attribute of some ancestor (White, Brown, Long, Cruikshanks, Good, Goodman, Olds, Longfellow, Doolittle).[20]

Of special interest to us in the present discussion is the fact that the appearance of certain types of family names at certain times is a record of certain important types of events—economic, political, technological, demographic and so on. Three examples of the correlation of social and name changes will be given.

The medieval proliferation and spread of craft names is a notable instance. This not only calls attention to a series of portentous economic-technological changes then occurring, but also shows what the important trades were at that time, as compared with the present, and in addition what trades have since disappeared. From the days of Charlemagne on, in Central, Western, and Northwestern Europe—but especially during and after the Crusades and the Commercial Revolution—there was a tremendous development of trade. This came with the new division of labor and specialization of skills; it was, in fact, an integral aspect of it, and resulted in the rise of towns and city industries. The guilds of the "free crafts" were an organized phase of this development.

Various characteristics of this multiplication of crafts are reflected in the names. One is the vast number and diversity of these names of the time, many of which have persisted far beyond the actual functioning of the trades, and are now "fossilized." In addition to those just mentioned above, the following have been widely represented: Mercer, Chandler (candlemaker), Seaman, Bricker, Carpenter, Joiner, Shearer, Fuller, Draper, Dyer, Carter, Bleecher (cloth bleacher), Walker (originally a cloth trampler), Shepherd, Farmer, Forester, Fowler, Leadbeater, Minter, Glover, Saddler, Tanner, Brewer, Miller, Baker, Collier, Snyder (cutter), Mason, Cooper, Currier, Gardner, Tyler, Arkwright, Steward.

Another feature is the evidence in the names of a relatively high degree of craft specialization. The modern *Smiths*, judging from the varieties of different specialties to be seen in the names of the medieval smiths, include descendants of blacksmiths, white-smiths, brown-smiths, locksmiths, silversmiths, goldsmiths, arrowsmiths. In connection with the practice of archery and the making of gear for it, we have to this day such names as Fletcher (arrowmaker), Bowmaster, Stringer, Arrowsmith, Bowman, Archer, Boyer (the man who makes or sells bows). The ecclesiastical names of the period and earlier, indicate a marked division of functions and statuses: Pope, Bishop, Abbott, Dean, Deacon, Monk, Priest, Chaplin.

The change of family names of an area may reflect another type of major social occurrence—namely *conquest*. The Norman Conquest, as we shall note in a later chapter, not only greatly enriched the vocabulary of the English with French words, but also brought a great influx of foreign names, as a new and permanent deposit: Bosanquet, Durand, Garrick, Martineau, Plimsoll.

Demographic change of profound proportions was repeatedly recorded in the vast diversification of family names in a country. Any telephone directory in the United States bespeaks the vast in-migration into our country, century after century, by peoples from the ends of the earth. The additions of new names indicate the successive waves of immigrants from different nations and regions of the world, as they settled different sections: Spanish, English, Dutch, French, German, Swedish, and then the peoples and names from southern and eastern Europe, from Asia Minor, and from Asia. Such a diversifying of names tells us much about economic contrasts and changes both in the country of departure and in that of admission, about changes in international conditions and relations, changing attitudes toward racial and ethnic groups in the country of admission, changes in national legislation with regard to the admission of certain racial stocks, and so on.

A related aspect of this change is the fact that the assimilation of immigrants into the United States has been evidenced in the Americanization of their names. For example, we note the appearance of German names in America from 1683 on, but we also note a progressive de-Germanizing of typical German family names; for example, Löwe to Lowe, Müller to Miller, Schmal to Small, Schmidt to Smith, Werner to Warner, Reuss to Royce, Weiss to Wise, Fuchs to Fox, Steinman to Rockefeller, Huber to Hoover. Mencken exhaustively analyzes the Americanization of Jewish, Norwegian, Swedish, Danish, Spanish, French, Italian, Chinese, Japanese, and other nationality surnames.[21]

5. *The Linguistic System as Partial Determinant of the Perceptual–Conceptual Processes of the Language Community*

a / The basic conception and its theoretical orientation: metalinguistics. In Chapter III we noted the function of language in perception, categorization, and thinking. We are now concerned with the fact that any language as a "going concern" *(as it functions at any given time)* is a powerful *determinant* of *what* its speakers perceive and categorize, *how* they *think, what* they *think about* among the myriad possibilities, and *what* is *important* and *valuable* and *real* for them. This set of facts and hypotheses also carries forward the analysis of the present chapter another very important step. The given language is not only a sociocultural index of the language community, as it is at the given time, and a record and inventory of the experiences of its speakers through time, but also, because of its unique development and conformation in these aspects, as compared with those of any other language, it has its particular body of words (vocabulary, terminology, or lexicon); its peculiar morphology, or kinds of words as they function as identifiers, classifiers, indicators of actions, modifiers (with their particular "form" characteristics, with respect to number, case, tense, gender, prefix, and suffix); its syntactical structure, whereby it puts all its given words together in its own particular scheme of orderly arrangement, as it states and explicates, and its semantic system, which carries its whole body of meanings, as expressed in its words, phrases and sentences. These inseparable features are peculiar in the forms they take in any language, even among languages of the same family, and the differences between unrelated language families (for example, English and Chinese) are so great as to give the novice in language study the notion that the languages that he does not know as his "mother tongue" do not demonstrate "standard" linguistic principles (which, of course, they do, in their own language communities).

Each language is a peculiar whole. Each language has its own pattern, independent of the patterns of other languages. Each language is, in a sense, a closed corporation, with its own laws, directives, and board of directors.

Particularly to be noted is the fact that each language has its own "spirit," "psyche," "ethos," "style," "inner form," "genius," "individuality," or "idiosyncracy," as different students put it. This is a product, even an expression, of the "cultural particularity" and the "spiritual personality," to use the terms that Vossler[22] uses of the language speakers through time. This is not a new discovery, as we shall see.

The peculiar "style" or "spirit" of the people is expressed in many ways: in their traditions and customs, their mores, their prevailing attitudes, beliefs, and opinions, their ideologies, their art—in fact, in most of their institutions, aspirations and goals. But this "style" is particularly reflected in and conveyed by the language: its vocabulary, morphology and syntax, its idioms, metaphors and analogies, even its diction and pronunciation—the "lilt" and "tempo" and "inflection" of its speakers. This individuality is not true only of languages that have sharp differences of vocabulary and grammar and diction, but also of those that are closely related—languages like Portuguese, Spanish, French and Italian. It is even noted sometimes among the speakers of the different regional dialects of the same language; Vossler, for example, speaks of "the transition from the Bavarian to the Suavian language spirit."[23] This so readily felt psychic difference between languages, and even between dialects or other "special" languages, is due to the fact that a language is "total of all the individual meanings that are expressed in it." Furthermore, "Every member of a language community develops a feeling for the habits and possibilities of psychic expression. For only those things can be meant and expressed in a language that are allowed by common use."[24]

Especially significant in our present discussion is the fact that the language as established by its speakers and as it stands at any given time turns upon them, "contains" them in its peculiar grammatical forms and semantic structure, fits them with much of the "style" of their culture, and regiments much of their thinking and acting. They are, in Dylan Thomas's phrase: "Shut . . . in a tower of words. . . ." Most persons, of course, are quite unaware of their dependence and subservience. This is because language is not only the means of almost all communication, but also the most elemental, omnipresent, inescapable, and powerful conditioning, shaping, even determining agency. Language, as we have seen, is an institutionalized system, which comes into being before all of its present speakers. It is a system into which they unconsciously fit, just as they fit into the determining patterns of the previously existing economic or political order. Each language operates as an instrument which guides its habitual users in observing, reacting and expressing themselves. It provides for the speakers a combination of attitudinal atmosphere and conceptual platform, which is spoken of commonly as their *Weltanschauung*. Each language "marks off" for its native speakers all of their "working" interpretations of reality—their interpretation of what they comprehend as essences, things, forms, processes, actions, time and temporal sequence, space and distance, quantities and qualities, and the manner in which they comprehend these. In considerable part, it provides its speakers, as members of a linguistic, and hence, of a common cultural community, with what they are aware of, what they imagine, believe, and feel, their ideas—in short what they think about and the way they think. It carries for its speakers their connotations and interpretations of what is existential, important and valuable in the universe.[25]

The language of a body of speakers has had their metaphysical word-picture of the world, their "stylizing" of it, *built into it* over the ages, and it tends to impose itself ever anew on posterity. The language has a tendency to structure their experience; it also patterns much of their overt behavior, as we shall see in later chapters. For the enduring community, the language couches what Durkheim called the "collective representations"—the collective representations of *all* of the "reality" of which the group is aware.

Concisely, then, each language is for its speakers a sort of ready-made set of spectacles[26] whereby they see the world, and a ready-made set of formulae whereby they state and interpret and live with *what* they see. To be born into a speech community is to acquire automatically these linguistic patterns. In effect, this means that the patterns operate as determiners.[27] Not only are the speakers unaware of this influence; they could not escape from it, and most would not care to, once they realized the nature of the metalinguistic situation in which they were "imprisoned," since their language gives the only "correct" view of things.

Any comparative study of culture shows that people derive very different pictures of the universe, depending on the language pattern in which their ideas came to be formulated.

This special area of linguistic study has come to be known as *metalinguistics* (or superlinguistics). The inventors of the term describe it as follows:

> This (the area termed metalinguistics) can be said to include the over-all relation of the linguistic system of the cultural totality. (p. 81).
> Metalinguistics includes the various matters often referred to as "ethnolinguistics," but is far more inclusive. Not only does it deal with WHAT people talk about and WHY, but also considers HOW they use the linguistic system, and how they react to its use. This leads further to the consideration of how the linguistic system affects the behavior, both conscious and unconscious, and the world-view of the speaker, and governs or influences the interactions between individuals and between groups. Linguistic behavior is, by definition, part of the overt culture, but the study of it as metalinguistics shows it to be not only a guide to the covert culture, but, in large part, the structural framework itself of the covert culture or sentiment-structure (p. 82).[28]

b / The Sapir–Whorf hypothesis: the major proponents and the essence of their contentions. The major formulation of the notion that the perceptions and thought and views of nature and of the world in general on the part of any given body of speakers is controlled, for the most part unconsciously, by their language is frequently spoken of in contemporary sociology, ethnology, and linguistics as the "Sapir–Whorf Hypothesis." It is thought by many to have been conceived by Edward Sapir in the 1920's of the present century; very similar ideas were developed by Korzybski at about the same time, and then given extended development by their major proponent, Benjamin Lee Whorf, in the 1930's. The root elements of the hypothesis, however, are much older.[29]

[1] *The ancients.* There is some evidence of this among the ancients. Ancient India, for example, was aware of the "inner affinity of language and the cosmic order," and of the significance of set patterns in control. Heraclitus (500 B.C.) and his followers were convinced, according to Cornford, that "the structure of man's speech reflects the structure of the world," and is "an embodiment or representation of it."[30]

[2] *Herder and Von Humboldt.* Greenberg points out that approaches somewhat similar to the Sapir–Whorf hypothesis may be found in modern times among European writers, and that these are "particularly strong in the German-speaking world," where they can be "traced back at least as far as Herder in the latter part of the eighteenth century." The great German philologist, Wilhelm von Humboldt, in the early nineteenth century presented the first definitive statement of the hypothesis. In his *Werke,* he stated: "Every language in each of its stages structures a complete world-view, in that it contains expressions not only for all the concepts which its speakers have of the world, but for all those which the world brings forth in it."[31] A little later in the same volume (p. 60), he presents the very essence of the idea of language as determinant: "Der Mensch lebt mit den Gegenständen hauptsächlich, ja . . . sogar ausschlieslich so wie Sprache sie ihm zuführt." (Man lives with situations primarily, yes exclusively, as language directs him.) Humboldt's influence is represented in a group of contemporary German scholars usually called the Neo-Humboldtians. Of the work of one of these, Professor Jost Trier, Ullman says: "His investigations revealed the existence of an inner universe of standards and ideals of distinctions and values enshrined in the linguistic medium; they located the concepts deemed sufficiently important to be given separate verbal labels; they reconstructed the general framework of thought and appreciation imposed by the vocabulary on the community, the unique prism through which past generations had viewed, interpreted and classified the various aspects of knowledge and intelligence."[32]

[3] *Korzybski.* Alfred Korzybski, a contemporary of Sapir and Whorf, in his *Science and Sanity,* first published in 1924, set for himself

the task of analyzing the structure of language, ranging from that of the insane to that of mathematical physicists, and of relating that structure to human behavior, to a theory of culture, and to history. One particular effort was to get the language of science accurately to state the nature of world structure as revealed by empirical study. This led to stress—among other aspects of language—the fact that a comparative study of the structure of different languages shows that they reflect the conceptions of the world held by those who developed the language, and that the languages as they stand "enslave" the "semantic reactions" of their users. Incidentally, Korzybski was much impressed by the work to date of the young man, Whorf, and made reprints of Whorf's articles available to his students.

Points of Korzybski's contention are somewhat as follows. Languages at best are only maps. Words are not the objects they represent. The structure of the language alone is the link which connects our verbal processes with the data of experience. Every language has its own peculiar structure, and in this structure it reflects the world as assumed by those who evolved the language. "In other words, we read unconsciously into the world the structure of the language we use." Furthermore, "every language has at its bottom certain metaphysics, which ascribe, consciously or unconsciously, some sort of structure to this world." The structure of an habitual language has tremendous power. Furthermore, "it is not an exaggeration to say that it [the structure of an habitual language] enslaves us through the mechanism of semantic reaction and that the structure which a language exhibits, and impresses on us unconsciously, is *automatically projected* upon the world around us."[33]

[4] *Sapir.* The classic statements of the metalinguistic position, of course, are those of Sapir and Whorf. Sapir in 1929 presented the key elements. Language is a guide to "social reality"; it powerfully conditions all our thinking about our social problems and processes. As human beings live in the objective world and the world of social activity, they are "very much at the mercy of the particular language which has become the medium of expression for their society." Language is not merely an incidental means of solving specific problems of communication and reflection; actually, the real world is to a large extent unconsciously built upon the language habits of the group. Each language represents a particular social reality. The "social patterns called words" affect even our simple acts of perception. "We see and hear and otherwise experience as we do because the language habits of our community predispose certain choices of interpretation."[34]

In further development of the basic thesis, Sapir states:

Language is not merely a more or less systematic inventory of the various items of experience which seem relevant to the individual, as is so often naively assumed, but is also a self-contained, creative, symbolic organization, which not only refers to experience largely acquired without its help but actually defines experience for us by reason of its formal completeness and because of our unconscious projection of its implicit expectations into the field of experience. . . . [Meanings are] not so much discovered in experience as imposed upon it, because of the tyrannical hold that linguistic form has upon our orientation in the world.[35]

[5] *Whorf*. Benjamin Lee Whorf (d. 1941), a student of Sapir, stands out, however, as the chief and best known proponent and expositor of the metalinguistic hypothesis. He has left an extensive and impressive body of writings in explication and illustration of his viewpoint.[36] In some of these articles we have the careful and detailed exposition of the theory of his position. The great bulk of them, however, are studies he made of North and South American Indian languages, which permit comparison of the cultures in general, the *Weltanschauung* and the languages in particular, and which serve as evidence of at least the relative validity of his thesis.

Most of the essential features of Whorf's contention are to be found in his article on "Science and Linguistics."[37] He points out that talking or the use of language is more than a process concerned strictly with communication—more than merely a linguistic formulation. The grammars of the different languages are not merely norms of conventional and social correctness, and guides to rational or intelligent thinking. "When linguists became able to examine critically and scientifically a large number of languages of widely different patterns, their base of reference was expanded." They discovered that

. . . the background linguistic system (in other words, the grammar) of each language is not merely a reproducing system for voicing ideas; but rather is itself the shaper of ideas, the program and guide for the individual's mental activity, for his analysis of impressions, for his synthesis of his mental stock in trade. Formulation of ideas is not an independent process, . . . but is part of a particular grammar, and differs, from slightly to greater, between different grammars (p. 212).

Whorf's classic epitomization of his contention is as follows:

We dissect nature along lines laid down by our native languages. The categories and types that we isolate from the world of phenomena we do not find there because they stare every observer in the face; on the contrary, the world is presented in a kaleido-scopic flux of impressions which has to be organized by our minds —and this means largely by the linguistic systems in our minds. We cut nature up, organize it into concepts, and ascribe signifi-cances as we do, largely because we are parties to an agreement to organize it in this way—an agreement that holds throughout our speech community and is codified in the patterns of our language. The agreement is, of course, an implicit and unstated one, *but its terms are absolutely obligatory;* we cannot talk at all except by sub-scribing to the organization and classification of data which the agreement decrees (p. 214).

We are thus introduced to a new principle of relativity, which holds that all observers are not led by the same physical evidence to the same picture of the universe, unless their linguistic back-grounds are similar, or can in some way be calibrated (p. 214).

Whorf then notes that this "rather startling conclusion is not so apparent if we compare only our modern European languages" since these are all Indo-European dialects "cut to the same basic plan." But when Semitic, Chinese, Tibetan, or African languages, or the native languages of the Americas, "where speech communities for many millenniums have gone their ways independently of each other and of the Old World," are contrasted with our own, the divergence in the analysis of the world becomes apparent. "The relativity of all conceptual systems, ours included, and their dependence upon language stand revealed."

The relation of language and human behavior is dealt with by Whorf in his article, "The Relation of Habitual Thought and Behavior to Language," written in 1939.[38] It is in language's ordinary everyday analysis of phenomena that we need to recognize its influence on other activities, cultural and personal.

The cue to a certain line of behavior is often given by the analogies of the linguistic formula in which the situation is spoken of, and by which to some degree it is analyzed, classified, and allotted its place in that world, which is to a large extent unconsciously built up on the language habits of the group (p. 137).[39]

c / **Supporting evidence.** A comparison of the many native languages of the Americas studied by Whorf[40] with each other, and also as they are examined in contrast to our language or the languages of Western civilization, tends to sustain the major contentions of this hypothesis. In the article of 1939 just referred to, Whorf contrasts our language, SAE ("Standard Average European") with Hopi, with respect to the very different kinds and uses of terminology and the correlated cultural differences. For example, the two languages show in their terms and the way in which their speakers use them, syntactically and semantically, marked differences in the conception of plurality and numbers, in awareness of time, in the nouns of physical quantity, in the terms dealing with the phases of temporal cycles, in the temporal forms of verbs, and in expressions of duration, intensity, and tendency. He brings out the difference by contrasting, in brief summary, the "habitual thought worlds" of SAE and Hopi speakers. By "thought world" he means "the microcosm that each man carries about within himself, by which he measures and understands what he can of the macrocosm."[41]

> The SAE microcosm has analyzed reality largely in terms of what it calls "things" (bodies and quasibodies) plus modes of extensional but formless existence through a binomial formula that expresses any existence as a spatial formless continuum related to the form, as contents is related to the outlines of its container. Nonspatial existents are imaginatively spatialized and charged with similar implications of form and continuum (p. 147).

> The Hopi microcosm seems to have analyzed reality largely in terms of *events* (or better "eventing"), referred to in two ways, objective and subjective. Objectively, and only if perceptible physical experience, events are expressed mainly as outlines, colors, movements, and other perceptive reports. Subjectively, for both the physical and nonphysical, events are considered the expression of invisible intensity factors, on which depend their stability and persistence, or their fugitiveness and proclivities. It implies that existents do not "become later and later" all in the same way; but some do so by grownig like plants, some by diffusing and vanishing, some by a procession of metamorphoses, some by enduring in one shape till affected by violent forces. In the nature of each existent able to manifest as a definite whole is the power of its own mode of duration: its growth, decline, stability, cyclicity, or creativeness. Everything is thus already "prepared" for the way it now manifests by earlier phases, and what it will be later, partly has been, and partly is in the act of being so "prepared." An emphasis and importance rests on this preparing or being prepared aspect of the world that may to the Hopi correspond to that "quality of reality" that "matter" or "stuff" has for us (pp. 147–148).

In the same article, he also indicates some of the "habitual behavior ("outer" and "inner") features of Hopi culture revealed in their language" as compared with "some impressions of linguistic habit in Western civilization," and also certain "historical implications" of the respective "language–culture complexes."[42]

Ancient Chinese, like most oriental languages, offers other instances of marked linguistic differences, which reflect in turn marked differences in *Weltanschauung,* as compared with our language and viewpoints. In line with Marcel Granet's early article,[43] Lindesmith and Strauss point out that the vocabulary of the ancient Chinese was concrete, specific, picturesque and descriptive. Almost all the words in it were used to evoke complex and specific images. Instead of using adjectives in connection with nouns, they included the whole description in one word. For example, they had seventeen words for various kinds and conditions of "mountains": one word for "bare mountain," another for "high mountain," another for "high mountain covered with vegetation," another for "a high and vast mountain." Furthermore, "Where the Occidental thinker can express his thoughts exactly and quickly, the Chinese had to do so by a kind of symbolization akin to poetic activity. The world thus appeared to the Chinese as a complex of particular aspects and images. Chinese thought, as reflected by the language, was oriented toward particulars, not toward generalizing or abstracting."[44] Similarly Merton points out[45] ". . . the Chinese language is not equipped to note concepts, analyze ideas, or to present doctrines discussively. It has remained intractable to formal precision." "Words and sentences . . . have an entirely emblematic character." "Just as the language is concrete and evocative, so the most general ideas of ancient Chinese thought were unalterably concrete, none of them comparable to our abstract ideas. Neither time nor space were abstractly conceived. Time proceeds by cycles and is round; space is square. . . . Techniques of the division and management of space . . . and the geometrical speculations which they presuppose are all linked with a set of social regulations."[46] The peculiar way of presenting time in Chinese might also be noted. The verb in English and Latin has time divided into past, present and future; China has four pasts at successively remote periods, periods from the present, a present and a future.

d / Some sociocultural implications. Even if language is only a partial determinant in the respects indicated, the metalinguistic hypothesis has certain profound social and cultural effects or implications, several of the more obvious of which will now be briefly discussed.

[1] *To know men you need to know what their linguistic usages mean to them.* Since these usages have such a significant influence on men's thought and social behavior, it is imperative that we know what linguistic items mean to them. The average man, when confronted with speakers of a different language, or sometimes even with speakers of

a different dialect, with their peculiar language structure and the correlated meanings they carry, "is likely to be nonplussed at first by what appear to him as fundamental deficiencies in intelligibility, or as outright departures from common sense, good logic, and good taste."[47] To "know" a person is to know how he thinks and how he interprets himself, his group and his world in his particular societal and cultural context; this, as we have seen, is revealed in and determined and limited by his language. Even intonations and emotional overtones, as well as specific connotations, have high pertinence as he reacts with his fellows. These facts obviously are very important in his contacts with members of other ethnic groups, with regional and national groups that speak a different language. Because of linguistic diversity and the correlative metaphysical diversity, there are vast possibilities not only of misunderstanding, but of complete lack of communication.

[2] *The meanings of words and phrases are dependent upon the social and behavioral function they perform.* This corollary to the proposition stated above has also been stated as follows by Mills: "Because language functions in the organization and control of behavior patterns, these patterns are determinants of the meanings in a language. Words carry meanings by virtue of dominant interpretations placed upon them by social behaviors. Interpretations or meanings spring from the habitual modes of behavior which pivot upon symbols. Such social patterns of behavior constitute the meanings of the symbols."[48]

[3] *A change of language of an individual or a group is a change of "world stance."* As has been at least implied so far, with the speaking of a language, as a cultural vehicle, go also the ideas and attitudes, the values, points of view and ways of life of its cultural community. A person speaking a language unavoidably participates to some degree in the ways of life represented by that language. A corollary of this is that a new cultural and social world, with new outlooks and demands and motivations, opens up for one who *really acquires* a new language. Pei has stated that "It has been fully established that a change in language on the part of an individual is attended by corresponding changes in gestures, facial expression, carriage, even humor and taboos."[49] Cherry states: "When I read French I . . . become as a different person with different thoughts; the language change bears with it a change of national character and temperament, a different history and literature."[50] This fact is observable in the case of bilingual speakers, as they pass from one language to another; they move from a world of one "style" and "psyche" and "ethos" to one in which these are quite different.[51]

With another language, one moves into another conceptual world: one notices new things and new categories of "reality"; one becomes aware of other values and other states of mind; one sees new sides of human sentiments, feelings, beliefs. According to an ancient maxim, "A man has as many souls as he has languages," and Wittgenstein has said, "If we spoke a different language, we would perceive a somewhat different world."

In this two-world situation also lies one of the great difficulties in *really learning* another language. Gray says: "Knowing a language is much more than possessing a thorough acquaintance with its grammatical forms, or than being able to read . . . it perfectly, or than having the ability to speak it fluently according to the rules of its best authorities. One may be amply qualified to do all this, and yet not really know the language so spoken or read. To possess true knowledge of a language is to feel it an integral part of one's self; it must not be 'foreign' in any sense."[52]

[4] *Language habits and traditions,* with all that they involve in the way of established and sanctioned vocabulary and grammatical and semantic structure, *may have a constraining effect on innovative thought.* In order to express new experiences, to develop new conceptions of reality—for example, in science and technology or in human relations —or to state new expressions of the human spirit, as in religion or aesthetics, it is necessary to have appropriate words and phrases with an ever-extending range of meanings. As we shall note in the next chapter, it is usually necessary to develop new words and other symbols to carry the new meanings or to give new meanings to some existing words. However, linguistic habits and traditions, like many others, are relatively rigid; consequently, there is nearly always a "lag" of language behind the demands made upon it by cultural and social changes. To be sure, the language patterns and the cultural milieu have grown together, constantly and reciprocally influencing each other, but as Whorf says:

> In this partnership the nature of the language is the factor that limits free plasticity and rigidifies channels of development in the more autocratic way. This is because a language is a system, not just an assemblage of norms. Large systematic outlines can change to something really new only very slowly, while many other cultural innovations are made with comparative quickness. Language thus represents the mass mind; it is affected by inventions and innovations, but affected little and slowly, whereas to inventors and innovators it legislates with the decree immediate.[53]

The effect of this is that language exists as a fixed frame of reference within which every intellectual effort, of people who are educated as well as those who are uneducated, must be made.

Attention must also be called to the inadequacy of language as the symbol of reality and in terms of the truncated view of reality that it gives. Symbols always in some respect or degree fall short of the reality they represent. The essence of this point is brought out by Katz: "Because of its symbolic nature, language is a poor substitute for the realities which it attempts to represent. The real world is more complex, more colorful, more fluid, more multidimensional than the pale words or oversimplified signs used to convey meaning."[54]

Related to these negative characteristics of language is a viewpoint voiced in an old saying: "Whoever speaks two languages is a rascal." It is also presented by Walter Bagehot[55]—namely, that another language alongside one's own brings about an intrusion of new ideas and new examples, and causes a confusion of one's consecrated concepts and codes.

[5] *Language has a determinative effect upon the range of perspective of individuals.* The significance for language users of metalinguistic structuring is evident, even within a given community, from a comparison between the much more limited cognitive and expressive world of the illiterate or poorly educated persons, with their small vocabularies and elementary syntax, and the cognitive and expressive world of the better educated circles, whose linguistic abilities permit them much more extensive awarenesses and perspectives, and a wider range and greater complexity of thought and action.

[6] *The problems of translation resulting from the metalinguistic situation.* As formidable as any of the effects so far mentioned of grammatical and semantic structuring of languages is the matter of translation from one language into another. Translation presents a situation of grave importance in a world of multiplied intercourse—economic, political, scientific, philosophical, literary and religious, voluntary and involuntary—between dozens of nations, most of which also form distinct language groups. In these contacts vast confusions, misunderstandings, conflicts—even nuclear world war—can result from some error, distortion or failure of communication. The difficulties encountered in the attempts to translate from one language into another are much more fundamental than they appear to be at first glance. The key problem of translation arises from the fact that each language is a complex unique system, whose structural and stylistic elements cannot be reproduced with complete exactitude of form, meaning and intent in any other language. As we have noted in the dis-

cussion of metalinguistics, every language provides its own specific and unique tools for expression and analysis, and to a great extent these determine for the speakers the problems they see and the solutions they find. The difficulties of translation are greatest between entirely unrelated languages—for example, the notorious difficulties of translating Chinese, or Bantu, or Vietnamese, or Hopi into American English. But there are many complications involved in translating between linguistic families within a major division of languages such as the Indo-European, for example, between the Germanic and the Romance languages, or even within families, for example, between French and Portuguese. Difficulties in translating some words and phrases of both ancient and modern languages are also commonplace. At the moment, one of the most crucial communication situations in the world involves the translation of English (as used in the United States) and Russian (as used in the U.S.S.R.) into each other, and into the other 2800 (plus or minus) languages of the world. In translating we are always crossing a greater or lesser barrier or "divide."

The factors that create the difficulties of translating between languages are numerous. There is, first of all, the diversity of the experiential worlds, historical and contemporary, of the users of the respective languages. Related to this is the diversity of their conceptual and semantic worlds. Particularly designative words—for example, "freedom," "democracy"—have very different meanings attached to them, as the result of the marked cultural (including the ideological and spiritual) differences between peoples.[56] In general, the wider the differences between the respective cultures, the greater the difficulty of achieving fairly accurate translation of their languages. There is also an array of complications attributable to the inherent differences of languages as systems, and these limit translation. The terminologies (vocabularies) may be quite different in what they refer to and what they categorize, depending upon the *Weltanschauung* of their speakers. Especially pertinent in this connection are the linguistic differentiations discussed earlier in the present chapter. Each language has its own morphological intricacies. Different languages sometimes lack parallel parts of speech. The syntactical structures always differ to a greater or less degree.[57] No two languages have the same range of meanings, nor are these meanings covered by comparable linguistic forms. The logical processes are not the same; it is almost impossible to transpose any logical idea unbroken (or even unbent) into another language. It is always very difficult to translate metaphors, images and idioms; these are often in themselves completely mystifying, even nonsensical, to the habitual users of another language. By no means least are the difficulties arising from the "spirit," "style," "soul," of the respective languages—non-structural, "internal" aspects—that almost defy even approximate reproduction in another language. Often, the most beautiful and telling phrases in one language seem to be despoiled of all their virtue or charm when rendered into another language. The practical or prosaic translator misses this delicate "inner" aspect of language altogether; but even the learned and sensitive comparative linguist has difficulty "externalizing" in one language the "inner" spirit of another.[58] Anyone with *Sprachgefühl* in several languages is quite aware of the difference in "spirit" and in both the categories and shades of meaning of the respective languages, as well as of his inability to express with exact sense in one language what he can so satisfactorily in another.[59]

Translation usually involves more than translating the text or utterance as accurately as possible. It is also affected by the purposes of the translator and the kind of material to be translated. Casagrande has distinguished the different purposes, and indicated the objectives of translation for each. The diverse purposes he has noted, with considerable reinterpretation of the objectives by the present writer, consist of: (1) the *pragmatic,* in which the emphasis is on the content of the message; (2) the *aesthetic-poetic,* in which the stress is on literary or aesthetic form; (3) the *linguistic,* where the interest centers around morphology and syntax; and (4) the *ethnographic,* where the prime concern is with the accuracy of the translation as a revelation of the ethnicity of its speakers.[60]

There is a saying: "Every translator is in part a traitor."[61] At any rate, he is a betrayer as far as exact restatement of precise content and exact representation of meaning, spiritual overtones, and other cultural nuances are concerned. The unhappy difficulties of the translator are condensed in the conclusion that, in effect, one does not translate *Languages,* one translates *Cultures.*[62] Hence, the pertinence of the statement: "Every translation is, strictly speaking, an interpretation, and an interpolation."[63] Thus in the end the "traitor" assumes a somewhat beneficent status in connection with the exceedingly difficult and portentous task of inter-people communication: he is not solely a mechanical transposer, but to some extent a creator, or re-creator.[64]

The dexterity, sometimes approaching legerdemain, that often has to be used, is indicated in the following quotations: "In translating the Bible into the Bulu language of the Cameroons, missionaries found that 'straightness' and 'kindness' were the closest they could get to 'righteousness' and 'grace,' while 'forgiveness' had to be translated into the Misketo Indian language of Nicaragua by 'taking-a-man's-fault-out-of-our-hearts,' and into Labrador Eskimo by 'not-being-able-to-think-about-it-any-more.' "[65]

Word comes from Rome that the publication of Pope John XXIII's recent encyclical *Mater et Magistra* was held up for two months because Vatican scholars had difficulty in translating into Latin some of the words and phrases there not originally encompassed by the language of ancient Latium. After truly heroic efforts, however, the job finally got done. "Atomic energy" came out *vis atomica,* and "radio and television" emerged as *radiophonica et televisifica.* But "the initial conquests of interplanetary space" required a more involved and colorful translation: *viae initiae per quas ad sidera ferar* which translated somewhat freely means "the beginning ways by which we are carried to the stars."[66]

There is now some prospect that electronic computers, using digital coding, may be used in turning one language code, at least in its written or alphabetic form, into another code in *its* written or alphabetic form. The American Air Force is said to have an electronic translating machine that can convert Russian novels and scientific texts into meaningful English.[67] So far the results of "robot rendering" are somewhat limited in scope and real accuracy of linguistic performance. A simple and factual one-to-one correspondence in vocabulary and structure is the best that can be achieved. The exact, entirely objective, and almost universal terms and formulae and other symbolic devices of scientific and technological language can be quite accurately transposed. But the operation is a purely mechanical one; as such, it is inconceivable that the machine would be able to translate the exceedingly important peculiar semantic and spiritual nuances attached to the symbols of one language into the symbols of another. The problem is especially difficult because, up until now at least, the metaphors, idioms, images, and other figurative expressions, and the peculiar meanings of certain words and phrases in particular context, are not caught and "sensed" by the machine, the "word-spell" is missed, and all these linguistic facets are not presented so as to reveal their peculiar stylistic and "inner" significance.[68] What can happen is indicated in the following: "A story is making the rounds these days about some scientists who designed an English-to-Russian translating machine. To test the device, they fed it the sentence, 'The spirit is willing but the flesh is weak.' Back came the translation: 'The liquor is good but the food is lousy.' "[69]

[7] *A note on the significance of language in the sociology of knowl-*

edge. Language is recognized as a fertile, in fact, indispensable subject of study and research in such specialized fields of investigation as semantics, anthropology, and psychology. Recently sociology has shown some awareness of its significance as a signal sociocultural product, and as a fundamental instrument and determinant in social behavior. However, in one special area of sociology in which language is so crucial—namely, the sociology of knowledge—there is almost no attention paid to it directly.[70] Nevertheless, the present viewpoint with regard to language as a crucial determinant of the processes of perception and conceptualization and of the establishment of the meaningfulness of the universe requires that at least the place of language in thinking about the nature of knowledge or the formation of knowledge (including the selection of items of knowledge), should be pointed out.

The sociology of knowledge is a special discipline within sociology. The term is used with a wide range of meanings. However, the basic contention is that knowledge is a social–cultural product, and that certain social factors influence (even determine) the mental productions of individuals, groups, and societies. It is essentially concerned with the relationship between thinking, knowledge (ideas), thought-styles, thought-systems and methods of thinking, *and* the existential (that is, the extra-theoretical, extra-cognitive, non-mental) historical and contemporary sociocultural factors. A little more specifically, Louis Wirth has suggested[71] that its main tasks are: to trace the bases of social judgments to their specific interest-bound roots in society; to note the types of concrete situation (for example, forms of social organization, including stratification system or status structure, power structure, quantity and quality of population, and also social-need situations and cultural levels), in which thought takes place and intellectual life is carried on; to show how the interests and purposes of certain groups (for example, social classes, political parties, ethnic groups, occupational groups, "intellectual-skill" groups, members of social movements) find expression in certain theories, doctrines, ideologies and intellectual movements; to discover the styles and methods of thought that are dominant in certain types of historical–social situations (as shown, for example, in Stoic thought in the third century B.C. and ensuing centuries in the east and central Mediterranean areas, early Christianity, the thought of the Renaissance, the Reformation, the French Enlightenment, socialism in the nineteenth and twentieth centuries, Utopianism in the early modern period and again in the nineteenth and twentieth centuries); to assess the role played by social institutions (political, economic, familial, technological) in the shaping, acquisition and transmission of knowledge.

In neglecting the relationship between language and the sociology of knowledge, we would be overlooking or slighting several important facts. The first is that language itself is one of the fundamental existential social conditions and influences; it is, in fact, prerequisite to the functioning of most of the others conventionally mentioned.

Second, when we are concerned with knowledge, we are concerned with the symbols that carry its content. We have noted repeatedly not only that the language of a people is their chief and most comprehensive symbolic system, but also that the meanings of all other symbols, if they are to become comprehensible to the people, must be translated into language forms. Werner Stark has stated that, without language, we can have no knowledge of things, for all of our knowledge is couched in words; our thought-processes consist in the use of words. "Even solitary and silent thinking is a kind of conversation. We really argue when we think."[72]

Third, we cannot sidestep the determinative influence of language structure upon thought, as brought out in the Sapir–Whorf Hypothesis, and as repeatedly demonstrated by comparative linguistic studies. Since all our information, knowledge, attitudes, and opinions are received through some act of communication, usually resolvable into language and couched in language, the structure of language is highly pertinent to the sociology of knowledge.[73]

Whorf asserted, it will be recalled, that the linguistic system is itself the shaper of ideas, the program and guide of the mental activity of the individual and of his analysis of impressions. His formulation of ideas is not an independent process, but to a greater or lesser extent part of a particular grammar. Later, in a passage not yet quoted here, he says:

> A person's thoughts are controlled by inexorable laws of pattern of which he is unconscious. These patterns are the unperceived intricate systematizations of his own language. . . . His thinking itself is in a language . . . and every language is a vast pattern system, different from others, in which are culturally ordained the forms and categories by which the personality not only communicates, but also . . . channels his reasoning, and builds the house of his consciousness.[74]

The principle extends beyond individuals as such. Groups and collectivities have their *general* thought channeled for them by the general language, but many of them—social classes, occupational (professional) groups, religious groups, scientists, etc.—have their "special" languages (to be examined at some length in a later chapter), which provide them with "special" perspectives, and operate as partial determinants of their thought processes, and as distinctive carriers of their special knowledge.

The language of the particular group is also an important factor in the "style" of their thinking as they respond to typical situations.

For the society, the language constitutes a vast but unique body of data, selected from the peculiar experience of the language community through its history, which forms both a shaping and a conditioning atmosphere, a kit of materials for its thinking and the means of getting what it thus knows in statable form.

Francis Bacon, three and a half centuries ago, pointed to a negative aspect of language that has direct bearing upon the sociology of knowledge. In connection with his discussion of the Four Idols, he denounced language as one of the most dangerous sources of deception. For him, it is the idol of the forum, verbalized illusions and prejudices that arise from the intercourse of men. He says: "Although we think we govern our words, yet certain it is that words as a Tartar's bow do shoot back upon the understanding of the wisest and mightily entangle and pervert the judgment."[75]

A further consideration of importance here is the already mentioned fact that the shortcomings of a language at any given time, with respect to the extent and variety of its terminology, morphology, syntax and semantic constructs, can have a limiting effect upon the kinds and range of thinking occasioned by new individual and social awarenesses, conditions and needs. Cassirer points out that the words of our language are originally created for a single and special purpose. But we cannot expect the descriptions and concepts made possible by these to be valid "when we pass the threshold of a new world"—for example, the structure of the atom or electron physics. There must be a change of words and fundamental concepts if we are to have more accurate "portraits of things." Otherwise, we "maintain a mere copy-theory of knowledge."[76]

The significance of language in the sociology of knowledge is thus by no means merely incidental; it is fundamental. Knowledge is always related to and to a considerable extent determined by the language learned and used. At the same time, knowledge may also be distorted and limited by it.

N O T E S

1 Cf. Mortimer Adler: "How to Read a Dictionary," *Saturday Review*, 23 (Dec. 13, 1941).

2 Both Sapir and Sturdevant have used the term "index." "In a sense, the network of cultural patterns of a civilization is indexed in the language which expresses that civilization." (Edward Sapir, "The Status of Linguistics as a Science,"

Language, 5 (1929), 207–214 (209).) "Vocabulary is a very sensitive index of the culture of a people." (Edward Sapir, "Language," *Encyclopedia of the Social Sciences* (New York: Macmillan Co., 1933), Vol. 9, p. 161.) "The words and phrases of a linguistic community . . . form a sort of index of the experience of all the members of that community." (Edgar H. Sturdevant, *An Introduction to Linguistic Science* (New Haven: Yale University Press, 1947), p. 123.)

3 Cf. Joseph H. Greenberg, "Linguistics and Ethnology," *Southern Journal of Anthropology,* 4 (Summer, 1948), 140–147.

4 Klineberg has summarized the "camel" terminology as follows: "There are said to be 6000 words connected in some way with 'camel,' including words derived from the camel and attributes associated with it. These include, for instance, names and classes of camels according to function—milk camels, riding camels, marriage camels, slaughter camels, etc.; names of breeds of different degrees of nobility of lineage, derivation from different lands, etc.; names of camels in groups, as several, a considerable number, innumerable, and with reference to their objects—grazing, conveying a caravan, war expeditions, etc.; as many as fifty words for pregnant camels, states of pregnancy, stage at which movement of the foetus is first felt, those who suckle and those who do not, those near delivery, etc." Otto Klineberg, *Social Psychology* (New York: Henry Holt & Co., 1940), pp. 44–45.

5 Georg Gerster, *Sahara: Desert of Destiny* (New York: Coward-McCann Publishing Co., 1960), p. 165.

6 "After consulting Gulliver on the function of his watch, the Lilliputians came to the conclusion that it was his God."

7 I am indebted for the major points in this paragraph to John B. Carroll, *The Study of Language: A Survey of Linguistics and Related Disciplines in America* (Cambridge: Harvard University Press, 1953), pp. 112–113.

8 Julian Samora and William N. Deane, "Language Usage as a Possible Index of Acculturation," *Sociology and Social Research,* 40 (May–June, 1956), 307–311.

9 These aspects have been brought out by James H. S. Bossard, "The Bilingual as Person—Linguistic Identification with Status," *American Sociological Review,* 10 (Dec., 1945), 699–709 (700).

10 Cf. George Herzog, "Culture Change and Language: Shifts in the Pima Vocabulary," in Leslie Spier, A. Irving Hollowell and Stanley S. Newman, *Language, Culture and Personality* (Menasha, Wis.: Sapir Memorial Publication Fund, 1941), pp. 66–74; G. D. H. Cole, *Essays in Social Theory* (London: Macmillan Co., 1950), pp. 219–220. One branch of the science of linguistics, etymology, is devoted to the history of words—the discovery of how a word came into being, and came to have the form and meaning it has today. It reveals much of social significance. Says John P. Hughes: "The course of this investigation often turns up a veritable treasure trove of unrecorded history, forgotten trades and traditions, the ways and conditions of life of other days, and choice archeological finds." (*The Science of Languages* (New York: Random House, 1962), pp. 205–207.) The comparative philosophy of the linguists also points to all sorts of social occurrences in the past among the whole train of speakers of the respective languages during their histories: the particular social circumstances of each people, the contacts of various kinds and under various conditions made by the people, migrations, all kinds of discoveries, inventions, borrowings, technological changes, and so on.

11 Note also: "In all efforts to reconstruct the past, he (the student of history) finds that words give *the light and shade* that is missing from the hard, clear-cut records found in the state papers and public documents, and hence he values them as an important accessory in the study of the past." Lucy M. Salmon, "Place-names and Personal Names as Records of History," *American Speech,* 2 (Feb., 1927), 228–231 (228).

12 Albert C. Baugh, *A History of the English Language* (New York: Appleton-Century-Crofts, 1957), p. 4.

13 Louis H. Gray, *Foundations of Language* (New York: Macmillan Co., 1939), pp. 10–11.

14 Cf. Richard T. La Piere, *Sociology* (New York: McGraw-Hill Book Co., 1947), p. 219.

15 From Margaret Schlauch, *The Gift of Language* (New York: Dover Publications, 1955), p. 274.

16 *Grundlegung einer Geschichte der Deutschen Sprache* (Halle: Max Niemeyer Verlag, 1948).

17 Hughes, pp. 81–87.

18 For a comprehensive treatment of "First Names" see Eloise Lambert and Mario Pei, *Our Names: Where They Came From and What They Mean* (New York: Lothrop, Lee & Shepard Co., 1960), pp. 15–19; H. L. Mencken, *The American Language* (New York: Alfred A. Knopf, 1945), Supplement I, pp. 462–525.

19 Mario Pei, *The Story of English* (Philadelphia: J. B. Lippincott, 1952), p. 131; Lambert and Pei, p. 52.

20 Cf. Ernest Weekley, *The Romance of Names* (New York: E. P. Dutton & Co., 1914), pp. 156–170; Lambert and Pei, pp. 71–72. At least all Western peoples and countries and many elsewhere, in so far as they have family names, reflect parallel derivations. For a comprehensive discussion of family names, see Lambert and Pei, pp. 71–125.

21 Mencken, *op. cit.*, pp. 396–462.

22 Karl Vossler, *The Spirit of Language in Civilization* (London: Routledge & Kegan Paul; (reprinted 1951), pp. 175–176.

23 *Ibid.*, p. 48.

24 *Ibid.*, pp. 47–49. See also Alfred L. Kroeber, "Total-Culture Pattern as Exemplified in Language," in his *Anthropology* (New York: Harcourt, Brace & Co., 1948), pp. 316–321. Virgil C. Aldrich has drawn together the "soul" peculiarities of different languages as set forth by writers of articles or chapters of books on the languages of different countries. See "Speaking the Same Language," *Ethics*, 65 (Apr., 1955), 213–217. For national characteristics as exemplified in language, see also A. A. Roback, *Destiny and Motivation in Language* (Cambridge, Mass.: Sci-Art Publishers, 1954), pp. 290–304.

25 The leading student of this area of linguistics has said: "We are inclined to think of language simply as a technique of expression, and not to realize that language first of all is a classification and arrangement of the stream of sensory experience which results in a certain world-order, a certain segment of the world that is easily expressible by the type of symbolic means that language employs. In other words, language does in a cruder but also in a broader and more versatile way the same thing science does." Benjamin Lee Whorf: *Language, Thought and Reality* (Cambridge: The Technology Press of M. I. T. and New York: Wiley, 1956), p. 55. In his discussion of these aspects of language, Kluckhohn states: "The events of the 'real' world are never felt or reported as a machine would do it. There is a selection process and an interpretation in the very act of response. Some features are highlighted; others are ignored or not fully discriminated." Clyde Kluckhohn, *Mirror of Man* (New York: Whittlesey House, 1949), p. 166. As to the effect, Ullman says: "The moulding influence of the linguistic medium of our 'conceptual' analysis of the world, and the linguistic nature of our 'concepts' themselves, are beyond dispute." Stephen Ullman, *Words and Their Use* (New York: Philosophical Library, 1951), p. 163.

26 Other figures used are "lens" and "prism," and "screen of linguistic stereotypes."

27 In the discussions, one finds such terms as "molders," "shapers," "groovers," "channelizers," "binders," "coercers," "enslavers."

28 George L. Trager and Henry L. Smith, Jr., *An Outline of English Structure* (Washington: American Council of Learned Societies, 1956). See also Henry L. Smith, Jr. and George Trager, "Metalinguistics," *ETC.: A Review of General Semantics*, 9 (Spring, 1952), 163–164.

29 John T. Waterman, "Benjamin Lee Whorf and Linguistic Field-theory," *Southwestern Journal of Anthropology,* 13 (Autumn, 1957), 201–211; Whorf, *op. cit.,* p. 171. See also Joseph H. Greenberg, "Concerning Inferences from Linguistic to Nonlinguistic Data," in Harry Hoijer (ed.), *Language in Culture* (Chicago: University of Chicago Press, 1953), pp. 3–19; Stephen Ullman, *The Principles of Semantics* (Oxford: Basil Blackwell, 1957), pp. 156–160; R. B. MacLeod's Foreword to Joseph Church, *Language and the Discovery of Reality* (New York: Random House, 1961), p. vii. For a pre-Sapir treatment of the viewpoint, with examples, see A. M. Hocart: "The Psychological Interpretation of Language," *British Journal of Psychology,* 5 (Nov., 1912), 267–279.

30 Francis M. Cornford, *From Religion to Philosophy* (London: E. Arnold, 1912), p. 192. Plato in the *Cratylus* discussed what might be called the psychology of language.

31 Berlin, 1948 printing, Vol. 6, p. 60. (Waterman's translation.)

32 *Op. cit.,* p. 159. For the ideas of another Neo-Humboldtian see Ernst Cassirer, *Language and Myth,* trans. Suzanne K. Langer, (New York: Dover Publications, 1946), pp. 1–17, 23–42.

33 Alfred Korzybski, *Science and Sanity: An Introduction to Non-Aristotelian Systems and General Semantics* (3rd ed.), (New York: International Non-Aristotelian Library Publishing Co., 1948), pp. 58–60, 87–90.

34 Edward Sapir, "The Status of Linguistics as a Science," *Language,* 5 (1929), 207–214 (209–210).

35 "Conceptual Categories in Primitive Languages," *Science* 74, 578.

36 See John B. Carroll (ed.), *Language, Thought, and Reality: Selected Writings of Benjamin Lee Whorf* (Cambridge: Technology Press of M. I. T., and New York: John Wiley & Sons, 1956), pp. 271–274. For earlier compilations see "Bibliography of the Writings of Benjamin Lee Whorf," compiled by Herbert Hockett in *ETC.: A Review of General Semantics,* 9 (Spring, 1952), 189–191, and the bibliography in *American Anthropologist,* 55 (Jan., 1953), 153–155.

37 This was originally published in the *Technology Review,* 44 (Apr., 1940), 229–231, 247–248. The points presented are taken from the reprint in Carroll (ed.), *op. cit.,* pp. 207–219.

38 See Carroll, pp. 134–139.

39 For an excellent concise summary of Whorf's views reduced to ten basic propositions, see Max Black, "Linguistic Relativity: The Views of Benjamin Lee Whorf," *Philosophical Review,* 68 (Apr., 1959), 228–238.

40 For the items see "Bibliography of the Writings of Benjamin Lee Whorf," compiled by Herbert Hockett in *ETC.: A Review of General Semantics,* 9 (Spring, 1952), 189–191 and in *American Anthropologist,* 55 (Jan., 1953), 153–155.

41 *Language, Thought and Reality,* p. 147.

42 On the contrasting ways in which the world is portrayed by Hopi and the western languages, see also the article on "Science and Linguistics" referred to above, esp. pp. 215–218. See also Whorf's "An American Indian Model of the Universe," *ETC.: A Review of General Semantics,* 8 (Dec., 1950), 27–33. On the difference between the linguistic structure and the correlated world view of the Hopi and the Navaho, neighbors for more than 400 years, see Harry Hoijer, "Cultural Implications of Some Navaho Linguistic Categories," *Language,* 27 (1951), 111–120. See also Dorothy D. Lee, "Conceptual Implications of an Indian Language," *Philosophy of Science,* 5 (Jan., 1938), 89–102, and "A Linguistic Approach to a System of Values," *Philosophy of Science,* 7 (July, 1940), 355–365. For other concisely stated examples and summaries of Whorfian studies, see Stuart Chase, *The Power of Words* (New York: Harcourt, Brace & Co., 1953), pp. 102–107.

The great majority of the anthropologists, linguists, and philosophers concerned with the intellectual and sociocultural influence of language accept most of the Sapir–Whorf hypothesis. Some point out, however, that it still poses a number of unsolved problems in theory and in empirical methods of verification. (See, for example, in the bibliography on "Metalinguistics and Language as Determinant" attached to the present chapter, the references to Brown, Capell, Carroll, Church, Fearing, Kluckhohn, and Rapoport and Horowitz.)

43 *"Quelques particularités du langage et de la pensée chinoise,"* Rev. Phil., 89–90 (1900), 98–128, 161–195.

44 Alfred R. Lindesmith and Anselm L. Strauss, *Social Psychology* (rev. ed.) (New York: Holt, Rinehart & Winston, 1956), pp. 227–228.

45 Following M. Granet, *Le Pensée Chinoise* (Paris: Le Renaissance du livre, 1934), pp. 37–38, 82, 87–95.

46 Robert K. Merton, "The Sociology of Knowledge," in Georges Gurvitch and Wilbert E. Moore, *Twentieth Century Sociology* (New York: Philosophical Library, 1945), pp. 366–405 (387, 388).

47 Lindesmith and Strauss, p. 226.

48 C. Wright Mills, "Language, Logic, and Culture," *American Sociological Review,* 4 (Oct., 1939), 670–680 (677).

49 Mario Pei, *The Story of Language* (Philadelphia: J. B. Lippincott & Co., 1949), p. 191.

50 Colin Cherry: *On Human Communication* (New York: John Wiley & Sons, 1957), p. 70.

51 "It would appear that even closely related languages differ in their inward spirit even more than in their outward form." Gray, p. 155. (Vossler also uses the term "inward spirit.")

52 *Ibid.*

53 *Language, Thought and Reality*, p. 156.

54 Daniel Katz, "Psychological Barriers to Communication," in Wilbur Schramm (ed.), *Mass Communications* (Urbana: University of Illinois Press, 1960), pp. 316–328 (316).

55 *Physics and Politics* (Intro. by Jacques Barzun, New York: Alfred A. Knopf, 1948), p. 63.

56 Says Malinowski: "Such German words as *Sehnsucht,* or *Sauerkraut,* or *Weltschmerz,* or *Schlachtfest,* . . . *Gemüt,* or *Gemeinheit* are not to be equated in any word in English, or for that matter, in any other European language. Such English words as 'sport,' 'gentleman,' 'fair play,' 'kindness,' 'quaint,' 'forlorn'—to mention only a few from a legion—are never translated in a foreign tongue, they are simply reproduced." Bronislaw Malinowski, *Coral Gardens and Their Magic* (New York: American Book Co., 1935), II, 12.

57 Vossler refers to translators as "form robbers" and "form breakers." (p. 179.)

58 The great literature of one language is difficult to translate because the conceptual, metaphor, and imagery systems cannot be exactly reproduced in the receiving language.

59 Lotz mentions that United Nations translators have observed that different languages seem to imply different attitudes; thus, according to them, the English pattern is pragmatic and inductive, the French generalizing and deductive, the Russian intuitional and particular. These differences make the common approach to a problem difficult. Lotz also notes this sort of problem among Bible translators, "who are faced with the problem of transposing texts embodying a Jewish–Christian ideology and a special ancient culture into languages associated with the most different societies." (John Lotz, "Linguistics," in Lynn White, Jr. (ed.), *Frontiers of Knowledge in the Study of Man* (New York: Harper & Brothers, 1956), pp. 207–231 (230).) On these qualitative aspects of translating, see especially UNESCO, *Scientific and Technical Translation and Other Aspects of the Language Problem,* Paris, 1957, Chap. 2.

60 Cf. Joseph B. Casagrande, "The Ends of Translation," *International Journal of American Linguistics,* 20 (No. 4, 1954), 335–340.

61 The original Italian form is *"Traduttore, traditore"* ("To translate is to betray").

62 Casagrande, p. 338. He states further in this connection: "That it is possible to translate one language into another at all attests to the universalities in culture, to common vicissitudes of human life, and to the like capabilities of men throughout the earth, as well as to the inherent nature of language and the character of the communication process itself; and, a cynic might add, to the arrogance of the translator" (p. 338).

63 William H. Werkmeister, *A Philosophy of Science* (New York: Harper & Brothers, 1940), p. 108.

64 In fact, Malinowski states: "Translation must always be the recreation of the original into something profoundly different. . . . It is never a substitution of word for word, but invariably the translation of whole contexts." (*Op. cit.,* pp. 11–12.)

65 Mario Pei, *The Story of Language* (Philadelphia: J. B. Lippincott & Co., 1949), p. 203.

66 John Scanlon, *Saturday Review,* 44 (Aug. 19, 1961), 45.

67 For a description of the machine samples of translation, and a discussion of many other aspects of machine translation, see Robert J. Clements, "Literature by Electronics," *Saturday Review,* 43 (July 16, 1960), 13–15, 39–40.

68 On these points see Anthony G. Oettinger, *Automatic Language Translation: Lexical and Technical Aspects* (Cambridge: Harvard University Press, 1962), pp. 104–126. The possibility that an error in translation by the Domei news agency of a message sent out by the Japanese government might have been responsible for the holocaust of Hiroshima is mentioned by Lincoln Barnett, *The Treasure of Our Tongue* (New York: Alfred Knopf, 1964), p. 292.

69 John G. Fuller, in "Trade Winds," *Saturday Review,* 45 (Feb. 17, 1962), 12.

70 One finds no reference to language in the synthesizing treatments of the sociology of knowledge in the flood of symposia of the last three decades, and Werner Stark alone mentions language among the systematic theoretical works in the field (*The Sociology of Knowledge* (London: Routledge and Kegan Paul, 1956), pp. 240, 278.) One recent exceptional instance of the recognition of the part of language is the section on "Linguistics" by Leo P. Chall in his treatment of "The Sociology of Knowledge" in J. S. Roucek, (ed.), *Contemporary Sociology* (New York: Philosophical Library, 1958), pp. 286–303, (293–295).

71 Preface to Karl Mannheim, *Ideology and Utopia* (New York: Harcourt, Brace & Co., 1936), pp. xi–xxx, with several interpolations and additions by the present writer.

72 *Op. cit.,* p. 240.

73 Cf. Chall, p. 293.

74 *Language, Thought and Reality,* pp. 212–213, 252.

75 *Advancement of Learning,* Book II. Quoted by Ernst Cassirer, "The Influence of Language Upon the Development of Scientific Thought," *Journal of Philosophy,* 39 (June 4, 1942), 309–327 (317). This article has a direct bearing on the present discussion.

76 *Ibid.,* pp. 319–320. Cassirer adds: "For the new language spoken by quantum-mechanics we have, so to speak, to find a general grammar and a general semantics" (320–321). A concrete instance of the cultural inadequacy of language to meet new conditions, and exemplifying a widespread situation among many of the underdeveloped peoples of the modern world, is found in the case of the native African élite. "When this élite wants to write poetry, or do scientific research, or make political speeches, or philosophize, it is obliged as a rule to use a European language. Friendship, family relationships, love-making can be handled in the vernacular; but little else." A quotation from Thomas Hodgkin in George H. Kimble, *Tropical Africa* (New York: Twentieth Century Fund, 1960), II, 385.

VII 🌿 Sociocultural Change
and Changing Language

Language presents a historical record of the culture of which it is a part. But history is a record of changes, and the recording instruments, if they are fairly sensitive to the changes and effective in presenting and expressing them, change also. We shall now examine the converse of the subject of the preceding chapter—namely, the change of language as sociocultural change takes place.

1. *The Necessity of Change of Standard Language*

Language must be a standard and self-perpetuating system, if it is to perform its strategic functions. As noted in Chapter V on "Language as a Social Institution," it must have the stability, both in time and place, that comes from being norm-governed. This is necessary so that words, grammatical forms and processes, and meanings may have currency as media of exchange throughout the area of use, and also that they may have approximately the same value for users tomorrow as they have today. Too rapid and too widespread alteration of language is a hindrance to communication which would then lend itself to confusion and misunderstanding.

The standard language, however, as an effective instrument through time and changing circumstance, cannot be strictly, completely and eternally formalized. If it is, it becomes static, and eventually doomed to petrifaction and death. For once the patterns of speech have become crystallized, they become functionally inadequate as soon as they fail to meet the increasingly different social and cultural demands made upon them by the ongoing and ever-changing community. A language full of archaisms of content and structure would not only give an over-simple and distorted conception of the world as it is; it would also lead to functional strains and tensions. There needs to be "linguistic spontaneity," "plasticity," "flexibility." Especially in a "going," developing, ever more complex society, the language must be continually moving in the direction of greater clarity, regularity, ease and pliancy of expression, and of extension and greater precision of terms and meanings. If this does not occur, we get instead what might be called a linguistic vacuum.

This means, in turn, that the diverse content and processes and meanings of the language system need to be forever checked, and different items—depending upon the circumstances—added, reselected, deleted, enlarged, strengthened and otherwise revised. Effective language can be thought of as an ever-refreshed "flow" in an ever-changing channel.

There are no perfectly static systems. For language, too, the only unchangeable law is the law of change. The change is slow at times, rapid at other times. A fairly alert person of seventy can set forth many profound linguistic changes—especially lapses, discards, substitutions and additions of terms—that have occurred during his own lifetime. And when one's own language is examined as it was commonly used a century ago, one finds it strange indeed.

> The English of the King James Bible or Shakespeare is unlike the English of today. The fourteenth-century English of Chaucer is intelligible to us only if we use a glossary. The ninth-century English of King Alfred the Great, of which we have contemporary manuscript records, seems to us like a foreign language; if we could meet English speakers of that time, we would not understand their speech, or they ours.[1]

A language cannot stand still if it is to survive, and to survive it must fulfill its social obligations. This means that it must continually change as sociocultural life itself changes. It is true that even the most dynamic linguistic system develops various functional encumbrances, and tends to resist change along certain—often important—lines. Every language also seems to show certain wayward tendencies. In spite of the fact that it is and must be highly institutionalized, it is nevertheless at times somewhat unruly, even intractable. For example, there is the tendency to slight certain rules and forms deemed important by the guardians. There is also the tendency to admit "impure" words and phrases and aberrant grammatical forms from the argots, slangs, and lingoes, and eventually to use them all as "correct."

We know, however, from many well-attested instances that, given time enough, every language in current use, even in the most remote and conservative communities, does succeed, by means of processes and devices, in accommodating itself sufficiently to the new elements of the environment, the new population elements, the new communal experiences, the new awarenesses, interests and needs—especially in so far as these relate to technical and social achievement—so that it is able to serve its basic general and societal functions. At certain times and under certain circumstances, these changes are glacially slow and barely distinguishable, even to expert students of language; at other times and under other circumstances, what has been referred to as a "linguistic revolution" is in process, especially in certain aspects of the language.

We shall now briefly deal with the general types of linguistic change that occur, and then more comprehensively examine the factors—especially the sociocultural events and situations—that relate to, and in many instances are responsible for, such changes.

2. The Main Types of Language Change

At this point, we shall merely present the most common types of linguistic change in outline form. Some of them will be discussed more extensively and illustrated in the next subsection, on the factors in linguistic change; others, because of their marked sociological significance, will be treated separately in some detail, and also in other contexts in later chapters.

It should be pointed out that, when a language changes through time, it is not by destroying or carelessly tampering with its fundamental elements, but by extending some and contracting others, as the occasion seems to require, thus functionally improving all of them. What this means is that the basic institutional nature of the language does not change much nor does it do so precipitously. It should also be kept in mind that the linguistic changes correlated with or caused by social changes first appear in speech (*parole*) and are only later incorporated into language (the linguistic system).

As language continuously adjusts itself to the ever-changing world, the amount and tempo of the changes it undergoes are usually very uneven. In general, the phonetic system, the morphological structures and the syntactic arrangements change very little and very slowly, as compared with the lexical fund. Of course, standard articulation, principles of word construction and syntax *do* change over a period of time, and some of these changes may be traced to determinable social factors, but the changes are few and slow, and usually made in the teeth of much resistance. It should be particularly recalled that phonology and grammar are the basic structural–regulative aspects of language, and concern themselves with the strictly coded parts. Furthermore, it is not so essential that they respond directly and immediately to the changing facts of society; in fact, if they did change much, rapidly and fortuitously, this would seriously interfere with the thought habits of the people. Any considerable or fundamental changes in these would also mean, in effect, that a new language had come into being—that the original language had been replaced by a different one. On the other hand, history shows that the vocabulary of a given language may sometimes be completely changed, without any notable alteration taking place in either its phonetic or grammatical structure. Moreover, changes in these features are usually very few in any given person's lifetime; for the most part, they occur over a span of generations. By contrast, vocabulary can change much and rapidly, both for individuals and groups. It does and must have a comparatively high degree of flexibility, malleability and extensibility. This means, first, that it is highly sensitive and responsive to the changes of the sociocultural world, however induced; second, that there must be names and other indicators and thought-counters for all that is newly experienced—the new objects, qualities, situations, places, persons, processes, interests, concepts, ideas, and perspectives, and that, correspondingly, the words standing for what has disappeared or become archaic must be dropped or take on new meanings. In this way, words ceaselessly come and go. Nevertheless, the basic word-stock remains much the same, since the "hard core" of ready-made and commonly known words must exist for day-to-day living. Finally, while words can accumulate almost without limit, no matter how numerous they may become, they must be used within the established systemic pattern.[2]

It should be noted that, while much of the resistance to language change is conscious and intentional, most (but not all) of the changes that do occur in the common standard language are unintentional, indirect and inadvertent.[3] They take place as the result of the sociocultural course of events; the ever-changing social situation creates conditions and circumstances which *pari passu* bring with them different kinds of language changes.

The main types of language changes follow.

a / The acquisition of new words for newly experienced aspects of human life. This consists of an increase in lexical volume and possible lexical complexity, *by the coining of new, enriching, non-synonymous words.* It takes various, not entirely mutually inclusive, forms.

Sheer creation, such as "Shangri-la," from Hilton's *Lost Horizon.*

Invention, that is, the making of new words by variously combining available roots and words—for example, in English, the copious construction of words out of roots and words from ancient and "dead" languages (Greek, "telephone"; Latin, "aqueduct"; Arabic, "algebra"; Hebrew, "Jehovah"), but also out of elements from other contemporary languages.

A special inventive device has been to adopt the name of the man who invented a new object or propagated it or contributed in some fashion to its existence, availability, prominence or success (for example, in connection with electricity, "ohm," "watt," "ampere").

The economizing process: (a) developing new words by the curtailing of old ones (for example, "canter" from "Canterbury trot," "spat" from "spatterdash," "tarp" from "tarpaulin," "exam" from "examination," "quad" from "quadrangle," "pub" from "public-house", (b) bringing about greater simplicity and ease of expression (for example, "horseless carriage" to "automobile" to "car").

Derivation: the process whereby an existing root is combined with established prefixes and suffixes so as to form new words, or a new word is formed out of two existing ones (for example, "protest" gives rise to "Protestant," and later to "Protestantism"; "fortnight" is simply a phonetic shortening of "fourteen nights").

Occasionally the process of derivation of a particular word can be traced back to some of its remote contributory elements. Thus "isolation" is a form of *insulation; insulation* is from the Latin *insula* (island); *insula* is derived from "in" and "salum"; *salum* ("the sea") means originally "the salt." Matthew Arnold put it accurately in his reference to "The salt-estranging sea" in the poem titled "Isolation."

The names for "woman" indicate chief functions in earlier times: "daughter" was a *milker* in the nomadic stage; the Latin "mulier" originally meant *miller, corn-grinder;* the English "wife" stems from *weaver,* as does "spinster"; "sister" comes from *sewster.*

The Latin word for "marriage" is "matrimonium," which means properly *motherhood;* to marry a woman was, in the Roman phrase, to lead her into motherhood—"ducere in matrimonium."

The word "classic" meant originally that a "classical" author is one whose works are to be studied in "class"; and only those works are proper for study in class which the difficulties of an ancient or foreign tongue render inaccessible without special study, just as those only are worthy of such study, whose excellence is sufficient to compensate the student for the time and labor so spent.

The word *preposterous,* in its Latin components, denotes a condition in which "hind-part is in front."[4]

Building new words out of existent roots and words by combination and blending. Examples of combination: back-country, breakfast, book-worm, boss-rule, boatswain, double-header, hairdo, know-how, loud-speaker, railroad, snowshoe. Blending: "flush," a blending of "flash" and "blush"; "brunch," a blending of "breakfast" and "lunch"; "smog," a blending of "smoke" and "fog"; "motel," a blending of "motor" and "hotel."

Forming new words by sheer analogy with ones already in use: for example, extension of "head" to "head of cabbage," "head of army," "head of class"; "disease," as physical ailment, from the old "dis-ease" which referred to discomfort of any kind; "motorcade" and "aquacade" coined in imitation of "cavalcade."

Functional change: a word used in a certain part of speech is transferred to another function: for example, "contact" (noun) used as "to contact" (verb).

The formation of terms through the metaphorical association of ideas: for example, "crane," based on the remote resemblance of the machine to a species of long-necked bird; "teeth" of gears associated with teeth of the mouth.

The authorization of vivid words of popular creation—words that come out of the popular vernacular: for example, fad, fun, freak, nag, pet, skid, swamp, snob, corny, cheese-cake, snafu, joy ride, wangle, strip tease, zoot suit, soap opera, jitterbug.

The addition to and incorporation in the standard language, as correct, of words and phrases from the sublanguages and "special" languages of the language community itself: acceptance of some slang and colloquial forms; intrusion of cant and jargon from the lower classes, even the demi-monde; transfer from local patois and regional groups; inclusion of items from internal ethnic groups; acceptance of words from new "prestige" classes (conquerors, scholars in a renaissance); acceptance of words formerly deemed "errors" or *gauche* or vulgar forms; adoption of terms from the "special languages" of occupational groups, trades and other special technical areas: for example, atomic language, oil well driller's language, medical language, gadget language, Hollywood language; terms from sports, for example, baseball terminology introduced into other departments of life; terms from the sciences.

Borrowing from across linguistic frontiers: the acquisition of "loan words," or the "naturalization" of foreign terms. This is a most extensive and general process of acquisition of words, accounting in the case of some languages (for example, English, Persian, Turkish) for over half of their vocabularies. For example, our American language includes thousands of words borrowed from other languages: American Indian (moccasin, papoose, squaw, totem, wampum); Negro (yam, goober, gumbo, voodoo, zombie); German (sauerkraut, wiener, frankfurter, hamburger, *Zeitgeist, Lebensraum, Weltanschauung,* beer); French (portage, cache, rouge, liaison, chauffeur, naivete, garage, camouflage, calaboose); Spanish (hammock, tomato, mustang, barbecue, plaza, adobe, canyon, lasso, corral, mesa, ranch); Chinese (tea, chow mein, shangbar); Japanese (kimono, jin-rick-sha); Malay (bamboo, gong); Arabic (sherbet, harem, coffee, algebra, zero, cipher, azimuth, zenith); Scandinavian (cake, curl, dirt, ill, happen, root, skin, sky, ugly, wing); Dutch (skipper, cruller, cole slaw, spook, boss, scow); Asiatic Indian (pundit, thug, curry, calico, punch); Italian (piano, allegro, andante, solo, soprano, bank, bankrupt, balance, traffic, spaghetti, florin).[5]

Converting specific into general terms. For example, in the United States, the frequent example of trademarks becoming general terms for a type of product. The term "thermos" is now applied to all vacuum bottles and jugs. An array of terms which have passed generally from proper to common nouns: Linoleum, Cellophane, Escalator, Deep Freeze, Aspirin, Milk of Magnesia, Kleenex, Celluloid, Scotch Tape.[6]

Making Loan-Translations: for example, "marriage of convenience" from the French *un mariage de convenance;* "Superman" from the German *Übermensch* (and the influence of Nietzsche).

b / Sematic shifts: This consists of changes in lexical meanings.

Giving old words and phrases new meanings or shadings of meanings: for example, present English *fee,* now a pecuniary charge for some service, originally meant "livestock," "cattle," "property," "money." English *meat* originally applied to *all food,* but now it means "flesh-food" or "edible food"; "angel" once meant "messenger"; "weird" once meant "destiny"; "anxiety" once meant literally a "narrow place"; "confer" once meant "to bring together"; "expire" originally meant only to "breathe out", later came to be connected with the occasion when one *last* breathes out, or "dies", and also came to be used to designate ending, as when a lease "expires"; "glamour", originally Scottish, was a corrupt form of "grammar," and has only recently come to be used as "enchantment" or "mysterious charm" or "delight"; "pen" originally meant "feather," then was applied to the primitive quill pen, and then to a writing instrument with a metal nib; "fair" used to mean "beautiful," now may mean "blond," or "equitable," or "morally just"; "chattel" formerly meant "cattle"—a species of movable property; "prestige" used to mean the tricks of a mountebank, instead of the awe and veneration assigned to nations and individuals; "urn" meant originally a receptacle for *urine;* "to foist" meant "to break wind silently." (Cf. the new shading of meaning which *Time* gives to such words as "mogul" and "tycoon.")

Sometimes words acquire new meanings by peculiar transformations. Hughes notes that, prior to 1880, the word *car* in English meant a kind of carriage—as in "jaunting-car"—and *Wagen* in German meant "a farm-cart." When the automobile was invented, a term was coined (Greek *autós,* "self" and Latin *mobilis,* "movable"), and such expressions as "gas buggy" and "horseless carriage" were used. In German, logical compounds were made: *Kraftwagen* ("power wagon") for automobile, *Lastwagen* ("load wagon") for truck, *Frachtwagen* ("freight wagon") for a railroad freight car. Now in German *Wagen* has become the common word for "car."[7] Monstrosities may occasionally appear, as new words become necessary. Note the German word for "garage": *Kraftwageneinstellehalle* (all one word, and without hyphens).

Extension of meaning of given words: "barn" once meant "barleyplace"; during the Civil War, "carpetbagger" developed from "carpet bag," and "copperhead" from the name of a snake; "stump" changed from a tree area to the idea of "political rostrum" or "political speechmaking"; "race" changed from the race track to politics; "antenna" changed from its zoological use (the antenna of bugs) to radio and television use.

Greater precision, specialization or contraction of meaning for given words: "lewd" once meant "ignorant."

Obsolescence of meanings: most of these examples are in the graveyard of words—e.g., words relating to such obsolescences as streetcars, or trades and crafts engaged in before mechanization and automation.

Idiomatic change: by idiom is meant those constructions peculiar to a given language which cannot be literally translated into another language, and the meaning of which cannot be gathered from their component parts. The idiom is a special aspect of the semantics of any language. Thus "look out," as most frequently used, does not mean "look outside," but "be careful."

The significant fact, at this point of the discussion, is that the process of obsolescence and the construction of idiomatic phrases go on all the time. New idioms, for example, appear when new words and word-combinations become available to state, uniquely and strikingly, an experienced—sometimes a newly experienced—thing, condition, or action. "Get away with" in the sense of "be able to do something in spite of obstacles," is a relatively recent addition to American English; to "put in orbit," when not referring to a space missile or space ship, but conveying the notion of "getting into action" or "placing under consideration," is a construction of the last decade.

c / Loss or replacement of words: usually comes with the obsolescence or disappearance from the culture of the cultural item which the word designated.

Dropping or disappearance of obsolete words and phrases, useless and meaningless in the present situation: for example, terms connected with falconry; the loss in English of "distaff," "flail," "fief."

Tabooing of particular words: (1) as knowledge increases and particular words are found to be erroneous; (2) as ethical changes occur, and there are new ethical sensitivities; (3) as linguistic "styles" change; (4) substitutions: for example, as in the case of euphemisms, the substitution of new words that do not evoke unpleasantness—*mortician* for *undertaker.*

Word obsolescence based on caprice of fashion or difficulty of use. This is the operation of the law of diminishing returns in the use of a given term (for example, it may be too long and cumbersome for the new era).

d / Phonetic change (especially over a period of time): changes in articulation and pronunciation. In most instances, these occur more or less unconsciously and slowly. For example, a slow but steady alteration, especially in the vowel sounds, has characterized English throughout history. Old English "stan" has become "stone"; "cu" has become "cow."

e / Grammatical changes: improvement in forms and processes. This consists in the reconstruction, supplementing and replacement of linguistic instruments that have proven to be clumsy, insufficient, overly intricate, capricious or difficult.

f / Changes in spelling. These occur slowly, but they are very considerable over a period of time. For example, Shakespeare's works are constantly being reprinted, but not in his own spelling or that of his age.

g / The continuous development of "special" languages, sublanguages, and new "styles" within the language, the words, phrases, and grammatical forms of which get into the standard speech or influence it (to be examined more fully in Chapters XII–XIV). For example, the languages of age and sex groups; occupational–professional languages; slangs (some temporary, some absorbed and normalized); class languages, with the emergence of new or changed classes; new literary "movements" and "schools," and changed "literary styles"; scientific–technological language specialties; argots and cants.[8]

3. *The Sociocultural Factors in Linguistic Change*

The language of a people records its history, but the language itself also has a history, which shows how its every development has been correlated with, if not always directly dependent upon or caused by, occurrences in the individual and collective life of its speakers through their history. The changes of society lead along a definite path. We shall now examine the major categories of factors in this continuous change of language.

Not *all* changes of language come directly as the result of social changes. Some can be explained as the result of strictly human characteristics—including human sensory and mental mischance, such as mishearing and misunderstanding, slurring and oversimplification of sounds, defective memory, lapses—that is, unconscious variations from a normal pattern (such as President Harding's "normalcy" when he wanted to say "normality"), or the use of wrong words (for example, Eisenhower spoke "extraneously" when what he was reaching for was "extemporaneously"), and sheer laziness in speech and writing. Nor are all of the society-related changes bound up with dynamic social and cultural changes. There is that aspect of change in language which comes quite unintentionally and without either inside or outside influence, implying some of the psychological defects mentioned above.

Sapir called this phenomenon "linguistic drift"—namely, the changes that come unconsciously as the speakers, over generations, fail to reproduce exactly the sound symbols, depart continually (though to a minor degree) from the pristine grammatical habits, and often bring about changes in the meanings of words and phrases so very gradually that the different steps in the process of transformation are undetectable, save when viewed with a very considerable time perspective.[9] There are also the continuous and unavoidable changes in man's physical environment, changes over which he is powerless, but to which he must symbolically, and especially linguistically, refer, and about which he must confer with his associates if he is to adjust to them. The seeds of linguistic transformation are often present in non-social and socially quiescent states.

The student of language finds, however, that the greater proportion of linguistic changes occur in a "social context," that many can quite accurately be said to be socioculturally determined, and that linguistic changes more or less parallel the historical changes in the intellectual and social situation of the people. In the main, it is societal and cultural developments, social conditions, social requirements, social influences and pressures, emanating from within and without the given language community, that mold the spoken and written language.

Many language changes are due to social, technological and educational changes that have produced cultural tension or upheaval, or have threatened to do so, and have thereby left linguistic *gaps* in the way of the absence of adequate words, phrases and meanings that now become necessary.

A second important fact is that language users make all sorts of contacts with other peoples, some of whom form other language communities. These contacts not only require new language, even force new language upon the given linguistic groups, but they also produce a rich, often fascinating, store of words and expressions indicative of attractive or profitable experience, some of which are taken over to enrich the languages.

We shall utilize the broad categorization of sociocultural factors just indicated, but with the full awareness that the two sets of factors are by no means completely and consistently either inclusive or mutually exclusive. Their items are, in many instances, inextricably interrelated, when viewed, as they must be, in the light of the inevitability of some kind and degree of communication between peoples who have any contact with each other, and of the cultural processes involved in diffusion-borrowing. Especially significant is the fact that, in modern societies, few presumably internal factors are entirely uninfluenced by external ones. For example, a modern people that is developing a host of new words and phrases and several special sublanguages, to cope with and facilitate their scientific-technological developments, would, at first glance, seem to be meeting an internal social problem of a communicative nature. No such development takes place, however, without copious influence from without. Furthermore, it is frequently almost impossible to determine the primacy or priority of the internal or external aspect of the change. This scheme is resorted to, however, because it seems to be a means of avoiding, or reducing the likelihood of, a hit-or-miss, pedestrian discussion of factors. It also enables us more readily to relate factors to *types* of language change.

It is not our province to deal with these factors in an intensive manner —e.g., to present exhaustive lists of words and phrases and other linguistic changes, as illustrations. Our function rather is merely to indicate the key significance of different types of sociocultural factors in these changes.

a / Strategic internal sociocultural changes and situations requiring linguistic adjustment. Such factors are innumerable, and of various degrees of pertinence. We will briefly indicate those that seem to have had special relevance in recent centuries in a society like our own.

[1] *Demographic changes.* Demographic changes within language communities and in contacting societies bring essential linguistic changes. While the elemental changes in population are of a biosocial and ecological nature, they all occur in a sociocultural context, and more and more of them are both effect of, and either cause or correlate of, societal and cultural factors. They include increases or decreases of population, new trends, changes in distribution, in spatial and social mobility and in composition—for example, the notable increase in the proportion of the children and the aged, or changes in the comparative proportion of the sexes, in the comparative numbers in racial and ethnic groups, in the ratio of urban and rural population, in location and density, as well as differentials in all these respects between different areas or nations, and a great variety of economic, political, and other problems. We have the development of such terms as "population explosion," "birth control" and its euphemistic forms: "family limitation," "planned parenthood," "death control," "sex ratio," "in-migration," "junior citizen," "senior citizen," "demographic balance," "optimum population," "underdeveloped countries," "metropolitanization," "urban sprawl," and so on.

[2] *Institutional changes.* The social institutions of a society, as

noted in Chapter V, are great clusters of essential, accepted and implemented ways of behaving socially. The fundamental division of operations in a society is among its major institutional systems. When a change takes place in any of the parts of these systems, there is also a change in the language used in connection with their operation. There is the emergence of special new words, of special new meanings for existent words, even of the necessity, in some institutional areas, of what amount to special sublanguages. There are also, of course, losses from the active vocabulary of some words pertaining to institutions, when these decline or when certain institutional characteristics or functions become less significant or disappear. With the decline of the institution of feudalism, for example, we have practically lost from usage such terms as *reeve, vassal, franklin* (that is, freeman). In every institutional sector—familial, economic, political, religious, recreational—words once used in the description of institutional behavior have been lost because of the disappearance of the related activity—for example, words involved in our former, rather simple, agricultural–village life and its economic, family, political, religious and recreational aspects.

Certain of these institutional areas will be briefly examined.

Scientific–technological factors. With the expansion of scientific knowledge, the language also expands. New terms are coined and borrowed; old terms are given special meanings that they have not had in ordinary language. Mathematical and other formulae, as well as vocabulary, are developed in order to symbolize and express new concepts, relations, and techniques. The different sciences develop what are essentially "special" sublanguages, including other than purely verbal symbols to facilitate their activities (to be discussed in Chapter XIII, Section 6). There is also a tendency for the newer sciences to take over terms from the older sciences, though with special applications and modified meanings. Changes in technology—which are essentially utilizations by man of his scientific facts, principles and techniques, in order to manipulate his physical, biological, psychological and societal environments—also bring a flood of linguistic changes. New types of man-made changes of the physical environment by the engineers must be named and described, and the techniques stated precisely; agriculture must have new names for new varieties of plants and animals, for new machines, new processes and so on; medical and pharmaceutical and other advances in health technology bring vast increases in nomenclature. In the "telephone area," we have such recent terms as "lineman," "switchboard operation," "telephone repairman," "station-to-station dialing." The automobile actually has occasioned the development of a copious special lingo, which has become part of common speech. With the "air age," and very recently the "space age," have come many new words (for example, "spacenaut" or "astronaut"). With the development of atomic science and technology, there has been a wave of neologisms: "nuclear," "nucleonics," "cryogenics," "atomic bomb," "reactor," "piles," "isotype," "nucleon," "chain reaction," "fission." Radar and supersonic speed have also produced a new language. "Automation" (itself a new word), along with the technologies upon which it depends, such as "electronics," has added all sorts of terms. It has even occurred to some people that some of our technology-related language has not kept up with our technological development, that it needs "streamlining." For example, the new verb "to teevee" has been proposed by various persons, not altogether jocularly, to replace the more cumbersome "to watch television," and "to vator," instead of "to take the elevator."

On the other hand, there has also been the decline and loss of older technological terms—in transportation, for example, the obsolescence of terminology relating to streetcars, steam locomotives, horses, wagons, buggies and harnesses.

Specifically we might note an array of terms and phrases more or less generally used that have been contributed or assigned fixed designative or descriptive meanings by two relatively young sciences, psychoanalysis and sociology. From psychoanalysis we have "syndrome," "tensions," "ambivalence," "escape," "compensation," "superego," "libido," "neurosis," and "psychosis," to mention only a few. With the rapid expansion and wide diffusion of sociology, and its increasing popularity and utility outside its own professional ranks (for example, by journalists and commentators), the word *sociology* itself, particularly in its adjectival form, is now extensively employed in connection with all kinds of social situations.

Sociology has contributed dozens of words and phrases—imports and inventions, though mainly standard terms given specific sociological connotation—now in rather common use, with approximately their sociological meanings, by those with a high school or college education. A small sampling presents an array of "socials"—"social structure," "social situation," "social distance," "social space," "social mobility," "social integration," "social hierarchy," "social heritage." There are "master terms" of sociology that are now widely used: "norms," "social systems," "racism," "reference group," "primary" and "secondary group," "folkways," "mores," and "institutions." Also by no means uncommon are imports, such as "dominance" from ecology, "charisma" and its derivatives from the German Max Weber, and "anomie" and its derivatives from the Frenchman Durkheim.

Political factors. Political changes also bring concomitant linguistic variations. Political-economic revolutions bring new words and phrases, new meanings for terms, and new modes of expression for the new social philosophy, the new or modified legal and administrative machinery, the new forms of economic production, exchange, distribution, consumption, the changed class structures and relations, the new types of relationship between governors and governed, and other social-organizational modifications. The French Revolution notably gave rise to a new terminology and semantics: "democracy," "legislature," "session," "citizen," "freedom." In the French, as also in the Russian, Revolution, there was in addition the production of political catchwords and catch phrases: "Liberty, Equality, Fraternity," or "Peace, Bread, and Land."

When Russia changed over from an aristocratic empire to the totalitarian U.S.S.R., there appeared a whole new vocabulary: Marxian terminology, new words to signify new ideological, technological and economic aspects of life, and new social-organizational forms and processes.

The change to a dictatorship not only brings words for ideological and administrative shifts, but also its crowd-catching slogans—for example, the grandiose verbosities of Hitler's Third Reich (*Lebensraum, Herrenvolk, Aryan Germany*).

A new political administration, coming into power as the result of orderly consitutional processes, but introducing minor governmental uniquenesses, also brings with it new political words, phrases, and slogans—for example, the host of new terms that came into existence with the new political viewpoints and activities of the New Deal and the New Frontier in the United States or, earlier, with the accession to power of the Labour Party in Britain.

New political conditions of an international nature require or induce new language: the burgeoning terminology for all sorts of international relations, procedures and organizations, including that of the United Nations, and such terms as "global war," "Cold War."

Economic factors. We need only call attention to the new language that has come into our society with industrialization: the new words and phrases for the new types of organizations and processes designed to conduct production and exchange, for the thousands upon thousands of new products with their type names and trade names, the changes in consumption (involving leisure, gadgets, vocations and so on), which affect the terminology relating to every department of life of the population. Worthy of separate mention is the changed terminology pertaining to urbanization: the words and phrases intended to indicate urban social–psychological characteristics, ecological conditions and processes, demographic characteristics and effects ("exurbanite"), revised forms of social institutions and new and revised social processes, social organizations and societal differentiation and structuring.

Religious factors. In spite of its conservative nature, religion changes continually in doctrine and in organizational forms. Historically, within peoples and nations, there have been both minor and major religious reformations, reflected in innovative ideas and organizations that had to be named, defined and otherwise linguistically expressed. In a nation in which great religious freedom prevails, there is a continuous appearance of new sects and cults, with their more or less unique theological and organizational forms, certain unusual ways of life and so on, for which new terminology also appears. There are, finally, the effects, evidenced in language, of the waxing and waning of religious dissension, of forms of attempted appeasement, cooperation and coordination among the diverse and divided religious elements, the influence of philosophies and psychologies.

[3] *The influence of innovative persons and "schools."* Distinguished (or, under the circumstances, perhaps conspicuous) persons—in literature, either polite or folk, in the daily press, on the radio or television, in special fields of intellectual endeavor—often develop new words and forms of expression which become part of the common language, sometimes permanently, sometimes only as a matter of a passing vogue.

The great literary "lights" frequently have an innovative effect upon the language. Their innovations in the way of enriched vocabulary and special expressional forms—such as the introduction of metaphorical phrases and similes, which are characterized by beauty, greater precision of meaning, or other enhancing features—become part of the standard language. One need only call attention to the influence upon the Italian language of the mighty literary output of the great Florentines, Dante, Petrarch and Boccaccio, during the first half of the fourteenth century. Shakespeare introduced a wide array of technical expressions and words for a wide range of subjects; he gave new meanings, new nuances and new values to words, and developed new bold "metaphors" and a bold new sentence structure, as well as a new poetic diction.[10] Jespersen points out that Shakespeare greatly increased the number of words in the English vocabulary, many of his unique expressions still being household words. As evidence, he notes the fact that Shakespeare used 20,000 words, as against 4800 in the King James version of the New Testament, and 8000 used by Milton.

In our own time, English has felt the influence of such men as Theodore Roosevelt, Ring Lardner, and Walter Winchell, not to mention "Churchillisms." The "linguistic whimsicality" of ingenious speakers or writers may make appreciable additions, often furnishing humorous as well as conceptual enrichment.

The names of individuals, conspicuous or notorious in some manner, or of certain of their products or characteristics, may become the basis for words of general currency—for example, "boycott" from the Irish landowner of that name, "quixotic" from Cervantes' *Don Quixote,* "Chesterfield," "Don Juan."

Great writers in such fields as philosophy, government, and the sciences and technologies have provided much "standard" terminology for discourse in their special areas. Many of their writings contribute to the traditional literary form, and function as models for the use, choice and arrangement of words and modes of expression; they enrich and enhance the standard language.

[4] *Linguistic and social reform movements.* Some linguistic change (or incitement to change) is the result of linguistic "reform movements" sponsored by formally or informally organized groups. They seek to, and sometimes do, bring certain improvements in the language—for example, by adopting a new alphabet (the Turks adopted the Roman alphabet under Mustapha Kemal Atatürk in 1928), simplifying the spelling ("phonetic spelling") or the grammar, reducing its lexicon ("Basic English"), standardizing certain meanings (as in some of the sciences), devising phonetic systems of writing to replace cumbersome, illiteracy-perpetuating scripts (for example, in some Asiatic countries). In the main, the effects of such linguistic reform movements have been limited, even negligible, and such changes as have been produced have come very slowly.

Social movements usually affect to some degree the language of those involved. We have alluded in the discussion of "Political Factors" to the effects upon language of communism, political reform movements (such as the New Deal), political–economic revolutions, and dictatorships.

[5] *Modified forms of social organization.* The changing structure of society, along with changing social attitudes and values, must be accompanied by appropriate linguistic forms. Changes in social differentiation provide examples. Pieris has pointed out that the European transition from a feudal to an individualistic order, from status to con-

tract, from *Gemeinschaft* to *Gesellschaft,* had its parallel in linguistic changes. This societal change was accompanied by individualism and democratization, which brought a devaluation of old statuses. The erosion of status relations was evidenced in a parallel lessening of the "snobbery of speech," and a devaluation and vulgarization of titles and forms of address. *Master* changed from a designation expressing lordship to its modern form *mister,* which is applied increasingly to all adult males; *Sire,* which originally meant king, became *sir; Ma Dame* (Dame originally meant high born) was contracted to *madam,* or even *ma'am.*[11]

In the stratification system, there is a continual fluctuation of social classes: the diminution or even disappearance of some, the waxing in proportion, prominence, and influence of others. In the Western World, particularly the United States, there is the shrinkage of the economically and culturally impoverished so-called "lower classes" as well as of the prestigious "upper classes," and the increase in size and economic and cultural influence of the "middle classes." While well-confirmed data are lacking, this seems to be bringing about a simplification of our English in some respects—for example, grammar—and a "leveling" and uniformizing of accent (although other factors are also potent in these changes). There seems to be a waning of the prestige of the special terminologies and accent of the highly educated or sophisticated population elements (for example, "Harvard" English).

There has been an obsolescence of certain occupations and, correspondingly, of their typical terminology; on the other hand, many new occupations have emerged, with their essential language.

The development of the bureaucratic form of structure and operation of large-scale organizations in almost all departments of modern life (government, business, education, religion, recreation) has necessitated an appropriate operational terminology, and has fostered the development of applicable descriptive words and phrases, such as "hierarchy of authority," "informational flow," "reign of rules," and the widely applied "organization man."

[6] *The appearance of new systems of ideas.* This takes many different forms. The society may undergo, for example, the rather far-reaching revision that results from an intellectual–cultural renaissance. This was the situation with respect to the West European Renaissance of the sixteenth and seventeenth centuries, and the French Enlightenment of the eighteenth. These brought new ideas in philosophy and science, new literary forms, new social values, attitudes, aims and plans —all requiring new language and a modification of meaning of much of

the old. The society may also undergo major changes in its reigning ideologies. Changes in political–economic ideology have been referred to above; there may also be changes in the majority religious ideology, as, for example, the transition in an area from predominantly Catholic to Protestant. The use of an influential new school of philosophy will give currency to new terms—for example, the considerable number of new terms introduced into our American language, at least at certain cultural levels and among certain social circles, by Existentialism, or earlier by Pragmatism.

[7] *Fads and fashions in language.* Related to the changes arising out of the appearance of "schools" and new systems of thought are changes brought about by fads and fashions in words. There is the eternal attraction exercised by novelty in language, as in attire, foods, music, architecture, art. There are powerful, sometimes irrational, passing vogues in language, momentary fads, whimsicalities of certain social classes (the "best society"), of categories or groups such as those of the motion picture, or the popular song, or the cocktail "crowd," or of certain conspicuous or notorious individuals. These arrest attention, and their speech forms may become for a while the fashion among portions of the population. Their popularity and the distinction which they are presumed to give, coupled with the compulsion exercised over some by fashion, may cause them to be widely imitated.

Some old words achieve for a time a special, almost faddish, new meaning and emphasis, through representing an adjustment to new realities or newly emphasized realities. The recent use of "pattern" in relation to individual behavior or social organization is a case in point. The term "image," in the sense of a posture or configuration or self-conception, is another.

Fashion introduces new words into the language, assigns a not always easily explainable prominence to certain words and phrases or groups of words and phrases, creates new and sometimes peculiar meanings for words and phrases already in existence, and usually banishes certain speech forms. The main effect of fashions in speech is, of course, upon its particular devotees. They add those forms that are "chic"; those that are not in fashion they dismiss as *passé.* There may be some small but permanent residue of terms and phrases and of new or revised meanings in the general language.

[8] *Such changes in the near future.* We have viewed these factors mainly as characteristic of modern complex societies like our own. Many of them now are becoming operative among the "underdeveloped" peoples, which constitute nearly two thirds of the population of the world. The magnitude of the linguistic problems and changes

that will unavoidably accompany the changes in other departments of their lives can be only dimly comprehended. The problems that the existent language structure of some of them present are many and great. Many of them are being suddenly plunged into modern technological, economic and political forms of action. Unlike Western peoples, among whom social changes (and the parallel linguistic changes) emerged over a period of centuries, these underdeveloped peoples now possess languages that are geared to very different sociocultural levels and a very different *Weltanschauung,* but which must suddenly produce, by construction and borrowing, a terminology that is utterly foreign in form and spirit.[12] Suffice it to say, there will be linguistic as well as population and technological "explosions" among them.[13]

b / The contacts with other cultures, peoples, and languages affecting a given language. There has hardly ever been a people or a language that has been sheltered from every outside influence. Today, certainly, no people anywhere have insurmountable physical or cultural walls around them. When peoples come into contact with each other, either peacefully or antagonistically, either face-to-face or through any of the means of spatially and temporally extended communication, their social and cultural activities unavoidably influence each other. Though seldom with equal reciprocity, objects (both natural and fabricated) pass from the one language community to the other, as do patterns of action— such as technical and economic procedures, political practices, religious rites, forms of individual conduct and so on. Since these activities are linguistically mediated, the respective languages come into contact, and this contact is bound to cause each language to react upon the other, particularly in the form of reciprocal borrowing. Such borrowing from across "linguistic frontiers," to use the terminology of the social linguists, mainly takes the form of the acquisition of "loan words," "loan translations," and "semantic loans."

We shall now examine briefly the major types of sociocultural factors that produce linguistic changes, primarily through direct contact between cultures, peoples, or languages. Because of the frequent interrelatedness of the phenomena, the rubrics used will by no means be entirely clear-cut or exclusive.

Some of the contacts are of an *incidental,* or even *basically unavoidable* nature. Listening to radio or television broadcasts across national or cultural and linguistic boundaries is usually an incidental contact. The contacts of speakers of different languages in a state of physical or geographic contiguity are inherently unavoidable. Nevertheless, the mere contact of peoples, in time, brings about linguistic osmosis and blending even more certainly than it does genetic mixing.

The vastly greater proportion of these contacts are *deliberate* on the part of one or both or all of the contacting parties. Most of the deliberate contact situations are of a more or less *peaceful* nature: (1) they may be engaged in for *mutually utilitarian* reasons, such as carrying on trade, political, educational, artistic, and other essential or desirable inter-people relations; (2) they may be such contacts as come with peaceful geographical, anthropological, and economic exploration, or such as may occur through peaceful invasion by different kinds of demographic, institutional, and cultural elements. The borrowing may be engaged in quite deliberately (3), in order to acquire necessary or enriching new words and phrases to express new meanings and to name and conceptually embellish new objects, situations and ideas, or (4), in order to adopt foreign language elements because of the prestige of the donors. Finally (5), these deliberate contacts may be, and frequently have been historically, of a *forceful nature*, accomplished through invasion of migrating peoples, military–political conquest, colonization, political annexation (incorporation of contiguous political entities), religious conquest "by the sword," and modern international propaganda.

Regardless of the type of contact, however, the words and phrases that *are* required are taken over *for good reasons:* convenience, indispensability, utility, prestige or compulsion.

A revealing procedure would be to note the major types of social and cultural *events* directly involving contact that have resulted in some degree of linguistic borrowing.

[1] *The settlement history of the particular people.* This reveals not only the construction of new words or the readaptation of old ones in order to cope linguistically with the peculiar climate, terrain, resources, and the economic, technical and other essential tasks associated with the new environment, but also with the language items borrowed from the indigenous, possibly aboriginal, inhabitants, especially during the early stages of the settlement process. Thus, for example, in North America since the 1500's, there has been the borrowing of words *from the Indians* (as noted above) by the Spanish, Dutch, French and English settlers. In our case, there have also been the exchanges between the successive increments of settlers, who may have been ethnically different, for example, in the area of New York City, Dutch to English, and then to a plethora of immigrant elements.

[2] *The spatial movement of people among other people.* Man takes

his speechways with him wherever he goes; his spatial movement, however, has taken and still takes various forms.

Migrations, frequently constituting invasion. While other than purely *intra*-national migrations have greatly diminished in the modern world, for a variety of physical, economic and especially political reasons, the migration of peoples in man's history, arising out of the stern necessity of avoiding physical or social catastrophe, has been a signal factor in the language exchange and development of peoples. Names, for example, migrate with people. They attach names from other places, or of persons or incidents of past memory, to their places of later occupancy. Place-names show that the Ainu of Japan, now mainly in the North, were at one time as far south as Central Japan. Place-names also give evidence of invasion, peaceful or forced: for example, some place names in Scotland show Celtic origin; Bismarck, North Dakota, was founded by German admirers of the "Iron Chancellor."

Explorations. Historically, the explorations of the adventurers of a country, and of its seekers for new routes, slaves, resources and territory, have brought about considerable borrowing of terminology. For example, the languages of the Spanish, Portuguese, Dutch, French and English, from the sixteenth century on, show innumerable examples due to such activity.

Emigration–immigration, or the peaceful movement of individuals and families, rather than peoples, from one spatial–political location to another, with the intention of permanent residence in the new location, has brought vast language exchange, especially during the last three centuries. One need call attention only to the assimilation of diverse immigrant ethnic, political and cultural elements in the United States, and the incorporation into American speech of new words and blending of speech forms that have come with the successive increments of immigrants from Northwest, Central, Southern and Eastern Europe, from Canada and Mexico, and even (to a considerably lesser extent) from the Orient. Conversely, immigrants in the new environment, with their new experiences and new needs and interests, have to communicate about them with each other and with their new associates. This requires for them much new language. As someone has put it: "Settle a group of Arab families in central Minnesota, and see what they manage to do about the weather or the 10,000 lakes."

Foreign travel and tourism. In the modern world, there is much international movement of a temporary and transient nature; it involves no intention of permanent change of residence, but is engaged in because of curiosity, for cultural enrichment, recreation or escape from boredom, or because it is "*the* thing to do." While most of this movement is hurried, and most of the contacts are therefore rather superficial, it does result in some occasional slight additions or substitutions of words and phrases. One should also note here temporary residence abroad for trade, political, educational and other purposes, on the part of relatively small numbers of people.

[3] *Foreign war.* Though each party in war is bent on the subjugation or even the extinction of the enemy, the war itself inevitably results in contacts between the parties involved, especially contacts with prisoners and with conquered civilians, and in negotiations between the contestants. Both sides do some borrowing of terms from each other, although a great number of variables in the actual situation will determine the number and kind of terms borrowed by the respective parties.

In the case of armies of occupation, the indigenous population and the members of the occupying army do much borrowing from each other, and the armed forces, on returning to their home country, bring not only brides, but foreign ways, including speech ways. In the main, however, it is likely—as in the case of G. I.'s in Japan, Korea, and Germany during the last decade—that much of the military-occasioned borrowing is of short-term significance.

[4] *Military–political conquest.* This has often been, in the past, the end-product of a successful foreign war. While both the conquerors and the conquered do some borrowing from each other, the actual circumstances here too determine the respective amount and kind. Invariably, however, the exchange transaction has been rather one-sided: not only have the conquered done most of the borrowing, they have also had the language of the conquerors imposed on them by law and police. This is partly for reasons of practical convenience or necessity: the conquered may have a variety of languages among them, and even if there is a main or widely used language, it may not have the necessary legal, administrative, technological and economic terminology. The imposition of a new language may also be used by the conqueror as a mark of conquest and absorption, since language is always an important symbol of a people. This sort of action is illustrated by the Germans' attempt to make their language compulsory among the conquered Poles, or among the French in Alsace–Lorraine.

[5] *The forcible inclusion of a foreign population element.* This is the obverse of conquest. We have in mind here the forcible introduction of a conquered people into the territory of the conquerors, as exemplified by the introduction of more than 15,000,000 Negro slaves into the Western hemisphere since the early sixteenth century, and the

forcible transportation of Dutch, Norwegian, Polish, and other workers into Germany by the Germans during World War II, to supplement their labor force. The "slaves" always have to learn some of the language of their enslavers, but they also leave deposits in the dominant language. One need only call attention to the addition of words of African origin to American speech, and the influence of the Negro upon the accent, pronunciation and intonation of the speech of the "Old South," not to mention the many other ways in which Negro culture has contributed to not only our American but also all other cultures with which it had contact.

[6] *Colonization and colonialism.* This has frequently followed conquest; it has, in fact, been a major objective of conquest. Not only does the process of colonization produce some influence on the colonizer's language, but often the language of the indigenous population provides many new terms for the language of the colonizers.

All extension of a given political hegemony, whether by conquest or colonization, by annexation, confederation or federation (to be discussed later in another connection), has its linguistic effects. The speakers of the non-official languages and regional dialects must have some familiarity with the official language, though this need will vary greatly with their social attitude, political position, physical location within the domain and so on. Unavoidably, the official language must make concessions in the way of avoidances as well as borrowing of terms from the other languages in the area of interdependence.

[7] *Economic relations, especially commerce and trade.* Here we have one of the most potent sets of factors in history. In the reciprocal borrowing of words and phrases during the course of these relations, the antagonism against the adoption of terms that arises, for example, out of political or religious pressure, is almost nonexistent. This is an area of "practical" interests; there is the inescapable utilitarian necessity that participants know some common names and phrases, and have some common recording devices. There must be reciprocally known and uniformly used names and phrases for natural and manufactured products, for tools and machines and techniques, and for occupations, whether with regard to the oilfield or the urban trading center, or in the conduct of technological and commercial correspondence. The language of every trading people, from ancient times on, has many words related to these aspects of inter-people trading and commerce.

Laird points out that, when England began to import continental economic goods, as well as continental ideas and manners, in the thirteenth century, it also imported *words* for the things along with them.

This occurred again in the fifteenth and sixteenth centuries. He notes that, in general, language moves along the current of the goods, not against it.[14] American English is rich in terms acquired through economic contact: "chocolate," "tomato," "copra," "kapok."

[8] *The invasion of a foreign religion or the change of religion.* Such invasion, whether as an accompaniment of military–political conquest, or in the form of forced ("by the sword") imposition upon a people by militant religionists, or by peaceful means, always has some effect upon the language of the invaded people. The given language of the invading religion is the *carrier*—the means of verbal and written expression—of the religion. If the religion is accepted to some degree, some of its language will also be. The spread of Islam from the seventh century on was accompanied by some degree of acceptance of Arabic, its linguistic medium. The introduction among different peoples of Buddhism, Hinduism, and Christianity has resulted in the introduction of at least some expressions from the languages carrying them.

Bloomfield has pointed out that, in the period of intensive Christian missionization of Britain by Roman Christianity from the seventh century onward, Old English borrowed Latin terms relating to Christianity, such as *church, minister, angel, devil, apostle, bishop, priest, monk, nun, shrine, cowl, mass,* and initiated Latin semantics in the way of loan-translations.[15]

With the religious terms will come a whole array of non-religious terms. The Spanish missionary penetration of the Pima Indians of the American Southwest, beginning about 1687, meant for them not only some Christianization, but also the acquisition of new techniques, foods and materials, and also substantial changes in their mode of organization. With all these, they borrowed designating Spanish terms. It is well known that terms relating to health, clothing, the gadgets, and many other features of Western culture have been introduced into various parts of the world by Christian missionaries.

[9] *Deliberate cultural interchange.* While this is not an entirely modern phenomenon, it has come to have special significance in our time, in so far as some of it has come to be conducted in a highly organized manner. Some cultural interchange—the interchange of art, literature, science, philosophy, religion, as well as the interchange of material objects and physical operations—inevitably comes with any kind of durable contact and, of course, there is also the corresponding linguistic exchange. Now, during times of peace, as the result of the ease of transportation and communication, and the relative freedom from political restrictions, there is a voluminous international exchange of

books, monographs, journals, radio broadcasts and motion picture and television films. Since World War II especially, there has come much studied and organized exchange. The extension of foreign aid and relief —as conducted, for example, by the U.S.A. and the U.S.S.R., requires the acquisition of some foreign language by the "aiders" if they are to be effective in their assistance, and usually a considerable body of new names and technical terms by those aided. There is also the growing tendency between countries to exchange students and teachers, as well as the exchange of scientists and technicians, not to mention the peaceful invasion of "underdeveloped" countries by the teachers and technicians from the "modernized" countries.

[10] *Sociologically significant variables in the linguistic change situations.* Thus far in this section, we have called attention to the major kinds of contact between peoples that produce linguistic changes. There is another sociologically important aspect of these contacts that has only been alluded to—namely, *the nature of the relations between the speakers of the respective contacting languages in the different kinds of contact situations.* While there is reciprocity, the respective borrowings are never even nearly equal. Different kinds and combinations of variables among the population elements in contact have different linguistic effects. None of the variables to be discussed operates independently, however. We have to examine them separately, simply for purposes of conceptual clarification.

The numbers factor in the "invasion" of foreign language into an area. Where the invaders are a comparatively small body, and the cultures of the indigenous and foreign elements are on approximately the same level, the invaders usually take on the language of the country. Numbers, for example, have counted greatly in the disuse or extinction of the languages brought to the United States by the immigrants. An important aspect of the situation is the fact that the immigrants came in small groups. They usually found their predecessors more or less Americanized, as well as often widely scattered and diffused among older stocks. The multiplicity of absolutely essential contacts with the speakers of the major or dominant language tended to foster disuse of their own tongue. Finally, marriage with persons of another foreign language or of the national speech encouraged the use of the national medium. Thus we have had a first generation of bilinguals among whom there is great resort to the mother tongue, but whose English is poor; the second generation tends to slough off its foreign tongue and speak fair English, though sometimes with an accent; the third generation becomes monolingual, having dropped the immigrant language altogether.

On the other hand, when the invaders are a large body coming *en masse* (historically, something like a Mongol invasion), or where the invaders come in floods over a period of time (the European settlers *vis-à-vis* the American Indians), the natives in considerable measure succumb to the language of the foreign majority, and the indigenous speech is regarded as servile.

In general, when two populations mingle, the speech of the more numerous prevails, even if it be that of the subject nationality, though a wide gap in culture may to some extent reduce the influence of the majority. However, enclaves ("pockets" or "islands") of the speakers of the language of the minority or lesser culture group may prevail for a long time—for example, the Basques in southwestern Europe, the Dravidians in India, and many native communities in Latin America.

The relative cultural and social–economic–political levels of the contacting peoples. Where the parties enjoy approximately the same standard of civilization, other things being equal, the reciprocity is likely to be more or less equal—for example, French, English, and Germans borrowing from each other in terms of convenience, utility, "style," and so on. Historically, there has also been great variation of cultural levels here.

A heretofore unmentioned aspect of invasion should be noted. If the people invaded are linguistically diverse, and great gaps exist among the strata and other functional segments of the population, the language of the highly cultured invader may come to be the language not of the masses but of strategically important functional categories. Thus, while the masses of India retained their hundreds of separate languages and dialects, English came to be the language of government, business, the upper echelons of the army, philosophy and science—of the educated, generally.

Another aspect of the comparative culture-level situation is important in our present world, namely, the variant level of technological–economic development. In such relations, the more technologically and economically advanced people are likely to provide the greatest number of terms that relate to complicated manufactured articles, to intricate machines, processes and techniques, to new occupations: for example, the terms used by native workers in the Iraqui and Venezuelan oil fields for items used in engineering, manufacturing and commercial processes, or by natives all over the world for new complicated biological or chemical products.

Social status and prestige factors. Social distances within a language community, as well as culture distances between communities, are important factors in linguistic change. In most societies, the speech of the people of the upper classes, or of the people who are admired under the value system, is imitated by those in the social echelons below them, for use in certain types of relations. As noted previously, however, there has been a tendency, in recent times, in the United States as well as in England for the growing middle classes to establish increasingly *their* speech forms as the dominant ones.

In general, however, where there is a considerable diversity of statuses, the dominant and privileged groups speak the "upper" language, and many kinds of pressure drive the speakers of the "lesser" or "lower" languages and lingoes to remodel their speech along the lines of the "upper" language. Ridicule and serious disadvantage may be the penalty for imperfections. Prestige is a powerful factor in language change, particularly the prestige of upper (or educated) classes. "Cultural words" or "imports" from a prestigious contacting culture or political entity, or the language of a dominant or admired ethnic element, are sometimes eagerly adopted. Thus, in the United States, the white man's languages were not only useful to the Indian, but also, after several generations of contact, a factor in his social position. Similarly, American immigrants not only found English essential in their social, economic and political relations, but also in many cases embraced it as quickly as they could, as a means of displaying the status which its knowledge symbolized. Fluent and correct English attested to their advanced state of acculturation.

In the relationship between different civilizations, words are frequently taken over by one people because the people from whom the loans are made possess a superior civilization. The borrowers consider the language forms of the superior people to be more elegant and dignified, while their own are deemed coarse. In such cases, the native language tends to be used only by the lower classes, and sometimes disappears altogether, at least from the writing of the culture.

Imposition by force. When a language has been forcibly imposed on a people by conquest or political maneuvering, a corresponding social–psychological situation is created. The imposed language is used in public relations and in the schools, but such transformation by pressure seems to invite violation of the dominator's decrees. There is usually a marked tendency for the controlled categories of people to use their language or mother tongue in the home and in other private relations, in their religious rites and ceremonials, at least to the extent that they are able to do so without incurring a penalty. This opposition to imposition is not only a matter of the rather widespread individual and group tendency to resist compulsion, but also of the desire for the retention and use of their own language, as far as is feasible, as a symbol and medium of their violated national (or ethnic) being.

c / **The conservatism of language.** We have indicated at some length the types of linguistic changes that occur and the major sets of factors in that change. While language does change—and changes greatly over a long period of time—it also shows pronounced tendencies to resist change.

In general, the history of almost any language will show that its changes have rarely come too rapidly. Actually, like almost all other institutions, language has a high degree of constancy and durability, even rigidity. Moreover, since it is regarded as such an indispensable thing by its speakers, it is protected, consciously and unconsciously, against loss, invasion or serious modification.[16] It is maintained by many students of culture that there is much less linguistic change than other societal and cultural change, and that the changes come more slowly. Certainly language is more resistant to *radical changes* than most other social phenomena. We never have in language the magnitude of upheaval in a short period of time that we have, and have had, in political–economic affairs—epochal changes in a generation, or even in a decade. The French and Russian Revolutions were followed by a new France and a new Russia, with profoundly modified ideologies and political and economic organization, yet the French and Russian languages continued with only slight additions and substitutions, lexically and semantically, to express the new conditions; as institutions, they remained fundamentally unchanged.

There is usually also some lag of language in relation to social and cultural needs. Since the time of Aristotle it has been recognized that language generally lags behind the development of thought. This has evidenced itself repeatedly in the lack of language capable of expressing the new ideas of philosophy, science, technology and art, but it has been equally obvious in almost every other department of social life.

The tendencies toward adjustive change and conservatism are continually, although variably, in evidence. A living language is thus constantly undergoing a rhythmic movement between fluidity and rigidity, and tends toward a "dynamic equilibrium," (although, as we shall note in the last section of this chapter, a perfect equilibrium is never achieved).

Our task now is briefly to examine the special types of conditions, pressures, techniques and institutions that make for the conservatism of language.

[1] *Physical and social isolation.* Isolation of the members of a

language community—whether physical or social, whether due to external natural factors or to social forces, or self-imposed—tends to preserve the forms of the language. Isolated peoples do not have contacts with other peoples and their languages, and this lack of contact reduces the likelihood of social change and the concomitant pressure for new language to cope with the changed conditions. Before the modern forms of transportation, which reduce the significance of distance and of geographical barriers, a people physically isolated by enclosed mountain valleys, deserts, peninsulas or islands, had languages that were often remarkably archaic. Indeed, they often presented "linguistic museums." The language of the Basques, who are confined among the valleys of the western Pyrenees—a language very unlike other European languages—has changed very little since Western linguists first became aware of it. American "mountain whites," "holed up" in the mountains of southeastern Kentucky, eastern Tennessee, and northwest Georgia since the mid-eighteenth century, brought with them from the middle Atlantic seaboard an English dialect and word forms from Elizabethan times and even earlier. Later some of these people moved to the Ozarks.[17] This language, like many of their other ways, remained relatively unchanged until the dynamic transformations of their lives that came with the military service draft of World War I, telephones, good roads, compulsory schooling, tourists and out-migration, and the exchanges between the out-migrants and the home folks. Until these exchanges, their language was that of a people whom one sociologist aptly referred to as "our contemporary ancestors."

The French of the French-Canadians is an instance of mainly voluntary social and cultural isolation. It has been *archaic* French, akin to the French of the late sixteenth and seventeenth centuries, when the French first came to the St. Lawrence Valley, and has therefore retained old forms of grammar, vocabulary, and idiom. The language of France itself, during the same time, has divested itself much more rapidly of moribund features. Other "linguistic museums" are (or have been until recently) certain areas in the Caucasus, the eastern Sudan and Ethiopia, New Guinea, Southeast Asia, and the eastern slope of the Peruvian and Ecuadorian Andes.

Attention need only be called to the fact that social or physical isolation of any body of speakers in the world today is less and less likely to be maintained, in the face of democratization, industrialization and urbanization, trade and travel, interrelated world economy, almost instantaneous nation-wide and world-wide communication, and both physical and social mobility of people. All these mean less and less unchanging language.

[2] *The institutionalized organization of language.* Because of its institutionalization language is a highly structured and conventionalized affair, with an established set of techniques that are intended to order and preserve it.[18] The general effect is to keep it from changing. Its vocabulary, or stock of words, is perpetuated in dictionaries. Although words are dropped and added, these often make their way but slowly into the general language. Grammatical—that is, the morphological and syntactical—structure and functioning, which rest on long-standing and sanctioned standards and codes, change even more slowly; in fact, they tend to persist indefinitely. The modification of meanings is often resisted.

[3] *Writing as a conserving agency.* Systems of writing, in all languages that have it, because of their peculiar structural and functional nature possess a greater rigidity than the primarily spoken set of symbols, and thus tend to exert a conservative influence. The mere act of writing a language tends to give rigidity to its lexicon, its grammar, and the related semantic organization of the language community.[19]

[4] *Literature.* A people with writing usually have a "literature," which has a somewhat separate conservative effect from writing *per se.* A literature implies a tradition that extends over several generations. Its works are significant cultural achievements: they are expressed by means of "correct" language; they point to the centrality of that language as a cultural instrument; they thus tend to fix and exalt the language in its written form, and to provide special sanctions for that form. The higher the value attached to the literature, the more likely it is that it will be looked upon as the proper, or even superior, form and presented as a model for correct usage.

One qualification should be made, however. Vendryes points out that historically the literary language of some people has sometimes been quite distinct from the standard language. The men of letters, poets or storytellers formed a caste apart, with their own traditions, customs and privileges. The result was that their products had the characteristics of a special language with relatively little linguistic influence. He mentions as examples the earlier Sanskrit literature of India and the language of the Greek epic.[20] It should be noted, however, that where literature is confined to a special social class or a very limited number of persons, its language remains relatively fixed and stationary, while the language of general intercourse changes more rapidly. On the other hand, where the literary language is widespread throughout the language community, it has the effect of dominating local dialects and special languages. Finally, the more intimately literature is associated with the life of the people, the greater is its chance of becoming a group asset and preserving the language in which it is written.

[5] *The lexicographers, grammarians, academicians and teachers.* These are the special "guardians" of language; like the guardians of rules and actions in other institutional areas, their influence is decidedly conservative. While the lexicon changes more readily and rapidly than the other institutional features of language, the lexicographers nevertheless "guard the words." Their special handiwork, the dictionaries, constitute a sort of *fait accompli* with regard to both volume and diversity of words and their stated meanings. It is obvious, of course—and without discredit to the lexicographers—that because of the continuous changes of language, dictionaries are nearly always in some measure behind the times when they are printed.

It is notorious that, under the influence of the grammarians, a language tends to lose much of its elasticity and responsiveness to the stimuli emanating from every aspect of social and cultural life. Some grammarians are sometimes irreverently but not inaccurately referred to as "administrators of commas."

The national *academies* (for example, *Académie Française*) have been instituted to guard the forms and meanings of words, to repulse intrusions, and generally to protect the language against mutability.

Finally, the teachers and the schools, especially the instructors of language, exercise a conservative influence.[21] Their function, of course, is to teach, and to teach in the *standard* language and not in aberrant or corrupt or otherwise unrecognized forms. Uniform language education is a necessity among a people. The instructors are human beings who often unconsciously engage in conservation of their own energy. As far as the case in point is concerned, this implies that teaching a fixed language, term after term, does not require new training and revision of teaching materials and habits. Many teachers do not want the existing language forms to change, any more than many ministers want their system of theology to change.

The services rendered by these "linguistic functionaries" or "bureaucrats"—the writers, the lexicographers and grammarians, and the schoolmasters—are of signal value. It is largely due to their combined efforts that we, or any language community of advanced cultural development, have a standard language. They have done for language what kings and other rulers or governmental bodies have done toward establishing and maintaining a monetary system. But their conservative influence is also well-recognized. They—as well as the laymen—need to be aware of the necessity of avoiding "sterile purity" and "frozen correctness."

[6] *Cultural and social-psychological contrast situations among contacting language groups and language communities.* While any kind of contact between peoples produces some cross-fertilization—as noted above—even peaceful contact causes the representatives of the respective cultures to be sharply aware of the uniqueness of their own culture, which is often thereupon interpreted as being superior. This frequently creates the possibility of antagonism, and certainly of resistance to borrowing many culture traits of the other groups, as well as of resistance to cultural identification with the "out-groups." Conversely, each group jealously seeks to maintain its cultural distinctiveness and autonomy.[22] Hence, there is an "in-turning" toward their own culture traits, a pride in them, an accentuation of emphasis upon them, a persistent desire to keep them free from contamination and change.

This cultural phenomenon has special application to the languages of contacting peoples. Invariably, the effects are of a conservative nature. We shall briefly examine several related aspects of the situation.

Linguistic xenophobia. Lewis refers to a kind of "linguistic xenophobia" (fear of the strange) prevailing in many linguistic communities —that is, foreign words are felt to threaten the unity of the group. Because of this social–psychological state, linguistic innovations, if not actively rejected, are at any rate far from welcomed. Even "when . . . the range of experience of a society widens and new forms of language become necessary, the immediate tendency . . . is to use the existing resources of the language before seeking new inventions."[23] The general effect is to seek to maintain the "purity" of the language.

Emotional involvement with the mother tongue. Language is a valued common possession of its speakers. Many persons, if not most, develop an emotional, prerational attachment to the language learned in childhood. It is the "mother tongue" of the members of the group. For each individual, whether or not he has reasoned it out, this native language is for him the carrier of what is familiar, traditional, and valuable; it is for him richer, more expressive than any other language. It was learned at his mother's knee; it is the medium whereby he acquired and has expressed the nursery rhymes, proverbs, anecdotes, family sayings, songs, prayers, catechism, and the important historical incidents. These in any other language would be "without flavor." Hence, the "purity" of this medium should be maintained.[24]

Language as a badge of group identity, distinctiveness, and solidarity. Ethnic and many other groups have a strong sense of being—almost always accentuated by contact with other groups—and do not want to lose their identity or their distinctiveness. They have an "in-group" feeling of distrust of other groups. No other institution gives the members of the group, or of the society generally, so strong a sense of being as does its language. The maintenance of its identity, and the conservation of it through the passage of time, depend upon the strength of its resistance to modifications of the forms of the language. As will be developed at some length in Chapter IX, the commonly possessed language is the crucial instrument in the maintenance of the solidarity, unity and competitive strength of the group.[25] It should also be noted that a minority that is discriminated against, socially excluded or depreciated—or even a majority group in such a situation—is more likely to retain its language peculiarities than one with social freedom and opportunity.

Haugen[26] points out that Norwegian immigrants to the United States, in spite of the force with which the economic, political and other social relations with their non-Norwegian neighbors were irresistibly pulling them toward bilingualism, tenaciously held onto Norwegian. They maintained it by means of such institutions as their branch of the Lutheran Church, their two colleges—Luther at Decorah, Iowa, and St. Olaf's at Northfield, Minnesota—their secular musical and athletic organizations, their "Sons of Norway" organization, their Norwegian-American Historical Society, and their Norwegian language press.[27]

Marked differences in cultural levels of the contacting peoples. This sharply accentuates the diversity factor as it operates among contacting peoples. A group of people of definitely higher culture located in the midst of a population of lower culture occupy a sort of "culture island" in a broad sea of different (and inferior) culture and language. Such a group will seek to protect its culture against degradation, dilution and pollution. An unyielding language is important among the institutional ways whereby they maintain their protective walls. As a well-known case in point, there is the rigid maintenance of the Dutch language by the successive generations of Dutch Afrikaners of Southern Africa, in order to preserve themselves in the ocean of Bantus. Similarly, the French in the St. Lawrence Valley, before their competition with the English stocks and the English language, were maintaining their cultural exclusiveness against the Indian tribes. Their rigidly maintained language was an important factor. Similarly, the Portuguese speech of Brazil is much more like that of the original colonizers among the Indians than it is like modern Lisbonese.

[7] *Political aspects.* As indicated in the discussion of writing above, a stable language is necessary for government. For example, constitutions, laws, ordinances, administrative rules and decrees and directives are in effect over generations of time and among people over wide areas; the language in which they are couched has to be fairly fixed and uniform. Thus legal language, especially, is notoriously conservative.

Another political aspect is the restorative and the "purist" efforts of the nationalists. Language is one of a nation's or a nationality group's most patent characteristics. The language of nationality groups has provided a rallying point for peoples bereft of nationhood, or for those who have never enjoyed the privileges of nationhood in the modern sense. When Poland lost her political freedom and unity in the nineteenth century, the people clung to their language as the last sign and element of their national character and unity. The stronger the efforts to prohibit the use of their language in public, the stronger, the prouder, the deeper their love for it, and the greater their efforts to use it surreptitiously. In Ireland, Gaelic, which had been consistently repressed for centuries, was resurrected and reestablished as an important badge of the new Irish states formed in the 1920's. Similarly, ancient Hebrew has been restored as the cultural and eventually the political language of the new state of Israel. Needless to say, it is only "pure" language, which usually means a long-standing language, that serves these purposes.

Historically, when a new accentuation of nationalism has come, it has sometimes been accompanied by special efforts to "purify" the language. Thus, the French Revolutionaries, among many other evidences of unity, insisted upon linguistic uniformity and undertook to root out of France all foreign languages and local dialects.[28] Notable also were Kemal Atatürk's efforts in the 1920's to purify the Turkish language of its Arabic and Persian loan-words.[29]

[8] *The family.* The family is the first medium of conveyance of the society's culture to the child. Not the least of its functions as conveyor is the transmission of the patterns and norms of speech. The plastic child, with his attention and development largely monopolized by his family during the months and years when the basic speech habits are formed, acquires his model of the mother tongue at the mother's knee. His language habits tend to become conditioned reflexes and second nature, showing themselves particularly in the fixing of language norms and of accent and intonation, and in the scope of vocabulary. Some of the family conveyance may be transmission of incorrect, inadequate and objectionable patterns, from the point of view of the criteria of standard or correct speech. Some of the "linguistic estate" may, during the later course of the individual's life, be overcome, improved or completed through training, or lost through atrophy; the "hard core," however, or the deeper layers of the language, are acquired during the early "family apprenticeship." These elements are firmly and durably rooted.[30] Thus, the childhood apprenticeship "constitutes the cornerstone of the individual's linguistic structure, and its relative stability accounts for the continuity of the fundamental linguistic tradition."[31]

It is also mainly in the family as a speech group that the individual acquires his *Sprachgefühl,* which is so potent in preventing language corruption, in maintaining intact the inner form of the language of the speaker, and in giving him his emotional bent toward his mother tongue.

[9] *Religion as a factor.* Historically, religion has been a decidedly influential factor in linguistic conservation. The language of the sacred books, of the rituals and ceremonies, of the religious instruction, and of the official functionaries in the performance of their duties, is itself almost a sacred thing. To change it is to impair the religion it expresses and mediates. There is, for example, the oft-expressed feeling of many English-speaking Protestants that the various Revised Versions, when stood up against the King James translation, somehow are not *The Bible* for them.

Pei calls attention especially to the conserving effect of religious *liturgical* language. As a spoken tongue, the liturgical language is often extinct, though it was the spoken tongue when and where the religion was originally established. Thus in India, Vedic persisted as the sacred tongue of Hinduism, and classical Sanskrit, long after its death as a spoken tongue, continues to be the official language of Buddhism. Avestan, the language of Zoroaster, is still used liturgically today by the Parsees. Hebrew, the official language of Judaism through the millennia, as we have just noted, is in the process of establishment as the language of Israel. Today, after an interval of a millennium and a half, Latin and Greek still continue to serve the western and eastern Christian churches, and for nearly that period of time the Arabic of the Arabian peninsula at the time of Mohammed has functioned as the official language of Islam.[32] The influence of these ancient liturgical languages is usually very considerable, since there is normally a carryover from the language of the religious services to the everyday tongue—a carryover which is felt in pronunciation, grammar, and particularly in vocabulary. The persistence of the King James version forms is well known.

There is adherence to religion-connected language when the speakers come to live under greatly changed social conditions. It is particularly notable that, when people migrate, they take along their religion and their language, and they want their religion in their old language.[33] The situation is well illustrated in the case of many immigrants to the United States: they brought their religion with them, and it was identified with their mother tongue. They persistently retained that language as the vehicle of their religion for a generation or more after they were otherwise Americanized. A common conclusion of students of American immigrants is that, while they welcomed much "Englishing" for both utilitarian and prestige purposes—especially along political, economic, and technological lines—they isolated themselves religiously, and felt no inferiority in retaining their old-country language as their religious language, or in resisting the invasion of English religious terminology.

4. The Tempo of Linguistic Change

A final consideration, suggested by the entire chapter thus far, and in a sense summarizing it, is the tempo of linguistic change. Tempo is related to the operation in time of all the factors involved in change. The dynamic factors are always opposed by those resisting change, so that the tempo or speed of change depends upon the degree to which the dynamic factors and other conditions inducing or requiring linguistic modification achieve ascendancy.

The speed of linguistic change is a relative matter; certainly it cannot be stated in absolute terms. There are historical periods when language changes very rapidly, and others when the change is relatively slow. At any given time, the tempo varies with the whole complex of influencing factors, internal and external, that affect the language community.

In general, linguistic change tends to slow down when social conditions are relatively static or slow to change. Important in this respect is the fact that, at the time, a people are in a state of physical or social isolation, engaged mainly in agricultural and sedentary pursuits, enjoying international peace and domestic tranquility, and free from physical or cultural invasion, and that their societal structuring and functioning is not undergoing marked institutional revision.

On the other hand, rapid linguistic change accompanies social and cultural upheavals and speedups as occasioned by invasion, conquest, international war, violent internal political-economic revolution, great intellectual ferment and ideological shift, interregional and international mobility, rapid technological change, industrialization and urbanization, and expansion and acceleration of international intellectual and economic exchange. Thus, as examples, Arabic has changed very slowly during the last millennium (yet is at present in a state of rapid change, especially in the way of vocabulary additions since World War I), while, during the same millennium, French and English have changed much and on occasions with marked acceleration, though they too have had their static interludes (for example, the Chaucerian era in England). In general, it can be said that the last fifty years have produced a greater volume and more rapid tempo of change in the world's leading languages than any earlier period of time of equal length.

As one contemplates the immediate future, two related facts stand out prominently regarding the relationship of world society and its languages. The one is that—with the multiple and multiplying contacts of users of the different languages, the words of all of them can be thought of as a sort of interlingual bank, upon which each can draw to enrich its own language as an expressional medium. The other—suggested by our present discussion—is that there are vast possibilities, probabilities, and some certainties of change in every language, as the result of the types of factors discussed.

N O T E S

1 Leonard Bloomfield, *Language* (New York: Henry Holt & Co., 1933), p. 281. Jespersen points out in connection with Shakespeare that his language differs in so many points from modern English that we need notes upon it, and several Shakespeare Dictionaries have been written to make it clear to modern readers. (Otto Jespersen, *Mankind, Nation, and the Individual* (Cambridge: Harvard University Press, 1925), p. 102.) Someone has said: "Each age must translate the classics in its own image—otherwise they die!"

2 Because of this ready responsiveness of vocabulary to sociocultural change and conditions, very many of our linguistic examples of linkage will be of a lexical nature.

3 Most institutions attain their efficacy through time because of such changes. (See Louis Schneider, "The Role of the Category of Ignorance in Sociological Theory: An Exploratory Statement," *American Sociological Review*, 27 (Aug., 1962), pp. 492–508.)

4 These instances of derivation are taken from George Willis, *The Philosophy of Speech* (New York: The Macmillan Co., 1922), pp. 41, 45, 47, 168.

5 For some of the principles involved in borrowing from other languages see Miles Dillon, "Linguistic Borrowing and Historical Evidence," *Language*, 21 (Jan.–Mar., 1945), 12–17.

6 Cf. "When a Trademark Becomes a Common Noun," *Saturday Review*, 45 (Aug. 11, 1962), pp. 33–34.

7 John P. Hughes, *The Science of Language* (New York: Random House, 1962), p. 16.

8 On the kinds of change that occur in language, see also Margaret Schlauch, *The Gift of Tongues* (New York: Modern Age, 1942), pp. 100–103, 111, 117, 119, 121, 230–231, 244–247, 249–251.

9 Edward Sapir, "Language," *Encyclopedia of the Social Sciences* (New York: Macmillan Co., 1943), IX, 155–168 (163).

10 Otto Jespersen, *Growth and Structure of the English Language* (Leipzig: Teubner, 1905), pp. 211–234.

11 Ralph Pieris, "Speech and Society: A Sociological Approach to Language," *American Sociological Review*, 16 (Aug., 1951), 499–505 (504).

12 The necessity and problem of coining new words for a new technological age are illustrated by a situation that arose when the Japanese were confronted with the fountain pen; the word they devised means "ten-thousand-year brush."

13 Cf. Mario Pei, "English in 2061: A Forecast," *Saturday Review*, 44 (Jan. 14, 1961), 12–14.

178   A SOCIOLOGY OF LANGUAGE

14 Charlton Laird, *The Miracle of Language* (Cleveland: World Publishing Co., 1953), pp. 89–91.

15 Bloomfield, *op. cit.,* p. 461.

16 This is reflected, for example, in the resistance to proposals made from time to time of certain reforms of English spelling and grammar so as to make the language, in the opinion of the proponents of change, more practicable, less inconsistent and easier to understand.

17 Among terms commonly used by them were *varmint,* a middle English word for *vermin, wrastle,* as used by Chaucer, *et* (to eat) as used by Shakespeare, Fletcher, Dr. Johnson and Pope, *pore* (poor) from seventeenth century England, and *withouten,* which goes back to the England of 1350. See Vance Randolph and G. P. Wilson, *Down in the Holler: A Gallery of Ozark Speech* (Norman: University of Oklahoma Press, 1953).

18 On the tendency toward conservatism of institutions in general, and reasons for the same, see Joyce O. Hertzler, *American Social Institutions: A Sociological Analysis* (Boston: Allyn & Bacon, 1961), pp. 136–149.

19 For a more extended treatment of both the positively and negatively conserving effects of writing, see Chap. XVII on "The Sociology of Writing," Sect. 6, p. 459.

20 J. Vendryes, *Language: A Linguistic Introduction to History* (New York: Barnes and Noble Reprint, 1951), p. 272.

21 It is probably true that the more highly educated people generally have a "purist" effect on language.

22 For the basic culture theory involved, see George Devereux and Edwin M. Loeb, "Antagonistic Acculturation," *American Sociological Review,* 8 (Apr., 1943), 133–147.

23 Morris M. Lewis, *Language in Society* (London: Thomas Nelson & Sons, 1947), p. 58.

24 Cf. Uriel Weinreich, *Languages in Contact: Findings and Problems* (New York: Publications of the Linguistic Circle of New York, No. 1, 1953), pp. 77–78; Einar Haugen, *The Norwegian Language in America: A Study of Bilingual Behavior* (Philadelphia: University of Pennsylvania Press, 1953), I, 234.

25 This is an aspect of the "Intergroup Tension Factor" which has been examined recently by social psychologists, sociologists and social linguists.

26 *Op.cit.,* pp. 33–40.

27 Haugen also points out, however (pp. 261–264), that by 1928 even the religious use of Norwegian had greatly declined, and that it has now practically disappeared.

28 Cf. Carlton J. H. Hayes, "Nationalism: Historical Development," *Encyclopedia of the Social Sciences,* II (New York: Macmillan Co., 1938), pp. 240–248.

29 This task failed, however, since these loans constituted over half of the Turkish language, and their loss would have hamstrung the language.

30 "With regard to people's native language it is indeed manifest that the period following the apprenticeship . . . , including systematic teaching in the schools, self-instruction through reading and imitation—wittingly or not—of specific models, can scarcely and only at the price of considerable effort alter, improve, or replace inveterate patterns of speech acquired during childhood." (Paul Schrecker, "The Family: Conveyance of Tradition," in Ruth N. Anshen (ed.), *The Family: Its Function and Destiny* (New York: Harper & Brothers, 1949), pp. 406–425 (412). We are indebted to Schrecker for most of the main points of the present discussion.

31 *Ibid.,* p. 414.

32 Mario Pei, *Language for Everybody* (New York: Devin-Adair, 1956), pp. 177–183.

33 This fact has been crisply put: "People prefer to confess their sins in the language in which they conceived and committed them." Everett C. and Helen M. Hughes, *Where People Meet* (Glencoe, Illinois: Free Press, 1952), p. 85.

VIII ❧ The Uniformation and Extension of Language: Historical, Contemporary

I. *Introduction*

This chapter is, in a sense, an extension of the preceding one. Here, however, we are not concerned with factors *inducing* changes in the way of the acquisition of new words, new grammatical forms, new pronunciations, and new meanings, or influences *retarding* changes along these lines—although these do actually appear among different portions of the populations affected by the kinds of changes about to be treated.

We are examining two social-linguistic processes of major importance, both operative historically and in our contemporary world—namely (1) the forces, processes and conditions making for the *uniformation of the language within the language community*—that is, a developing common or standard language gaining ascendancy over, incorporating elements from, or replacing, local or regional dialects, slangs, occupational jargons, class and other "special" sublanguages—and (2) *the extension of some languages into different language communities,* incorporating many, if not all, of the people of these other communities into the given language "empire," or making the "imperial" language a bilingual necessity at least among some segments of the population of the "invaded" areas.

Four general and closely related facts stand out in connection with our present study, facts which have been demonstrated in the past, and have direct applicability in the present and the near future. The first is that the totality of populations speaking a given language is an ever-changing figure: some language populations are increasing, while some are decreasing, even becoming negligible in number, or actually disappearing as a language community. Thus, in the United States, as we will note in greater detail below, the number of speakers of a common "Americanese" ("United States as she is spoke") is coming to include almost the entire population, overriding areal dialects, the languages and patois of racial and nationality and class groups, and many slangs and jargons.

The second fact is that there is continual change in the geographic spread of a language. Internally, the dialect of one of the larger or more culturally or politically strategic or dominant communities can replace the other regional dialects and become the universal standard language in the geographical area, as has repeatedly happened. Externally, a language can invade other language communities and spread across a continent or even, here and there, across the world. There can, of course, also be a geographic shrinkage of a given "Empire" language. Between the seventeenth and the early twentieth centuries, English spread to what were to become the United States and Canada, to the subcontinent of India, to Australia and New Zealand, and to portions of Southeast Asia, including Ceylon and the Philippines. In recent decades, however, it has been losing ground in India, Pakistan, Ceylon, and the Philippines, as these countries return to one or more of their own languages as official "standard." English is, at the same time, making giant strides in Western Europe, Japan, and Latin America as a "second" language. Russian, for centuries confined mainly to certain European provinces of the old Russian Empire, in recent decades has spread throughout Eastern Europe, the Asiatic portions of the Soviet Union, and apparently in Red China.

A third important general fact that lends special pertinence to our present task is the one that Jespersen called attention to more than a generation ago—namely, that the modern tendency is toward greater and fewer language unities, instead of the older multiplicity and splintering of languages because of meager and physically or socially separated populations.[1] Indeed, today, in the large, extended, complex societies, there is an enormous tendency toward having a "standard" language prevail for all population segments and all geographic divisions.[2] There is also the attention unavoidably paid to the present-day language "empires" (for example, by the United Nations), the extension and increasing international importance of some "empires" and the shrinkage of others, and the recurrent interest, based on the pain-fully obvious need of ending the "language traffic jam"[3] of the world, by the use of a single language for international or even world use, whether this means granting hegemony to an existent, naturally de-veloped "empire" language or adopting an artificially and deliberately constructed one, such as Esperanto or Interlingua.

A fourth fact, closely related to the third, is that languages can shrink in importance and in the number and geographic spread of their speakers; they can even die out altogether and be superseded by other languages. For the purpose of our present study, this simply means that, when some population element—a racial or nationality minority, a regional group, a politically conquered or absorbed people, a social class (or classes), a functional category (political officials, business men, philosophers, scientists, and so on)—adopt, as the case may be, the "common" language of the community, or the highly utilitarian "empire" language, their special group languages diminish in importance and in their utility to them, and may even wither and eventually die. There is much evidence that this too is happening in the world today.[4]

We are here mainly concerned with the factors involved in the uni-formation and extension of a language or, in reverse, in the shrinkage or death of some of the competing languages and sublanguages. We shall find that quite a few of the factors inducing or retarding linguis-tic change are operative in these processes. But here they operate *in a different cause-and-effect context*. They may still produce changes of the sort discussed in the preceding chapter, but what we are now particularly interested in is the effects of these same factors in *also* bringing about the uniformation of language in the given language community, the dominance of an "empire" language in certain areas in process of becoming "empire" areas, or the acceptance of the "empire" language as a second special utility language by some seg-ments of the "invaded" population.

Finally, we shall note that both the internal uniformation and th° extension of empires are due mainly to circumstances outside languages themselves. For example, the languages that become star° or that build empires, are not necessarily the "easier" ones to u° learn. What happens occurs in accordance with certain known cal principles, and is due to more or less determinable soc. factors.

2. *The Sociological Principles Relating to the Acceptance of New Cultural Features*

The uniformation of language within a given area, whether as a purely local phenomenon or for the world as a whole, the spread and wide acceptance of some languages as against some others, and the accommodation of contacting languages with each other—all these involve fairly well-known sociological principles of cultural diffusion and acceptance.

The acquisition of any kind of new culture elements by a given group, area or society comes about in the course of the sequential processes of culture transportation, contact and exchange. The processes are fundamentally processes of give-and-take among the people who inter-act—processes of mingling, unequal giving and selective taking, and partial merging of culture elements, ranging in complexity from single traits to whole patterns, and in space from immediately adjacent peoples to all the peoples in the world accessible by any means of communication. The processes are directly affected both by the density and the gravity of communication—that is, by the amount and intensity of communicative contact with other peoples and cultures, and by the dominance and imperativeness of communication in the lives of the people, individually and collectively.

Intentionally or not, lending and borrowing are sure to occur, re-gardless of whether the contacts are friendly or unfriendly, and regard-less of the similarity or dissimilarity in numbers or in cultural level of those contacting, or the forcefulness or dominance of the respective peoples or cultures. Nevertheless, as we shall note shortly, the differ-ential situations have marked effects on both giving and taking.

The processes of spreading and giving are known as the *diffusion* processes. The culture elements (ideas, objects, practices) are dis-seminated *from* a culture center or culture region *to* other culture groups across space and over time, through many different communica-tion channels and agencies of contact. The contacts may be *brief* or *sustained, direct* or *indirect*. The exchange of cultural elements may be *intracultural* or intrasocietal—that is, *within* the framework of a single culture or larger society, or *intercultural* or intersocietal—that is, be-tween one culture or society and another.

From the point of view of the absence or presence of design on the part of the *donor* or disseminator, the process may be (1) *natural, un-conscious, spontaneous* or *incidental*—that is, a gradual and undirected infiltration of elements, as facilitated by geographical proximity, random migration, trade and commerce, travel, press, radio and television; or (2) *purposeful*—that is, a matter of deliberate and often aggressively pursued efforts by such procedures as missionization, certain forms of education, or other organized procedures of indoctrination and prose-lytizing, colonization or conquest.

The borrowing or receiving and acceptance processes are counter-parts to the diffusion processes. They involve the action of the *recipients* of the new and foreign culture elements, as they take over certain elements from other cultures or societies as the result of their interaction with them, and as they adopt and incorporate these elements into their own culture system.

As in the case of diffusion, so also the borrowing or acceptance of culture elements may range from spontaneous, even unconscious, imi-tation to high-pressure adoption by way of organized instruction or by the threat or use of force.

Diffused culture elements—whether they are single traits, complexes, or patterns—are seldom taken over by the receiving or borrow-ing people, with complete passivity, by pure addition or *in toto*. Invari-ably, the adoption is of a *selective nature,* with respect to the amount and kind of items borrowed; usually there is some modification of form and reinterpretation of meaning; finally, the adoption of different items occurs at varying rates. Many diffused elements are actually *rejected* in whole or in part, for reasons mentioned below. Thus, the adoption may take the form of (1) acceptance with slight modification, (2) substitution in part of the new for the old, and the corresponding dis-carding of the passé old, or (3) fitting the new into the old.

A number of factors, by no means mutually exclusive, are involved as this relative and graded borrowing and acceptance occurs:

[1] *Spatial location and distance.* Groups, cultures or societies con-tiguous to the point of origin or dominance of given culture elements are likely to borrow them first. Even in the modern world, physical contiguity of the transmitting and receiving cultures is still a factor in the borrowing of culture, but it is rapidly losing its determinative signifi-cance with the increase in ease of transportation and communication.

[2] *Cultural differences and antagonisms.* Both within a people and between cultures and societies, the presence of sharp culture differences, especially if they involve avoidances and antagonisms, will create bar-riers and cut off or curtail borrowing.

[3] *Similarity of diffusion and receiving culture.* When the cultures are very similar and on nearly the same level, there is likely to be a mutual ability to comprehend and utilize each other's culture elements;

very often there will result a two-way exchange, and a harmonious fusion of many culture elements. Where there is great difference in culture kind and level—for example, as between preliterate and highly civilized peoples—the simpler peoples as possible borrowers have a more or less limited comprehension of elements of the higher culture and a correspondingly limited ability to appropriate them.

[4] *Attitude toward foreign culture elements.* For a variety of reasons, peoples vary greatly in their hospitality to foreign practices, objects, and ideas. An attitude of superiority or exclusiveness or one of defensiveness, or the inability to comprehend meanings and utilities, may create great obstacles in borrowing. On the other hand, crisis conditions, revealing the inadequacy of existing instrumentalities and procedures and producing widely recognized needs, may create a great demand for new things and ways.

[5] *The utility and compatibility of foreign culture elements.* If the newly presented element promises distinct utility, profitability, and efficacy under existing conditions, it will be taken over. In order to be accepted, an item must have some demonstrable advantage alongside items of habitual or familiar usage. Closely related are the factors of compatibility and radicalness. If the traits are in line with the major interests or circumstances, or the prevailing "run of attention" of the receiving group—if they are "fit"—they have a good chance of acceptance. If they are "out of line" or radical, they are likely to be blocked or rejected altogether.

[6] *Relative prestige and dominance.* The relative prestige of the donor and receiving groups is a factor of significance. Under most conditions, a group which recognizes its social inferiority will be more likely to borrow from its superiors than its superiors will be to borrow from it. With respect to given categories of culture items—foreign and domestic—if they are practically equal in political, economic, intellectual or other utility and prestige, they normally continue side by side.

[7] *Degree and level of organization of the respective cultures.* This is closely related to the preceding factor. If both cultures are equally "strong" or "weak" in organization, there is not much likelihood, other things being equal, that many of their elements will displace each other; they are more likely to exist side by side relatively unchanged. But if the factor of organization differs greatly in strength, the weaker will be constrained by a variety of circumstances to make compliant changes, unless it is able completely to withdraw from contact.[5]

These principles and factors relate directly to the processes of linguistic uniformation *within an area* (including "one world") and the special and increasing acceptance of certain few dominant languages. Most of the principles are demonstrated by concrete historical instances.

3. The Factors in Uniformation Within the Language Community

By uniformation we mean the process or complex of processes continually going on in every language community to establish and maintain a "standard" or "common" language among the population. While dialects and patois, special languages and sublanguages, may and do exist among the occupants of a given sociolinguistic area, it is absolutely essential that there be an areawide *common* language as the fundamental means of communication between all the different regions and all the different population elements—such as ethnic groups, social classes, occupational groups, urban and rural elements, age and sex groups. The people from the different territorial parts of the country and from all of the socially and culturally differentiated elements, in their contacts with each other, soon learn to avoid forms of speech that are misleading or unintelligible to other members of the group. The greater the area, the more diversified the people, interests and activities, the greater the need for areawide cooperation, order and efficiency of operation, and the more intensive the communication in the community—the more essential is a common, universal, uniform language. In order to have social unity, there must be linguistic unity.

The "standard" or "common" language develops under a variety of circumstances. The "base" or "core" portions of what is to be a given "standard" language have, historically, usually been derived from some favored dialect or local language of the area, or from the language forms of a social class (even a lower-class lingo), or the language of a control or other special functional group of the area, or the language of a conquering people, to mention only the more frequent sources. This, then, through the course of the generations, is subjected to continual revision—additions, subtractions, grammatical and semantic modifications, including the incorporation as "respectable" or "correct" of colloquialisms, humorous and slang forms, and all sorts of specially developed, functional forms from within, as well as the borrowings from without, noted in the preceding chapter. Thus, in ancient Greece the dialect of Attica spread and became the basis of the "Common Greek" (*Koiné*) of the Hellenic peninsula, Thrace, Asia Minor and the Eastern

Mediterranean, Alexandria, Sicily and Magna Graecia. Latin, the language of the city of Rome and the immediate province of Latium, became the predominant language of Italy and eventually of the Empire. Standard French emerged from *Francien,* the original dialect of Île-de-France and the area centering about the islands of the Seine within Paris. It came to extend all over the European areas where French is spoken, through the power of the French kings prior to the Revolution, and it functioned as the language of the official classes, the gentry, the Army, the law courts, and the schools, universities and the Church, in so far as Latin was not employed. Standard English stems from the East Midland (London) dialect, which was the language spoken at the Court in the fourteenth and fifteenth centuries, served as the speech of the educated and ruling classes, and then came to be regarded as the most elegant and refined type of English.

Standard Spanish is descended from the northern Castilian dialect, which dominated the Galician dialect in the west, the Catalan in the east, and a group of central dialects. Standard German grew from the language that Martin Luther used in his translation of the Bible, which in turn was the archaic administrative written German used in intercourt relations among the German states, and at the time the only variety of German understood and used (to be sure, by a very small and specialized population segment) in the areas occupied by Germans.

Once a standard language has come to prevail in an area, it has a high degree of "staying power," and tends to dominate or even overcome all other languages coming into the area. In the case of the United States, one notes the continuing preponderance of "English," despite the infusion of African languages with the slaves, or the introduction of Western and Northwestern European languages in the eighteenth and nineteenth centuries or, in the nineteenth and twentieth centuries, the languages that came with the immigrants from Southeastern and Eastern Europe.

An important point, to be fully demonstrated below, is that almost all of the historical circumstances and influences which explain the predominance of the language that is taken as the base, and which also provide the reason for its having spread over the area of local speech, *are external to language itself.* They are mainly determined by special types of social conditions prevailing in each country, although these different types usually combine in a particular way in each instance.

The more important determinative factors, historical and contemporary, in the uniformation of language will now be briefly presented. Undoubtedly, the classic presentation in English of such factors is that of Otto Jespersen.[6] His thesis is that "Linguistic unity depends always on intercourse, on a community of life, whereby the chief roughness of different dialects are smoothed down" (p. 46), and that "This intercourse may be assisted or brought about in various ways." It may be added that, conversely, sharp separations, segregations and avoidances among the regional and ethnic and class groups of a language community, however caused, are likely to impede the dominance of standard language, and make for the retention, even the increase, of dialects, patois, and foreign languages.

We will draw on Jespersen's study for types and examples of determinative factors, but we will also add factors revealed by a sociological examination and present additional recent or contemporary examples.

[1] *War and military service.* Jespersen mentions war as "causing the mingling of populations from different parts of the country" (p. 46), and either the dominance of the official language of the army or a more or less uneven blending of the dialects represented among the contacting military personnel and civilian population. He also refers to military service (pp. 61–62) as an instance of intercourse moving toward the formation of a common language. For example, not only did the system of conscription in Germany in the late nineteenth century itself draw together into the military forces recruits from every part of the country, but the government also made it a rule to move employees about as much as possible. Thus, their own language became more polished through the rubbing off of its local peculiarities.

Wagner has noted that "adult males who have served in the Russian, Mexican, or Indian army go back to their villages speaking some Russian, Spanish, Hindi, or English respectively." Also, "For generations, speakers of national languages have filtered back into the dialect-using villages of France, Germany, and other European countries from the armies. Their presence has helped to extinguish local dialects altogether."[7]

In the case of the United States, all of our wars have served to effect greater internal social and linguistic uniformity. But with the beginning of compulsory military service in World War I, heretofore physically and socially isolated populations—such as the Appalachian and Ozark "mountain whites" and the Louisiana Cajuns—racial groups, such as the Negroes and Indians, and various "hidebound" and incompletely assimilated nationality elements were drawn into the common stream. During the war and immediately afterwards, there were also popular movements to stamp out the use of foreign languages, especially German, within the country.

[2] *Intermarriage.* Jespersen mentions intermarriage between persons

from different villages and regions, each with their different dialects, as an important historical factor. The very marriages themselves, of course, indicate some breakdown of difference. In most cases, both parties use the standard language instead of their separate dialects in their communication with each other, and it is also the language taught their children. In the United States intermarriage between representatives of different nationalities and different regions and, to some extent, between representatives of different social classes has, in general, had a uniformizing effect.

[3] *A common religion.* Great religious festivals and assemblies among peoples with a common religion have drawn people together from far and wide and required a mutually intelligible speech among them. In ancient Greece there was the widespread attendance at the oracles of Delphi and Olympia. A sacred book can have a similarly unifying effect: Luther's translation of the Bible, with its choice expressions which are not the sole property of any particular district, had great influence among the German peoples, Catholic as well as Protestant. The Koran aids in maintaining the purity of Arabic in every Islamic country. A great church, with its common spoken rituals and exposition of doctrine, its common organizational (or administrative) language, its publications, its assemblies of clergy and laymen, is a unifying power.

[4] *Language for governmental purposes.* The chances of a common language being evolved are much better in an area in which a single government is in effect. In the first place, every government must have a *language of administration* in order to carry messages to all the inhabitants of the country. At any given time, most states have resorted to a single language for such purposes, although Switzerland has succeeded for several centuries in being a compact national state with four official languages. In most instances a political language, once established, has gained in influence as a general language for many other purposes.

Uniformity of language is most likely to occur where there is *a markedly centralized government,* as was evident in the early Roman Empire with its official Latin overriding the other Italian dialects, and later similarly in France, and to a great extent in England.

Though they had long been politically disunited, the pre-nineteenth century German states were drawn toward linguistic unity by the new necessities of political communication. Even before Luther's time, there was the Saxon "chancellery-language," which was imitated by other Chancelleries, including those of Austria, and which became a sort of common official "written language." The very striving toward unity among the German states affected not merely the written, but also the spoken language.

Historically, *political unification through the conquest of the territory* has occasionally been an important factor in the unification of language. The conquerors, in imposing peace and order, have at the same time imposed their language along with other features of their cultures. In the case of the Roman conquests, as of those by other nations later, Rome's language became not only dominant but "standard," in so far as it became the official language, the language of literature, the medium of commerce and of religion, and the only road to office or social preferment.[8]

Political unification through annexation of contiguous areas, and through confederation or federation of political entities has had, and has now, a markedly positive effect upon linguistic uniformation. Where these occur, there is a nationwide need for an administrative and legal terminology, the necessity for a common language for use in the governmental assemblies and bureaus, as well as in the army and other organizations. Furthermore, with the decline of border barriers and other political obstacles to movement and exchange (such as visas and customs), and the extension of over-all political boundaries, there is a greater ease of interregional travel, migration, trade and exchange of "culture." The tendency toward a uniform American English within the closely federated and ever more politically interdependent United States needs no exposition. The extension of German, and to a lesser extent of Hungarian, by way of the Austro-Hungarian Empire's complex of "nations" is well known. Within recent decades, there have been several notable efforts to establish a common language in newly combined political areas that have had a diversity of languages. Though there are some seventy recognized languages among the diversity of races and nationalities within the area of the U.S.S.R., Russian has been established as the common as well as the official language of the entire Soviet Union. India, under the new constitution and the successive Five-Year Plans, is trying to set up Hindi as the nationwide language among its fifteen major languages and hundreds of dialects and tribal languages.[9] China has some nine major dialects and hundreds of lesser ones. Prior to the Communist regime, Mandarin was understood to some extent by about two-thirds of the Chinese, who used it as a second language but retained their own dialects locally. An effort is being made to overcome the confusion of tongues by making Mandarin officially the standard language. In all three of the above cases, the officially designated "standard" is taught in the schools.

[5] *Writing, printing, literacy, and literature.* This complex of closely related factors has been of great importance historically in standardizing language. Writing has a conserving effect, as we noted in the preceding chapter. It also has a marked *uniformizing* effect. Also applicable here is the fact that it is a rather durable conventionalization, stabilization and systematization of speech forms. To this should be added, finally, the fact that writing, because of its wider use and influence in temporal and spatial communicative exchange, as compared with the fleeting and unrecorded spoken word, must also be universally standard within the ongoing language community, if it is to fulfill its reason for existence.[10]

Print and printing are a further development of writing, and have a correspondingly further stabilizing and uniformizing effect on language. Writing and print in a language community help to promote universal *literacy*—that is, the ability to write and to read both script and print. So long as these proficiencies are confined to the few, the language of the literate or educated portion of the population may be quite different from that of the masses of the people. But when literacy expands and includes more and more people, these people must have a standard language as a medium of expression. This development was copiously demonstrated by European peoples from the sixteenth century on; its necessity at present, among the millions and millions of underdeveloped people who are striving for political, economic, social and technological "modernization," is universally recognized.[11]

Standard language is most definite and best observed in its written and printed form—namely, the *literature* of the people—and that literature is, in turn, very important in the rise of a great common language. As Jespersen points out,[12] it is possible for a literary society to arise before the birth of a written language; there can be an oral body of lore before there is a written one—for example, the language of the Irish sagas in the Middle Ages. But a written literature has the standardizing advantages of writing in general. Furthermore, in literary intercourse, the writers *use* a given, existing standard language. The literary use, however, is never quite like the local dialects, unless the writers deliberately seek to depict these in some artistic or scientific manner. In addition, the literary works are ordinarily addressed to a wider audience than the spoken word, and hence tend to utilize "correct" language.

[6] *Centers of administration, trade and culture.* The rise of such centers within the given area of interdependence and communication, as history has repeatedly demonstrated, has had great influence in

establishing the standard language for the area. We have already referred to some of these local areas, towns or cities as sources of the dialect which became dominant. In most cases, the reason why the dialect became the standard language was that the place, town or city was a center of government, trade, art, science, philosophy, literature or education, or usually some combination of these. Athens, considered from the point of view of this type of factor, was the political, artistic, philosophical and literary center, and established the "standard" language which, from the fourth century B.C. to the ninth century A.D., served as the medium of expression for Greeks everywhere. Latin, which became the standard language of Italy, and for a while of the whole Western World, was essentially the language of Rome, the dominant political capital. As a consequence of its peculiar location at the first fordable and bridgeable place above the mouth of the Tiber, as well as of the significance of the Tiber and the Tiber valley as a route, Rome also controlled much of the north-and-south and also east-and-west trade and travel across Italy. Standard English developed from London: the court resided and operated from there; noblemen and traders and politicians from all districts gathered there; most literary people gravitated to the city and exercised their influence from there. Standard Russian is based on the Moscow dialect, standard Japanese on the Tokyo dialect.

Historically, universities as centers of learning and investigation have had a uniformizing effect, in addition to functioning as a main agency in both linguistic innovation and conservation. The universities have not drawn their students exclusively from one district. In some countries—for example, Germany prior to World War I—it was customary for students to attend several universities in turn. The students thus lost their localisms and developed a tolerably uniform language.

In recent centuries, the universities have taught in the standard language of their country, promoted its use, and been guardians of its correctness. They have also been the source of most of the textbooks, and of much of its literature in the fields of science, philosophy and art, and in the technologies; hence their profound effect on the ever-developing "standard" terminology in these areas.

Cities themselves, as they have become more numerous, and have increased in size and in the proportion of the total population living in them, have had a uniformizing influence. They have attracted their population from the entire surrounding area and beyond, and have intermingled these elements, which had to have a common discourse. As the result of the "collected" nature of their population, they have had a wide area of communication—between the residents of the city and their districts of origin. Urban populations also tend to be more physically mobile, and consequently to engage in interregional migration more than do rural populations. The modern metropolitan area, as a source of all kinds of influence, and as the place of all kinds of social and cultural exchanges, need only be mentioned here.

[7] *Upper-class influence.* The common language of a people has occasionally been, to a considerable degree, a class language, particularly an *upper-class* language. This, too, follows naturally from social conditions. The upper classes, especially in the past, have traveled more and mixed more with people of similar standing from other parts of the country. The members of the upper class are usually more highly educated and have a wider range of interests that call for some form of exposition. They also usually carry higher prestige, and their ways are thus likely to be imitated—if the social system permits this. The English upper class, for example, met in London on visits, and at each other's homes in the different parts of England; some of them patronized the arts and sciences; many were interested in the expansion of the Empire; their sons, from all parts of England, attended the "public schools" (the boarding schools for the upper-class boys).

In our American society, communication *among* our social classes is an important factor in our linguistic unification. Among the important factors in this connection are democratization, permissive social mobility, almost universal literacy, and popular education available to most, even at the higher levels.

[8] *Universal education.* When the people of a political entity develop an organized system of popular education compulsory for all children, they *must* have a standard language; the instruction simply cannot be in a multiplicity of dialects or lingoes, if it is to serve its fundamental social and cultural functions. The effect of universal schooling is the extension of common educational opportunities to all levels and elements of the population, and a consequent weakening of regional dialects. In the United States, the linguistic uniformizing aspects have included emphasis upon speaking the standard language, and the ability to write the common system of writing. There has also been the tendency toward universalization of certain items in the curriculum in schools all over the United States, and a relative uniformity of textbooks. The uniformation has been further expedited by the movement of children from school to school in different regions of the country, as their families have engaged in interregional migration; because of the great likelihood of migration of the publicly educated during their late "teens"

and "twenties," there has been a growing necessity for the schools to prepare children for life anywhere in the country. The influence of the educational system (with its standard language) has been greatly extended to the ever higher educational levels because of the ever more pressing necessity of high school and, increasingly, college education, in terms of economic, and especially occupational, competitive proficiency.

There has been a likelihood in the United States in the past that children of first-generation (and sometimes later) immigrant families would speak the common "English" at school and on the street, and the "foreign" language at home. Such bilingualism, however, while it still exists here and there, is declining rapidly with our greatly curtailed immigration. It is a rather well-established general fact that in modern societies whichever language comes to dominate the educational system gains thereby an enormous advantage with regard to its propagation.

In a country in which general education is universal and more or less uniform, local or class, "foreign" or otherwise non-standard idioms, words and pronunciations are to be laughed at as uneducated, "queer," or even "vulgar," and the young, usually sensitive to peer acceptance and approval, seek to abide by the common standard.

[9] *Technological and economic uniformizers. Facilitation of transportation* within a language community has always been a potent uniformizing influence; in fact, it has been a basic factor, along with other uniformizers to be noted shortly. In Roman days, the great highways and military roads counteracted dialect-splitting and multiplication. Today, the automobile provides contacts everywhere within the nation between people from all parts of the country, from different ethnic groups, and from different educational, economic and cultural levels. Air transportation has speeded up these processes. Every development of transportation is a more extensive and accelerated means of contact among people. It also makes people aware of their speech divergencies, and encourages efforts to avoid what now turn out to be "eccentricities" of speech.

Areawide commerce and trade for millennia have required that all who are engaged in these activities—the producers of the exchanged commodities, the money-changers and bankers, the sellers and buyers at all levels—have common terms for their products, services, techniques and media of exchange, and know precisely one another's products, prices and other conditions of exchange. For this, a fairly common language has been essential. The territorial expansion of industry and commerce has usually been paralleled by a similar expansion of the language. In our society, the uniformation of our language has been aided by journeys throughout the country in search of work, and the interregional mobility of people that arises out of fluctuating differentials in economic opportunity; by the extension of trade areas and the intensification of interregional trade; by the mechanization of agriculture and the movement of the surplus rural population to urban business and industry.

Mention need only be made of the uniformizing effect of *mass communication.* "Mass printed matter"—such as newspapers of wide (in some instances national) circulation, the mass circulation journals (for example, the "news" and "picture" weeklies), and the paperbacks and "pocket" editions of books in the United States, Canada, and most of the countries of Western and Central Europe—these now reach almost everyone, are for almost everyone, and seek to be linguistically comprehensible to everyone. The radio and television announcers of the wide regional and nationwide systems must of necessity utilize a fairly common (for the "mass of the masses") vocabulary, grammar, intonation and pronunciation, and standard meanings for words and phrases. Nor should the great increase in interregional long-distance communication by telephone be lost sight of as a factor. In general, it seems that, with the geographical expansion of listening, there is need for a greater uniformizing of the speech forms that people listen to.

[10] *Physical and social mobility.* Both the physical and the social mobility of persons tend to bring about uniformation of language. As people move more widely through physical space, they need a more uniform language throughout that space. The greater the volume of physical mobility in such an area, the greater is the likelihood that local individualities (for example, dialects and ethnic group languages) will subside. Social mobility also works as a uniformizing factor. As people shift laterally or horizontally, and assume membership in different groups or organizations of approximately the same social stratum, they find former group linguistic "specials" or idiosyncracies a handicap. When they move up the social ladder, they discard, if they possibly can, lower-class linguistic stigmata.

[11] *Social–psychological factors.* Conformity to and maintenance of the dominant language of the community is aided by several social–psychological situations. Of importance is *language loyalty,*[13] which is closely akin to loyalty to nation. Their common language is a most important symbol of the group; as such, it assumes a high position in the scale of values of most of its users, as a contrast to other languages, and to

its own aberrant or corrupt forms. In terms of this principle of language loyalty, the language is something to be "defended." It causes the people to rally themselves and their fellow speakers, consciously and explicitly, in its behalf; to display protective mechanisms against its change, especially its perversion—in short, to fight to maintain its purity.

The *social prestige* factor is important not only in impelling the speakers of sublanguages or of "foreign" languages within the language community to embrace the standard language, but also in causing *all* speakers, in spite of their linguistic or ethnic ancestry, to seek to speak "correctly." To speak in any other than the correct form is often interpreted as due to lack of education and sophistication, as a form of cultural uncouthness or as an indicator of inferior status. Correct speech habits are a social asset; they are of vast utility in the achievement of various kinds of "success," and in playing the vertical social-mobility "game."

Conclusion. uniformity in the United States. As we conclude the subject of linguistic uniformation, it can be pointed out that the people of the United States, as a language community, have demonstrated linguistic uniformation over a large geographic area, among peoples highly diversified racially and ethnically, and in a relatively short period of time —probably heretofore unequaled. The older immigrant languages (along with their related bilingualism) have largely disappeared from the daily speech of the immigrants' descendants. They are now being studied as "foreign" languages by many of these descendants; the languages of more recent immigrants are in process of extinction. There are a few "pockets of resistance"—some Canadian-French in the Northeast, the Germans of Pennsylvania, some of the speakers of Spanish of the Southwest—but these are negligible, numerically and socially. Among the immigrant stocks, the utility and necessity of English overcame their conservative attitudes toward the old-country languages as something precious, familiar, traditional. In their economic activities, they had to speak to speakers of English when they bought from and sold to them, worked with them, and so on. Politically, they had to become familiar with ordinances and laws, taxes and taxation, voting and legislation, the courts—and all this had to be done in English. Socially, they could not avoid common interests or association with their English-speaking neighbors and associates in almost every extra-family activity. The secular press, the American public school system, traffic signals, as well as a myriad of other unavoidable contacts with English, drew them into the English orbit. The immigrants and their descendants had to live in the omnipresent new world into which they had introduced themselves. They had to be congruent with it; they had to know its "ins and outs"; they had to "learn to think" in the American language. Before they knew it, they were using the common speech-patterns of the community.

We have noted the tendency for regional and class distinctions of speech to become fewer and less sharp. Factors that have been already noted are pertinent here: ready and speedy transportation to every nook and cranny of our land; ease of transcontinental physical movement without political obstacles; far-flung political unity, and increasing governmental centralization; almost instantaneous mass communication, by means of a variety of highly efficient media; nationwide trade; the decline in the proportion of the lower classes and the numerical, economic, and cultural burgeoning of the middle classes; the marked decline in illiteracy; the increasing uniformity of curricula in the elementary schools, public and private, throughout the land; the increase in the proportion of the population achieving "higher" education; the importance of "correct" speech for the achievement of "success."

4. The Spreading of Some Languages and the Development of Linguistic "Empires"

There have been notable instances, for at least the last four millennia, of certain languages that have extended beyond the borders of their original language communities into other, sometimes quite remote, areas where they became, if not always the first language, certainly the essential auxiliary language of large numbers of people. In recent times, and in the present "One World," this phenomenon is demonstrating itself in a most significant manner, as several standard languages have been, for more or less determinable reasons, and at the expense of many others, extending beyond their original geographic and cultural borders; they have built, or are in the process of building, extensive "empires" or far-flung "commonwealths." As notable instances from the past, we can observe the sway of Aramaic, some twenty-five centuries ago, as the *lingua franca* of the entire "Fertile Crescent"; a little later, the rise of the vulgarized Attic dialect, the *Koiné,* which was to dominate the east Mediterranean area and much of the Middle East from the fourth century B.C. to the end of the ninth century A.D.; Latin, the vernacular of the early city-state, Rome, becoming first the language of Italy, then that of the Roman Empire, and for centuries the common language of the Western World; Chinese flooding the vocabularies of the Koreans, Japanese, and the peoples of Inner Asia and Southeast Asia for centuries;

the hegemony of the Arabic of the Koran among the ethnically and regionally diverse peoples of the Mohammedan "belt" of the world; in the thirteenth century and later, the spread of German eastward; from 1500 A.D. on, the extension of Spanish, Portuguese, French, and English; today, English or Anglo-American and Russian have widely extended their usage, as will be specifically indicated in Section 5 below.

As in the case of the uniformation of a language *within* a community, the spread and dominance of the "empire" language does *not* depend to any significant degree upon the qualities of the language itself: its aesthetic features, its grammatical simplicity, its euphony or ease of pronunciation, the qualities of its semantics or of its system of writing, its ease of spelling or the extensiveness of its vocabulary. Some of these features do to some extent exist among some of the "empire" languages. But the wide use of a language, sometimes extending to remote continents and peoples, has been and still is largely due to a combination of social, economic, religious, political and military factors. For purposes of exposition, we shall now present several of the most historically important *types* of factors, or significant types of correlation, between linguistic universalization and particular situations.

It should be noted, however, that as a given language comes to spread and to some extent to assume a dominant position, it does not necessarily wipe out the languages of the invaded areas. There may be different degrees of merger, as well as compromise, among the contacting languages. Often there has been a kind of coexistence, the "empire" language being used in government and commerce, and possibly in the area-wide science, technology, religion and literature, while the indigenous languages persist in the more private and traditional departments of life. For example, after more than three centuries of contact with Spanish and Portuguese, in various areas of Central and South America and Mexico, the native languages still coexist with them. It also seems to be a fact that, for quite a while after the contact, the invading and colonizing language has been more likely to prevail in the cities, while the native or older forms of speech have tended to persist in the villages and the back country.

a / The essential technosocial prerequisites for the spread of a language: transportation and recent transspace communication. The migration of a language depends in the main upon the migration of its speakers and the key aspects of their culture; the amount and extent of this, and the resultant amount of contact and communication, rest basically upon transportation facilities across geographic space, on land and sea. The vast language "empires" of history, like political-military empires, had to wait upon the discovery and development of land routes across plains, steppes, tundras, plateaus and deserts, up and down river valleys, and over or around mountain ranges; the emergence of domesticated transport animals and wheeled vehicles; the development of water transportation—first fluvial, then on inland and coastal seas, and finally, with the invention of the astrolabe, compass, sextant and the fast-sailing vessel, on the oceans. In very recent times, they have had the advantage of ships and vehicles propelled by steam and internal-combustion engines.

In more recent times, as will be noted in some detail in Chapter XVIII, the various technological devices which use electricity, and make possible not only intra-continental but worldwide communication—such as the telegraph, the telephone, radio, and television—have, in part, diminished the importance of transportation, or have compensated for some features of it, as they have increased the range, speed, volume, and persistence of the impact of language upon the speakers of other languages.

While the availability of transportation facilities has not been, and is not now, a *guarantee*, most of the typical factors involved in the development of language "empires," both historically and contemporaneously (to be briefly examined below), are still nonoperative without the adequate transportation of speakers across physical space. Electrical energy, wires, and air waves are mainly supplemental aids to linguistic migration and penetration. The explorers, conquerors, colonists, diplomats, administrators, traders, missionaries and tourists, the books, machines and other agencies that transmit literature, art, philosophy, scientific principles, technological technics and techniques, and forms of social organization—all of which are potent linguistic carriers—must, to begin with, be transported.

b / The major conditions affecting the spread of language.

[1] *The extension of political and military power.* This has been, and still is, a major factor in the development of linguistic empires.

One of the most common forms of the extension of political power has been conquest–colonization. Military conquest has usually been the prerequisite to colonization, which, in turn, has usually meant more or less permanent conquest. Always the conquerors–colonists took their language with them and maintained it in as pure a form as they could; always some of the conqueror's language was adopted by the native population, under duress or because of its utility, prestige and the social rewards connected with its employment.

One of the richest examples of colonization as a factor in cultural, including linguistic, diffusion is Greece. The people of Greece—as a consequence of its strict geographical boundaries, its limited agricultural land and other natural resources, and its burgeoning population—early outgrew their food supply; they had to "strike out," to move their surplus numbers to accessible and conquerable places of opportunity for livelihood. By around 700 B.C., they had some 700 colonies, established by the different city-states, in Macedonia, the Black Sea area, Asia Minor, the islands of the eastern Mediterranean, North Africa, Sicily and the southern third of Italy (Magna Graecia), as well as the Mediterranean coast of Spain and France. Each of these colonies was an outpost, a point of transmission, a broadcasting station for Greek culture in general and the common Greek language in particular.[14] In the fourth century B.C., there was the development of the Macedonian Empire, which reached its peak with Alexander the Great. The old Greek world was overwhelmed in a few years by this whirlwind conqueror. Not only was the military and political power of Macedon extended further in Europe, Asia and Africa; under his successors, this power was followed by trade, the arts, Greek learning and thought, the Greek way of life, and, of course, by the basic medium for all these, the Hellenistic Greek language.

The Latin language followed in the tracks of Roman conquest and *imperium,* spreading to Carthage and other parts of North Africa, across the Alps to Gaul, to the Iberian peninsula, to Britain, to the Rhine country and the Danubian areas, and to some extent competing with and even replacing the *Koiné* in the eastern reaches of the Empire. In almost all of the central and western parts of the Empire, the indigenous languages were displaced by Latin; only the vernaculars of Britain and Germany escaped this fate. A special type of agency in this spread was the Roman *colonia*—that is, lands assigned to veterans of the Roman army, who were located in conquered territory, with a form of municipal government to hold them together. These Roman *coloniae* also served as centers for the diffusion of the new ways of life and thought introduced by the Roman legions, administrators and traders.

The Latin which was diffused throughout the provinces of the Empire was not "classical" Latin, but that spoken by the common people, vulgar Latin or *Lingua Romana.* The modern Romance languages stem from this far-flung living language.

In the 1200's, German moved eastward with the conquests and colonization efforts of the Teutonic Knights. During the last four centuries, Spanish and Portuguese have moved into Latin America with the *conquistadores* and have become the dominant political, economic, scientific and cultural languages in their respective areas. Dutch spread to New Amsterdam in North America for a while, and to South Africa, Southeast Asia and one area in South America. French expanded to parts of North and Cenrtal America, Southeast Asia and Africa. There has been a slow, but recently forced, acceleration of the extension of Russian into Asia and scattered points elsewhere. And, of course, there has been the development of the greatest of all recent language empires, English, which has spread with English conquerors, colonists, diplomats, administrators, traders and scholars to the Americas, the Indian subcontinent, Southeast Asia, Africa, Australia and New Zealand. The more important aspects of these instances of massive linguistic migration, penetration and establishment, as the consequence of the extension of political hegemony by conquest and colonization, are widely known, and need no further explanation here.

The numerical relation of conquerors and conquered, and their respective cultural levels, present two situations which have affected the tendency to domination by the conqueror's language. If the conquerors are more numerous and enjoy a higher standard of civilization, their language may completely dominate the language of the conquered. Thus, the great bulk of European colonists and immigrants who came to the Western Hemisphere destroyed or pushed aside the original inhabitants. While some of the Amerindian languages survive to this day, as we have previously noted, they have had very little effect on the European languages introduced, especially English, Spanish, Portuguese and French, and they are steadily losing ground. On the other hand, if the region conquered is already densely populated or the conquerors are few in number, and if the vast masses of the people are of a markedly different culture, or are determined to maintain their separate individuality and nationality, then two closely related things may happen: first, the "empire" language may be adopted by certain elements of the population as their auxiliary language, for civil and military administration, international trade, mass communication (if they have it), science and philosophy, for some of their nationwide literature and some of their higher education; second, as a consequence of the political and cultural prestige of the speakers of the conqueror's language, it may become the main language of the upper classes of the subject (colonial) people. Both of these possibilities are illustrated by the position of "English" in India, Pakistan, Burma, Ceylon and regions in Africa.

Three other observations are pertinent with regard to the relation between linguistic extension and the factor of political control. The first has to do with the linguistic effect of changes of political control. Historically, two situations have been apparent. Although at first glance they appeared to be quite inconsistent, actually each has been determined by a special complex of circumstances. In one type of situation, language change came with the change of political control. Thus, in England, with the invasion of the Normans, Norman-French prevailed as the political, and to a considerable extent as the upper-class language for two centuries. But, with the decline of Norman rule, Norman-French was rather quickly ousted by English. English was the language of the masses, the language by which the traditions were perpetuated, while Norman-French was to some extent the imposed language of the conqueror. The other possible situation has been one in which, even though the political power may change to the extent of complete extinction of the conqueror's control and the formation of a new state, his language—once foreign, but by this time thoroughly established, at least for important parts of the population—continues with little change. This, of course, has been the situation with respect to Spanish, Portuguese, French and English in the New World, and English in many other parts of the world, as the respective conquering and colonial governments have lost control.

A second observation has to do with the practice of *Sprachpolitik*— that is, the policy of deliberate and forcible extension by the conquerors of their language over their subjects, this extension being enforced with penalties. The Germans have for centuries been pursuing this policy; within recent times, they have attempted to force German upon the Poles of East Prussia and the parts of Poland conquered by them. Recently, also, the Russians have attempted to force their language upon the people of the former Baltic states, as well as in parts of the vast areas over which they have established military-political control. *Sprachpolitik* is almost invariably resisted—the reason for this is plainly the "language-loyalty principle" discussed in the preceding chapter, as well as quite comprehensible group attitudes of antagonism to control by force.

By contrast, the Romans did not impose their language upon their subjects by force; in the main, they maintained a policy of cultural, including linguistic, self-determination. This "paid off," however, in the form of rather free and wide acceptance of their language.

My third observation is that there have been notable historical instances of the extension of a language through the exercise of international political power and of the influence of its speakers, short of the political control involved in conquest and colonization. France, for example, from the Treaty of Westphalia (1648) till the collapse of Napoleon, was the dominant European political power. Its language, more than that of any other among the European powers, was the language of political communication, the language in which treaties were written, the language of diplomacy—the latter international use of French prevailing through the nineteenth and into the twentieth centuries. Since the days of Elizabeth I, the English of Great Britain has had wide political sway not only within the British Commonwealth of Nations, but almost universally. The extension of English today is in part due to the world political influence of the United States, just as the extension of Russian beyond its traditional borders has been due to the power of the U.S.S.R. in the contemporary world.

[2] *The international extension of economic activity.* Historically, the extension of trade and commerce has often accompanied the extension of military-political empire, but there has also been the vast reciprocal penetration of lands and people by the products, financial credits, agricultural, industrial and commercial techniques and other economic features of peoples and nations, quite apart from conquest, colonization and extension of political control.

As noted in the preceding section, there must be a common language serving as a means of communication, if trade and commerce and other economic activities are to be successfully conducted among the population segments and areas within a language community. The same necessity is equally cogent in connection with the conduct of economic activities across continents and oceans.

As some people or nation extends its trade and commerce, or becomes an important agent of inter-people, international and intercontinental trade and commerce, its language, or adaptations of it (for example, in the form of "pidgins"),[15] usually becomes the communicative medium for economic transactions. In ancient times, Latin accompanied the Roman trader, and came to be essential to the complex economic production and exchange carried on among all the far-flung portions of the Empire and beyond. In recent times, the international use of English has come to be at least as far-flung as the financial sway of the British pound or the American dollar. At the present time the dominance of the material civilization of the United States in many parts of the world—its gadgets, clothing, cigarettes, soft drinks, automobiles, industrial techniques, drugs, and so on—has been a factor of stupendous significance in making English the leading language of world commerce. Quite a bit of English accompanies the economic and technological assistance rendered by the United States. Such facts as these have suggested to many the utility of English as their first auxiliary language.

[3] *The spread of a great religion.* This has been a notable factor in the spread of a language, although the language thus spread has usually not taken the place of the main speech of the great mass of people affected. There is, however, one notable instance of this.

Arabic, which was originally restricted to the Arabian peninsula, has become a world language by reason of the fact that it is the spoken and written language of Islam. Mohammed and his militant followers, from the seventh century on, have spectacularly spread the Islamic religion to vast regions of the earth by military conquest as well as less violent missionization. By contrast with Christianity, Mohammedanism has never proselytized in translation. The Koran, wherever it was used, by mullah and common worshiper alike, had to be read and chanted in the language of the Prophet himself. As a result of this religious expansion, Arabic became the popular language of North Africa and the states of the Near East (at present, Syria, Jordan, Lebanon and Iraq). It was also diffused into parts of Europe itself (for example, the Iberian peninsula and the Balkans, where traces of it still linger), and into the Indian subcontinent and Southeast Asia. Arabic has also had much influence in Persia, central Africa, Madagascar and dozens of lesser areas and cultures. The effect of Arabic is felt wherever there are Muslims. While spoken Arabic has split into a diversity of spoken dialects, the classical Arabic of the *Koran* is still the common literary language everywhere in the Arabic-speaking world, regardless of the local spoken forms. Moreover, in most of these countries, Mohammedanism has been more than a creed; it has been an impelling way of life, and almost everywhere a foster-mother of learning. During medieval times, in southwestern Europe as well as in the North African and Asiatic Mediterranean littoral, Islam carried Arabic as the language not only of scripture, but also of science and revived classical learning. In the contemporary world, Arabic is by no means the language of all Muslims. For example, only a minute percentage of the Muslims of Pakistan, India, Turkey, and Iran can either read or speak Arabic.

Buddhism, starting from India, has carried a knowledge of Pali or of Sanskrit long distances, but it has remained a scriptural and learned language, used mainly by monks and scholars, and has not changed or displaced the speech of the far-flung adherents (in Tibet, Southeast Asia, China, Japan). In India itself, there is nothing to indicate that the spread of Buddhism had any determinable effect on the development of the Indian languages.

The relationship between the development of Christianity and the spread of Latin (and Greek in the East) is well known. Latin flowed, along with the builders of the Roman Empire, to its farthest reaches, and after the establishment of Christianity in the Empire, its missionaries, using Latin as their main language, themselves extended their activities wherever the *imperium* prevailed and beyond, thus making Latin the official sacred as well as the official political and leading secular utilitarian language.

In recent centuries, Christian missionaries, penetrating to the ends of the earth, have been instrumental in spreading, in a limited way, the use of certain modern languages—notably English, German, French, Spanish and Portuguese. In general, however, in the modern world the uniformation of language and speech across linguistic borders is not so much associated with the spread of religion as it is with political control, commerce, and the spread of the arts and sciences.

[4] *The spread of the arts, sciences, technologies and ideologies.* The spread of a language, as a medium for communicating the arts, sciences, technology or ruling ideology of a given culture or, more extensively, of a type and level of civilization, has an effect somewhat similar to that of religion. That is, the language seldom becomes a substitute speech for the masses of the population involved, but rather exerts its influence mainly in specialized areas of life and interest, or else some words or phrases or other "special-language" features are adopted only by those functioning in the particular area of interest or activity.

Historically, a language whose literature has been widely studied because of the art, philosophy, science or other culture elements enshrined in it has had a strong influence on the languages of the peoples making contact with it. Latin exerted such an influence throughout the Middle Ages, because of the old literature of Rome and, as noted, the spread of Roman Christianity. Greek became important anew with the Renaissance. French has exerted great influence through the prestige of its literature and culture during the last 600 years. This occurred, first, during the twelfth and thirteenth centuries, when the victorious Crusaders carried it to Jerusalem, Antioch, Cyprus, Constantinople, Egypt and Tunis. In the seventeenth, eighteenth and nineteenth centuries, French penetrated abroad, through the force of its explosive new ideas. The vast expansion of the sciences, philosophy and the arts by the *philosophes* and Encyclopedists (often they were the same persons), and of the concepts of freedom and the rights of man, of democracy and democratic government in general, by the great political philosophers of the Enlightenment and the Revolution, required, on the part of all who could comprehend these, a knowledge of the linguistic medium in which they were expressed. This, of course, applied mainly to the upper classes of the communicating world.

Between the beginning of the ninth and the end of the fifteenth century A.D., Arabic had a considerable influence in Europe as a result of the fact that great Muslim (as well as Jewish) scholars had kept the ancient Greek and Hellenic learning—its arts and sciences—alive, while Western and Central Europe was suffering its cultural and political "Dark Ages." Scholars of northern and western Europe had to acquire a knowledge of Arabic, as well as Latin, at a time when Moorish Spain was the flower of European culture—according to Charles Haskins, the incubator of the Renaissance—and sole custodian, not only of philosophy in some of its major forms, but more particularly of all of the mechanics, medicine, astronomy and mathematics of the ancient world.

The language, or at least the special terms, of a people that is producing technological developments must, of necessity, be adopted by those accepting the technics and techniques. In remote times, the acquisition of agricultural and pastoral techniques favored the expansion of the languages of those peoples who incorporated these techniques into their economy, and who increased in numbers, wealth, and power through the possession of their superior food-producing techniques. In recent decades, the languages of the more technologically developed peoples have spread to many other areas. Not only their material technology, with its superior machines, gadgets, techniques and consumer goods, but also their social-organizational and psychological technologies have come to be widely used and, unavoidably, the language by which it was necessary to name these elements and describe these agencies and techniques had to accompany the technologies.

Certain particular technological developments in communications, usually occurring among peoples already highly developed culturally, have fostered the extension of the languages of these peoples. The development of printing in ancient China seems to be a case in point: the utilization of printing by the leading European cultures, after it had been introduced from the Far East in the fifteenth century, has been a factor of pronounced importance in the universalization of their languages through their mass media.

Historically, the spread of an attractive or vigorously propagandized social-political-economic ideology has also created some demand abroad for the major language in which it is couched. Mention need only be made of the attractive ideology of the French Revolution and its effects upon the spread of French as a language, or of the high-pressure international inculcation of Communist ideology in relation to the spread of Russian.

International tourism has come to be a factor of some significance in the spread of some languages. Americans, for example, have visited overseas countries annually to the extent of some 2,000,000 in recent years, not to mention millions of visits made by Americans across the Mexican and Canadian borders. This means that American English has been learned to some degree and come to be used by the transportation, hotel, motel, restaurant, guide-service and amusement personnel, in almost every place widely visited by American tourists. American tourists have come to be both *demanders* and *suppliers* of English in non-English-speaking countries.

5. *Language for "One World"*

A major consideration concerning the uniformation and extension of language is that of a common world language for interpeople communication and action. Ever since men became aware, in ancient times, that there is some correlation between the diversity of languages and misunderstandings, separations and dissensions (even unto war) among men, there has been the wish that all mankind might talk the same language.

The crucial issue of an international, universal language—one designed to be spoken, understood, read and written by all peoples of the earth—is relatively recent, however, as a practical necessity. The problem was not quite that urgent back in the seventeenth century, when it was first given some conscious thought. It became immediate only in the nineteenth century, with the development of the "One World." The present situation poses several considerations of marked sociological and psychological, as well as linguistic, pertinence.

a / "One World." The new world that began to emerge about five centuries ago, but which has especially developed in the present century, is a contracting, interrelated and ever more crowded world. With the development of transportation—particularly the jet plane—space and time have shrunk, so that even remote people are at most only a few hours from each other, as against the weeks and months of former times. All of the peoples and nations are more dependent upon each other for the material things of life than were the inhabitants of a village a hundred years ago; it is a "share-the-wealth" world, and the so-called "curtains"—Iron, Bamboo, Dollar—only accentuate and illuminate that fact. Culturally, many of the residues of the intellectual, humanistic, religious, political, commercial, scientific–technological, agricultural and industrial revolutions of the Western World since 1450 have come to penetrate and increasingly to influence all the rest of the world. This "one world" has arrived at the point where regional problems cannot be solved piecemeal and in isolation; even national problems and actions are the intimate and vital concern of every other nation. For the individuals living in it, the world has broadened: its peoples, nations and regions are tied one to another by exchange of goods, services and ideas, by their mutual friendships and mutual suspicions, by their very antagonisms and conflicts. The whole world is a small island today, in which all of its people are thrown together in a multiplicity of ways, and in which all of their activity—good or bad, peaceful or hostile—now proceeds on a more or less integrated basis.

At the same time, the world has become a vast "whispering gallery." The ever-developing means of communication by land, sea, air and air waves have multiplied with surprising rapidity, and have reached a high degree of efficiency and penetrative power; they have wired the world into a single vast and intricate circuit. The *possibility* has been created of the activities and opinions of all the world being known almost everywhere in it, instantaneously and simultaneously.

Finally, it is a world becoming ever more crowded with people. With the world population increasing by more than 65,000,000 persons a year, and all indications pointing to the fact that it will increase at an even greater rate during the decades ahead, "standing room" becomes scarcer and scarcer, and people are thrown together more and more. As they meet and interact, they must communicate; whether or not they do it effectively is another matter.

b / The multiplicity of languages. Although the possibility of international communication exists, some linguists, social scientists, and people involved in practical ways in international activities contend that communication—and with it the free flow of cultural goods— is not what it can or should be. While there are other factors that threaten or curtail adequate communication for living in One World, the key factor seems to be the multiplicity of different languages in the world. What seems to be needed for the vast number of linguistic social units, in the opinion of many, is a few languages that are widely understood, or even a single worldwide language for worldwide communication—a language as widespread as, and coordinate with, the common communicating area. The world community, it is contended, can function effectively and peacefully, only when peoples can readily talk to peoples. Actually, because of the multiplicity of languages, we have in considerable measure a "defeat of communication" and a state of disturbing "world confusion," and this constitutes "something of an anachronism in an age of electronic revolution and jet-propulsion."[16]

[1] *The large number.* The number of languages spoken in the world today is a more or less undetermined figure. Precisely how many there are, we cannot say. One reason is the lack of adequate information on the languages of certain regions, particularly South America and parts of Africa and the Western Pacific. Another more fundamental reason is that, even where our information is adequate, it is sometimes difficult to determine whether the speech of two groups should be counted as separate languages, or only as different dialects of a single language. A third reason is a reflection of the problems—linguistic, sociological, political and ecological—that are involved in defining the boundaries of language communities. The boundaries are not sharp. There is nearly always an imprecise prenumbral band, taking in both sides of the presumed boundary in which "mixture" of the adjoining languages occurs. Sometimes the people in this overlap are bilinguals or polyglots. There is also the assumption that the boundaries of a speech community coincide with political boundaries. In Scandinavia, for example, Danish, Norwegian and Swedish, though mutually intelligible, are regarded as different languages because of their political status. But this relationship is by no means general. There is the classical exception of Switzerland which, even though it is a closeknit single political unit, includes speakers of four different languages: French, German, Italian and Ladin (or Rhaeto–Romance). In the subcontinent of India, the new political boundaries have not prevented the overlapping of languages, nor has the new political alignment facilitated the counting of their respective speakers. Finally, the number of languages does not remain constant even in a short-term perspective. Languages of some of the smaller social units of the earth are waning and dying; it is possible, on the other hand, that some new languages are forming.[17]

As the result of these difficulties, we find a considerable lack of precision among the experts regarding the number of languages in the world. For our working conception, we have to depend upon such statements as the following: "The students of linguistics have identified at least 2500 active and differing speech communities, not counting dialects."[18] "The number of languages spoken in the world today is some three or four thousand. Precisely how many we cannot say."[19] "Inventories of languages of the world usually list from three to four thousand spoken languages."[20] "There are some 2800 languages in the world, according to the French Academy of Science."[21] "There are in spoken use throughout the world today, according to our most reliable linguists, 2,796 separate languages, exclusive of dialects."[22] "They (the experts) can still only guess at the number of existing languages: somewhere between 3000 and 6000."[23]

The "splintered" state of languages spoken among mankind is brought out in various anthropological and demographic studies. It is estimated that there are, or until recently have been, over 1000 languages among the Indians of the Western Hemisphere, most of which do not have more than a few hundred or a few thousand speakers. Voegelin calls attention to the large number of languages among North American primitives,[24] showing some sixteen language families, which include within them about ninety distinct languages. For example, the Algonquian family includes thirteen languages, the Athabaskan nineteen, the Uto–Aztecan ten. It is estimated that in South America there are 558 major languages, belonging to 94 groups; Quechua, the language of the Incas, is in the lead with some 4 million speakers scattered from Ecuador to northern Argentina.

More than 800 different languages are said to be spoken in Africa. In Abyssinia alone, some 70 languages exist among the different racial stocks. About 500 languages are used by various Negro tribes south of the Sahara, the leaders being Hausa in Nigeria with some 14 million, and Swahili in East Africa with around 18 million speakers. Hundreds upon hundreds of languages exist in Asia. In Burma alone, 18,500,000 people speak 126 different languages and dialects.[25] Indonesia has 200 provincial languages.[26]

In spite of these statistics, there is considerable difficulty in determining, at any given time, the number of speakers of any particular language, even the leading ones of the world. A cursory examination of the estimates reveals, however, that in spite of the vast number of languages still existing, the great bulk of the people of the modern world speak a relatively small number of "key" languages. Even the languages with 1,000,000 or more speakers probably do not exceed 200 in number, one of the latest estimates being 130; many of these are remote and little known.[27]

There is also a notable tendency, stressed by Jespersen, and mentioned above, toward a diminution in the number of languages in the world.

The world's truly significant languages, from the military, economic and political standpoint, now number less than one hundred, and among these only thirteen or fourteen have 50,000,000 or more speakers. This means that the possible world languages are relatively few; those that there are already have a large number of speakers and, in certain instances, intercontinental extension.

[2] *The major contemporary speech communities.* The data will be compiled by the present writer from a number of sources, and the respective speech communities will be ranked according to the approximate number of their speakers and users.[28]

English. English is the most widely spoken language in a mutually intelligible form and the most widely used of all contemporary languages. It is the mother tongue of some 285,000,000 speakers in the British Isles, North America north of the Rio Grande, and Australia and New Zealand. It is quite readily understood by approximately 250,000,000 more in India, Africa and elsewhere, and is the "second" language of somewhere between 50,000,000 and 125,000,000 more. While an effort is being made to change the situation in India, it is still the government language of some 700,000,000 of the world's people. It is the most widely read language; more of the world's printed matter —newspapers, journals, books—is in English than in any other language. English is the leading commercial and broadcasting language of the world, and has increasing sway as the chief diplomatic and scientific–technological language of the world. The speakers and writers of English are distributed over the entire globe.

Chinese. About 600,000,000 people speak the nine major dialects of Chinese—dialects that almost amount to a family of more or less distinct spoken languages, some of which are practically unintelligible to speakers of the other regional languages. However, it is estimated that about 300,000,000 speak variants of Mandarin—the dialect of North China, the language of the former Imperial Court, and the official language of present Communist China. Cantonese ranks second with something above 100,000,000 speakers. In spite of the large number of speakers, these are almost all within the boundaries of China, which is only a portion of a continent.

The languages of India. The speakers of the languages of the subcontinent of India amount to some 480,000,000. The 1951 Indian census reported 845 languages and dialects, including 63 non-Indian tongues. There are about 200 separate languages, belonging to four different families of speech. However, more than nine tenths of the population reported that one or more of the fifteen main languages (each having more than nine million speakers) was their mother tongue.

About 12 million persons spoke one or another of the 23 tribal languages, 18 million used one of the other 24 languages, and some 3 million named one of the 720 dialects.

The fifteen main languages are recognized as "languages of India" by the Constitution. But Hindi, which is to be *the* official language under the Constitution and the Five-Year Plans, is spoken by about 160,000,000 and, if the closely related Urdu is included, the speakers of the leading common language amount to around 200,000,000.[29] It is estimated that 75,000,000 speak Bengali, the second ranking language. The great bulk of the speakers of these Indian languages are in India itself; only a few million are elsewhere—Southeast Asia, east and south Africa, Central America.[30]

Russian. There are said to be some seventy recognized languages in the U.S.S.R. Among these, Russian (including the closely related Ukrainian and Byelorussian) is spoken by some 150,000,000, and understood as a "second" language by as many as 100,000,000 more within the U.S.S.R. and among its satellites. Russian has been until recently a restricted language, but is now expanding as has been noted. It has become a necessity for scientists everywhere.

The other contemporary languages, or closely related group languages, with 50,000,000 or more speakers using each as their first or important auxiliary language, are herewith listed, in descending order, and according to the most recent estimates:

Spanish, with around 140,000,000 speakers, is the language of Spain, and the leading language of Latin America, where it has the great bulk of its speakers and is the official language of 18 of the 22 independent American nations.

The speakers of the closely related *Indonesian* family of languages amount to about 105,000,000 and are confined almost entirely to Southeast Asia. The distinguishable separate languages, as noted above, add up to about 200. The leading tongues are Javanese and Malay—Javanese being the language of about 30 million. The new nation is attempting to establish Behasa Indonesia (meaning literally "the language of Indonesia") as the official and legal common language, to supersede the many different dialects. While the local schools continue to teach the provincial languages, Behasa is now compulsory for them all.[31]

German is the language of some 100,000,000. It is spoken mostly in Germany, Austria and a part of Switzerland, although there are also speakers in lands of German immigration: the United States, Argentina, Brazil, Chile, Uruguay.

Japanese has an estimated 95,000,000 speakers, mostly in the Japanese archipelago, with only a few scattered millions elsewhere in east Asia and some of the islands of the Pacific, and in Brazil.

Arabic is spoken by around 80,000,000 people throughout the Muslim "belt" of the world. It is spoken on the African continent from the Mediterranean to the Sahara and from Morocco to Egypt; in most of the countries of the Middle East: Arabia, Yemen, Syria, Jordan, Lebanon, Iraq; as an auxiliary language, by African Negroes, East Indians, Indonesians, Turks, Chinese, Albanians.

Portuguese is spoken by about 75,000,000 persons. It is, of course, the language of Portugal, but the great body of its speakers is in Brazil, where it is the most widely spoken first or second language and is the official language. It is also spoken in the Portuguese empire, including the Azores, Angola and Mozambique in Africa, and in small colonies (or former colonies) on the coast of India and in the Indonesian islands.

French, with 65,000,000 speakers, is practically as widespread among the territories of the world as English, though the number of its speakers is very much less. In addition to being used in France itself, it is one of the official languages of Belgium and Switzerland and is spoken in Europe by large numbers of educated people of all countries. In the Western Hemisphere, it is official in Canada, Haiti, French Guiana and Guadelupe, and is spoken widely by the educated people of Latin America. It is the administrative tongue in Morocco, Tunisia and Algeria, and is also spoken in Equatorial Africa, French West Africa, Madagascar, Indochina, Samoa, Tahiti and other scattered islands in the Pacific and Indian oceans. It is also a widely read cultural language.

Italian is spoken by about 55,000,000 persons in Italy, North Africa, and points in the Western Hemisphere.

It is significant to note, both from the point of view of supremacy, and as a notable aspect of the development of linguistic "empires," that six of the thirteen or fourteen leading contemporary languages of the world, and the languages of greatest intercontinental extension and influence (English, Spanish, French, Portuguese, Italian and Russian) are European in origin. The first four have become mainly Euro-American; Russian has become Eurasiatic.[32]

c / The presumed need of greater world linguistic uniformation: the arguments pro and con. Even though "One World" exists in a number of signal respects (despite the "Iron Curtain"), and while several of the language "empires" are almost worldwide in extent and their languages are spoken by sizable fractions of the world's people, many social linguists and other students of world society contend that the contemporary world still lacks adequate, accurate and sufficiently uniform linguistic communication. This situation, these proponents note, exists at the very time when there is increasing recognition of the utter indispensability of worldwide, clear-cut, mutually intelligible discourse. This communication is needed in a multiplicity of momentous areas of modern social life, which have become inter-people, international, and intercontinental—areas such as political relations (including intergovernmental, diplomatic and world-government relations), business and world trade, science and technology, philosophy, art, medicine, drugs, literature, labor relations, workers' relations, world health planning and administration, scholarship and teaching contacts (especially in view of the increasing exchange of teachers and students), international economic and technical assistance, travel and tourism—as well as for the demographers and social statisticians, in their planning for resource utilization, for international conferences and international mass communication (press, radio, and television), export films, missionaries, aerial transportation—and even, ironically, for soldiers.

One of the great problems recognized by students of modern affairs (and to be treated specifically in Chapter X) centers around the fact that the multiplicity of languages operates as one of the powerful centrifugal forces keeping humanity asunder. The linguistic situation in this respect is similar to—in fact, usually correlated with one or more of—the other "Great Barriers" among peoples: nationalism, economic competition, ideological conflict, race and nationality prejudice and dissension, diversity of religious convictions, and the major free-world–communist world cleavage. Thus the problem of linguistic diversity relates directly to the problem of mutual understanding and of unity and peace among the different peoples of the world. Failure of complete understanding because of linguistic difficulties provides a fertile soil for suspicion on the part of one body of speakers with respect to another, and this, of course, further retards mutual understanding and peaceful and profitable interaction.

Such situations, in the opinion of some students of the social aspects of language, point to the desirability, indeed the necessity of a universal language, or a few international ones. A universal or common language, as the concept is used by most of its proponents, does not necessarily mean one used exclusively by all persons and groups—that is, to the exclusion of all other languages. The language they have in mind is one for worldwide, or at least, wide interpeople use. Most people— that is, those who would not have the universal language as their mother tongue—would probably use their own mother tongue for *intra*-group or *intra*-national communication, and the universal language for extra-group and extra-national communication.

The wide use of a single or a few languages, which could be easily understood and used by all (or many) peoples and nations, would do much to promote inter-people understanding. It would also tend to place everyone on nearly the same footing. This would abolish or, at any rate, greatly reduce the feeling of inferiority on the part of both (or all) of the parties of speakers who speak the others' languages, usually hesitantly and often poorly, sometimes not at all, or have to depend upon translation—which, as has been noted, is at best somewhat hazardous. It should also be pointed out that a universal language would not be a guarantee of world understanding, order, cooperation and peace. The bitter fact must be accepted that universal communication also makes possible the keener revelation of differences, the wider extension of prejudices and antagonisms, the stirring-up of rivalries, the spread of propaganda and other false or misleading doctrine, the mental and ideological manipulation and exploitation of peoples on a world scale.

This critical consideration, however, does not offer grounds for denying the fact that inter-people communication, which is as adequate and accurate as possible, while it may not be a guarantee, is a strategically necessary condition for inter-people amity, prosperity and peace, or that a universal or widely used language is a gateway to, and a potent instrument for, worldwide communion and understanding, the application of principles of worldwide action and of effective opinion. In all candor, however, it should be kept in mind that, in the last analysis, world unity of peoples is not a matter of a common culture or a common language; rather, it rests on the activation of a few strategic values —shared respect, shared information, shared decision-making.

d / The essential linguistic and social features of a universal language. We have used the term "one or a few languages" several times. Let us briefly examine some of the essential linguistic and social features of a possible (and generally usable) international language.

Linguistically, it must meet: (1) the *manipulative* needs of mankind, which means especially that it must be an efficient means of political, economic, scientific and technological intercommunication and management; (2) *declarative needs*—that is, it must permit identification and description of all items of significance in worldwide discourse, and make for clarity, simplicity, adaptability, conciseness and precision of statement; (3) *semantic needs*—that is, clear, universally accepted and universally used meanings. It must also (4) *engage the feelings, loyalty and will,* as well as the *thought and action* of those called upon to use it.[33]

Goad presents five functional essentials of a universal language: (1) *phonetic and literary clearness,* so that it is distinctly heard when properly pronounced; (2) *ease*—that is, relative simplicity and regularity of its grammatical construction; (3) *conciseness*—no excess of polysyllabism; (4) *expressiveness*—that is, its vividness and wealth of homely and familiar associations, and (5) its *power of assimilating foreign words* without doing violence to its own tradition.[34]

The existence and effectiveness of any one-world language, however, also depends upon certain non-linguistic conditions. First, there would seem to be the need of an awareness upon the part of the peoples of the world of the basic unity and mounting interdependence of all mankind. Despite the obviousness of the facts of "One World" presented above, there is still widespread myopia regarding them. Second, an awareness of the needs that call for universal linguistic communication is essential; yet those needs are still recognized by only relatively few of the world's inhabitants.[35] Men will have to relate the language to the satisfaction of basic needs of an economic, political, or scientific nature; especially, in the light of recent events, its importance in relation to *security* as affected, for example, by electronics, nuclear fission and the possibilities of mutual destruction.[36]

Third, and quite concretely, in the opinion of many, the "one" language seems to hinge in considerable part upon an effective set of world political machinery to decide upon it, promote it in all educational institutions the world over, prescribe it for economic, political and scientific intercourse, and itself use it in all of its deliberations and administration. It would seem that a world language can exist only in a world political society, whether this comes about by evolution or by compulsion through world conquest. "Evidently one language depends on 'one world,' not 'one world' on one language."[37]

The actualizing of a world language rests upon both the favoring and the hindering factors, the more significant of each of which will now be briefly noted.

e / Factors favoring one universal language. The following are among the important factors favoring a universal language:

[1] *The incentives* to uniform world communication are stronger than ever before. They flow from the needs for inter-people and intercontinental discourse in strategic areas of relations mentioned in the

preceding section. The self-interest of individuals, and the reciprocal advantages to be derived by all kinds of groups and organizations, may prove to be powerful factors. These are "straws in the wind." The cosmopolitan character of modern scientific work has resulted in some standardization of terminology in a few "empire" languages. These relatively few languages have come to be used more and more in the presentation of original scientific contributions. This has been increasingly done in English during recent decades. The tendency to use one language—English—in commercial relations and business correspondence has already been noted. International aviation, as a matter of necessity, has already produced a highly technical worldwide language based on English, with a minimal vocabulary of about 800 words, to be employed for radiotelephone communications connected with instrument flight. Politics also, on an international level, over the generations has developed something in the way of a common vocabulary to enable rulers, diplomats and other governmental agents to deal with each other in an orderly and comprehensible manner.[38]

[2] *The spread of a common civilization among all its peoples is a characteristic of the contemporary world.* What is labeled as "modernization" is occurring among the two thirds of the population of the world designated in the United Nations terminology as being more or less "underdeveloped." The process of "modernization" is that of the the development of a people from a "folk" or "folk-agrarian" society to the modern industrialized–urbanized–technologized–statized society characteristic of the more "advanced" twenty to twenty-five percent of the world's people.[39] Most of the features of modernization are universally desired and acquisition of them is proceeding everywhere in the world to some degree. Through its scientific, technological and economic development, its enhanced physical productivity, its high standard and plane of living, its development of education, its more effective, nationwide political life, and its greater cultural sophistication, to mention only the more outstanding features, modernization both: (1) enhances the possibilities of one language through the development of universal interests and a common way of life, and (2) posits a large body of common needs, most of which can be met satisfactorily only through international activity.

[3] *The physical technology*—the "machines" or physical means— by which a universal language may grow and live now exists. These are the devices (printing presses, teletype, typewriters, telephone and telegraph, radio and television) that broadcast the written and spoken word, and make intercourse easy, rapid, frequent and planetary (possibly interplanetary in the not too distant future). Today, the machines of

language, especially the telecommunications devices, by binding mankind into a single communicating area, are beginning to make a single common speech possible. Says Lewis: "When New York and Moscow can speak daily to each other, and even, through television, face to face, can read the same books and newspapers, and see the same films, does it seem beyond possibility that at some future time one language may become their common tongue?"[40]

[4] *Modern social technology* also favors the development of a world language. In the preceding section it was pointed out that "one" language seems to hinge on an effective set of world social and political machinery. There is some evidence that we are "on the way" along these lines. We had the example recently of a semi-formal organization that, after extensive research and experimentation, drew up the International Language for Aviation (ILA) indicated above. Several agencies are concerned with the production of uniform terminologies within the several sciences for international use, notably the International Organization for Standardization, in the area of the physical and biological sciences, and UNESCO, which is concerned with the social as well as the physical sciences. The United Nations may, in time, develop beyond a world agency for debate and negotiation and become a world government— even of the federated kind. It might then recognize, promote, and utilize one universal language, instead of the four or five "empire" languages now utilized in its activities.

f / Hindering and negating factors. In the case of a great majority of the world's speakers, the adoption and use of a world language will mean either substituting it for their own national language, or adding it as a second language to be used in their extra-group communication. Either of these situations poses certain problems.

[1] *The resistance factor.* As noted in Chapter VII on "Sociocultural Change and Changing Language," there is always a resistance to change within a language on the part of its native speakers. It has also been commonly experienced that the main body of speakers of a given language resist the adoption of a "foreign" language as their *main* language. As the result of this attitude, even a world language as a second or auxiliary language would suffer at the hands of many people.

[2] *Exacerbated nationalism.* Excessive devotion to nationalism at the present time greatly hampers interlingual communication. This too is not a technical difficulty, but a matter of hostile attitude. For millennia there has been a national–cultural devotion to the group's own language as a supreme badge of their nationality, and a jealousy and suspicion of other languages as, in part at least, violations or implied

criticisms of the group's own language. In recent centuries, the speakers of given "empire" languages have exercised at least a quiet (though still perceptible) resistance to the supremacy of other "empire" languages. During the last four decades, concurrently with the growth of international communication and interdependence, there has been a striking increase in the efforts to preserve and cultivate national or ethnic group languages, not merely as means of communication, but especially as superior expressions of their cultures and as means of sharply distinguishing themselves from other groups. Well-known instances of such languages are Gaelic, Russian, Canadian-French, Hebrew, Hindi, and Mandarin. At the moment, also, it is somewhat difficult to envision the great powers setting aside national jealousies sufficiently to permit them to elevate another nation's language to international rank.

[3] *Translation.* As will be noted at greater length below, it is inconceivable that in the near future a single language will be spoken as the sole language of the peoples of the world. Hence, most peoples will be speakers both of the world language and of their own language, as their most frequent mode of speech. This raises the question of translation—which, in turn, involves the fact that each language is a unique system of elements that cannot be reproduced with complete exactitude of form and meaning in another language.[41]

Several other negative implications of the translation problem emerge when we face the possible fact of a world language in operation.

[4] *Experiential diversity and expressional and semantic confusion.* A given language is a product of the experience of *one* particular people. It reflects this given body of experience, not universal experience. The different peoples of the world still live under very diverse conditions; hence, they have very many different experiences. Would not a universal language—particularly if it were *not* the mother tongue—therefore provide a given people with limited means of expressing their own experiential backgrounds, as well as their current experiences with the world? The importance of common experience as the real basis of effective communication must be recognized. If one single language were used to express these diverse experiences, evaluations and outlooks, given words would be used with very different meanings. Particular bodies of speakers would be unable to express themselves exactly in the world language, and they would have some difficulty fully comprehending it. Thus, both speakers and receivers would be apt to be frustrated in their expression and comprehension, and basic misunderstandings could (and quite likely would) occur.

Related to this is the fact that all those people who were not native speakers of the world language would be living to some extent in *two* linguistic worlds—which would mean two somewhat unlike experiential and expressional worlds.

[5] *Cultural pluralism and varying* **Weltanschauung.** The widespread, possibly exclusive, use of a single language also has inherent in it a weakness from the point of view of culture theory. Language, as has been noted, is both a function and a medium of culture. But we have no world culture nor any single culture as yet, only the cultures of many different peoples. Realistically, and consistently with the findings of the social sciences on the question of culture, we are forced to accept cultural pluralism. Cultural pluralism, however, means a variety of languages as instruments of a diversity of culture systems.

One implication of this is that no world language would "fit" the entire world; it would not express and reflect the experience, the psyche and ethos, the *Weltanschauung* of the people of the different cultures prevailing in the world.

A further implication of cultural pluralism has to do with certain possible humanistic and spiritual effects of one language, if it purveyed a single "standard" body of attitudes, meanings and interpretations. If this were to result, the effects would be appalling—even tragic. All the different peoples would be "run in a common mold." Instead of enriching uniqueness and diversity, a universal all-alikeness and "deadlevelism," with the accompanying cultural stuffiness and stifling of spirit, would be quite conceivable.

g / The pidgins as auxiliary languages. The pidgins are one existent type of international or inter-people language. They are "natural" auxiliary languages, which serve millions of users in various parts of the world. Like the "creolized" languages, they are "mixed" jargons. The "mixture" or "blend" results from the meeting of the national language of a people of high culture—in most instances, one of the languages that we have referred to as "imperial" languages—with the language of slaves, peons, or other submerged classes, or of a people of a very different ethnic and linguistic stock. The new idiom has a strong base in the imperial language, but it is sufficiently different to warrant its classification as a separate new language. The two types of mixed languages are different, however, with respect to coverage. The creolized language is the only form of speech among the mass of the native population *within* a country. Haitian Creole, for example, is a crossing of French and of various Negro languages of the "former slaves"; it has expanded functionally, so widely that it is used in written form in the press and in literature.

The pidgins, on the one hand, are "mixed" languages, used among peoples from different speech communities for intergroup and inter-people communicative purposes. They are fairly efficient workaday vernaculars, and enable contacting people with very different cultures and very different mother tongues to get along with each other in certain limited areas of activity—to trade with each other, to work with each other, but also to maintain ethnically mixed marriages. While there are many pidgins, the more notable now are the pidgin English used along the coast of China and in the ports of Southeast Asia, Taiwan, Korea and Japan; the Melanesian or Pacific pidgin English (*the Beach-la-Mar*) used between whites and natives in much of the South Pacific; the pidgins of Africa, which are mainly mixtures of English, French or Portuguese and the native regional languages; and *sabir,* a mixture of French, Spanish, Italian, Greek and Arabic, used in the Mediterranean area. A significant North American pidgin was the Chinook jargon which formerly flourished on the Northwest Coast as a means of communication between white traders, whalers and trappers and the Indian tribes of the area.

While these pidgins are minimum languages, they are not just a hash, a corruption without any rules or grammar; they are institutionalized, as any "going" language must be. The English pidgins, for example, have a reduced and simplified grammar (with declensions and conjunctions eliminated); they also have reduced vocabularies, with the meanings of some of the words extended, however, far beyond the original English use. But these, like the other pidgins, have a true linguistic structure and are languages in their own right.

Their regionality, their peculiar hybrid nature, and their usefulness for only limited purposes precludes the likelihood that any of them will ever be considered as a world language.[42]

h / The likelihood of a world language as a common auxiliary language, and the possible type. While several students of the world linguistic situation sustain the hope that one worldwide language will eventually replace the multiplicity of existing tongues, and function as the single and universal basic means of communication, the candid ones, sternly facing the realities of the situation, are of the opinion that what we can have, and most likely will have, is one language which will serve as the chief auxiliary or second language, learned and used by increasingly larger proportions of the world's population as the One World bears in upon them. Almost everyone will continue to know and to use the existing national tongues for everyday regional use, but many—certainly all those with intellectual and social interests beyond their national borders— would also acquire, if it is not already their native tongue, the single, most widely known and widely used common medium, with supremacy over the many mutually unintelligible tongues. The common language would function as the interlanguage, or bridge-language, between the separate language groups for inter-people and international exchange.

The choice of a world language lies between a "constructed," "engineered," or "artificial" language, on the one hand, and an already established "natural" language, either in its existent form as one of the leading imperial languages, or in a simplified form of the latter.

There has been an interest in deliberately constructed languages for interlingual or worldwide use at least as far back as 1629, when Descartes founded the idea and devised the first such language. It is estimated that about 600 have been attempted since, but few have advanced very far beyond the blueprint stage. Those with a full structure have been variously constructed: some have been attempts at blending or combining certain elements of different ancient (particularly Latin) and modern languages; some have been considerable modifications, especially simplifications, of certain national languages; others have attempted a completely artificed *a priori* language. In fairly recent times, Schleyer's Volapük, first devised in 1879, developed several offshoots and received considerable attention for a time, although it is now receiving little. Among the most prominent constructed languages advocated at the present time are Zamenhof's Esperanto, first presented in 1887, Plano's Interlingua, founded early in the present century, and in somewhat revised form recently promoted by Alexander Gode, Jespersen's Novial (1928), Ogden's Basic English in the 1930's and Interglossa in 1943 by Hogben.

The constructed languages have failed to arouse much interest. Even the one which is most widely known, learned, and spoken, and most energetically promoted—Esperanto—has a limited use and a small (although most devoted) following. The Esperanto movement is divided into numerous international, national, and local groups, and those who speak it and understand it are scattered widely throughout the world; according to the estimates of the best available authorities, the number of Esperantists in the world runs somewhere between 6,000,000 and 8,000,000. It is practically the only constructed international language used and spoken in the world today.[43]

It would seem that if the world is to have a single international auxiliary language, it will have to be one of the great natural imperial languages; possibly we shall have to settle for several of these languages. Such selection is unlikely to come about by any formal international agreement, but rather as the result of its spontaneous adoption and use by more and more peoples, in meeting their diverse extra-national communicative needs. Only a very few of the natural languages are likely to achieve this worldwide utility and use. Some of the languages with large numbers of speakers—for example, Mandarin, Malay–Javanese, and Hindi—can be ruled out of consideration at the present time because they are highly local, not even universally spoken within their own nation, and are quite unintelligible to the speakers of other languages, even in their world region. Others, such as Spanish, German, Portuguese and Italian, while used here and there in the world at large, have a relatively small number of speakers and rather specialized users. The fact that Arabic is so directly and almost exclusively connected with the religion of Mohammedanism precludes its ever becoming a general world auxiliary language.

The two languages destined to be most likely utilized in world discourse, on the basis of present facts, circumstances, and trends, are Russian and Anglo-English. Russian, as the original and official language of twentieth-century world Communism, is rapidly and aggressively gaining increasing acceptance. It is still, however, centered on two continents.

Anglo-English, to begin with, has a long "head start" over all of the other imperial languages. As we have already noted, it is the mother tongue of more people than any other language; even more important, from the present viewpoint, is its massive worldwide use as the auxiliary language for political, diplomatic, commercial, scientific, mass-communication and other purposes. It can also be pointed out that it is the native language of two of the world's great powers. It is the language most widely and strategically distributed over the earth's surface; it is, in fact, used as a native language on at least four continents. Laird has pointed out that the countries speaking it "have more political prestige, more military strength, more international trade, more productive potential, more wealth, more of almost everything that goes to support language than half a dozen of (the) nearest competitors."[44]

English is the language that is most widely taught, studied and read. It also has the advantage of having been the subject of research in hundreds of studies of methods and materials for teaching it as a foreign language.[45] It contains by far the most extensive literature, both in the original and through translations. Of no mean significance is the fact that it has been in the recent past, and is in the present, the vehicle for not only the thoughts, but also the feelings and emotions, and the traditions and values of more real men and women than any other language. As has been well said, "English is the key to more doors than any other language."[46]

As a language, Anglo-English has both favorable and unfavorable features. (1) From the standpoint of suitability and adaptability, it has proved itself in the following ways: (a) Its *vocabulary* is not only the most abundant and the richest in variety of expressional possibilities—adequate to almost every need—but it is also the most international—more international, in fact, than Esperanto, which is usually especially recommended in that respect. (b) Its *grammar* is relatively simple, with little unnecessary elaboration of declension and conjugation. Its construction is fairly straightforward and logical: for example, it does not have the complication of sex being attributed (through gender) to inanimate things. (c) As *a means of expression,* it is precise and concise for political usages (commerce, government, science, technology), and is capable of an infinite distinction of shades of meaning for literary purposes (*belles-lettres,* philosophy).

(2) It also presents defects and difficulties: (a) There are many irregularities in its verbs. (b) Its plural nouns are peculiarly difficult to master. (c) The divergence between its forms in speech and in writing is greater than in any other western language. (d) Its accenting is often uncertain and wavering. (e) It contains many homonyms, that is, words with the same or very similar pronunciation, but with different spellings and meanings. (f) Its orthography is frequently unphonetic—that is, there is a lack of relationship between the spelling and the pronunciation of words. (g) Some of its spelling is quite irrational, and some of its idiom incalculable. While these defects are serious, it should be recalled that none of the other leading imperial languages come as near as it does to meeting the specifications of an ideal or even a "model" language.[47]

If world linguistic communication procedure "boils down" to the use of one of the leading imperial languages as the main auxiliary or second language for the great bulk of the world's people, then linguists and social scientists must be prepared to face some of the problems of bilingualism (or even of trilingualism), as well as the distinct social and cultural gains emerging from it. These will be examined in Chapter XV, especially Section 5.

N O T E S

1 Cf. Otto Jespersen, *Mankind, Nation, and the Individual* (Cambridge: Harvard University Press, 1925), p. 45.
2 This unification tendency, of course, is not inconsistent with the fact, to be developed in Chap. XIII, that there are certain differentiating and specializing processes going on in most of the great languages, which are by no means due to isolation or lack of internal or external communication.
3 Cf. Mario Pei, "Ending the Language Traffic Jam," *Saturday Review*, 44 (Sept. 9, 1961), 14–16, 51.
4 The decline of a language does not always coincide with its inefficiency, its vulgarization, or the political, economic, religious, educational or other functional preferability of another language. It may come with the loss of its speakers in the given area as the result of their absorption into some other population, the prohibition of its use by government or conquerors, or the loss of prestige resulting from the loss of its typical speakers.
5 These principles have been taken in part from Joyce O. Hertzler, *Society in Action: A Study of Basic Social Processes* (New York: Dryden Press, 1954), pp. 83–88. For an excellent survey of principles with a massive array of further references, see Elihu Katz, Martin L. Levin and Herbert Hamilton, "Traditions of Research on the Diffusion of Innovation," *American Sociological Review*, 28 (Apr., 1963), 237–252.
6 *Mankind, Nation and Individual from a Linguistic Point of View* (Cambridge: Harvard University Press, 1925), pp. 38–83.
7 Philip L. Wagner, *The Human Use of the Earth* (Glencoe: Free Press, 1960), p. 45.
8 For an excellent discussion of uniformation of language by conquest, see Robert E. Park, *The Immigrant Press and Its Control* (New York: Harper & Brothers, 1922), pp. 21–25.
9 In India there has long been a proverbial saying to the effect that the speech changes every few miles.
10 Cf. Leonard Bloomfield, "Literate and Illiterate Speech," *American Speech*, 2 (July, 1927), 432–439.
11 For a comprehensive treatment of the uniformizing and many other sociocultural effects of writing, printing and literacy, see Chap. XVII on "The Socology of Writing."
12 *Op. cit.*, p. 51.
13 This point is an extension of Sect. 3, p. 172, of the preceding chapter. The present treatment of language loyalty is in large part dependent upon Uriel Weinreich, *Languages in Contact: Findings and Problems* (New York: Publications of the Linguistic Circle of New York, No. 1, 1953), 98–104.
14 It is, of course, equally true that the colonies also constituted "listening posts," whereby the Greeks selectively acquired all sorts of culture elements from these diverse peoples and civilizations—a fact of no mean significance in accounting for the scope, catholicity and richness of Greek culture.
15 On "pidgins," see Sects. 5, g below.
16 Joshua Whatmough, *Language: A Modern Synthesis* (New York: St. Martin's Press, 1956), p. 51.
17 These difficulties have been described in part in Charles F. Hockett, *A Course in Modern Linguistics* (New York: Macmillan Co., 1958), pp. 7–8; John Lotz, "Linguistics," in Lynn White, Jr. (ed.), *Frontiers of Knowledge in the Study of Man* (New York: Harper & Brothers, 1956), pp. 207–231.

18 Stuart Chase, *Power of Words* (New York: Harcourt, Brace & Co., 1954), p. 5.
19 Hockett, p. 7.
20 Lotz, p. 209.
21 Wladimir S. and E. S. Woytinsky, *World Population and Production* (New York: Twentieth Century Fund, 1953), p. 51.
22 Mario Pei, *One Language for the World* (New York: Devin–Adair, 1958), p. 5. On p. 196, Pei refers to "2,796 natural tongues, and 600 or more constructed languages." Later, he writes: "Man Talks in 3000 Tongues," *New York Times Magazine*, Nov. 6, 1960, p. 62.
23 *Time,* Feb. 24, 1961.
24 C. F. Voegelin, "North American Indian Languages Still Spoken and Their Genetic Relationships," in Leslie Spier, A. Irving Hallowell and Stephen S. Newman (eds.), *Language, Culture, and Personality* (Menasha, Wis.: Sapir Memorial Publication Fund, 1941), pp. 15–40.
25 Cf. Mario Pei, *Language for Everybody* (New York: Devin–Adair, 1956), pp. 223–230.
26 Dorothy Woodman, *The Republic of Indonesia* (New York: Philosophical Library, 1955), pp. 297–300.
27 Pei, p. 33; *Time,* Feb. 24, 1961.
28 The major sources from which these approximations have been compiled are: W. H. Nicolls, "The World's Languages," *National Geographic Magazine,* 84 (Dec., 1943), 689–700; Mario Pei, *The World's Chief Languages* (London: George Allen & Unwin, 1949), pp. 15–17, 25–39; Wladimir S. and E. S. Woytinsky, *World Population and Production* (New York: Twentieth Century Fund, 1953), pp. 51–54; Stuart Chase, *The Power of Words* (New York: Harcourt, Brace & Co., 1954), p. 5; Mario Pei, *Language for Everybody* (New York: Devin–Adair, 1956), pp. 26–42; Mario Pei, *One Language for the World* (New York: Devin–Adair, 1958), pp. 10–19; Maurice Parmelee: *The History of Modern Culture* (New York: Philosophical Library, 1960), pp. 136–138; *Time,* Feb. 24, 1961.
29 India's Constitution of 1950 provided that during the first fifteen years of independence, English as well as Hindi would be official languages, English having "associate status," since it had been the language of the elite, of government and commerce, and the only language link among all sectors of the population since the establishment of British rule. In 1963 the Indian Parliament decreed that Republic Day, January 26, 1965, was to be the official date of the inauguration of Hindi as the sole official language of the nation. The officialization of Hindi has been fought by the non-Hindi regions, chiefly the populous southern states, ever since the Constitutional announcement. The effort fully to institute Hindi on the official date resulted in anti-Hindi rallies, some conspicuous suicides of protest, the resignation of several cabinet ministers, and bloody riots, with a death toll of sixty or more, during January and February. The Prime Minister, in a broadcast on February 11, 1965, promised non-Hindi states in South India that they could go on using English as long as the public considered it necessary.
30 On the language situation of India, see Wladimir S. Woytinsky, *India: The Awakening Giant* (New York: Harper & Brothers, 1957), pp. 6–7; Kingsley Davis, *Population of India and Pakistan* (Princeton: Princeton University Press, 1951), p. 157; "New Tower of Babel," *U. S. News and World Report,* Feb. 3, 1956; Harold L. Geisert, *Population Problems in the Development of India and Southeast Asia* (Washington: Population Research Report, The George Washington University, 1961), p. 19.
31 Cf. Woodman, pp. 297–300.
32 These are Indo-European languages. Recently it has been pointed out that these languages are spoken by the majority of the world's inhabitants. "Of the world's present population of about three billion, over half speak languages of the Indo-European family, and if to this total we add languages of a somewhat similar structure, such as the Semitic and the Ural-Altaic, we come close to

covering three-fourths of the world's people." Mario Pei, *Voices of Man* (New York: Harper and Row, 1962), p. 31.

33 These points are, in part, from Morris M. Lewis, *Language in Society* (London: Thomas Nelson & Sons, 1947), pp. 65–68.

34 Harold E. Goad, *Language in History* (Baltimore: Penguin Books, 1958), pp. 16, 18–19, 22–23.

35 Note, for example, the opposition or, at any rate, the general indifference, to the teaching of foreign languages in the elementary schools of the United States, even on the part of such presumably informed and alert groups as PTA's.

36 "A supra-national secondary language will not make much headway unless those who are called upon to learn it are convinced that it will contribute to their desired ends." Lewis, p. 67.

37 Cf. Whatmough, p. 54.

38 Cf. Whatmough, pp. 54–56, 60.

39 For a detailed analysis of "The Modernization Pattern," see Joyce O. Hertzler, *The Crisis in World Population* (Lincoln: University of Nebraska Press, 1956), pp. 38–44.

40 *Op. cit.,* p. 68. See also Whatmough, *ibid.,* p. 52.

41 For a presentation of the more important linguistic and social problems of translation, see Chap. VI, Sect. 5, p. 128.

42 On pidgins see Sidney J. Baker, "The Literature of Pidgin English," *American Speech,* 19 (Dec., 1944), 271–275; Joseph Bram, *Language and Society* (New York: Random House, 1955), pp. 56–58; Louis H. Gray, *Foundations of Language* (New York: Macmillan Co., 1939), pp. 36–37; Robert A. Hall, Jr., *Hands Off Pidgin English* (Sydney: Pacific Publications, 1955), and "Pidgin Languages," *Scientific American,* 200 (Feb., 1959), 121–132; Melville M. Jacobs and Bernhard J. Stern, *Outline of Anthropology* (New York: Barnes & Noble, 1947), pp. 286–287; Charlton Laird, *The Miracle of Language* (Cleveland: World Publishing Co., 1953), pp. 286–287; Mario Pei, *The Story of English* (Philadelphia: J. B. Lippincott & Co., 1952), pp. 167–175; Uriel Weinreich, *op. cit.,* pp. 69–70, 104–106.

43 On artificial languages, see Otto Jespersen, "Nature and the Art of Language," *American Speech,* 5 (Dec., 1929), 89–103; Herman Colletz, "World Languages," *Language,* 2 (1926), 1–13; Frederick Bodmer, *The Loom of Language* (New York: Norton, 1944), pp. 448–518; John C. Flugel, "Esperanto and the International Language Movement," in *Men and Their Motives* (New York: International Universities Press, 1947), pp. 159–213; Mario Pei, *The World's Chief Languages* (London: Allen & Unwin, 1949), pp. 580–583; Mario Pei, *One Language for the World* (New York: Devin-Adair, 1958), pp. 87–105, 132–175; H. Jacob, *A Planned Auxiliary Language* (London: Dennis Dobson, Ltd., 1957).

44 Charlton Laird, *The Miracle of Language* (Cleveland: World Publishing Co., 1953), p. 285.

45 *Saturday Review,* 44 (Oct. 7, 1961), 29.

46 Maurice Parmelee, *op. cit.,* p. 1083. Note the following statement by Dr. Kofi Busia, a former leader of the Opposition in Ghana's Legislative Assembly, when he spoke in the Assembly in March, 1957: "The English language has not only enabled us to communicate with our fellow countrymen of different tongues and tribes, but has also prepared us for effective membership in the wider community of nations to which we now come as adults and no longer as wards." (Quoted in George H. Kimble, *Tropical Africa* (New York: Twentieth Century Fund, 1960), Vol. II, 368.)

47 On Anglo-English as the world language, see Janet R. Aiken, "English as the International Language," *American Speech,* 9 (Apr., 1934), 98–110; Maurice Parmelee, *The History of Modern Culture* (New York: Philosophical Library, 1960), pp. 1083–1084; Mario Pei, *The Story of Language* (Philadelphia: J. B. Lippincott Co., 1952), pp. 302–308; Michael West, "English as a World Language," *American Speech,* 9 (Oct., 1934), 163–174.

IX ❦ Language as a Centripetal
Factor in Human Societies

One of the major concerns of sociology is with the factors contributing to group unity, solidarity, integration and cohesion, on the one hand, and the differentiation (including stratification), splitting, separation and antagonism within and between groups, on the other, as well as with the processes involved in the respective types of situations. Hence one of sociology's major interests in language is the part it plays in both these sets of processes. Language functions as a cause in each case and also, conversely, shows in itself typical effects of these respective social situations. We shall henceforth refer to these as the centripetal and centrifugal aspects of the group functioning of language.

The centripetal aspects to be examined in the present chapter are its group-unifying and -solidifying effects, its efficacy as an assimilative agent, and its relationship to nationality and the nation–state.

1. *Language the Social Unifier*

Language serves effectively—in many instances, more so than any other sociocultural agent—not only as a way of enabling persons to function as members of a group, but also as the binding, integrative and solidarity-producing factor within and between groups.

First of all, it should be recalled that *it is the elemental functional agent in any group*. As noted in Chapter IV, any social unit, as an operative combination of human beings, must have a communications network. This is a primary essential for its formation and maintenance. By means of the "net," the members express their ideas and emotions, increase and exchange their many forms of information, reach understanding and consensus, and carry on all their joint activities. Without this "net," which takes in every form of communication between two or among more members, the group would be nonexistent, and the persons would form a mere random collection of human beings.

Language, as we have repeatedly noted, is the basis of all *human* communication. Thus, the very functioning and survival of the group depends upon the adequacy, extent and accuracy of its language. More specifically, it is the medium of every cultural, social and societal action of the members of a group—all that they have culturally inherited or recalled from the past, or have consciously or unconsciously devised; all of their collective spiritual life; all the institutional principles, norms and organizational instruments that enable them to function effectively as a going concern; all that they direct and do in the immediate present; all the forms of their co-ordination and correlation of activity; all that they anticipate and plan for the future. As it was classically put: "People who speak the same language find it convenient to live together."[1] *Pari passu,* most peoples have demonstrated both *loyalty* and *obedience* to their languages.

Second, language has great effectiveness *as one of the major welding agents of human groups,* both in space and time. It should be noted at the outset that common language is not the sole determinant of the unity and cohesion of groups.[2] Mention need only be made of the common geographical setting in which the people are located, with its mountains, valleys, streams, plains, deserts, and its highways and cities; race and color; community through intermarriage; the common physical needs and the instrumentalizing scientific, technological and economic institutions; its political beliefs, politics and aims and agencies for internal order and peace; its common religious interests and organizations; its educational system; its common culture in general; its distinctive psyche, ethos, and pathos. All of these interplay with language and contribute to it as a cultural stream. But the fact must also be stressed that the common language is the tool which *makes all these conditions, institutions and activities effective* as unifying and solidifying factors. Some of these may fail; language remains.[3]

The effect of *language as a unifier goes far beyond its instrumentalizing of these other factors.* In itself, it creates a union, a "speech fellowship,"[4] a strong collective consciousness, a set of precious binding relationships. Actually, persons who speak the same language are united by the very fact that they do so. As a mother tongue, it is made up of words and phrases that are idiomatic, personally significant, expressive of the group's historical experiences and values, its precious memories, common sentiments, great associations, fond traditions, its vicissitudes and triumphs. Those things that are artistically common in a language— its style, the evidences of taste, its peculiar usages (such as its word sounds and rhythms, or its metaphors)—these make the psyche and ethos of its speakers concrete. The language enables the members of the group to "come to terms" with their own incentives, to discuss, develop and pool their values, opinions and aims, to compose their divergences and incompatibilities, and to overcome the uncertainty and incoherence of their motivations. Furthermore, it cuts across geographic distance and barriers, across economic-political-cultural regions, political factions and parties, class barriers and other social differentiations and distances, and religious differences, as it encourages community of interest and action and paves the way for unities and alliances.

It seems to have been a most important factor in the creation of "consciousness of kind" everywhere through time, and this consciousness of kind has almost invariably produced a "consciousness of unity." The people with whom one habitually, continually and perennially communicates by means of one's mother tongue constitute one's primary community; one feels a kinship with them. As individuals, we have a sense of communion with them. Our common speech inspires mutual confidence, sympathy and rapport. These fellow-speakers are "our kind of people." Every member of our group has the feeling that he is speaking a language different from that of neighboring groups. Those who do not speak our language—even our dialect—are in some measure "outsiders" or "foreigners," "strangers" or "barbarians." Because communication with them is not easy and precise, and because reciprocal understanding is therefore weak, the speakers of other languages with whom one has contact are often regarded with suspicion as to what they are thinking and saying. Differences in speech divide groups; similarity in speech reinforces group loyalty, morale and solidarity. The latter determines group affiliation, and—what is of special sociological pertinence—marks off the out-group from the in-group.

The converse of the above principle is also a rather well-established social fact—namely that, as facility and uniformity of language develop among diverse people, unity also develops among them. Likewise, the isolation from other groups resulting from language differences gives the members of each particular group a sense of distinction.[5]

The common language creates and maintains an almost unconscious sense of community among its speakers, wherever they may be. An American, placed among a group of associated foreigners, will spontaneously gravitate toward an Englishman, who speaks his language. Similarly, the sound of one's mother tongue usually rings familiarly and pleasantly in the ears of the American tourist in Paris, Athens or Hong Kong, of the Latvian or Latin-American immigrant in the United States, of the refugee wherever he may be; it invites the union and communion of its speakers.

In general, almost all kinds of groups—families, clans, locality groups, ethnic groups and nationalities, political entities, including states and federations—are held together by it. Under modern conditions, its cohesive effect is vastly greater than that of religion, and perhaps paralleled only by law and government, education and common economic enterprise. Furthermore, in modern societies it is quite apparent that there is more and more that needs to be talked about and written about. Correlated with this is the fact that language today covers wider areas of interest, need and concern; thanks to modern means of transportation and communication, a given language can prevail over ever wider areas of the world as an expediting and unifying agent. More specifically, there is the fact that, historically, political, economic and cultural consolidation has usually brought language consolidation. Finally, as was hypothesized in the preceding chapter, the extension and the increasing intensity of social intercourse over ever wider areas will make for an ever wider uniformity of speech.

Finally, the common language also serves as *an effective means of identifying and classifying a people or a society, and as a potent symbol of the social unity and solidarity of those who speak it.* The language is a readily and universally observable badge of cultural similarity—especially of distinctive values, ideologies, aims and ways of life. It identifies and classifies its speakers, and sets them apart from the speakers of other mother tongues, or even of other dialects or "special" languages. By means of it, we determine whether a person is an American or a Spaniard, an Alabaman or a Vermonter, one of the highly or the less well-educated. Through this designation and labeling, the speakers of a common language recognize each other wherever they may be and hence are enabled to safeguard their common culture and group life. Similarly, the stranger is identified by his defective speech— for example, how he pronounces "ich" in German, or the "x's" in Spanish, or "thither" in English.

In primitive and old world societies, especially, through the ages, languages have been used as symbols of intertribal or local differences, on the one hand, and of intra-tribal unity on the other.

2. *Social Assimilation and Language*

a / The community language as assimilative agent. Throughout history, the immigrants, the cultural minorities, the conquered or captives, and any other strangers in the midst of any group (especially any community), have always presented the sociological problem of sociocultural assimilation—that is, the merging of these people, with their diverse cultural and societal conditioning, into the common culture and the functional life of the resident community. Anything that tends to break up the segregation and classification of population elements, and produces allegiance to and use of the common culture heritage, thereby tends to facilitate assimilation. Language, as the most crucial and universally used feature of a given cultural heritage, is directly significant as an assimilative factor.[6] This is due to the fact that a real assimilation of foreign elements cannot be secured simply by inducting them into the new political order and the new economic, religious and other particular social processes.[7] They need to become part of the *whole* social process—which rests basically upon free and adequate communication and upon the ability and the incentive to communicate over wide ranges of subjects. The common, dominant or indigenous language is the basic communication equipment.

Other conditions, of course, must also prevail. These include such economic conditions as wide markets and non-discrimination in employment; wide and ready physical mobility in the pursuit of desirable regional, economic and other life conditions; opportunity for political participation; freedom from rigid social stratification and social distance and, conversely, freedom of social opportunity and social mobility; access to all levels of educational opportunity. As in the case of group unity and unification, language is also the facilitator of all these conditions. What is more, with the acquisition of the common language (its lexicon, syntax, idioms, the conception of reality and the *Weltanschauung* evidenced by its peculiar structure), there comes the learning of the subtler aspects of the surrounding cultural and social world: the underlying values and attitudes, the elements of the "spirit" and "style" behind the ways of the larger social life, and the unlearning of old, now alien, forms. Assimilation becomes easier and more rapid, the greater the similarity and compatibility of the mental and social equipment of persons in both the dominant and foreign groups. Linguistic similarity and compatibility—a common *Sprachgefühl*—is the key expediting agency. In general, the enculturation of persons is only possible as they learn to speak and understand the language of the cultural community.

b / Language as an index of assimilation. Correlated with the role of language as the primary assimilative agent is the fact that it also serves as one of the most accurate, as well as the most conspicuous and usable, indices or measures of social assimilation. Perhaps one of the most revealing indications of assimilation in the United States has been the rather rapid adoption of Anglo-American by groups that had originally had a different mother tongue. In our country, as elsewhere where a bilingual or multilingual situation has existed, the successive stages of language usage—namely: (1) the use of the foreign language only; (2) the use of both the foreign language and the national language; (3) the use of the national language only—have provided one of the main measures of degrees of assimilation.

In general, though, in the United States, an immigrant has ordinarily been considered assimilated when he has acquired fair competence in the use of our language, for this has enabled him to acquire all the important features of the social rituals, informal and formal, of the community (including the indigenous nuances of meaning), and to participate without personal embarrassment because of "uncouthness," and without encountering prejudice or "distance" attitudes in the common life.

To be sure, adoption of the indigenous language by the newcomers proves neither that those who have made this adoption have relinquished all other former distinctive traits, nor that they have been fully accepted by the larger population. They may have still other characteristics, which somewhat estrange them. On the other hand, especially in the United States, not much obloquy has attached to bilingualism; in fact, it has been deemed a token of cleverness in some circles. The ability to speak American, the common language, to be designated as truly "Americanized," has been deemed more important than the fact of having discarded the Old World language.

The changing of a "foreign" family name to one more compatible with the major ethnic or national forms may also be looked upon as an evidence of assimilation. In this country, the fact that Huber has been changed to *Hoover,* Zimmerman to *Carpenter,* Norskog to *Norwood,*

Langlais to *Langley,* St. Cyr to *Sears,* Schneider to *Snyder,* or Jaeger to *Hunter,* means that the individuals or families that have done this changing are now rather well "Americanized." Their self-images and the images they seek to present of themselves have come into conformity with those regarded in the community as more conventional.

3. *Language and Nationality, Nationalism and Nation*

The preceding examination of language as a social unifier and a potent assimilative agent, while important in itself, also points to principles of marked pertinence, in connection with the function of language in the maintenance of nationalities, the development and persistence of nationalism, and the formation and operation of nations. These are matters of vast significance in understanding some of the most conspicuous social, ethnic, political and linguistic occurrences and trends during the last two centuries; they are also being rather widely demonstrated among the rising peoples and nations of the contemporary world. An examination of them points particularly to language as a factor of profound political importance.

a / The meanings of the major terms. It is essential at the outset that we clearly distinguish among the major trends involved in our discussion. *A people*—not to be confused with *people,* that is, merely some sort of designated category of human beings—is a loose aggregation or collectivity of persons, who have several objective characteristics, such as a common territorial residence, a common language, common traditions, customs and habits, and common historical experiences and memories. Thus we may have the American people, the Jewish people, the English-speaking people, the "colored" peoples. A people may include a variety of races, nationalities, or nations.

A *nationality* is a much tighter, more unified and uniform grouping. It does not necessarily exist as a primary, or even as a societally organized, group. But its members are bound together by an array of specific ties, such as the possession of a present or past common territory (a "homeland"), a belief in their common origin, a history and destiny, the desire to share a common life. They have a high mutual regard and a pronounced sense of "we-feeling" on the one hand, and on the other a sharp sense of difference and demarcation from other nationalities. While they do not have complete uniformity of cultural traits, they do have a common culture; there is a general conformity among them to certain common values, to a body of common thoughts, prejudices, feelings and sentiments, to common customs and traditions, and usually to their special forms of such basic institutions as language, religion, ethical ideas and morality, recreation, home and family patterns. When juxtaposed, or in competition, with other nationalities, they usually aspire to and engage in a movement toward cultural, economic, political and territorial autonomy and integrity. Economic independence, political unification and power, and territorial hegemony—although frequently present as nationality aims—are not essential or universal components, as will be noted below.

A *nation* is a nationality or a combination of nationalities that has achieved separate statehood, with all that that implies in terms of ideology, structural organization and operation. It is a "body politic." Specifically, it is a population with a common government peculiarly and exclusively its own and with complete territorial establishment and control over all inhabitants along certain essential lines.

Nationalism is a "state of mind," often resulting in or attempting to become a social movement. It involves a body of principles or doctrines that reflect the goal of making a nationality into a nation, freed from the domination of alien powers and possessing political autonomy and the effective unity, solidarity and supreme loyalty of its members.

b / Nationality and language. A nationality, as just indicated, is a continuing group bound together by some combination of common beliefs, values and patterns of action. Language stands out as the one distinguishing trait that the whole nationality does and, in fact, must have, and as probably the strongest single reenforcing factor in nationality.[8] When a nationality has a common religion, that is usually an equally strong force, but its members do not always have the same or even closely similar religious views. The members of a nationality may change, or have changed for them by outside forces, their locality, the government controlling them, the religion they nominally follow and various other patterns of behavior; although those bonds may be broken, however, language and tradition still hold.

Formal political action has, in recent times, operated on the basis of the close relationship between nationality and language. Throughout the nineteenth century and into the twentieth, the designation and reconstruction of nationalities were effected mainly on a linguistic basis. These nationalities that gained their independence in the break-up of Europe after World War I were all primarily language groups. Moreover, at the Paris Peace Conference following that war, it was established that people were not to be discriminated against because of their language, and minorities were to have unrestricted use of their own languages. There is thus much point to this formal criterion.

Language is usually the carrier of the common culture of the nationality—especially those portions of the culture that continue through the generations. It is the fundamental agency in the expression and preservation of the special spiritual and sociopsychic qualities of the nationality group. The proverbial expressions of the people, the old saws or rhymes, the songs, the deeply embedded metaphors, even the traditional uses of the most ordinary words, together form an important part of the psychological matrix in which nationality persists. The language is the means whereby it preserves its intellectual inheritance, not only through word-of-mouth transmission but also through its literature. If the language is an old one with fine literary traditions, rich in emotion and thought, with every word possessing a long life history, pregnant with deep and varied associations, it is much more powerful as a binding force than a newer language.

In general, its common language is the most durable feature of a nationality group. This is brought out in a Welsh national song:

> If the enemy has ravished the Land of Wales,
> The Language of Wales is living as ever.

Similarly Czech patriots had a saying: "As long as the language lives, the nation is not dead."

The common language functions as a *symbol* and *identifier* of nationality, as well as being a carrier of it. This has been exemplified historically. For example, it was largely through the preservation of the Polish language that the Poles retained their common identity for 150 years under Russian, Austrian, and German domination. The retention of a traditional tongue is often the principal aim of those who wish to prevent any kind of ethnic group from losing its integrity and identity, while the loss of that language (as we have already noted in a general way, during the discussion of assimilation) is taken to be a measure of assimilation with another group.

As Sumner and Keller pointed out more than a generation ago, language is so characteristic of human groups that the very adjective descriptive of nationality is employed as a noun meaning the group's language. They observe that, when we use the term "English" alone, we refer to the English speech, that most distinguishing English thing; "französisch" does not mean the French religion, nor does "español" mean the Spanish government. It is unnecessary to say "la langue française," since the adjective is enough.[9]

Not only nationalities, but whole societies are often designated by their general language. The name Chinese, for example, refers to a language (or a closely related complex of dialects), as does the name Russian, and many others.

The sociological significance of language among nationality groups has been especially revealed in the history of immigrants into the United States. It has been repeatedly noted that there has been a marked tendency for aliens who speak a foreign language to congregate in groups—in "language pockets"—in rural areas or in certain sections of the larger towns and cities. The common language was a symbol of their group identity and stability; it was for them a comforting and unifying factor, and it gave them status in their own consciousness. It brought them into relation with long-standing kinfolk, and sturdy and familiar social–cultural bulwarks. It was the means whereby they expressed their hopes and fears in their social isolation and strangeness, their means of communication and communion with others "in the same boat," and especially the means of meeting their helplessness and their lack of adjustment, of discussing their new needs and their new ideas.

c / Nationalism and language.

[1] *The recency and the essentials of nationalism.* Nationalism itself is a relatively modern phenomenon. While some nationalist phases and elements can be found much earlier—for example, in England during the reign of Henry VIII—the French Revolution has with good reason been widely accepted as the conventional watershed marking the turn to the "age of nationalism." Both the thought leading to the Revolution and the action of the Revolution itself established principles and essential forms of social behavior. Nationalism burgeoned as one of the major political–philosophical concerns of the nineteenth century. First arising in Western Europe, it has since spread over much of the earth. A product of historical development, it emerged, along with democracy and industrialism, as a resultant of the advances in transportation and the consequently increased mobility and contact of peoples, the extension and intensification of communication, the international (even intercontinental) expansion of economic exchange and, by no means least, increased political and military contacts. It especially reflected the growing awareness of the necessity of and the advantages to a people or a nationality, of political organization in an age of growing economic-political-ideological-military rivalry. It rests basically on a nationality, or several territorially or culturally intimately related peoples or nationalities, who seek to gain or maintain autonomous (usually *politically* autonomous) development. The members of the nationalistic

group, often rather extensive, deem themselves uniquely united by similarities and compatibilities such as common territory, common or similar descent, common culture (especially common customs and traditions), literature and folklore, a common *Volksgeist,* a common social organization (including common institutional forms), often a somewhat common political experience and aims, and especially, with few exceptions, a common language. Not all of these are present in every given instance. There are occasional cases where nationalism exists without any corresponding political expression.

While nationalism among a given people or nationality may be a mere body of sentiments and hopes, its signal feature in this age of nationalism has been its dynamism. Though sometimes inept as it has appeared among some peoples, in most instances it resolves itself into a social movement which seeks to achieve the sociocultural independence of the group. This, in turn, usually rests upon the political independence and operational autonomy of the group. The central objective is thus the establishment of the group's own centralized form of government over a distinct territory.

[2] *The place of language in nationalism.* A nationalistic group takes pride in its native characteristics. Among these the mother tongue has the especial love and loyalty of the group. The members prefer it above all others as the language they thoroughly understand, in which they feel "at home." It is for them a "given," a natural fact; it is also an enriching and ennobling heritage and possession. They equate love of language with love of the homeland. Their language is a symbol of themselves as a unique, continuous, united and aspiring people. It is for them both the medium of maintenance and the superior reflector and banner of their national character. In fact, of all the institutions that mark the nationalistic group, language is the one of which the members are most conscious and to which they are most fanatically attached. It is something to be defended against encroachment. A rather widespread nationalist slogan is: "One country, one people, one language." Likewise, for all outsiders, language is not only the most obvious means of identification, but also the touchstone of the character of any group, and the key to its self-contained existence.[10]

Because of the centrality of language in group integration and maintenance, it has often been a bone of contention between majority and minority nationalities and nationalistic groups within a country. Language is usually the first object of attack on the part of a political power which is seeking to suppress the individuality or the rising cultural and political consciousness of a suppressed or minority people, seeking to "denationalize" them. The dominant majority or the political organization tries to extinguish the language of the subject people, or at least tries to forbid its use and to impose its own language upon them. Linguistic suppression has included special efforts to censor or suppress the nationality press.

While practical considerations may enter into these efforts directed against the language of culturally different and socially and politically "troublesome" ethnic and nationalistic groups, they arise mainly from the well-attested fact that the pride, integrity, honor and prestige of the group is closely attached to their language, and from the belief, on the part of both dominator and dominated, that continued use of the language will contribute to the group's survival and expansion.

The reactions of the oppressed to these suppressive efforts are much the same wherever they occur. The oppressed oppose the efforts of officials who forbid the use of their language in their schools and churches; they struggle to maintain their nationality press. Patriotism frequently, under these circumstances, centers about their determination to maintain their despised language in their homes and for other semi-private intercourse, even though its use may be forbidden and punished. During the last century, no nationality group in Europe would allow its language to be quietly extinguished, as were Iberian in Spain or Celtic in Gaul during Roman times; they all opposed strenuously any legal or military prohibition of the use of their language. Along the same lines, the literary revival of folk speech among the European peoples has always been a prelude to the revival of the nationality spirit of a subject or suppressed people. Finally, the agitators for nationality unity, or the leaders in maintaining it, have regularly used the common language as a primary uniting appeal.

It should be noted, however, that before the age of nationalism, language was rarely stressed as a factor upon which the prestige and power of a group depended, nor was it made an object of political or cultural struggle. In Greek and Roman times, there was no strong language consciousness or language discrimination, nor was there any conscious effort to impose a national language on other nationalities within the extending national areas of influence or conquest. In fact, the wars, laws and prohibitions about language that have appeared during the last century—for example, in Alsace, Lorraine, Belgium, Schleswig-Holstein, Poland, the Tyrol and Czechoslovakia—were unknown in the past.[11] In modern times, however, once a people has had its sense of nationality awakened, it stands guard over its group language. Especially when it is under oppression or in conditions of conflict, a group is likely to defend its language as its own peculiar heritage, lest the group identity be lost with it.

Such efforts to retain the group language have occasionally been quite successful in preventing the eradication of a nationality or a nationalistic group. During the last century and a half, the Poles, as noted, were held together by their language. Language prevented the total obliteration of Lithuanian nationality; it kept the people from becoming Poles, Russians or Germans. Similar retention of nationality through language prevailed among the Czechs, Hungarians, Croatians and Serbs. The two Balkan peoples who best maintained their distinction, the Roumanians and Albanians, did so, in part at least, by keeping their folk tongues free from Slavic or Greek influence.

[3] *Nationalistic movements and language revivals.* The close relationship between nationalism and language is brought out in the frequently noted fact that many nationalist movements of recent times have been at the same time a linguistic and literary movement. The language has been an important rallying-point for a people seeking the privileges of statehood. Beginning in Wales in the latter part of the eighteenth century, and among other peoples in Europe during the nineteenth and early twentieth centuries, there has been a series of revivals of folk languages, each of which has been the prelude or parallel to a nationalist movement. Of importance have been the movements in behalf of Norwegian and Danish, the Celtic revivals in Brittany, Ireland, Scotland and Wales, and the nationalistic efforts in behalf of Polish and Czech. In the present century, there has been the stress upon Gaelic in the Irish separatist movement, and upon the folk tongues of the different nationalities involved in the break-up of the Austro-Hungarian Empire, not to mention the revival of Hebrew in connection with the development of Jewish nationalism and the reestablishment of Israel.

Park has noted, as evidence of the correlation of nationalistic and linguistic revival, that the exile, the refugee and the immigrant have often been the *first* to manifest national-language consciousness. The movement for the revival of an ancient Irish language, Gaelic, may be said to have had its origin in Boston, at the hands of the Phil-Celtic Society, organized there in 1873, three years before Gaelic attracted the attention of scholars in Dublin.[12] The Lithuanians, Poles, and others in the United States have had somewhat similar attitudes toward their respective languages.

The occasional linguistic revivals in the modern world seem, at first glance, to be somewhat paradoxical, for this is an age of intercommunication and interdependence, increasing universalism and cosmopolitanism; all sorts of physical and cultural barriers are therefore now becoming inconsequential. The revivals would seem to imply the resurgence of a sort of national–cultural provincialism, and the attempt of the people to imprison themselves in their own language. The sociopsychic and sociological conclusions, however, must be that nationalities and nationalism persist, and not necesarily as anachronisms; that people do cherish their historical heritage; that, in trying to preserve their identity and achieve or maintain their autonomy, they are struggling to avoid being lost or absorbed in the mass. Nor have these revivals been solely revivals of language and of nationalistic political aspirations; they have frequently also been the key to the *intellectual awakening* of the common people of the ethnic groups. These intellectual awakenings have been fostered by increasing literacy and by a new awareness of the great writings in the past in the mother tongue and the great historical events depicted, as well as by a contact with the larger world which has invited comparisons with other peoples and sometimes suggested separate political identity.

d / The nation and language. Our final task in connection with the centripetal function of language is to indicate its role in the modern nation. This, in the main, is a logical consequence of the immediately preceding discussions.

[1] *The operation of language in a nation.* Political union in the form of the nation–state is usually the consummation of nationalistic endeavors. Correlatively, such union often creates an effective political body out of heterogeneous elements. At least as far back as Turgot, language has been recognized as one of the, if not the, most essential element of nationhood. According to Herder, the national language was the guardian of the national community and the matrix of its civilization, and hence a sacred instrument.[13] Historically speaking, each nation —however diverse as to component nationality elements, regions with their dialects, and social strata—has desired to have a national language, not only as a symbol of unity, but also as a means of maintaining social and cultural harmony and stability. Most important of all is the utilitarian significance of a common language for demographic and regional elements in communicating with each other, and especially for conducting the nationwide political, economic, scientific–technological, military, literary and educational activities. Generally speaking, the people who compose a single nation must think together about all manner of things, and the common language is essential as their *currency of thought*. Actually, many—although by no means all—nations do have their own language, but in most cases the languages preceded the

nation, and in some cases the language community extends beyond a given nation or nations.

[2] *Two historical instances.* Two significant instances will be presented, one European and one American, of the recognition of common language as an important factor in national development.

One is the case of France. From the fifteenth century on, the French were developing a feeling of nationalism and national unity. In so doing, they sought to enrich, ennoble and purify their language as a national cultural heritage and political instrument. It was with this intent that kings promulgated their language laws, and Richelieu founded the *Académie Française*. It was in France that the state for the first time undertook the organization of a unified language. As Vossler points out, the Revolution continued what the monarchy had already begun. In 1790, the national assembly published a manifesto which sought to arouse in all districts "a holy emulation" to eradicate all dialects, provincialisms, patois and jargons, for the sake of national unity.[14] One of the intellectual leaders of the Revolution expressed a widely held thought when he said: "We have revolutionized the government, the habits, the customs, commerce, and thought; let us also revolutionize the language which is their daily instrument." "Citizens," he exclaimed, "the language of a free people ought to be one and the same for all! . . . It is treason to *la Patrie* to leave the citizens in ignorance of the national language."[15]

The American instance is the emphasis which Noah Webster, author of the famous *Webster's Blue-backed Speller* (first published in 1783) and compiler of our first dictionary, placed upon a uniform national language as an indispensable prerequisite of independent nationhood. He said: "A national language is a bond of national union." Henry Steele Commager, in a perceptive treatment of Webster's general ideas as well as his specific major works, has indicated the ways in which Webster's work helped to cement our nationalism and our nation.[16] Commager asserts that Webster "contributed more than any other single person to a uniform American speech, and to the avoidance of those differences in accent and vocabulary that might proclaim differences in background, in class or in region." This Webster achieved in considerable measure through his speller, his grammar and his dictionary—but especially the speller. Commager quotes Jefferson Davis as writing: "Above all other people we are one, and above all books which have united us in the bond of common language, I place the good old Spelling-Book of Noah Webster." From the beginning, the United States has been physically extensive and regionally diverse; its people have represented many races and nationalities, different cultural backgrounds and levels, and different class systems. But Webster, with his stress upon common sense and prevailing common usage (the "general practice") as against the resort to the "culture-tongue" as the basis of the national language in most European countries, successfully promoted a generally usable language, that today has wider *uniformity* among more people than any other language—a truly national language.

[3] *The language situation in the new nations struggling for national unity.* While there are exceptions (to be noted immediately below), modern states have the greatest national unity and greatest operative efficiency when they are linguistically united; they seem to "do better" that way. Hence, there is a persistent tendency, where multilinguality exists, either to attempt to establish one language as the national language, or for the politically interdependent language communities to set themselves up as separate political units.

The diversity of languages discussed in the preceding chapter is one of the major complications at the present time among most of the "underdeveloped" peoples, or other nationalities or combinations of nationalities, which have recently developed nationalistic consciousness and are trying to unite nationally. This situation is particularly acute among the peoples of Asia, Africa and Latin America.

Among many of these peoples the prevailing vernaculars are mutually unintelligible, mostly non-literary and often limited to small districts. Wide differences exist between the language of the government, the cities and the upper classes, on the one hand, and the language or languages of the countryside, on the other hand.

As a result of these linguistic situations, the internal communication essential to political functioning, and especially to the greatly needed political unification and consolidation, as well as for internal economic production and exchange, is seriously impeded. The uniformity and consistency of public education, the expression of technical ideas, the transmission of knowledge from other countries, even the presentation of their more or less common cultural traditions—these are almost impossible.

Among the Asian peoples that are now attempting to achieve national unity, India, China, Pakistan, Ceylon, Thailand, Indonesia and the Philippines present conspicuous examples of attempts to wrestle with the language problem. Among most of these, there has been an effort to establish one (or at most two) of their many languages as the national language, by constitutional fiat: Hindi in India, *Kuo Yü* (national language) or the "Mandarin" variant of the Peking dialect in China, Urdu and Bengali in Pakistan, *Bahasa Indonesia* in Indonesia, Tagalog in the Philippines. But an observer comments that a long leap separates inscription on the statute books from general acquiescence.[17] Emerson examines India's problems at some length. He points out that language-community feeling has often been stronger than Indian nationalism. In fact, of the fourteen states established as of 1955–56, the bulk represented consolidated linguistic communities with their own languages; both Bombay and the Punjab were deliberately established on a multi-lingual basis.[18]

In Afghanistan, India, Indonesia, Malaya and Pakistan, there is the added serious obstacle to unification in that there is the existence side by side, in the same cities and regions, of several languages with highly developed literatures and separate cultural traditions.[19]

The nations now coming into being in Africa south of the Sahara are likely to be plagued with language problems as acute as those confronting India and some of the other Asian countries. There are some widely used languages, such as Bantu in the south, Swahili on the east coast, and Yoruba in the west. But the territories in which these languages are spoken are interspersed with numerous dialects, and also include peoples with separate and diverse nationalistic aspirations. All of the potentially national areas include several languages. For example, more than 200 languages and dialects have been reported in the area of the former Belgian Congo alone. Furthermore, the languages or dialects actually spoken in many instances embrace relatively small numbers of people, thus making even more difficult the development and establishment of a single national language.[20] Nigeria, a complex of 50,000,000 people, which recently achieved independent political status, is trying to carry on with five major languages, yet millions of Nigerians use innumerable other languages and dialects; Ghana has four main languages, but there are many dialects among these. An additional complication lies in the fact that the few African languages that exist in written form have been constituted since the appearance of Westerners; in a number of instances, the writing systems have been devised by Westerners. Thus, none of the combinations of peoples seeking national unity has the unifying linguistic advantage that the system of writing provides in China.

In the Western hemisphere, south of the Rio Grande, the great bulk of the population is still Indian and has tribal languages, although in the Caribbean Islands and in northern South America there are peoples descended from Negro slaves, who have a number of mixed dialects. In so far as these countries do have one widely used language among their multiplicity of languages and dialects, that language is the cultural language of the European invaders: Spanish for most of them,

Portuguese in Brazil, French or English in parts of the central area.

What are these multilingual people to do about selecting a language or languages for their political administration, for the statement of their legislation and the conduct of their courts, for carrying on their economic affairs and their mass education? Will it be one or several of their indigenous languages, or a European language? Obviously, the social problems and human costs of establishing a national language where a multiplicity of languages exists are grave and great.

[4] *Qualifications regarding national linguistic uniformity and national unity and operation.* It should be pointed out that these generalizations should be tempered or qualified in the light of certain historical facts. First, common language is not the only strategic item in the development of nationality and nationalism. As noted above, common religion has been and is an important factor in certain instances. The common territory of the area of political jurisdiction is of almost equal weight with language, as a unifier. "America the Beautiful" is probably the hymn most widely used at American public gatherings. Closely related to community of territory are the common memories of sentiment-laden historical events—the trials and tribulations of the extension of frontiers, physical hardships endured, wars and battles won and lost, great heroes and great successful social movements, great cultural achievements. The factors so much expedited by language—namely, political administration, military organization, economic exchange, the common educational system and the national literature—are so potent that they may actually more than compensate for any degree of linguistic diversity.

Thus, in the second place, it is possible to have national unity, a fervent patriotism and a great devotion to their nation among the citizenry, even though they may consist of several different linguistic communities. In other words, national units and language units are not necessarily identical. Switzerland consists of four nationality elements: the Germans, French, Italians and Rhaeto-Romans. Each of the four speak their own language and cultivate loyalty to it without, however, aspiring to such nationalistic goals as political independence. In fact, Switzerland has been one of the outstanding examples of national political cohesiveness during the last four centuries. Here the different language groups have communication facilities and other binding forces of such strength as to permit them to cooperate politically with the other Swiss language groups more than they do with the speakers of their own language in other nations.[21]

In Belgium, there is political unity among the speakers of French and Flemish; in Canada, among the English- and French-speaking elements, who are separated by religious differences; in South Africa, there is the precarious union of the speakers of Afrikaans and English. The Soviet Union is an explicit union of "nations" which are also language groups, each with a considerable degree of linguistic autonomy, even though "Great Russian" is the *lingua franca* of the whole Union. In the old Austro-Hungarian Empire, the different nationalities spoke German, Italian, Czech, Polish, Serbian and Roumanian, to mention only the more important languages; and its break-up and disappearance was not connected primarily with its diversity of languages. In each of these instances, there has been some combination of unifying elements sufficient to hold the people together as a nation. Among the important factors operative in different number and combination in the instances indicated have been some strong common needs, common habits and common wealth, common symbols, experiences and memories, some common social institutions and institutional relations and activities, a common quest for security and common national goals, common efforts to elevate group prestige and make it secure among the nations, often intimate cross-nationality personal associations and, in some instances, definite and unmistakable police pressure.

In the third place, as noted briefly in the discussion of the language community in Chapter II, a given language community may include several independent nations. Thus, the English speakers of the world include at least six sovereign peoples: British, American, Canadian, Irish, Australian and the people of New Zealand. Spanish is the official and cultural language of nineteen nations: Spain, Argentina, Chile, Uruguay, Paraguay, Boliva, Peru, Ecuador, Colombia, Venezuela, Panama, Costa Rica, San Salvador, Honduras, Nicaragua, Guatemala, Mexico, Cuba, the Dominican Republic and the American territory of Puerto Rico. German is the language of four peoples with traditions of separate identity: the two German states, the Germans of Switzerland, the Austrians and the Luxemburgers. Portuguese is the language of Portugal and Brazil; Arabic is the language of an array of old and new nations extending across the Muslim belt of the world.

In spite of these exceptions and qualifications, the fundamental principles still prevail among most of the nations of the world: (1) nationalities are usually linguistic groups; (2) language maintenance, autonomy and revival are almost universal features of nationalism; (3) a common language has been, in the great majority of instances, not only essential to the operation of a nation, it has also served as a symbol and agency of unity.

NOTES

1 Emily G. Balch, *Our Slavic Fellow Citizens* (New York: Charities Publication Committee, 1910), p. 410.
2 For a discussion of this qualification, see Max Weber, *The Theory of Social and Economic Organization*, trans. A. M. Henderson and T. Parsons, ed. T. Parsons, (Glencoe, Ill.: Free Press, 1947), pp. 138–139.
3 Though the point will not be developed here, it is also a fact that social coherence and cohesion, however achieved, also favor a common language.
4 This happy term was used by John R. Firth, "Personality and Language in Society," (British), *Sociological Review*, 42 (Sect. One, 1950), 37–53.
5 Instances of the use of language differences as a basis for determining strangeness and out-group membership will be noted in the next chapter.
6 Ludwig Gumplowicz in *Der Rassenkampf* insisted upon the importance of a common language in securing the assimilation and amalgamation of ethnic elements, for only by common speech are men "men" to each other.
7 For an excellent discussion of the major cultural and social factors in assimilation, see Karl W. Deutsch, *Nationalism and Social Communication* (New York: John Wiley & Sons, 1953), pp. 132–135.
8 It should be noted that linguistic descent is a clearly demonstrable evidence of nationality descent. Particularly notable, as shown in nationality studies, is the fact that, while language is not a universal aspect of nationality, it is the only criterion available for statistical purposes.
9 William G. Sumner and Albert G. Keller, *The Science of Society* (New Haven: Yale University Press, 1927), I, 357.
10 It is worth noting that the development of philology—the science which is concerned with the elements, laws and principles of language, and sometimes aptly referred to as "the biography of nations"—has had its main development since the middle of the eighteenth century, when language began to be represented as the key to the most essential characteristics of peoples and their cultures. In fact, the development of philology parallels the development of nationalism. Cf. Max H. Boehm, "Nationalism: Theoretical Aspects," *Encyclopedia of the Social Sciences* (New York: The Macmillan Co., 1938), II, 231–240 (235).
11 On the recency of language as a major cause of dissension, see Karl Vossler, *The Spirit of Language in Civilization* (London: Routledge & Kegan Paul, 1951), pp. 117–119; Hans Kohn, *The Idea of Nationalism* (New York: Macmillan, 1944), p. 6.
12 Robert E. Park, *The Immigrant Press and Its Control* (New York: Harper & Brothers, 1922), pp. 49–50.
13 Kohn, p. 431.
14 *Op. cit.*, pp. 126–127.
15 Mentioned in Carlton J. H. Hayes, *The Historical Evolution of Modern Nationalism* (New York: Macmillan, 1931), pp. 64–65.
16 Henry Steele Commager, "Schoolmaster to America," *Saturday Review*, 41 (Oct. 18, 1958), 10–12, 66–67.
17 Rupert Emerson, *From Empire to Nation: The Rise to Self-assertion of Asian and African Peoples* (Cambridge: Harvard University Press, 1960), p. 139.
18 *Ibid.*, p. 143.
19 Cf. United Nations, *Report on the World Social Situation*, (Department of Social Affairs: New York, 1952), pp. 76–78.
20 Emerson, p. 145.
21 Cf. Deutsch, *op. cit.*, p. 71. See the especially revealing article by Kurt Mayer, "Cultural Pluralism and Linguistic Equilibrium in Switzerland," *American Sociological Review*, 16 (Apr., 1951), 157–163.

X ❦ Language as a Centrifugal Factor in Human Societies

Language is the great unifier and sociocultural assimilating agent; it is a crucial factor in the coherence and persistence of most ethnic and naturalistic groups and the nation–state. But, under certain rather common and widespread conditions of contact and interaction, it is also a great divider and separator of human categories and groups, a factor in ignorance, suspicion and misunderstanding between groups, a block to cooperation and unity, a basis for social discrimination and segregation, and a source of cultural, societal and political antagonism. The "linguistic loyalty" and "linguistic allegiance" that bind the speakers of a common language together function as potent separators of the speakers of different languages. To be sure, there are other centrifugal forces. Today humanity is being torn asunder by such powerful factors as nationalism, industrial competition, ideological conflict, ethnocentrism, race prejudice and race discrimination, religious convictions and the like. Prominent among these factors, and functionally interrelated with all of them, is language.

It should be kept in mind, however, that while differences in language contribute to the centrifugal tendencies and relations just referred to, these non-linguistic factors, when they prevail within or between communities, can and often do promote and perpetuate language *differences*—for example, between the inhabitants of different geographic areas, between all sorts of special interest groups (occupations, professions, criminal elements, age groups, and so on), between ethnic elements and between social classes, as well as vast inter-community, inter-people, and international linguistic differences.

The relationship between language difference and social and cultural separation and antagonism is usually an ambivalent one.

I. *The Multiplicity of Languages and Difficulties of Communication*

Before examining some of the more important and more typical aspects of this, one basic situation should be mentioned. Attention was called in Chapter VIII to the multiplicity of languages and dialects in the contemporary world. These thousands of languages and dialects have sociological and social-psychological factual significance, because almost all kinds of intra- and intergroup differences and separations are in greater or lesser measure consequences of the kind and amount of intercommunication between the respective population elements. The *many* languages are *different* languages—different systems of interhuman communication. Each of these systems is more or less unintelligible to the users of most of the other systems. Hence, there is an absence of communication between these disparate groups of speakers—which, in turn, means impaired or limited interaction—and this absence leads to the dissociating and disorganizing situations just mentioned. The Curse of Babel still causes confusion, division, social misfunctioning and strife among mankind.[1] The members of the human race are members of many different language groups and communities, and are without ready communication among each other, because of these linguistic differences. Just as a common language usually makes for mutual comprehension and unity, so difference of language can lead to lack of understanding, misunderstanding and disunity. As E. B. Tylor put it nearly a century ago: "Those who are ignorant of one another's language, it has been said, are to one another as though they were dumb."[2] In certain respects, the thousands of languages and dialects spoken in the world today not only distinguish groups, including entire nations and peoples, in certain crucial ways, but even tend to pull them apart.

Particularly pertinent at the moment, as noted in the preceding chapter, is the way in which the multiplicity of languages and dialects within many of the countries of recent nationhood or of peoples striving for statehood creates divisive obstacles. The multilinguality among them not only separates the different regions and segments of the population, but also frequently maintains dissociation—that is, these elements do not want to associate because of recognized, even cherished, differences.

2. The Interplay of the Different Kinds of Isolation, Language Diversity and Social Separation

The different kinds of isolative conditions and agencies affecting human beings, individually and jointly, create marked differentials in the opportunity of human beings to communicate with each other; this, in turn, means that these isolative factors constitute barriers and handicaps which exclude people from exchange and participation with each other. A very significant social and cultural aspect of isolation–exclusion, however brought about, is the fact that it contributes directly to the development and maintenance of language differentials both within and between language communities. These intra- and intergroup language divergences, conversely, function as barriers and hindrances to understanding, reciprocity and joint action, and hence as factors in social, psychic and cultural isolation, separation and exclusion.[3]

We need to be aware of the nature of the different kinds of isolation as they affect language, and to be conscious of the fact that these different forms usually operate in some degree of combination with each other, as well as of the effects of language differences upon individual and social isolation.[4]

We shall first briefly indicate the geographical, physiological–psychological, ethnic–racial and societal conditions that contribute to the development and maintenance of intra-group and intergroup linguistic differences and gaps, and consequently have dissociative and disorganizing social effects.

a / Geographic location, distance and topography. The surface of the earth, the basic physical factor, has had profound intra-group and intergroup linguistic effects. Historically, it has created various inaccessibilities, barriers and distances within language areas.[5] People isolated physically from each other by mountain chains, forests, vast stretches of tundra, swamplands, deserts, arms of the sea, or wide rivers have *not* shared a general trend of thought and action, and their languages have shown differential features.

The geographic extent and the physical barriers and distances of the area within which a more or less common language has prevailed have been basic, although not exclusive, factors in the splitting of the language in time into somewhat distinctive languages. The more immediate effect, however, is the formation and development of *dialects,* that is, regional variants of the main language—somewhat divergent as to phonetics, formal characteristics, vocabulary and pronunciation—which may develop (and often have done so), into separate languages. The existence of dialects is, in some degree, a horizontal division of the language community (or nation), and when there are many or sharply different dialects, these have a separative effect; they may, in fact, lead to the dissolution of the larger group (for example, the nation) into smaller component parts.[6]

As the result of their physical isolation and general sociocultural retardation, some people retain a dialect which has marked peculiarities, as compared with the standard language of the larger area, and which, though colorful and quaint in its archaisms, is a definite handicap in communication, thus contributing to the "backwardness" and cultural isolation of its speakers. Our own American Appalachian and Ozark Highlanders, prior to World War I, were notable instances.

While some of the great languages of the world are intercontinental today (notably English, Spanish, Portuguese and French), the evidence points to the fact that they originated and had their fundamental development in specific and separate areas of the earth, and the greater proportion of them are still in large measure geographically localized.

The availability and effectiveness of the means of overcoming the handicaps of geographic isolation and distance, and of developing wider cultural, economic and political contacts is, today, for most of the world, closely correlated both with the uniformation and the decline in number of distinct linguistic groups in the various areas, and with the degree of modernization of their inhabitants.

b / Sociocultural isolation, discriminatory and disorganizing factors. A number of sociocultural conditions affecting language and reflecting both intra-community and intercommunity linguistic differences, as well as certain characteristics of language themselves, also have sociocultural separative effects; at any rate, they limit free, easy and effective inter-person and intergroup communication.

[1] *Ethnocentrism and language.* Ethnocentrism, with its in-group amity and out-group enmity, and its group-egoism (our group as the superior group, as against all others), has been reflected in the attitudes and correlated actions of the members of a given group toward the languages of other groups—attitudes and actions which often produce

marked isolative and centrifugal effects. In fact, ethnic intolerance, discrimination and hostility have probably been based on the linguistic as much as on any other cultural factor. Conversely, the retention of a language, under competitive conditions, has been an important means of evidencing and maintaining ethnocentric attitudes and objectives.

Intercommunity aspects of ethnocentrism. The use of a different language as a criterion for "foreigners" and "out-group membership" has long been recognized, and is a copiously demonstrated historical fact. People who were able to make themselves intelligible to each other often called themselves "The Speakers" or "The People"; those who spoke a strange tongue they spoke of as "The Jabberers" or "The Strangers." The Greek word *barbaros,* which meant "strange" or "foreign," and in consequence "rude" and "ignorant," probably had its source in the idea of stammering, stuttering, babbling unintelligibly. Other people had similar derogatory epithets. The Slavs labeled themselves "the intelligible men," but called the Germans with whom they came into contact *niemci,* "the mutes," people who could not make themselves understood. Sophocles used the expression "tongueless" for the barbarians as contrasted with the Greeks.[7] There is also the classical account in the Book of Judges, where we are told that a "different" pronunciation of the word *shibboleth* was the cue for the slaughter of the barbarous Ephraimites by the Israelites.

Intra-community aspects. Those minorities within a community who are either ignorant of the language spoken by the great majority, or who speak it only with difficulty, feel (with good reason) more or less isolated. In the United States, unassimilated ethnic elements, speaking foreign languages, have found themselves frequently not only in a state of physical segregation from the majority, but also suffering social and cultural separation, discrimination, estrangement and "distance." These different speech groups were much more effectively separated than dialect groups, because they spoke *different* standard languages, not merely variations of a common tongue.

The different language has almost everywhere also functioned as a "badge" of the minority group, along with such other features as physical appearance, nationality, religion, customs and social class position. Moreover, their "foreign" language has served as a pointedly obvious representation and form of expression of most of these other peculiar minority-group characteristics.

The minority-group language has been related to both the horizontal and the vertical social distance of its speakers from those of the majority language: (1) *horizontal,* in that the members of the "foreign" minority group have often been either involuntarily or voluntarily segregated residentially from the majority and from other minority groups, and have also (before they were assimilated) often been separated by the assignment to them of particular occupations; (2) *vertical,* in that minorities, foreign-language and racial, have invariably been assigned lower social status, and hence, were members of the lower social strata.

[2] *The "special" languages of the language community.* Every standard language and every language community has, and has had from early times, within it a whole host of "special"—in some instances, "secret"—languages of *societal* origin and determination.[8] These are the peculiar variants of the common language, developed and used by the members of *special interest* (not minority) groups and categories in their communication with each other.

While most of these special languages exist for the sake of precision and facility of discourse within the particular group of speakers, who have been specialized in one way and for one reason or another, they are also monopolistic, "inclusive–exclusive" agents—that is, they function among the members of the group, on the one hand, as a precious means of identifying and inclusively enjoying a relationship with one another as special creatures and, on the other hand, of marking and excluding the non-speakers. As such, they estrange their respective groups of speakers from each other in their correlated social relationships, and interfere, in some instances quite intentionally, with the ready access of the members of the respective groups to each other; in general, they set their speakers apart from the larger society, by fostering and maintaining horizontal social distance.

[3] *The literate–illiterate cleavage.* Ever since there has been writing, there has been a sharp cleavage between those who have been able to use it and those without this ability. This rests in part on the fact that the literary form of the language permits forms of expression, and a range of universality and durability of expression and understanding among its writers and readers, that do not exist with spoken language. Furthermore, the written language is likely to be the formalized mother tongue, while much of the spoken language consists of the regionally or locally diverse dialects or of the lingoes and jargons. Finally, both historically and contemporaneously, the literary language has been and is the main medium of communication of the *educated* classes, and has set them apart —in amount and uniformity of knowledge, in breadth and richness of cultural contact and understanding—from the illiterate classes, with their limited and localized interests and comprehension. Where there is, among a people, such a divergence between folk and literary lan-

guage, the effect is to retard the development of the non-literate population, and to hold down their intellectual and social level.

One of the classic examples of this is China, until two decades ago,
where the *literati* and the rest of the population lived to a great extent
in two separate worlds. Medieval Europe provides a similar illustration.
But the situation has tremendous pertinence today. It is seldom realized
that fully half—possibly as much as 60 per cent—of the world's
population can neither read nor write. This means, in general, that communication with these people is possible only through the spoken idiom,
with its vast diversities. This illiterate–literate gap is an especially crucial
aspect of the state of affairs prevailing among the great body of underdeveloped peoples in Asia, Africa and Latin America who desire
"modernization." The illiterates of a given people are not only functionally and structurally divorced from their own literate compatriots,
but have a woefully truncated understanding and possibility of participating in the intellectual, scientific–technological, economic, political, and
ideological movements and activities of the interlocked and shrinking
modern world.

[4] *Certain eccentricities of meaning of the words and phrases of a
given language.* The diverse meanings of given words in different contexts, and the ambiguities of meaning of given words that hold true for
different classes and conditions of men, have a separative effect through
the resultant failure of communication to be ready and accurate. Nouns
such as "democracy," "civilization," and "education" have different
significance for different conditions and categories of men; nouns like
"freedom," "happiness," and "progress" are interpreted differently by
almost every individual. Very many words lie open to an infinite variety
of interpretation.

Each language has its own peculiar colloquial and idiomatic words
and expressions. Only those who understand the particular social context of the terms as used have a workable knowledge of them, for many
of these peculiarities reflect a meaning quite at variance with the literal
meaning of the words themselves. "Cool" is an expression for various
jazz idioms, and has nothing to do, in this context, with temperature.
"Get on the ball" is an expression commonly associated with pitching
in baseball; in the contemporary usage of some persons it represents a
directive to greater effort or efficiency. "Look out" may sometimes mean
the exact opposite of its literal meaning—in short, to duck, run, look
away, or beware.[9]

Vastly complicating the task of mutual understanding is the lack of
lexical precision in most languages: given words or words with identical

sounds may have very different meanings. These are the many words with homonymous meanings. The same symbol or word may thus have very different referents: for example, "human ear," "ear of corn." The word "hand" is used in a variety of meanings: his "hand" (part of the human body), "hour hand" (a very different object: part of a clock), "all hands on deck" ("hands" as persons), "a good hand at gardening" (a person proficient at gardening), "he held a good hand" (at cards), "he got the upper hand" (some advantage). Similarly, note the uses of "bar": "iron bar," "bar to progress," "he should be behind the bars," "studied for the bar," "let down the bars," "bar of music," "sand bar," "candy bar," "mosquito bar," "bar sinister," "bar none," "ordered drinks at the bar." Identical words may have different meanings when used as noun or adjective or verb: "sound" may be used as a noun meaning "noise," or as an adjective meaning "healthy." We can have a "set of people" and we can "set a hen." The myth of the one-and-only meaning is also demonstrated in the word "strike," when it is used as a verb, not to speak of its use as a noun: "the workers voted to strike for better pay"; "he promised not to strike her again"; "it is not easy to strike a match on glass"; "the batter did not strike out."

Words of the same sound (but different spellings) are likely to have different meanings: "flower" and "flour." We are also sometimes confused by synonyms: one sense, with several different names for it.

The ambiguities of speech that often produce some breakdown of communication and are potentially conducive to misunderstanding were discovered by Alice, in talking to the wilful Red and White Queens:

> Here the Red Queen began again. "Can you answer useful questions?" she said. "How is bread made?"
> "I know *that*!" Alice cried eagerly. "You take some flour ———."
> "Where do you pick the flower?" the White Queen asked. "In a garden or in the hedge?"
> "Well, it isn't *picked* at all," Alice explained, "it's *ground* ———"
> "How many acres of ground?" said the White Queen. "You mustn't leave out so many things."[10]

In general, it may be concluded that language differences and gaps, however produced and developed—whether as a matter of different language systems altogether, different dialects, sensory, physiological or physical defects or handicaps, special-interest group variation, literary differentials or eccentricities of language itself—tend to create or foster difficulties of discourse, and hence impair communication and tend to produce misunderstanding or entire lack of understanding, reciprocal suspicion, often some degree of antagonism, always some degree of social separation, and always the blocking of common participation and cooperation.

Linguistic differences, whether they are a consequence of isolation or a cause of it, serve to perpetuate isolation. They result in what might be referred to as societal and cultural "hospitalism."[11] Even within a general language community, the differentiated groups and categories of speakers function to some extent in different culture contexts: words have different meanings attached to them; situations are differently defined and evaluated; data are differently interpreted, and different conclusions are drawn from the data. The different sets of speakers occupy different "universes of discourse," which means that to some degree they operate in different universes of experiencing, conception and action. In a very real sense, there prevails between them a "difference" and often a conflict of philosophies, which keeps them apart. This key factor was pointedly presented in one of the favorite themes of the late, socially perspicacious cartoonist, Webster, as voiced in the words: "They don't speak our langwidge!"

3. *Some Social and Social–Psychological Separative or Antagonistic Effects of Language*

The two-way relationship between language and social situations also shows itself in certain of the former's social and social–psychological separative or antagonistic effects.

a / The very ease of communication, including facilitation through language uniformation, can accentuate social separation and antagonism. In general, as has been indicated previously, difficulty of communication, in the way of "breaks," "gaps," and "blocks"—whether these are brought about by uncontrollable physical or social circumstances, or by deliberate individual and group action—encourages social separation and antagonism. It is equally possible, and quite likely under certain conditions that, where ease of communication prevails among separated and dissident groups, the social separation and conflict can become even sharper for a while, as each group becomes more readily and extensively aware of the other's thoughts, feelings and actions. From racial opposition in the United States, and also in South Africa, it seems to be evident that uniformation of language as between the racial elements and among the many regional dialects, as well as increase in literacy, have been a very important factor, at this stage of the conflict between the respective racial groups, in increasing rather than diminishing the antagonism.

In the earlier stages of active group conflict, better and more uniform communication increases the knowledge of the groups about each other. This is especially true of more oppressed and disadvantaged elements in the situation. They learn of the advantages and amenities enjoyed by the dominant group, of the internal weaknesses and the errors of the other group, of their own proper social rights and their own strength; they learn that they are in a constantly improving position for developing strategy and action. If this stage of the conflict is satisfactorily resolved, then the continual maintenance and even further easing and improving of communication may aid in bringing about a state of relative amity and unity.

b / The effect of efforts to suppress a mother tongue. In the past, and to some extent in the present, conquerors have attempted to stop the use of the native languages of conquered elements. This has usually taken the form of prohibition by law of the use of the native language in school, press, or pulpit. Such a policy has, of course, been intended to make the conquest secure, and to promote social "uniformity" and political "solidarity." For example, Germany under Bismarck, in 1872, decreed that German should be the language of instruction in the Polish schools, and that the police should close any public meetings where speeches were made in any language other than German. In the early years of the present century—in the Ukraine, in Russian Poland, in the Baltic states, and in Lithuania—the languages of the peoples were forbidden by the Russian Empire.

These procedures, however, have had opposite social and psychological effects from those intended by the conquerors. In fact, many oppressed peoples have refused to use the language of the oppressor, as an evidence of their independence and resistance. The German efforts provoked violent resistance, which had to be put down by force. The Russian efforts similarly aroused in the people a strong desire to violate the ban on their language in every way possible. The masses of the people in the border provinces not only used their own language in the privacy of their homes, but also surreptitiously read and maintained the folk speech as a literary language. The fact that what they read was contraband only added zest to the reading of it. The Polish hated the Germans, above all as conquerors, but they equally hated the German language as an evidence of that conquest.

It has frequently been the case that attention to the mother tongue of a people has remained nonexistent until attention has been focused on it. It is the efforts to suppress it that make it crucially important. Then, the latent language loyalty and allegiance come to the fore. Moreover, the prohibitions make the banned language an effective unifier of its native speakers, because for them it is at least a symbol of their spiritual independence. In general, such suppressive tactics do not, in the short run, foster assimilation; on the contrary, they accentuate antagonism.[12]

c / The disruptive effect of learning the language of a more advanced civilization. While these effects were noticeable with the spread of Greek and Roman civilization, they are of special pertinence in our present world as the young men and women of the underdeveloped peoples have learned Western languages. The knowledge of these languages has opened up vast bodies of literature which present new and attractive social values, objectives and practices. Teeming as they are with "seditious" thoughts, the young people who come into contact with them are not slow to apply them to their own problems. At the same time, this separates them from the older population elements.

4. *The Deliberate Use of Language for Separative Purposes*

Another important sociological aspect of language as a centrifugal social vehicle is its deliberate use (or misuse) for purposes of discriminating against other groups and categories, isolating and excluding others, and even creating and increasing social conflict.

a / Linguistic intolerance. There is, first of all, the more or less conscious and deliberate separation from the speakers of other languages, which is due to that "linguistic intolerance" that is manifested in an aversion to languages other than one's own, and often in the depreciation and deliberate avoidance of their speakers. The "naive monoglot" regards speakers of other languages as something less than human, and even the better tutored often think of them as at least "foreign," quite likely as creatures of lesser knowledge and inferior culture. This attitude, which is not always subtly expressed or gently exercised, ranges all the way from the exalted stance toward other languages and speakers of the members of the English-speaking Union or the *Académie Française* to that of certain American G. I.s abroad, when they are confronted with the reality of foreigners and their incomprehensible tongues: "Why the hell don't they talk American?"

b / The retention of a "foreign" or "minority" language within a country to prevent or at least forestall the assimilation of its speakers. The editors of the immigrant, foreign-language press in the United States, during their period of greatest influence prior to the 1920's, sought to use the press as a means of preventing assimilation. By means of their newspapers and journals, they endeavored to keep the interests and activities of their readers focused on the home country, and separated from those of America.[13] In French Canada, the influence of the French has been great in preserving the French language and French tradition and customs, and in blocking the absorption of French-descended people into the larger Canadian life.

c / The language of concealment. Languages of concealment, contrived by many different kinds of groups, function as limitations upon or even barriers to communication, understanding, cooperation, organization and planning. They do, as they are intended to, separate (and divide) their members from all others.[14]

5. Language and Political Divergence and Conflict

In recent times, reference has occasionally been made to a new field of study, "political linguistics," which is concerned with the political implications, uses and effects of language. An aspect of this situation, long sensed, is the close relationship between linguistic and political divergence and linguistic and political conflict. The upsurge of nationalism during and since the eighteenth century has especially focused attention on the political significance of language, fostered a new interest in languages and correlated language and nationalistic aspirations and activities.[15] In recent times there has emerged an aggressive nationalism, which has sought to disseminate and exalt its own "national" language, and to demean and suppress other languages. We shall briefly examine several phases of the relation between linguistic and political divergence.

a / Language, itself, has often been the object of international and political cleavage and antagonism. As between peoples or nations the conflict springs from the fact, already noted in the preceding chapter, that language is usually identified with national pride, honor and prestige, as well as with tendencies toward national survival and expansion. Linguistic differences, again and again, have thwarted or beclouded intercommunication, and have been a source of international misunderstanding and a block to peaceful and useful action. Even with the assistance of the best translators, the United Nations Assembly and the Councils still have interlingual problems. Historically, linguistic differences have been utilized by warmongers and other international troublemakers to promote their own ends.

b / Language differences have had internal political separative effects. Markedly different dialects—or, even more certainly, the prevalence of separate languages within a nation—have tended to dissolve the nation into smaller, separated, component parts, a process which has seriously jeopardized the greater national idea and unity. The Ottoman Empire and the Austro-Hungarian Empire are well-known cases in point.

In multilingual nations, there have often been efforts to promote an "official" language for legal affairs, administration, the press and general education, through the schools, sometimes the churches, and sometimes by governmental ukase and under police enforcement.

Lotz has presented several contemporary examples of internal political complications arising out of language differences. In Norway, much national energy is spent on disputes between the proponents of two very closely related language forms, the *riksmål* and the *landsmål,* which are roughly correlated with the political attitudes of the Conservatives and the Left. In free India, as we have noted, attempt has been made to redraw the administrative map along linguistic lines, thus showing that language takes precedence in this subcontinent over geographic and economic factors. The Soviet Union is a federation of fifteen "republics" which correspond in considerable part to the major language differences within the Union.[16]

c / National dissolution along linguistic lines. So great is the political importance of linguistic differences that, when multilingual and ethnically complex nations have been dissolved, the dismembering has been along linguistic lines. At Versailles (1919) after World War I, the Austro-Hungarian Empire was divided along linguistic lines, although this was somewhat obscured by the use of the word "ethnic." With the dissolution of the Ottoman Empire, there also occurred a great shuffling about of "Greeks" and "Turks" into their respective new political domains. After the Second World War, there was a wholesale expulsion and relocation of minority groups on the basis of their languages.

6. *America's Linguistic Provincialism*

A final pressing problem of vast practical significance, involving grave separative effects, has to do with the chronic American neglect and ignorance of foreign languages. There is an almost universal inability (recent immigrants excepted) to speak a foreign language, even among our educated people and, in notoriously many cases, among our political, economic, and cultural representatives abroad. Though it is not quite so serious as the speech lack, we also have among us a most limited ability to read other important languages. This situation exists in spite of the fact that only the Soviet Union compares with us in our involvement in the affairs of the world. We are very much involved in the linguistic aspects of international contact, communication and action, as the result of the prominent part we do take—and possibly must take—in foreign aid, both our own and the United Nations programs, and in the education of other peoples all over the world, and because of our strategic place in diplomacy, the worldwide police duties of our military, our role as leader of the "free" peoples in the "Cold War," and our own vast economic interdependence and exchange ("foreign trade"), and as a by-product of the extensive tourism abroad on the part of our citizens who, in a very real though informal way, function as American representatives and diplomats. And this is to mention only the more important among our foreign involvements.

Our chronic neglect of and poverty in foreign languages have put us behind a "language curtain," and have woefully handicapped us in our intercourse with the citizens of the world; they have, in some measure, isolated us from the world along the lines just indicated, intensified our insularity and parochialism, and led to considerable ineptness in our interaction with other peoples and nations.

Of serious concern is the fact that the great majority of the American citizenry seem to be unaware of the importance of a knowledge of and facility in the use of other languages, especially those of the leading peoples, now that they are unavoidably participating, both positively and negatively, in the affairs of practically all of the peoples of the world. Many Americans—and well-educated and often strategically situated persons and categories among them—even seem to take a smug pride in their antipathy to things foreign, including languages, and in their linguistic isolationism and "dumbness" (in the sense of their being unable to speak). Some persons still demean the teaching of foreign languages in our schools and colleges, dubbing such instruction "frills" and "impractical," and attempting to discourage or prevent its inclusion in the curriculum.

Since Pearl Harbor, we have attempted to repair this in a small way. For our own public representatives abroad, we have such training agencies as the Army Language School at Monterey, California—possibly the largest language training center in the world—where some five hundred instructors are offering intensive instruction in twenty-nine Western and Eastern languages, the Navy Language School at Anacostia in Washington, D.C., which provides instruction in six major tongues, and the State Department's Foreign Service Institute, which is equipped to teach some thirty languages. Other government agencies have, or are in the process of setting up, special language and area training programs. Foreign languages are getting back into the schools—even at the elementary-school level, in some scattered instances. But even at the college level, we are still "short" in the amount and diversity of language instruction given and required, and in the number of different languages for which training is provided.

In the meantime, and in rather sharp contrast to our tongue-tied condition, the Soviet Union, more than any other contemporary nation, is keenly aware of the importance of foreign languages, both for its representatives abroad and for its citizens. Young Russians start studying foreign languages at the age of twelve. Various state efforts to encourage adults, including those of the European satellites, to learn other languages are thought to be quite successful. Much stress is placed on English; it is estimated that about 10,000,000 Russians of all ages are studying English. The Communists appreciate fully the force of language as an instrument of indoctrination; they are showing the world that words, especially in the people's own languages, may be far more effective than bombs.[17]

N O T E S

1 "The whole earth was of one language and one speech. . . . And the Lord said, Behold the people is one, and they have all one language; and this they begin to do [building the tower to heaven] and now nothing will be restrained among them; which they have imagined to do." To break down this powerful, arrogant union, the Lord resorted not to arms, nor did He invoke the destructive powers

of his Cosmos. He simply smote the people with the inability to understand each other's speech. "Let us go down, and there confound their language, that they may not understand one another's speech. So the Lord scattered them abroad from thence upon the face of the earth: and they left off to build the city. Therefore is the name of it called Babel; because the Lord did there confound the language of all the earth: and from thence did the Lord scatter them abroad upon the face of all the earth." *Genesis* 11:1–9.

2 *Researches into the Early History of Mankind* (London: J. Murray, 1870), p. 34.

3 For example, the adult in a foreign country with a different speech is excluded from much that goes on there.

4 As an excellent example of the interplay of geographical obstacles, variations in language and cultural diversity, see the description of the "Several Spains" by W. B. Fisher and H. Bowen–Jones, *Spain: A Geographical Background* (London: Christopher, 1958), pp. 102–106.

5 As noted in Chap. VIII, the modern space-neutralizing means of communication and other technological and socioeconomic and political developments have tended to have a uniformizing effect, but "linguistic geography" still has a great pertinence for many phases of language study.

6 For a more extensive analysis of the nature, formation and sociological significance of dialects, see Chap. XII, Sect. 5.

7 Cf. Tylor, p. 34; Hans Kohn, *The Idea of Nationalism: A Study in Its Origins and Background* (New York: Macmillan Co., 1944), p. 7; Ralph Pieris, "Speech and Society: A Sociological Approach to Language," *American Sociological Review,* 16 (Aug., 1951), 499–505 (499).

8 These will be dealt with more comprehensively, both as sociocultural products and as functional agents, in Chap. XIII. They are mentioned here because of their separating effects.

9 The examples are from Julian Samora and William Deane, "Language Usage as a Possible Index of Acculturation," *Sociology & Social Research,* 40 (May–June, 1956), 307–311.

10 Lewis Carroll, *Through the Looking Glass* (Philadelphia: John C. Winston & Co., 1923), Chap. IX, p. 207. A newspaper report some years ago described how a recruit broke ranks during maneuvers and plunged into the *woods at his left,* after an officer had shouted, "Bear to the *right!*" The recruit explained, "I'm afraid of bears." (Mentioned by Bernard F. Huppé and Jack J. Kaminsky, *Logic and Language* (New York: Alfred A. Knopf, 1956), p. 13.)

11 This is the apt term referring to the effects of isolation, especially with respect to the seclusion from communication, which was developed by Rene A. Spitz, "Hospitalism," in *The Psychoanalytic Study of the Child* (New York: International Universities Press, 1945), I, 53–72.

12 It should be noted, however, that peoples whose languages have been successfully suppressed or supplanted have practically ceased to exist culturally or politically.

13 Cf. Robert E. Park, *The Immigrant Press and Its Control* (New York: Harper & Brothers, 1922), pp. 55–57, 79–88.

14 For a more detailed discussion of languages of concealment see Chap. XIII, Sect. 4. A distinctly separative effect is also achieved by the use of language in the form of demeaning, derogatory and abusive words and phrases, its manipulation for purposes of misinformation and the strategic use of silence and censorship. These will be discussed primarily as linguistic devices used in social control, in Chap. XI, Sect. 7.

15 Cf. Clarence A. Manning, "The Menace of Linguistic Nationalism," *South Atlantic Quarterly,* 44 (Jan., 1945), 13–22.

16 John Lotz, "Linguistics," in Lynn White, Jr. (ed.), *Frontiers of Knowledge in the Study of Man* (New York: Harper & Brothers, 1956), pp. 209–211. The converse of the major point of the last two paragraphs should also be recorded,

namely that political separation, however it occurs, encourages monolingual development among the separated elements. Says Leonard Bloomfield: "It is estimated that, under old conditions, a new political boundary led in less than fifty years to some linguistic difference." (*Language* (New York: Henry Holt & Co., 1933), p. 343.)

17 This section has been suggested in large part by, and all of its specific facts have been taken from, the telling article by Jacob Ornstein, "Our Tongue-tied Generation," *Saturday Review,* 43 (Nov. 26, 1960), 15–17, 38–39. On the desirability of bi- or even multilinguality for persons living in the modern world, see Chapter XV, Sect. 5.

XI ❧ The Language of Social Control and the Social Control of Language

Language is a dynamic factor in human life. Its effectiveness extends quite beyond its general determinative influence in perception and conception. It is a primary factor in what is known in the social sciences, especially social psychology and sociology, as *social control*. Throughout history, language has been manipulated as a highly effective tool in social control.

1. *The Sociology of Social Control*

Social control is one of the primary concerns of sociology. The reasons for the existence of social control, the basic forms it takes, the functions it performs, will now be briefly set forth. Whenever there is interaction between two or more human beings, there is some control unconsciously or consciously exercised. When we think of *social* control, we mean the way in which social power and social influence, as exercised by individuals and groups, function to regulate, direct, adjust and organize the social conduct—the beliefs, thoughts and feelings, as well as the overt behavior—of other individuals and groups.

We members of society, in our various interactions with each other, in our person-to-person contacts and through our many informal and formal combinations, as well as in our different capacities and positions, influence each other's conduct, sometimes for our own good, sometimes for that of others.

Social control involves processes, procedures, techniques, programs and other social instrumentalities for bringing about—by suggestion, persuasion or compulsion—actions of a positive or negative nature. It seeks to induce desired, prescribed and expected actions and operations in some instances; in others, it prohibits, constrains or prevents unsocial, anti-social or unwanted behavior. As has been implied, there is a given range of conscious intention. Much of the control to which we submit, however, is unconscious; we may be said to live in an "atmosphere of control" created by our culture, which conditions us and incites us to response from birth to death. Much of it is conscious and intentional and is exercised with specific conformity-producing objectives. We conform, differentially as individuals and groups to be sure, to the requests and commands of others, to fads and fashions, the dictates of public opinion, advertising, organized propaganda, to the requirements of the organizations of which we are voluntary or involuntary members and to the chartered and societally enforced requirements of our social institutions.

Social control is both personal and impersonal. Personal control is seated in and exercised by persons, dead and living. Among the dead are our ancestors, great rulers and leaders, great misleaders, heroes, reformers, idealists, deliverers, statesmen and so on; among the living, every associate with whom we have some degree of communication—friends and fellow group members, or opponents—is influential. But, more specifically, there are such categories as those of contemporary leaders and misleaders, parents, children and other relatives, teachers, employers and employees, officials of organizations, persons of high social status and influence, directors of mass communication agencies or of social movements, and persons with learning. By impersonal control, we mean mainly group control, both that of primary or face-to-face groups, such as the peer group, the family, the neighborhood and cliques, and of secondary groups—groups that are mainly organizations for specific purposes, such as the religious, occupational, educational, economic, civic, military, and political organizations that conduct the major operations of communities.

Finally, attention should be called to the objectives of conscious social-control action. Social-control techniques and instruments, like all other techniques and instruments, are ethically and purposively neutral. They may be used to fulfill quite different objectives: personal, anti-social, asocial or social. Of the three major categories from this point of view, the *first* consists of *the exploitative and predatory controls*. Much control is exercised by individuals and groups for the specific purposes of advancing their own special interests and ends, without regard for the interests of those controlled or the effect of the control upon the well-being of the community or society as a whole. The *second* major category consists of *regulatory and maintenance controls*. These are used in the interest of individual and social well-being. They solicit, require and attempt to produce social order—that is, harmonious, co-ordinated and correlated interactions—and to proscribe and restrain anti-social action. The *third* major category consists of the *reorganizational controls*. Throughout history, deliberate efforts have been made, for good or ill, to remold the human social world. This is the control exercised in the course of social movements—such as reform movements, dictatorships, social revolutions, and, more recently, through scientific social planning—for example, by corporations, local communities, states, national and international organizations and nation-states.

2. *The General Significance of Language in Social Control*

Language is a basic medium in social control, and is directly involved in every aspect of it; in fact, social control is one of language's elemental reasons for existence.[1] In different social contexts, language is a factor exercising evocative, creative, propulsive and restraining power and thereby an influence on the beliefs, motives and actions of individuals and groups.

In everyday affairs, words and phrases are used to inform and apprise, to inspire and edify, to arouse and provoke, to persuade and dissuade, to intoxicate, amuse and entertain, to praise and flatter, to confuse, distort or conceal meanings, to insult and vilify, to intimidate, to exploit, to corrupt, and even to destroy others. Words as names, as epithets, and in the form of descriptive phrases, are used to label persons, groups and categories of persons; they also label things, acts and incidents. As such, they have both negative and positive psychic and social effects.

Different types and combinations of words, oral and written, variously used, are the key agencies in the manipulation and regulation of people in the interests of individual and social well-being, order and prosperity, and in the socially constructive enlargement of the comprehension and social participation of persons as individuals and as members of the community. By means of language, feelings, sentiments and cogitations are aroused, directed and canalized; beliefs, viewpoints and valuations are fostered; opinions and preferences are formed; and social conventions and societally essential social behaviors are maintained.

In various forms and guises, they are also the means whereby the harassers, exploiters and enslavers of men—the selfish egoists, organizations of many kinds, dictators, some propagandists, some evangelists, and so on—have conducted their activities, regardless of the social or ethical qualities of their objectives. As Disraeli put it: "With words we govern men!"

The mere control of the information made available to individuals and groups—which is always conveyed in some linguistic form or symbolic form translated into language—goes a long way toward determining the nature of their appraisals and prescriptions, their preferences and objectives and, hence, their behavior. The "bondage to words" is a stark social reality.

One of the specially significant social-control features of language as such is what is referred to as "word grip." The verbal act—an utterance in the form of a word or a phrase, or a sequence of these—coupled with the manner in which it is uttered, is capable of setting in motion a force which influences, even controls, persons and situations. "Words are acts . . . and they function as acts."[2] Certain words and phrases, depending in general on the fact that they pertain to certain emotion-charged, or crisis-laden or controversial areas of life, exercise this hold on people. In the typical American community the response to such words as "American," "democracy," "honesty," "booster," "knocker," "success," "average man," "practical," "common sense," "radical," "conservative," "atheist," "community spirit," "red-blooded" or "expert" can be predicted.[3] Some words have a pleasure or comfort or "lullaby" value; others, such as "Don't" and "No," have a "scare" or pain value. The semantic quality which the words themselves possess is important: "stink" is distasteful to us, "idyllic" is pleasing, "love" has pleasing connotations, and "hate" is sinister.

The tonal quality of the utterance directly affects the power to control or influence. This depends on (1) *volume* (loudness or softness); (2) *pitch* (deep or high tones on the musical scale, monotone or pitchlessness); (3) *quality* (smooth, rotund, harsh); (4) *tempo* (fast, slow, jerky), as well as all these in various combinations.[4] Hence, the manner of issuing the utterance—the vocal pattern—is of vast importance.

Sound and rhythm fascinate us: we associate them with pleasing or distasteful things and conditions, and they act directly on our deepest feelings. Melodious and soft "accents" soothe us, percussive sounds disturb us. We respond differently to changes in rhythm from smooth to explosive sound, and to variations in intensity.[5]

Different words have different character; they are used in different expressional contexts and with different emotional intent. Thus, to use a simple illustration, the English words "horse," "steed," "nag," and "gee-gee," all mean the same thing in the sense that they all refer to the same animal, but the emotional coloring is different in every case. "Horse" is the everyday word with the least emotional context. "Steed," on the other hand, belongs to the language of poetry and is dignified and majestic, while the occasionally used "gee-gee" is a playful nursery word.

Finally, it should be noted that there is a marked difference in the control effectiveness of spoken and written words. Spoken words have tonal qualities plus the qualities that are given by physical gestures. Written words require very different techniques: they can use no shadings and variations of meanings and intent of the sort that inflections and gestures can give; they have to depend on style, underlining, punctuation, metaphor and so on.[6] Usually, "the spoken word acts more effectively, more hypnotically, than the written word."[7]

Because of these features of language and the effectiveness of language in the various respects mentioned earlier, it itself also has phases that need to be avoided or controlled in the interests of individual and concerted well-being.

3. *The Magical Power of Words*

Before we take up the more important social-psychological and sociological aspects of the dynamism of speech in social action, it is desirable that we consider the nature of the belief in the magical power and influence, for good or ill, of words and phrases, over and above their strictly pragmatic effectiveness—a belief that has prevailed almost universally from earliest times. It still enters into social linguistics in one form or another. We find it curiously blended with scientific interpretations of the effects of language. Not infrequently, it is used along with scientific cause-and-effect explanations and descriptions, by highly intelligent and educated people who seem to be unconscious of their primitivism.

The significance of words as social instruments, and as the vehicles of meaning, has been briefly noted.[8] The term "word" is also used in a more mystical and extended sense in the WORD, the *Logos,* the all-encompassing expression for language as the identifier of all that is experienced, as carrier of all that is imagined, believed and known, as the means of controlling things, events and persons—even as a supreme creative force itself.

a / The religious significance of the WORD. The WORD has had central religious significance as identification with Deity, as the essence of Being, and as the creative tool of Deity. This is pointed to in Victor Hugo's proclamation: "Le mot, qu'on le sache, est un être vivant . . . le mot, c'est le Verbe, et le Verbe, c'est Dieu." The Word has been presented in most of the great religions as the essence of wisdom, the primary[9] source from which all Being is derived, the instrument employed by the Creator when he established the universe. The Sumerians and Babylonians regarded the Word as creative wisdom. In ancient Egyptian theology, the primary force of "the heart and the tongue" was attributed to the creation-god Ptah, whereby he produced and governed all gods and men, all animals, and all that lives. In the Hindu Veddas, the *Aum* or *Om* is the mystic symbol—the "word of words"—embodying in itself the essence of the Veddas and of the universe. One of the fundamental principles of Brahma is that "the world originates from the Word." This ineffable potency is also indicated by the Christian John when he begins the Fourth Gospel with the statement:

> In the beginning was the Word,
> And the Word was with God,
> And the Word was God.
> The same was in the beginning with God.[10]

In *Genesis* we are informed that all things came into existence through the utterance of their names by the Creator. "God called the light Day, and the darkness he called Night" (1:5), "And God called the firmament Heaven" (1:8), "God called the dry land Earth; and the gathering together of the waters called he Seas" (1:9). Then he created the First Man and assigned to him the task of naming (giving identity to) beast and fowl: "The Lord formed every beast of the field and every fowl of the air; and brought them unto Adam to see what he would call them; and whatsoever Adam called every living creature, that was the name thereof" (2:19).

Language has been the avenue for creating sublime images of deity:

Tao, Jahveh, Allah. Such words have profound holiness; they become untouchable and sacrosanct: "Thou shalt not take the name of the Lord, thy God, in vain."

b / The essence of word magic. The essence of word magic in the control of reality lies in the mysterious identity of the verbal symbol and the non-verbal fact. The word is much more than "a mere piece of verbiage"; it carries vast power. The power of the specific word derives from the qualities, good and evil, that are believed to inhere in the relevant aspects of the world to which the word refers. The very word creates an entity that now exists in reality. Thus the word and the thing are indissolubly one. Furthermore, it is not only an indicator but, properly used, can function as a trigger to and a formula for action. A person or a group gains positive magical power over some phase of reality by coining a word for it, or by properly using the right word for it; it may thus enjoy "good luck." If one says certain other categories of words, which have ominous power, or uses words relating to presumably sinister entities and situations, one incurs great risks, and may suffer "bad luck." To curtail the effectiveness of certain categories of "bad" words, they are specially tabooed. Because of this magical value, then, words can be used for purposes of enchantment or exorcism and, conversely, for visiting curses upon others.

Thus different categories of words have different kinds of mystical significance. Some bring boons of different sorts, some of these words actually become objects of religious reverence. The use of others, because of their connection with sinister or awesome things and situations, or holy and sacred beings and objects, is adjusted to or controlled by innumerable circumlocutions and bans. In general, as a result of the recognition of the supreme potency of words, men through the ages have "worshipped words," as Francis Bacon put it, in his discussion of the "Idols of the Forum."

4. *The Special Control Significance of Names*

Words give the power to name things, persons, groups, events and situations, and then the name itself becomes the expression of the mysterious essence of the real or imagined entity. A name does several things. First, it identifies, denotes or signifies something, comes to be descriptive of it, and thus takes it out of the realm of the unknown or the amorphous. A nameless thing is something vague, incomplete, uncanny. According to the ancient Babylonians (and also the ancient Hebrews, as we have just noted), as among many others since, "that which had no name did not exist, and its existence commenced only when it received its name."[11] Especially significant is the fact that this naming gives reference power over that to which it refers. Second, the name assigns that to which it refers to some meaningful and established, or in some instances new, classification or category of "knowns." This also distinguishes what is named from other classes of items; the name thus marks the boundaries of the thing. Third, in all cultures, the name is thought to be (and logically and pragmatically is) a definite part of the person or thing to which it is attached. Fourth, by means of this identification and classification, the thing, person, and so on is not "secret" or "fugitive"; it is known and fixed as real: the name and it are inseparable. Hence, it is vulnerable to all who can name it; he who uses its name has manipulative power over it.

We are here concerned with the functions which the names and naming of persons, social categories and groups perform in human relations, particularly those involving contrasting social statuses and social control. Of special significance is the fact that manipulating names is used as a means of manipulating persons, groups, social situations and social relations. This popular belief in the manipulative power of names is reflected in the fairy-tales, songs and traditional legends of many peoples, and in the presumed effectiveness of their many kinds of sorcerers.

Names of persons, as of all other entities, are devices born of the need to introduce order in human relationships. Among both primitives and moderns, *an individual has no definition, no validity for himself, without a name.* His name is his badge of individuality, the means whereby he identifies himself and enters upon a truly subjective existence. My own name, for example, stands for *me,* a person. Divesting me of it reduces me to a meaningless, even pathological, nonentity. As Louis Adamic put it so well:

> Taking a man's name away from him may permanently harm his personality or even destroy it. It is done for punishment in some penitentiaries where persons are given numbers, and its effect on convicts is almost worse than incarceration itself.[12]

The "reputational" names we give persons affect them greatly. Giving a "bad" name tends to intimidate the recipient; it may even make him a social outcast. A "good" name gives him a "lift" within himself, and brings him favor among his associates. A grandiloquent name given to "anyone with something to give away" is a form of flattery, and often a way of very successfully "using" that person.

By acquiring (learning) the names of objects, animals and other people around him, the individual also acquires an objective consciousness—a consciousness of himself, in contrast to and *vis-à-vis* all other entities.[13] His accumulation of names is a gauge of his individual and social growth.

Individuals have no social status without names. The name of a person at any given time in his career, indicates his sex, age group and family status. In many cultures, it also shows his occupation. Among us, a man's name has all sorts of nationality, class, minority–majority and historical–cultural identifying connotations. Hierarchy in an organization, community or society is reflected in the general names assigned to the incumbents of the different ranks (*peasant, middle class, aristocracy*) and the titles given to the holders of the more exalted ranks (*Sir, Lord, President, Emperor*).

There is a long-standing superstition that knowledge of the name gives power over the thing, because of the absolute and necessary nexus between the thing and the name. Moreover, according to magical thinking (which is now also seen to have considerable pragmatic significance), *by knowing the name of a person, and by using it in certain ways, one gains power over that person.* This has several aspects. Many primitives hide their names; some are especially afraid of mentioning their names to strangers, for they deem their names to be part of their being, and they do not wish others to gain power over them by knowing their names. Among moderns, anonymity is sought as a way of avoiding apprehension and responsibility. It is used as a means of controlling an undesirable situation: one escapes from it through the obliteration of the nominally identified self. Change of name is utilized for somewhat similar ends. To change one's name or to assume a secret "organization name" was a rather widespread practice for people going "underground" politically—for example, in the totalitarian states in the decade of the 'forties and, at the present time, for Communists in the United States.

Being able to speak familiarly to a great man achieves a certain power over him. When lesser folk call him "Jimmy" or "Teddy" or "Jack," they possess a part of him. As the result of this identity of person and name and of power and name, the utterance of certain names—for example, those of the dead, of kings, of deities and devils— may be dangerous and hence is often tabooed.

Among both primitives and moderns, *the name is frequently viewed as something self-existent.* For example, it is hoped that a person who has been named after an eminent man or an ancestor (Lincoln Jones, John D. Rockefeller, IV) will inherit his qualities.

An especially intriguing sociological aspect of names is the *relationship of the change of name and the change of identity, of ego, and of the social status of the person.* A name carries with it certain evaluations made by the named one himself, as well as the evaluations of others regarding him.[14] A change of name invariably means some change in these evaluations. Even a voluntary change of name involves some change of identity of the person, for himself as well as among others. Such change affects his ego, and the claims he and others make upon his ego. For example, there is a new release of spirit and a new self-conception when a person of immigrant descent emerges as an American after discarding his foreign or minority-group name (often correlated with social inferiority and discrimination) for a highly regarded American name (*Przwilski* to Price). The new name, usually a more conventional or prestigious one, also becomes a social asset and may open heretofore closed social doors to the individual.

The effect on personality is also brought on in the correlation between changes of names and turning points in the life-cycle of the individual. At puberty, the primitive lad receives a new name; upon obtaining it, he has ceased to exist as a child and has been recast, in his own consciousness and in the eyes of the community, as a man. When a woman takes her husband's name upon marrying him, she undergoes certain transformations of ego, as well as leaving the circle of her original family and assuming the status of married woman, as her new name shows.

A change in name may sometimes reflect an important change in the relationship of the individual to his social environment; witness the cataclysmic name-changes in the Bible—Jacob to Israel, Saul to Paul.[15]

In the entertainment world in the United States, there has been abundant evidence of the attempt to present a new "image" of one's self to the public by changing one's name. Some of these changes are readily understandable:[16] for example, Issur Danielovitch to Kirk Douglas, Frances Gumm to Judy Garland, Doris Kappelhoff to Doris Day, Frederick Bickel to Frederic March, Rose Louise Hovic to Gypsy Rose Lee, Margarita Cansino to Rita Hayworth, Izzy Itskowitz to Eddie Cantor, Sam Goldfisch to Sam Goldwyn, Benny Kubelsky to Jack Benny. Regarding one notable instance *Time* says: "Frederick Austerlitz was just too hobnailed a surname to weight the light soles of Fred Astaire." Other changes, not quite so explicable, and perhaps not changing the image significantly, are Edythe Marrener to Susan Hayward, Virginia McMath to Ginger Rogers, Helen Beck to Sally Rand, Ruby Stevens to Barbara Stanwyck.[17]

The nicknames ("Joe Bananas," "Mr. Big," "The Old Man," "Sol the Beak," "Jimmy Blue Eyes," "Charlie Bullets," "Silk Shirt Jimmy," "Weatherbird") used or applied to underworld characters are not mere playful, fanciful, or colorful "monikers," though many are decidedly apt in one way or another, and give some "image" to those so designated. The important point is that mobsters, hoodlums, and other criminals must be identified among their associates. But, for them, names are dangerous and identify them to the law enforcement officers and to the public. Their actual names are not likely to be exchanged, even among friends. Nor are they to be used casually on a telephone that might be "bugged." Hence, a hoodlum may go through a dozen aliases, shedding names like old suits, to confound the law. But he must be known among his cronies, and to them he is known by his nickname, which serves almost as a code.

A final aspect of the use of names in social control concerns what is referred to as "name-dropping." This consists of mentioning with a casual air, as though they were acquaintances or even close friends, the names of a prominent person or persons of well-known special competence, authority, or other particular importance in the social situation involved. The purpose is not only to enhance the prestige of the name-dropper—"prestige by association," so to speak—but also, on occasion, to awe or possibly intimidate or otherwise control the person to whom he is speaking or writing.

5. *The Social Efforts to Control Certain Categories of Words*

One sociologically significant aspect of the dynamism of language is a concomitant of the widely held assumption noted above—in many cases deeply rooted in superstition—that words have the "power" to alter things, situations, and the course of events, for good or ill. This phase is that *certain words,* depending upon what they refer to, *are themselves subjected to social control.* By manipulating the words, men think that they can, in some measure, manipulate the disagreeable or sinister reality to which they refer. Some kinds of words are avoided, or their use is censured. The word or name is prohibited so that the power (especially for evil) of the person or entity named, or the awefulness of the thing or the category of occurrence, or the social obloquy of the unconventional act, is not visited on the utterer of the word. Other words, by means of rhetorical and metaphysical devices, are made to yield to forms of circumlocution in the way of "softening" them, or of substituting "sweeter" or "more respectable" or "safer" expressions for them.

a / The tabooing of words. Certain words are interdicted, forbidden, or made untouchable.[18] Most societies taboo certain things and also the performance of certain acts, at least under certain circumstances. To a certain extent the things that should not be touched and the acts that should not be committed should not be mentioned either.

Another underlying principle seems to be that we can avoid knowledge of, or even experience with, a disagreeable or feared reality by refusing to name it. Certain types of words are superstitiously believed to entail mysterious evil consequences. In the area of religion, the utterance (in most contexts) of the names of deities and devils has been tabooed. For example, there is the avoidance of the name of God in Brahmanism, Judaism, and Islamism. Some words are deemed blasphemous and are interdicted. The words for certain dreaded or evil conditions are sometimes proscribed—for example, the word *cancer*. Recently an educated acquaintance of mine was heard to remark: "Don't say it! Don't say it! You'll bring it on."

On the basis of reigning convention, certain words are made untouchable and are banished from the vocabulary of well-brought-up persons, because they relate to persons or acts which are deemed "immoral," or because they deal with unpleasant or shocking or indelicate aspects of life. Their employment is an evidence of coarseness (*gaucherie*) or "bad taste," and one who uses them places himself in an exposed or vulnerable position. So the technique of social pretense is adopted. There are such generally tabooed words as *bastard* and *bitch* and *whore* (when these are used to indicate human beings). Many particular words relating to the sex act, defecation, urination, vomiting and expectoration are deemed "obscene" and may not be pronounced among the "respectable" or appear in writing. The famous "nasty four-letter words" in the English language, while ancient and persistent in their use at certain social levels and under certain conditions (for example, in armies), bear such a stigma that many "proper" people avoid uttering them. They rarely appear in print, and are not listed in leading dictionaries, for example, the *Oxford English Dictionary* and Webster's *Unabridged*.[19]

Among many others, the direct term *death,* certain names for clothing (for example, *pants, undershirt*), or for parts of the human body (*legs, guts, breasts, bottom*), or for certain diseases (*syphilis*) or physiological conditions (*constipation*) or certain surgery (*breast cancer, prostate*), or for certain animals or insects (*skunks, lice*) are interdicted.

b / Controlling the situation by euphemisms. Most men come to recognize that there can be no avoidance of or escape from most realities, however sinister, awesome, fearsome, obscene, indelicate, or contrary to reigning conventions they may be believed to be. Nor can they dispense with the concepts attached to or the meanings of the realities; they must have words for them. Therefore, while certain of these ominous words may be more or less effectively tabooed, there is the almost universal practice of using some kind of figurative paraphrase, a disguising metaphor, a toned-down or "dry-cleaned" name that keeps them neutral or remote, or of digging up an obsolete or obscure term to replace the proscribed word, or to veil it and render it more innocent. In these ways, the linguistic situation is socially controlled, not by avoidance or proscription, but by conventionalized subterfuge and substitution, and by other appeasing circumlocutions. Usually, also, it is felt by many that, in their using the more conventional word or phrase, the gravity or indecency of the thing, person, situation or occurrence is somewhat lessened. At any rate, the "nice" word sounds better.

Such less offensive words are known as *euphemisms.* People have developed substitute names for their gods that made them less vulnerable to possible supernatural power. Among Jews and Christians, there is the second Biblical commandment, which forbids us to take the name of God in vain; although this is interpreted with varying degrees of stringency, it is still an active force in our speech habits, both positively and negatively. The ancient Hebrews used such substitutes for *God* as *Adonai* and *Jahveh*; we use *the Almighty, the Supreme Being.* Many today, in writing, do not use *God,* but *G-d,* or *G—;* in speech, they use some of the circumlocutions mentioned below.

In English, there are many euphemisms for *death* and for everything connected with it. *Death* itself it referred to by such symbols as *the end, asleep in Jesus, Gone to Glory, called beyond, dissolution, departure, release; dying* as *expiring, passing away, breathing one's last* or, in the beautiful expression, *entschlafen, going to rest.* There are also such humorous, flippant, or slang forms for *to die* as to *pop off, hand in one's checks, push up the daisies, kick the bucket, go to Davy Jones's locker, wink out, croak; to kill* is expressed as *liquidate, bump off, rub out, burn* or *take the hot seat.*[20] In connection with death and dying, H. L. Mencken observed:

> A *mortician* never handles a *corpse;* he prepares a *body* or *patient.* This business is carried on in a *preparation-room* or *operating-room,* and when it is achieved the patient is put into a *casket* and stored in the *reposing-room* or *slumber-room* of a *funeral home.* On the day of the funeral he is moved to the *chapel* therein for the last exorcism, and then hauled to the cemetery in a *funeral car.* . . . . The old-time shroud is now a *négligé* or *slumber-shirt* or *slumber-robe,* the mortician's work-truck is an *ambulance,* and the cemetery is . . . a *memorial-park.*[21]

It might be added that the installment buying of funerals is referred to as *Layaway Plans,* and in some instances as *Sunrise Plans.*

Some vocations, seeking to have their aura "stepped up," have been elegantly dressed up with "hifalutin" and presumably more dignified titles—for example, *mortician* for *undertaker, life underwriter* for *insurance agent, realtor* for *real estate agent, mason laborer* for *hod carrier, ecdysiast* for *strip-teaser, beautician* for *hair dresser, tonsorial artist* for *barber, landscape architect* for *gardener, sanitation man* for *garbage man, prostitute* or *lady of the evening* for *whore.* Somewhat related is the recent penchant for important-sounding, executive-type titles. The *janitor* is now an *engineer of sanitation;* the *usher* is an *audience guide,* the *dog-catcher* a *canine administrator;* a *supervisor of missing dogs* is an *animal controller,* or *officer in charge of dog law enforcement.*

There is an array of dry-cleaned terms for human physiological states, processes, and functions: *perspiration* for *sweat; intoxication, inebriation, under the influence of liquor,* or *being three sheets to the wind* for *drunkenness; expectoration* for *spit; throw up, regurgitate,* or *unswallow* for *vomit.* In English we have been put to it to find an acceptable designation for the *latrine.* We have called it variously the *privy,* the *water-closet,* the *lavatory,* the *bathroom,* the *rest room,* the *powder room* (or such jocular terms as *Heifer's Corral,* or *Little Boy's Room*). Our neighbors also use subterfuges. The Germans, for example, operating on the not uncommon principle that a foreign word does not have the same threat of indecency or unconventionality that a colloquial term does, get out of the difficulty by using French words: *pissoir, toilette, closet.* As far as the human body is concerned, it is more refined to have an *abdomen* than a *belly, limbs* instead of *legs, derrière* instead of *bottom, bosom* instead of *breasts, intestines* or *bowels* or *alimentary canal* instead of *guts, dentures* instead of *false teeth.*

We sometimes use "cold and clinical" or "antiseptic" or "scientific" terminology to refer to some taboo matter. A recent prize example, the use of which can be meaningful only to the well-informed, is the phrase "a therapeutic interruption of pregnancy," instead of the more offensive term "voluntary abortion." Also, *niacin* does not sound so bad for some people as *nicotinic acid.*

Almost every area of social life provides examples. The studied use of ambiguous or deceptive words in social-economic-political propaganda is called (by its users) *dialectical strategy.* When a nation engages in a war, or otherwise moves in on some other country or area, it is *a just war of liberation,* and its purpose is to *liberate* the conquered people. Conquest is a *rectification of frontiers.* The slave camps of torture are called *labor camps* or *reeducation camps. Relocation camp* seems to be nicer than *concentration camp.* An economic *depression* somehow isn't quite so bad if we call it *recession, readjustment, rolling adjustment, deflation* or even *disinflation.* Farm product *surpluses* become *excess reserves.* An *S. O. B.* in any department of life is not as bad as a *son of a bitch; for crying out loud* takes the blasphemic touch off *for Christ's sake,* nor is one who *veers from the truth* or is a *prevaricator* as reprehensible as a *liar.* It is not so disconcerting to be concerned about *human relations* as about *race relations,* or about *juvenile delinquents* as against *child criminals,* or about *senior citizens* as against *the aged.* And if one is still in a state of distraction as to how to control "naughty" words, he can forget it all more respectably in a *cocktail lounge* or even in a *tavern* than he can in a *saloon,* or he can get himself invited to a *canape party* or an *hors d'oeuvre party,* or he can mix his own *cheer* (or *poison*) with ingredients obtained at the *House of Bottles.*[22]

It should also be noted that words are used as rhetorical devices for speaking ill of something. This is called *dysphemism* or *cacophemism* and is illustrated when we call our clothes *duds,* a horse a *nag* or an *old plug,* a female member of the race a *bitch.* (On dysphemism, see Eric Partridge, *Slang Today and Yesterday* (London: Routledge & Kegan Paul, 1932), pp. 14–16.) There is also the resort to the peculiar sort of exorcism of attempting to make objectionable things disappear by giving them bad names; for example, when we call a troublemaker a *Bolshevik,* he may "shut up," and, in effect, disappear from the scene; or if we call one who is disrespectful of or misuses the property of others a *Communist,* he may mend his ways. An additional feature of linguistic taboo should also be noted—namely, the emotional "kick" which some persons seem to get from violating it, such as the sophisticate at a cocktail party, or some modern poet parading his "earthy realisms," or small boys inscribing "four-letter words" on sidewalks and walls.

c / The manipulation of oaths, profanity and expletives. Men everywhere have used curse words to give form and force to their malign wishes, and swear words to back up vows and establish veracity. We still retain some of the oaths, especially for solemn religious and political occasions, but both curses and oaths have their widest use in profanity and as expletives. While the original purpose or meaning of many of these long-standing formulae has often been forgotten, the terms themselves have been remembered and, because of their powerful original connections, men feel that they gain emphasis by using them, especially as expletives, to give forceful outlet to their emotions.

The most effective curses, oaths, and expletives involve the use of the names of God, saints, holy places, and also devils. But since the profane use of these words actually is blasphemy, or borders on blasphemy, the sinister effects of which must be avoided, oaths and profanity are among the forbidden categories of words in most social circles. However, like many other kinds of forbidden words, they are widely resorted to, but in toned-down, or disguised forms and this, it is felt by the users, makes them "safer." This is actually, of course, an extension of euphemism to another class of words. We have much of what Burges Johnson has aptly referred to as "bootleg profanity" or "Deaconic swearing."[23] For example, "Christopher Columbus!," the clergyman's expletive on the golf links, has all of the psychic intent and emotional force of profanity.

Hell is still used as a curse, as an expletive, and as a kind of bearing down. Some are told to "Go to Hell," but others are euphemistically informed to "Go to Blazes" or "Go to Halifax." In being forceful, I paid "a hell of a price," "raised hell" and refused with "Like hell I will!" Instead of the use of "God" as exclamation, we have *Gad, Gosh, Golly, Jove, Godfrey, Egad;* there are also such substitutes for "Lord" as *Lordy, Lawsy, Lawk* for Jesus, *Jeminy, Gee, Gee Whiz, Gee-willikens, Jeez,* and for *Christ, Cricky* or *Cripes.* Instead of coming out with a straight *Damn,* there is resort to *drat, blast, darn* and *dang.* In place of *Goddam,* there is *goldarn, doggone, consarn,* and *goshdarn.* And there are a thousand ingenious variations of all these.

d / The manipulation of "good words" for good ends. In the control of words for desired individual or social ends, we find among many peoples the proper manipulation of "good words," especially in the form of right verbal formulae: These, it is believed, if spoken or written, are powerful enough to keep evil away, to cure sickness, or bring good —"a bettering of facts"—to him who knows them and applies them. We frequently hear: "Say it, and bring it about!"[24] We tell the distressed or sick child that she is "a little angel"; the highly criticized property holder is eased by being called "an excellent citizen"; to make a place a "sanctuary" is enough to keep away the enemies or the devils.

e / The humorous use of language. Language is also used to make one laugh in certain kinds of situations. Not only jokes and funny stories, but such verbal tricks as puns, malapropisms, spoonerisms, childish speech, and other intentionally wrong forms or departures from standard language, or humorous and sometimes cleverly coined words and phrases, supply control outlets. They are effective because they make a double exposure on the mind. They are used in several ways: (1) To lighten or ease grave situations, or to serve as a means of surmounting restrictions. Thus a seasonal respiratory curse may be made slightly more endurable by referring to it as "the hay-fever sneason," and an upset stomach is easier to endure as the "colly-wobbles." Many euphemisms are more effective because of the humorous turn that they are given, for example, the humorous ways of referring to certain bodily functions or the places where these functions are exercised; the humorous ways of referring to the Devil, such as "Old Harry" and "Old Nick," or the reference to "Hell" as a "warm climate." (2) Humorous verbal creations may also be used to bring out, sometimes in biting fashion, certain special facets of meaning—for example, the term "the clique-claque principle," in reference to the fact that, in university faculties, there are often cliques, the members of which function as claques for each other, or an allusion to the United States Senate as "the cave of the winds." (3) A humorous term or phrase may also be used as a form of critical characterization—for example, the term "payola" or "goldbricker," or "He's not a singer, he's a vocalamity." (4) A sportive verbal construct may also be used as a concise and precise form of reference—for example *hobohemia*.

6. *Language in Dynamic Social Action*

Aware of the magical and pragmatic *power* that inheres in language (including names) we address ourselves in the remainder of this chapter to certain key aspects of language as a dynamic factor in social life. Of immediate significance is the fact that words and phrases and sentences and sequences of all these, properly used, function not only as guides to social action, but also as dynamos and engines. Men have long been aware of the effect-achieving impact of language.[25]

a / General aspects. Malinowski, in his classic treatment, stressed the fact that "Language is primarily an instrument of action, and not a means of telling a tale, of entertaining or instructing from a purely intellectual point of view." He concluded that "words in their primary and essential sense *do act, produce,* and *achieve,*" and pointed out that there are "two peaks" of the dynamism of words: "One is to be found in certain sacred uses, that is in magical formulae, sacramental utterances, exorcisms, curses and blessings, and most prayers." The second climax of speech dynamics is found in "the direct pragmatic effect of words."[26]

Most of what happens socially—that is, over and above a man's own limited fields of personal action, is mediated by language, incited and propelled by language, instructed and programmed by language, directed and controlled by language.

Language plays its pristine function of control in personal relations. In the relatively simple relationship of two persons with each other, one, by setting the verbal context of the verbal situation ("A fine morning," "Good to see you," "I'm terribly sorry"), creates the context of action, and not only permits but even compels complementary action, thus directly but not always voluntarily exercising power over the other.[27] More obvious is the use of language by one person as a deliberate means of manipulating the other person for his own personal ends: the servant by words and tones "using" the master, even though he may hate him; the student using polite expressions of flattery to secure a grade; the panhandler or beggar using sad or whining tones for a "handout"; the eight-year-old talking his mother into a dime for an ice-cream cone. In our conversations and letters, we try to impress on others our experiences, attitudes, feelings, beliefs and ideas; we make requests for services; we even try to "club" our respondents, by flattery, into meeting our commands and directives.

Right words, appropriate time-tested phrases, and more complexly organized forms of speech—the proper ritual verbalisms—are powerful agents of effective change in *social* action and interaction. By means of them, as Hayakawa has put it, ". . . we influence and to an enormous extent control human events." He continues: "It is for this reason that writers write; preachers preach; employers, parents and teachers scold; propagandists send out news releases; statesmen give addresses."[28]

Words may be used to shape people's beliefs, prejudices, fears, ideals, and aspirations. They are used to arouse wonder, indignation and horror. They are a profound means of influencing the thoughts of persons. They can stir the energies of persons and groups, and stimulate all manner of individual and social behavior. They are used in making pleas and requests for action. They are the instruments whereby men and their organizations issue their directives—informally and formally— to each other.

In our modern intercommunicating and interdependent world, there rages a "war of words," as various kinds of interest groups and authority groups devise and manipulate language to persuade, direct, mislead, confuse, exploit, enslave or regulate people. Especially significant is the "battle for men's minds" now being waged by the leading peoples and nations on the respective sides of the conflict between the world's two great opposing ideologies, as they seek to influence the beliefs, opinions, emotions, attitudes and actions of the opponents, the neutrals and the friendly groups.

Language is the basis of the operation of those major instruments of social order and efficiency, the social institutions. The institutions are, in effect, systems of traditional and recorded language. Education, for example, is the socialization and training of the individual, in large measure through language symbols. The public opinion and edicts and laws so important in government are partly a matter of language. Economic institutions function through stated plans, directives, contracts, and so on. The sacred books, the theologies, the traditions and rituals of religion would be nonexistent without language. In fact, much of the "institutionalization" of the forms of social control in all of the departments of social life consists in the rather precise statement, and thus the cultural establishment, of the values and purposes dominating the particular area of social action, the codes, the forms of structural and functional organization, the positional privileges, responsibilities and duties, directives and commands, and the penalties for disregard or infraction of institutional rules and required behavior.

Some of the more important types of social control will now be briefly examined.

b / The functional forms in person-to-person control. Persons use words with various connotative and emotional effects in their efforts to get other persons to act, or to refrain from acting, in certain ways deemed desirable or undesirable by the utterer. Most of these, of course,

can also be (and are) used by groups. Persons control each other by
praise, that is, by "expressions of hearty approval in sincere and appropriate terms."[29] We praise each other as an expectation of some
future behavior favorable to ourselves—by oral and written language,
in face-to-face speech, and by letter and printed page. What many
people of a community praise is the expression of a reigning value and
a desired goal of behavior. Such, for example, are evidenced by means of
inscriptions (including epitaphs), testimonials, resolutions.

We also control each other by means of *flattery,* that is, by "artful
commendation or compliments, by heaping up exaggerated tributes, by
offering unreasoning and undeserved praise," in brief, by "laying it on
thick," by praising gone "on the loose."[30] To control others by
flattery, we make exaggerated compliments, endure unjustified or in-
temperate criticisms or even profanity directed against us, avoid giving
and accepting annoying advice, listen with an air of eagerness to the
"golden" (and other) words of the person being flattered, abuse and
ridicule his rivals—in general, produce "sweet-sounding words" for the
person being controlled.

Gossip, the deliberate peddling of pestilential items about another
by word of mouth or in written or printed form, is another widely used
means of manipulating others. It enhances the variety and, by contrast,
the self-esteem of the gossiper; it enables him, in a vicious but highly
effective way, to intimidate and hurt his victim and to gain some revenge over him. It also, however, serves in some measure to prevent
departures from the accepted social code, for the juiciest subject matter
of the gossips is usually reputed departures from the norms.

Satire is the mixture of humorous review *and* criticism of the ways
of another; it requires a degree of artistry if it is to be used effectively.
The material is the foibles or faults of the person satirized, which are
depicted in a humorous, ironic or fantastic way. It succeeds because
people fear ridicule.

The *threat,* most often in the form of a verbal expression of an intention or determination to inflict injury upon or bring harm or deprivation to another, is used to proscribe or prescribe certain action for
others. The threat usually contains reference to some form of punishment for the nonconformist.

c / Functional forms in collective control. The linguistic forms used in
the control of people as individuals, groups and masses may be classified
as to those which are socioculturally (1) *unorganized,* that is, not drawn
up by and for the use of organizations, and (2) *organized,* that is, those

which are so drawn up. They may also be categorized on the basis of their social-control functions—that is, as to whether they are to effect social regulation and maintenance in the interests of order and well-being, or are to be used for social exploitative or predatory purposes. These two major categories will overlap somewhat in our present treatment.

[1] *Some historical organized forms, especially proverbs.* Before discussing the linguistic forms used in the more formally organized controls of modern advanced societies, we wish to note briefly that preliterate and prescientific societies had devices such as myths, legends, stories, songs, parables, sayings, admonitions, mottoes, aphorisms and proverbs to state and perpetuate their values and goals, and to indicate and prescribe the directives for getting them into action. Each form is important both linguistically and sociologically. However, of these, the proverb has been especially important as a verbal controlling device. It is ancient and has been well-nigh universal; it has been largely superseded by other control forms of modern societies, but is by no means extinct or useless.

In proverbs, we have traditional observations of popular origin about human reactions to different kinds of situations, these observations being based on long folk experience and discussion. They are condensed language forms: the facts and principles are presented in short sentences, often in quaint or striking figurative, pithy, even pungent form. They have been referred to as "nuggets of wisdom" and "capsular knowledge." Cervantes defined a proverb as "a short sentence drawn from long experience."

Proverbs are widely accepted group definitions of typical human and social situations. They reflect the values, the group morality, the attitudes, feelings, opinions, explanations, interpretations and life-goals of the people, as these have formed and crystallized through the centuries. They are so convenient, omnipresent, "pat" and true that they function as channelizers of beliefs and attitudes, and as substitutes for thought about different types of situations; they can thus even block new, fresh looks. Those who use proverbs extensively have their thinking both guided *and* confined by them, since they take away the necessity of individual generalization and explanation. Many go beyond mere individual responses in their suggestions and implications, and serve as important agencies both in voicing and in controlling public opinion; they are quoted to quell individual expressions of divergent opinion. What is especially important in the present context is that they usually imply an appropriately compliant belief, attitude or action; in many instances, they suggest formulae for action and perform as inciters to and controllers of action in the type of situation involved.

[2] *Important contemporary organized forms.* In modern societies like our own, social control for regulatory and maintenance purposes has become a highly organized matter, because the societies themselves are so complexly organized. The societies have huge populations; the relations of the people are largely of a secondary and impersonal nature; there is a vast division of labor; most cooperation is carried on by organizations; there is much social distance between population elements, arrayed at graded hierarchical levels, and much social and physical mobility. While the primary controls are by no means nonoperative, of necessity the secondary group controls—formally organized and organizationally established, maintained and enforced—play a greater and greater part in social action and social order.

These secondary controls are of many varieties and are mainly conducted by organizations. Each of the social-control procedures involves some particular kind of mastery of human relations, purposes and processes. Each type of control has its *special and essential form of discourse,* determined by its area of relations and the particular type of function to be effected. Among the different forms of special discourse for the purpose of influencing or controlling people through organizations are the language of the stated law and that of the judges and the law-enforcing agencies; the language of command, drill and giving orders; the language of instructions; the language of speakers to popular audiences; the language of debate in deliberative or public-informational assemblies; the language of leadership and officership; and the language of salesmanship, promotion and advertising.

Formal collective directive language. A category of central importance in the directing of human action in complex societies consists of those *formally stated* prescriptions, appearing along with collective sanctions, which try to impose standard patterns of behavior upon individuals and combinations of individuals, in the interests of the whole group. Such regulatory control language is found in the constitutions, the laws and rules, and the oaths of office of all sorts of organizations, including nations and their subdivisions; in the decisions of the courts and administrative bodies; in contracts and in marriage vows; in induction rituals, for example, the assumption of citizenship in a state, or of membership in an organization.[31]

These language forms are often solemnly stated in rather ponderous and intricate prose. They not only direct action, but also add effective connotations, because they are so weighted with social importance; they are often part of or are accompanied by ritual and ceremony; some are also accompanied by prayers, and include appeals to supernatural power ("So help me God!"). Almost all of them state requirements in the way of compliant behavior, which requires discipline on the part of the performer, and the violation of which brings censure and, in many instances, formal punishment.

The language of organizations. Organizations, as they conduct their maintenance and regulatory functions in their communities, use certain types of language in conducting the different types of activity essential to their effective and continuous operation. While this particular language has many different aspects (to be examined briefly in Chapter XIII), some of these have social-control significance—notably, the language used in giving clear-cut instructions and advice on the lines of action being pursued or to be pursued, or issuing orders, which is also a phase of the language of command and subordination (to be touched upon below). They are a form of directing and controlling action, since they point to accomplishment targets.

The language of command, obedience and subordination. A special form of language used in organizational control is the language of command and subordination. This language is also important in person-to-person control, for example, parental commanding, but it is mainly involved in the operation of organizations, especially those that conduct major institutionalized functions: political, military, economic, religious, educational. It shows its typical features most clearly in work and military organizations.

A command is given in a situation of crisis. This does not necessarily mean that the participants are confronted with catastrophe, but simply that something must be done immediately. The command is an expression of authority; it consists of an order to obey, to act in a certain way. Its purpose is to inhibit, halt or correct one line of action, and prepare the way for or initiate another. Dynamic response is thus anticipated; it is, in fact, the main reason for the command. The commander must be master of the situation; he must control or dominate.

The command itself must be given in a short, decisive and clarifying manner. In general, as Dubin points out, "The language of command tends to be highly precise, relatively impersonal, and effectively descriptive." He also notes that "it tends to be concise in its expression, and the symbols in which it is couched tend to be uniquely appropriate to the organization."[32]

The command always implies compliance—which is, in effect, subordination to the commander. The subordinates have their own language, which they use in communicating with their organization superiors. Says Dubin:

> This language of subordination is one of the most visible aspects of authority and status relations in work organizations. "Sir" and

"Mister" are common parts of the subordinate's language. Equally common are the attitudes of "speaking only when spoken to," and posture of rapt attention to the boss's words. Still obvious, but at the gestural level, are head nodding in automatic agreement, tensed bodily positions indicating obeisance, rising from a seat when the boss enters, or ceremonially following him in walking.[33]

The language of social movements. The effective development of social movements—especially social reform movements, social-economic-political revolutions, and dictatorships—depends in considerable part upon the use of appropriate language. This is apparent at each *stage* of development.[34] In the period of aggravation and incubation, there must be ever more clear-cut verbal formulation of the grievances and grounds for unrest and dissatisfaction. Otherwise the discontent never reaches expression as a unifying and marshaling force. In the period of initiation and discussion, there is the "speechifying" of the leaders, as they agitate, preach and harangue; the debate, pro and con; the circulation of promotional literature, including the movement's own journals and pamphlets; the rallying-cries, incorporating slogans, mottoes and catchwords; the "fighting" words, directed against the opponents; and the language of the assemblies of the proponents of the movement. In the period of organization, the ideology must be stated with some specificity, and the policies, plans and program of action must be set forth in language which is precise as to statement and of appropriate functional form. In the final period of institutionalization, the principles of organization, the structure and functions of the agencies, and the rules of operation must be clearly stated in the constitution and by-laws, and in all instructional materials. The directives at the various levels of organization, and the other organizational procedures noted above in the language of organizations, must be appropriately stated. If it is a movement that turns into a new or sharply-revised political agency, there will be the necessity of developing a body of law, or an overhauling of the relevant portions of the existent law.

The uses of language in social movements are multiform. A few special ones can be mentioned, such as the elimination of derogatory terms (*nigger,* in civil rights movements); the development of special terms or meanings (*citizen,* in the French Revolution; *comrade,* in movements of socialism and communism); switching to a common language in a reformatory or nationalistic movement (administrative *German* by Luther in the early Reformation, *Gaelic* by the Irish, *Hebrew* by the Zionists).

One kind of social movement, which has become very prominent in our world during the past four decades, and must be touched upon here as a type for brief examination—namely, dictatorship—presents different uses of language, as dictators and their hangers-on attempt to control the public and maintain their power. Several prominent features will be briefly presented.

Most of the dictators-to-be and their followers have insinuated themselves and their ideologies and objectives into the people (their victims-to-be), by campaigns of inflammatory and fanatical speeches. For a year before he took over, Louis Napoleon conducted an intensive campaign of speechmaking. Millions of persons now living recall the demagogic orators of the dictatorships of the nineteen-thirties—notably, Hitler, Goebbels, Mussolini, Atatürk—who had been trained in the most psychologically proficient techniques of rabble-rousing and influencing all who could or had to listen through the controlled right of assembly and and controlled radio. The violent, almost hysterical, histrionics of Mussolini and Hitler are particularly to be remembered. More recently, we have had the performances of the "word-fighter" Castro in Cuba.

Most dictators, both while "on the rise" and after in power, have had wide resort to "intoxicating," emotion-charged words and phrases (which might be referred to as "Basket Phrases") as ready crystallizations of their ideologies and purposes. The appealing phrases have been a means of integrating the populations, and of advancing the national well-being—as they conceived it. All sought to use these as doubt-allaying slogans, as inciters to enthusiasm, and as a means of keeping group emotion at an evangelistic pitch.[35]

A special linguistic device, the grandiloquent *title,* whether assumed by the dictator or his clique or granted by his followers, has been widely demonstrated among dictators and dictatorships. These titles have made the dictator an almost mystical symbol of authority, leadership and national greatness; they have stimulated loyalty, focused allegiance and made childlike submission a joy as well as a duty. Thus Mussolini was "Il Duce" and Hitler "der Führer"; Kemal Atatürk in 1922 was given the title "Ghazi" (the Victorious), and later "Atatürk" (Chief Turk).

The control of public opinion—of all agencies of education, information, and mass communication—through the control of what is uttered, written or printed has long been a strategic social procedure of dictators. Modern dictators especially have completely controlled journalism, radio, cinema and television from personnel to output, in order to hold the people from within by selecting the thought materials at their disposal, by shaping their convictions and by keeping constant control over their emotions. Quite paradoxically, the greater literacy and more widespread reading habits of modern peoples—which are essential for the successful operation of a democracy—also enable the dictator to work his nefarious ways. Through a completely controlled and thoroughly propagandized press, he influences all who read or listen. Dictators also use catchwords to catch people, threatening slogans, derogatory "labels" for potential dissenters and, of course, edicts, orders, and so on.

Most dictatorships use *censorship,* which fundamentally consists of keeping out of the country, or of suppressing, any words or ideas that they do not wish the people to see or hear—words that might lead to doubt, suspicion or recalcitrance on the people's part. Meerloo has called attention to the fact that a sort of word-taboo exists and spreads under a dictatorship. Not only are certain words a burning brand in behalf of the dictator and his rule; there are others that may have wide appeal and may also have an explosive counterrevolutionary effect. He fears the appearance of such words—"free" and "freeing," words suggesting freedom, liberty, independence, self-sufficiency—and he tries to cut down their currency. He is possessed by a form of *logophobia* (the fear of words).[36]

Other governmental manipulation of language. As stated above at various points, there have been occasional efforts on the part of governments to control the language, or certain aspects of the language, that is used by the people of the country. A noteworthy recent development has been the marked revision of the spelling systems of several countries. Potter has pointed out that "Within living memory Sweden, Denmark, the Netherlands, Russia, and Czechoslovakia have made substantial changes in their official orthographies. The Ministry of Education at Prague even went so far as to prescribe rules of word order."[37] Several recent dictators have manipulated the writing systems. The Chinese system was greatly simplified under the direction of Sun Yat-sen after the revolution of 1911. Under the dictatorship of Mao Tse-tung, Mandarin Chinese (or Gwoyev, the Peking variety) is being given an alphabet to replace the numerous pictographic characters. In Turkey in 1928, Mustapha Kemal Atatürk replaced the Arabic alphabet and script, which had been in effect since the adoption of Mohammedanism by the Turks, with the Latin alphabet. He established its use by fiat, not only making instruction in it compulsory in the schools, but also reprinting every schoolbook and changing every public sign.

7. The Kit of Verbal Control Tools

In concluding this discussion of language in its relation to social control, we shall briefly describe some of the more common and widely used types of verbal-control devices used by individuals and groups to dominate, positively or negatively, other persons or groups. These special types of instrumental words and phrases, as they are used, control the "targets" (the recipients) in various ways. Some (the inciters) are mainly provocative–propulsive in effect, evoking emotion and leading to intended positive or negative action. Some exercise control by way of the state of exaltation they produce in those conditioned to them. Others (the destroyers) control through their destructive effects, or through the fear of destruction or harm effected by their use. As has been pointedly said, in this connection: "Words are weapons."[38] Still others (the neutralizers) control by withholding ideas, information or other inciters or exciters, by deliberately misinforming people or by lulling or bullying people into a state of apathy or ineptitude. Some of them may have several effects, depending upon the social context in which they are used. Some of them are occasionally used in combination, or alternately or sequentially to heighten the effect. However, the nature of each, as mainly used, will be concisely delineated as one of a rather formidable kit of verbal tools—long devised and long used—available for social-control purposes.

a / The inciters and destroyers. Many words are emotion-charged symbols. All sorts of emotional values—those related to love, sympathy and affection, on the one hand, and to hate, discriminatory attitudes, anger and pugnacity, on the other—are attached to them. Many also carry with them a body of myth, illusion and imagery. Words thus arouse emotional associations and stereotypes of beliefs and ideas; they function as powerful provocatives to emotion-loaded, belief-dominated action. What is more important at this point is that words and phrases are deliberately used to set off emotion, to bring positive or negative emotional responses, to provoke strife or efforts at retaliation, to induce or to propel to intense expenditure of energy, and so on.

Name-calling is one of the most widely used and most potent procedures in social control by words. Individuals and groups from time immemorial have called each other names, not only to evidence feeling states, but also to influence the others for good or ill. Name-calling, like many other verbal controllers, is intimately connected with word magic. If you call a person a "good" name, you feel that you have favored him; if you call him a "bad" name, you feel that you have hurt him. In either case, you wished to do it.

Names and phrases can be most appropriately categorized as *honorific* and *humilific*. (a) The honorific name or phrase usually implies that the recipient significantly conforms to some popularly developed value-judgment regarding a type of social relationship. It is intended to be complimentary, elevating, even exalting. We call the person "citizen," "hero," "savior," "thinker," "philanthropist," "pundit." The different names also advertise the values of those qualities and actions that the community stands by. A name that points to a "good" action constitutes a sort of beacon light for all affected in the particular conduct area. Names in general (in some measure, by their nature) suggest or incite to a relevant behavior. A good name has the effect of praise; it often gives the recipient a "lift" of personality; it is sought and fondly accepted by most. The principle recurs several times in the *Book of Proverbs,* the best known statement being: "A good name is rather to be chosen than riches."

Closely related to "good" names and phrases are the positively provocative "halo words"—those emotion-charged symbols arousing love and affection which "set up" the individual or group for patterned response: "Darling"; "Deutschland über Alles!"; "England for the Englishman"; "Great Benefactor."

(b) The humilific name implies that the target or the victim falls far short of important reigning values and conventions, and has engaged, or is about to be engaged, in reprehensible behavior. Humilific names —apparently much more widely resorted to than the honorific—are terms of disrespect, disgust, contempt, reproach, abuse, hatred, repudiation and vilification. They are intended to be derogatory, depreciatory, degrading, denigrating, often intimidating—even mentally, spiritually and socially hurtful. The victim is a "parasite," "coward," "traitor," "Red," "Communist," "trash," "Un-American," "Radical," "parlor pink," "heretic," "nigger-lover," "do-gooder," "egg-head," "warmonger." A form of named activity may be "socialism," "socialized medicine."

In our *Gesellschaft* society, humilific name-calling is particularly notable among groups, especially political, economic, religious and majority–minority groups.[39] In general, the more standard "bad names" are convenient, easy, readily available means of "whipping" your enemies or those you wish to hurt. Calling a "bad" name is often a form of revenge. The fear of a bad name is a potent factor in the behavior of persons: a bad name may bring a flood of gossip or other dishonoring notoriety. Everyone fears being the victim of vicious name-calling, whether it be done crudely or with suavity, for it is difficult to defend oneself against a "bad" name, however unjust it may be, and also to hound down the name-callers and throttle them. A "bad" name is something to be avoided and resisted. Among the widely used derogatory and abusive words and phrases are the "fighting words," the "poison words," the "smear words." Language in the form of opprobrious epithets and derogatory descriptive words and phrases is widely used as a means of "branding" or adversely labeling or stereotyping persons and objects, categories, groups and organizations, acts and incidents, ideas, beliefs and philosophies. Even more specifically, these language forms are used against other persons, individually and by categories and groups, to direct and canalize the feelings and sentiments of at least some portion of the community against them, and to foster prejudices and hostile attitudes—in short, to "hurt" the victims psychically and socially, and even to inspire antagonistic action directed against them.

Among these derogatory forms are the "fighting words," many of them unprintable. They consist of terms and phrases so full of contempt and hatred that, if the recipients fully understand their import and are in a position to respond, the utterance of the words almost automatically under the conventions invites, even requires, efforts of retaliation, physical or verbal, on their part. Many of the common epithets and invectives that are hurled at opponents—the verbal and written brickbats—are of this type. The term S. O. B.—even used in high places—is a notable example. The "poison words" ("nigger-lover," "white trash") are those whereby individuals or groups assassinate verbally those whom they fear or do not like; they constitute the fine art of smearing at its peak. There are also the "scold words," the *Schimpfworte* ("bureaucracy" and "bureaucratic," "anti-administration," "heathen"), the "hate words" ("boche," "scab"), and the words used in depreciating minorities ("mick," "kike," "heinie," "hunky," "wop," "chink," "greaser," "nigger"). Most of these words can set off action just as readily as a bull is set off by a red flag.[40]

The damaging effect upon the person against whom malicious and vicious language is visited is potentially so great that legal control is provided. The law of slander (derogatory speech) and the law of libel (derogatory writing) define such action and provide for redress through suit for damages.

All manner of special pleaders, propagandists, promoters and publicists, most demagogues, politicians and organization leaders, and all who fear, despise and hate other human beings, individually or as other categories and groups (and who is *not* included here in some respect?)—these people use such invectives as proven means of heightening the effect of their contempt and of vilifying those they fear and hate. They are powerful agencies in the exercise of "man's inhumanity to man."

Nonetheless, these derogatory verbal devices—indecent, brutal and unjust as many of them are—are usually warnings that certain kinds of behavior towards others are held to be improper or even antisocial. Many of them, as used, also consciously or unconsciously imply the desirability or necessity of mending their ways, on the part of those to whom they are addressed. Some, as has been noted, are tremendous in their potential dynamism.

In the United States, social and ethnic groups have coined innumerable derogatory terms and sayings to refer to other groups. A recent study uses the term "ethnophaulisms," derived from the Greek roots meaning to disparage an ethnic group, a term originally developed by A. A. Roback to refer to such terminology.[41] The author develops five cogent generalizations relating ethnophaulisms and ethnocentrism as evidenced in the United States, and concludes with the surmise that "ethnophaulisms are essential to the existence of such forms of ethnocentrism as chauvinism, pejorative stereotypes, scapegoats, segregation, and discrimination."[42]

b / The bamboozlers, tranquilizers, and neutralizers. Nietzsche suggested long ago that words can also be used as masks. Many words and phrases are used, or more accurately misused, to deceive people, to distort facts, to conceal intentions and purposes. Others are used to intoxicate, to hypnotize, to mystify people in order to manipulate them. Orators and demagogues, propagandists and publicists, advertisers and sellers, politicians and preachers utilize these exploitative forms.

[1] *There is the misuse of certain important words that have ambiguous meanings as variously used.* The same word, as Voltaire observed, does not always signify the same thing. Well-known words of this sort are "justice," "liberty," "freedom," "democracy," and "truth." Words and phrases such as these—fine in most of their connotations— can be deliberately and knowingly distorted, or invested with certain specialized or perverted meanings and associations, and manipulated as vehicles of confusion, misrepresentation, seduction and exploitation.[43]

Meerloo points out that most craft and professional jargons were originally intended to exercise a magic impression on laymen. He notes that modern scientists and technologists—and he might have especially stressed pseudo-scientists—devise or greedily accept magic words and phrases, sometimes imported from outside their area. These are used for a number of purposes, such as: (1) to mystify the ignorant, (2) to hide their lack of knowledge and their unsolved problems, and (3) to cover up their more personal and emotional involvements. To illustrate the latter point, he gives an example from psychology: "It is . . . more neutral to talk about libido than about sexual urge."[44] Mention might also be made of the use of "siblings" instead of "brothers and sisters." There is also the widespread use of modern sophisticated words to cover secrets —for example, by presidents and other governmental officials in press conferences, by corporation officials regarding corporate conditions, procedures and plans, by diplomats, by "brass" connected with research and use of atomic energy, and so on. Through words and names, some things are deliberately made more obscure, instead of clearer.

[2] *The use of language for misinformation.* Attention need only be called to the tendency, in fact the persistent practice, of all sorts of groups—gossips, cliques, majority and minority groups, competitive organizations, internal and worldwide ideological groups, nations and combinations of nations—in their vying with each other, to employ language in order to repress facts and suppress truth, to present deliberately misleading partial or "loaded" information so as to spread false doctrine, and to use stereotypes, illusions, myths and other distortions of knowledge as a means to misinform people and to confound their loyalties and convictions.

[3] *The language of concealment and defense.* Various groups and population elements have special languages, usually in the form of rather carefully artificed modifications of the standard language, actually amounting to sublanguages, the express purpose of which is to conceal from outsiders the intent of what they want to say to each other. Thus, "thieves' language" is the special argot whereby thieves conceal their ways and means of action, protect themselves from the public, and expedite their own exploitation of the public. Other criminal argots have similar masking functions. In commercial establishments, the detective ("store dick") and sales staff have special signs and nonstandard words to indicate suspected or actual pickpockets and shoplifters. Upper classes devise linguistic forms and mannerisms to distinguish themselves from the "common rabble." Some of the professions affect some terminology to enhance the mysteries of their craft. There is the solemn verbosity of lawyers and diplomats who thereby are able systematically to conceal their actual thoughts and feelings. In fact, prolixity is cultivated in the traditional language of diplomacy, the function there being to mask the direct clash of personality.

Some dentists, feeling themselves somewhat on the defensive scientifically as against regular medical practitioners, make a great show of highly technical medical (or pseudo-medical) terminology, quite incomprehensible to the hapless victim in the chair, in order to conceal their feeling of inferiority. There are those who have concluded that the occasional pompous verbiage of some philosophers and theologians is used to conceal their factual uncertainty.

Some of the languages of concealment do have favorable general social effects (for example, in criminal detection), but all of them are employed primarily in order to deceive others.

Secret languages are also used for purposes of defense and protection. Individuals and groups resort to "double talk" for such purposes. People may call others names as a way of defending themselves. As Ichheiser has pointed out, when a person calls another a "parasite" or a "swindler," he does not necessarily persecute or commit aggression, but is rather defending himself.[45] Other forms of linguistic action are used defensively. When individuals indulge in gossip, they are frequently drawing fire away from themselves; when they slander, they are often detracting attention from themselves to the presumed foibles of others; when they lie, they are trying to "get out from under"; when they use curse words or profanity, they are relieving self-tension. Groups sometimes use similar tactics for similar reasons.

[4] *The use of language in certain ways to lull, paralyze, or bully people into certain states desired by the manipulators.* Different techniques in using language and different linguistic forms are used. (a) *The monotonous repetition of words and phrases* has a paralyzing effect. Robert Owen said, "Never argue; repeat your assertions." (b) Conversely, there is the bullying effected by *noisemaking,* or what Meerloo calls "Magic-Shouting."[46] By the use of loudspeakers and amplifiers, with their loud noises, the illogicality of the words and sentences uttered over them is hidden, doubt and criticism are beaten down and the fear or hesitation of the shouters is evaded or masked. Many can remember the tactics of the Nazis—especially Hitler, Goebbels and Goering—and the Italian Fascists—especially Mussolini—in this regard: the shrieking at the people at frequent mass assemblies; the continual bombardment on the streets and in public places by public address systems going full blast; the shouting at prisoners and enemies as a prime weapon of intimidation. Mere loquacity on the part of individuals may reduce their listeners to victims. In general, under the pressure of repetition and shouting, in the case of large numbers of individuals, the mind submits; it escapes into apathy and empty conformity.

Closely related is (c) *the strategic use of silence*—the refusal to communicate—as a way of "cutting," or even excommunicating, the person or group to be hurt or disciplined. Even to sophisticates, silence and a refusal to respond are powerfully disconcerting, even threatening— sometimes more so than downright contradiction or denunciation.

Akin to the use of silence is (d) *the use of censorship*. It has been mentioned above as a device used by dictators, but it is a form of social control by means of language control, which is ancient—at least as old as Rome of the fifth century B.C.—and has existed in all known societies. It has prevailed wherever some person or group has been able to exercise some influence or authority in the situation over the transmission of communicative materials. Fundamentally, it consists of deleting or limiting the content of any medium of communication by those exercising some sphere of authority, informal or formal. It is a sort of forced mental isolation of the recipients, a control by deprivation of that which is objectionable for one reason or another to those who control the issuing of the information. To put it simply, censorship is an attempt to control potentially "bad" situations by keeping the related suggestion or fact-carrying symbols (mostly in the form of words) from the sensitive and susceptible listeners, readers, or viewers. Censorship levels today range from that exercised by individuals over other individuals (for example, by parents or teachers), through that exercised by cliques, vested interest and pressure groups, and almost all of the different kinds of institutional organizations (for example, economic, educational, religious), up to that exercised by the supreme governments, particularly in the administrative and military departments. It has come to be increasingly organized during the last four centuries.[47]

The witchery of words and phrases in beguiling, spellbinding or stampeding people is demonstrated in (e) *the use of catchwords and slogans* by agitators, politicians, religious persuaders, advertisers and all others who endeavor to catch the public. The *catchword*—"peace," "honor," "liberty," "prosperity," "economy," "home," "mother"—is usually a vague but emotionalized term which arouses emotion, thwarts reflection and replaces tiresome thinking. It has a "pushbutton" effect, like Pavlov's dogs secreting gastric juice at the sound of the bell. It discharges certain special feelings and sets off a given reaction associated with it.

The *slogan* is a *catchline*. It is a "trigger" or "catch" phrase that labels and stereotypes social objectives and definitions. It, too, functions as a stimulus to arouse known social attitudes and produce conditioned responses and, if repeated often enough, allays doubt, suspicion and criticism, and smothers or substitutes for independent thought. Some seem to have an almost hypnotic effect.

Lumley, in his classic analysis of slogans, has called attention to the characteristics of a good slogan: it is simple to understand, easy to remember, pleasant to repeat; it often has alliterative and rhythmic qualities; it is brief and easily repeated; it has aptness, is affirmative, and appeals to the curiosity, the sentiments, or man's love of a pun; finally, it appears to summarize a profound idea. Its use in advertising is widespread and well known.[48]

In the political area of life, slogans have been abundantly cultivated: "Liberty, Equality and Fraternity"; "Fifty-four forty or fight"; "Cape to Cairo"; "America for Americans"; "Restore the land to the landless"; "Make the World Safe for Democracy." The advertisers of the modern world, as everyone is aware, promote their wares in print, by radio and on the television screen, by slogans, as do social movements of all kinds and all sorts of organizations.

In general, catchwords and slogans are so widely resorted to because they are such effective means of getting people to "walk in step."[49]

N O T E S

1 Allport and de Laguna, four decades ago, asserted that the control of others rather than the desire to communicate was the chief cause of the origin and development of language. Floyd H. Allport, *Social Psychology* (Boston: Houghton Mifflin Co., 1924), pp. 193–194; Grace de Laguna, *Speech, Its Functions and Development* (New Haven: Yale University Press, 1927), p. 41.

2 Bronislaw Malinowski, *Coral Gardens and Their Magic* (New York: American Book Co., 1935), II, 54.

3 This list is largely from William Albig, *Modern Public Opinion* (New York: McGraw-Hill Book Co., 1956), p. 111.

4 From Elias T. Arenson, "Language and Semantics," in Joseph S. Roucek (ed.), *Social Control* (New York: D. Van Nostrand Co., 1956), pp. 223–239 (227).

5 This point has been suggested by Joost A. M. Meerloo, *Conversation and Communication: A Philosophical Inquiry into Language and Human Relations* (New York: International Universities Press, 1952), p. 62.

6 Arenson, *op. cit.*

7 Meerloo, p. 60.

8 Chap. III, Sect. 1.

9 The German term *ursprünglich* carries this meaning better than the English *primary*.

10 *John* 1:1–2. In the recently published *New English Bible,* this reads: "When all things began, the Word already was. The Word dwelt with God and what God was, the Word was. The Word, then, was with God at the beginning."

11 Edward Clodd, *Magic in Names and Other Things* (London: Chapman & Hall, 1920), pp. 50–51. See also Chap. VI, Sect. 4, above on "Names as Cultural Recordings."

12 Louis Adamic, *What's Your Name?* (New York: Harper and Brothers, 1942), p. 74.

13 Cf. Mario Pei, *The Story of Language* (Philadelphia: J. B. Lippincott & Co., 1949), p. 72.

14 Anselm L. Strauss, *Mirrors and Masks: The Search for Identity* (Glencoe, Ill.: Free Press, 1959), pp. 15–30.

15 John Lotz, "Linguistics," in Lynn White, Jr. (ed.), *Frontiers of Knowledge in the Study of Man* (New York: Harper & Brothers, 1956), pp. 207–231 (230–231).

16 Cf. the revealing article "Egos" in *Time Magazine*, Mar. 23, 1962, p. 73.

17 The changing of a "foreign" or "minority-group" name to one more like dominant group names—as an evidence of assimilation, and as an aid in upward social mobility—has been discussed. In either case, the change to a more prestigious name relieves the individual of sensitiveness, and often makes possible a wider and easier mingling with the majority.

18 On word-taboos among primitive people, see Robert M. Estrich and Hans Sperber, *Three Keys to Language* (New York: Rinehart, 1952), pp. 1–13. Note the following instance of word taboos among a tribal people: Malays dislike uttering the word *harimau*, or more commonly *rimau*, meaning "tiger." They believe that if the word is used by them during the daytime, it will be impressed upon the subconscious mind of the tiger, at that moment dreaming in the jungle. Thereafter, they consider that they will be in great danger from the animal, which will seek them out and kill them. "The Malays prefer to use fancy names such as *Tok Bĕlany* ("the striped prince") or *Si-Pudong* ("old hairy face"). . . . The village Malays that I met preferred the word *dia* ("he") or avoided mentioning the tiger directly by name." (A. Locke, *The Tigers of Trengganu* (New York: Charles Scribner's Sons, 1954), p. 162.)

19 It should be kept in mind that these sex or excremental functions are not obscene in themselves, for they are a normal part of living, and are generally subject to the solicitude of relatives or close friends or to ordinary inquiry from a physician. The determinant of obscenity lies in the attitudes and prudishness of the people.

20 Cf. Louise Pound, "American Euphemisms for Dying, Death, and Burial," *American Speech*, 11 (Oct. 1936), 195–202.

21 H. L. Mencken, *The American Language* (New York: Alfred A. Knopf, 1945), pp. 287–288.

22 This tabooing and these euphemisms *do* make communication about certain subjects less reprehensible, and hence easier, for many people who are sensitive to certain conventions and *mystiques*. Many euphemisms, however, are so specially veiled that only the well-initiated get their full import. Some also, as we will point out in Sect. 7 below, in effect produce deceptions by means of ambiguous words. It is important to note, with particular reference to Chap. XIV, that euphemisms are frequently employed as a test of class and taste, and hence as a basis for discrimination and selection or exclusion.

23 Burges Johnson, "The Oath Interjectional," in Charles B. Jennings, Nancy King and Marjorie Stevenson (eds.), *Weigh the Word* (New York: Harper & Brothers, 1957), pp. 133–138. The writer is indebted to this work for several points in the present paragraph.

24 In his analysis of the use of "good words," Irving J. Lee says: *"The mechanism takes this form:* to say the word is to bring about a new condition to change the make-up of the 'thing.' This magical change, widely sought in our society, may seem as the attempt in general to replace the *evil*, the *undesirable*, the *difficult*, the *useless*, the *dangerous*, the *negative*, the *painful*, by the "good" words, so that the statement will be assumed to make the thing better in itself as well as better in the attitudes of the listeners or hearers." (*Language Habits in Human Affairs* (New York: Harper & Brothers, 1941), p. 162.)

25 As Clifton Fadiman has put it: "Words are not only words. They are motors, often prime motors."

26 *Op. cit.*, pp. 52–53, 214.

27 Ernst Becker, "Socialization, Command of Performance, and Mental Illness," *American Journal of Sociology*, 67 (Mar., 1962), 494–506 (495, 497–498).

28 S. I. Hayakawa, *Language in Thought and Action* (New York: Harcourt, Brace & Co., 1949), pp. 100–101.

29 Fredrick E. Lumley, *Means of Social Control* (New York: The Century Co., 1925), pp. 56–80.
30 *Ibid.*, pp. 81–108.
31 Cf. Hayakawa, p. 106.
32 Robert Dubin, *The World of Work* (Englewood Cliffs, N. J.: Prentice-Hall, 1958), p. 345. See also Lumley, pp. 315–338.
33 *Ibid.*, p. 345.
34 For a sociological analysis of social movements see Joyce O. Hertzler, *Society in Action* (New York: Dryden Press, 1954), pp. 361–380; C. Wendell King, *Social Movements in the United States* (New York: Random House, 1956).
35 Incidentally, it might be noted that, in certain instances, not only did the charisma of the dictator enhance his words, but also, conversely, the mystical power of his "sacred utterances" added to his charisma.
36 Cf. Meerloo, *op. cit.*, p. 77. On the social control as exercised by some of the important dictators of history, see Joyce O. Hertzler, "Crises and Dictatorships," *American Sociological Review*, 5 (Apr., 1940), 157–168; Joyce O. Hertzler, "Totalitarian Ways of Life," in Joseph S. Roucek (ed.), *Social Control* (2nd ed.; Princeton, N. J.: D. Van Nostrand Co., 1956), pp. 525–544.
37 Simeon Potter, *Modern Linguistics* (London: Andre Deutsch, Ltd., 1957), pp. 162–163.
38 Everett C. and Helen M. Hughes, *Where People Meet: Ethnic and Racial Frontiers* (Glencoe, Ill.: Free Press, 1952), p. 139.
39 Says Meerloo, "Find a new label of vilification and you can fascinate huge masses of people. Propagandists and publicists are master craftsmen in coining magic names. Orators and demagogues exploit them." (*Op. cit.*, p. 75.)
40 For abundant American examples of derogatory and abusive terms, see H. L. Mencken, *op. cit.*, Supplement I, pp. 597–598, 673. See also F. W. Boardman, Jr., "Political Name Calling," *American Speech*, 15 (Dec., 1940), 353–356.
41 Erdman B. Palmore, " 'Ethnophaulisms' and Ethnocentrism," *American Journal of Sociology*, 67 (Jan., 1962), 442–445.
42 It should not be thought that ethnophaulisms, and what they mean in the way of ethnic and racial discrimination, are to be found only in the United States. They are an almost universal linguistic phenomenon, wherever ethnic contact and sharp ethnocentrism exist. Roback, in his *A Dictionary of International Slurs* (Cambridge, Mass.: Sci-Art Publishers, 1944) gives lists of ethnophaulisms from more than twenty-three different languages. (On the use of derogatory racial terminology, see Daniel Katz and Kenneth W. Braly, "Racial Prejudice and Racial Stereotypes," *Journal of Abnormal and Social Psychology*, 30 (July, 1935) 175–193; Daniel Katz and Kenneth W. Braly, "Verbal Stereotypes and Racial Prejudice," in Theodore M. Newcomb and Eugene L. Hartley (eds.), *Readings in Social Psychology* (New York: Henry Holt & Co., 1947), pp. 204–216.)
43 On such uses of "justice," "freedom," and "democracy," see David Spitz, *Patterns of Anti-Democratic Thought* (New York: The Macmillan Co., 1949), pp. 3–4.
44 *Op. cit.*, p. 75. Meerloo says that scientific words are also used to take away the magic and mystery of feelings and thoughts (pp. 75–76).
45 Gustav Ichheiser, "Structures and Dynamics of Personal Relations," *American Sociological Review*, 8 (June, 1943), 302–305 (304).
46 *Op. cit.*, pp. 108–110.
47 For an excellent treatment of modern censorship, see William Albig, *Modern Public Opinion* (New York: McGraw-Hill Book Co., 1956), pp. 235–258.
48 The writer recently saw the following catchlines in Germany: a soft-drink advertisement with "Für Leute von Heute," and a potato chip advertisement, "Knuspisch frisch für jeden Tisch."
49 On catchwords and slogans, see Lumley, pp. 158–184; Albig, pp. 103–104; Meerloo, pp. 97–99.

XII ❧ Social Differentiation and Linguistic Specialization in the Language Community: I. Theoretical Orientation; the Dialects

1. *The Place and Nature of the "Special" Languages*

Alongside the current tendency toward the increasing generalization and standardization—even stereotyping—of language is the equally significant fact that there is a growing tendency toward differentiation and specialization of speech forms and the development of sublanguages within many language communities. In brief, the general language is also spoken in a considerable number of ways for a considerable number of well-determined sociological reasons.[1]

In the light of the astounding variations and divergences that occur, one may speak of the "worlds of words" within a language. Each language has its own Tower of Babel. The different geographical areas—even in modern mass societies, with their ready physical mobility and universality of communication—still have their peculiarities of vocabulary, pronunciation and idiom. Almost every category of persons, and almost every social group or other subsection of society, whether out of particular interest or special function, or other special circumstance, has some individuality of terminology, phrasing and articulation in its intra-group, inter-member communication. The range is from a secret term or two used by a pair or by the members of a simple friendship clique, through the "special" languages of families and households, the different economic and social segments of the population—the language of the drawing room, the middle classes, the tenement districts; of age groups—for example, "teenagers" and sex groups; of the "half-world" and underworld; of the many diverse crafts and professions and of the specialized functionaries of institutionally organized activities—the sciences and technologies; business, commerce and industry; advertising and journalism; the Church, its theology and ecclesiastical orders; medicine and the physicians; the law, the courts and the legal profession; politicians and political parties; the educators; bureaucracies and bureaucrats in every area of organized activity—of the art world, the stage, the sports and their devotees; of "hobby-riders"; of some of the fraternal orders, students, war and the military, ideological groups. There would seem to be almost as many subforms of language as there are subgroupings within modern society.

All these special skeletal languages or sublanguages (or subcultural languages, as they are variously referred to) are in some significant (though not always profound) aspect departures from, or in certain respects specialized modifications of, "standard" language. They sometimes differ so much among themselves that we as individuals may know one or a few of them quite well, and yet know almost nothing of others. In brief, some are not only unintelligible, but are also without interest to outsiders; most are readily comprehensible only to the initiated; some, as we will note, are intended to be "secret."

These specialties are not independent languages, but rather specialized adaptations of the standard words, with their standard definitions and assigned meanings, that are part of the general or base language system of the community. They are special currents in the main stream of language. None of the "special" languages can exist by themselves, without the nourishing stem of the general language of everyday life; they are based upon and utilize the framework of the larger society's language. They must use the modes of word formation, the general grammatical structure, the phonetics, the vocabulary and the semantics of the language of the whole community. The standard language tends to keep the "special" languages from "going overboard" in their development of eccentricities and neologisms. Too great a departure from it means that the special language becomes incapable of conveying meanings, even for its speakers.

2. *Mainly a Characteristic of Complex Societies: Historical Trends*

There have been some "specials" at all levels of civilization and at all times, particularly the areal dialects, the family and clan lingoes, those of the sex and the age groups, and those of certain recurrent "professional" functionaries, such as magicians, medicine men, priests. But the great diversity and volume of specials is a phenomenon of modern, complex societies.

Societies with small populations and a low technological level—such as food-gathering societies, simple agricultural societies, or societies in which the social systems are relatively lacking in social and cultural inequalities—these societies usually have a single pattern of speech with only minor speech variations, mainly in the choice of words, tone, and style of delivery, and these are merely a matter of individual eccentricity in the use of the common language. But when pastoral and agricultural societies appeared, with socioeconomic systems of the kind that flowered in later Neolithic and subsequent times, they were characterized by larger populations, social inequalities, pronounced social stratification, some group specialization of labor, and urban–rural distinctions. With these societies came a very considerable divergence of speech forms within the speech community.

The great quantity of special-group sublanguages in a society, however, is characteristic of the complex societies of recent times, with their vast division of labor, multiplication of special interests and specialization of function. The ever more differentiated segments of the population, persons in the multiplying institutionalized areas of societal life, the ever increasing and diversifying special categories of technicians, scientists, organizational functionaries and devotees of special and new foci of interests, do have—must have—their own precise forms of discourse for denotative, descriptive and operative purposes. This means, especially, that the technical argots and jargons and the special languages of organizations have proliferated *in kind* and *in number* among the areas of interest and activity in which they are employed.

3. *The Major Types of Special Languages*

The various types of "special languages," or differentiated sets of speech forms and usages, correspond to the different structural–functional forms of social groups and categories of the population of the language community or nation. Each autonomous grouping and each category of the population with distinctive interests and functions has something in the way of special identifying language forms. It is natural that something as fundamental as language should be a sort of analog of the variety and totality of characteristics that constitute the individuality of each group and functional category of persons. Both the groups and the correlated special languages can be variously classified. A sociologically and linguistically useful general categorization involves the distinction between the horizontal and vertical "special languages."[2]

The *horizontal specials* are those of the different geographic areas— regions and localities within the regions. The population elements, with their particular sociocultural characteristics, are distinguished from each other by their different locations on the land surface of the general domain, and by their special functions in ecological relations. We shall examine, as major examples of horizontal or areal "specials," the dialects of different localities and regions, and the somewhat differentiated rural and urban speech forms.

The *vertically* divided specialisms are those of different groupings and categories within a given area. These are the special language forms and usages of the different biosocial groups, the ethnic groups within the larger area, the different crafts, professions and callings, groups with particular knowledge, the different institutional organizations and functionaries, groups that are ideologically secret or socially deviant, segregated or otherwise special-interest or specially constituted, or of specially functional social groups that are distinguished from each other by vertical lines of separation and functional diversification.

A very important third category of special languages consists of *those of the different social layers or levels of the population as arrayed in vertical social space*—the specialties corresponding to the stratification system of the society. This stratification system is a fact of profound sociological and linguistic importance. In the United States, as elsewhere, language reflects class distinctions and is used to maintain such distinctions.

The array of special languages to be examined will be functionally classified under these three general categories and then briefly analyzed as to their structural–functional place in the social system, their characteristic forms, their major social functions and social effects, and the trends regarding their increased or declining usage and significance.

4. *The Language Forms at the Different Levels of Usage*

Before we go into a more detailed analysis of the social nature and function of the more important varieties of special languages within a society, it is desirable to keep in mind the distinction, not always clear in discussions of different linguistic forms, between (1) the different types of areal, special-interest, and special-function group forms and usages, in some instances amounting to sublanguages and "marginal" languages, on the one hand, and on the other, (2) the speech forms that constitute different levels and variants of correctness and quality.

In this section, we shall briefly note certain generally used structural–functional forms of any language, which, in the main, constitute some departure from what is deemed to be standard or correct. They reflect levels of usage of a language. They may be involved in both the horizontal (dialect) and vertical (special-group) "specials," and also in the speech forms of the different social strata.

Vernacular speech, as distinct particularly from literary language, is "everyday speech"—"familiar English," to use Partridge's term—spoken in the common, repeated relationships of people and in the conduct of the widely shared activities of life. It is the sort of language that almost all of us use when we go shopping, talk to the neighbor across the hedge, ride the bus, or talk to the furnace repairman or to the teller in the bank. Most significantly, it is the form of speech transmitted by parents to children, the form used in the home and the local peer group, the language of "culture as it is lived."[3]

Vulgarisms, found in all languages, but by no means resorted to by the entire population, are expressions decidedly incorrect and in bad taste. Their use is a mark of ignorance, low breeding or deliberate salaciousness. Partridge has distinguished between two kinds of vulgarisms: "(1) *illiteracies,* that is, words and phrases used only by the illiterate and used incorrectly; and (2) *low language,* which consists of expressions avoided by the polite and decent, at least in polite or decent company."[4]

Colloquialisms are, in the main, an aspect of the vernacular. They are expressions which, while not usually accepted as standard speech, and below the literary grade, are yet above slang, far above cant, and stand altogether apart from vulgarisms. Perhaps the most pointed feature of colloquial speech is that it is not "dignified" but informal, an "old shoe" sort of expression considered appropriate to familiar conversation, but generally avoided by cultivated persons in formal writing and in public and formal speaking. Some of the speech employed in the family, among good friends, and on ordinary occasions, even among educated people, includes colloquialisms. Colloquial speech varies greatly from class to class, group to group, family to family, and individual to individual; it even varies according to the persons being addressed. In general, colloquial speech is simpler in syntax than standard speech, occasionally uses words which are local or otherwise "special," and has more unconventional pronunciation and enunciation.[5] Slang words frequently rise to the rank of colloquialisms.

Slang is a very ancient and apparently universal phenomenon of psychological and social as well as linguistic pertinence. It is language below the level of formal correctness of standard educated speech, appearing in both vernacular and literary language forms. In the primary sense, it denotes expressions that are viewed by the guardians of "correct" speech as inelegant or exaggerated in their imagery, unconventionality and grotesqueness, or as less respectable forms current among the coarser, ruder or more eccentric parts of the community. As the prodigious breeder, not only of many colloquialisms, but also (as history shows) of many words and phrases that continually revivify and expand standard language, it merits more attention than has been given to the other below-standard speech forms.

The most distinctive feature of slang as a special form of expression is that it owes its origin to the creative urge, and its use to the desire to break away from the commonplace, the stiff or stuffy, the drab or trite, as imposed on us by the conventional community. Slang is always innovative, always a manifestation of the sense for novelty in the psyche of a people, always new, non-standard expression showing originality of terminology and phrasing. It consists, concretely, of newly contrived words and figures of speech (most of them produced for their own sake, but some as substitutes for tabooed words), of reconstructed and sometimes mutilated or misapplied old words, and of current words and phrases employed in some new special sense. There is a wide resort to metaphor—that is, the use of one idea or image to point to another.[6]

In our society, slang is a cosmopolitan matter, in both emergence and usage. It comes into being in considerable part by a sort of "spontaneous generation," from all levels of society and many of the different cultural types of the population: from the cants of the half-world (for example, circus folks and hoboes) and the underworld, from the jargons of the crafts, from teenagers and college students, from the stage, from sports (including middle- and upper-class golf, for example, *nineteenth hole,* to *stymie*), from journalism, from radio and television gag writers, from minority ethnic groups. Some of it starts in the linguistic ingenuity and whimsicality of one individual—Walter Winchell, G. B. Shaw, Ring Lardner. It is common to, or at least understood by, the vast majority of the population, and used, in varying degree and circumstances, by most of the population.

Slang seems to appear for a variety of social, psychological and social-psychological reasons. Sumner long ago suggested that slang was a sign of the flexibility and exuberance of a people, when he said: "A people who are prosperous and happy, optimistic and progressive, will produce much slang. It is a case of play. They amuse themselves with language."[7] Roback hints that some find in it an outlet for their rebelliousness;[8] the slang of teenagers and of some college students, or some of the half-world and underworld, is a protest against the restraints imposed by formality and convention. Especially significant is the fact that some of it fills real communicative needs: it brings to light delicate nuances for which the standard tongue has no mode of expression; it provides a metaphorical name for an object or concept that is new to the generality of people (for example, *ghost-writer*); it gives many people concreteness for the abstract and earthiness for the idealistic; it provides escape from clichés and longwindedness, and it breaks up the monotony of too formalized a discourse (for example, a classroom lecture is frequently relieved by a slang word or phrase). As Carl Sandburg put it, "slang is language that takes off its coat, spits on its hands, and goes to work."

Slang tends to satisfy a number of emotional and intellectual needs of individuals: as an expression of sheer high spirits—just for the fun of it (language, according to Jespersen, as "linguistic exuberance"); as "linguistic sport and luxury"; as an exercise in wit or humor— slang as "jesting language" with humorous (*old soak*) or facetious (*gink* or *bird* for man) connotations; to be picturesque, startling, sparkling, vigorous, pungent, tangy in expression, even at the cost of inexactitude. The unconventional phrase is an occasional form of relaxation. In relations with others, it helps, under certain circumstances, to reduce solemnity, pain or tragedy; like colloquialisms, it eases the way for smoother social contacts, by putting the speaker in tune with his companions and inducing a sense of friendliness and intimacy.[9]

By no means least is the fact that much slang has real social utility. It is forever changing, continually adapting itself, providing new and often illuminating words and phrases suited to the occasion or to the questions of the moment. In some of its forms, it has been an effective instrument in social control, being used for exalting or lampooning persons and events. In fact, it reveals much of what is going on, especially with respect to the various groups that are in some way affecting our society at a given time.[10]

Of great social importance is the fact that it meets the necessity for frequently renewing the vocabulary of a rapidly changing society, if communication is to be efficient and adequate. To be sure, its expressions do not at first appear in the dictionary. Furthermore, as with many other innovations, much of it is ephemeral: thousands of its creations recede and vanish. But in spite of the high mortality rate, slang (along with dialects and scientific technological jargons) is one of the major sources of new language. Its terms get into the colloquial language and then into the dictionary, and in time are accepted as good usage. Surprisingly much of standard language has evolved through slang, in richness, in variety and appropriateness of terms and forms, and in greater lexical and semantic proficiency. Says Mencken of slang, in this connection: "It is, in fact, the most powerful of all stimulants that keep language alive and growing."[11]

Many expressions that we now accept as eminently "correct" can be dated by decades or even by centuries as slang. Few people, for example, are aware that such terms as *methinks, encroach, purport, subject matter, workmanship, selfsame* were once slang, and attacked as such. Even slang terms of lowly social origin—from criminals, the lower classes, the humbler occupations, the back country, minority ethnic groups—as well as items which have been deemed vulgarisms, in time and under the proper circumstances (which will make the terms apt and revealing expressions) will seep upward by a sort of capillary attraction and survive as respectable colloquialisms, having become "standard" and permanent, even "literary."

Slang is of ever-increasing importance in our country. Its production and its inclusion in our American English has probably achieved the ultimate in linguistic swiftness. Moreover, while some of our slang is highly local or of groups, increasingly much of it comes to be language-wide during its vogue. These situations rest, of course, on the all-pervasiveness and universality of modern communication.

A *patois* is a distinctly illiterate speech belonging to the lower classes. Those who speak the *patois* understand the cultural form of the general language, but speak only its special form. The kind of English spoken by former Negro slaves in the United States, or the present "French" spoken by the Negro peasantry of Haiti, are instances of this.

5. *The Horizontally Differentiated Special Languages*

The horizontal special languages consist of, first, the regional and local-ity dialects, and, second, the rural–urban distinctions.

a / Dialects.

[1] *The nature of dialects.* Dialects are variant forms of the com-mon language, usually limited to particular geographical areas of the community. Specifically, they are *areal* linguistic specialisms of the larger community. The examination of language by areas has come to be a subject of profound importance. In fact, the social linguists now have the term "linguistic geography" or "geographical linguistics," to refer to the branch of linguistics devoted to the distribution and arrangement of languages throughout the earth. An important endeavor of the lin-guistic geographers is the field study of dialects ("dialect geography"). These investigators develop *dialect maps,* on which the approximate boundaries of the adjacent dialects of the larger community are de-lineated by lines known as isoglosses.[12] These boundaries are drawn on the basis of criteria of difference which involve such readily determin-able aspects of dialect speech as the dominance of particular words and certain pronunciations and intonations. In some instances, students of dialects have developed "dialect grammars" and "dialect dictionaries."

Dialects reflect one important aspect of the fact that, when the geo-graphical distribution of language forms is plotted, they fall into more or less definite spatial patterns and denote "linguistic areas."[13]

There can be no absolutely clearcut line between varieties of dialect speech. There is always a penumbral area along the isoglosses, where there is "borrowing across the border" and the adjoining dialects blend with each other. Furthermore, dialect boundaries are continually shift-ing and fluctuating.

In general, however, each dialect usually corresponds to a given territory and to most of its given population. The variations of dialectal forms may range from purely local to regional manifestations. The dia-lects themselves deviate from the norm of the language in distinctive peculiarities of vocabulary and idiom (word usage), accent, intona-tion and pronunciation, and usually only limited difference of gram-matical forms. In most language communities, dialects do not differ so much from each other as to be unintelligible to the speakers of other dialects.[14]

Dialects are confined to the vernacular and are chiefly oral and orally transmitted. They do not enter into the standard written language of the community, except in poetry, plays, short stories and novels depicting regional situations, or in the direct reporting of conversations.

[2] *Historical factors in the formation and maintenance of dialects.* A dialect is a variety of a language which arises from peculiar local or regional conditions and historical circumstances. Perhaps the most important general fact is that dialects are the product of *isolation,* physical and social. Physical isolation may be due to geographical barriers, such as forests, mountains, deserts or bodies of water, although bodies of water, even in the days of primitive water transportation, also encouraged contact and linguistic uniformation.[15] Social barriers (such as political-administrative boundaries, colonial isolation, political restrictions on travel), technological or traditional factors which restrain physical mobility, or sharp class or caste distinctions which tend to separate the strata of the population socially from one another, have also been potent factors. Predominance of rural life is almost universally a factor in the maintenance of dialects; they are stronger among people who cling more closely to the soil than among those who engage in urban occupations, in trade and commerce, and so on. Length of settlement has also been an important maintenance factor: those sections of the United States, for instance, that have been settled the longest have had the most distinctive speechways. In more recent times, the fact that educational facilities are not available over the entire area of the community, or are not equally accessible to all classes and all ethnic elements of the population, has been one of the most significant factors in the retaining of speech localisms and regionalisms.

In the United States, dialects of the different localities and regions have also been affected by the European places of origin of the original colonial settlers, and later of the immigrant stocks (English in New England, French in the South, Spanish in the Southwest, German, Scandinavian, Italian, and so on, in the Central states); the presence of certain racial elements (Negroes in the South, Indians in the West); the major types of industry carried on (the lumbering country, the "cow country"); deliberate social isolation (for example, Pennsylvania "Dutch" and other "hard-shell" religious groups); in some instances, by seemingly deliberate social affectation (for example, "Brooklynese," as against the speech of the rest of New York City).[16]

[3] *Sociocultural significance of dialects and trends affecting dialects.* As Sapir pointed out, no known language, unless it was artificially preserved for liturgical or other non-popular uses, has ever been known to resist the tendency to split up into dialects.[17] His own linguistic

"drift" occurring among a physically isolated body of speakers, the contacts in the area with other ethnic elements, the necessity of developing technical and other special terminology and semantics for successful living in the area, the peculiar contacts and conditions produced by barter and trade, internal political conditions, exogamic marriage, and war, as these have affected the people of the given area, have been factors.

Equally significant, and by no means inconsistent with the above, is another general fact—namely that, when a community has been cut up into a large number of dialects, there is a tendency for one of the local dialects to become accepted as the favored or desired form of speech within the larger linguistic community.[18] The economic and political dominance of the speakers of the ascendant dialect, their greater cultural prestige, and other similar factors have been influential. This approved local dialect became the symbol of cultural values, and spread at the expense of the local forms of speech. It functioned as the *primary* language of the larger area, its former fellow dialects now being considered as *secondary* forms of speech.

Closely related to this is the quite general contention among linguists that most "standard" languages are direct developments from particular dialects of former languages.

Historically, dialect has been the medium, and perhaps also the symbol, of the culture of the people in a larger community or nation. Dialect has been the inimitable ingredient, a distinguishing aspect of the ballads, tales, myths, and whimsies of the people.[19] When dialect disappears, for one reason or another, much of the folk culture also disappears.

Dialect has certain sociologically significant relationships to the class structure of a community. In the first place, the upper classes, while often committed to the use of upper-class jargons as prestige symbols, are decidedly lesser reflectors of the dialects of their locality or region. As a general rule, they approach the standard speech of the greater language community, whenever any care in speaking is indicated. Upper-class Southerners do not use Negro or "Cracker" dialect, nor do upper-class New Yorkers use "Brooklynese." Conversely, the lower classes—with less or no formal education, little or no outside or literate culture contact and, usually (except for a few occupations) less physical mobility—use dialect continually and in concentrated form. Dialects have, in fact, been mainly a function of the lower social strata.[20]

At the same time, in most countries in the past, it has been necessary for the upper classes to be practically plural lingual. They have used the standard language for formal purposes (literature, religion, correspondence, public addresses), but employed the local dialect for more familiar uses among themselves, and especially for communication with the lower classes.

As in the past, we have in the modern world some instances of the breaking up of a major language into many dialects, with the increase of political nationalism among its speakers. Laird presents a signal instance. In Central and South America and in the West Indies, the fact that Spanish is rapidly breaking up into dialects is greatly impairing Latin-American unity. There has been some endeavor to stem the movement by teaching Castilian Spanish in the schools, but Laird concludes that Spanish will continue to break up until the Latin Americans have enough political, commercial, and social community to stop the trend.[21]

In the main, however, in the large, populous, technologically advanced, politically integrated and urbanized countries of the world, there has been a tendency for dialects to weaken and to grow fewer. It is unlikely that dialects and localisms will disappear, but they have less and less utility, and are being pushed farther and farther into the background. In the United States, we still have the persistence of certain kinds of localisms,[22] but dialects are withering. In France standard French, and in Great Britain standard English, have succeeded most of the dialects, leaving only a few unassimilated areas of non-standard speech, the holdout languages in France being Provençal, Basque, Breton, Alemannic German and Flemish, and in England, Welsh and Scots Gaelic.

The shrinking of dialects is due to an increasing number of ever more potent factors, which are causing all spatial sections and all population segments increasingly to employ "standard" language—or, in the case of the United States, what Mencken called "General American." These factors are of a social-economic, technological, political and educational nature, and have been presented in some detail in Chapter VIII, Section 3. By means of these factors there has been a great weakening of regional social and cultural isolation.

The ever more persistent effect of these factors is to bring about a "homogenization" of speech in the United States and countries like it. John Steinbeck, in his book recording his observations on a tour across the northern tier of states, down the Pacific Coast, across the southern bottom, and then up the Atlantic Seaboard, says: "It seemed to me that regional speech is in process of disappearing. . . . Just as our bread, mixed and baked, packaged and sold without benefit of accident or human frailty, is uniformly good and uniformly tasteless, so will our speech become one speech."[23]

It would seem that, if a country of the modern world wished to maintain its dialects, it would have to meet the following conditions: (1) have a sedentary and economically and politically self-sufficient population in all areas; (2) avoid the development of all means and agencies of modern transportation; (3) withhold general public schooling and foster illiteracy; (4) exclude all segments of the population from the influences of mass communication.

b / Rural–urban differentiation. For some 7000 years, since cities began, societies with cities have distinguished between the rural and urban portions of their area, as well as between the categories of persons occupying the respective portions of the area. In so far as this is an areal distinction of people, it is not based on region or locality as such, but on rural versus urban residence and activities in the whole language community, and also within its regions and lesser geographic areas. The occupants of the rural and urban areas have always had something in the way of speech specialisms, which have rested fundamentally on the composition and the ways of life of the respective populations. The urban population is usually more heterogeneous as to ethnicity, economic features, occupations, social strata, education and religion. Consequently, almost every kind of language specialism can be found in at least a large city, and few of these can be designated in themselves as characteristically urban. The rural population in most communities, on the other hand, is usually ethnically more homogeneous, although not necessarily from community to community over wide areas; social–economic class spread and variation is usually less, although here too there are glaring exceptions; educational facilities have been poorer in quality, and have offered less variety of educational opportunities. Most important of all has been the fact that most people in rural communities have had a common and homogeneous way of life, built around agriculture. In fact, the rural population, which is generally thought of as consisting largely of agriculturists, could also be looked upon as an occupational group, with some features of their linguistic specialisms determined by their special occupation. This agricultural way of life historically caused the people to live in greater spatial isolation. Their life was more static and uniform, and less susceptible to the factors making for change and diversification. In most respects, rural people have been more conservative in the values they have adhered to, their attitudes toward change, their institutional life.

These facets of the rural way of life have affected the language of the people. In fact, many urbanites (who are rarely students of linguistics) think that they can detect a ruralite by his speech, both in what he talks about, and how he says it (grammatical forms, pronunciation, vocabulary).

The characteristic talk is largely concerned with agriculture and, as such, with nature—especially land, the seasons and the weather—with crops and livestock, the daily routines, planting and harvesting. Urbanites and ruralites often have different terms for the same things or occurrences.

The city dweller everywhere is unlikely to know the taboos of farm life—that the *bull, ram, stud,* and *boar* are rarely called by those names among farmers and almost never when women are present. And if he (the city dweller) speaks of castrating animals, the urbanite will usually say *castrate* (or possibly *geld*), never *cut, change,* or *alter.* Many city dwellers have even said that they thought a boar was an entirely different animal from a *hog.* And only a person who had had some experience with animals would certainly know what a *shote* is, or would refrain from using *pig* and *hog* synonymously.[24]

As to speech forms and habits in themselves, a study of the speech habits of farm children thirty-five years ago reported that many of them spoke indistinctly and carelessly, and made frequent use of provincial words and pronunciations.[25] A decade later a well-known rural sociologist said, with respect to the various facets of rural language:

The language of farm people has been simple, practical, and often abbreviated. Colloquialisms are primarily rural; old forms of speech persist in isolated areas; the rural character in fiction employs crude forms of speech; farm journals usually do not contain the elaborate forms of rhetorical expression that are found in sophisticated magazines read by the upper strata of the urban community.[26]

Apart from the marked relation of language to agriculture in the rural regions, there is much more areal localization of language in rural areas, while city language tends to be whatever is the common language of the larger area—with, of course, the multiple "specialisms" of the cities as adaptations. This is due in considerable part to the fact that ruralities have been more physically isolated and less part of the "stream of things." Hence their "specialisms" are more likely to be those of the immediate areal locale of their speakers. In Latin America, the greater proportion of the urbanites speak Spanish (Portuguese in Brazil), while the ruralites, including the Indians, speak local languages–dialects, ethnic group patois, and tribal languages. In the Arab world, the city dwellers for the most part speak Arabic, while the rural populations speak dialects or tribal languages. Even in the United States, as was noted in the discussion of dialects, regional and local dialects are much more in evidence in rural than in urban areas. The ethnic-group "specials" have also usually persisted longer in settlements in the rural areas.[27]

At present, however, in the United States, as is also true for some of the other linguistic specialisms, the differences between rural and urban speech forms and habits are diminishing. Educational facilities and opportunities for rural children which approach those of urban children in availability and quality; better education of the parents of rural children; the almost complete assimilation of foreign elements; the breakdown of localism (and with it, the weakening of local dialects) and especially, the greater contact with the city by automobile and the influence of the radio and television—all these have worked in the direction of uniformity with the nationwide ordinary speech. The tendency is for the technical terminology of agriculture alone to remain as a distinctive feature. Urban–rural linguistic differences still prevail, however, in the less urbanized areas of the world.

N O T E S

1 On these two opposing tendencies in the "American symbol system," see W. Lloyd Warner, *American Life: Dream and Reality* (Chicago: University of Chicago Press, 1953), pp. 45–47.

2 Cf. Stephen Ullman, *The Principles of Semantics* (Glasgow: Jackson, Son & Co., 1951), pp. 12–13; William J. Entwistle, *Aspects of Language* (London: Faber & Faber, 1953), pp. 30–32; Mario Pei, *Language for Everybody* (New York: Devin-Adair, 1956), pp. 51–66.

3 Cf. Margaret Lantis, "Vernacular Culture," *American Anthropologist*, 62 (Apr., 1960), 202–216; John J. Gumperz, "Speech Variation and the Study of Indian Civilization," *American Anthropologist*, 63 (Oct., 1961), 976–988. What Basil Bernstein describes as "public language" is much like what is here called vernacular speech but is not identical in form and usage with it. ("Public Language: Some Sociological Implications of a Linguistic Form," *British Journal of Sociology*, 10 (Dec., 1959), 311–326. Distinction has been made between (1) "formally correct English" which is used chiefly for serious and Important occurrences, whether in speech or writing, (2) "fully acceptable English," for informal but well-bred conversation and correspondence

—"standard, cultivated, colloquial English," and (3) "popular or illiterate speech," *not* used by persons who wish to pass as cultivated, save in order to represent uneducated speech, or to be jocose. (See H. L. Mencken, *The American Language* (New York: Alfred A. Knopf, 1948) Supplement II, p. 385.) Hans Kurath distinguishes three levels, and assigns them to their respective main locales: (1) "cultivated speech," which is most widespread in urban areas, and tends to be national or regional in character, (2) "common speech," the language of the large middle class, and (3) "folk speech," which is found in rural areas. The second and third levels are speechways of relatively unschooled people, who read little, travel little, and acquire their language largely by ear from the older generation in their immediate vicinity. ("The American Language," *Scientific American,* 182 (Jan., 1950), 48–51.)

4 Eric Partridge, *Here, There, and Everywhere: Essays Upon Language* (London: H. Hamilton, 1950), p. 52.

5 Cf. Eric Partridge, *The World of Words* (London: George Routledge & Sons, 1938), pp. 191–192.

6 George Willis, *The Philosophy of Speech* (New York: Macmillan Co., (no date given, but about 1922)), pp. 194–196.

7 William G. Sumner, *Folkways* (Boston: Ginn & Co., 1907), p. 141.

8 A. A. Roback, *Destiny and Motivation in Language* (Cambridge, Mass.: Sci-Art Publishers, 1954), p. 308.

9 Fifteen reasons for the use of slang, as given by M. Alfredo Niceforo, have been presented by Eric Partridge, *Slang Today and Yesterday* (London: Routledge & Kegan Paul, 1959), pp. 5–7. Several of the reasons given by the present writer were suggested by this list.

10 Cf. Hugh D. Duncan, *Language and Literature in Society* (Chicago: University of Chicago Press, 1953), pp. 110–111.

11 *Op. cit.,* p. 647.

12 For example, see Hans Kurath, *A Word Geography of the Eastern United States* (Ann Arbor, Michigan: University of Michigan Press, 1949).

13 An important sociocultural factor is involved in the intensification and uniformation of the particular features of the dialect. This factor is reflected in what is known as *the principle of density,* which rests on the fact that the inhabitants of the area talk much more to each other than to persons who live elsewhere, while each speaker is constantly adapting his speech habits to those of his interlocutors.

14 In some instances, however, some of the dialects of a people or nation of vast extent, or with formidable barriers between its regions, may be so far apart in certain respects that they are almost incomprehensible to the respective bodies of speakers. In China, for example, a quarter of a century ago, although the Northern and Southern dialects were simply etymological variants, they were so divergent that the speakers often had to resort to pidgin English in order to understand one another.

15 Even small watercourses, however, have served as linguistic dividers. Einar Haugen tells of one of his American-Norwegian informants who said that, in Norway, "Every time you crossed a creek, there was a new language." (*The Norwegian Language in America: A Study of Bilingual Behavior* (Philadelphia: University of Pennsylvania Press, 1953), II, 336.)

16 Cf. Hans Kurath, "The American Language," *Scientific American,* 182 (Jan., 1950), 48–51.

17 Edward Sapir, "Dialect," *Encyclopedia of the Social Sciences* (New York: Macmillan Co., 1931), XV 123–126 (123).

18 *Ibid.*

19 Cf. Everett C. and Helen M. Hughes, *Where People Meet* (Glencoe, Ill.: Free Press, 1952), p. 118.

20 Cf. Mencken, pp. 107–109.

21 Charlton Laird, *The Miracle of Language* (Cleveland: World Publishing Co., 1953), p. 27.

22 One example is the varying names of given foods. Cakes made of cornmeal, for example, are variously called: *johnny cakes, corn cakes, hoe cakes, corn dodgers.* There is also Kurath's gleaning of the local words for *seesaw*: the Rhode Islanders used to call it a "dandle," the Marylanders "cocky horse," the coastal North Caroliners "lucky-horse," the Western North Caroliners "ridy-horse," the Black Islanders "tippity-bounce," the Cap Codders "tilt," the natives of the Connecticut Valley "tinter," the Hudson Valley natives "teeter-totter," and the Bostonians "teeterboard."

23 *Travels with Charley* (New York: Viking Press, 1962), p. 96.

24 Raven I. McDavid, "Dialect Geography and Social Science Problems," *Social Forces,* 25 (Dec., 1946), 168–172 (171).

25 Bird T. Baldwin *et al., Farm Children* (New York: Appleton & Co., 1930), Chap. 16.

26 Paul H. Landis, *Rural Life in Process* (New York: McGraw-Hill Book Co., 1940), p. 101.

27 Occasionally a rural dialect may become the standard and even the national language of a people. Professor Peter A. Munch describes the conditions in Norway under which the *landsmål or* "country language," which had come to be the standard norm for rural dialects by the 1840's, came to have ascendancy over the *riksmål or* "state language," and in the 1880's was adopted by the *Storting* as the official language of Norway. (*A Study of Cultural Change: Rural–Urban Conflicts in Norway* (Oslo: Aschehoug & Co. (W. Nygaard), 1956), pp. 46–48.)

XIII ❧ Social Differentiation and Linguistic Specialization in the Language Community: II. The Special Group and Technical Languages

1. *The Vertically Differentiated Special Languages*

As noted earlier, the vertically differentiated special languages are group, not areal, terminologies and sublanguages. They are numerous —almost as numerous as the different types of groups in which human beings associate themselves and communicate with one another by linguistic means. They are, of necessity, suitable to the composition of these groups and to their particular functions and ends.

The speech specialisms in this second category range from a small glossary of technical or other special-interest or special-function terms that are used by some groups, to practically a completely separate language, for others. More specifically, as "special" languages in relation to the common language, they are specialized terminologies of various sorts: some of the terms are specially invented, or else are common terms that have been given special meanings; some involve special pronunciations of common terms; few involve any marked change of standard grammar.

Categorization of the different forms cannot be clear-cut. Because there is overlapping of characteristics and functions of the different categories of groups, there is also some overlapping and interfusion of their special linguistic instruments. Some separation into major classes of forms, however, is essential to an understanding of their place and function in the society, as well as of the parallel linguistic characteristics of the special languages.

The following categorization of vertically differentiated special languages rests upon a classification of the groups which use them, with special reference to the sociologically significant characteristics and functions of the speakers.

2. *The Biosocial Categories and Groups*

Here we are concerned with the language peculiarities of two biologically-determined categories of the population: the sex groups and the age groups. The two sexes and the different age groups are distinct in their societal position and function and in their cultural importance in the social order.

a / The specialisms of the sexes. The dissimilar roles, and hence different tasks and interests of men and women, as well as of male and female children, call forth different rules governing their behavior. This often implies different connotations for certain kinds of terms, as well as some specialization of vocabularies and usages. Segregation of language by sex groups has been especially marked among primitive people. The Caribs of the Lesser Antilles had what amounted to two distinct vocabularies: the one was used by men, and by women when speaking to men; the other was used by women when speaking to each other and by men when repeating some saying by women. The men had expressions which the women understood but never pronounced themselves, and the women had words and phrases which the men never used; if they did so, they were laughed to scorn. The councils of war did not admit women, and were conducted in a special jargon into which women were never initiated. Thomas has given other instances of sex-determined usages.

> In Madagascar there are terms proper for a woman to use to her own sex, others for women to men, and for men to women. Amongst the Guaycurus (of Brazil) the women have many phrases peculiar to themselves, and never employed by men; the reason being that women are "barred" by the men. So in Surinam (in Fiji) . . . there are many words which it is *tabu* to utter in female society. In Micronesia many words are tabooed for men when conversing with women. . . . In Fiji again, women make their salutations in different words from those of men.[1]

Frazer and others have noted that, among some of the American Indian tribes, there were differences of language between men and women, and that these took the form of different words and usages for certain occasions and certain kinds of relationships; in the latter category, for example, he noted the special forms of speech used between a woman and her son-in-law.[2] An observer of the Chuckchi relates, "When I was trying to learn their language I found that young men did not know the names of some parts of the house frame, household utensils, and instruments for dressing skins. 'Ugh,' they would say, 'I don't know, that is a woman's business.' "[3]

In Japan, for centuries, girls have learned a rich, flowery vocabulary, while boys employed a ruder and more limited one. There have also been male and female word patterns.[4] Thomas also reported in 1909 that "In Japan female writing has quite a different syntax and many peculiar idioms; the Japanese alphabet possesses two sets of characters, *katakana* for the use of men, and *hiragana* for women."[5]

In general, major differentiations of language between the sexes of a society are rare. Contact between the sexes is so continuous and so extensive that sharp differences cannot long be maintained. Nevertheless, in spite of all kinds of social, economic and political equalization of the sexes in our society, men and women still have particularities of discourse along some lines, which create some difficulties in "carry-over" and complicate the process of exact communication at these points. Differences in language style according to the sex of the speaker are not uncommon. Men are amused by some female expressions, especially as they reflect certain differences in the conception of some of the conventions. They are perplexed by "women's meanings," and some of the talk of the "women's world," which they are apt to dub "hen cackle." In fact, some subtle "distances," reflected in meanings, speech content, and speech form still prevail between the sexes. The cartoonist Briggs based some of his most telling pieces on such situations. Some remaining differences are slight accentuations of taboos of certain language forms among the sexes. Many women eschew profanity and "tough talk"—forms of speech presumed to be confined strictly to males—and are shocked by the use of them. There is also still some distinction in our culture in the manner of greeting appropriate for men and women, and other special forms reflected in speech are used in some of the codes of courtesy as between the sexes.

But in general, with the legal equality of the sexes, the vast employment of women, the fact that the sexes increasingly perform the same kinds of work, and the participation of women coequally with men in all sorts of community and national activities, most of the sharply distinct functional divergences between the sexes—such as are conducive to or require speech specialization—have grown weaker or disappeared. The embracing of "male talk" by women has sometimes come to include "vulgar" language, especially in certain social circles. There is also the tendency among some women to exaggerate male "gutter talk."

b / The age-group specialisms. The successive stages of the human life-cycle are reflected in terms carrying specific age connotations. Both primitives and moderns have "terminologies of age," such as "infant," "child," "adolescent," "grown-up," "mature," "aged." While these or parallel terms do not divide the life-span of the individual in the same fashion in every language or every society, nevertheless every such word is part of a system of differentiating people as to age status, and as such carries established connotations of appropriate behavioral standards for each rank and for relations between the ranks, as well as connotations of the privileges and courtesies extended to the respective age categories. In brief, with respect to age, as well as other social and demographic distinctions, vocabulary has been used as a tool for locating persons behaviorally, by establishing reference points for social norms and for different kinds of social relations and social action.[6]

Vendryes has pointed out that sometimes people belonging to different generations have employed different sublanguages. Among the Masai in East Africa, the masculine population was divided into two classes, each of which had strict rules forbidding the use of certain foods—for example, parts of animals that were *tabu* to the aged—and consequently the use of related words.[7] Among primitive peoples, language was definitely related to the rites of passage—for example, as will be noted in connection with the discussion of secret languages, the acquisition by novices of the adult secret language during initiation rites. In some primitive societies, somewhat mysterious special speech forms have been used by the elders to keep the young "in check." Special terms have been used for address to the aged.

Even in a modern society such as ours, both sexes, as they assume the statuses and roles of each respective age–stage, with its related functions, responsibilities, and privileges, also unconsciously assume a host of new terms to enable them to converse about and deal with the new contingencies. Each age–stage is a period in which persons have distinctive social experiences and tasks, by virtue of the particularities of that period in their life-span, and consequently—and of necessity—it has its appropriate speech elements and forms. There is the speech of babies and young children, limited in vocabulary and imperfect in grammar and pronunciation, the language of adolescents, the special terminologies essential to young married people and to parents, "middle-age talk," and the rapidly expanding terminologies about and by the "old folks."

A remarkable study has been made recently by the Opies, which reveals in a most penetrating and comprehensive manner the special language of children.[8] It is based on information collected during the years 1951–1959 from five thousand children attending seventy schools —primary, secondary modern, and grammar, rural and urban—in different parts of England, Scotland and Wales, and one school in Dublin. It is a disclosure of the lore and the language natural to these schoolchildren *when out of school.* The authors believe, and it would seem rightly, that their extensive sample is representative of the child population as a whole. The language they describe is the special language of some seven million inhabitants of Britain but, as the authors indicate, is largely unknown and certainly unheeded by the other six-sevenths of the population, which constitute the adult world of the island.[9]

The study presents, with copious examples, the major types of the children's linguistic forms. These, it should be noted, are in large measure representative of the *types* of most children's language almost everywhere. Notable are: jokes; tricky phrases for inflicting pain on others and setting self-incriminating or embarrassing traps; riddles; rhymes (some of them mildly indelicate) for various occasions and events; their "oral legislation" (for example, the speech forms involved in positive affirmations, in their swopping, secret keepings, and so on); nicknames for different categories of things and persons; epithets; jeers for different offenses of associates; dishonorific names and phrases for spoil-sports, fools, dunces, and so on; the words and phrases used in the child's discourse for "calendar celebrations" (for example, April Fool's Day, May Day, Hallowe'en, Christmas, St. Valentine's Day, Easter); their special terms for referring to friends, enemies, and the opposite sex; the sniping language of partisanship (for example, the terms used regarding Catholics by Protestant children and vice versa, and the reviling language used in village and school rivalry); the jokes, terms, and phrases used with respect to those in authority (school teachers, police); and situations involving authority (tardiness, playing truant, receiving beatings).

A conspicuous form of age-group special language also found in England by the Opies, and worthy of special attention, is the "secret"

322   A S O C I O L O G Y   O F   L A N G U A G E

or "private" argot so often developed by children and teenagers. This is a conversational language which consists of slang elements, of decidedly unique grammatical forms (for example, "pig latin"), and "secret" words. Being unintelligible to the uninitiated, it serves effectively for the cherished special discourse and special forms of social interaction for those "in the know." It is used to impress the age-fellows on the "outside" and, it is usually hoped, all ranges of adults as well, with the importance, the mystery and the exclusiveness of the given group of adolescent speakers.[10]

3. The Speech Differentiations of Ethnic Groups Within a Community

Ethnic groups are groups within the larger community that show conspicuous differences by virtue of being racial or national minorities, or which otherwise show marked cultural, and often especially religious, differences as compared with the rest of the community. They are usually minorities in the larger population. As long as they exist in a community, a state of biculturism also exists, though this is most sharply felt among the minority group members. They may speak peculiar blends of the common language of the larger community and the original ("mother tongue") language of their social or nationality origin, or they may have distinctly different languages from that of the majority. In many instances, the ethnic groups with their peculiar dialects or their distinctly different languages live in particular, often segregated, urban or rural areas of the larger political entity.

Until foreign-speaking ethnic groups lose their mother tongue completely as they become culturally assimilated, there will always be some plural lingualism. This will be particularly true among the minority, who are unable entirely to avoid interaction with the majority, but outsiders who have dealings with the minority will also have some degree of use of the minority language.

On account of the vast migration and intermingling of mankind, instances of speech differentiations of ethnic groups within larger linguistic or political entities have been numerous throughout history. In the United States we have the Mennonite groups of Pennsylvania, speaking their peculiar blend of Rhineland German and eastern colloquial American-English, known as "Pennsylvania Dutch." Also the geographic clustering of foreign-language-speaking immigrants (Czechs, Swedes, Poles, Norwegians, Germans, Italians, Finns, Canadian French) and their descendants, often for several generations, has also been a commonplace phenomenon in both rural and urban areas. The first generation confined itself largely to the home-country language. Later generations took on American-English rapidly, at first using many old-country terms and an unmistakable accent (for example, "Milwaukee German," "Swedish-American," "Czech-American"). However, by the fourth generation, the "foreign" eccentricities had practically disappeared, and unilinguality prevailed. In certain parts of the Southwest, particularly in New Mexico where it is an official language, a considerable number of people of Mexican descent continue to use Spanish, and bilingual proficiency remains essential.

Historically, the speakers of Yiddish, who lived in many nations, used a language largely confined to the ghettoes and distinct from that of the various nations in which they resided. The speakers of the French *patois* that is mainly found in Quebec and in the adjoining portions of Ontario are a minority element, although sizable, of predominantly English-speaking Canada. The Basque language of southwestern France and northern Spain, and the Breton language of Brittany in northern France are not dialects of Spanish and French, but historically distinct languages.

As a consequence of spatial isolation and social segregation, whether imposed or voluntary, the different minority language or the special blend or dialect may prevail for a long time among members of the group, and may often even be cherished as a mark of their distinctiveness. But the tendency in modern nations is for ethnic specialisms to yield to uniformation pressures.

However, where a minority language persists, its speakers may suffer serious consequences. This is cogently brought out in a study by E. Jacques Brazeau, with regard to the situation of French-Canadians in Canadian plural society.[11] His general view is that in Canadian society, where English is the sole language that has currency in all aspects of social activity, people of different tongues have unequal opportunities for work. As a result, French-Canadians, in order to obtain jobs, have had to develop adaptability; many have learned English—especially clerical, administrative, and even highly technical vocabularies—in order to work. There is unemployment among those who have not learned English.

Brazeau also touches upon some broader implications for the speakers of the minority language in a majority–minority situation. Several consequences follow from the dominance of one language in a plural society. There is, first, a limited utilization of the potential skills of those who do not know the dominant language; second, the speakers of the other mother tongues are disengaged from important aspects of social reality; third, there may be an unequal development of the various groups' human resources. He hypothesizes also that, within the context of a social organization that gives precedence to one language in a plural society, the secondary languages become less adequate media of socio-cultural life than the dominant language. For example, there are areas of activity in which a pool of knowledge, oral or written, is not readily accessible in the minority's tongue. As a consequence, their language in these areas is likely to be poor in content, and their information dependent upon translations which are neither plentiful nor good.

4. The Language Specialisms of Groups Stressing Concealment or Secrecy of Action

Special variations of the common language are used by different categories of persons for the purpose of concealing or deliberately misrepresenting their intentions and activities. Here we wish to ex-amine two important types of secret languages or lingoes, especially with respect to their nature and their usage for the secret purposes of the groups employing them. These are: (1) those languages that are developed and maintained by groups in order to enhance and support their mystery, exclusiveness and grandeur, and are linked with almost all kinds of secret societies, and (2) those that have been developed and maintained in order to carry on the group's activities without revealing either their intentions or their activities to outsiders, especially so as to escape their comprehensions and detection. These latter include mainly the cants of the halfworld and underworld.

a / The secret languages of secret societies. Most of the known social systems—primitive, ancient, medieval, modern—have had secret or-ganizations within them, in some instances playing a very important part in the maintenance of social control. As Sumner and Keller noted many years ago, the secret languages have been a conspicuous and central part of the stock in trade of the powerful secret organizations in all ages.[12]

[1] *Primitive secret societies.* The secret languages of primitive secret societies are part of a complex of special organizational features: the men's house; restricted prestigious membership; secret lore; special

signs and symbols; mystifying and magical sacred formulae; special rituals and ceremonials, especially initiation rites; oath-taking; age classes and hierarchies; sharp distinctions between the sexes; differential special social power and influence; an array of taboos.

In most primitive secret societies, the special secret language was known only to the initiated members of the societies. Instruction in it and its adoption by neophytes was an essential feature of the initiation rites. Of particular pertinence was the fact that no novice became a full member until he had acquired the secret language. The privilege of using the magical language was a sort of badge of the achievement of adult status; with it, the initiate acquired new identity and significance, even power. The secret language of most primitive societies was carefully guarded for the use of members. In fact, the revelation of the secret terminology was tabooed, and violations were punished by ostracism and more extreme measures.

Novices also acquired new names during the initiation rites—a lasting reminder of the great change that had come over them. The sacredness of such names was impressed on the boys. The names were usually secret, knowledge of them being confined to the initiated members.[13]

As with most "special" languages, these secret languages of primitive secret societies have been variations of the common language. For example, careful linguistic examination was made of the secret lingoes of the Eskimos and the Dakota Indians, and it was found that they were usually the ordinary speech modified by: (1) unusual accentuation, (2) the introduction of figurative and symbolic expressions, and (3) the addition of archaic words and phrases.[14] Specimens of secret languages have also been recorded in Nigeria, on the Congo, and elsewhere in Africa. Thomas has made this comment about their forms:

> Broadly speaking, we may say that we find languages of three types: (1) old languages retained for cult purposes only; (2) languages made up in part of words from other dialects, in part of other elements; (3) languages in which the ordinary language is changed by the addition of a prefix or suffix, by a change of class in the noun, by a change of vowel, or a change of consonant.[15]

One of the primary objectives of these secret languages of primitive secret societies seems to have been to mystify the uninitiated and those ineligible for initiation within the tribe, as well as all outsiders.[16]

The more specific social and psychological utilities of the secret languages of the primitive secret societies, however, can be summarized as follows: (1) they gave the initiation rites an air of mystery, and impressed the initiates—the future responsible participants in the operation of the tribe—with the gravity of their maturity; (2) they provided the members with a specialized terminology not only to conduct the affairs of the society, but also to enable them to carry on their different social-control functions, especially over children, those not accepted or initiated, the other sex, and outsiders; (3) they were a means of identifying responsible, trustworthy fellow tribesmen, and, conversely, of detecting non-members (possibly enemies); (4) they were a means of maintaining the exclusiveness of the members, which among most peoples enhanced the social prestige of membership, titillated their vanity, and was a source of gratification and self-esteem to them;[17] (5) they gave the speakers special social power within the group, as well as in their relations with foreigners.

[2] *Contemporary secret societies.* There are a large number of recent and contemporary secret societies that have taken the form of fraternal orders; some political groups, such as the early Tammany Hall; semipolitical organizations, such as the Ku Klux Klan; religious organizations, such as the Rosicrucians, and certain secret societies of evil intent, such as the Molly Maguires of the nineteenth century, the Black Hand of the early 1920's, and the contemporary Mafia, which maintain private languages pretty much for the same reasons and to conduct the same functions as those of primitive secret societies.

We shall briefly note some special linguistic features of American fraternal orders.[18] While the number of these societies and the membership in them are declining, a sizable portion of the population, both male and female, are members. The secret language is, of course, calculated to lend an air of mystery to the order and, by setting the members apart, to aid them in retaining their fraternal exclusiveness. It is also the language used in the rituals, in describing and using the society's symbols, in defining and pursuing its special interests, and sometimes in naming some of its organizational and operational features.

The conditions of secrecy of the fraternal orders place certain restrictions upon the speech behavior of members. For example, they "must not write, print, or impart verbally any of the secrets relating to passwords, ritual, or other secret features. These are supreme taboos of secret fraternalism."[19]

The analytical observer is also struck by certain linguistic features which are unique without being secret, especially their resort to magic names. There are the grandiloquent names of the societies with such forms as "Fraternal Order of," "Knights of," "Benevolent Order of," "Royal Order of," "Imperial Order of," implying in some instances non-democratic conceptions of the order vis-à-vis other ones. Gist points out that the names fall into patterns. One of the most familiar involves reference to some "animal or bird": Elks, Eagles, Moose, Owls, Orioles, Buffaloes, Beavers. Another is found in numerous orders of "knighthood": Knights and Ladies of Security, Knights of Pythias, Knights of Malta, Knights of the Ku Klux Klan. Somewhat similar are the names referring to "royalty": Royal Arcanum, Royal Order of Lions, Royal Neighbors of America. Other names reflect "the exultation of a romantic past": Ancient Free and Accepted Masons, Ancient Order of Shepherds, Daughters of the Nile, Ancient Order of Druids, Veiled Prophets of the Enchanted Realm. Some have as part of the title "son" or "daughter," or perhaps both, if of mixed membership; Sons of Norway, Daughters of America, Sons and Daughters of Liberty. The terms "independent" and "improved" appear also: Independent Order of Foresters, Improved Order of Red Men.

One organization employs for its name a symbolic device the complete meaning of which is kept secret from outsiders. There is a woman's order known as P. E. O., the letters of which, according to the different opinions of outsiders, refer to the phrases "protect each other," or "put education over," the latter being suggested by one of the group's major activities.

Local installations of some of these organizations, corresponding to the names of the over-all order, have such names as Hive, Grotto, Aerie, Forest, Grove, Commandary, Camp, Tabernacle, Drove, and Castle.

Flamboyant titles of officials have a peculiar ring in a land where officials are "servants": Eminent Grand Commander, Worshipful Master, Exalted Ruler, Noble Grand Architect, Mighty Chosen, Most Excellent Commander, Imperial Wizard, Supreme Chancellor.[20] The Ku Klux Klan, in conveying the association of special meaning and power, has such awesome titles as Genii, Grand Dragons, Hydras of Realms, Kleagles of Domains, Grand Titans and Furies of Provinces, Exalted Cyclops and Terrors of Klantons.

Most fraternal orders have a "stepping-up" process, which consists of achieving consecutively higher "degrees" through a succession of complicated ritualistic requirements. The names of these degrees have an air of their own. The initiate of the Knights of Pythias goes through the first three degrees as successively "page," "esquire," and "knight"; in the Improved Order of Red Men he takes, in order, the "degree of adoption," "hunters' degree," and "warriors' degree."[21] The organizational climate of the fraternal orders is a unique one, recognizable by many features, not the least of which is its special terminologies and other speech patterns.

b / The secret language of the halfworld and underworld. This language is usually called *cant*. However, *cant* is used in two senses. The one is for an affected, hypocritical, or ostentatious religious or solemn language, used insincerely to gain a reputation for goodness or piety. The other usage—that of the social linguists, and the one most appropriate to our purpose—is that it is the more or less barbarous *secret* language used by the halfworld and underworld: gypsies and carnival folk, and especially prison inmates, thieves, pickpockets, shoplifters, beggars, hoboes, card-sharpers, confidence men, swindlers, safecrackers, drug addicts and drug traffickers, racketeers, gangsters, white slavers and prostitutes, and other criminal elements and their associates and hangers-on, such as "fences" and "spivs."[22]

As is the case with most of the other intra-language specialties, cant is not a separate language with a syntax of its own, although some of the sentence structures impress the outsider as indeed bizarre. It is rather a secret vocabulary, or glossary, intended to be understood only by its highly cohesive and carefully initiated group of speakers. But its secrecy extends only to such things, actions, processes and ideas that, to the underworld, are important. Hence, in the main, only certain words are secret.

While it has marked utility as a technically effective and economical internal communicative device, the main purpose of this cant is to conceal from and deceive and mystify all "outsiders," in order successfully to exploit them. Its users do not wish to have their intra-group activities, directives, intentions or other "inside" information known by the larger community, especially by their intended victims and the law-enforcing agencies, nor do they wish to expose themselves to detection and arrest. Thus its usage is both exploitative and defensive. But it has other sociological significance. Its speakers are outlaws—people "outside the pale" of acceptance and respectability. Their special speech, as it is used, thus has the function of showing bravado and the speakers' revolt against the main body of society with its normal language, as well as of maintaining solidarity among its speakers.

Each branch of the underworld is apt to have its own terminology which, to some extent, is known to the corresponding branch in other countries. At the same time, certain words and phrases and meanings are common to all or nearly all of the categories of people, while others belong only to related categories, such as panhandlers and hoboes, or white slavers and prostitutes.

These special terminologies include words used to refer to types of crime and criminals, to the techniques and tools used in their activities and the materials involved, and especially to the other categories of persons and the social institutions to which they become related in their nefarious activities—"fences," the victims or customers, the law, the police.

Much of cant rests on the systematic switching of the meanings of generally known words. Thus jewels become "ice"; stolen jewels sought by the police are "hot ice"; heroin is "snow"; a drug addict is a "snow bird"; a lawyer is a "mouthpiece"; a weapon is a "persuader"; a revolver is a "gat" or "iron"; to kidnap is "to snatch"; a payroll is a "snatch"; the payoff man in the numbers racket is the "banker"; to hit with a blackjack is "to sap"; a victim or intended victim of a confidence man is a "mark."[23]

The extent to which the cant of the underworld has infiltrated our vernacular is evidenced by such words as the following, most of which no longer require an explanation or translation for most people: "to gyp," "third degree," "to bump off," "to hijack," "trigger man," "take a powder," "take the rap," "take for a ride," "clip joint," "hot stuff," "fix," "muscle in," "scram," "throw the book at."

5. *The Special Technical and Organizational Languages of the Major Institutional Areas*

We now take up the array of technical languages sometimes referred to as jargons.[24] Every work group of a trade, craft, calling, or profession; every art, science, technology, business, industry, sport or game, hobby, or religious group; every ideological group or cult of whatsoever kind; every "school of thought," and standardized organizational activity—all these have their special terminology. This consists of names and other descriptive and definitional words, of idiomatic phrases, and other symbols for the objects, conditions, facts, interests, values, ideas, principles, processes and techniques, relations, combinations, purposes, pursuits, products and other technicalities and specialties with which the group personnel is concerned. Unequivocal names are given to objects and to events that ordinary language does not always describe adequately; sometimes ordinary words are specially used or are employed with a special meaning; sometimes special terms are borrowed from other languages or are invented.

These special technical languages are not generally used by the rank-

and-file members of the community, for they are not familiar to or clearly comprehended by outsiders. Like the secret languages, they are distinct from the language of the home and the neighborhood, and are ordinarily learned after childhood, often as the result of conscious and practised effort. The groups and categories of people concerned with these special languages function in the different major institutional areas of society. We shall briefly examine these special terminologies and usages under the headings of the institutional areas in which they operate. Before doing so, however, we wish to depict, as a general background for this examination, the sociologically significant features, especially the roles—not sharply distinct—of the special technical languages, as they function in three very general and recurrent, but by no means mutually exclusive, types of functional group. One or more of these types—often all three—are to be found in almost every major institutional area of social life. These are work groups, large-scale formal organizations or bureaucracies, and ideological groups.

a / Common features and functions of work groups and their languages. The special languages of work groups—which range from functionally conjoined associates engaged in conducting the simplest crafts to those in the highest professions—are the means whereby the personnel, all experts in some respect, habitually communicate with each other as they carry on their occupational functions. These languages are definitely not for communication with other work groups or with laymen, and they are largely unknown to outsiders.

The primary purpose is to convey precise information with respect to the common affairs of the group. Each occupational language consists of a body, sometimes quite extensive, of detailed, specially selected (frequently also specially invented), arbitrarily used, descriptive and analytical terms. There is specially contrived nomenclature and phrasing: in some instances great conciseness, in others great prolixity of expression. Such a set of devices is an absolute necessity if ambiguity and incompleteness are to be avoided, and specificity, exactness, adequacy and precision are to be achieved. It permits quick and accurate communication among group members, and usually works in the interest of economy of action. In general, it assists the group as a functional entity. In brief, each work group has a well-developed system of "talk" that is peculiar to it, and meets its specific needs; each new occupation soon develops one. This is the "shop-talk" aspect.

Another significant aspect of the occupational jargon is that it serves to identify the member of the occupation, to relate him to his occupational fellows, and to distinguish him from those outside the occupation. As such it serves as a bond and is an important factor in the maintenance of group unity and the sense of what has been called "colleagueship."[25]

The converse of this is the fact that the occupational jargon is used as a stratagem to keep the layman in ignorance, in order to enable the work group to carry on its affairs and functions without the intrusion or interference of outsiders.[26] One of the most important obligations of colleagueship is the use of double talk—that is, talking in one frame of reference to one's clients or society at large, and in a different frame of reference to one's colleagues. This is in most cases not a matter of "fooling the client," but rather a means of effectively dealing with him. A doctor might be able to tell the patient very little, if he had to use strictly scientific language; he might even alarm him. He must therefore use language on the patient that the latter will understand. The police use a highly specialized language among themselves, which is very different from the language they use with the public. The functions of this private police language, as Westley points out, are as: (1) a shield against the possible attacks of a (usually) hostile public and newspapers; (2) a protection from criminals, who would profit from knowledge of internal police affairs; (3) a protection of their own persons on those occasions when their use of violence has exceeded that which is legally permissible, or when political corruption has been involved.[27] The peculiar interests, needs, and functions of almost any work group require that they be able to discuss their clients, patients, customers, and so on, in a precise and objective manner among themselves, to recount to each other their occupational uncertainties, mistakes, perplexities and problems (to "let their hair down"), and to reassure each other and back their faith in themselves, individually and collectively. This requires that they speak in such a manner that, if they were overheard, their speech would not disturb or disillusion the client or outsider, simply because it would not be understood.[28]

It is, of course, obvious that occupational jargons, especially those that are highly esoteric, even though they may be contrived in order to withhold information from others, may tend to block communication with other occupations and sometimes with employers, as well as with laymen or the public at large, whom the occupation serves and upon whom it is dependent for support and justification for its continued existence.[29]

b / The language of bureaucracies. In order to appreciate the main characteristics of the language of bureaucracies, it is essential that we understand their particular structural–functional features and the place in society of bureaucracies themselves. They are large-scale formal organizations—the special, highly developed, complex form of conducting the large enterprises that have come to be characteristic of huge and specialized societies like our own. This form of organization governs almost all important large-scale operating entities, whether they are governmental, semi-private, or private. All governments and governmental agencies, business and industrial organizations (especially in the form of corporations), educational institutions and systems, religious organizations, professional and occupational associations, larger recreational and athletic organizations and even large-scale criminal enterprises are organized on formal principles. They carry on functions of wide significance *to* the public, and most of them *for* the public, or for large segments of it, whether they are themselves public or private organizations.

Bureaucracy is the almost universal system of conducting large-scale divided and specialized, but joint activities, which involve numerous and highly differentiated and departmentalized personnel. Among the personnel there must be precision, reliability and continuity of performance, and adequate coordination and control.

Structurally, the bureaucracy takes the form of a pyramid, consisting of horizontal layers of administrative and technical personnel. As we move vertically from the top to the bottom of the pyramid, we usually find not only an increasing number of lesser administrative officers and departments, but also a larger and larger number of personnel. At each level, the personnel is vertically divided into different but related tasks and specialties.

There must be authority, or assigned power, to determine principles of procedure, make decisions, give and enforce commands and instructions, specify and assign tasks, and to supervise and guide the entire personnel, so as to maintain the organization as an efficient instrumentality of action. This formal authority is hierarchically organized and specialized for each rank. It is relayed downward from each level to the ones below it, through the successive layers of the administrative pyramid. The channels between layers must permit the free flow of authority, or there will be confusion and conflict. This means especially that there must be *channels of communication* through which principles, decisions, orders, instructions, suggestions and all sorts of other pertinent information can be transmitted to all elements of the organization. Without communication, there can be no organization.

Although there is much informal communication, from the point of view of operation, formal communication which uses the established lines of authority is more important. Such communication flows in various directions: much of it flows downward, from upper to lower levels, in the form of transmitted decisions and orders; some of it goes upward in the form of general decisions of the rank-and-file membership, or of information and suggestions, sometimes solicited, from the lower ranks of operating personnel. This upward-and-downward channeling of information can be likened to flow from the respective ends of a funnel. Some of it also occurs *laterally,* from person to person and from department to department within each scalar level, in order to facilitate cooperation at that level. In general, the communication involving authority is downward; that involving the flow of information is both up and down through all the levels, and every way within each level.

Most activity on the part of the bureaucracy is highly specialized, and the language used—oral and written—is of necessity highly specialized, each functional type of bureaucracy having a highly unique type of special language of its own.

Probably the best way to characterize, in a general way, the special language of bureaucracies is to consider it from the point of view of the language: (1) for internal use and (2) for external use.

[1] *The language for internal operation.* The special language for internal use takes two fairly distinct forms: (a) language designed to convey all sorts of information, including general instructions, and to conduct all sorts of discussions and affairs within and between ranks and departments, and (b) the language of the management or administration of the organization.

The language of internal exchange of information and for discussion is, in the main, the special technical language of the experts and of "expertise," as determined by the type of special functions which the bureaucracy performs in and for society. It consists of special names, phrases and other vocal or visual symbols (sometimes special pronunciations), used in connection with materials, principles, bodies of knowledge, values, beliefs, instruments, processes and techniques, factors in the environment, rituals, objectives, purposes of endeavors, plans and programs of the personnel. One need only refer to the highly diversified specialty of language, depending on whether the large-scale formal organization is political (a government bureau), religious (a specific denomination or sect, with its own theology and beliefs), educational (a school system), industrial (for example, engaged in the production of optics, electronic materials, automobiles or biologicals and pharmaceuticals). There is often also a great differentiation between divisions and departments of great organizations—for example, the manufacturing divisions of General Motors; the colleges, the major subject-matter divisions, and even the departments of a university; the major branches of the Army—as well as between the several operative levels, as the result of the lessening degrees of expertise in the successively lower ranks.

All large-scale organizations also have their language of general instructions. This is to be found in the instructional manuals issued for all ranks and specialties of the managerial and technical personnel. Governmental bureaus and departments, political parties, industrial and commercial concerns, trade associations, religious organizations, educational organizations, trade unions—all have their own "how-to-do-it" books.

Essential also are the rules for operating the deliberative assemblies of the directors, the stockholders or others representative of the membership, and the meetings of the administrative and technical staffs. This is the language of *Roberts Rules of Order*.

The language of administration or management is probably much more "standard" as to general type, from one kind of bureaucracy to another, than is the language used in internal exchange of information. This is the language of the governing techniques of the organization; it is primarily concerned with the exercise of authority. The principles, purposes, procedures, rights and duties, and rules of operation must be established and continually modified by the governing board. This is the language of decision-making. Decisions must be transmitted in comprehensible and technically appropriate form to all ranks and departments of personnel. The multiple codes and the related instrumentalizing bodies of rules covering all suborganizations, relationships and operations must be precisely stated and interpreted. Special instructions, orders, directives and commands must be issued; these will vary greatly in tenor, style and method of presentation, depending upon the typical functions of the organization—for example, whether they are issued in a military organization, a penal institution, a great religious body, a university or an industrial or commercial organization. The language of administration is also involved in the establishment and maintenance of sanctions, in the statement and execution of such matters as the bases for advancement and salary increases, for rights, privileges and benefits and, of course, for warnings and penalties. The essential activities of planning, policy-making and programming must be set forth in language comprehensible to the types and levels of specialists inside the organization, to interested non-specialists connected with the organization—such as members of the board of trustees or stockholders—and to outsiders, even the public at large. Every large-scale, formal organization has to have various sorts of managerial language forms, differing in terminology, and specialty and style of phrasing, because of the differences in their respective purposes and "targets."

These varied forms of special organizational discourse differ—as language—in directness, precision and terseness of statement, in intricacy and prolixity, in use of or freedom from metaphor, in repetitiousness, in the emotional charge they carry, in the elaboration of concepts and meaning, and in style (to mention only the more important differences).

On account of the many specialized work groups in a large organization, it is often necessary to translate the ideas, directions and orders of management into a language that is more compatible with the particular jargons of the different groups within the enterprise. Furthermore, different segments and levels of the personnel may attach very different meanings to the same words and statements, and use them in very different circumstances and contexts. Hence, especially in a large organization —such as a university, a huge industrial complex like General Motors, or a research organization—it may be necessary for the spokesmen of the departments and the specialists to be interpreters of their occupational or scientific language to management and to those in other specialties.[30]

While all formal organizations, of necessity, have their rules for the conduct of their deliberative assemblies, as noted above, mention should be made of the almost stereotyped language that is used at meetings of this sort—board meetings, conferences of administrators, meetings with stockholders and organizational conventions. Some of it can be said to have become "ritualized," as is also the case, for example, with respect to some oaths and other verbal forms widely used in courts, in the public utterance of religious creeds, and in the vocal conduct of the mass.

[2] *The language for external use.* All large-scale formal organizations, both public and private, have obligations to the public and are dependent upon it for custom and support. They need to convey information about their contributions to the public, convince it of their justifiability, and appeal to it for support. Because of their specialized nature, these statements of objectives and alleged contributions must be translated into terms that are comprehensible and attractive to the general population. Sometimes, it also seems necessary to withhold information, or to present it in a disguised manner; it is often, therefore, carefully selected as to content and form.

Bureaucracies are sensitive to their status with society at large. They do not wish to offend any special-interest groups, or to take any action that will prejudice their own important interests or objectives. Hence, they develop systems of double-talk whereby rulings and policy announcements are issued, but without providing any clear statement for the public at large.[31] This might be called the language of "protective coloration"; the principle applies both in protection against the public's awareness of internal affairs and in what is released to the external world.

While specialization often tends to extremism, the prolixity of bureaucratic language has come to attract considerable attention, and some of it has invited such designations as "officialese," "bafflegab," "gobbledegook." The bafflegab of some government bureaucrats is especially noteworthy. The vogue among them seems to be to say what is said in the most complicated, cumbersome, stilted, longwinded, and absurd manner possible. Here is a recent example of a stupefying prolixity of "75 cent words": "In the current stages of the ongoing post-attack productivity study, the identification of the enervating effects of a decreased caloric diet upon physical productivity indicates the need to plan, pre-attack, for adequate caloric food stockpiles." What is meant here is that soldiers should have a square meal ready for them after fighting.[32]

c / The language of ideological groups and "schools of thought." An ideological group is a collectivity of people, sometimes widely scattered, who hold to a common ideology. While the precise nature of ideologies differs somewhat in the different areas of social life in which they are found, in general an ideology consists of a set of established, interrelated beliefs about some matter of major concern—usually also a matter of controversy—to some portion of the people making up the society. The belief purports to describe the existence of things as they are and, usually, as it is hoped they will be. The central, thematic belief is elaborated, supported, and sometimes implemented by official creeds, which state the basic beliefs and values; by way of myths and legends, which historically explain their origins or existence, and thus validate group beliefs, practices and events; by interpretations and statements of present and future purposes; by stated programs of action toward achieving their ends (for example, the "class struggle"); by rationalizations and justifications; by rituals of varying degree of formality for both group and public ("out-group") consumption. Frequently, in the history of a social movement of greater or lesser magnitude, their main use is to justify certain social philosophies and to promote certain concerted action on the part of numbers of individuals, such as will carry into effect the tenets of the ideology. The ideologies are believed to be right or good by the people of the groups holding to them; usually their role is to seek to increase the number of "true believers."

Every institutional area of social life has its controversial, often conflicting, ideologies and ideological groups. This can be seen from the mere listing of some of the more widely known ideologies of the present period: Capitalism, Communism, Socialism, Nationalism, Familism, Ruralism, Militarism, Pacifism, Internationalism, Unionism, Deweyism, Authoritarianism, Racism, Anti-Racism, Catholicism, Protestantism, Fundamentalism, Mormonism, Impressionism, and Positivism (in science and philosophy).

Ideological language is the language of the "isms." This gives it certain characteristics. First, there is its *declaratory and descriptive aspect:* the language forms that "carry," or serve as the "vehicles" for stating, the beliefs, values and purposes of the ideology. This is seen in specially invented words and phrases, common words and phrases given special meanings and "coloring," and other symbolic forms— depending upon the sociocultural area of functioning. (This, of course, is what every special language consists of, to some extent.)

The other aspect is responsible for some of its uniqueness—namely, its *purposiveness.* Ideologies prevail in areas of difference of belief— areas of contradiction and controversy. This is a fact of central importance in their existence, in the structural–functional forms they take and, of special significance here, in the linguistic forms and styles that they utilize. The language of ideology has the kinds of words, the sentence structure, the figures of speech, the tonal stressing (in its oral form)—in general, the effort to use the "word magic" of the special pleader, the proselytizer, missionary and evangelist, the defender of a philosophy or of some way of life, the aggressive justifier, the promoter and salesman, the propagandist, the social reformer and, in some cases, the misleader and the rabble-rouser. This language can take the form of slogans, derogatory names for the opposition, epithets, double-talk, sometimes well-devised obfuscations of terms and ideas, ear-catching "ritualistic" phrases (sometimes very vague as to their real meaning). It is not the language of reporting and explaining, but that of controversy and debate, a means for exerting social-psychological power.

The special languages of "schools of thought" are closely related in structure and purpose to those of ideological groups, because these "schools" are also generally of a sectarian and "splinter" nature. They consist of a separate body of devotees, within a larger area of thought, belief or practice, who collectively maintain a distinctive system of similar views, or share the same particularistic spirit, principles, canons, precepts and opinions or advocate the same particular methods within a general area of thought or practice. They are to be found especially in philosophy, theology, art, medicine, politics and economics—for example, the Existentialist school of philosophy, the Barthian school of theology, the Keynesian school of economics, the Abstractionist school of painting, the osteopaths in medicine. They carefully, and often militantly, present their distinctive constructs and points of view. For this they need and devise special languages—specially invented terms, and especially contrived meanings for terms—in order to depict their special viewpoints and their departures from the beliefs, ideas and practices of the larger area.[33]

6. Some Distinguishing Features of the Special Languages in Different Institutional Systems

We take up, finally, the instances of the technical sublanguages of some of the major institutional areas. In all cases, these special languages have developed the forms they have in order to meet the peculiar functional requirements of their respective institutional systems.

a / The special languages of the economic order. The economic order obviously needs many special utility languages, most of them with technical characteristics, in order to enable all the different divisions and specializations of occupations and industries—in fact, every functionally diverse area of the complex economy—to operate effectively. In general, the special languages of the economic order are primarily those of work groups and of the administrative and technical levels and departments of bureaucracies, whose characteristics were discussed in the introduction of the present section. While work groups perform in offices and service departments of schools, colleges and universities, churches and other religious organizations, governmental agencies, welfare organizations and so on, they are especially significant in that area which is designated as *economic*—the work groups in banks, construction, factories, wholesale and retail trade, and communication and transportation. Next to the area of government, the bureaucratic form of structural–functional organization is most common; it appears with most of its typical characteristics in the multiple and varied economic activities of modern society, especially in *corporations*.[34]

As in every other major area of social life, the special economic languages must have specific nomenclatures, specially pointed phrases and figures of speech, sometimes special gestures and other non-verbal symbols. These sometimes exist in more or less secret and abbreviated form, in order to enable the personnel to communicate about: (1) the materials used in the economic activities; (2) the instruments used; (3) techniques and technologies involved; (4) the performance of the technical operations; (5) the control and manipulation of personnel; (6) the categories of human beings involved in all of the functions, levels and types of relationships: co-workers, officers, owners and suppliers, customers, patients or clients, competitors, the public; (7) all economic and functionally related services performed at the different levels and divisions of the economy.

The economic languages, being those of a truly pivotal system of institutions, contribute a tremendously extensive, varied, complicated system of discourse. The major subdivisions of the economy—agriculture and forestry, mining, trade and commerce, manufacturing, construction, transportation,[35] and finance—each have distinct special terminologies. Within each there are further specializations: for example, the "specials" of cotton farmers, wheat farmers, and livestock farmers, or of the sheep men as distinct from the cattlemen.[36] A whole industry will have its own "industrial language," for example, the steel industry, electronics, automobiles, aeronautics. In the field of finance, there is the language of accounting, of the banks and trust companies, the stock and produce exchanges, the Federal Reserve System, the investment houses. In the field of commerce, there is the language about the commodities involved in buying and selling, the language of importers, jobbers, wholesalers and retailers, the language of marketing.[37]

Involved in all the major areas of the economy, but also operating as distinct specializations, are the languages of advertisers and advertising, public relations, the labor unions (when they operate as bureaucracies, justify themselves to the public, confer with and carry on opposition against management), as well as the language of mechanization and automation and of other recent developments in industrial technology.

Overlapping with some of the language of the political order is the language of property: the rights and privileges pertaining to it, its ownership and ownership practices, its inheritance, transfer, use, sale and rental. Increasingly obvious, even to the general public, is the difference in the economic language of a *capitalist* as against a *socialistic* or *communistic economy*.[38]

b / The special languages of the political order. The language of political institutions has several "special" functional aspects.

There are first of all the readily recognized language forms which depict or reflect the ideological pattern or express the basic political doctrine of the particular governmental system—whether it be democratic, communistic, totalitarian or monarchistic. This is the verbalization of its political mythology and philosophy. Each political ideology has its stereotyped words and phrases, its pointedly stated slogans and catchwords, its simplified expressions of the basic ideas and values of its political philosophy; these function more or less as incantations. The basic relationships and basic postulates of the state find their characteristic expression in preambles to constitutions, and in the utterances of and documents from "founding fathers" and "statesmen." The Soviet Union has such a typical expression as "the Dictatorship of the Proletariat." The American government seeks ". . . to form a more perfect union, establish justice, insure domestic tranquillity, provide for the common defense, promote the general welfare, and secure the blessings of liberty to ourselves and our posterity." The French as a political entity believe in "Liberty, Equality, and Fraternity," while Americans contend that all men have the right to "life, liberty, and the pursuit of happiness."

These aspects of political language recur again and again in public papers intended for both national and international consumption, in the public addresses of politicians and political officials, in the press on the occasion of political commemorations and national holidays, and in controversy with representatives of other political ideologies and doctrines. The outstanding feature of many of the speeches is the simple repetition of these mythical and doctrinal elements in the form of emotion-charged clichés.[39]

Second, there is the language of the political formula—that is, the language which describes and prescribes in detail the structure of the particular political society. It consists of the "basic public law," as expressed in the Constitution. It elaborates in specific detail the make-up and functions of the agencies, and the areas of jurisdiction and duties of the functionaries, necessary to put the political doctrine into effect as a form of government.

Third, there is what Lasswell calls the "miranda,"[40] that is, the symbols of sentiment and of identification with the ideology and doctrine. The function of these forms is to arouse admiration and enthusiasm and to strengthen political faiths and loyalties. They repeat, elaborate and apply the essentials of the doctrine and formula. In the United States, for example, we have such "key words" as "rights," "freedom," "democracy," and "equality." Sentiments of loyalty cluster around these terms, and bind the citizenry together. Akin to the key verbal symbols are the maxims or slogans, the terse string of words, that we repeat again and again, such as "freedom of speech," "trial by jury," "Bill of Rights," "equality of all before the law."

Fourth, there is what has been well called "the language of power."[41] This is the aspect of political language that probably first occurs to people as a consequence of its direct effect upon them. Much political language is used to state rules and laws, present the obligations inherent in the oaths of office, register decisions and verdicts to be carried into effect. The purpose of much of it is to control: to plead, convince, enlist, admonish, compel, restrain people. "Speechifying"—resting upon the supposed magic of the "word" before the "crowd"—and "explanation" (for example, the President's News Conferences) are ways of informing, persuading and captivating the citizenry.

Language is also used for such political ends as being a stimulus to action—especially in the ordering or commanding the action, as a means of developing and manipulating the allegiances and loyalties of the members of the political community, and as a way of proposing and endorsing issues and actions; it is used to conceal information from, and to hoodwink, persons and groups both at home and abroad, and to calumniate both internal and external opponents.

The main portion of the language of power is the language of administration, that is, the language of officialdom and of the different types of bureaucracies involved in conducting the functions of government. One type of administrative language consists especially of *the vocabulary of rulership*. In a democracy, this is the blend of terminology intended to convey, in the utterances of the "rulers" (President, governor, mayor), the ideas of authority, omniscience and benefaction, and at the same time of "servantship."

The language of political bureaucracy takes several forms. One important category is the language of the governmental agencies that bring pressure on the citizenry and regulate and control it, in so far as certain actions must be prevented and prohibited, and certain others encouraged and requested. This is the language of directing, ordering, demanding and commanding—discreet and tempered in a democracy—and the language of threats and penalties. This language, by its nature, attaches special and specific meanings to key words. It cannot be equivocal.

Another type of bureaucratic language, by no means completely separate from the preceding, is that used by departments and bureaus as they conduct their functions, both internally and in dealing with the public. The special jargons of the government bureaus in such areas, for example, as agriculture, commerce, health, foods and drugs, social work, education, meteorology, communications, physics, involve almost every other technical language. Of necessity, if they are to function properly, they must have their own vocabularies and standardized ways of defining, explaining, recording their activities, and especially of communicating internally, as they conduct their operations and report them to the public. But some governmental bureaucrats supremely epitomize bureaucratic "officialese," "bafflegab," and "gobbledegook," as has been noted above.

Fifth, there is the language of the political parties and politicians. The political parties more or less skillfully use all sorts of "party symbols," not the least of which are their pat phrases, slogans and catchwords. They have non-flattering names and verbalized allusions for the opposition. The politicians have their own special "rhetoric." Both the content and the delivery of their fulminations are polemical and controversial by nature, invariably stereotyped around those modes that are presumed to be effectively persuasive appeals, depending, of course, on their viewpoints: "radical," "reactionary," "violator of states' rights," "regimentation," "socialism." The parties and the politicians try to manipulate the terminology of the ideology in their own behalf. The language of the "hustings" is, under some circumstances, the language of "defense" of policy or action, and this necessitates, on occasion, a language of circumlocution and studied vagueness.

Sixth, there are the related special languages of the law, the courts and the lawyers. Legal terminology, which is used in such important instruments as all manner of laws, public regulations and ordinances, in contracts, wills, the decisions of courts and the statement of legal propositions, should of necessity have specificity, clarity and exactness of meaning and usage. It should concentrate upon what is essential in the assertion, and isolate the constant from the variable features. Huntington Cairns has pointed out that most lawmakers and jurists have sought to meet these criteria. The Roman classical jurists, for example, developed a special professional form of speech that sought simplicity and exactitude, and therefore "eschewed rhetoric, neologism, metaphors, unusual words, archaisms, and emotion," and called things only by their technical names.[42] The history of English common law exhibits efforts to realize similar objectives. The terminology of Anglo-American law, according to Cairns, shows extraordinary precision. As a technical language, it permits highly abstract analyses; at the same time, it is applicable to the concrete affairs of life. It has provided essential nomenclature to cover new situations.

In general, the language of law is a relatively highly developed special system of discourse. Here too, however, the special language, at the hands of some legislators, jurists and lawyers, not infrequently becomes the victim of verbiage—vague, uncertain, ponderous, voluminous, awkward, even unintelligible. It is sometimes far more obscure than the abstract legal principles which it states.

Seventh, and finally, there is the highly conventionalized special language used in the practice of diplomacy, which, in turn, consists of conducting negotiations between governments by their designated representatives, the "diplomats." The special forms that oral and written diplomatic language take are the result of the essential functions of diplomacy. It is the language of maneuver, of a competitive game; words and phrases and documents are the pawns in it. It has a common vocabulary and uses somewhat standardized forms of phrasing, known to the diplomats of all countries. It is also the language of ceremonial, which is usually "set" in form and often quite stilted. It is marked by the formal use of names and titles, and conformity to conventional rules as to form of address and correspondence. The play of power and the threat of its use is inherent in diplomacy; this is reflected in the fact that its language carries connotations of power. The show of power in the language, however, is carefully manipulated, even veiled, since one of the functions of diplomats is to avoid open breaks or conflict. Thus, it is especially a language of persuasion. Finally, it is cautious, discreet language—cautious as to what and how much is revealed, and the manner and style of its presentation. This may at times involve deliberate resort to obfuscation and, preferably, suave lying.

While it is often obscure to the layman, the special language of diplomacy is not ambiguous to the trained and experienced diplomats of most countries of the world; if it seems to be so, it is a commonly practiced ambiguity, which is so well known that it conveys quite standard meanings and indicates typical intentions. Of course, much "diplomacy" today is couched in non-diplomatic language, that is, in the language of *power and propaganda.*

c / The special languages of the military system. Although the military systems of modern nations are a subdivision of their executive–administrative branch of government, they are so massive in terms of personnel involved, so ubiquitous, and expend such a large proportion of public funds, that there is much justification for focusing special attention upon them as vast governmental structural–functional agencies by themselves. The military system has been the most highly organized, the most consistently glorified, and usually the best supported of the activities of government. The military system has its *raison d'être* in war—the waging of war and the defense of the nation against war. Its fundamental function is to operate, if possible, as a sufficiently powerful social machine to intimidate, repel, weaken, even destroy other nations. Essentially, it is the most highly institutionalized use that mankind has yet devised of force and of the utilization of manpower, resources and every known science and technology.

The main special languages of the military system are those of a huge, complex organization. Certain other special languages of sociological interest and concern are almost incidental to the organizational language, namely, the colorful lingoes of the men in the ranks— "soldier language."

The language of the system as such is a variant of the language of bureaucracy. It might be pointed out in passing that the military organization is probably the archetype of bureaucratic structure, and its operation the epitome of bureaucratic organization. Readily recognizable as peculiarly characteristic of the language of military organization is the prominence of the language of hierarchical arrangements: the language of one-way transmission down through the levels of orders, instructions and commands; the language of obedience and deference of lower to higher ranks, of titles, of forms of address; the language of the rules and codes that actuate performance and tie the ranks and departments together into a complex instrument. Especially significant in this connection is the language of command, as it flows from commander-in-chief to the major divisions (Army, Navy, Air Corps), and then down through the successive levels of commissioned and non-commissioned officers and technical grades to the men in the ranks ("staff-and-line" language).

Equally essential and prominent are the special technical languages: the terminologies of the physical, psychological and social sciences and technologies utilized; the language of military maneuvers on land, sea and in the air; the language used to name, describe and manipulate equipment; the language of ballistics (the science and technology of projectiles), of logistics (the moving and supplying of armies), of communication, including codes, ciphers and the deciphering of military intelligence, of diplomatic maneuvering by the military. Worthy of special mention is the language of military maneuver—of tactics and strategy. In an age of highly technical specialization and mechanization (automatization) of warfare, this language, both oral and written, has also become highly technical; as a result of the fact that maneuver involves communication and cooperation with a diversity of other specialized personnel in split-second operations, language must also be, of necessity, concise and precise. A jet crew communicating with one another, with other crews, and with the ground and ships at sea, has to be able to use the minimum, but at the same time, the applicable terminology.

Finally, there is the language of the sentiments, attitudes, beliefs, myths, legends and ceremonials of the military system.

The language of the soldier—the man-in-the-ranks—is, of course, related to the other special languages of the military system. But it is above all a special group language: the language of a body of persons who are, to a considerable extent, separated from the main body of the citizenry, engaged in at least potentially hazardous functions, and subjected to special conditions of association and existence, as compared with those of normal civilian life.

The soldier's language has utilitarian aspects. It includes what Elkin has referred to as "convenience expressions": convenience designations, such as "sun-tans" and "jeep," and convenience abbreviations, such as "CO" for commanding officer, or "OP" for observation point. The convenience expressions the soldier uses relate to expected details of living, military objects, routinized army jobs, or accepted army phenomena.[43] His language, in its various manifestations, reflects especially his psychological states, and his social-psychological and sociological conditions. Some of it is the language of tension-release—expletives, epithets, the wide resort to the "four-letter words" and figures of speech, some of which "get the pressure off his chest" but are not acceptable in polite society. Much of his inelegant, even obscene, language is designed to enable him to endure what he hates or fears, but cannot change. The medical officer becomes a "butcher," a hospital a "butcher shop," and a casualty list a "butcher's bill." The cook becomes a "gut burglar" or "belly robber," and rations are called "crap" or "garbage." The strict officer is called an "iron-ass," and trying to please superiors is "brown-nosing."[44]

Elkin notes how the language of the soldier reflects his total self-image: (1) his image of solidarity with other men in the Army ("G.I.," "Joe," or "Mac"), (2) the image of freedom from certain of the customary restraints of civilian society (the omnipresent obscene-word prefix), and (3) the image of strength and virility ("sweat out," "blow one's top"). His language also includes many terms which reflect his attitude toward his officers and authority in general.

The humor element is sometimes blended in with the technically essential terminology as when, in soldier language, "big wheel" is used for top sergeant, "fruit salad" for the decorations (medals) of officers, "whizzbangs" or "buzzbombs" for rocket bombs, or when certain fellow soldiers are referred to as "gold-brickers" or "sack artists."

d / The language of sports and entertainment. Every sport and every form of entertainment has its special and often flamboyant terminology, some of which is clearly comprehensible only to its active participants and devoted followers. The more prominent American sports—such as baseball, football, basketball, prizefighting, wrestling, golf and tennis—as well as most minor ones; the prominent games—such as bridge and poker and other games of chance (including public gambling)—have their special terms, sometimes many in number, which cover every technical aspect of the sport or game: players and their positions, rules, things played with, techniques of performance and misplays. For instance, Paul Coburn lists for basketball, in his *The Sports Description Handbook,* sixty-six terms for throwing the ball into the basket, of which the following are samples: "cages a toss," "flicks it through," "rings up a deuce," "flips it in," "pops the ropes," "spears the net," "hits the target," "gift throw," "gratis heave." Such terms as "bulldogging," "crowbait," "jughead," are clearly determined and economical terms for rodeo people. Hunters and fishermen have their special terminology for the creatures of interest, their special characteristics, habits, and habitats, as well as for their own equipment and procedures. The stage—operatic, legitimate theater, musical, burlesque, vaudeville, nightclub—and the screen, radio and television have rich, copious, well-adapted linguistic means for communication regarding their internal functions, equipment, personnel, relations with spectators and patrons. These are exemplified in such journals as *Variety,* or in the highly esoteric terminology characteristic of Hollywood.

e / Family language. The general institutional language of the family system of each culture is more or less unique, in keeping with the special characteristics of the family and kin-relationships in each culture. It is a cluster of determinable names and forms, including the names of the different categories of family members ("father," "daughter," "sister"); the special terms for types and degrees of relationship, which differ in different family systems (for example, the terms for "father's brother," "mother's sister"), "cousin" (in Russian, this means literally "tribesman"), "in-laws"; the exclusive language of sex intercourse of the marriage partners; the special systems for naming offspring; the special terms of endearment; the series of words in formulae of politeness applying among different classes of family members.

There is also the private language of families. Almost every family has a special terminology, which reflects ancestors outstanding for one or another reason, as well as long-standing family customs and traditions. Families may develop special terms and phrases that are understood only by the members. These often originate in experiences which the family considers unique and prefers to recall with the special overtone or mood of the experience.[45] Even a baby's mispronunciation may become a dear family term. Husband and wife often develop little phrases so intimate and subtle that only they can understand them. The language of different families may vary with the specific language patterns of the parents—regional, social, vocational and other similar idioms.

f / The language of religion. This is the special language concerned with the "sacred" as opposed to the "secular," to use Durkheim's terms,[46] the holy in contrast to the profane. It is used by the devotees to state their religious beliefs, describe their sacred things, and prescribe and conduct their religious rites. Each language community has an array of special religious terminologies, as varied as the types and numbers of religions and subreligions functioning in it. Here too language is the essential utilitarian tool for expressing and recording all the aspects of the religious experience, as well as the religious beliefs and formulae, of the respective religious groups; it serves as the reflector and index of religious diversity.

Each religion is unique in its beliefs, creeds, doctrines and dogmas. This means, more specifically, that each religion is somewhat unique in its theology—that is, its reasoning about supernatural power and deity or deities; its mythology, legends and mysteries; its eschatology, for example, its beliefs about death, resurrection, immortality, end of the world, final judgment and state after death; its cosmology and chronology; its teleology, that is, its interpretation of final causes; its apologetics and ideology, that is, its body of justificatory facts and truths; its interpretations of human worth and human destiny on earth and in eternity, and its conception of rewards and punishment here and hereafter; its doctrines and formulae of salvation, its conceptions of sanctity or sacredness, and what it taboos, permits or requires as duties from its devotees. There are special set names, phrases, figures of speech and forms of address for all these aspects and meanings, and specific ways of using many of the more general terms.

Distinctive language is used in the rites, rituals and ceremonies of religion: its liturgy or worship (for example, masses), the formal utterances of its professional functionaries, its prayers and incantations, appeals to the deity, sacrificial and sacramental performances, purification rites, birth, baptismal, marriage and death rites, recitals of creed and confessions of faith, festivals, hymns and chants, benedictions—even its pilgrimages. There are, for example, the different "styles" and taboos regarding the utterance of the name of the deity. Prayer, especially public prayer, has its special phrasing and tonal quality. The sermon, quite apart from its distinctive religious content, is patterned as to form, and is delivered with a distinctive tonal quality and gesture. Some peoples or countries have liturgic languages that are entirely different and separate from the language of daily use—for example, Hebrew among the Jews, Sanskrit in India, Latin in Roman Catholic countries, Old Church Slavic in Southeastern Europe and Syriac in Asia Minor.

The individual devotees in their private religious practice use characteristic linguistic forms for expressing awe and obedience, love, reverence and homage, for appeasing the deity and making atonement.

Almost all religious groups—world religions, churches, denominations, sects, cults—are more or less formally organized. Those so organized have a body of language, usually extensive and distinctive, for their structural and functional features. There is the language relating to its authority and its ecclesiastical and territorial organization—for example, the titles, jurisdictions, duties of the various levels of its professional personnel, and the designations of its regions, districts, local parishes or congregations; the language of its forms of covenanting, church law, book of discipline, codes of conduct; the names and directions for use of its physical paraphernalia (edifice, altars, pulpits, sacrificial and worship instruments, the costumes and vestments of its specialized functionaries); the language of its lay organizations. The languages of each aspect and form of organization differ, as the forms themselves do. Most religious groups also have their special missionary and propagandist terminology, their language of defense and offense against non-believers and skeptics. Important in most religions are the names of their founders, prophets, messiahs and great promoters.

In our country, vast diversities of religious language are revealed, as we compare that of Catholics, the almost infinite array of Protestants, Jews, Mormons, Christian Scientists, Ethical Culturists and Humanists, Trinitarians and Unitarians, Fundamentalists and Modernists, theists, deists and mystics. We also have to include the language of atheism and agnosticism, and of orthodoxy and heterodoxy. Within our American Protestantism, there is the special organizational language of each of the three forms of church government: congregational, episcopal, and presbyterian.

There are occasional instances of the major religious groups of a country being separated from each other by major linguistic differences. In Canada, for example, the great bulk of the Catholics are the French-speaking French-Canadians, while the Protestant majority is English-speaking.

g / The world of art and its special languages. In the world of the fine arts, cognizance must be taken of two kinds of special languages: (1) the symbolic means of conveying aesthetic experience to others, and (2) the technical language of each art. With respect to the first type, it should be noted that each art is a "language" in the sense that it is a somewhat systematized way of communication; in this instance, a way of conveying aesthetic experience to others. Various kinds of symbols are used in art, such as physical shapes, lines and other marks, colors, combined masses, rhythmic motions, sounds, words and phrases, and combinations of these. By means of these, the aesthetic sensations, emotions, imaginings, conceptualizations, desires and ideals of the artist are recorded and made available to all others who are attuned to their reception and comprehension. Viewed socially, each art is a medium or vehicle for portraying and interpreting the impulses and yearnings, the emotional and intellectual currents, the great perplexities and great intuitions, the imaginative and spiritual resources and achievements of its time. The artistic product is thus a kind of "writing."

The second kind of special language of art is *its technical language,* the body of special terms by means of which the "specialists" in the world of art—the artists, the art connoisseurs, the art critics, and those who market art communicate with each other. Each art as a technique, as a means of producing a type of product, has its special terms (1) for the materials or media it works with, whether that be stone or paint or colors or sounds or words, or human organs, muscles and movements; (2) for its processes and techniques and methods of execution and for its technical capacities and skills; (3) for its special values, attitudes and perspectives; (4) for the tools, instruments and other equipment used in its processes of creation and presentation; (5) for the conditions of work and performance; (6) for the criteria of quality; (7) for the interfunctional relations of artists, performers, managers, displayers, patrons and audience; (8) for the market for artistic wares; (9) for its current emphases, styles, movements and trends. Each major form of art—graphic, pictorial or plastic, musical, literary, dramatic, terpsichorean, architectural, as well as the host of applied arts—will have its own particular variant terms for these technical aspects, terms which are peculiar and appropriate to its medium and expressional techniques. Within each art field, there are often special "schools" (for example, "schools" of painting in the graphic art area, of poetry in the literary area, of architecture), or cliques holding to similar values, styles, forms, and so on, each of which has a certain distinctive terminology to distinguish its special beliefs and practices from others prevailing in the art area.

h / The language of the jazz community. Lying midway between the special languages of sports and entertainment and those of art is the special language centering around jazz music—the language of the "jazz community."[47] This consists of the closely related vernaculars of the jazz creators and musicians; of the publishers and distributors of printed jazz music and the personnel of the jazz record industry; of the broadcasters of jazz by radio and television; and, by no means least, of the great body of jazz addicts. This special language, with its peculiar functional subforms among its various categories of users, is one of wide currency. Listening to jazz is a major form of entertainment or of passing time on the part of millions during the many hours it is presented daily on radio and television and in the playing of records. Though jazz is of American origin, it has come to have an almost universal acceptance, now being widely played and enjoyed in Europe, Australia, the Soviet Union, and even in some of the back country, not to mention the urban areas, of Latin America, Asia, and Africa. It has been enfranchised by "highbrow" culture and has been played with increasing frequency in Carnegie Hall and by symphony orchestras; many symphony programs, in fact, are very likely to include a jazz number.

There are substantial sociological and social-psychological reasons for jazz language, as there are for jazz itself. Gold has pointed out in his insightful study that the people who created this singularly American idiom did so as the result of the peculiar conditions surrounding the development of modern jazz.[48]

Jazz itself was a "music of protest" on the part of its Negro originators and its early Negro and white developers. Its language was "an impish rebellion of people largely deprived of formal education."[49] Mezzrow has also suggested that the language served as an ego-booster in that it provided its relatively uneducated users with a complicated and more or less secret language comparable to that of such specialized professionals as doctors and lawyers.[50] For both its creators and players and its many devoted listeners, jazz in its various forms serves several different (and at first glance seemingly inconsistent) functions: an emotional stimulant, a tranquilizer or even narcotic, a medium of escape from self or boredom. In general, as in the case of most of the other special languages, it functions as a sort of inner-circle code and keeps the jazz community separated from the general public.[51] The "circle," however, as has been implied, has come to be one of vast circumference.

The jazzmen and jazz addicts employ a colorful and highly esoteric language. This special jargon is "jive," though the term is also used to refer to a form of jazz music. The devotees are "hipsters." Some jazz music is *sweet,* but some *hot;* the *hot* may be "jive," or "swing," or "be-bop." The devotee or player of the hot variety is a "hepcat." A "clambake" or "jam session" is a gathering of hot musicians at which the different instruments may "swing" or "jam," that is, freely be improvised with; for example, there may be "bend" or special effects from the brass section, and the whole effect can be "cool" or sensational. The musical instruments have special names: among those for piano is "box," for the double-base "bull fiddle," for trombone "sliphorn," for French horn "pretzel." Among the performers of the different instruments, the drummer is a "skin-beater," the guitarist a "whanger," the trumpeter a "Gabriel." Among the addicts a dance is a "cement-mixer," a girl is a "chick" or a "witch," and "whacky" is to dance wildly; thrills are "kicks"; having fun is "balling," sex is "jelly," and to be "hep" is to be aware of things.

i / The language of science. Scientists found long ago that some of the language in daily use is of very limited value in dealing with science. In their respective fields, they have had to construct highly specialized terminologies and skeleton languages to meet their specific purposes. In fact, the justification of the formation of special technical languages is strongest in the language of science, for here we have the sharpest accentuation of the strategic need for specialized languages, and also the most highly developed case of standardized particularity and precision of terminology, phraseology, grammar and other symbolic devices, as well as of consistency in usage. It is the most exacting and exclusive among the technical languages. Furthermore, it constitutes one of the most striking instances of the sociocultural significance of language —its part in the formation, presentation and recording of human knowledge and investigative methods, and in the description, prescription and direction of human technological activity.

[1] *Reasons for the language of science.* The language of science is in part necessitated by the fact that the knowledge of scientists transcends the capacity of lay language to state it and record it. This knowledge —which consists of identified factual data, definitions, axioms, principles, hypotheses, theorems, postulates, taxonomies, allegations and interpretations—is unintelligible and hence valueless, if it is not precisely, accurately and uniformly stated and recorded for its present and future users and beneficiaries. The fact that the investigative and experimental techniques of science must be conducted with the utmost precision is another factor. To describe these, to have findings resulting from their employment available for testing and utilization by others, and to enable these methods to be exactly and accurately replicated by others, requires that they be stated and recorded in "scientific" language. The instruments used in scientific research must also be accurately and uniformly named and described, and directions for their operation must be clearly and widely comprehensible. Hence, every scientific discipline must develop and maintain a special language adapted to its nature. This is, in fact, one of the first steps in the development of science itself, and the continuous improvement and supplementation of this language represents an essential part of scientific work. So special is scientific language that the meaning of a technical term in a scientific language often cannot be derived or guessed at from the meaning of the same word as it is used in ordinary language.

Each separate science has a vocabulary peculiar to itself because of the type of phenomena with which it is concerned. To a recognizable extent, there is a chemical language, a physical language, a biological language, a sociological language, as well as others within the general framework of the languages of science.

Included in the language of science, as in all large-scale institutionalized activities, is also the special terminology dealing with the roles of its functionaries, the language of its bureaucratically organized professional associations, its financial foundations and research institutes, not to mention all the corporate organizations that carry on the extensive technological activities based on science.

[2] *The common features of the languages of sciences.* While each science and nascent science has its special terminology and other com-

municative symbolism adapted to its own special purposes, all the languages of science, *as instruments of science,* have certain features in common. (a) The language of science has *directness and precision of expression;* it must avoid vagueness and ambiguity at all costs. Hence, it seeks to be consistent in its use of terms and precise in its syntax. Unlike the language of the arts, it avoids figures of speech, the use of metaphor and hyperbole. (b) It is *objective;* it cannot be subjective (that is, highly personalized), intuitive, or speculative. (c) In the light of science's function—that is, since it develops its theory in order to impose order on what appears to be chaos—its language is *discriminative and specific* as to the name, feature, and category of referents in any given statement; it is *logical in its presentation.* (d) Scientific prose is *unemotional;* ideally it does not show a glimmer of feeling and warmth; it expounds and explains without producing—or intending to produce—"a quickening of the pulse." (e) Unlike the languages of some of the arts, with their widely inclusive nature—for example, poetry with the many connotations it adds to given words and its resort to metaphor, allusion and simile—the language of science is highly *exact and exclusive:* exact in its meanings, and exclusive of any other than these single and specifically assigned meanings. For the same reason, it should have, and in most instances does have, a high degree of *semantic consistency.* (f) It is highly formalized, conventionalized or *standardized, as to connotations and meanings of words,* and as to its *style of expression;* scientists as cooperators must of necessity use words and all other pertinent symbols in a rigorously specified manner. The terms used must always have *standardized referents.* (g) It is *cautious,* not flamboyant, arbitrary, or dogmatic. Science is always aware that "the evidence is not yet all in." (h) Its style is usually *economical*— that is, no more language is used than is essential to clear and adequate presentation. It would usually take much more language and many more involved sentences for a scientist to communicate the same facts and meanings to a layman than it does to a fellow scientist. (i) Historically, scientific words have had a high degree of *permanence,* as well as singleness of meaning, and marked *constancy* in form and function, as compared with so many ordinary words. Always, of course, the durability has rested upon the appropriateness of the words in meeting the terminological needs. In general, the words of science have precise and unchanging meanings and a lack of misleading and distorting associations. (j) The language of science presents *public* knowledge regarding its area of investigation; the information is not of a confidential or privileged character.

[3] *The sources of scientific language.* There are three main sources

of the elements—mainly the vocabulary—of scientific language. (a) First, there are the *borrowed words*—the words borrowed from ordinary language, but given a new and special meaning by the scientists, although the scientific meaning usually bears some resemblance to the meanings in everyday life. Examples of such borrowed terms are: *force, energy, work, power, mass, velocity, weight* as the physicist uses them, *life* as the biologist uses it, *time* as the mathematician or the astronomer uses it, *salt* as the chemist uses it, *status, role, authority, community* as the sociologist uses them. This borrowing leads to some confusion, especially in the social sciences, since the listener or reader does not always know whether the word is being used in the common or the scientifically specialized sense. (b) Some words are *imported* from foreign languages or from foreign countries, because they are so admirably suited for inclusion in the special vocabulary of science. They are usually taken into the language without much change in spelling or meaning. Latin has contributed *atlas, axis, bacillus, cortex, fulcrum, genus, humus, larva, nucleus, ovum, pelvis, species, vertebra;* from the Greek we have *genesis, larynx, nectar, stigma, thorax.* The scientific languages of every country show numerous inclusions from the scientific languages of other countries, sometimes as the result of pioneering scientific work in the country of source—for example, the borrowing by American scientists of German and other European scientific terms, in almost every science, a half century ago, or the recent borrowing by other countries of American nuclear-science terminology. (c) Probably the largest group of special words used in science are *invented* by the scientists themselves for their own purposes. The advance of science, especially during the last century, has been so rapid, and its extension into new, heretofore untouched areas of investigation so great, that neither the common language nor the language of the ancients or of contemporary foreigners could supply sufficient words for its needs—the scientists *had* to contrive useful names for all of the newly discovered phenomena. Invented terms are, for example, *infrared, anabolic, katabolic, intracellular, ultraviolet, quadruped, monoxide.*

[4] *Parallel development of science and scientific language.* The language of science clearly reflects and records the changes in science. The reasons are clear. As the methods of science are extended to new areas of concern (for example, nuclear physics, psychology, sociology), there must be the appropriate language for naming, defining and conceptualizing what has been discovered. New language is necessary as the scientific "knowns" in any established field increase in number and kind. As science penetrates existing areas of investigation in increasing

"depth," and as the "knowns" become more specific and exact with regard to form, function and behavior, the more specific and exact, and at the same time, the more comprehensive must become the linguistic and other symbolic forms of connotation, expression and recording. Furthermore, as a science advances in its conquest of its phenomenal field, there is a noticeable refinement in its language; its statements become more purely designative, better confirmed and better systematized, and its concepts are presented in more standard terms. Thus the very additions to the scientific vocabulary and the logical and semantic "tightening up" of the language, as these changes appear in time and space, usually reflect the development of the sciences themselves in scope and method, in new specialties and intensities, in conceptual integration, and in new localities of the earth.

[5] *The tendency toward universality of the languages of science.* Partly as a consequence of the fact that the phenomena with which the sciences are concerned occur independently of any physical or political boundaries, that scientific procedures and knowledges are markedly similar wherever scientific investigation is conducted, and that the diffusion of scientific techniques, theories and products occurs, by intention or otherwise, on a *world* scale—for all these reasons, the scientific languages are tending to become increasingly similar and mutually comprehensible among the cultures and nations of the earth. In fact, science is probably more international than any other sociocultural activity. This universality is further brought out by the fact that the scientific prose of any one people can be translated into the language of another equally scientifically advanced people more readily and accurately than can any other prose. Involved here is not only the universality of science, but also the greater uniformity of style (simplicity, specificity), of meaning (fewer nuances of meaning), and a conception of the essentials of presentation among the scientific writers of the world.[52]

[6] *The contention that scientific language is obscure or prolix.* The charge is occasionally made by laymen that the language of science is obscure, while some scientists prefer to think that the language of other sciences is unnecessarily prolix. As to the first contention, it should be said at once that scientific speech and writing is never deliberately obscure. Science deals with complex phenomena and, as noted, it must have many special or specially used terms for these. Furthermore, scientific terms, in many instances, cannot be simple, monosyllabic words. It is often economical, with respect to the use of essential words for a concept or for the name of a substance or object, for example, a chemical compound, to have a multisyllabic, even a multi-hyphenated com-

pound word. For the specialist or other informed person, the single compounded scientific term may take the place of a paragraph of as many as 200 words that would be used in ordinary description. Thus, it is frequently a case of *multum in parvo*. A paragraph of scientific reporting which is highly meaningful and useful to a scientist in a given field may be hopelessly obscure to a scientifically uninformed layman, or even to a scientist in a different field of knowledge and investigation. It is even likely that the incomprehensibility of scientific language to non-specialists and the non-initiated has grown with the rapid development of science and technology during recent years.

As to the second charge, it should be noted that, in a rapidly developing new science, there may be a seeming tendency toward verbosity —a "mess of verbiage." This may be an actuality to some extent with regard to *some* of its theorists and proponents. But it is essential to have names and other symbols, and particularly reasoned conceptualizations, in order to be able to refer to the discovered principles and the other new products of observation and experimentation. A new science is engaged in devising suitable and adequate tools, which may seem new and strange to some. This new science is in process of abandoning "educated guesses" and individualistic conceptions and procedures, but, while such conceptions and procedures may not be adequately standardized and integrated, and may not have the desired precision as instruments, they do have something tremendously worthwhile to say. Only to the wholly uninitiated can this language of a new science be dubbed "empty verbosity," "gobbledegook," or "esoteric symbolism."

[7] *Mathematics: the basic idiom of science.* Mathematics is the basic denotative system whereby all of the sciences to a greater or lesser extent express the quantities, forms, arrangements, and magnitudes of their respective categories of natural phenomena. By means of its body of rigorously defined, self-consistent, specialized and precise written symbols, signs, and abbreviations, now almost international in their application, mathematics can disclose in exact, economical, logical, and unbiased and unemotional manner, free from many complicating linguistic features (for example, those of grammar), the characteristics, relations, and operations of scientific phenomena.

The signs and symbols used as media have various origins, and have developed over a long period of time, though the greater portion of those now in use are the product of the period since the invention of printing. Within the twentieth century they have been universalized and standardized; however, they are undergoing rapid further development at the present time. Among them are standard linguistic signs such as letters of the Greek alphabet plus some from Hebrew and Old English alphabets, with capital and lower case letters used with different signification; Arabic and Roman numerals; a great number and variety of specially invented signs (for example, parentheses, brackets, angle indicators, indicators of subtraction, addition, multiplication, division, square and higher roots, subscripts, and dozens of others). These are variously combined, depending upon the descriptive or analytical problem at hand.

Mathematics is a language which depicts the quantitative properties of the universe. By means of its devices and procedures it can deal with the problem of numbers as applied to enumeration, mensuration, and computation; spatial properties of linearity, shape, angle, area, distance and volume (mass) can be analyzed and concisely presented; forces and energies and movement can be designated and calculated; sequences, periodicities, series of occurrence, and rates and amounts of change in time can be established; the relations of quantities, magnitudes and forces can be exactly equated; the integration and differentiation of properties and magnitudes can be calculated; masses of items can be statistically sampled; and probabilities and chain reactions can be predicted. These are only major types of contributions; there are hosts of others varying from problem to problem and science to science.

The scientist uses these mathematical operations to describe things, processes, events, and relations; to evaluate and correlate the variables in given situations; to provide the basic data for his theories and to enable him to refine and check them; to qualify his postulates and theorems and generalizations or laws; to present his formulae of action. Needless to say, every technology also uses the sub-language of mathematics.

Most mathematical language can be put into words, but this would be a very awkward and uneconomical procedure. Mathematics, therefore, is a form of "shorthand." Directly related is the additional fact that, in all of the special areas where it is used, mathematical language makes up for the lacks of ordinary language; for example, it is not subject to the same kinds of semantic risks. It might also be noted that mathematical language and formal logic often disclose or point up weaknesses or "mistakes" in ordinary human logic.

The language of mathematics has undergone new and extensive development in very recent decades under the impetus of the theoretical and practical problems posed by nucleonics, jet-age (or super-mach) aeronautics, and the exploration of outer space.

Another development relating to the language of science and technology is the peculiar electronic communication of the modern computers. The basic function of computers is the processing of diverse, complex and quantitatively vast information. The data, in various "computer language" forms (perhaps as many as fifty such "languages"), are given to the computers which translate them into "machine language." In the process the different parts of the computers give each other information; "talk" to each other about this information; talk back to each other ("feedback"); give each other directives; and then give the answer.

j / The language of sociology. Brief mention of certain aspects of the special language of sociology, the science of major orientation in this volume, is in order. This language is, first and foremost, the language of a body of professionals.[53] This is a group devoted to the analysis of human society: its structures and functions, its systems and patterns of action and interaction, and the host of diverse conditioning and determinative factors. Sociology, like all sciences, must have an appropriate and adequate terminology and style of communicating its discovered facts, theoretical formulations and methodological procedures. As a rather new science, its terminology is not yet as highly standardized as is desirable in a science, nor has it achieved as great a degree of conceptual integration as have some of the older sciences. Furthermore, the terminology and the style of presentation of some of the sociologists has been forbidding. The terminology has sometimes been imprecisely ("loosely") used; the writing has been verbose and obtuse (on occasion apparently employed in order to mystify and to "show off," as children do with their "secret language").

The language of sociology, nonetheless, seeks to conform to the general principles governing the language of science, and it is achieving most of them in a large measure. The standardization of terms and the integration of concepts is occurring rapidly. In recent years some of the books in sociology and many of the articles and research reports in the professional journals have come to consist of clear, "lean," and "muscular" prose. And some of the craftsmen have used the language with grace and stylistic felicity. There is at least a "semi-institutionalization" of "sociological rhetoric," to use Page's apt term.[54]

k / The language of medicine. A special technical language, involving features both typical and extremist, is the language of medicine. The rapid and extensive advances in medical science and technology have required the continuous construction of new nomenclature and technical description. Many old terms have ceased to have clear meaning and have been discarded. When new knowledge pertaining to the health of human beings—physiological, anatomical, chemical, bacteriological, psychiatric, ecological—has been discovered, or new techniques of treatment and control have been invented, there must be some new language for the description and manipulation of these advances. While this may not be in terms of the common language of the lay public, it soon becomes standard within the professional area. There are today, for example, many varieties of heart impairment, of pneumonia, of cancer, each of which must be distinctively named, described, and treated.

The language that some physicians and dentists use in their professional intercourse with laymen, whether these be patients or simply members of the public, is sometimes carried to the point of extreme specialism, quite beyond the requirements of precision and facility of discourse. It should be remembered that the receiver of a communication, if he is to derive information from it, must be able to understand it. When your physician tells you that you are suffering from "bilateral perorbital hematoma," and means only that you have a black eye, he is giving you an accurate anatomical–physiological description, but he is not enlightening you very much. Note also this instance of "medicalese": The patient "suffered a bilateral digital amputation" (lost two fingers), with "a resultant diminution of digital dexterity, the end product of same being a severe limitation of his pre-operative ability." The conclusion must be that the effort is being made to mystify the public with respect to the highly technical and esoteric nature of their knowledge and performance, and to create an aura about their profession.

1 / Other special languages. Though the above treatment of special languages is extensive, there are a considerable number of other such sublanguages in our culture to which we have not given attention. The existence of all of these is also due to their functional importance to their coterie of speakers. Some of the languages are unique, because of the dramatic eccentricities or even the pathological characteristics of their speakers. Some are of recent appearance—the novel speech forms, for example, of a striking new technological development. Among these heretofore unmentioned sublanguages are those of railroaders, taxi, bus and truck drivers, workers in oilfields, nurses and hospital attendants, policemen and detectives, the personnel of the mass communications industries (newspapers, magazines, radio and television), those in the production and distribution of motion pictures, college students ("collegiate speech"), school teachers, social workers, or those in pathological groupings, such as homosexuals.

Notable instances of recent, and as yet largely unrecorded technical "specials," are those of the Air Force and "missile-ese." The Air Force man does not say "Okay" or "No" in response to inquiries, instructions, or the imparting of information; he says, "Roger," or just "Roj." Special equipment has special naming, which does not follow the standard terminology for the item; for example, certain complexes of electronic components are called "black boxes." Initials are widely used. Some stand for jobs, e.g., "ac" for "aircraft commander"; some for conditions, such as "aocp" for "aircraft out of commission," and some for techniques, such as "jato" for "jet-assisted takeoff." The airman has many nicknames or phrases peculiar to his craft: his home base is "the home patch," his plane is "the bird"; the pilot is a "tiger," "jock" or "hero"; his cockpit is his "little office"; when he retracts the plane's wheels on takeoff, he "sucks up the gear"; when problems arise, conditions are "hairy." When all is well, he sums it up in two words: "No Sweat."[55] The missile men at Cape Kennedy and other missile bases have a spoken and written language which is a hodgepodge of scientific jargon, test pilot slang, Madison Avenue-ism, corrupted idiom and verbal innovations concocted to fit the occasion. An example: "The launch sent the three-stage vehicle, a second-generation configuration, on a nominal trajectory . . . the command module programmed, staged and optimized its attitude in the automatic mode—all well within the defined parameters." There is much substitution of special terms for standard words and phrases: "vehicle" or "booster" instead of "rocket"; "space-craft," but never "satellite." To fly a normal course a rocket must "program through a normal trajectory," and if it fails, it "aborts" or "falls short of its goal."[56]

These heretofore unmentioned special languages, and those which have only recently emerged, also have sociological and social-psychological reasons for existence. The terminology of each is a functional blend; it reflects several factors, depending upon the sociocultural context in which it operates as the expressional medium—such as providing utility and efficiency of expression, advancing the occupational or other proficiency of its speakers as a group, maintaining secrecy in communication, functioning as a form of self-flattery, enhancing the exclusiveness and the presumed prestige and superiority of its speakers as a collectivity, providing special identification among out-groups and mutual admiration within the in-group.

N O T E S

1 William I. Thomas, *Sourcebook for Social Origins* (Chicago: University of Chicago Press, 1909), p. 521. See also Otto Jespersen, *Language: Its Nature, Development, and Origin* (New York: Macmillan Co., 1922), pp. 237–238; William G. Sumner and Albert G. Keller: *The Science of Society* (New Haven: Yale University Press, 1927), IV, 1161; Uriel Weinreich: *Languages in Contact* (New York: Publications of the Linguistic Circle of New York, No. 1, 1953), pp. 93–94.

2 Sir James G. Frazer, "Men's Languages and Women's Languages," *Fortnightly Review,* 73 (Jan., 1900), 79–90.

3 Wilfred D. Hambly and Charles Hose, *Origins of Education among Primitive Peoples* (London: The Macmillan Co., 1926), p. 287.

4 Joost A. M. Meerloo, *Conversation and Communication: A Psychological Inquiry into Language and Human Relations* (New York: International Universities Press, 1952), p. 71.

5 *Ibid.*

6 Cf. George Herzog, "Linguistic Approaches to Culture and Personality," in Stansfeld S. Sargent (ed.), *Culture and Personality* (New York: Viking Fund, 1949), pp. 93–102.

7 J. Vendryes, *Language: A Linguistic Introduction to History* (London: Kegan, Paul, Trench & Trubner, 1925), p. 257.

8 Iona and Peter Opie, *The Lore and Language of Schoolchildren* (Oxford: The Clarendon Press, 1959).

9 *Ibid.,* p. v.

10 Professor Henry Angelino of the University of Oklahoma made a study of "The Argot of the American Adolescent," based mainly on findings in Norman, Oklahoma. The following are a few instances of special terms with their meanings: "ancient"=parent; "bag"=a girl who is not too attractive; "bell me"= call me up; "bomb"=a girl who is very attractive; "diploma man"=student; "drip"=someone you don't like; "evil eye"=teacher; "flip lip"=wisecracking person; "id"=romance, courting; "loopy"=something dumb.

11 E. Jacques Brazeau, "Language Differences and Occupational Experience," *Canadian Journal of Economics and Political Science,* 24 (Nov., 1959), 532–540.

12 William G. Sumner and Albert G. Keller, *The Science of Society* (New Haven: Yale University Press, 1927), I, 558. (For their treatment of "Fraternities and Maturity Usages," see pp. 525–560.)

13 Most of this discussion of the secret languages of primitive secret societies has been derived from Hutton Webster's classic *Primitive Secret Societies* (2nd ed.) (New York: Macmillan Co., 1908), pp. 40–43. See also Ralph Piddington, *An Introduction to Social Anthropology* (New York: Frederick A. Praeger, 1950), I, 207–213.

14 *Ibid.,* p. 43.

15 N. W. Thomas, "African Secret Societies" (*Hastings Encyclopedia of Religion and Ethics*), II, 301.

16 It is interesting to note that our term "mumbo-jumbo" is often used for language that is unnecessarily involved and difficult to understand—that is, for gibberish. The original Mumbo Jumbo was an African secret order with a complicated private language centered around a mysterious deity (or demon), *Mama Dhiombo,* who was greatly feared by the women.

17 "In all ages secrecy and mystery have been favorite, successful, and also cheap devices for securing prestige." Sumner and Keller, p. 2148.

18 We shall draw entirely upon the classic study by Noel P. Gist, *Secret Societies: A Cultural Study of Fraternalism in the United States* (Columbia, Mo.: University of Missouri Studies), Vol. XV, No. 4 (October 1, 1940).

19 *Ibid.*, pp. 9, 93.

20 On names and titles see *ibid.*, pp. 55–58.

21 *Ibid.*, pp. 65–68.

22 The term *argot* is frequently used interchangeably with *cant*. In French it stems from the language of malefactors, and it was used originally in English to designate such special language. Some important linguists still use *argot*. Mencken, for example, says that "every trade, profession, sport and hobby has its argot," and lists samples of the "argots" of sixty-nine occupations (*The American Language* (New York: Alfred A. Knopf, 1948), Supplement II, p. 731). For total treatment of argots, see pp. 731–777. In the present discussion, we shall use *cant* for the lingoes of malefactors.

23 For an excellent and extensive glossary of terms used by professional criminals, see Edwin H. Sutherland (ed.), *The Professional Thief* (Chicago: University of Chicago Press, 1937), pp. 235–243. On underworld cant, see also Ruth S. Cavan, *Criminology* (New York: Thomas Y. Crowell Co., 1948), pp. 138–141; Eric Partridge, *A Dictionary of the Underworld, British and American: Being the Vocabularies of Crooks, Criminals, Racketeers, Beggars, and Tramps: 16th–20th Centuries* (London: Routledge & Kegan Paul, 1950); Eric Partridge, *Here, There and Everywhere: Essays Upon Language* (London: H. Hamilton, 1950), pp. 84–88, 97–115.

24 *Jargon*, as used in the past, has meant many different kinds of language: a confused unintelligible language (gabble, gibberish); a strange, outlandish, or barbarous language (of foreign or uncivilized people); a hybrid or mixed language (such as the pidgins). It is now, by most linguists, used as the name for the technical sublanguages of every occupational, organizational, institutional, and other special-interest and special-function group, and nearly every special branch of knowledge. (Cf. Eric Partridge, *The World of Words* (London: George Routledge & Sons Ltd., 1938), p. 198; Joseph Church, *Language and the Discovery of Reality* (New York: Random House, 1961), p. 119.) However, some eminently respectable students of language still use it in the sense of *gibberish*.

25 For a recent statement see Edward Gross, "The Obligations and Rewards of Colleagueship," in his *Work and Society* (New York: Thomas Y. Crowell Co., 1958), pp. 235–241.

26 Cf. Wilbert E. Moore and Melvin M. Tumin, "Some Social Functions of Ignorance," *American Sociological Review*, 14 (Dec., 1949), 787–795.

27 William A. Westley, "Violence and the Police," *American Journal of Sociology*, 59 (July, 1953), 34–41. See also his "Secrecy and the Police," *Social Forces*, 34 (Mar., 1956), 254–257.

28 Cf. Gross, pp. 238–240.

29 Carl R. Rogers and Fritz J. Roethlisberger, "Barriers and Gateways to Communication," *Harvard Business Review*, 30 (July–Aug., 1952), 46–52; Robert E. Lane, "Businessmen and Bureaucrats," *Social Forces*, 32 (Dec., 1953), 145–152.

30 This has been suggested in part by Robert Dubin, *The World of Work* (Englewood Cliffs, N. J.: Prentice-Hall Inc., 1958), p. 342.

31 Cf. Richard T. La Piere, *A Theory of Social Control* (New York: McGraw-Hill Book Co., 1954), pp. 216–217.

32 Quoted in a *Chicago News* World Service Release of July 18, 1962. That bureaucratic jargon is not a peculiarly American phenomenon is illustrated by the examples of British bureaucratic language provided by Eric Partridge, *Chamber of Horrors* (New York: British Book Center, 1953). Other facts

and instances of bureaucratic language will be brought out below in the discussion of the specialized languages in some of the major institutional areas of social life.

33 For a somewhat different classification and treatment of the different specialized sublanguages of the typical community, see Part Three, especially pp. 242–269, of Marcel Cohen, *Pour une sociologie du langage* (Paris: Albin Michel, 1956).

34 Cf. Wilbert E. Moore, *The Conduct of the Corporation* (New York: Random House, 1962).

35 See Fred W. Cottrell, *The Railroader* (Stanford, Cal.: Stanford University Press, 1940), pp. 117–139.

36 "I once overheard a sheepman, whom I was visiting, giving instructions to his herder. I could not understand what they were saying, so strange was their vocabulary," William F. Ogburn, "Influences Affecting the Future of Sociology," *Social Forces*, 38 (Oct., 1959), 3–7.

37 Note the following words and phrases used by economic experts with special reference to business conditions, as reported in the single issue of August 1, 1960 of *U. S. News and World Report*: "Inventory build-up," "inventory accumulation," "inventory readjustment," "inflationary pressures," "deterioration of profit margins," "plant-and-equipment expenditures," "patterns of gain," "hesitancy in the market," "capital facilities," "built-in stabilizers," "expansionary forces," "economic climate," "economic atmosphere." Experts on the stock market in the same journal (August 8, 1960) used such terms as "profit-margin squeeze," "market was vulnerable," "high price structure of the market," "eroding of the dollar's value," "bull-market highs," "turn-around in profits," "investor confidence." (See also "The Language of Business" from *Fortune Magazine*, Nov. 1950; reprinted in Charles B. Jennings, Nancy King, and Marjorie Stevenson (eds.), *Weigh the Word* (New York: Harper & Brothers, 1957), pp. 91–99.)

38 Sometimes there is an amusing "gilding" of crafts in their special uses of language. Kay Nelson in a little piece on "The Language of Beauty" pointed out that the hairdresser is now a stylist or a coiffure designer; instead of having customers, beauty shops have clients, patrons, or even patients; hairdos are inspired, created, conceived—*not* done. (*Saturday Evening Post*, July 14–21, 1962, p. 62.)

39 This has been aptly referred to as "oracle language," issued as "we turn our political prayer wheels." See Joost A. M. Meerloo, *Conversation and Communication: A Psychological Inquiry Into Language and Human Relations* (New York: International Universities Press, 1952), pp. 74–75.

40 Harold D. Lasswell, "The Language of Power," in H. D. Lasswell and Nathan Leites *et al., The Language of Politics* (New York: George W. Stewart, 1949), pp. 2–19.

41 *Ibid.*

42 Huntington Cairns, "Language of Jurisprudence," in Ruth N. Anshen (ed.), *Language: An Enquiry into Its Meaning and Function* (New York: Harper & Brothers, 1957), pp. 232–269.

43 Morroe Berger, "Army Language," *American Speech*, 26 (Dec., 1945), pp. 258–264; Frederich Elkin, "The Soldier's Language," *American Journal of Sociology*, 51 (Mar., 1946), 414–422.

44 Hugh D. Duncan, *Communication and the Social Order* (New York: Bedminster Press, 1962), pp. 410–411.

45 Hans Gerth and C. Wright Mills, *Character and Social Structure: The Psychology of Social Institutions* (New York: Harcourt, Brace & Co., 1953), pp. 281–283.

46 Emile Durkheim, *The Elementary Forms of the Religious Life,* trans. J. W. Swain (Glencoe, Ill.: Free Press, 1947), pp. 37–42. See also "The Religious Significance of the WORD," in Chap. XI, Sect. 3, of the present work.

47 Alan P. Merriam and Raymond W. Mack, "The Jazz Community," *Social Forces,* 38 (Mar., 1960), 211–222.

48 Robert S. Gold, "The Vernacular of the Jazz World," *American Speech*, 32 (Dec., 1957), 271–282.

49 *Ibid.*, p. 272.

50 Milton Mezzrow and Bernard Wolfe, *Really the Blues* (New York: Random House, 1946), pp. 8–9, 14.

51 Merriam and Mack, p. 218.

52 At the same time, the continuing lack of facility in the languages of other scientifically advanced people upon the part of many scientists still has an adverse effect upon the advancement of science in the modern world. Many scientists are ill-equipped in languages. Such a lack is a more serious barrier to research than is commonly assumed; it makes for parochialism in research.

53 As of 1963, the members of the American Sociological Association—the true "card-carrying" professionals—as listed in the official *Directory*, numbered over 7200. The number of persons teaching sociology at the high school and college level, or conducting research of a sociological nature under the auspices of many different organizations, or otherwise interested in or dealing with social phenomena in a sociological manner, but not formally connected, probably far exceeds the membership of the Association.

54 On this subject, see Charles H. Page, "Sociology as an Educational Enterprise," in Page (ed.), *Sociology and Contemporary Education* (New York: Random House, 1964), pp. 3–39 (3–9, 37–38). In this volume see also pp. 52–54, 128–130. Cf. David Dressler and George W. Korber, "A Comment on the Language of Sociology," *Pacific Sociological Review*, 5 (Spring, 1962), 36–40; Severyn T. Bruyn, "Rhetorical Devices in Sociological Analysis," *Sociological Quarterly*, 5 (Spring, 1964), 101–112.

55 From an Associated Press release of May 29, 1964.

56 From a United Press International report by Alvin B. Webb, Jr., released November 11, 1963.

XIV ✺ Social Differentiation and Linguistic Specialization in the Language Community: III. The Languages of the Social Classes

A feature of language with both causal and effectual significance, so important as to merit special treatment, is its association with a society's stratification system. This feature very definitely involves patterned linguistic *and* societal differences of a separative nature, and the discussion to follow has direct relationship to Chapter X, "Language as a Centrifugal Factor in Human Societies." But the subject has even greater pertinence in the present framework of analysis, because of the fact that the speech and other language habits of the different social strata of most societies tend to have characteristic forms, which are so much in contrast with each other as to merit designation as "special" languages of the general language.

1. *The Correlation of Social and Linguistic Stratification*

Social stratification has to do with the fact that individuals and groups in all societies are to some degree hierarchically typed, ranked and socially spaced and divided as horizontal layers or strata. Society can thus be conceived of as a layer cake.[1] While the strata are complementary, they are unequal in one or more ways, according to the current yardsticks of evaluation of the given society. Prestige, esteem, honor, privileges and rights, responsibilities and authority are unequally assigned; they exist in a series of higher degrees among the successively higher layers. While there is a relative equality of members within each of the layers, there are distinctions of higher and lower, superior and inferior, between any two of them.

The different levels or layers of a stratification system are characterized by differences in regard to a considerable number of aspects of the way of life. Notable in our American society, where stratification takes the form of a class system, are differences in cultural values; income, wealth, and forms of property; occupation; location and type of residence; patterns of consumption, especially as that is displayed in personal grooming, price of attire, and in the price and taste of home furnishings; types and levels of education and of the schools at which it is attained; taste in reading, radio and television programs; political opinion, affiliation and influence; patterns of family life and sex attitudes and behavior; manners and morals and esthetic taste; religious attitudes, types of religious organizations belonged to, and amount and kind of social participation; types and number of informal and formal organizations belonged to, other than educational or religious ones; and other sociocultural attributes. Members of the same class meet with each other more frequently at informal get-togethers (visiting, playing games, parties); they participate in more of the same kinds of formal organizations with each other; the members of the same class look upon each other as "the same kind of folks" and feel more comfortable with one another.

The fact of primary significance in our present study is the one that Jespersen pointed out—namely, that the social stratification of a country also leaves its marks on the language of the persons of the different strata.[2] There is some degree of linguistic differentiation corresponding to and correlated with the social layers themselves. In fact, the outstanding situations, structural forms, social functions and processes of social stratification are reflected in the linguistic forms and processes of a given community or society. This is due to the fact that the speech patterns of each social class are a part of its all-pervading cultural behavior, and, like their other behavior patterns, are always to some extent formal and stylized. People live in their social class intuitively, habitually, and *verbally*.[3] The language shows class differences, based on combinations of differential educational, ethnic, economic, political, aesthetic and religious factors.

What happens in the way of change in the stratification system directly affects the linguistic system. The *amount, nature or form,* and *rigidity* of social stratification varies in a given society from one era to another;

it also varies from one society to another at any given time, as does the underlying value structure and supporting ideology. Variation in these features in a given society is reflected in the different speech forms, conventions and habits of the different strata.

A converse aspect of language and stratification will also be noted below—namely, that certain aspects of language are utilized to indicate and sustain one's position in the stratification system.

The type and amount of linguistic stratification depends, for its sharpness and persistence, upon the rigidity of the social stratification system. Historically, the stratification systems have been rigid almost everywhere and at all levels of civilization; the language of the upper, middle (where they existed), and lower classes have shown marked differences; both social and linguistic stratification have been zealously maintained, and not always solely at the instigation of the upper, presumably favored strata. In most of Western civilization, social position was much more "closed" prior to the seventeenth century than after. Then, the leaven of democratic ideas and ideals began to be effective, and the various equalizing "freedoms" began to be available to more and more segments of the population. In much of the contemporary world, however—especially in the more underdeveloped portions—the stratification systems, while yielding to democratizing and equalizing pressures, still have a considerable degree of rigidity; in some areas, ancient and deep-seated caste systems still prevail, and assignment to a social class is determined by one's heredity. When stratification is rigid, the linguistic forms of the speakers of the different "estates," classes or castes show great differences; these differences persist, and the different forms do not diffuse very rapidly from stratum to stratum.

On the other hand, in modern, open class societies, such as our own—with free compulsory elementary and secondary education and easily obtained opportunities for higher education, with relative equality of economic opportunity for all, with a wide range of vertical social mobility and a considerable amount of it in actuality, and especially with mass vocal and written communication—class differences in language become less and less sharp. Nevertheless, the remaining differences between classes with respect to the kind and normal level of education achieved; economic variations, such as blue-collar, white-collar, professional, or administrative occupational status; differences in sources and amount of income and in the kinds and levels of consumption; kinds of associations and organization membership; ethnic and racial backgrounds and degree of assimilation; and to some extent differential regional conditions, as they affect these factors—all these still conspire to produce class differences in language, though, as we will note, they are diminishing. There is still a tendency for each class to develop its own distinctive kinds and qualities of usages and its somewhat particularized universe of discourse.

2. The Kinds of Distinctions Among the Strata in the Use of Language

We are particularly concerned with the differences of language form and usage to be found among the social classes—that is, the class variations of and departures from standard language.

The fact of stratification in every community has introduced a special or qualifying conception of standard speech—namely, the notion of "correct" speech. This consists of the forms of standard speech that are used by the educated and privileged and otherwise prestigious elements of the population—the "ruling and cultured classes." This language is "good," "right," "high" (*Hochdeutsch*), "grammatical," while the speech forms employed by the members of the lower strata are termed "bad," "incorrect," "vulgar," "rustic," "low," or "uncouth." Some of the major kinds of differences between the languages of these strata, historical and contemporary, will be briefly examined, the more obvious ones first.

a / In grammar. The syntax of the common man is of an elementary variety, as contrasted with that of the more cultured person; he violates more of the rules and principles of "standard" grammar.

b / In pronunciation, accent and intonation. Variations along these lines are noticeable even in the United States, where class divergences in speech are relatively moderate. The speech, in these respects, of the men congregating in a workingmen's tavern is quite different from that of the habitués of the Harvard Club.

c / In volume, range, and richness of vocabulary. The linguistic environment of the respective social classes varies greatly: that of the lower classes is one of relative linguistic poverty, as compared with the opulence of that of the upper classes. Thus, in the stratification system of a society where a single language prevails, the speech of the upper classes usually will be superior in correctness and richer in its expressional facility. Particularly significant is the fact that the *vocabulary* of the upper classes is much more extensive, including words that reflect more categories of knowledge and interest, and many more synonyms and figurative terms, such as permit more precise, elaborate and colorful statements. That of the lower classes, on the other hand, shows limitations in these regards. Divergences in vocabulary are usually the single most noticeable feature of the linguistic stratification.

d / In "style" and "taste" in the selection and use of words and phrases. There is often wide variation in the resort to euphemisms, the use of slang and argots, in precision of use of the various "correctnesses" of grammar and pronunciation, and in gracefulness, adroitness and cultural "flair" in the selection, combination and enunciation of words and phrases.[4]

e / In the use of writing and in reading. The upper classes have more formal education and are more literate. In general, they write more: they send more letters, keep more records, use writing much more in meeting their social obligations. Usually, they also read more, and what they read is more diversified as to areas of interest, and on a higher cultural level.

f / In the ways in which a given object, relation or event is experienced and communicated by the respective social classes. It has long been recognized that what the members of the different social classes experience in identical situations, what they say as they respond to these situations, and how they say it, may differ very considerably. Several recent studies tend to demonstrate these facts. In the United States, as Schatzman and Strauss[5] have pointed out, class differences—especially those between the lower and middle classes, to which they devote themselves in their study—are more than differences in preciseness of grammar, in vocabulary, the ability to elaborate or literary style. This is illustrated especially in communication situations which involve the naming, identifying, defining, classifying and conceptualizing of experienced objects, acts, conditions and events. As indicated, in the modes of speaking which revealed their respective capacities for organization of perception and thought, the two classes show marked differences in "(a) the number and kinds of perspectives utilized in communication; (b) the ability to take the listener's role; (c) the handling of classifications; and (d) the frameworks and stylistic devices which order and implement the communications."[6]

In England, Basil Bernstein has been conducting an investigation into sub-cultural and social class influences upon behavior, especiallly language behavior and learning. In one report[7] he addressed himself to the contention that there is a fundamental difference between the middle class and the working class, in social perception and sensitivity to the structure of objects. The middle-class members possess an awareness of the importance between means and long-term ends; behavior is oriented to certain values but with a premium on individual differentiation within them. They show the ability to adopt appropriate measures to implement the attainment of distant ends by a purposeful means-end chain. Furthermore, the middle class demonstrates an instrumental attitude to social relations and objects. Its language structure mediates the relation between thought and feeling regarding social relations and objects. Moreover, the middle-class language "is rich in personal, individual qualifications, and its form implies sets of advanced logical operations." Space, time and social relationships are explicitly and extensively designated. "The connections and interrelations between means and distant ends are stressed." In general, the "attitudes and conditions are distinctive characteristics of the cultural environment in which the middle-class child learns about his world and develops his speech modes."

By contrast, and because of the more impoverished working-class environment and the more limited reaction to experience, the working-class child takes a "non-instrumental attitude toward social relations and objects." He shows "resistance to extensions of vocabulary, the manipulation of words, and the construction of ordered sentences"; he has "a preference for descriptive responses," and "is oriented towards the cursory examination of a series of different items." His language is limited to expressive symbolism and a public language.[8]

In a second report Bernstein is explicitly concerned with the fact that he found entirely different *modes* of speech within the lower working class and the middle class.[9] In this study, too, he noted different emphases. "The . . . forms of language used progressively oriented the speakers to distinct and different types of relationships to objects and persons, irrespective of the levels of measured intelligence." Bernstein presents certain "suggestions" which are sustained by his study. The typical dominant speech mode of the middle class shows perceptual activity and a theoretical attitude towards the structural possibilties of sentence organization. This facilitates the verbal elaboration by the subject of his sensitivity to the implications of separateness and difference, and points to the possibilities inherent in a complex conceptual hierarchy for the organization of experience.

The more limited speech forms of the members of the lower working class in general "discourage the speaker from verbally elaborating subjective intent, and orient the users to descriptive rather than abstract concepts."

In offering a somewhat hesitant explanation, Bernstein points out that "the normal linguistic environment of the working class is one of relative deprivation." The mode of expression of the working-class child may be a matter of learning. Early in life he acquires speech forms which create and reinforce in him limited dimensions of the significance of things, which, in turn, limit the type of stimuli to which he learns to respond. In contrast, the middle-class and upper-class child acquires a more complex conceptual hierarchy for the organization of experience. For him a value is placed upon early verbalization and the ability to describe, conceptualize and classify in some detail.

g / In the use of different languages by the respective classes. This differentiation will be examined in greater detail in the next section; for the record here, it is noteworthy that, in the past as well as in the contemporary world, there are notable instances of the upper and lower classes actually using *different* languages in their daily intercourse, or dialects so different as to be practically incomprehensible. In Britain, for example, during the time of the Norman Conquest, the upper classes spoke French; the lower classes spoke Old English, in its various regional dialects.

In some instances, the class languages have been so dissimilar that a separate interclass language has been used for communication between members of the classes. For example, in the Pacific region, the "pidgins," among their many users, have served as an interclass language. The great bulk of the people have spoken their own tribal languages and dialects, and the upper classes (the top officials, the educated) have spoken European languages; the pidgins have been used as the interclass and interpeople means of communication.

h / Greater upper-class uniformity; lower-class differentials and specialisms. It is also probable that the upper classes throughout a language community or country are more likely to speak the same language —that is, one which is similar as to range and quality of vocabulary, grammar, pronunciations, idiom, and the like—while, among the lower levels, the speech may be sharply split into local and regional dialects, occupational argots, slang, and brogues.

3. Language as Reflector of Social Stratification

From the sociological point of view, we are especially interested in the manner in which class differences in language reveal themselves in the social life of the people of the speech community. There is much evidence that the speech forms and daily usages of persons function rather effectively as symbols of class position. Indications of these class differences in language take several forms (to be discussed in the present and succeeding sections). Here we are concerned with the manner in which language generally reflects the stratification system. It does this chiefly in two ways: first, there are indications in the speech of any single person of his position in the status system; second, there are the reflections in the linguistic system of a community of that community's class structure. These we wish to examine briefly.

a / The reflectors of social position in the speech and the reactions to speech of the individual. As a London councilor put it long ago: "Every man carries his caste mark in his mouth."

Each class speaks "its own language"; it has its own distinctive forms of expression and its particular universe of discourse. The class position of the individual is indicated in the main by the way he performs, according to the distinctions in language just mentioned.

The speech of the English cockney is his hallmark. He shows a characteristic choice of words; he actually has words that the upper classes do not have, uses words that they taboo; he has his own grammatical forms (thought by the upper classes to be mis- or un-grammatical) and, most obviously, he has a vastly peculiar pronunciation and intonation. Alongside the "public school," or Oxford or Cambridge, or other "upper-estate" language of the members of polite and highly educated society, with its strikingly different vocabulary, grammar and accent, the cockney brogue seems to be a distantly related, almost foreign, tongue.

At the other extremity of the English class system, the aristocracy has a special language—especially marked in accent and vocabulary—which distinguishes it from the language of the lower classes. In 1955, Professor A. S. C. Ross attracted great interest with his presentation of what he called "U-words," that is, words used by the British "Upper Classes," and "non-U words," which are shuttled back and forth among the lower classes. The same theme was more fully developed in a controversial book by Nancy Mitford.[10] The "U" speech in considerable part inheres in the "U" character of its speakers. The "U" *accent* can be taught to lower-class persons, the *speech forms* never perfectly; there will always be slips. "Your 'a' or your 'serviette' is showing" is one of the most crushing rebuffs a social climber can suffer in England. And as Denis W. Brogan commented in a review of the book,[11] "To say 'toilet' or 'mirror' marks you as not to the manner or manor born." The peak in U-usage cannot be attained by those who are not aristocratically born; that is the blessing of the *"Natural* U-users," who always know the right words and accent, because the accent they use and the words they favor are, by that very fact, U.

The fundamental principle, of much wider relevance and applicability than the English situation, is succinctly put in the phrase: "A misplaced "h" is sufficient to betray a man's breeding, his education, his social class."[12]

The situation in the United States presents fewer sharp contrasts than in most countries. All classes speak roughly the same, except that the better-educated upper and middle classes have better diction and grammar, and use a more extensive vocabulary.[13]

Nevertheless, in so far as there are levels of American-English, they correspond to a large extent to the social levels, and reflect the status of the speakers. In general, even in the countries where the stratification system is highly fluid and open, the speech forms, especially those of the upper educational and economic levels, are also used as *status symbols.*

The stratum position of a person can in part be determined by the way he addresses his equals, his inferiors, and his superiors. This has long been the case in rigidly stratified societies. In the languages of many of these, there are special terms of address to indicate the class status of speakers and of those spoken to. Members of different castes, where a caste system prevails, sometimes have to speak indirectly to members of other castes. In some societies, persons of high status may not talk at all about some things that others talk of constantly.

This sort of thing also demonstrates itself in flexible, open-class societies, in the use or non-use of conventional titles or forms of address, in the relative formality of conversational exchange, and in the volume and tone of voice. The young white-collar bank clerk speaks to the chairman of the board in certain unmistakable and identifying ways, and vice versa—in spite of democratic pretensions. In the United States, one frequently notes the almost unconscious address of the term "Mister" to an upper-class person, or one who appears to be a person of distinction, even though the nature of the occasion may not require it.

The members of the different classes attach different connotations to given words and have different emotional reactions to them. The starving European peasant of the eighteenth century put a very different meaning on the word "bread" from the one Marie Antoinette did ("Why don't they eat cake?"). In the United States a member of the working class reacts very differently to such words as "scab" or "labor union" from the way a member of the employing class does.

The ability to write and read is evidence of high status in some societies. In India, for example, a country where the great majority of the people have always been illiterate, the ability to read has been— the situation is changing somewhat today—a symbol of Brahman caste membership.

The class of a person in a generally literate society can be in part determined by how much he reads and what he reads. As noted above, the upper classes do more reading, and this holds true for complex advanced societies, as well as for the less developed ones. Various studies also show that the upper classes tend to read printed material of a culturally higher level than that read by the lower classes. A recent detailed study,[14] involving the class system of greater New Haven, showed that, of class I (the highest), 51 per cent read the *New York Times,* and a sizable proportion read such magazines as *U. S. News and World Report, Harper's, The New Yorker,* and *Saturday Review.* "At least four such 'quality' magazines came into over 53 per cent of the class I homes" (p. 83). Class V (the lowest) showed a very small proportion of readers. None read the *New York Times,* but 28 per cent reported that they occasionally read the *New York Daily Mirror.* Few in this class read magazines; *Life,* which Zechariah Chafee referred to as "for those who can't read," was the most popular. Some 16 per cent read escape fiction, the women being especially devoted to the "true confessions" variety, and the men to "western" fiction (pp. 127–128).

The subject matter of discourse often indicates class position. The educated, the cultivated, the elite, the men of affairs are much more likely to discuss politics, religion and economic matters, to speak and write and read about art and literature, especially poems, lectures, plays, operas and symphonies, novels.

The class of a person may be determined in part by how he describes and analyzes objects and events, thus revealing his habits of perception, conceptualization and the organization of experience. The Schatzman and Strauss study referred to above suggests a set of criteria to enable one to determine class by way of what is revealed in the respective speech forms and speech content. This study shows, among other things that, almost without exception, any description offered by a lower-class respondent is seen only through his own eyes, while the middle-class respondents show much wider and more numerous perspectives. Lower-class persons "displayed relative insensitivity to disparities of perspective," while those from the middle class recognize diversities, qualify summaries, use illustrations, meticulously locate and identify places and persons in great complexity and detail. Members of the lower class show very limited classificatory ability, and apparently are able to think only "in particularistic or concrete terms," while middle-class speech is "richly interlarded with classificatory terms"—is, in fact, "organized around classification." The lower class do not give long, well-organized, tightly knit descriptions, but rather give segmental or limited ones, while "without exception, the middle-class respondents imposed over-all frames of their own upon the entire interview and had a master-frame and many subsidiary frames."

Bernstein's English studies also point up the fact that certain speech-habits and speech-forms identify the middle class as against the lower working class. The middle-class speaker can be detected by the evidence in his speech of discrimination, of perceptual activity and of theoretical constructs; by evidence of an awareness of the relationship between means and ends; by the ability to verbalize about and mediate between thought and feeling; by the ability, as indicated in his somewhat elaborated speech, to conceptualize, to qualify, and to engage in advanced logical operations. The lower working-class person, on the other hand, is revealed by his limited and relatively unchanging vocabulary, his addiction to simple description rather than abstraction, and the absence of qualifications and subjective elaborations in his speech.

b / The reflectors of class structure in the linguistic system itself or in the several languages prevailing in a community. Grammar forms in some languages, depending upon who is addressing whom, may reflect status distinctions. In German, for example, but not in English, there is a multiplicity of personal pronouns to express the graded attitudes toward the person addressed. One uses *du* for equals or familiars, *sie* for superiors.

Almost all languages have special terms for status incumbents and status roles which indicate degrees of status and respect. The educational, intellectual or occupational headman is the *magister,* the *master,* the *maître,* the *maestro,* or the *Meister.* There are the names of different castes (for example, in India, the *Brahmans, Kshatriyas, Vaisyas,* and *Sudras*); distinguishing terms, such as *aristocracy* and *peasantry;*

respect titles, such as *sahib* in India, *effendi* in the Near East, *sire* and *lord* in England, *Herr Professor Doktor* in Germany.

Some languages have, or have had, special language forms in referring to the different social ranks. Ancient Japanese required the use of certain special adjectives in connection with the doings of highly placed personages and forbade the application of "ordinary" adjectives. The Koreans, at least until recently, were said to use more than twenty verbal forms, according to the social rank of speaker and listener.[15]

The number of languages or sublanguages in a community spoken by the different strata, and the variations among them in form and circumstances of usage, has been an important historical reflector of the stratification situation. The class or caste of the person has been symbolized in part with respect to whether he knew only his own or also one or more other languages. In some markedly aristocratic societies, the upper classes—who sometimes also were of a different race or nationality—have known and used one or more foreign languages, while the lower classes, the peasantry, were confined to the indigenous language, or even to their own dialect of it.[16]

Through the seventeenth, eighteenth, and even into the nineteenth century, the upper classes of many European countries spoke "cultural" French in addition to, or in preference to, their own "rude" native language. The old Russian Court spoke French and, before 1914, English as well. In Siam, the court-centered nobility spoke French rather than the national language or the regional dialects of the commoners. Prior to World War I, about 60 per cent of the people in Transylvania in the old Austro-Hungarian Empire spoke Roumanian, while the literary, military, and land-owning classes spoke Magyar or German. Similarly, along the eastern boundary of the German Empire, the peasants spoke only Polish, while the dominant classes spoke German.[17]

In Ceylon, during the British period (1795–1947), the Westernized elite used English in professional life, in schools, and in conversation amongst friends, sometimes even in the home.[18] Today in Haiti, all classes speak the patois known as Creole, but the middle and upper classes—a decidedly minor portion of the population—speak French. In India, the educated, scholarly, administrative, scientific and leisured upper castes speak English, often as their main language, at any rate, in addition to Hindi or their other regional language, while the illiterate masses speak only the regional languages, or only their tribal or village dialects.

Some societies have maintained distinctive "patrician" and "common" forms of speech and also stratum-graded forms of address, as well as different forms of speech used in class relations. In Polynesia, the chiefs of some of the islands, including Hawaii, had a special form of court language which was kept secret from the commoners and which, incidentally, was also used in speaking to and of the gods.[19] In Samoa there was a chief's language, used exclusively when speaking to a chief, whether he were addressed by another chief of a rank inferior to his own, or by a person of low rank. But when the chiefs addressed persons of lower rank, or when they talked of themselves, they always used ordinary language.[20]

In Java, at least until recently, as many as five different graded vocabularies existed: *Ngoko,* used by an individual of low status in talking to his equals, and by one of higher status addressing his inferiors; *Kromo,* used by a person of inferior rank in addressing his superiors, and by individuals of the higher classes in talking to each other; *Madyo,* a mixture of *Kromo* and *Ngoko,* with the addition of some terms peculiar to itself, used by persons of low status in talking to each other formally, and also employed by persons of superior rank in addressing older individuals of lower status, and by merchants and servants of nobles in addressing each other; *Kromo-inggil,* used by persons in referring to the personal attributes or property of a god, or of a very superior individual; and *Boso-kedaton,* the idiom of the royal courts, used by all men of the court in addressing each other or when referring to the ruler, but never in addressing the latter.[21]

4. *Language as an Agent in Maintaining Social Distance and Social Position*

The hierarchical differentiations of language not only reflect social stratification; they also have the effect in themselves of maintaining the stratification system. Historically, some of the features have been studiously utilized, especially by the upper strata, to maintain social distance and to preserve their monopoly of what have been deemed superior culture elements and their prized social position.

a / Ever since writing was discovered, **it has had the effect of maintaining stratification through the social distinction and social functioning that are attached, respectively, to literacy and illiteracy; facility in its practice has been used as a means of maintaining status.**[22]

b / The existence of diversely specialized speech, amounting to sub-languages within the language, among the different strata of the community, and also the use of a foreign language by the elite as against the vernacular of the masses, tend to maintain the class system; they have been used by the upper strata to protect and preserve their position. The result of the linguistic bifurcation, as coordinated with the distinction between the elite and the common people is, in effect, to build a screen, if not a wall, between them. It not only reflects a sharp social segmentation and separation but, on the basis of our present social-psychological knowledge, and our knowledge of the part that language plays in perception, conceptualization and socialization, we can say assuredly that the situation is bound to produce marked differences in the development of personality, in experiencing, in immediate conditioning by the social and cultural environment, and in thoughtways.

The use of a highly specialized variant of the general language or of a foreign language has often meant, for the upper strata, a means of distinguishing themselves from the "common rabble," and of maintaining exclusive possession of their exalted position. Referring to the situation in Haiti, and the use of French there by the upper classes, who are ruling classes in government and economic affairs, Everett and Helen Hughes say: "By conducting all public affairs in French and by discouraging the common people from learning French, those on top keep a monopoly of many positions, including that of translator in courts and other public offices. A language and literacy barrier limits competition from the lower classes, just as a race line may do elsewhere."[23]

The existence of sharp class lines and their persistence may show up in certain structural forms of the language. In India, where much of the traditional caste system persists (in spite of official disapproval), there are all sorts of language forms correlated with acts of domination and deference in the highly formalized relationships between the castes.

c / The emphasis upon "correctness" and "elegance" and "style" of speech by the upper layers, and the resultant "cultivated" or "high society" or "drawing-room" (once upon a time, "court") **speech,** has been, among other things, an effort clearly to identify the speakers as members of the elite. Moreover, this has usually been accompanied by strenuous endeavors to protect themselves against the intrusion of the coarser language of the middle and lower classes. That their efforts have carried an element of insurance is to be seen in the recognized sociological fact that the attainment of such refined language, both oral and written, requires much leisure, special training, and coaching—opportunities and possibilities that the lower classes do not have. Such speech does quite definitely have the effect of excluding the lower classes from the rarefied higher social altitudes.

It should be noted that minorities, which are usually assigned lower social status until they are assimilated, have used their own language to maintain social and cultural distance as a means of self-defense against the larger society or nation—that is, in order to avoid loss of cultural identity and to preserve group unity and integrity. This is shown in the persistent use of Yiddish by the Jews in the Ghettos of eighteenth-century Europe, and the use of the "old-country" language by first-generation immigrant groups in the United States.

d / An upper-class language, more or less uniform from one locality to another within a country, and in occasional instances cutting across national lines, has been a means of unifying and consolidating upper classes. The speech of the lower classes has usually reflected their physical and social isolation and relative immobility, and hence has been a matter primarily of local, often quite divergent, dialects. The upper classes, on the other hand, have had a much greater uniformity of language. This has been due to such factors as the greater similarity of education among them, wider physical circulation, more frequent and more extensive contacts with the elite from other areas (as they assembled at each other's estates, at the court, at spas), a greater similarity of cultural values and goals and of interests, their use of writing and resort to written correspondence with each other, their enjoyment of a common literature, and, in general, a much greater similarity in what they talked and wrote about. Thus, for example, the English spoken by the educated upper classes anywhere in Great Britain is much the same, but the lower class speech still to some extent consists of dialects, jargons, and argots. Sociologically significant is the fact that this greater uniformity of language among the upper classes has in itself been an annealing factor.

In medieval times in Europe, the almost universal use of Latin by the ruling estates bound them together in many ways. In early modern Europe, the use of French as the court language permitted aristocrats, whatever their national (or regional) antecedents, to associate with one another, and thus gave them the sense of belonging to a truly international superclass. Moreover, the ability to speak French amounted to an international prerequisite to and verification of elite status. In order to pass as an aristocrat, the incumbents of, and the aspirants to, top status had to speak French.

Today, English as spoken by an upper-class educated and cultured

Englishman, Canadian, Australian, American, Hindu, Pakistani, Iranian or Japanese creates a common consciousness and a basis for cultural camaraderie that extends beyond ethnic, political and religious lines.

e / Names have been and are used as means of maintaining social space. In many societies, calling a person by his given name involved certain positional, moral and legal relations, including certain social responsibilities toward that person. Especially significant at this point is the fact that the free and mutually acceptable use of the given name ("Bill" or "Joe") has evidenced a considerable degree of intimacy, similarity, even equality of status between the speakers.

Conversely, one can "hold off" a person from undue intimacy and from invasion of the status distinction by refusing the use of his or her given name, and referring to that person instead as "Mr." or "Miss" or "Mrs."

5. *Language and Social Mobility*

We shall note two aspects of the relation between language and the movement up and down through the social layers.

a / Language itself, in some of its forms, **moves up and down the social ladder.** In all cultures and eras, there has been some intercommunication between the respective strata of society; the words and other speech forms they have used could *not* be confined to certain social levels of language. Thus, there has been in the past and still is a noticeable tendency for linguistic elements to be *upwardly* mobile. Frequently, items from the patois, of slang, argot, and even the cant language-forms of earthy terms thought of as vulgarisms, as well as other bits from lower-class vernaculars, which had been initially snubbed by the upper classes, have moved upward, by a sort of capillary attraction, into the patterns of upper-class speech, become standard and respectable, and been accepted by polite society. Sheard gives the following as examples of "low," "unworthy" words, used only by lower ranks in eighteenth-century England, which have come to be included in present day refined, regularized vocabulary: *banter, begot, enthusiasm, flimsy, flirtation, fop, gambling, hanker, humbug, jilt, mob, shabby, shuffle, snob, stingy, touchy.*[24] Within the lifetime of many contemporaries, such terms of lowly origin as the following have become respectable and standard: *sucker, jalopy, to grouse.*

It is equally a fact, much more palatable to many, that words, grammatical forms, particular expressions, pronunciations—in fact, all sorts of refinements, correctnesses and specialized terminologies, as used by the upper classes and by scientists and other esoteric specialists—have percolated down into the "standard" language of the language community, and even into the speech of the lower classes. In modern advanced societies like our own, with universal and compulsory education at ever higher levels for more and more people, and with populations that are almost completely literate, there seems to be a greater influence of upper-level language upon the common language, a much greater uniformation of language at the standard level, and thus less and less "corruption" of language.[25]

b / A second aspect of the relationship between language and social mobility—an aspect which is of greater concern to us at this point—is the fact that **persons aspiring to upward social mobility use language, particularly "correct" or "prestige" language, as an elevating instrument.** Status seekers, even in the relatively rigid societies of the past, have been aware of the importance of this agency; but there was comparatively little vertical social mobility until recent times. However, in an open-class social system, with its freedom and opportunity for upward movement, the resort to language as a means of social achievement is especially significant.

The basic fact is that the speech (vocabulary, correctness of grammar, accent, intonation, style) of polite, educated, prestigious superior society is one of the strategic hallmarks of social acceptance or non-acceptance in that society. Hence those who want to reach the higher altitudes of social space must drop their lower-class language—or at least discard the most glaring "giveaways" of lower-class forms—and as soon as possible become adept in the speech usages that are in favor in the cliques or strata to which they aspire, for such speech signifies success and preferred status. Facility in its use is essential in order to create for others the impression that the speaker does indeed belong to a higher social class. Correct habits of writing are also involved, of course.[26]

The actuality of the importance of upper-class language for people "on the up" is reflected in the speech of the *arriviste,* with his overdoing of certain words, tenses, and accents, and in the language of hangers-on and servants of the elite (butlers, valets, for example, P. G. Wodehouse's Jeeves). The ambitious young scholar from a backwoods section of the country who affects a Harvard or Oxford accent is amusing at times, especially on those occasions when he forgets to use his newly acquired accent.

In the United States, the changing of family names has been an interesting aspect of the relation of language, social stratification and the penchant for upward social mobility. Names of persons and families are changed for many reasons. One rather prominent reason among us has been the revision of family names, which indicated membership in less favored ethnic or minority groups, especially immigrant groups somewhat discriminated against, so that they might conform to the names of majority or prestigious or powerful population segments of the community. The instances are legion—people of German descent changing their names from *Pfoersching* to *Pershing*, *Schmidt* to *Smith* or even *Smythe*, Jews changing *Kabotnik* to *Cabot*, *Levy* to *Levitt* or *Lee*, *Stein, Weinstein, Finkelstein* to *Stone*, Czech names like *Dolezal* to *Dalzell, Jelek* to *Gillette* or *Jellicoe, Pribyl* to *Preeble*, the Italian *Bianchi* becoming *White*. The educated and socially and economically ambitious among these foreign-name groups have been especially prone to name changing.[27]

6. *A Resumé of the Sociocultural Significance of the Special Languages*

The special languages reflect certain significant characteristics of associated human beings as well as certain important social situations and occurrences.

a / Their ubiquity and universality point to the general fact that, **whenever social circumstances lead to the formation of a distinct group within the whole body of a society, or of distinct common characteristics and functions for a category of the population, the people involved will tend to develop, or deliberately devise, speech forms of their own.** More specifically, the specialized languages of vocational groups, social-economic classes, sex and age groups, and all sorts of organizations, underscore not only the significance of fluid and effective means of communication in the operation and maintenance of groups, but especially *a tendency for and an ability of groups to fit their speech and writing to their experience, their special interests, their peculiar communicative needs, their objectives, the peculiarities of their internal organization, and their positions and functions in the larger society.* It emerges rather clearly that the main reason for the existence of most of the special languages is to be found in the utilities which they provide to their users for achieving their recognized individual and group purposes and functions. By no means the least among these utilities is the monopoly of a special means of communication, and in some instances of control or defense, which possession of the languages bestows on their particular bodies of speakers.

b / The fact that the members of the special language groups share their speech only among themselves, and cannot or will not do so with others, **has both exclusive and inclusive effects.** The special language assists in keeping the distinction between member and non-member clear, and identifies the members of the in-group in contrast to the out-groups, setting them definitely apart from all others. Closely related to this is the fact that the special language has *a cohesive, solidarity-producing effect among its speakers*. It symbolizes the strength of the ties between them and serves as a "prop to in-groupness." Thus the speakers strengthen their ties with each other, and may even make their joint activities more effective. The group language also often serves as an aid in the maintenance of morale, and possibly as a means of gaining prestige for group members in the eyes of non-members.

c / The element of secrecy has its distinct social significance. The more secret "specials" satisfy the desire for the concealment of their intentions and activities on the part of group members, and thereby provide anonymity and security. Many of the other special languages, however, also have a certain element of deliberate secrecy about them. Some groups affect secrecy in their special lingo as a way of enhancing their exclusiveness and their mutual esteem and solidarity. Any kind of secret is "between we-uns"; it usually flatters we-uns and is "against you-uns."

The element of secrecy has definite utility in some circumstances. The sales personnel of a particular department of a large store, for example, use secret forms to inform each other, in the presence of customers, about certain facts that the circumstances require shall be unintelligible to these same customers. The secret features of the special languages of certain work groups, such as the police, as has been noted, provide a similar utility.

d / The fact that most of the special languages to some extent exclude outsiders from the group of speakers, and isolate and dissociate the members of the respective groups from each other, has already been noted above. Especially significant is the correlated fact that **some of them are so esoteric in one way or another that they tend to block, or**

at any rate seriously to complicate communication between the groups, and thus create a degree of "confusion of tongues" in the communication. This is certain to interfere with some exchange of mutually essential information, to foster ignorance along some lines, produce misunderstanding and lead to friction.

Especially notable today is the fact that some of the special technical languages of certain strategic craft, professional, scientific and technological groups are growing steadily more specialized, refined and complicated, and hence are less translatable into the common language of the vitally concerned general public. This tends to block the general acquisition of important information—for example, with respect to health, nuclear fission, space, the highly technical destructive instruments of potential national enemies.

Bossard has pointed out that linguistic labels, as exemplified by the special languages and minority-group languages, are among the most common devices people use against each other. They are particularly effective as instruments of oblique attack or of depreciation.[28]

e / As civilization advances, it becomes necessary to develop capability in an increasing number of special languages. In less complex societies, the roles of most persons are relatively few, and they do not require a knowledge of very many of its special languages. For most people, the local dialect, their class argot, and one or two organizational jargons suffice. But with the extension of interests and diversification of activities that come with "development," the greater becomes the need to know and use the "specials" related to different interests and activities. In India today, for example, as a man's range of life extends respectively from the local, single-village level, to the subregional, then to the regional, and finally, to the all-India level, with an accompanying extension of his interests, knowledge, viewpoints, and activities, his need for the command of the parallel diverse forms of speech increases.[29]

f / To the social linguist and the social scientist, the special languages serve as **"windows" upon the sociocultural peculiarities and particularities of their speakers as a group or category**—whether they are criminals, "senior citizens," bus drivers, or sociologists. They reveal the major "inner" preoccupations and concerns of their members, their special outlooks on the surrounding and contacting world. Being among the most important tools in justifying the existence and accomplishing the ends of the group speakers, the special languages reflect the values and norms of the group speakers, something of their structuring as a group, especially the functions of their group in the larger society, something of their rites and routines, and much about their relations with other groups and categories of the population.

The special languages also show that, the more specialized or more exclusive such groups are, the greater the probability that their language will show marked peculiarities, of which the members of other groups are distinctly aware, as well as peculiarities which make it relatively incomprehensible or useless for other groups.

g / Some of the special languages show **extremist tendencies, which have definite psychological and sociological aspects.** Some become so involved, pretentious, verbose, complicated and obscure in their terminology, and so full of circumlocutions, that they border on the ridiculous. This extremist verbiage, several instances of which have been noted above, is often referred to as gobbledegook. This development may be the consequence of one or more several factors: the desire (1) to impress the uninitiated with the esoteric or otherwise highly specialized nature of the activity; (2) to advertise one's affiliation with a particular group; (3) to give the initiated an inflated sense of the weight and importance (which may be quite small in actuality) of group membership and participation; (4) an often unconscious wish to be different from the crowd; (5) a deliberate desire to keep outsiders or the public ignorant as to what the group means or is (or is not) doing; (6) a sense of insecurity about the actual importance of one's calling or group, or a sense of being "under fire," which invites efforts at defense.

h / Even a cursory examination of the speech habits of individuals shows that **the special languages are not mutually exclusive as far as any particular individual is concerned.** In other words, almost every person belongs not to one but to several speech groups. The given American college student, for example, not only belongs to the general English speech community, but speaks the American version of English. In addition, his "American" shows up as a midwestern (or other regional) dialect (sometimes with slight evidences of ethnic-group accent); he is adept at special college slang; as a senior, he is probably beginning to show proficiency in the specialized jargon of his major subject. The adult American male enjoys some secret terminology with his family, and other secret terminology with other members of his sex; as a banker, he is proficient in the elaborate jargon of the world of finance; he speaks the argot of golf, revels in the protected jargon of the Masonic Order and, as a paying patron of the local art museum, has some adeptness in the "arty" lingo. The Amish of Lancaster County, Pennsylvania, use what almost amount to three different languages: (1) "Pennsylvania Dutch," which is a curious blend of Rhineland German and Eastern Pennsylvania American, is their common everyday speech, the speech used among kin, friends and neighbors; (2) Biblical High German is used in their sermons, hymn-singing and reading of religious literature; and (3) vernacular American-English for their communication with "outsiders."

i / The changes in the kind and volume of special languages over a period of time, and the changes within particular current special languages, reflect both the types and the volume of social changes of almost every kind. We have already noted that the weakening of dialects and socioeconomic class languages as the means of mass communication, universal education and increased physical and social mobility have come to affect almost every locality and every population segment of a modern society. There is, in addition, the obsolescence and disappearance of some occupational jargons, and the wholesale disappearance of antiquated terms from within some of the technical languages, as the objects or techniques or circumstances to which they were once attached have disappeared. Ethnic group *patois* have almost disappeared in the United States, as their speakers have become socially and culturally assimilated.

On the other hand—and this is so obvious as to require only brief mention—the new special languages, or the great variation in or extension of terminology in current special languages in certain areas of life, point to an intensification of interest in these areas, to inventions, discoveries or other creativeness in the field, to individual and social needs created by changes in the special area or interdependent areas, such as require description, analysis and treatment. The vast increase of special languages of new occupational and special-knowledge groups, as scientific and technological advances occur; the continuous development, revision and diversification of the organizational languages, as bureaucratic forms penetrate new areas of life; changes in the languages of philosophy and the arts, as "schools of thought" and "styles" come and go; the diversification of slangs, as special-interest cliques and groups increase—these are all cases in point.

j / Finally, while the special languages have certain negative sociocultural effects, they also have definite **positive effects, especially in the way of enriching the common language and keeping it fluid and fit as a communicative agent,** abreast of the different social and cultural developments that are taking place. Thus the language of the community not only maintains its efficacy as the basic tool in meeting the necessities and whims of communication, but also extends the range and quality of daily intergroup communication.

As noted above, although slang is a linguistic aberration as it stands at any given moment, it has been a prodigious breeder of words and phrases that continually revivify and expand standard language. It is a common fact that our present American-English shows massive infusions from the scientific and technological special languages—for example, from those of medicine and pharmacy, or from those of airplane pilots, space scientists and technologists, electronic and nuclear physicists, psychologists and psychiatrists, and sociologists. Other notable contributors have been the languages of the special crafts (the sailor's "half seas over," "to tack"); the fine and applied arts; the sports ("stymied," "play ball," "neck and neck," "behind the eight ball"); the stage; finance and the stock exchange ("hedging," "liquidate," "bullish," "bearish"); religion (Biblical terms, the coinages of popular evangelists); the military; jazz; even the cant of criminals. Of these, the languages of science and technology have doubtless been the most productive of all the group languages. Pei estimates that "fully half the words in our language . . . are of scientific or technological origin."[30] Savory points out that, for 500 years, words of science have been pushing their way into the language of everyday life. In fact, there are so many, and these are so generally used, that few people think of them as scientific, specialized, or unusual.[31]

Nor is the enrichment from other special-language areas a new effect. Historically, the great religions have had a powerful influence upon the common languages of their devotees, even though the latter may have been speakers of diverse languages and dialects. One need only mention the common words in the languages of the Muslim world that are derived from classical Arabic, the written and priestly language of the religion; the intrusion of Latin words of the Church in Europe into the many vernaculars; the words from the sacred texts of Brahmanism in Sanskrit and Pali in the dialects of India; the terminology borrowed from Martin Luther's German translation of the Bible or from the King James English version.

Giants of literature have sometimes been the medium for introducing terms from special languages into the common language. Shakespeare, for example, drew on trade language, legal language, theological language, naval language, military language, official language, and even on the language of fools.

Enriching contributions from the special languages make it possible for all speakers of the common language to expand their horizons, to comprehend and to communicate about all manner of new things and occurrences. These contributions aid us in our individual speech. The interesting conversationalist avoids prosiness by sharpening and coloring his speech with words and phrases taken from the professions, sports, radio and television, the Fourth Estate, the arts, and even from those of the halfworld and underworld.

N O T E S

1 The stratification systems of the world today differ somewhat as to structural type, as they also have historically, owing to differences in the social and cultural organization of the societies. The most widespread general contemporary designation, however, is "class system."

2 Otto Jespersen, *Mankind, Nation, and the Individual* (Cambridge: Harvard University Press, 1925), pp. 141–148.

3 Richard Hoggart, *The Uses of Literacy* (London: Chatto & Windus, 1957), p. 29.

4 With respect to the English working class, see, for example, Hoggart, pp. 74–75.

5 Leonard Schatzman and Anselm Strauss, "Social Class and Modes of Communication," *American Journal of Sociology*, 66 (Jan., 1955), 329–338.

6 *Ibid.*, p. 330. (For data and details, see the study.)

7 Basil Bernstein, "Some Sociological Determinants of Perception: An Enquiry into Sub-Cultural Differences," *British Journal of Sociology*, 9 (June, 1958), 159–174.

8 On Bernstein's concept of "public language," see "Public Language: Some Sociological Implications of a Linguistic Form," *British Journal of Sociology*, 10 (Dec., 1959), 311–326.

9 "Language and Social Class," *British Journal of Sociology*, 11 (Sept., 1960), 271–276.

10 Nancy Mitford, *Noblesse Oblige: An Enquiry into the Identifiable Characteristics of the English Aristocracy* (New York: Harper & Brothers, 1956).

11 *Saturday Review*, 39 (July 28, 1956), 17–18.

12 Ralph Pieris, "Speech and Society: A Sociological Approach to Language," *American Sociological Review*, 16 (Apr., 1951), 499–505 (500). On English speech patterns as indicators of class position, see T. H. Pear, *English Social Differences* (London: George Allen & Unwin, 1955), Chap. 3; Roy Lewis and Angus Maude, *The English Middle Classes* (New York: Alfred A. Knopf, 1950).

13 Cf. Bernard Barber, *Social Stratification* (New York: Harcourt, Brace & Co., 1957), p. 151.

14 August B. Hollingshead and Frederick C. Redlich, *Social Class and Mental Illness* (New York: John Wiley & Sons, 1958).

15 Cf. Karl Vossler, *The Spirit of Language in Civilization*, trans. Oscar Oeser (London: Routledge & Kegan Paul, 1951), p. 94.

16 Apart, of course, from some bilingual lower-class persons on the borders between language communities.

17 Leon Dominian, *The Frontiers of Language and Nationality in Europe* (New York: Henry Holt & Co., 1917), p. xiii.

18 Ralph Pieris, "Bilingualism and Cultural Marginality," *British Journal of Sociology*, 2 (Dec., 1951), 328–339 (333).

19 William G. Sumner and Albert G. Keller, *The Science of Society* (New Haven: Yale University Press, 1927), I, 493.

20 *Ibid.*

21 From R. Kennedy, *The Ethnology of the Greater Sunda Islands* (a manuscript), referred to by William I. Thomas, *Primitive Behavior* (New York: McGraw-Hill Book Co., 1937), p. 84.

22 This subject, under the heading, "The Literate–Illiterate Cleavage," has been developed in Chap. X, Sect. 2.

23 Everett C. and Helen M. Hughes, *Where Peoples Meet* (Glencoe, Ill.: Free Press, 1952), p. 34.

24 J. A. Sheard, *The Words We Use* (London: Andre Deutsch, 1954), p. 309.

25 On upward and downward mobility of language see Sheard, pp. 309–310.

26 Cf. Uriel Weinreich, *Languages in Contact: Findings and Problems* (New York: Publications of the Linguistic Circle of New York, No. 1, 1953), pp. 78–79.

27 On the subject see especially Louis Adamic, *What's Your Name?* (New York: Harper & Brothers, 1942).

28 James H. S. Bossard, "The Bilingual as a Person—Linguistic Identification with Status," *American Sociological Review*, 10 (Dec., 1945), 699–709.

29 Cf. John Gumperz, Jr., "Speech Variation in the Study of Indian Civilization," *American Anthropologist*, 63 (Oct., 1961), 976–988.

30 Mario Pei, *The Story of English* (Philadelphia: J. B. Lippincott & Co., 1952), p. 209.

31 Theodore H. Savory, *The Language of Science: Its Growth, Character and Usage* (London: Andre Deutsch, Ltd., 1953), p. 56.

xv ❧ Language and the Individual

In Chapter VI we examined language as a revealer of a people's social and intellectual history and of their peculiarly distinct style, as well as a partial determinant of their perceptual–conceptual processes and of their *Weltanschauung*. In the present chapter, we shall be concerned with the relationship of the social system of language and the *individual* as a social person.

It should be pointed out at the outset that individuals are the focal elements in the linguistic process. They are, in the last analysis, the *senders* and *receivers* of all messages transmitted linguistically or by other signs and symbols. The social-linguistic aspect of this is the speaker–listener situation. It has been succinctly developed by Carroll in the form of a diagrammatic model, the essential features of which will be outlined, although with some adaptations by the present writer.[1] (1) The reason for the existence of language is that the individual has communicative intentions; he has some "excitatory intention" to transmit information that consists of sensations, perceptions, memories, thoughts, concepts or even images. (2) These intentions he formulates or *encodes,* on the basis of his own particular experiential and cultural repertory, and according to the principles and rules of the language, as he, in his particular sociocultural context, has been conditioned to use them. (3) He thus produces his message, utilizing standard linguistic forms and procedures. The message may be couched in formalized vocal sounds, formalized marks on a page or other standardized symbolic gestures or objects. These, however, in order to convey meaning, abide by the regularities of the linguistic code observable in the speech community: the regularities called words—the lexicographic features—and the regularities of the structural utterance, with its distinctive phonetic, morphological and syntactical features. (4) The receiver (hearer, listener) takes this message apart; he *decodes* it by means of his rule-established linguistic habits, but also as he is affected, in his discriminatory responses to it as an individual, by his auditory or perceptive ability, his intelligence, his knowledge and his particular awareness of, training for, reception of or interest in the given message. (5) Finally he, the receiver, upon decoding the message, achieves his own interpretation or understanding of the intentions of its sender, and acts upon the message, but always according to his own "sets to respond." These aspects of the behavior of the individual in the linguistic situation will have pertinence throughout the discussion.

We shall deal briefly with language, with respect to a number of intermeshed ways in which it affects the person as a member of his society: how it enters into the development of his self; how it socializes him and otherwise affects him as a societal participant; how it orients him in time; how it frees him and binds him in his self-realization; how its lack, or the impairment of his facility in its use, impairs his socialization and social participation; how it reveals signal facets of his personality; how it enters into and reflects his social position and roles; how it indexes his breeding, his cultural stance and quality.

1. *Language in the Personal and Social Life of the Individual*

Language, itself a unique human social product, is the basic tool, not only in the development and maintenance of the individual as self and person, but also in his *enculturation*—that is, his introduction to, conditioning by and interiorization of the cultural heritage of his society—and in his *socialization*—that is, his acquisition, by way of social experience and training, of proficiency as a well-functioning participant in all of the social groups, small and large, primary and secondary, informal and formal, to which he belongs.[2] These two basic, jointly operating, developmental and adjustive processes begin very early and continue throughout life, as the individual is continually shaped and reshaped as a functioning integer of his society. From the first moments of consciousness, language plays a strategic role in these processes.

a / The acquisition of language by the child. While the strategic significance of language in the life of the human individual continues throughout his life, it is especially highlighted and focused in the linguistic,
psychological and sociocultural development of the child. The development of language facility rapidly advances the child beyond his nascent
condition as an undisciplined organism, and fits him for human status
among the creatures of the earth, for human behavior and for socialization and enculturation. As his linguistic ability advances from stage to
stage during his growth, his range and depth of proficiency in these
areas are extended. The early unfolding of his speech facility also provides us with a key to the understanding of his humanness and his social
and cultural fitness.

We shall not go into an extensive and detailed exposition of the stages
and forms of the linguistic development of the child. A massive literature
of both theoretical and experimental studies on the subject is available.
While the stages of language development are by no means identical in
every child, since both the children and their social environments vary
greatly, and while much still needs to be learned about the acquisition
of language by the child, the main features normally are something like
the following.[3]

The infant and child live in all-encompassing physical and sociocultural
environments. A fundamental aspect of the latter is the "verbal environment."[4] As he learns to speak, he grows into the language world around
him; by means of it, he discovers himself and becomes a full-fledged
socialized and encultured being. Since he does not have language
facility at birth, however, and without it his humanness is at first only
partial, he is for some time relatively unsocialized.

The earliest noises made by the infant are simple crying and screaming
sounds, mainly of a reflex nature, and involving purely affective conditions. They are sounds uttered largely in response to conditions of comfort and discomfort, especially the latter, as products of stomach
contractions, wetness, fatigue, pain, and so on. These sounds are
relatively undifferentiated during the first few days, but soon differences
can be distinguished—for example, a cry of hunger as against one caused
by a pinprick. These simple cries are supplemented, usually by the third
month, by cooing, gurgling, and babbling; this continues until the end of
the first year. The latter are expressive sounds, uttered for their own sake,
as play. They show some phonetic variation—vowel sounds at first; then
a little later consonants—and evidence considerable experimentation.

This early activity appears to be largely "random" in character. During the second six months—in some cases earlier—the child becomes responsive to vocal stimuli, shows some discrimination and, what is of special importance, begins to imitate sounds from his environment, especially those made by his parents and siblings. As time passes, the imitation of sounds becomes surer and more exact, and intonational imitation grows more certain and more precisely articulated. Near the end of his first year, he shows verbal understanding, as he associates sound, act and object through repeated experience. At about this time, he begins to respond in specific ways to conventional speech, and to utter conventional words as a means of dealing with specific situations. Because of the reactions of associates, especially parents, to his utterances, his own sounds begin to contain "meaning" for him; they take on a social character. Usually early in his second year, he begins to produce verbal utterances which involve more or less standard vocal patterns and sound variations, in order to express himself and to communicate specific messages to others.

The child's first spoken words are usually syllables or repeated syllables such as *mama, wawa, dada;* the use of other words soon follows. For the most part, the infant's first words are employed as sentences, rather than as single words; they do service as one-word sentences ("ball" may mean "there is the ball," "where is the ball?," "I want the ball," depending on the intonation). The development of sentences and phrases follows. During the second and third years of life, the child learns the grammatical, syntactical, and stylistic rules of his language. He now has a by no means final, but at least fair, degree of language proficiency. This development of linguistic facility puts the child in a position to receive and to carry forward his historical and continually changing culture. He is also prepared to act as a socialized human being, one fully participant in his various groups and relationships. What are some of the signal early effects in these respects?

b / The role of language in the enculturation of the individual. The enculturation of the individual consists primarily of his acquisition of an intellectual and behavioral orientation in his physical and social universe. This, in turn, consists in his attainment of identifications, categorizations, working concepts, and the standard meanings of all manner of things, events and situations, before he can act appropriately. However, the first significant enculturating effect on the child as he acquires his language flows from his use of words, especially when he makes the momentous discovery that things have names. The very act of naming designates an object or attribute or relationship as a specific and restricted part of some whole. He discovers that these words more or less correspond to aspects of the real world around him; they carry the meanings of the items that he has experienced or that have been pointed out to him. The word-stock also provides him with indicators of the categories of things, their different kinds and qualities. Thus he becomes conscious of scope and variation in the nature of things. For him, now as a child and later throughout his life, language has ceased to be a chain of sound; it has become the representative, the surrogate of reality. By means of it, the objective world has been created for him; he has awareness of things in their specific modes of existence, their specific qualities and their relational characteristics.

In Chapter III we took note of the general functions of language. Several of these are of particular concern at this point, in that they are directly involved in the enculturation of the individual. The words of his language not only mobilize the individual's attention toward the world around him, but also provide him with frames or guides for perception. The different combinations of words and distinctions between words provide him with the diverse meanings of things. They function as the key agencies in the development and conduct of his conceptual thinking, and in the growth and maintenance of his powers of specific description, objective reference, assignment and refinement of meaning, interpretation and generalization, and abstraction.

To revert more specifically to the child: by means of language he becomes conscious of the actuality and distinctions of time and space—very important aspects of advance in the life of the child. He refers first to the present, and then to the past and the future. He becomes aware of such spatial distinctions as large and small, long and short, near and far. With regard to time and space, he comes to be able to conceptualize the extent of each, to explore the part played by people and activity in each, and to project his own thinking into the past and the future, in real and imagined objects, places and events near and far. With language he also takes on such critical categories as those of number, action and quality. These comprehensions he utilizes throughout his life.

By means of the questions he asks, the child not only satisfies his needs and obtains action on his behalf, but becomes able to deal with absent and imaginary situations, to obtain information and satisfy his curiosity about that which he experiences—not only the names of things, but also the why and how of things, their purposes and goals and ends.

In sum, it is in talking about his world—in verbalizing reality—that the individual achieves a full consciousness of it—that is to say, learns about it; in this way explains his experience with it. The world's properties and conditions become part of the schematic framework in which he lives. He comes to terms of some sort with the world, which thus becomes more or less manageable by him. Especially significant in connection with enculturation is the fact that, as the individual's experience is verbalized in the form of standard language forms, it comes into accord with established schemata of his group—that is, the principles whereby experience is organized into knowledge.

Language has wider and other equally weighty effects for the individual, whether child or man. These we shall treat briefly as the effects for the individual as a self, and the effects in his socialization.

c / Language and the individual as self. There is an integral relationship between language and the self: consciousness itself, the consciousness of self, the content of self and the growth of self.

Consciousness itself on the part of a person—psychic awareness of being in the world—is not identical with the mere formation of reality-contact—for example, sensitiveness to light and sound, heat and cold and substance.[5] Consciousness is behavior that uses symbols. It seems to consist operationally of the identification and interpretation of the items of the milieu (for example, when coming out from under the influence of an anaesthetic or waking from a deep sleep). Such identification and interpretation, as has been observed, is a matter of at least inner gesturing, usually but not necessarily verbal, on the part of the individual, but gesturing in terms of significant, meaning-laden symbols of the group.

Closely related to individual consciousness is *consciousness of self*. This largely depends on the language world into which a person is born and which he has made his own. It results from the verbalization by the individual about himself *vis-à-vis* the objective world, especially his human associates—a verbalization made by and to himself, and also by means of his communication with others. The very "act of communication," as Cooley[6] put it, sets up the individual as a human being—humanizes him, so to speak. The process of expressing himself linguistically about what he experiences—face to face with others or silently in imagined situations—gives the individual an awareness of self as an independent entity, distinguishable from all other entities.[7] As the individual specifically identifies, categorizes, conceptualizes and objectifies the items of his universe by words, phrases and sentences of the language he has learned, he finds self to be a peculiar and separate personal existence, yet at the same time a participant in the total context. This significant aspect of language is exemplified when the child learns his own name, and comes to use it regarding himself in distinction to others, thereby accentuating his separate identity and independent existence. In addition to awareness of and response to his name, his sense of self—other identity is also reflected in his use of such pronouns as "you" or "me," such phrases as " 'I' am 'Jimmy,' " " 'You' are 'Tommy.' "

To view the matter from a slightly different angle, when a person speaks, it is always, though in varying degree, an act of creation, involving himself as an existent personality. To speak is to *be oneself* and *know oneself.*

Language plays a significant part not only in the consciousness of self, but also in the closely related *development or construction of self.* As Mead has pointed out, language and self develop together in social situations. We do not intend to add to the already numerous detailed syntheses, interpretations, and applications of the Mead hypothesis, but simply to point to the skeletal features that relate language to the development of self.[8]

The self is not initially there; it is something that has a development. It appears in the process of social experience and activity; it is essentially a social structure. But what is the nature of this process by which the individual can get out of himself experientially, and take an objective, impersonal attitude to himself, in such a way as to become an object to himself?

The individual becomes an object to himself only by becoming aware of the attitudes of other individuals toward himself, within a social environment or context of experience or behavior in which both he and they are involved. There are two stages in this development. In the first stage, "the individual's self is constituted simply by an organization of particular attitudes of other individuals toward himself and toward another in the specific social acts in which he participates with them"; but, at the second stage, the self is constituted also "by an organization of the social attitudes of the generalized other or the social group as a whole to which he belongs" (p. 158). Mead goes on: "These social or group attitudes are brought within the individual's field of direct experience, and are included as elements in the structure or constitution of his self, in the same way that the attitudes of particular other individuals are; and the individual arrives at them, or succeeds in taking them, by means of further organizing, and then generalizing, the attitudes of particular other individuals in terms of their organized social bearings and implications. So the self reaches its full development by organizing these individual attitudes of others into the organized social or group attitudes." It thus becomes "an individual reflection of the general systematic pattern of social or group behavior in which it and the others are all involved" (p. 158).

The process, however, involves more than being in a social group, being affected by others and affecting them. The individual not only takes up the attitudes of others, but acts toward himself as others act; he takes the different roles that the others supply; he acquires the responses that are common to all.

But "the peculiar character of human social activity is formed in the process of communication" (p. 145). Communication occurs by some sort of "gesture"; it is the beginning of social acts; it consists of stimuli exerted by an organism and the adjustive responses made to them by another organism (pp. 43, 145). When the gesture has "some idea behind it," and "it arouses that idea in the other individual, then we have a significant symbol" (p. 145). When we have a symbol which answers to a meaning in the experience of the first individual, and which calls out that same meaning in the second individual, then the gesture "has become what we call 'language' " (p. 46). Language is the essential medium by which a personality is constructed; it is the mechanism by which stimuli are exerted and responses are carried out. It is the means whereby attitudes are aroused in the other; it mediates the activities that give rise in the individual to the processes of taking the role of others (pp. 75, 162, 171, 260, 268, 335). In so far as he can take the role of the other, he can, in a measure, look back at himself from that perspective, respond to himself, and so become aware of himself as an object—achieve self-consciousness.

Language is also very important in providing the *content and dimensions of personality*. It is for the individual an inescapable, ever-present environment which presents him to and orients him in all of the other environments that have some meaning to him—cosmic, natural physical and biological, sociocultural, supernatural, even imagined environments. What the group is "aware of" and "knows about" the various environments is mediated by the language to the individual throughout his life. The language that he uses thus not only functions as his agency in utilizing his universe, and as his medium for thinking as he does; it also canalizes his expression of it in considerable part, and gives him much of the content of what he thinks about and reflects on as important, in his self-behavior. The particular network of words possessed by the individual, in a very real sense, may be said to be the measure of his universe and, correspondingly, to establish the limits to which his innate potentialities may carry him. Related to this is the importance of the amount and range of his own language in determining the range of his ability to identify, classify and think, perceptually and emotionally to react to what he experiences.[9] This in turn is an important factor in the orienting of self to the potentials of his world, and in the development of the various facets of his personality.

It is well to point out that language facility is a matter of education, informal and formal. For the child, for example, the degree of richness and precision of parental language is a major influence in shaping the quality and quantity of the child's vocabulary and the accuracy of his grammatical expression during his growing years. This linguistic development continues under the influence of language instruction in his schools. We know that performance in intelligence tests is seriously affected by verbal facility; in fact, size of vocabulary and precision of expression seem to be major factors in achieved and measured intelligence.[10]

An uneducated person—a partial illiterate—is known by his speech, or rather by his want of speech; he is incapable of understanding a large portion of the words of his own language, as it is used today; he shows marked disability in participating in the intellectual and spiritual life of his community. "Language may be compared to the keyboard of a musical instrument. . . . An educated person is like an organ in which all the keys are connected with the pipes, and all the stops are in working order; whilst an uneducated person is like an instrument in which half the keys do not speak, and many of the stops are lacking."[11]

A further significant aspect of language in the development of self is *its part in the growth of the self*. The self is a continual development—a continually new synthesis and integration. As it develops, it becomes a registrator of the manifold verbal symbols that depict each new aspect of reality that comes to the person. On the other hand, the individual must be able to use this equipment with confidence, to use language freely so that he can live and act expansively. If you hedge in his language, you hedge in his development: you take away most of his ability to grow with new experience.

The number of sublanguages of his own mother tongue and the number of foreign languages with which an individual is familiar are potent factors in the make-up, richness and extent of his personality. The "special" languages an individual knows, as was pointed out in Chap. XIV, Sect. 6, are means whereby we constantly identify him with particular social groups. Each one he knows is a "window" on some significant segment and activity of his society and age. For example, when the layman acquires some new scientific or artistic or religious terminology, or even comes to understand some of the argot of criminals, he has gained new insights and has extended his experiential and cognitive horizons into these other areas of interest and activity.

Having proficiency in one or more national languages other than his own makes the individual a participant in as many new cultural worlds, with their different values, attitudes, interests, institutional forms, styles of life and world views. It is fundamentally true that he who is adept in two languages lives in two worlds, and his experiential and cultural insights and reach are extended correspondingly.[12] These insights are integral to his personality enrichment and stature.

> As many languages as someone speaks,
> So many times is he a man.[13] (*Charles V*)

Similarly, Schopenhauer is said to have remarked that, every time he learned a new language, he gained a new soul.[14]

A significant converse aspect of the linkage of persons and language is the part that persons play in the *maintenance of language*. A language is a socially contrived system of habits of speech and the use of related symbolic forms. This systemic complex is learned by "persons," that is, people who are members of a society. What is more important, however, is the fact that language is actively and somewhat consistently maintained, transmitted and modified through time, by the individual performances and the interactional activities of persons. As Firth points out, when a person speaks, he fuses into a single verbal creation habits, custom and tradition—the elements of the past—on the one hand and, on the other hand, the element of innovation of the moment by himself as a particular personality. All persons, in some degree, share in this creation; of special significance is the fact that, as all speak together, they maintain this ever-changing system and with their descendants perpetuate it in time.[15]

d / Language and the socialization of the individual. Certain specific contributions of language to the continuing socialization of the individual, in addition to their part in the development of the social self, merit attention.

It is by means of its own language, with its particular structure and its own unique body of meanings, that *the society indoctrinates the individual with its "history" and its basic operational principles and rules*. He thus acquires the accepted facts, as well as the beliefs and myths, about its career in time—items which it is expected he will accept, exemplify and continue as a member. Through language, the essential knowledge for social behavior is gained and the characteristic mental habits and social interests are inculcated. By means of it, the social values, attitudes, ideas, traditions, ideals, ideologies and goals are defined and made conceivable for the individual, and internalized by him. As noted in Chapter XI, the behavioral principles and all the rules governing prescriptions (requirements) and proscriptions (prohibitions) are instituted in specific forms of language and instilled by means of it. The society by that means effectively maintains all of its major controls over the members, individually and collectively.

Language is *a potent social instrument used by the individual in his relations with his associates.* The child early becomes aware of that fact. He finds that, by the use of certain sounds, words, phrases and sentences, he can declare himself, he can bring upon himself types of attention from others. Some vocalizations enable him to bring about some changes in his environment that are desired by him; others, he discovers, result in unwanted types of reaction. He becomes aware of his ability to direct and manipulate others, and he uses language to do so. As his language facility develops he gains new insights into himself and acquires increasing control over his own behavior—especially the ability to direct it in conformity with learned social standards by conversing with himself about it. By way of the expressions of others, he develops sensitivity to the approval and disapproval of others, and responds more coherently and consistently to the expectations of others.

Language plays an important part in *the assumption of social roles by the individual, and in his performance of these roles.* While he may not be conscious of that fact, he acquires in specific verbal form the definitions and specifications of the roles for the different types of social situations in which he is involved. He outlines verbally his behavior in each role, and imagines the response (of either an approving or a critical nature) of possible others. He thus "rounds out" his conception of his various roles and at the same time internalizes them.

By means of language, the individual *obtains information regarding the social organization of his society,* especially its institutions and the functions they require of him.

By means of language, the individual *learns about the system of social rank of his society, and his place in it.* Through it, he not only acquires the manners, mores, rituals, and economic traits of his own social class; being immersed in the "special" language of his class, he acquires *its* vocabulary, accent, pronunciation, idiom and metaphor.

The very use of the common language of his group has a socializing effect upon him: it binds him to his co-speakers. Furthermore, as was noted in an earlier chapter, the speech community, by contrast with other communities, has a certain *esprit de corps,* which enhances the feeling of "belongingness" of the individual and favors actions valued by the community.

In general, it is only through language that the individual can live with other people, do their bidding, influence them to do his bidding and engage in teamwork with them.

2. *The Part of Language in the Orientation and Range of the Individual in Time*

Not only does the individual become aware—as a child—of the actuality of time, and acquire the verbal means of distinguishing its phases; throughout his life, language is the means whereby he orients himself toward the past, present, and future of the stream of time—something that subhuman creatures cannot do. He relates and locates himself with respect to the life of his ancestors and other predecessors, which has been preserved for him in traditions, legends, and written records. It is, of course, by language that he adjusts to and cooperates with his contemporaries. He relates himself to his children, even to his remote descendants, as the culture he has learned (and possibly augmented in some measure) is projected into the future by linguistic instruments. He can achieve a sort of sociocultural immortality through the remembrances and recordings of others, including later generations, about him. As he formulates eschatological doctrines and religious beliefs, he achieves some orientation with eternity.[16]

3. *Language as a Means of the Freedom and the Enslavement of the Individual*

The individual is ensured a considerable degree of freedom by means of the possession of language. First and foremost, it gives him the means to express himself—which is of immeasurable value in the development of human personality. Language also frees him, in part, from his own instincts; he can draw on the accumulated knowledge of his civilization, as he lives his life more or less consciously. He can profit by the experience of others, past and present. He does not have to solve anew every problem that was ever faced by his ancestors. Language can free him to some degree from engulfment in complete uniformity: by means of it, each man can specialize. Furthermore, language provides a variety of channels through which the individual may develop his manner of expression; he can do so in an uncommon, fresh, even eccentric manner —a manner individual and proper to him as a particular person.

At the same time, his language to some extent enslaves the individual. While any individual use of language is in some measure an outcome of individual conditions and behavior, and may in some part be an act of original creation, the language is that of his speech community, and his actual language performance is basically a matter of conditioning. He may have much individual "flair" and "style," but he uses an institutionalized medium, which has conditioned not only his speech behavior but also his intellectual behavior. He cannot avoid drawing upon the vast body of established words and structures—which may have a stultifying effect on him. Departure from established expressional forms may be regarded as eccentric. There is always the possibility that the individual sees the world of the past and the world around him "through a screen of linguistic stereotypes."[17]

Furthermore, through linguistically recorded knowledge, the individual is bound by the experience and conclusions of others; he is forced into a sort of experiential and cultural straitjacket. The language couches in somewhat fixed forms the representations of things, events, relations. It also binds him by ancient and sanctified phrases to the ideological attitudes of his group and his society. It not only integrates him with his society as it is, but ties him to it as it is. The individual is by no means an entirely free agent in speech matters.[18]

4. The Effects of Lack of Language or Impairment of Language Facility Upon the Socialization of the Individual

When the individual, for one reason or another, is unable to talk competently to himself or to communicate readily with others, he is diminished as a self to himself and to his associates. This is the other side of the shield of the relationship of language and the individual. There is a definite interplay between the lack of language or the impairment of the individual's language ability and the impairment of his personality or the deficiency of his sociocultural participation. Any inadequacy in language facility, whatever its cause, results in a truncated personality and an incompletely socialized individual; any impairment of the normal social life of the individual during the early years of life, when competence in language is developing, means a somewhat corresponding deficiency of language ability. The more common situations will be briefly noted.

Those who are individually subnormal along the lines to be immediately discussed are always somewhat crippled in linguistic ability, in spite of the best training; they are also lacking in social proficiency. The *feebleminded,* whether their mental retardation is the consequence of injury, disease or congenital deficiency, range from the vegetable-like idiot to the near-normal moron. The different levels of mental processes among the mentally deficient are accompanied by corresponding levels of sign behavior, ranging from the simplest gestures and mumblings to fairly normal mother-tongue speech. The mental level of the individual affects his learning ability, and is revealed in his capacity to organize behavior abstractly. Especially significant is the fact that these differences of mental ability and communicative behavior also result to some degree in isolation of the respective categories of individuals—in the case of idiots, almost complete isolation—from the social and cultural life of the community, and some inability to enter into it.

Sensory defects, such as blindness and deafness, limit the ability of the individual to learn the general language and hence to communicate freely; they reduce or retard mental development and learning ability, interfere with social contact, restrict the acquisition of culture, and in some measure impair or limit the personality development of the individual. The blind, the deaf and the blind–deaf (as revealed, for example, in the well-known cases of Helen Keller and Laura Bridgman) must have special training, if they are to learn language and develop the ability to participate in the life of the community.

The blind and the deaf, in spite of their otherwise full mental and physical competence to participate with their fellows, are kept from full and free social activity by their sensory handicap. This has various effects, depending upon the particular persons: some feel greatly frustrated by their functional limitations and their dependence upon others for certain services; some, especially among the deaf, develop anxieties and suspicions on the basis of *presumed* efforts on the part of the non-afflicted to ignore or avoid them; others withdraw even more than necessary because of their handicap; some lapse into apathy. Often there is a deleterious personality effect.

Both the blind and the deaf, because of their handicaps in general communication or their own special forms of communication, live in a world apart, a subculture, a community within a community. In modern countries, both receive a segregated education. The deaf have their own manual methods of direct communication, such as the language of signs, or of finger spelling, or a combination of these. As the result of their peculiar mechanical nature, they have a special symbolic and syntactical structure. The blind have their special limiting ways of writing and printing. Both the deaf and the blind suffer a greater or lesser degree of vocational exclusion. Both have special mutual-interest organizations (national and local), their own journals, and exclusive activities. Desirable as these are in an immediate sense, they contribute to some extent to the future isolation of their users from the larger community.

Lindesmith and Strauss summarize the situation well, when they point out that neither mentally retarded nor blind or deaf individuals "can enter into the stream of symbols which characterize the human community."[19]

Some students of speech disorders (such, for example, as stuttering, lisping, and cleft palate) have discovered that these disorders may affect personality in various ways. Notable are self-defense and anxiety tensions, aggressive behavior among some and withdrawing or avoiding tendencies among others, feelings of guilt and inferiority, fears and discouragements, and personalized resentments.

The extreme social isolation of children, which results in a lack of language development, is the key to their stunted mental development and cultural retardation. We have well-authenticated cases of children who were neglected or abandoned at an early age, and who survived alone or with only occasional contact with another human being. Kingsley Davis has presented the cases of Anna and Isabelle, two victims of extreme neglect.[20] While the two cases differ markedly in certain important respects, when they were discovered at around six years of age, both were unable to speak, and both seemed to be in a state of mental retardation. Both, however, in the social environment of the special schools for retarded children and as influenced by training efforts, developed a degree of language capacity—a capacity that could never have been realized in the original condition of isolation. Davis says of Anna, when she was over ten years of age and just before she died: "She talked mainly in phrases but would repeat words and try to carry on a conversation." As both acquired some speech ability, they also grasped to some degree the world of cultural meaning.

We have also accumulated during recent centuries cases of feral children and adults—human creatures lost at an early age, who lived, up to the time of discovery, with animals or in complete solitude. The "wolf" children, Amala and Kamala, of Northern India are noteworthy cases.[21] These feral individuals, when found, were without language or any other forms of human cultural development. All showed great difficulty in learning even the most rudimentary speech, and acquired but a slight and imperfect command of the content of culture.

In general, it can be said that these feral, or otherwise isolated persons, had had no experience on the human level and no social intercourse on the symbolic level; even after discovery and the assumption of social interaction, they had difficulty developing facility in symbolic communication and cultural behavior.

Two types of behavioral disorder—aphasia and schizophrenia—acutely affect the language performance, self-actualization and social participation of the individual. The term "aphasia" refers, in a general way, to the loss or disturbance of language responses in the individual. It may be brought about by cerebral injury, hypnosis, or traumatic experiences. It manifests itself in: (a) disability in pronouncing words clearly and in using them in a grammatical and orderly manner; (b) inability to use or understand words as names of objects or qualities; (c) difficulty in understanding the speech of others; (d) inability to grasp the general meaning or import of symbolic patterns—for example, being unable to see a joke in a cartoon, or to "get the point" of what has been said or written. The sufferer has the inability to identify objects, to reason effectively with himself, to convey consistent ideas to others orally or in writing, to make sense of what he hears or reads. As a result of this disturbance of his language function, his whole inner life is impoverished and unrealistically simplified; his freedom of thought and voluntary action are largely lost. He has lost his basic means of self-orientation: he is without adequate means of formulation of his relationships to other persons or to the physical world, especially when it is conceived and considered abstractly; he is unable to come to grips with normal social requirements. In a very real sense, he is in the world but not of it.[22]

Schizophrenia has various phases. For our present purpose, it is sufficient to say that schizophrenics suffer impairment of thought processes and marked disturbances of social relations; they have lost contact with society. The language of the schizophrenic particularly reveals his distraught and bizarre state. Its outstanding aspects as presented by Church are: (a) "word salad": an incoherent jumble of real words, which is meant to make sense; (b) asyndetic speech: juxtaposition of more or less related terms taking the place of normal linkages; (c) metonymy: the use of idiosyncratic approximation ("I have menu three times a day"), or of a personal idiom which the listener must translate, since ordinary words have been given a unique signification; (d) alien intrusions of disturbing ideas or extraneous associations, and the combining of words in unconventional ways; (e) defective generalizations; (f) neologisms: invented words; and (g) often a fusion of two related words, as in "steam-sails."[23] Lindesmith and Strauss say: "Conversation with a schizophrenic leaves one with the feeling that both he and you have been talking past each other."

5. Language as the Index and Revealer of the Individual

Another important aspect of the language of individuals has to do with language as the reflector and measure of a man as a person and as a member of his society, and also as an example of his culture.[24]

For the given individual, the structure of his language is something like a ready-made suit of clothes that he cannot avoid wearing. His linguistic behavior—like his use of leisure, his family practices, his manners, dress, and consumption style—is learned, habitual, socially standardized and subject to normative control. Yet there is always some individualization of a language by members of the speech community, some particularity in each person's use of it. Each has his own personal way of "wearing" the prefabricated garment; each speaks the language in his own style; each thinks with it in his own fashion. Each member of the speech community may be said to possess his own *idiolect,* his own personal variety of the language system, his own particular way of speaking his mother tongue—as distinct, for example, from his dialect, or common "special" language, which he shares with all the members of his ethnic or areal or special-interest subgroup. Hence, it can be said, with some degree of justice, that there are just as many idiolects, just as many varieties of a living language, as there are speakers of that language.[25]

While we know little about the relative influence of the *average* individual in producing changes in the standard language of his group, attention should be called to the possibility. The influence of innovative persons or "schools" was discussed in Chapter VII, Section 3a. Each of us, however, in some microscopic degree may introduce innovations, most of which arise inadvertently, and many of which may be looked upon at first as aberrations. At any rate, as Sapir has suggested, every individual, along with his linguistic compatriots, is a direct participant in the innovative tendencies that constitute the "drift" of the language.[26]

The linguistic behavior of the individual is affected by, varies with, and serves as important evidence of his own peculiar personality characteristics, his early and later socialization, his significant group memberships and identifications, his social roles and statuses, and others among his social circumstances. When a man speaks, he is verbalizing a portion of the subjective and objective schematic framework within which he orders his life; he is translating into words his individual propulsions, his innate and acquired abilities, his sociocultural patterns and reactions.

a / Language as the vehicle of individual personality characteristics. That a man is revealed by his speech was classically put by Ben Jonson long ago: "Language most shows a man. *Speak that I may see thee!* It springs out of the most retired and inmost parts of us and is the image of the parent of it, the mind. *No glass renders a man's form and likeness so true as his speech."*[27]

When a person speaks, he tells us not only about the world as he experiences it, but also, through both his form and his content, about himself. This relationship can be expressed in the hypothesis that the *verbal style* of the individual serves as a vehicle for and indicator of his *personality style.* Numerous classic studies have pointed to the fact that there is such a thing as personality style: each personality has its own inimitable "flavor" and "flair," its own peculiar dispositions and forms of expression, its own degrees and ways of achieving definiteness and effectiveness in its relations with others. Important affective constituent elements of personality style are the level of intelligence and intellectual power, and the cognitive style of the individual, the kinds and intensity and stability of his feelings and emotions, his special expressional characteristics, the nature and strength of his propulsions and inhibitions, the features of his physical and mental health (or ill-health), his beliefs, prejudices, insights and values, his loves and hates, his frustrations and satisfactions, his "artistry," his sense of humor, his taciturnity or garrulousness, his confidence in himself or lack of it, his sense of inferiority or superiority.

These and other stylistic features of self, in various combinations, are reflected in the language of the individual in a variety of ways:

1. The quantity and variety of vocabulary and the particular vocabulary preferences shown; the personal choice of words.

2. The grammatical form and syntactical order.

3. The complexity of sentence structure.

4. The length of sentences.[28]

5. Accent; the inflections, intonations and pronunciations used.

6. Monotone or rhythm and variations of tones; changes of pitch and timbre.

7. Such properties as stridency or mellifluence, strain or relaxation,

gruffness or kindliness of tone, flatness or expressiveness, fluency or fragmentation of output, blocking, the dominance of such affective qualities as irony, gentleness, warmth or whimsicality.[29]

8. The omissions and substitutions used; the speech inhibitions.

9. The directness or indirectness of speech.

10. The facility (free flow) or halting nature of the structural organization of the individual's speech: for example, "the tendency to garble word sequences, to leave sentences unfinished (whether hopping from idea to idea or by letting sentences trail off), to be sidetracked onto tangents, and onto tangents of tangents, and to try to tell things wrong end to."[30]

11. "Slips of the tongue"—lisping, stuttering, and other speech disorders—as reflectors of mental disorders.

12. The tendencies to repetition, circumlocution, allusiveness, circumstantiality, and the like.

13. The logical quality and sequence of ideas, and the degree of consistency and coordination.

14. The kinds of ideas presented, their sharpness, the level of abstraction revealed, the special association of ideas.

15. The ignorance or avoidance of, or the imaginative use of, certain terms and phrases, the use of metaphor, idiom, vivid figures of speech, analogies, "sugar-coated" words, clichés, platitudes, puns, slang, euphemisms, vulgarisms, conservatisms.

16. Pomposity, apology, modesty or straightforwardness in manner of speaking.

17. Whether the individual talks much and says little, or talks little or moderately and says much ("rings bells").

18. The imitation of prestigious or admired persons.

19. The adaptability and suitability of the language used to each particular situation.

To the well-known phrase, "Style is the man," can be added, "His speech reveals his style." The whole matter was concisely summarized by Sapir:

> The fundamental quality of one's voice, the phonetic patterns of speech, the speed and relative smoothness of articulation, the length and build of the sentences, the character and range of the vocabulary, the stylistic consistency of the words used, the readiness with which words respond to the requirements of the social environment, in particular, the suitability of one's language to the language habits of the person addressed—all these are so many complex indicators of the personality.[31]

b / Language as the revealer of the individual's locale, his social roles and position, and his cultural level. The language or the "special" languages of the individual also provide hallmarks by means of which he can be located on social, societal, and cultural coordinates—his locale, his social place or places, his functions in the social organization of his society, his cultural level and range.

[1] *The individual's dialect labels him areally.* The fact that a person speaks with a high pitched voice and nasal twang identifies him as coming from a certain section of New England. The speech of the born-and-bred Texan has equally recognizable characteristics.

[2] The way a person speaks and writes is also, to a considerable extent, *an index of his family breeding and upbringing*—of its level of cultural refinement and its attention to standards.

In many instances the language of the person—what he expresses and how he expresses it—also reflects the kind and quality of his intelligence.

[3] The special terminologies and sublanguages which a person uses *show his particular interest-group orientations and his group affiliations.* They indicate whether he is "butcher, baker, candlestick maker"; "doctor, lawyer, merchant chief"; "rich man, poor man, beggarman, thief." The speech forms used in different circumstances reveal whether the person is a scientific or technological specialist, and if so, what kind he is; whether he is a teenager, a religious cultist, a sports devotee, a "hick" or illiterate, a "highbrow" or an "aristocrat."

The language of an individual—especially his accent and pronunciation, the stresses and tempi of his utterances, his use and misuse of vocabulary, certain peculiarities of grammar, and sometimes dominant preoccupations with certain subjects—sometimes reveals *the ethnic group membership or ethnic background of the individual.* Certain stock phrases and catchwords may reveal, perhaps unintentionally, the speaker's ideological affiliations. The individual's proficiency of "special" vocabulary, terminology and phrasing, or lack of it, is evidence of whether he is an outsider, a novice or a thoroughly initiated member of groups in which he participates.

The language of the individual is in some instances a declaration of his social-psychological place among the members of the group. For example, his manner of speaking often reflects attitudes of dominance, equality or subordination with respect to other members of the group.

[4] Closely related to the group-identification function of language for the individual is the fact that the special languages he speaks *reveal some of his roles and statuses, both in the larger society and in the*

special groups to which he belongs. These languages are reflectors of function. However, since social functions are differentially and unequally evaluated, some of the "special" languages—particularly those bound up with the major occupations and preoccupations of the speakers— indicate strategic roles and serve as indices of status. Some of them, for example, the "Park Avenue" lingo, the esoteric jargon of some "professionals," the cant of a nortorious crook, are cherished as *symbols* of social status.[32]

Within the group, the degree of success with which the individual manipulates his group's sublanguage is an important criterion of acceptance and place. When you master your major "special," you are admitted to the secret mysteries and benefits of the group or order. One who lacks proficiency, for example, the teenager who is unfamiliar with the current teenage argot with its gags and catchwords, is "out of things." A member of the group who is careless with the "special" is usually somewhat suspect.

[5] The language of a man is also *a measure of the range and level of his participation in his community and his culture.* A culturally facile and sophisticated person usually has parallel linguistic proficiency, depth, and range. The amount and variety of his vocabulary determine the extent and range of his expression, apprehension, understanding, and particularly of his cultural perspectives; it also determines, in general, his cultural participation and contribution. A person with a limited vocabulary lives in a restricted world; the one with an extensive vocabulary lives in a wide world, one with many vistas. Likewise, adequacy of one's syntax presages the ability to express one's thought accurately. Conversely, limited language tools do not permit a wide range of awareness, of viewpoint and interest, of knowledge, thinking and action. Hence, the language facility of the individual, while it is not a guarantee of high cultural contribution, is usually accepted by most people as the indicator of the cultural potentialities of the individual. The extent of his universe is directly correlated with the extent of his universe of discourse.

Speak, that we, your associates, may know thee!

N O T E S

1 John B. Carroll, *The Study of Language* (Cambridge: Harvard University Press, 1953), pp. 88–94.
2 This distinction is found, among others, in Joseph Bram, *Language and Society* (New York: Random House, 1955), p. 23.

3 For some select items on the acquisition of language by the child, see the appended bibliography. Two of the best, most cautious and most comprehensive syntheses and digests of what is confidently known are: Morris M. Lewis, *Infant Speech: A Study of the Beginnings of Language* (2nd ed., New York: Humanities Press, 1951), and Alfred R. Lindesmith and Anselm L. Strauss, *Social Psychology* (rev. ed., New York: Holt, Rinehart & Winston, 1956), Chap. 6, "The Acquisition of Language and Reason," pp. 159–196. Dependence upon these two sources of information is herewith acknowledged. An excellent earlier concise treatment is to be found in Erwin A. Esper: "Language," in Carl Murchison (ed.), *Handbook of Social Psychology* (Worcester, Mass.: Clark University Press, 1935), pp. 417–460 (433–443).

4 This excellent term was used by Joseph Church, *Language and the Discovery of Reality: A Developmental Psychology of Cognition* (New York: Random House, 1961), pp. 86–87.

5 Cf. Clemens E. Benda, "The Linguistic Bases of Consciousness," *ETC.: A Review of General Semantics,* 16 (Spring, 1959), 343–355.

6 Charles H. Cooley, *Human Nature and the Social Order* (New York: Charles Scribner's Sons, 1910), p. 49.

7 "Emerson says somewhere that "the man is but half himself; the other half is his expression"; this is literally true. The man comes to be, through some sort of expression, and has no higher existence apart from it; overt or imaginary, it takes place all the time." (*Ibid.,* p. 57.)

8 For Mead's classical presentation of the relation of language to self-development, see George H. Mead, *Mind, Self, and Society* (Chicago: University of Chicago Press, 1934), pp. 42–226, 268–289, 300, 335. The pages indicated for the quotations from Mead immediately below refer to this work. See also his "Thought, Symbols, and Language," in Kimball Young, *Source Book for Social Psychology* (New York: Alfred A. Knopf, 1938), pp. 341–346; and his "Language and the Development of Self," in T. M. Newcomb and E. L. Hartley (eds.), *Readings in Social Psychology* (New York: Henry Holt & Co., 1947), pp. 179–189.

9 This is clearly brought out in the language history of the child. A child introduced early to a wealth of language, and taught to discriminate between the meanings of words, to use them with beauty and clarity, has decidedly better possibilities of developing a rich personality than a child of meager and careless speech experience.

10 Robert E. L. Faris, "Reflections on the Ability Dimension in Human Society," *American Sociological Review,* 26 (Dec., 1961), 835–843 (839–840).

11 George Willis, *The Philosophy of Speech* (New York: The Macmillan Co., 1922), p. 214. See also pp. 206, 207, 210.

12 The deficits of duo-linguality under certain social and cultural conditions will be discussed in the next chapter.

13 Quoted by Joost A. M. Meerloo, *Conversation and Communication* (New York: International Universities Press, 1952), p. 68.

14 In the same connection, Mead said: "A person learns a new language, and as we say, gets a new soul. He puts himself into the attitude of those that make use of that language. He cannot read its literature, cannot converse with those that belong to that community, without taking on its peculiar attitudes. He becomes in a sense a different individual." (*Mind, Self, and Society,* p. 283.) Mario Pei has called attention to the pragmatic advantages—"another string to his bow"—which that man has who speaks another language besides his own. For example, it aids him in commercial exchange, in his international political understanding and activity, when he travels for pleasure, in his scientific and technological awareness and understanding and, above all, in his cultural relations, understanding and participation. See *The World's Chief Languages* (London: George Allen & Unwin, 1949), p. 11.

15 The content of this paragraph has been suggested in part by John R. Firth,

"Personality and Language in Society," *Sociological Review* (Brit.), 42 (1950), 37–53 (46, 49–50).

16 These ideas have been suggested in part by Arnold W. Green, *Sociology* (New York: McGraw-Hill Book Co., 1960), p. 71.

17 Cf. Green, pp. 72–75. See also Walter R. Goldschmidt (ed.), *Exploring the Ways of Mankind* (New York: Holt, Rinehart & Winston, 1960), Introduction to Chap. II, p. 67.

18 Cf. Robert M. Estrich and Hans Sperber, *Three Keys to Language* (New York: Rinehart, 1952), pp. 337–338.

19 *Op. cit.*, p. 140.

20 Kingsley Davis, "Extreme Social Isolation of a Child," *American Journal of Sociology*, 45 (Jan., 1940), 556–565; Kingsley Davis, "Final Note on a Case of Extreme Isolation," *American Journal of Sociology*, 52 (Mar., 1947), 432–437. See also Kingsley Davis, *Human Society* (New York: Macmillan Co., 1949), pp. 204–208.

21 J. A. Singh and R. M. Zingg, *Wolf Children and Feral Man* (New York: Harper & Brothers, 1942). See also Arnold Gesell, *Wolf Child and Human Child* (New York: Harper & Brothers, 1939).

22 For a more comprehensive treatment of aphasia, see Lindesmith and Strauss, pp. 140–152, from which the above has been largely derived. See also Kurt Goldstein, *Human Nature in the Light of Psychopathology* (Cambridge: Harvard University Press, 1940), and the classic by Kurt Goldstein: *Language and Language Disturbances: Aphasic Symptom Complexes and Their Significance for Medicine and Theory of Language* (New York: Grune & Stratton, 1948).

23 Church, pp. 159–162. See also Lindesmith & Strauss, *op. cit.*, pp. 152–155.

24 On the relationship between name and personality, see Chap. XI, Sect. 4.

25 On idiolect, see John B. Carroll, *The Study of Language* (Cambridge: Harvard University Press, 1953), p. 10; Simeon Potter, *Modern Linguistics* (London: Andre Deutsch, Ltd., 1957), p. 123; Charles F. Hockett, *A Course in Modern Linguistics* (New York: Macmillan Co., 1958), p. 322.

26 Edward Sapir, *Language* (New York: Harcourt, Brace, and Co., 1921), Chap. VII.

27 Quoted by Sidney J. Baker, "The Pattern of Language," *Journal of General Psychology*, 42 (Jan., 1950), 26–66. (Italics added.)

28 Suzanne K. Langer has noted that the use of words is always an index of an individual's intellectual power. The vagueness or precision of the distinctions he can draw between one thing or another, and the range of what he knows is shown in his choice of distinct words for things, and in the number of different words—the range and size of his vocabulary—he uses. ("Philosophy: The Growing Center," in Lynn White, Jr. (ed.), *Frontiers of Knowledge* (New York: Harper & Brothers, 1956), pp. 257–286.)

29 Most of these qualities are from Church, p. 190.

30 Church, *ibid.*

31 Edward Sapir, "Language," *Encyclopedia of the Social Sciences* (New York: The Macmillan Co., 1943), X, 160. A converse aspect of the relation of language and the personality of the individual should not be lost sight of. As has been noted several times, especially in Chap. VI, Sect. 5, the specific language that the individual uses helps to determine his mental processes and his cultural milieu. This, in turn, helps to govern the development of his personality. The language of people may thus have a direct part in establishing patterns of personality characteristics.

32 For an extended discussion of speech and reactions to speech as reflectors of the social position of persons, see Chap. XIV, Sect. 3, p. 372.

XVI ❧ Plural Lingualism in the Modern World

While the necessity of using more than one language in daily intra-community social intercourse is rapidly diminishing within the United States at the present time, the ability to use more than one language is an increasingly important aspect of the linguistic situation in almost all parts of the modern shrinking, interlocking, and ever more crowded world. As for many Americans, our parents, grandparents, or great-grandparents spoke two or more languages with varying degrees of proficiency in their local communities because it was unavoidable: they *had* to speak English in addition to the ancestral tongues they brought with them from abroad. In the decades ahead, we Americans, like almost all other peoples, will need auxiliary languages in our multiplying inter-people contacts and international relations (as noted in Chapter VIII, Section 5). Especially noteworthy is the fact that most of the more or less underdeveloped, but newly emerging, peoples of the world in Africa, Asia, and Latin America, who together comprise a majority of the population of the world, now face, and will continue to face for some time, the necessity of using two or more languages. In their efforts to achieve internal political unification, they will face their multiple tribal languages and regional dialects. In attempting to carry on as members of "modernizing" nations, they may continue to speak their tribal language, but they will also need some degree of proficiency in their dominant national language, should one come to be established, and usually in one or more of the "empire" languages of the world. They will need to be able to use these other languages in their governmental activities, industrial employment and economic exchange (both internal and external), their increasing urban life, educational activities, utilization of mass communications—in fact, in the conduct of most of their social activities and organizations beyond the family (what with cross-marriages, even within some families). In general, there is a very great likelihood that most of the six billion persons in the world of the year 2000 will have to have some proficiency in one or more languages in addition to their mother tongue.

The standard term in linguistics for the use of more than one language is *bilingualism* (or trilingualism). Strictly defined, it is "native-like control of two languages."[1] A bilingual person is one who is able to speak his mother tongue and another language with "equal" or "approximately equal" facility. As Haugen puts it, "Bilingualism . . . is understood here to begin at the point where the speakers of one language can produce complete, meaningful utterances in the other language."[2] The true bilingual, according to strictly formal linguistic conceptualization, has two *idiolects,* or two distinct and separate sets of speech habits. In systematic terminology, "A bilingual person can be said to have two coding systems for his intentive behavior and two sets of decoding responses leading into interpretive behavior."[3]

If the terms *bilingualism* and *bilingual* are to be used as strictly defined, particularly in the sense of equal facility in two languages, several difficulties present themselves. In the first place, as Bloomfield has pointed out,[4] one cannot define a degree of perfection for a person in another language than his mother tongue; perfection of command, or "equality" of facility, is a relative matter. Second, most polyglots (persons with some facility in several languages) belong primarily to *one* speech community, and have only partial control of any other language;[5] whereas persons with even approximately equal facility in the two or more languages they use are, in spite of all claims and pretensions to the contrary, markedly exceptional. Furthermore, the two languages of the bilingual person usually play somewhat different roles in his life, the one ordinarily being the *home language,* while the other serves various other purposes—intellectual-cultural, economic (occupational, trade), religious and so on. Third, as indicated above, there is a need in the modern world for *some* capability in one or more languages other than the mother tongue on the part of millions, even billions, of people, both as individuals and as members of groups. The filling of this need does not require complete equality of proficiency in the other language(s), even if this were determinable or possible. What is required of most people is not, for example, the ability to translate exactly, but sufficient communicative facility by means of the other language(s) to conduct ordinary daily activities in the world as it is. Some cross-people and cross-cultural linguistic communicative ability—even that acquired through only one or several years of school instruction—is far better than linguistic isolation or ineptitude through ignorance. Fourth, there are many areas (and even local communities) where several languages are used, and where the different segments of the population have some facility in the other languages; yet in them nothing approaching bilingualism or polyglotism in the strict formal linguistic sense prevails. The several population elements have differential facility in the use of the several languages.

In our sociological treatment of the use of more than one language by many persons in the community, we find "bilingualism," as strictly defined, to be of limited use; it does not apply to many actual linguistic situations in the contemporary world that we have to accept realistically, nor is it realizable in a practical way, except among a very small and exceptional minority. Therefore, the terms "plural lingual facility" and "plural-language community" will be used here. While this is more cumbersome terminology, and some may object to revising a long-standing concept, the terms are more accurate, in that the implication or requirement of "equal" or "approximately equal" is not involved. The terms are also more inclusive of the multi-language situations actually prevailing in so many communities of the world today. Obviously, "bilingualism" is one particular form of "plural lingualism"; the latter, however, also includes various degrees of practical, or existent (though not "perfect" or "equal") facility in more than one language. "Bilingual" and "bilingual community" in their standard linguistic sense will be used where and when they can be considered to apply. The numerous situations involving several languages in given communities, and differential facility in their employment by different portions of the population, as well as the preparation for some degree of proficiency in cross-language activity, call for this more widely applicable terminology.

A brief examination of the social circumstances, past and present, that produce some proficiency in more than one language, of the functions, social correlates and social effects of such proficiency, and of the conditions that make it desirable or indispensable—this will focus new attention upon, and place in a new perspective and relationship, several important aspects of the sociology of language that have been examined in earlier chapters.[6] It also calls attention to the bearing of plural lingualism on the individual, with regard to problems of social adjustment, of psychological, social and cultural deficits and boons that accrue to him, and of certain inevitabilities as to, if not full bilingual parity, at least some facility in more than one language for the socially conscious and competently participant citizen of the world of communication we now live in.

We shall briefly examine the sociologically significant aspects of plural lingualism from two points of view. The first is *intra*-community plural lingualism, the form almost immediately envisaged when the term is mentioned, and the form to which the major part of previous investigational attention has been devoted. The second is plural lingualism in a very different dimension—namely, *inter*national (or perhaps, *trans*national) linguistic facility, which heretofore, when it has been given any attention, has been brought into discussions of language more or less obliquely, as a centrifugal factor; the difficulties and unlikelihood of a single universal world language, either natural or artificial, and the necessity of communication for the rising tide of international and inter-people interaction. The more outstanding social and individual aspects and effects of all these will be noted.

1. *Intra-Community Plural Lingualism: Nature and Extent*

Intra-community plural lingualism is a phenomenon that grows out of the juxtaposition and interaction of speakers of different languages *within* a single community—that is, a combination of interrelated individuals and groups functioning together within a given territory. The community may be a nation or a lesser (politically consolidated) area or region; it may be a functionally demarcated geographic–economic area, urban, rural or jointly urban and rural; it may even be a neighborhood. The plural lingual community has come about as the result of invasion by speakers of a foreign language, through military conquest or occupation, colonization, the invasion of a religion (missionization by the cross or by the sword), through immigration and even through deliberate importation of forced labor, by indenture or by employment inducements. Most of its typical characteristics also occur where peoples speaking different languages are juxtaposed at physical, political or ethnic borders.

The United States, through most of its history, has been a nation of many diverse linguistic population segments and areas. The Federal

Census, as recently as 1940, indicated that some 21,996,000 persons, or one out of almost every five white persons living in the United States, was reared in a home in which some language other than English was the principal one spoken during the years of early childhood.[7] The amount of plural lingualism has greatly diminished since then.[8] In fact, most of the mother tongues or "first" languages, other than English, which occupied positions of appreciable importance a quarter of a century ago, such as German, French, Italian and the languages of the Scandinavian and Eastern European countries, have greatly declined; the speakers of only one, Spanish—and that by way of Mexico and Puerto Rico—have increased in number. Despite the diminution of the proportion of the population which is bilingual according to the Census of 1960, there were at that time in the United States still some 20,000,000 speakers of languages other than English. We still have areas where plural lingualism is a noticeable sociocultural feature. In New York City, one American in ten is a Spanish-speaking person, of Puerto Rican background. Louisiana has about 400,000 French-speaking "natives." A large portion of the population—those of Mexican descent—in New Mexico, Arizona and certain areas of Texas and California, speak various Spanish dialects. There is also still some fluent German spoken in the Midwest, Italian in many big cities, Chinese and Japanese especially on the West Coast, and Russian, Polish and Scandinavian scattered throughout the country.

Elsewhere in the world today, as indicated above, there are vast areas occupied by awakening, politically and economically transitional peoples, whose diverse ethnic elements, amounting to millions upon millions of persons, with their numerous languages and dialects, are trying to function together as political entities. Specific representative areas are Brazil, with its Europe-descended elements (Portuguese, German, and Italian), its Japanese population, its Negro tribal elements and its Indian tribes;[9] South Africa, with its English and Afrikaans, its Asiatic Indian, and its Bantu and other Negro tribal elements; India, with fifteen major languages, the cleavage between those who speak English and the vast masses who do not, the multiplicity of tribal languages and of dialects within these. Among some of the newly established nations in Africa and Asia, it would seem that not merely two languages, but a *multi*linguality will have to prevail for some time if they are to endure—for example, the roughly 200 different, often antagonistic, tribes, jealous of their specific traditions and ways, including their language, who are attempting to function as the Congo Republic.[10]

It should also be recalled that several contemporary countries of the world are *officially* plural lingual: Flemish and Walloon French in Belgium; French and English in Canada; Czech and Slovak in Czechoslovakia; Swiss German, French, Italian and Romansh in Switzerland; Afrikaans and English in the Union of South Africa; Serbian, Croatian and Slovenian in Yugoslavia; in the Soviet Union, each of the sixteen Republics has its own language, which is semi-official, and all of the 145 or so major and minor tongues have political standing.

2. Significant Sociocultural Variables and Facts Regarding the Plural Lingual Community

Plural lingualism within any given area poses a variety of problems both for the community as a social system and for the plural lingual individuals as personalities. The types, extent, and gravity of the problems depend upon the relevance and the particular configuration of sociocultural factors that prevail. Each community has its own peculiar structural and functional character. Correspondingly, the variables involved in the plural lingual situation of each community present a unique configuration and constitute a specific context for plural lingual behavior. The variables or factors, however, fall into typical categories —types that seem to be almost universal in plural lingual situations. Certain facts stand out, which reflect cause and effect in the operation of the factors, taken singly or in combination. These facts point to certain conclusions regarding plural lingualism as a social phenomenon, some of which also have a considerable degree of generality. None of the variables are sole determinants, and they vary greatly in influence in different situations. Nor do given facts relate solely to given factors; hence there will be some overlapping of facts as the result of the frequent intermeshing of variables.

a / The size of the respective groups or collectivities of speakers usually differs. Ordinarily, when the segments of the population that speak two or more different ancestral tongues are approximately equal in size, both language groups will have to speak both languages. Where there is a great difference in size, the larger group may be almost entirely monolingual and able to ignore, or do without, the language of the small group in most of its activities. Conversely, only by the self-imposition of the most extreme social isolation (aided by the quite unlikely ability to preserve adequate physical maintenance under the circumstances), can a very small number of speakers of a language, immersed in a vast sea of speakers of another language, preserve its separate language, or get along without the major language. The smaller group—the smaller it is, the greater the likelihood of this—finds its efforts to preserve its ancestral tongue "a losing battle," especially through the generations.

This highlights the fact that, in many communities where several languages are spoken, the greater proportion of the interacting persons are monolinguals; they speak only the dominant language. Only the speakers among the numerical and ethnic minorities—the immigrants, those brought in under compulsion, the "native" or indigenous population—need to be able to use two languages.

b / The linguistic bifurcation may vary in permanence. The *permanence* of plural lingualism rests upon the fact that it exists as a long-standing, established, quite generally accepted (though not necessarily condoned) and relatively enduring linguistic relationship. We have, for example, the durable, official, and socially rather successful plural lingualism of Canada, Switzerland, Belgium, South Africa and the American Southwest, mentioned above, as conspicuous instances. These have endured, in several instances, for centuries; the variables are more or less in balance; both (or more) languages are usually politically and culturally acceptable, at least in certain contexts; the speakers of the several languages are *institutionally* accommodated to one another.

In a community of long-standing plural linguality, the situation may come to be regarded as quite normal. This, in turn, affects the degree to which the bilingual is viewed as usual or unusual. As Bossard noted in his classical study of two decades ago:

> To be bilingual in the heart of the Pennsylvania German belt is to be what the great bulk of the people are. The bilingual is the normal person, operating with persons who are bilingual. The same is true in the French Acadian settlements in Louisiana, or in the Spanish settlements of New Mexico. *It is the vogue to be bilingual. This is quite different from being bilingual in an area which is largely, or almost wholly, unilingual.*[11]

The fixity and acceptance of the bilingual or plural lingual situation does not necessarily mean, however, that the members of the respective linguistic groups look upon each other as cultural or social equals. This is especially true where the different linguistic groups are at the same time sharply differentiated social strata, resting upon racial, religious or caste differentiation.

The second, or *temporary* type, involves a plural lingualism, even a bilingualism, where the factors in the situation point toward the disappearance of the forms existing at the moment, and the likelihood that the speakers of the socially or culturally "inferior" language will be (or are in the process of being) assimilated to the larger community in a matter of several generations. This disappearing type of plural lingualism is especially exemplified among most of the non-English-speaking immigrants to the United States, Central and Western Canada, and Australia. In these instances, the immigrants have entered the countries voluntarily as individuals or families; they have existed at first as uninitiated cultural elements; in many instances, they have been looked down upon and have felt themselves to be cultural inferiors. At the same time, these societies have offered social and cultural opportunity—even invitation. Social acceptance and social advancement were presented as possible, the latter even as expectable. In these instances, however, acceptance and free and full participation have been linguistically determined. One language—that of the dominant and socially and culturally important majority elements of the population—was acceptable. All others were "foreign" and frowned upon, and in most instances had pretty much disappeared by the third generation of immigrant stock.

These two contrasting types of plural lingual situations are actually the poles of a continuum. Most concrete instances, as they exist at a given time, can be located somewhere along the continuum. The *permanence* of the location, however, is a relative matter. Plural linguality may disappear in a rather short time for certain age or class elements, or areal segments of a plural lingual group, with numerous and varied types and combinations of social changes. On the other hand, a heretofore monolingual group or area may find some degree of plural linguality essential, desirable or unavoidable, for a large number of possible reasons.

c / The plural lingual community may be one of relative cultural homogeneity or it may be one of considerable differentiation. In some instances, even though the languages or dialects of the respective population elements differ, their traditional cultural ways and social life may be much the same. This is the situation in some Swiss communities, as among some adjoining tribal peoples in Africa, Asia, and Latin

America. The language "badge" is thus the single factor, or one of a few diverse factors, in social relations. Apparently, the plural lingual situation is not highly correlated with sociocultural diversity or separation. In the great bulk of the plural lingual situations, however, the linguistic difference is paralleled by social and other cultural diversities —sometimes extreme and of long historical standing, and in some instances marking racial diversities as well.

Bilingualism or plural lingualism in a community is usually, though not always, accompanied by biculturalism. In most instances, as has been noted, a given language to some degree reflects and embodies the culture; in fact, it is an expression of it. The culture often carries the name of the language through which it is expressed. This is not to say, however, that there is an inherent relationship between language and culture. As noted earlier, a common culture can be shared by people who speak unrelated languages. It is also a fact that speakers of identical or similar or related languages may have cultures that have notable differences; for example, those of the different groups of speakers of French or Spanish the world over.

Nevertheless, within the usual context of factors and conditions, in the great bulk of plural lingual situations the language and the culture of which it is the carrier are directly related. The mother tongues involved are integral parts—"traits"—of the historical cultures of the respective bodies of speakers. Each language acquires what Sapir has called a "condensation symbolism."

Thus the great bulk of plural lingual situations constitute contacts between different cultural groups. This entails biculturalism, or the participation in two cultures, as well as in two languages.

The speakers of the respective mother tongues in the plural lingual community are identified with the correlated culture. The members of the community impute to each other a mutual cultural alliance, on the basis of a common ancestral tongue. The speakers so identify themselves in contrast to the speakers of the "other" language, and thus set themselves off from the latter. "Outsiders" are people who speak a different language and have a culture that differs in important respects. Similarly, in order to determine the culture of an individual, one first identifies his main language.

The juxtaposed cultures may be quite different. The "other" culture group may (usually does) have significantly different cultural features, such as religion or education (as in Eastern Canada), or a different status (the old long-standing population segments, as against the immigrant elements), or it may be of a different race (the Japanese in

Brazil), or represent urban–rural or other marked regional differences by comparison with the different ways of life involved.

d / An extremely important situation that often prevails is that the bodies of speakers of the different languages current in the community may have social and related cultural superiority-inferiority differences among them—such as those of class, ethnicity, race, religion, and occupation. Differences of social, political and economic power, influence, standing and opportunity may also differentiate them.

Where such conditions exist, *the "superior" or "dominant" language is usually that of the socially "superior" and "dominant" population elements.* It is the language of the officialdom, of all the major social institutions and their organizations—particularly the language of the main property holders, the managers of the major industrial and commercial establishments, the political officials, the civic leaders, the patrons of culture. In some cases, it is the language of the dominant, though not necessarily the most numerous race, the language of most *public* communication, of those who control the opportunities for employment and social advancement.

Knowledge of the vernacular of the "inferior" population elements does not of itself qualify a person for any of these public positions. On the other hand, the language of the socially superior and the dominant has high utility in the community. It is, in fact, a necessity for active participation in community affairs; its speakers have prestige, they are socially advantaged and preferred. Thus speakers of the language or languages of the inferior population elements will be under a personal and social compulsion to learn and to use the language of the dominant elements in all relations and activities. Usually, they come to use the superior language, in time giving up their own language altogether.

When social "inferiors" persistently adhere to their own language, and try to ignore or avoid the "other" language, it is under the force of conceptions of their own superiority, or of an exclusiveness based on religious or other crucial cultural reasons—such as the desire to maintain their ethnic identity (the Pennsylvania Dutch)—or a belief in their higher cultural level (for example, by equating higher culture with higher "race"—as is true, concretely, of an enclave of Europeans in the midst of Africans or Asiatics).

The upshot of the superior–inferior situation, involving social evaluation as it does, is that *it can produce at least social strain, if not some social conflict,* between the respective elements. This situation, combined with that of the usually prevailing biculturalism with its cultural cleavage, can produce a "schism of the body politic," to use Pieris's term—an endangering of the relations of the population elements involved.[12]

Closely related to the situation of social inequality is the fact that *the juxtaposed cultures, as represented by the respective bodies of speakers, are rarely accepted as "equals."* Usually, if the culture of one group of speakers is held to be superior in the given context of circumstances by the greater portion of the population, their language will also be considered to be the superior and aspired-to language. Speakers of the languages of the lesser culture groups will be viewed as culturally inferior. This differentially affects the self-conceptions of the respective groups of plural linguals. It causes the superior to expect the inferior to embrace the language of his superior culture, and to use it in all his relations with him.

A corollary of the fact just discussed is that *the languages of a plural lingual community are often identified with different social statuses.* As just noted, the language of the dominant culture or socially powerful population elements is usually given more social acclaim. Thus, in many a plural lingual community a social process is in operation whereby people are assigned status within the prevailing status system, partly, at least, on the basis of their adherence to or departure from the socially ranking language of the community. The language minorities, for example, immigrant or ethnic groups, are regarded as being of lower social status, by virtue of their "foreign" language.

The correlation of language with social status varies, however, from community to community, and in terms of the operation of particular sets of factors. For example, to have established social prestige and high standing in the community, even though one speaks the "foreign" language, is a guarantee of high status. In plural lingual Arizona and New Mexico, the prestigious indigenous Spanish-speaking "Old Families" are on a social parity with any English-speaking elements of the population, and their high social position lends distinction to the Spanish language.[13]

On the other hand, the lowest strata of the speakers of a "foreign" language in the community are usually particularly disadvantaged. They are the slowest to acquire facility in the socially and culturally dominant language. Among the factors involved are their more limited social circulation, as compared with that of their linguistic compatriots of higher status, their more limited economic and educational opportunities, the greater likelihood of their physical isolation (even segregation), their more limited social goals, and their restricted cultural range.

Another frequent aspect of the sociocultural position of *the speakers* of the "foreign" or "other" language is that *they are usually somewhat marginal in cultural performance, as compared with the speakers of the main language,* and are therefore usually socially peripheral rather than part of the central body. They have been referred to as "cultural hybrids." Many such people have been made keenly aware of their cultural marginality, which may have positive motivating effects, but may also deleteriously affect their personalities, especially threatening the unity of their personalities.

Whether or not this state of marginality exists depends upon the particular social situation, especially the degree of establishment and reciprocal acceptance of the bilingualistic situation. Even bilingualism, however, does not necessarily entail cultural marginality. For example:

> In Java, the noblemen speak Ngoko, the commoners Kromo. But the two orders understand each other's language, and each uses the other's language in addressing him. In this case, bilingualism is an integral part of the cultural set-up, social stratification being reflected in a linguistic bifurcation.[14]

Here the two languages are two established and generally accepted aspects of the same culture. Marginality exists where and when the culture of the speakers of the "other" language is regarded as "foreign" and possibly of lesser repute, even viewed with suspicion, and its carriers likewise depreciated.

The situation with respect to cultural equality or inequality of the respective language groups also *affects the attitudes of tolerance or intolerance regarding the use of the two or more languages in the community.* If the groups of speakers of the respective languages are relatively "equal" along social and cultural lines, there is usually a concomitant tolerance for each other's languages—for example, the reciprocal tolerance of both English and French among many of the people of Eastern Canada. Conversely, the long established elements, the ethnic majority, the culturally dominant elements may and usually do react somewhat intolerantly to "foreign" languages in their midst. However, if the speakers of the reputedly inferior language or languages are potentially capable of more or less equal social and cultural participation and, in the main, are aspiring thereto, there may be temporary tolerance of or condescension to their "inferior" language. This has been the attitude of many Americans to the ancestral languages of immigrants.

e / Another set of facts and factors has to do with **the linguistic behavior of the minority linguistic group in its intra-group relations and in its relations with the members of the majority.** There is wide variation in the use of the ancestral language and the majority language by the members of the ethnic minority group, depending on who is in contact with whom, and under what circumstances. In brief, each language used by the minority plural lingual comes to be identified with certain fields of interpersonal relations.

Barker studied the plural linguals of Mexican descent in Tucson, Arizona.[15] While his findings were specific as to the particular community, they may have a more universal significance. He found that his Mexican-descended plural linguals used the ancestral language on some occasions and in certain circumstances, and English on others; on certain occasions, they alternated between one language and the other.

Four such linguistically identifiable relations were readily distinguishable: (1) In the field of intimate or familial relations, Spanish was almost universally used. It was the language of early childhood, the language used by parents to children in the home, and employed in close friendships, in parish social life, and in the ceremonial relationships of the Mexican–American community. The ancestral language thus was directly identified with family background and minority group membership. (2) In the field of informal relations among the members of the Mexican–American group with one another, rapid shifting from one language to another was common, the two languages sometimes being used in the same sentence or phrase. This was especially true of the younger native-born portion of the population. Barker observes that this switching may have been due, first, to the fact that the speakers felt that the context or subject they were discussing could be better and more easily expressed in one language than in the other, and, second, in other instances, their choice may have been dictated by their feeling that what they were trying to say simply could not be expressed in the other language. (3) In the field of formal relations among the Mexican–Americans, including many types of economic relations and some formal social relationships, English was widely used. One of the main reasons for the substitution of English for formal Spanish was the fact that the children did not learn formal Spanish at home. Their language for formal uses was the English they learned at school. Thus, for many children, English came to be identified with most types of formal relationships. The exceptions were events in the Mexican community with a religious or patriotic social context, in which formal Spanish was customarily used. (4) In the field of Anglo–Mexican relations, English was the standard language. Even when the Mexican–Americans knew that the "Anglos" they were addressing spoke Spanish, they almost always used English.

In general, two points stand out. One is that the ancestral language of the minority plural linguals tends to be used rather persistently in the more restricted contexts: in close family relationships, in private prayer and self-conversation, in conversation with friends and other intimate informal events, and in precious, ancient, family, primary-group and nationality-group ceremonials. The other point is that the language of the majority is used, as far as possible, in their relations with them. These may, in fact, be the poles of a continuum of typical usage of their two languages by the plural linguals.[16]

f / The factors in the weakening of the immigrant ancestral language. There has been a tendency for plural lingualism to disappear among the descendants of immigrants in the United States in a matter of two generations; when the ancestral language is retained by some individuals, it is primarily for sentimental or cultural reasons. Presentation of the factors in the disappearance from usage of the foreign language epitomizes some of the other facts just discussed. The ancestral language weakens for a number of reasons.

Some factors tend to bring about erosion and disappearance. As a consequence of the special features of the new sociocultural (even the physical) environments, the ancestral language, having been developed in a different milieu, lacks the words and expressions necessary to activity in the new situations, thus creating a need for a new vocabulary which will be able to describe and state new facts. Their economic pursuits, their involvement in the political life of the community, their new experiences in sports and games and in school subjects, conspire to bring about what Haugen calls "The Great Vocabulary Shift."[17] Another item in the erosion of ancestral language is the fact that the social and cultural disorientation of the immigrants undermines their inertial resistance to excessive borrowing of items from the dominant language. This often brings about a progressive dilution and corruption of their ancestral language.

More important, however, is the fact that the social and cultural position and functions of members of the immigrant stock change with successive generations. Most of these changes greatly favor more and more resort to the major community language. Both through everyday intercourse and through education, they cease to be bicultural, become culturally assimilated, and perform culturally through the medium of the main language. In the absence of legal ethnic discrimination, and with the weakening of whatever community discrimination there has been and increasing cultural absorption, generation by generation, the tenacity with which out-groups retain their language as a precious symbol of their existence relaxes and the language itself all but disappears. In order to profit by economic and educational opportunity, to overcome their social and cultural marginality and move toward equality status, by achieving upward social mobility, they come to believe that they should not display their immigrant tongue, and that they should instead develop high competence in the dominant language. In general, it can be said that the immigrant language tends to disappear because it loses its functional importance, socially and culturally.

3. *The Plural Lingual Individual*

Attention has been called in the preceding chapter to the close relationship between language and the personality structure and behavior of the individual. The language of the individual reflects his personality style, his major interests and preoccupations, the major groups to which he belongs, his social statuses and roles, his cultural level, his social class, as well as his defects and disorders and his social impoverishments. It was also pointed out that a knowledge of and facility in more than one language gives the individual distinct personal and cultural advantages. Here we shall briefly examine the sociocultural boons enjoyed by the bilingual or plural lingual in his plural lingual community. Moreover, the plural lingual situation also produces distinct psychic and social problems for him to contend with; these too will be briefly examined.

a / Social gains from plural linguality for the individual. The plural lingual individual, however meager his facility in the "other" language or languages, has *some* measure of ability to communicate with the members of the groups who do not speak his language; since interaction with them is unavoidable, some form of communication is essential. Some facility in a second or third language also provides, as we have noted, a degree of insight into other cultural worlds, even though these insights are sometimes resisted. Whether the individual likes it or not, is aware of it or not, the social and cultural perspectives he acquires by means of the "other" language are broadening, enriching and sometimes illuminating, with regard to the other culture.

While these boons may accrue to some extent under any kind of status relationship between the respective linguistic groups, they are most likely to occur where and when the social relations and the respective culture levels are those of relative equality.

b / The sociocultural and psychic strains of the plural lingual individual. The actual language situation, however, is usually *not* merely one of essential cross-group communication or of profitable exchange of culture, but also, in many instances, one in which several of the social and cultural conditions discussed in the preceding section prevail. This means that the representatives of the respective language groups, though they are in most cases functionally interdependent, interact as social unequals. These conditions create a variety of strains for the participants, especially the members of the less advantaged groups.

The bicultural situation in which he finds himself. The plural lingual is a person who usually participates—though differentially—in two cultural systems and two sets of social ways. This situation poses for him two closely related problems. The first is the fact that participation in a bicultural situation rarely carries with it equal or reciprocal cultural proficiency. However, in order that communication may be a real exchange of approximately equally understood meanings, the persons who speak the "other" language should have considerable proficiency in the related "other" culture. This proficiency implies insight into the inner and subtle features, a "feeling" for it, an understanding of its religious and familial and other deeply ingrained institutional values, traditions and beliefs, as well as linguistic proficiency in vocabulary, grammar, pronunciation and idiom, so as to express the culture. Usually, neither side has these proficiencies in full measure. Thus, to use a phrase resorted to earlier, the speakers of the different languages, like schizophrenics, may frequently be talking past each other to some extent rather than to each other.

When this bilingual–bicultural situation ceases to exist, it is because the members of one or the other group of speakers have been exterminated, deported or assimilated.

Closely related to this problem of differential cultural proficiency is the fact that there are usually expressions of a certain sort which the bilingual or plural lingual can accurately and satisfactorily state in his ancestral language, but which he cannot adequately translate into the other language. This inability to translate freely from one language to another is particularly serious for the minority group member during the earlier stages of assimilation. It impairs his communicative ability in general, and particularly his relations with the majority members. He is embarrassed by his inadequacies of understanding and expression, and has a sense of incompetence and inferiority arising out of his realization that he is only a "part man" in the main language.

The *second problem* is based on the fact that the *speaker of two languages lives with two different sets of cultural perspectives*. Each language—both "mother" or "home" tongue, and "other"—is part and symbol of a given culture. And, as Bossard points out, the language reflects the essence of its culture in such a way that another language cannot serve as a substitute.[18] When the bilingual shifts from one language to the other, he can often actually feel the change. In this connection, Church mentions the interesting fact that the truly bilingual person, who is accomplished in both languages, may undergo a transformation in personality, taking on the national characteristics that go with his second language.[19] He reports the case of an adult and presumably educated bilingual, who used French, his paternal language, for logical and technical discussions, and German for emotive expressions and literary discussions, switching from language to language as the topic of conversation changed.[20]

The fact can also be stated that the individual who has *Sprachgefühl* in two languages is capable of living and thinking in the spirit and style of each related culture.

The problem for the individual grows out of the fact that he has to do more than merely express himself in one language or the other. He lives in two, not always compatible, cultural worlds. This requires that he try to integrate within himself a dual cultural situation—a task which the monolingual never even quite envisages.[21] As the bilingual switches his speech from one to the other language, he also, in order to be fully effective in his communication, supposedly switches from one cultural content, style and spirit to the other. This requires large knowledge of the second culture, a cultural dexterity, that few have. As an example of the task involved, one need only mention the English-speaking American trying to switch to the culture world of the native speakers of Swahili or Hopi, or of an Eskimo dialect.

The bilingual thus must always be socioculturally and psychologically oriented in two different worlds. They are seldom a "merged" system for him. He has a "divided linguistic allegiance" and he lives a divided perceptive and cultural life; in certain respects, he is therefore a "divided man." Thus, just as the bilingual community may to some extent suffer a "schism of the body politic," so the bilingual person may suffer a "schism in the soul."[22]

Loyalty to the ancestral language. Another situation of strain for the bilingual, or plural lingual, in some instances, is the fact that he has a deep loyalty to the language he learned first, the ancestral language or mother tongue. This loyalty tends to persist in some degree among many plural linguals, in spite of all manner of new allegiances and conformities, and causes him to resist any interference in this regard. First, he has a strong functional attachment to the mother tongue: it is his first acquired language; he has a mastery of it, and an ease in its use that he is only rarely likely to equal later on for any other tongue; he feels comfortable with it; he can express his inmost thoughts and feelings with it. It also stands for and has been a medium for expressing many personal and private experiences. Second, he has a cultural loyalty to it: it is associated for him with group traditions, customs, experiences, ceremonies, values, mores, beliefs and institutional ways.

The recent immigrant—a minority group member—who is only beginning to be assimilated, has a strong loyalty to the ancestral language, even though he is also strongly motivated to become part of the new society and culture. His very frustrations in the new milieu may cause him to adhere to the mother tongue as something that he is certain of. The transitional generations in assimilation usually have a diminishing overt loyalty to the language of their ancestors, although they often retain it covertly. The accomplished, "true" or "complete" bilingual, skilled in the other language, "at home" in the other culture, in effect the "equal" of the speakers of the other language, nevertheless still tends to retain his loyalty to the tongue learned at his mother's knee.

The plural lingual as minority group member. Attention was called to the aspects of the social and cultural superiority–inferiority situation in the plural lingual community. The speakers of the respective languages are acutely affected, especially those who speak the language of minority or otherwise socially and culturally "inferior" groups.

This situation of strain is demonstrated by different sorts of protective devices resorted to by the socially "inferior" plural linguals. The devices seem to be evidence of the fact that the mother-tongue speaker of the minority language often seems to feel a psychological as well as social subordination.

(1) There is, in some cases, the avoidance of all but the most imperative formal relations with majority group members. (2) Minority group speakers are frequently shy about speaking their ancestral tongue in the presence of members of the majority. (3) When they speak the majority language, they seek to do so as meticulously as possible: they use correct "other" language words and grammar, try to overcome their accent, make their voice sound like that of the "others," guard against inferior-language borrowing. Slips may give away their minority origin. (4) When they

speak to majority members in the majority language, they do so in a quiet, restrained manner, thus behaving inconspicuously and avoiding ridicule or slight. (5) Those moving up the social ladder may especially try to abandon their ancestral speech in favor of the majority language: in the presence of "superiors," they may even deny that they speak the "inferior" language; they may try to select their friends from among the majority; they may withdraw from kinship and other "native groups."[23]

In summary: many a plural lingual is a sort of "split personality." (1) He has to live in two different cultures; (2) he has to switch from one culture to the other as he switches from language to language; (3) he may also have to live on two different status levels—as an equal with his linguistic counterparts, and as an inferior among the speakers of the majority or dominant language.

The problems of the plural lingual child. These and other strains to which the plural lingual is subjected are sharply focused in the plural lingual child. There is, first, the fact of the double linguistic task. The acquisition of two languages and of facility in their use, in an environment where two languages are necessary, often imposes a considerable task upon the child.

The ease or arduousness of the task, however, depends upon the particular combination of variables existing in the situation in which the child learns his several languages. Where the plural linguality is a rather normal matter, where there is reciprocal tolerance between the ethnic elements and social relations are amicable, where there is no marked discrimination on cultural grounds and the two or more languages are more or less equally used in the activities of the community—then the task of learning two or more languages is not so difficult, and usually not so likely to produce serious strains. Under such circumstances, while the children may receive formal instruction in the community's language in the schools, they also have the advantage, under the conditions of ready interaction, of the highly efficient "aural-oral" acquisition—the instructional form which is now widely recommended as the most effective way of learning a foreign language, whether as a child or as an adult. There are today areas in Europe—such as certain sections of Poland, Switzerland, Germany, France and Italy—where children grow up with a mastery of two or three languages, apparently learning them with ease and without great social or psychic strain.

However, if the plural lingual child does *not* live under such a favorable combination of circumstances—and, in the majority of situations, they are *not* favorable in most bilingual communities—then the child is under a double strain.

(1) The child has a double adjustment task, since he operates in two different and sometimes incongruous social, as well as linguistic, frameworks. First, he must switch back and forth from one language to the other, and the social circumstances are such that, in order to avoid censure, he must be able to express himself adequately and acceptably in each. Second, he functions socially in two very different worlds: he must know the language of the home and intimate kinship circle, as well as the nationality group, but he must also know the language of the outside world—the school, the street, the playground and the gang. As he becomes more and more involved in extended relations in wider and wider circles, his personality is increasingly shifted from the setting of the ancestral ethnic group system to that of the majority society. The incongruity of the ancestral language in the wider context grows on him.

(2) The child has to adjust himself to the majority–minority, social superiority–inferiority situation in the community, in so far as this affects his two languages. The two languages, he soon discovers, differ in social acceptability. The inferiority of his home language becomes especially poignant to an adolescent. But as soon as he becomes conscious of the differential assessments of language and related culture and prestige, he avoids speaking his mother tongue among members of the "superior" categories; he develops acute consciousness of his "foreign" accent when he is speaking the majority language, and he seeks to correct it. To avoid linguistic *faux pas,* and to give other evidences of facility in the use of the socially acceptable language, are necessary not only in order to maintain the child's social position among his fellows, but also to assure and protect his confidence in himself. Perhaps equally weighty is the fact that this protects him against that social ridicule which children can visit so viciously upon the variant, linguistic or otherwise.

4. *The International Plural Lingualism of the Year 2000*

a / The communication need. As we face the world of the year 2000 —assuming that it escapes extinction by nuclear explosion—certain assumptions seem to be quite justifiable in the light of present trends. With our progressively speedier forms of transportation, the space–place–time factor will have been reduced to a tiny fraction of what it now is. There will be six billion or more people in this physically limited area, instead of the present three billion. These people, as individuals and as participants in all kinds of groups and organizations, will have

multiplied contacts and interactions with each other. There will
ɛr more numerous, complex and crucial interdependencies, and
ɪe possibility of greater and more frequent antagonisms. In such a
..ɯ, communication will have increased in geometric ratio as compared with the present. The whole world will have become a community
of many diverse peoples, cultures and nations, in which adequate, accurate, mutually intelligible discourse will be not only desirable but
absolutely essential.

The problem we are now concerned with has to do with communication between the representatives of communities, regions, nations, ethnic
groups, peoples and cultures of *the world;* in brief, language facility for
intra-world communication. More specifically, facility in several languages will be necessary for political understanding and political relations (including intergovernmental, diplomatic and world government
relations), for business, industry and international trade, for science and
technology, for the application of medical knowledge and skills, the
development and uses of drugs and medical appliances, and the planning
and administration of world health, for exchange of demographic information and population control, for the production, understanding and
exchange of philosophy, art and literature, for scholarship and teaching,
for labor relations and workers' relations, for ideological persuasion, for
international economic and technical assistance, for pleasure, travel and
tourism, for intercontinental transportation and world-wide mass communication. By no means least is the importance, for a whole complex of
military reasons, of knowledge of the languages of potential enemies. At
the same time, accuracy and adequacy of understanding, and hence of
communication, while not a guarantee of world peace, is a prerequisite
for it. World peace may involve a "fail-safe" line in people-to-people
communication, beyond which it *must* go, as well as one involving international military operations beyond which action *dare not go.*

b / The place of plural lingualism. How conduct this inter-people,
international cultural exchange? For centuries, linguists have discussed
and constructed artificial languages—Volapük, Esperanto, Interlingua,
and others of lesser renown—which they hoped might have universal
use. But none of these has "caught on," partly because they are purely
instrumental, and possess little or no historical–cultural symbolic significance. It is the candid opinion of most students of the situation that
it is utopian to hope that such a language would have a wide enough
adoption the world over to serve as a world language.

There seems to be no great likelihood, for a number of political, ethnic and other reasons, that any of the major "empire" languages of the world will come to be used exclusively, or to the considerable exclusion of the other "empire" languages. Nor does it seem probable, at the present time, that any world power will be able to force its language upon the peoples of the world, whether friends or foes, as a sole means of communication. There seems to be no tendency for "native" languages to die out, or for nationalities and nations to give up the languages that identify them. If anything, as was noted in Chapter VIII, with the increased emphasis on nationalism, there have come organized movements, not only to preserve mother tongues, but even to revive some that had tended to atrophy as practical languages (for example, Gaelic and Hebrew). Many languages in current use will continue to be used.

What seems to be likely is that some of the present great internationally used languages—perhaps not more than five or six of those discussed in Chapter VIII—will come increasingly to provide adequate means of communication for the greater part of the essential and desirable inter-people and international dealings. These will not replace or be a substitute for the ethnic, regional or national languages of individuals and groups, but will be their auxiliary or second or third language. Instead of world unilinguality, there will be plural linguality, involving mainly, as one or more "other" languages, these "great" languages.

This plural lingualism of the near future will not only be confined to diplomats, foreign traders, foreign aiders, the missionaries for ideologies, the international aristocracy and the like. It will be essential for the great bulk of the "common men," for all persons—if they are not to be culturally isolated, illiterate, unconscious of what is going on in the modern world, and incapable or ineffective in all activity, individual or group, that involves inter-people or international relations. All who expect to be understanding, informed and participant citizens of the kind of world we live in will need this ability. Many of the tribal and underdeveloped people will find it necessary to know and use a more generally used language. The self-interest of individuals the world over, as well as their reciprocal needs and the advantages to be derived by them as members of groups and organizations, will dictate this wider linguistic facility.

Many Americans, with their chauvinism and international myopia (combined with what has been termed their "linguistic illiteracy" and "linguistic idiocy"), seem to be unconscious of the fact that international plural linguality is already not only desirable, but actually existent among many people in strategic areas of the world—business people, politically involved persons, scientists and technologists, the cultured classes of, for example, central Europe, Latin America, Japan, India, Southeast Asia and parts of Africa.

c / Sociological orientation regarding international plural lingualism.
Some features of international plural lingualism are similar in operation
to those of intra-community plural lingualism. There is still some uncertainty regarding the effect of others. In general, however, it can be assumed that international plural lingualism presents some dimensions that
are quite different from those of the intra-community variety.

The gains. There is the extension, by means of plural linguality, of the
cultural insights and proficiencies of the individual, as each additional
language that is acquired opens new "windows" upon new worlds. For
individuals and groups, there are various practical utilities already mentioned above, as well as the fact that the "other" languages make it
possible to be sharers of the economic, political, scientific, technological,
philosophical contributions and characteristics of the "other" people.

One of its signal social advantages, which also exists in intra-community lingual situations, is its social and cultural welding effect. Plural
lingual proficients bind together the respective groups of speakers and
their cultures.[24] Says Haugen:

> They form a link, a bridge, perhaps we should say a channel of com-
> munication between groups. Groups which would otherwise cen-
> trifugally part company and rotate around axes of their own are kept
> in contact by bilinguals who span the linguistic borders. Such links
> are increasingly important in a larger world of discourse.[25]

Closely related is its effect in maintaining the adjustment of peoples to
each other. Diverse elements are enabled to "get along" with others.
Knowing Russian enables many diverse peoples within the Soviet Union
to get along with each other; it also helps peoples outside to "carry
on" with the Russians. Similar integrative benefits accrue to peoples
through the use of English, Spanish, Arabic and the other "Empire"
languages.

Likely problem situations. Several problem situations present themselves.

There will undoubtedly be a continuance of the myopic notion that
the sole reason for the use of the tribal or national language is as
an evidence of unity, uniformity, solidarity and effective and complete
acculturation within a country, and that plural linguality will (or does)
impair that solidarity, induce cultural dilution and possibly constitute
a degree of cultural apostasy. Both have been a factor in particular historical situations in the past. There is no reason, however, for believing
that the latter situation is likely to prevail generally; enjoyment of two
cultures does not necessarily mean that one is a traitor to one of them.

In the past, in some plural lingual situations, the languages used were directly related to conditions of inequality as between nations—to social dominance–submission and cultural superiority–inferiority. This has produced mixed behavior. Some have eagerly embraced the language of the powerful and "superior" peoples and countries. The socially ambitious and upwardly mobile, as noted above, have looked upon it as the indispensable means of advancement. Some have regarded the "higher" language as a patent of "higher" culture. Others again—those proud of their culture, despite their present comparatively depressed social or cultural position—have resisted the "higher" language. In the present world, many of the people of the until recently "colonial" areas of Asia and Africa will *need* to use one or the other of the "Empire" languages, usually languages that have been associated with colonial extension and involved in their erstwhile economic and political exploitation, or at least in the dominance exercised over them. Some of these newly-developing, but formerly colonially subjected, peoples may have a sharp antagonism to these languages, in spite of their contemporary usefulness.

Another complicating condition, unfortunately still present, is the chauvinistic attitude of some groups among those people who regard themselves as superior, and hold themselves aloof linguistically as superior. In our case, this has been aptly referred to as a "combination of the Fortress America Spirit and of the English Supremacy," and is reflected in such clichés as "Who needs any of those funny languages anyway? All intelligent people speak English," or the belief that in this-or-the-other country, "Everybody speaks English; so don't bother to learn the language!" The result of this is a wall of separation between Americans and vital sections of other nations.[26]

As in the case of intra-community plural lingualism, the problems relating to unequal facility in the use of the respective languages also exist here. Under any conditions, if the communicator is of inferior ability in the use of the "other" language, there is a greater likelihood of inadequate, incorrect or confusing expression in the other language, and accompanying inexactness of meaning. This always produces some sort of "cross-up." In some types and levels of inter-people communication, this could have tragic consequences.

Basic operational considerations. In spite of the difficulties that inhere in inter-people or international plural lingualism, the vast gains accruing from it, and especially the fact that it is increasingly imperative for many of the individuals and functional groups all over the world, points to certain fundamental implemental and operational considerations.

Basic, especially for Americans, is the proper psychological orientation. The plural-linguals-to-be need to develop a conviction, a positive attitude, toward knowing one or more of the other worldwide or world-important languages or, for some purposes, some of the lesser languages. This is quite possible, *if* people see that it is to their private self-interest —to their social, economic, political and cultural advantage.

A second important consideration is the fact that individuals and persons as members of groups will have to exercise some selectivity in the choice of second and third languages. In the *intra*-community situation, the residents have no choice; the "other" language is that of the other ethnic element, interrelation with whom is unavoidable. While there is this element of inescapability in some international situations, in most it does not prevail, and persons will have to choose. Obviously they will not be able to learn all of the (to them) important languages, nor will they all learn or use the same combination of languages for their trans-national or trans-cultural discourse. Which will be learned and employed will depend upon the special substantive, areal and functional needs, concerns and interests of the particular individuals, categories and groups, and also (and especially) upon the specific social and cultural utilities which the different major languages will provide in pursuit of particular purposes.

Finally, this plural lingualism imposes specific educational obligations upon the peoples and nations. These auxiliary languages, in the great majority of instances, will have to be systematically taught. While the "other" language is often taught at various stages of the educational ladder, in intra-community situations, some contact is unavoidably made with the other language, regardless of the age of the person, and some acquisition spontaneously occurs. In the situation involving an international language, the bulk of its speakers—its "native" speakers— usually reside in a different culture area, even on a different continent. Moreover, the possible or anticipated contacts with the "other" speakers or areas may take place at some time in the future. Yet these contingencies should be prepared for. In fact, in preparing for the future in the present kind of world, adequate instruction in foreign languages is as important as instruction for adjustment to and survival in a world that has been recast by nuclear and space science and technology.

The importance of a knowledge of foreign languages was clearly revealed during World War II, when the military services, with the assistance of professional teachers, inaugurated language training programs for some of their strategic personnel. Perhaps there has been some realization of the fact that *all* personnel is now strategic. At any rate, since the War, foreign languages have staged a comeback in the United States. Their instruction has been promoted by numerous linguistic and educational committees, commissions and associations, and much attention is being given to instructional policies, principles and procedures. We need to salute and encourage this new interest, greatly extend the number of students to be included, and increase the length, depth and richness of the instruction. Nonetheless, attention by Americans generally to the importance of foreign languages and to their instruction is still pathetically limited, and the typical attitude remains shortsighted and parochial, as was noted in Chapter X, Sect. 6.

Several aspects of language teaching, of sociological and social-psychological relevance, will be indicated.

In the first place, the great bulk of the population has little or no awareness of or concern about the necessity of proficiency in foreign languages. A sense of urgency needs to be developed, and favoring attitudes and motivation toward such learning need to be built up. The well-known fact needs to be stressed that we Americans have lagged in our knowledge of foreign languages, and that a considerable number of the countries of the world with whom we are associated have for some time placed far greater stress in their educational systems than we have upon the systematic development of proficiency in other leading languages. They have viewed this instruction not as a more or less esoteric exercise at the secondary school or college level for the relatively few, but as a stern necessity, for cultural and utilitarian purposes, for as many as possible.

Second, the instruction should be given in the most effective manner that we know. Traditionally, our formal teaching of foreign languages has been a part—and often a very secondary part—of high school and college education. Now it is rather widely accepted by experts that this instruction should be given at all levels, but should start with young children, five-year-olds and earlier. It is now recognized that normal youngsters can easily learn several languages. Children have a plasticity and a readiness for the learning of additional languages that almost amounts to acquisition by osmosis. According to the "New American Method," at present highly regarded, and jocularly referred to as the "aural-oral" method, the child's early instruction should consist of hearing and speaking the words and phrases and sentences. Thus he spontaneously develops a familiarity and facility with the language. He automatically acquires the "feel" of it, instantly recognizing a word or phrase and its meaning, without the process of translation. The traditional memorization and analysis of grammatical construction, in so far as it is needed, comes at later stages of instruction.

Third, it is obvious that the instructors should know the structure and history of the language, and be able to speak it fluently and correctly and to use the most widely accepted pronunciation. It should be noted that the United States still has a "reservoir" of persons who have a "native" facility in other languages—for example, German, French, Spanish, Chinese, Japanese, the Scandinavian languages, even Russian—to utilize in giving this instruction.

Fourth, during the course of the instruction, the student should achieve a substantial understanding of the history, culture and typical folk attitudes and sentiments of the main body of speakers of the language. Among us, a great deal of the instruction at the higher levels beyond the "mechanics" of the language has been devoted to developing familiarity with certain select literary "classics" written in the language. Any "educated" person should have some knowledge of these, and most persons are capable of profiting from them; what is more, some of the classics may epitomize certain features of the culture and the people. But they do not present many of its characteristic and often crucially important features. The proficient user of another language, as he interacts with the "native" speakers, also needs awareness of the history of the people, their peculiar and precious traditions, their pleasant and bitter memories, their customs and beliefs, their typical reactions in different socially important situations, something of their major social institutions, their cultural style and forms, their interpretations of life and the universe (*Weltanschauung*), and so on. If he does not have this, he will miss much of the utility and fun of the use of the language, and may as a result fail to communicate clearly and without social mishap.

N O T E S

1 Leonard Bloomfield, *Language* (New York: Henry Holt & Co., 1933), p. 56.
2 Einar Haugen, *The Norwegian Language in America: A Study of Bilingual Behavior* (Philadelphia: University of Pennsylvania Press, 1953), I, 6.
3 John B. Carroll, *The Study of Language* (Cambridge: Harvard University Press, 1953), p. 99.
4 *Op. cit.*, p. 56.
5 Charles F. Hockett, *A Course in Modern Linguistics* (New York: Macmillan Co., 1958), p. 8.
6 See, for example, the factors in the contacts with other cultures, peoples and languages, as they imply the use of additional languages by persons and groups, in Chap. VII, Sect. 3; the effects of the spread of linguistic "em-

pires" on the need for plural lingualism, in Chap. VIII, Sect. 4; the relation of the multiplicity of languages and dialects—regional, national, continental and global—to plural lingualism, in Chap. VIII, Sect. 5; pidgins and creolized languages as "second" languages, in Chap. VIII, Sect. 5; speech differentiation of ethnic groups within a plural society, and the unavoidability of plural lingualism, in Chap. XIII, Sect. 3; the implications of plural lingualism in some stratification systems, Chap. XIV, Sects. 2, 3, and 4.

7 Federal Census on Mother Tongue for 1940.

8 The position of the Census Bureau has also changed. In 1940, the question involving bilingualism asked for the language spoken in earliest childhood. In the 1960 Census, mother tongue was defined as the principal language spoken in the person's home before he came to the United States.

9 Most Latin-American countries have somewhat similar ethnic–linguistic conditions.

10 For data on the language splintering of contemporary peoples, see Chap. VIII, Sect. 4.

11 James H. S. Bossard, "The Bilingual as a Person—Linguistic Identification with Status," *American Sociological Review,* 10 (Dec., 1945), 699–709. (Italics added.)

12 Ralph Pieris, "Bilinguality and Cultural Marginality," *British Journal of Sociology,* 2 (Dec., 1951), 328–339.

13 George C. Barker, "Social Functions of Language in a Mexican–American Community," *Acta Americana,* 5 (July–Sept., 1947), 185–202.

14 Pieris, *op. cit.,* pp. 329–330.

15 Barker, *op. cit.* (See also his "Growing Up in a Bilingual Community," *The Kiva,* 17 (Nov.–Dec., 1951), 17–32.)

16 With respect to the Tucson Mexican community, Barker says: "For individuals in the Mexican community, these fields [the four fields of social relations just mentioned] may be represented as a kind of continuum, at one end of which are the intimate relations with others of Mexican descent, while at the other end are the purely formal relations with 'Anglos.' In between are formal and informal relations with people of Mexican descent *outside* the family, and in some cases with Mexicans from Mexico." He points out that this continuum in social relations is paralleled by a continuum in language usage. At one end of this linguistic continuum, Spanish is dominant in the speaker's contacts; at the other end, English is dominant. In between are the Spanish dialects and the various mixtures of the two languages. ("Social Functions of Language in a Mexican Community," p. 197.)

17 Einar Haugen, *The Norwegian Language in America: A Study of Bilingual Behavior* (Philadelphia: University of Pennsylvania Press, 1953), I, 74–97.

18 *Op. cit.,* p. 700.

19 Joseph Church, *Language and the Discovery of Reality: A Developmental Psychology of Cognition* (New York: Random House, 1961), p. 28.

20 *Ibid.,* p. 92.

21 Haugen, p. 3. See Haugen's discussion of "The Bilingual's Dilemma," pp. 1–12.

22 Pieris, *op. cit.,* p. 336.

23 On protective devices, see Barker, pp. 196–200; Bossard, pp. 703–704.

24 It is of course conceivable, and sometimes a fact, that under some conditions the very opposite occurs.

25 *Op. cit.,* p. 7. Haugen mentions Latin in the Middle Ages as a case in point. As one of a bilingual combination, it "became the expression of supralocal unity," and the link in tying groups together that would otherwise have been mutually isolated. (*Ibid.*)

26 From Fred M. Hechinger, "Foreign Languages Stage a Comeback," *Saturday Review,* 46 (Feb. 26, 1963), 64–66, 89–91 (64, 90).

XVII ❦ The Sociology of Writing

There has been frequent reference to writing throughout this study. This is inevitable since a system of writing, among all peoples who have it, is a vitally important, inseparable phase of their linguistic system. At the same time the basic differences between spoken and written language and, correspondingly, the special or significantly variant sociocultural functions performed by, or capable of being performed by and with writing merit some special consideration. What follows is a brief but systematic treatment of its peculiar symbolic and communicative characteristics, its late emergence in cultural and societal history, the apparent circumstances of its appearance, and certain sociologically pertinent features, utilities and effects. Almost every sociologically significant aspect of language in general has certain distinctive functions in its written form.

1. *The Place of Writing in Language*

While language and writing are clearly related, they are not identical. Writing is a late and special development within language. Language, in essence, is an invented and arbitrary system of controls, whereby human vocal sounds (speech) are definitely patterned and given specific meanings. Writing is a supplemental and artificed set of techniques. It consists of a standardized system of visible marks or objects, designed to serve as graphic representations of speech; the meanings of the marks, in turn, are also agreed upon by the people using them. All other formalized symbol systems among human beings have their foundations in the original, basic spoken language; they are thus *secondary* symbolic systems. Writing is the most widespread, the most extensively elaborated and the most socially important of these secondary systems.[1] By means of it, the reader of the marks obtains visual impressions through which he interprets the author's verbalized meanings. In the end, writing is simply a sufficient set of symbols to depict the range of utterances, with the signs carrying meanings arbitrarily established by culture, by usage. In effect, it is itself a surrogate or a symbol of speech, or as Pei puts it, "A system of writing is *a symbol of a symbol.*"[2]

2. *What Writing Does*

The "invention" of writing, while not as epochal an event as the invention of speech, was far more important than may be suspected. Writing gave to language a scope and many utilities that speech does not have. The first basic fact in connection with the development of writing is that speech, as a means of communication, requires a primary or face-to-face and temporally synchronized relationship between the sender and the receiver of the messages. Speech thus presents distinct inadequacies as a form of communication between persons in secondary or non-face-to-face relationships, or in situations in which the sending and the receiving of the message take place over an interval of time. The second basic fact is that, unassisted, the human memory cannot be depended upon for full and exact recall, and that messages transmitted by human intermediaries, by word of mouth and from person to person, inadvertently suffer some distortion of fact, meaning and intent. What are the signal supplemental functions that writing adds to language?

Writing makes possible communication across wide physical space; that is, it makes possible communication in secondary relationships. The range of the unaided human voice is very limited spatially. With the development of writing, people in communication with one another were no longer limited only to those within "earshot" and "eyeshot"—that is, those within the range of direct hearing or the simple relay of sound signals (for example, drum beats)—and those within the range of gestures or other directly seen signs. With writing, which is capable of transmission in many forms, people are enabled to send and receive messages across vast spaces, to and from other people whom they have never met in person, and perhaps will never meet. The messages can be carried intact and uncorrupted. If the senders and receivers, whether individuals, groups, or organizations, have mutually comprehensible systems of writing, and effective physical means of transporting or transmitting the writing or its derived or substitute forms, there are no spatial limitations upon their exchange of messages with each other.

With writing, messages can be carried through time. The communicators need not be in immediately synchronous relationship. The messages can be transmitted far beyond the moment of conception by the producer, and even beyond the life span of individuals and groups; they can be transmitted from generation to generation, and from one social and cultural era to another.

A related aspect of considerable significance is the fact that a person can transmit messages to himself for later use or consideration. Thus the sender of a written message can at some later time become the receiver of that same message.

By means of writing, all kinds of information intended to be made available to others, across space and time, can be more accurately stated than if it were orally relayed by human intermediaries. Oral communication is more or less imperfect. The spoken word is spontaneous in its very essence; as noted above, it is subject to distortion, even when efforts are made to retain the exactness of the message. Oral transmission depends upon human recall, which is faulty in most persons. Spoken utterance involves certain problems of reception and interpretation in the speaker–listener situation: hearing, attention, precision in verbal repetition, pronunciation and so on. The repetitions are subject to many variations, either unintentional, through forgetfulness or misunderstanding, or wilful, through the desire to misrepresent or to improve. Hence, there are marked difficulties with regard to the exact and precise reproduction of the form and intent of the message.

Writing, on the other hand, in both form and content, implies care and attention. To a considerable degree, it overcomes the deficiencies of the spoken word. The written message read by the receiver ten thousand miles away or two millennia later can be the very same document produced by the conceiver, or it can be reproduced exactly, word for word, phrase by phrase. The written statement has tangibility, uniformity and definiteness; it avoids "personalization" of the message by the oral-aural intermediaries, and is not hearsay or surmise.

Writing is also a more deliberate mode of expression. It can be erased, replaced or amended. It can even be destroyed entirely, without incriminating the writer. An incidental related gain in this connection is the fact that people often find that their thoughts are clarified and systematized, and that necessary qualifications and extensions appear, when they subject them to the more rigorous tests of exactness and completeness demanded by the written form.

Closely related to accuracy as a feature is the fact that writing gives a degree of durability, even permanence, to the message. The spoken word is ephemeral; it "dies a-borning." Its effect must be immediate, or there is no effect. One of the outstanding functions of speech (as pointed out in Chapter III), is to serve as an aid to social memory. In fact, without speech, there is no way of identifying and describing events—real and imagined, natural, sociocultural and supernatural, and no way of perpetuating this information for future use. But if this lore is handed down verbally from generation to generation, there is the likelihood that it will be incomplete, and also the possibility of its being distorted (not necessarily deliberately) as time goes on. Graphic representations, on the other hand, are physically "crystallized" words. They are engraved on stone or clay tablets, inscribed on parchment and paper, bound in scrolls and books, stored in various kinds of safe depositories. As such, they are records that may last unchanged for thousands of years. They provide a "storage" function. Without speech, no history; without writing, no permanent records.

Writing also assists in overcoming the limitations of the human mind, especially the limits upon the quantity and variety of materials that human beings can remember. In brief, the written message or report, or the accounting of things and events, can be much greater in volume and detail than one transmitted by oral means. It is the difference between the twenty-four or more volumes of the *Encyclopedia Britannica* and "what one small head can hold." In general, writing serves as a sort of external memory, supplementing what people can remember in quantity, variety and detail, and through time.

Finally, the visible, durable conventionalized marks which constitute writing, and the fact of its wider comprehensibility (for example, as compared with spoken dialects), give the message an objective, public character that it does not have until it is converted into writing. Writing, once executed, can be permanent and conspicuous. It stands by itself, by contrast with the fleeting and intangible spoken word.

Most of the functions performed by writing are highly advantageous to mankind, in accordance with the almost universally accepted values regarding human and social well-being. By its very nature, however, it suffers from several disabilities. It lacks certain expressional facilities usually found in speech. Writing is, in some respects, relatively clumsy, lengthy and slow. The written message lacks those nonverbal props which add so much flexibility and force to speech—such as gestures and facial expression, variation in the pace and rhythm of the utterance of the words and phrases, manipulation of pitch, tone and articulation. There are a dozen ways of saying "Yes"; it may take a lengthy paragraph to convey the spine-chilling effect of one piercing scream. If speech is transcribed literally into writing, much of its informational and expressional effect is lost. Possible double meanings and nuances of meaning, which in conversation can be taken care of by gesture, facial expression or intonation, are with difficulty translated into written words, phrases, clauses and sentences. Writing tries, in part, to compensate for these weaknesses by a complicated paraphernalia of punctuation, capitalization, italics, blanks and other special printing devices.

3. *The Recency of Writing and the Restrictedness of Literacy*

In spite of the advantages of writing, as seen from our point of view as members of a complex and literate industrial society, it is a very recent invention of mankind. Man has had fully developed speech for hundreds of thousands, perhaps for a million, years. But all languages have been spoken, through nearly all of their history, by people who could not read or write. True writing began in China, Mesopotamia and other portions of the Near East, and Egypt, between 8000 B.C. and 4000 B.C. It has been applied only in very recent times to most of the languages that are spoken today. Most of the 3000 or so of the languages of the world still have no writing; many linguists believe that those that do have writing constitute as little as five percent of the total.[3]

As late as a century ago, millions of people in the civilized countries could not read or write. In fact, through most of the history of writing itself, among the peoples that have had it, facility in it and the regular use of it has been a prerogative of only certain special and privileged population segments, such as some professionals (including priests, scribes, scholars and scientists), government officials and some members of the upper classes. This situation prevailed in Western Europe until as recently as a century and a half ago. Today, the proportion of people who can read and write in China, India, the Arabic areas, Southeast Asia, Africa, and Central and South America is relatively small, though strenuous efforts to overcome illiteracy are being made in most of these areas. Around the middle of the present century, according to the comprehensive UNESCO report on world literacy, the phenomenon of illiteracy has not been confined to any particular part of the world or group of countries; it exists everywhere, although in greatly varying degree.[4] As to the over-all world situation, the study reports:

> It is estimated that there are about 700 million adult illiterates (out of 1,587,000,000 "adults," reckoned as persons 15 years of age or over), in the world today. They represent about 44 per cent of the total world population 15 years old and over. Almost half of all the countries and territories (97 out of 198) are believed to have 50 per cent or more illiteracy among their adult population. In about one-third of all countries, there are at least a million adult illiterates in each country. Such, in broad terms, is the magnitude of the problem of the world literacy in the middle of the twentieth century.[5]

The "ability both to read and to write a simple message in any language"[6] varies greatly among the different regions and peoples of the world. Sample regions, with the percentage of illiterates among the population 15 years and over (as of the early and middle 1950's), follow: Africa, 80–85 per cent; North America, 3–4 per cent; South America, 42–44 per cent; Southwest Asia, 75–80 per cent; Southeast Asia, 65–70 per cent; East Asia, 45–50 per cent; Northern and Western Europe, 1–2 per cent; Southern Europe, 20–21 per cent; the U.S.S.R., 5–10 per cent.[7]

When the United States became a nation, barely 20 per cent of the people knew how to read and write; as late as 1840, when literacy was first recorded in the Census, only 40 per cent of the population of the United States was literate.[8] In recent decades American literacy–illiteracy has been mainly defined in terms of schooling. As of about 1950, it was estimated that we had somewhat above 10 million "sheer or near illiterates" in the adult population—that is, people without the equivalent of a fourth grade education, who either could not read, or were unable to understand what they read, well enough for the purposes of good citizenship. Of these about 4,200,000 were foreign-born, and 2,700,000 were Negroes. The most recent data, based entirely on school enrollment,[9] states that the number of persons 14 years and over with less than 5 years of school completed was 8,179,000, or some 6.3 per cent of a population of 14 years old and over that amounted to 129,295,000 persons. The report mentions that such persons are sometimes referred to as "functional illiterates." Of the non-white population some 2,310,000, or almost 17 per cent of a total of 13,528,000, had less than 5 years of schooling.

4. *The Main Historical Forms of Writing*

The study of the actual forms which writing systems have taken historically is primarily a concern of linguists. The anthropologists and sociologists, however, are also interested in them as groping inventive efforts to contrive adequate communicative instruments under given sociocultural circumstances, as products of particular eras and peoples, as instrumental systems of various degrees of functional efficiency, and also as examples (especially in the case of the most universal system) of progressive improvement as, during the course of its diffusion, successive peoples took it over and adapted it to their own peculiar needs.

a / Subwriting. From earliest times, even in the most localized primitive groups, men had to do some communicating with others who were beyond the range of hearing or of seeing any signs they might make, as well as the necessity of transmitting information to others later in time. In brief, they needed some means of transcending the space–time limitations of immediate face-to-face spoken and gestural language.

True writing, as observed above, consists of standardized graphic devices carrying conventional meanings. Some indicators or reminders of a non-graphic nature, at a level below that of writing, have been used and are still being used, under certain circumstances. These consist of object symbols of one kind or another, which may be referred to as pre-writing, or embryo writing. Certain marks on a tool have indicated whose property it was; stones or other natural objects have indicated land boundaries. In addition to such property marks, men have used mnemonic signs—signs which, though not able to express thought itself, did serve to represent thought, and were capable of functioning as guides and "reminders," as memory aids. The branch placed in a certain way on the ground proved useful as a direction or road mark; the knotted rope (for example, the Peruvian *quippos,* or looped cord), the vari-colored cords, the notched stick, the West African native's use of corn, feathers, stones, sticks, cowries in various combinations, the American Indian's wampum, the fire-and-smoke signal, wigwagging, the string around the finger—all conveyed orders or information which the initiated could interpret.

These property marks and mnemonic signs were probably the starting points of writing. But they had limited utility because they permitted only a limited combination of signs for representing relations between ideas, and they could not be developed into a system of writing, on account of the materials of which they were made, which did not permit practical improvement.[10] Nevertheless, they were representational objects which conveyed messages.

The most perfect form of writing thus far devised is alphabetic writing. Historically, there have been several other systems. Each of these has presented means of depicting graphically—that is, by means of different kinds and combinations of marks—what the makers of the marks intended to convey. Such methods have constituted, generally speaking, early stages in the development of writing.

b / Pictographs. The earliest of these forms consists of the most natural way of visibly communicating information—namely, by means of realistic pictures, in the form of drawings, paintings, carvings and so on.[11] Small children resort to crude drawings to express themselves and to convey ideas to others. Prehistoric men left drawings, paintings, and etchings (known as petroglyphs) on the walls of caves, some as early as 35,000 B.C., and they, as well as more recent primitives, made inscriptions on bone, stone, ivory and other materials.[12]

A step beyond the use of simple drawings or inscribings is systematic pictographic "writing," which consists of the use of somewhat conventionalized pictures to represent objects, actions, events and relations, with a definite consensus existing among the users regarding the meanings of these figures. By combining these figures, it became possible to record continuous thought; a coherent and connected tale could be told. The North American Indians, for example, used relatively plain but widely recognized and understood pictures in describing battles, hunting and raiding expeditions, military parties on the march, buffalo hunts. While these records and messages in somewhat standard picture form had the advantage of being permanent, and some of them transportable, they were limited in scope and accuracy.

Although the pictographic principle persists in some measure in all of the more sophisticated non-alphabetic systems of writing, the pictographs are now supplemented by marks designed to add detail, or are modified in various ways, sometimes to the extent of having other conventionalized marks replace them, though these still represent the picture. They also have phonetic values incorporated in them, so that graphic figures also portray sounds of the spoken language.

A direct derivation from the pictograph, used to add a new and essential expressional element, is the device sometimes known as the picto-ideograph. It is a pictorial symbol whose function is to denote qualities and abstractions. But this leads to a discussion of ideographs.

c / Ideographs. The use of ideographs is the next refinement in the functional development of writing. The number of picturable objects is definitely limited, and it is quite impossible to represent adequately many spoken-language words and many thought-concepts by means of pictures. Ideographs originated as picture symbols. Several of the great early writing systems retained some picture forms to represent both tangible-picturable and some intangible-nonpicturable things, actions, processes and ideas. These pictures, however, in order to fulfill these various expressional functions, became so idealized as to their meaning, so modified in form, so stylized and generalized (sometimes qualified or supplemented by additional marks), and so conventionally combined, as to have a significance quite apart from that of their original pictographic form and meaning. In effect, they no longer resembled pictures.

An ideograph is a drawing, or "character," to use the more technical term. It is a rigidly conventionalized mark or set of distinctive marks, sometimes quite complex. It represents not a sound, nor even a word, but an idea—an idea about matters both concrete and abstract. Thus the conventionalized drawing of a dove stands for "peace"; the drawing of a man with protruding ribs represents "famine," and an eye with tears dropping from it, "sorrow." Max Weber has given examples of the derivation of ideographic meanings. In ancient Egypt, the sign for "government" was the Pharaoh holding a stick in his hand; the Chinese character also identified "governing" with the handling of a stick. In China, the handling of the stick was, in turn, identified with the "regulation of waters." The Chinese character for city meant "fortress."[13]

d / The great transitional or mixed-method systems. These are transitional, not in any evolutionary manner, but in the sense that in their structures they show the change from representational (pictographic and ideographic) writing to phonetic writing; they are mixed in that they combine, in varying degree, pictures or abbreviations of pictures, ideographs and forms of these to represent sounds.

Different peoples in various parts of the world—Sumerians and Babylonians, Egyptians, Hittites, Chinese, Aztecs and Incas—developed systems of writing that utilized pictures, or graphic devices which were abbreviations of or substitutes for pictures; they also used ideographs extensively. Writing that was chiefly ideographic, however, presented a fundamental difficulty: it did not have a way of substituting any image for the sounds used in spoken language to name the object or idea. Hence, several of them, particularly the Assyro-Babylonians and Egyptians (but others also, to varying degrees), isolated certain characters and gave them a phonetic value. Thus the characters in these writing systems had a twofold value: they represented the picturable object or idea, and they also had phonographic significance. The given character (a representation of a human eye, for example) came to represent the same sound under all circumstances. It no longer represented the object or idea to the sight; instead, it stood for a sound that carried meaning to the ear, it was the *name* of some object or idea. This was a distinct gain in ease and quality of communication. The commonest linguistic result seems to have been a set of syllabic symbols, each one of which denoted one syllabic sound. But these name-sounds were uttered as words. Thus the figures or characters came to stand for whole words: they became "word signs," and not object or idea signs. Because of this fundamental feature, Bloomfield decries as "misleading" the term "ideographic" writing, saying that it would be better to use "word-writing" or "logographic writing."[14]

Chinese is a contemporary example of a widely used writing system in which both pictographic and ideographic features play a large role. Single unit symbols usually stand for things. The unit symbols are put together to form words for non-picturable conditions, events and concepts: for example, the combined pictographs for "sun" and "moon" give "light"; "woman" plus "child" gives "good"; three combined figures for "woman" gives "gossip"; "dawn" appears as a sun floating above a horizontal line; sun and moon together make "bright." These figures, made up of from one to several simple pictures, are "words." By combining characters, it is possible to form more and more complicated and abstract concepts. In Chinese also, to some limited extent, in order to cope with the inadequacies of pictorial and ideographic representation, some characters were introduced that have phonetic significance. Like other logographic systems, Chinese employs a large number of characters. Among present Chinese words, there are 214 "classifiers," one of which is sure to be found in any character in the language. To be able to read at all in Chinese, one must know the meanings of 3000 different characters. Familiarity with some 7000 characters is essential to read a Chinese newspaper intelligently, and a really literate person must be acquainted with a great many more of the 40,000 characters that appear in the biggest Chinese dictionary.[15]

In the case of Japanese writing, which developed from Chinese, the symbol—which was originally of a pictographic-ideographic nature—stands for a syllable. Thus, a large number of words can be represented by a much smaller number of signs than in Chinese.

The so-called hieroglyphic writing of ancient Egypt consisted of over 500 distinct characters, which were conventionalized pictures; many of them actually denoted the names (instead of the meanings, as in Chinese writing) of the objects, actions, concepts, and so on, which they represented. Devices resting on phonetic distinctions were used to indicate specific meaning, when the picture might have several interpretations—for example, the figure of a man with his hand to his mouth might be either "eat" or "silent." Later Egyptian writing became more and more phonetic, with standard characters coming increasingly to represent certain syllabic or word sounds.

Cuneiform, probably originally devised by the Sumerians, was the most widespread and most historically significant writing system in the ancient Near East, with a history covering at least three millennia B.C. As an international graphic medium of communication, it was second only to the Phoenician–Greek–Roman alphabetic system. Graphically, through most of its history, it consisted of wedge-shaped marks in conventionally patterned arrangements. It began as pictures; then the pictographs developed into conventional linear drawings. As a consequence of the prevalent use of clay tablets (though other inscribing materials were also used), the linear strokes acquired a wedge-shaped appearance, being pressed into the soft clay with the slanted edge of a stylus. Thus, curved lines disappeared entirely. In its main established form, it consisted of around 600 characters. Cuneiform developed sound symbols representing syllables to denote grammatical elements. It is worthy of note that the speech of the people was largely monosyllabic.

Though ideographic writing makes it possible to represent intangible and non-picturable objects, events, and relations—including abstract concepts—it has serious limitations, even with phonetic additions. It is cumbersome, difficult to execute, because of the necessity of knowing so many characters, circumscribed in expressional and descriptive ability, and somewhat inexact. As Vendryes has pointed out, it leaves too much to be supplied by the imagination and easily creates "a system of ambiguities." Especially important is the fact that, since it can use only word-order, it has no means of expressing grammatical notions—such as the distinction between individual and species or between noun and verb, tense, mood, negation and so on. To indicate these fully, it would have to add all sorts of special signs—which would multiply the number of ideograms to infinity, and make writing practically unusable. It was not an adequate intermediary between the language of thought and the spoken language, in which all kinds of ideas are expressed; it did not provide an economical way of substituting images and sounds for one another.[16]

e / **Alphabetic writing.** With the alphabetic system, the ultimate functional level of writing to date is reached: ultimate in terms of the simplicity and the smallness of the number of basic written characters, as well as in terms of convenience, suitability, adaptability, manageability, versatility, learnability, portability. Compared with the transitional systems, it is the most simple form of writing, suitable for any spoken form of expression. As Brown observes, the representational forms of writing clearly demonstrated the limits of their usefulness in the ancient societies. These latter expanded in size and complexity, and as their repertory of abstract ideas expanded, a more economical and facile form was needed.[17] As noted above, there was a clear tendency in the transitional systems for some symbols to become more schematic and less like their referents. The new orthographic economy that developed dropped ideographic connotations altogether, and advanced beyond the stage of syllabic sounds. With these systems, the phonetic principle in orthography came fully forward; there was a real reunion of speech and writing.

In alphabetic writing, each of the basic symbols denotes—arbitrarily, not representationally—one of the unit consonant or vowel sounds of the spoken language. As Kroeber puts it, ". . . it operates on the principle of a letter symbol for each minimal acoustic element of speech."[18] In linguistic terms, there is one symbol for each phoneme, and the phonemes of a given language, as has been observed earlier, are relatively few in number. When these pure minimum-sound symbols, which are true letters (amounting, in all, to no more than two or three dozen simple signs), are consistently used, then "all the characters for syllables, words, objects, ideas, and 'determinatives' or classifiers can be discarded; and anything that can be spoken can also be written, and with complete intelligibility."[19]

The alphabet was invented by a Semitic people in the Near East, previous to 1000 B.C., and possibly as early as 1800 to 1500 B.C. All later alphabetic systems are variants on this. The letters for most sounds in any form of alphabet resemble the letters in some other alphabet; they are often derived from the letters of the original alphabet. In most instances, the names of the letters are very similar. Thus, the Hebrew *aleph, beth, gimel* and *dalith* correspond to the Greek *alpha, beta, gamma* and *delta,* and to the Romans' and the A, B, C, and D of English.[20]

The alphabet, with some alterations, has spread all over the world, displacing all other writing systems except the Sinitic (mainly Chinese and Japanese). The alterations—which do not depart from the basic principle—are due in part to the need of fitting old alphabets into new languages with somewhat different sounds, or to adapt them to language changes. Some modifications have also come about through efforts at reform or stylistic improvement, or as the result of just plain wear and tear. The appearance of the alphabet and these changes in it thus exemplify certain basic processes of cultural change.[21]

In the original Semitic locale, the alphabet was used by the Phoenicians, the Hebrews, and the Arameans. The ancient Greeks took over the Phoenician system, making certain changes in it, and developing a number of regional variations (for example, in Miletus, Attica, Corinth, Chalcis and Lydia). From the Greeks, the alphabet spread to the Mediterranean peoples, the Romans receiving it, apparently, through the mediation of the Etruscans. The Romans, too, developed several somewhat distinctive forms (Chalcidic, Etruscan, Umbrian, Oscan, Faliscan and Latin). In the Middle Ages, alphabet-writing, based on Greek and Roman models, spread to almost all the peoples of Europe. The alphabets of eastern Europe stem mainly from the old Greek alphabet, largely as the result of its use by the Eastern Church; the Roman alphabet was the basis for those of the people of central, western and northwestern Europe who accepted the western version of Christianity.

It is noteworthy that there is an Arabic alphabet, originating from the original Semitic form, which spread with the Koran to most of the Mohammedan areas of the earth. Developments of the original Semitic alphabet also appear in the Armenian alphabet, and in the Sanskrit writing of India and its descendants in southwest Asia.

Several specific advantages of alphabetic writing should be mentioned. It is a great economy for the individual, since everyone learns to speak before learning to write. After he has memorized the relatively simple characters of the alphabet, he can substitute letters for the sound elements; then he can spell, and hence read and write.

For the culture generally, in addition to the advantages mentioned above, the great flexibility of the alphabet, which makes possible the efficient expression of all kinds of meaning, is one of its signal socio-cultural features. New words to denote new objects, processes, and meanings do not need to have separate new complicated figures devised for them (as in cuneiform or hieroglyphic writing); they can be contrived at once, in immediately intelligible graphic form, out of two or more of the—in the case of English—twenty-six letters of the alphabet. Words of compounded complexity, carrying a whole portmanteau of meanings, can be coined (such as the German word *Bezugweltanschauungsgesetzlehre* which was presented three decades ago, as a substitute for the "Relativitätstheorie" made famous by Einstein). The possibility of creating words is almost infinite.[22]

Alphabetic writing has survived—in fact, it has flourished and been extended for three and a half millennia, notwithstanding the increasing complexity and range of communication, the development of much new knowledge, intellectual and technological revolutions, and (especially important from the technical point of view) the introduction of printing and of the typewriter, as well as the extensive use of shorthand. Furthermore, from the Greek period to the present, while there have been all sorts of adaptations and some revisions, nothing new has happened in the inner structural development of the alphabetic writing of the western world. This attests to its suitability for various eras and cultures, and seems to confirm its position as an ultimate system of writing.

5. *Writing as an Earmark of Civilization*

Now that we have noted the recency of writing in the history of mankind, and some of the features of its development as an efficient instrument of communication, it is appropriate that we briefly assess its significance in the career of man on earth, locate it in man's social and cultural evolution, and indicate some of its major sociocultural features and effects.

The functional significance of writing in man's social and cultural life was succinctly put by the historian, James H. Breasted: "The invention of writing and a convenient set of records on paper has had a greater influence in uplifting the human race than any other intellectual achievement in the career of man."[23] Mirabeau, Kant, Carlyle, Renan and countless more recent scholars have expressed the belief that the invention of writing marked a major turning point in the cultural history of peoples. Thomas Astle phrased it well a hundred and eighty years ago: "The noblest acquisition of mankind is SPEECH, and the most useful art is WRITING. The first eminently distinguishes MAN from the brute creation; the second from uncivilized savages."[24]

The significance of this invention is so great that the cultures which have a written language are called "civilizations," whereas those that do not are referred to as "preliterate," "nonliterate" or "primitive." That writing is at least one of the major earmarks of civilization— possibly even its benchmark—is the conclusion of most anthropologists,[25] and of the social scientists who know about language, as well as of various philosophers.

Civilization is a state of great cultural complexity. The significance of this fact in relation to writing is brought out by Faris:

A preliterate society can have a culture only as complex as can be carried in the minds of the living generation. With the acquisition of writing this limit is removed, and civilization of unlimited complexity is made possible. The fund of knowledge stored in print and accessible to the population is a major component of the framework of collective ability.[26]

Writing is not held to be a "cause" of civilization. But it is a fact that, everywhere in the ancient world, writing was the invariable accompaniment of certain ecological conditions, and especially of certain cultural developments that are the inherent and integral ingredients of the state of civilization. Outstanding among the latter are: the development of government; the arts, philosophy and science; the division of labor and the specialization of occupations—including the appearance of some of the professions, commerce and industry and metallurgy; extensive means of transportation on land and water; the domestication of animals; an agriculture developed well beyond the use of simple tools and methods; and producing for a market. Writing is always present when a people have reached a state of civilization; correlatively, it seems that civilization cannot exist without writing. Each is dependent upon and contributes to the other.

This fact was made pointedly clear among the people of the Middle Ages when they emerged from barbarism, just as it is in the world today, in the efforts of the so-called underdeveloped peoples to achieve the highly developed social and cultural state to which they aspire. The latter are aware of the fact that there is a direct relationship between the ability of their people to write and read, their general level of literacy, on the one hand, and on the other, their relative level of cultural and social proficiency, their national status and the image of them held by other peoples and nations.

The significance of writing for civilized life rests upon the typical but peculiar communicative requirements of a civilized people, and upon what writing has made possible, in the way of the activities and accomplishments that characterize such sociocultural life.

a / Civilized societies usually consist of relatively large populations, which are also spatially extended. Persons, groups and organizations are no longer confined to those of the local, primary, self-sufficient community, but are often far removed geographically from each other. Yet they must exchange diverse information, and conduct a great volume and variety of joint activities, if they are to function together as an economically productive and politically ordered and secure society, and otherwise maintain their common social and cultural life. Nothing other than written means of communication makes this possible.

b / In a civilized society, **many of the most important human relationships are of a secondary nature, and are conducted by means of secondary forms of communication.** Relationships tend to become more impersonal, anonymous, formal and contractual. The social as well as physical "spacings" and "distances" are greater than in most primitive societies; they require media for the harmonization and ordering of life, with efficacies far beyond those of face-to-face communication. There are more segmented interests, more special-interest groups, more diffuse and secondary relations and secondary groups. Daily, face-to-face verbal communication becomes more and more private, and is confined to a limited number of specific or special relationships and interests. Most of the wider and more important contacts, relationships, and exchanges are mediated through writing, or through instruments based on writing.

c / A civilized society has **a large and growing body of knowledge and other intellectual and artistic products,** which it hopes to preserve and transmit to later generations. Its body of knowledge—the result of long experience and long intellectual achievement—is too extensive, too complicated or exact, or too important in its significantly stated form, to be stored in native human memory or transmitted by word of mouth. This corpus of information is incorporated in a general literature; literature, in the full sense of the term, can exist only when the culture has writing. Much of this literature is kept in libraries— that is, in special places where books and documents are collected, carefully cared for, catalogued and made available to readers. Notable ancient instances were the Royal Library at Nineveh, established under Ashurbanipal (668–626 B.C.), the library of Aristotle (384–322 B.C.), the Museum of Alexandria, begun by Ptolemy I about 280 B.C. (this was the chief library of the ancient world), and the library of Lucullus in Rome in the first century B.C. All modern civilized peoples have their private, organizational and public libraries.

The following are the kinds of intellectual achievements, whose recording, and possibly much of whose development, rests fundamentally upon writing.

[1] *Scientific–technological knowledge must be accurately stated and durably recorded.* This knowledge consists of such things as: (a) an accumulated and cumulative body of discovered facts and constructed principles and theories; (b) the investigative, particularly the experimental, technics and techniques, whereby old knowledge is tested and new knowledge achieved; (c) the whole complex of technical information, of formulae, procedures, rules and organizational activities essential to conducting the actual technological (applied) operations, along with knowledge of the facts and of principles and procedures. Very important here, as in certain other areas of civilized life, is the construction of symbolic systems for coping with problems of time. This involves locating and orienting specific occurrences, synchronizing and coordinating processes and connected events, and designating duration and sequence. Central to this complex is a body of astronomical data, based on observations over a period of time, as well as some sort of calendar, which all civilized peoples have. Closely related to the time complex is a system of measuring, counting and calculating, which involves at least the knowledge of arithmetic and geometry and a body of mathematical data. Neither the means for dealing with time, nor these mathematical devices are possible without writing.

[2] *A body of philosophical wisdom* which incorporated interpretations of the universe—its nature, powers, causes, operative principles and ends—and interpretations of man, his function and destiny, of the meaning of life, of common ethical and aesthetic principles, could not be maintained without writing. Writing in its various forms has come to be more and more important for us today, as the essential medium for the presentation of abstract ideas. In a world of new philosophies and revised ideologies, of ever-advancing sciences and the extension of science to new areas of concern, such as nuclear and space technology, of the development of mathematics and quantitative meanings for dozens of new uses, of cybernetics—in such a world, the volume of abstract ideas has come to be tremendous. In abstract ideas, concepts are complexly inclusive and refined, and the logic is carefully constructed; the volume of words is great as compared with those used for the expression of any simple idea, and the words must be

used with a high degree of semantic exactitude and grammatical precision, if the distinctiveness of the idea is to be kept clear. We soon get "lost," if we depend upon the mere oral organization of such ideas. In order to develop them and to set them forth in clarity and essential detail, to make them comprehensible and usable for others, they must be put down in writing.

[3] *There is also a vast body of religious lore,* with its theology, theogony, eschatology, and so on.

[4] *A socially utilitarian literature* is invariably found, along with accounts of the historical, ethnic, economic and political development of the peoples. A preliterate people have only legend, not recorded factual history.

[5] *By no means least is an aesthetic literature,* which consists of the culture's poetry, drama, fiction, songs, ballads and so on. In fact, writing in itself has had aesthetic value, and is one form of art among civilized peoples.

d / Much of the complex societal life of a civilized society must be **conducted by means of large-scale and geographically extended formal organization.** The regulation of activities must be of a highly institutionalized nature. This organization and regulation extend far beyond that which can be accomplished through the orally transmitted mores, traditions and customs, or through the local social organizations of preliterate societies.

Civilized societies are politically organized. Their principles and purposes of formation and operation are stated in constitutions or other written documents (even though they may claim to have an "unwritten" constitution). Governmental organization extends over many people, and often over a wide area. Administrative orders, reports and regulations must be accurately and specifically stated and disseminated throughout the land. A uniform body of codified law prevails over the entire political area, so voluminous, complex and detailed that any thought of its being preserved through digital triggering—for example, the Code of Hammurabi, as compared with the Ten Commandments—is preposterous. The decrees of the courts must be published. Many other kinds of impersonal and wide-range social controls must be maintained. Historical records must be kept of kings and governors, of reigns and administrations, of diplomatic agreements and activities.

Developed economic life demands writing. Information about economic resources, about wealth and income, must be accurately presented and preserved. For political as well as economic purposes, moreover, censuses of the population—the human resources—are taken, and the data classified. Commercial and marketing operations, accounting practices, financial and credit procedures, the units of value in the exchange of goods and services (which usually involves a monetary system) require a variety of special forms of writing. The kinds of property, real, corporate and personal, must be designated, and their physical and monetary dimensions precisely recorded. The agreements and promises (contracts) involved in all transactions must be fully and accurately stated and carefully preserved.

Certain general organizational essentials, which cannot exist without writing, are found in the social organizations of civilized life, whether these be political, economic, military, scientific–technological, religious or educational. The jurisdiction and activities of these usually extend over wide areas, and involve many people as functionaries and beneficiaries. Their purposes, principles and basic operative procedures must be clearly stated. There must be extensive sets of rules and regulations—many of them in the form of formal laws—indicating what is required, permitted and prohibited in a great variety of operations and relationships. These rules and laws must be known by many people, often over wide areas; to ensure this, they must be preserved in exact form. The activities and accomplishments of the organizations must be accurately and fully recorded for both present and future use. Since these organizations are bureaucratically organized, directives, instructions and functional information must be transmitted, both vertically and laterally, between the various layers of specialized and hierarchized personnel. Orders must be accurately stated and transmitted, and the information that is exchanged must be exact and full.

6. *Sociocultural Aspects of Writing*

In our examination of the relationship of writing to the cultural level of civilization, it has been obvious that writing has played a strategic role in social and cultural development. A more detailed examination of certain of the more sociologically significant among its functions and effects is a primary objective of the present treatment.

a / The recording function of writing and some of its effects. The fact that writing makes possible the production of exact and permanent records has already been touched upon.[27] It should be recognized that the records of language itself cannot go back beyond the invention of writing and the first written documents. Documents and inscriptions from the past give us the only evidence we have of the nature of the languages of different eras and areas, and of the progression of languages. In order for us to study given languages and dialects, and particularly in order to compare different ones, including those of illiterates, we must have them as recorded in written form.

We are especially concerned with the fact that the recording function has great importance in itself, both socially and culturally. Several notable aspects will now be briefly examined.

[1] *The social economy of explicit records.* When the ideas and accomplishments of past generations are preserved in written records, each new generation does not have to find out all these things anew by trial and error, by study and experiment. Instead, it has at its disposal a body of knowledge greater in amount, and also much more complex and abstract, than could be remembered and accurately transmitted through verbal means. Every child in a literate society grows up in a sociocultural environment in which most of what is deemed important, past or present, is in writing. Each generation, therefore, does not have to start from scratch; it can "take off" from recorded knowledge gleaned from the voluminous experiences of many peoples, as well as the foolishness of many others. Furthermore, if records can be transported, writing makes available information that has been conceived and preserved by people of other epochs or from remote regions. This often provides a basis for important new and useful knowledge. In both instances, the records reveal the mistakes and the failures that have been suffered and paid for by others, as well as their great positive achievements. These experiences come to the newcomers almost as a gift.

[2] *Writing permits, in fact encourages, a rapid, progressive and elaborate accumulation of knowledge, thus promoting discovery and invention.* In all eras and areas that possess writing, the written word has increased in a number of ways the likelihood that discoveries and inventions will be made and will become culturally effective.

Written knowledge, unlike mere remembered lore, makes possible the rapid and extensive development of the *culture base*—that is, the total accumulated culture heritage, framework or matrix of the specific society. If the culture base is broad, it contains many varieties and a great number of culture materials. These may suggest new discoveries; they are available for that combining and recombining which is the essence of invention. With the progressive accumulation of knowledge so greatly aided by the writing of it, these two processes of discovery and invention can occur at a rate nearly that of the exponential principle.

Another related aspect is the fact that what is discovered and invented at a given time and place may not be pertinent to what is then being sought, or it may be incomplete and deemed useless, or it may not be utilized because of social resistance. If it is recorded in permanent form, however, it will not be lost or forgotten; it will continue to remain available for other or later students, investigators and inventors. For these, it may be highly provocative; in fact, it may trigger wholly new sequences and varieties of discovery and invention. Such records have made possible the great advances in the technical knowledge of recent and contemporary man, and have thereby given rise to the great spurt of growth during the last three or four of the thousand millennia that man has existed on the earth.

Of pertinence also is the fact that bibliography and extensive reading in the area of interest is the first and fundamental step in experiment and research.

[3] *The progress of nations.* It is obvious from our discussion of the relation of writing and civilization that, as the result of the recording of the history of peoples and nations, each people can profit by its own mistakes and those of all other peoples of whom it has knowledge.[28] Each society, of course, also has the record of its own past achievements and those of others to build upon. These recorded facts provide the possibility, if they are properly used, for the social, economic, political, legal, scientific, philosophical, technological and artistic progress of the people or nation.

b / Print, printing and paper. In the beginning, all records were manually produced by the use of pen, pencil, or stylus; documents and manuscripts were represented on clay and wax tablets, sheets of papyrus, vellum or parchment. They could be duplicated only by laborious copying. In Alexandria before the Christian era, one could buy a copy of a manuscript by a great author, but at a high price. Monks spent a good part of their lives copying manuscripts. It was not until printing was developed that the world of letters rapidly moved forward. Probably about the sixth century A. D., the Chinese began to print a group of characters from wood blocks; by the tenth century they had begun keeping their records in that way. The Romans also used wood blocks. Gutenberg, Faust, and others improved upon the Chinese method by a system of movable metal type in manually operated presses. Tremendous advances have come since the fifteenth century, such as modern power presses, linotype, monotype, teletype and photo-offset. The importance of paper in this advance is often overlooked. The older materials were unsatisfactory in quality, while the main manuscript materials such as vellum and parchment were insufficient in quantity for the new mode of printing by mechanical devices. First developed in China around the first century of the Christian era, the making of paper from macerated rags reached the Arab world during the eighth century and became established in the West by the thirteenth. With the aid of certain rather recent mechanical and chemical advances, wood pulp—a material that exists in great quantity—and other vegetable matter came to be used, whereupon paper became cheap and abundant. Print and printing have correspondingly advanced and increased.[29]

Two major gains accrued immediately as the result of printing. First, printed letters are standard in their conformation, and hence much less liable to error than handscript. The services of handwriting experts in deciphering handwritten documents are not needed for the printed page. Second, the printing press and paper made possible for the first time in human history the comparatively cheap, easy and voluminous reproduction of written matter. Once the type was set up, a thousand copies could be run off with but little more labor than a hundred. The metal in the type could be used over and over again, so that the cost of casting it could be spread over the printing of many books. As a consequence, a steadily rising number of books and pamphlets were made available to all who had learned to read.[30]

The sociocultural effects of printing have been great. It had certain important *effects upon language itself*. It greatly accelerated the tendency of writing in general to reduce the enormous number of dialects that still prevailed in most areas, and instead encouraged the use of the national language. Thus, the area over which persons could communicate with each other effectively was widened. Furthermore, the printed words, beheld by many people over a wide area, tended to standardize the spelling and the grammatical forms of the given language, encouraged greater uniformity in punctuation and capitalization, word and syllable division and paragraphing, as well as continually recalling standard pronunciations and meanings. These tendencies and effects are also likely to occur in the present underdeveloped countries, as the rate of literacy goes up there.

The increasing availability of printed materials *brought about a cultural revolution which has been under way for several centuries, and is still in full swing*. Printing has brought students from all portions of the literate world into contact with each other and, through the resulting awareness of what has been accomplished, has tremendously stimulated both the dissemination of existing knowledge and efforts toward the acquisition of new truths.

Some of the most important cultural developments of recent times can be attributed in considerable part to printing. The rise of science, for example, was stimulated by it. The works of the great scientific thinkers of antiquity—for example Aristotle and Ptolemy—and of medieval times, have now become the heritage of many literate men. Subsequent scientific findings have been accurately stated and preserved in readily available form. Printing greatly enhances the storage capacity of writing, so that printed records have become a much more capacious storehouse of knowledge, upon which any would-be discoverer or inventor can draw at will. La Piere, among others, has pointed out that the printed word also leads to vastly extended and rapid diffusion of inventions and discoveries, both within societies and between societies. In so far as a greater number share the knowledge and are stimulated by it, the chances become greater that new insights will be gained and new combinations of knowledge will come about.[31]

Printing has *made possible and encouraged secular aesthetic and religious literature.* Popular education, with its dynamic effects, is inconceivable without printing. The literate individual today can be "rich" in as many literatures—philosophical, scientific, artistic, religious, and so on—as he has reading proficiency in. He can enjoy, in his intellectual life, "the dimensions of a large library."

Print is the *means of gradually introducing and incorporating into the language, for a wide circle of readers, new items in process of becoming standard,* such as new scientific, economic, political and technological terms, modifications of spelling, and new colorful forms of expression.

Social movements have been greatly facilitated by print and printing. The leaders of such movements have long been aware of printing as a highly efficient instrument both for inaugurating and for maintaining them. The great reformers of the Reformation, Calvin and Luther, were quick to seize upon print as a means of carrying on their efforts. The great men of the Reformation stressed the desirability of men being able to study the Bible themselves; the necessary corollary of this was that men should be taught to read. The Protestant churches have thus encouraged literacy and printing.

Dictators have dominated the press, in order to control the issuance of information and, through it, public opinion. Richelieu established the first French newspaper as a means of influencing public opinion, and surrounded himself with a small army of writers whose business it was to produce appropriate treatises. Cromwell also used the press, as did Napoleon who, by means of it, issued propaganda so lavishly that a saying appeared among his subjects: "False as a bulletin." The dictators of the present century have controlled the processes of journalism from personnel to output.

In the hands of authoritarians, printed materials become instruments of government propaganda. Paradoxically, it is the existence of a greater literacy than had ever before existed, which has enabled the dictators of recent centuries, through a controlled and thoroughly propagandized nationwide press, to influence everyone who reads. Modern linotype machines and high-speed presses vastly increase the volume of printed "dope" that can be issued.

The freeing effect. At the same time, having the accounts of events and the statements of knowledge and belief in written (especially, printed) form makes possible a greater degree of detachment from them and a more critical attitude toward them than is likely to be present if they are presented in the rapid flow of face-to-face verbal discourse. They can be carefully and deliberately reviewed in documentary form after the event. Having materials in written form also tends to free the recipients of communications from the immediate visible or audible personality effects of the sender—for example, the shouting, emotionalism, gesticulation or striking physical characteristics of a demagogue, or the personal or verbal wiles of a charmer or manipulator.

c / The uniformizing effect of writing among a people. The uniformity and unity of a people are more or less encumbered by barriers in the form of tribal languages, dissimilar spoken dialects and other sharp internal variations in speech, as has been noted. But the written or "literary language" as it is found in books, journals, and newspapers is usually standard throughout the language community. By means of writing, the common beliefs, ideas, values, ideologies, rules and laws, as well as the resultant standardized measures for collective action, are preserved and widely disseminated; opinions are recorded and shared over the entire area.

Historically, writing has been the durable outward symbol of a culture. All of the great cultures, ancient as well as modern, have had their identifying writing systems. Nations have been unified by them. It is in part because of this fact that conquerors have so frequently attempted to destroy the writings of the conquered—the "book burnings."

History also demonstrates the fact that a common writing system has frequently effected a considerable degree of cultural uniformity and social unity between peoples and nations.

d / Writing as a conserving agency. Writing has conserving effects upon itself as a system and upon communication in general.

In the first place, in order to carry out any of the basic functions discussed in Sect. 2 above, *writing must be thoroughly stabilized and systematized:* word-spellings, vocabulary, and grammatical forms must be relatively unalterable and unmistakable. For if two different receivers across space get what seem to be somewhat unlike messages when these were supposed to be identical, or if a generation cannot make sense out of its predecessors' writings, or if an individual writes himself a confusing message, the written language has lost its basic justification and function. It must be unyielding to momentary fancy and pressure in its entire structuring and usage.

A second aspect has to do with the fact that *societies* that have writing —and they are the complex and culturally advanced ones—*depend upon it to help systematize and make explicit the bases of the social, economic and political life of the people:* its codes of law and organizational operation, directives and contracts, standardized knowledge and published instructions for carrying on its activities. A writing system which was chaotic or unpredictable would make these functions impossible to execute.

A third aspect of writing as a conserving agent is of a *dysfunctional nature.* It seems to be inevitable that, when any form of speech becomes written language, it loses much of its linguistic freedom. All forms of speech have their rules and usages, as has been indicated repeatedly; in a written language, the forms become much more constant and stereotyped so that, finally, "words and phrases are adjudged to be good or bad, not by their power, clarity, and aptness of expression, but by the external criterion of correctness." There is a tendency to fix spelling,[32] grammar, punctuation and pronunciation; to discourage the assimilation of picturesque and vigorous elements from outside; to cripple free and spontaneous powers of word creation; to fail to abandon words —especially in historical, religious and epic compositions—that are no longer used in daily speech. The written symbol system achieves predominance, almost tyranny, over the audible one.[33]

A fourth, and perhaps the most important stabilizing influence of writing, is the fact that *in its printed form,* it *makes for the fixation of meanings.* They are thus maintained uncorrupted and unmodified over large stretches of time and space.

As a result of this quite understandable, and in most instances essential, conservatism, "the conventions of writing remain unaltered even though the speech-forms have undergone linguistic change."[34] Written language is thus much more likely to have archaic features than spoken language, which must meet the hourly circumstances of its speakers, and which is usually being invigorated by colloquialisms, dialects, slangs and the newly developing special sublanguages. There is a tendency thus for a written language to represent the language as it was spoken rather than as it is spoken.[35] Hockett comments that "people are more conservative about writing systems than about any other human institution . . . even religion."[36]

e / **Writing and social differentiation.** In the great ancient societies, and until very recently almost everywhere, most of the people could not write and read. Even today, as noted above, in most of the countries of Asia, Africa and Latin America, there is a vast disproportion between the literate and the illiterate.

Writing, it seems, was originally developed by the priests as a means of keeping temple accounts, recording economic revenues, rights and obligations, and registering governmental events. In general, through most of the history of writing and reading, they have been the accomplishments of numbers of the upper and middle strata or their specially trained hirelings, and they have been employed for the use and benefit of the upper and middle strata.

The main population elements enjoying these proficiencies were: the members of the priesthood, at least at the higher levels; the upper rank of kings, nobles and administrative officials and their scribes and clerks; the scholars, some of the "scientists," including astrologers and soothsayers, engineers and certain specialized craftsmen, mathematicians and the members of other such learned professions; the upper level of economic producers and some of the commercial traders. Thus writing and reading were a specialty and prerogative of the very few, perhaps not more than one per cent of the population of ancient societies.

Historically, the small minority who could write among most peoples developed as a highly strategic and influential segment of the social structure. They kept the commercial, religious and political records; they wrote, read and interpreted the laws; they conducted the administrative and diplomatic correspondence; they produced the literature; they maintained the intellectual tradition of learning and formal erudition, which differed fundamentally from the much lower level of intellectual and social life of the illiterate masses.[37]

Writing, in the main, served the ruling and possessing classes as an exclusive instrument useful for maintaining their property rights and perpetuating their social power. Furthermore, the peasantry and the artisans had almost no possibility of learning the cumbersome and complicated art of writing, for this required formal education and specialized training. In fact, some of the ancient priesthoods sought, by their complicated writing, to preserve their vested interest and their badge of social prestige, through keeping the knowledge of writing from the common people. Writing thus helped to create, intensify, and perpetuate a division of society into two portions—among which, the number of people, on the one hand, and the privileges and social power, on the other hand, were in inverse ratio to each other.[38]

Several important technical factors are significant in this situation. First, the already mentioned weaknesses of the pre-alphabetic forms of writing (especially the "mixed-method" systems) were in part responsible. They were cumbersome, consisting as they did of hundreds and thousands of separate, complex characters that had to be learned, and usually required practice and dexterity for their execution. Only those with highly specialized tasks that required writing could have had the incentive to engage in the laborious learning of the complicated art of writing (the great masses of the people were serfs or peasants engaged in manual labor), and only those with leisure could devote the necessary energy and time to it. Such libraries as existed were connected with the temples and courts; in view of their inaccessibility and the very limited amount of literacy, they were altogether useless to the overwhelming majority of the population.

The alphabetic system, with its small number of simple characters and its ready learnability, changed the situation somewhat. But another important restrictive factor still had to be resolved.

Second, before printing, regardless of the nature of the writing system, the reproduction of written materials, as noted above, was a matter of laborious copying by hand by priests and scribes. This meant that these materials were costly, in view of the time and labor involved in their production; only a few people could pay the price for them. It meant also that written materials were scarce. Because of their cost and scarcity, even had there been widespread literacy, they would have been available to only a very small and select portion of the population. The invention and use of printing and paper broke this monopoly of the privileged and the few; many could enjoy and employ what had once been a very restricted possession.

f / Writing, printing and democracy. While writing and printing are not guarantees of democracy, they are an indispensable means to it. Democracy rests on an informed citizenry. The invention of the alphabet made it possible to produce writing that many more could read, in so far as the reading of what had been written became easier to learn. The alphabet thus democratized both writing and reading. With the invention of printing and cheap newsprint, informative materials could be produced in great quantities and at low cost. Wherever printed matter is readily available, literacy tends to spread, even to become practically universal among an entire people; this means that almost everyone becomes capable of informing himself. As a result of the speed with which printed materials can be produced and transported, important issues quickly and easily become matters of nationwide discussion; public opinion can "shape up." Thus truly democratic government is made possible, over wide territories.

g / Literacy, full social participation and education. Attention has already been called to the vast extent of illiteracy in the present world. The illiterate is deprived of most of those activities that are indispensable, if he is to have a full social and cultural life today. The elimination of illiteracy, especially among the host of underdeveloped peoples, is one of the most urgent tasks confronting mankind. "Functional literacy"—that is, the possession of knowledge and skills in reading and writing, such as will enable the individual to engage effectively in all those activities in which literacy is normally assumed in his culture or group, is a minimal requirement in every department of life everywhere today.[39] The individual needs to be literate in order to meet most of the practical needs of daily life, to improve his standard of living, to raise his economic status (particularly with respect to carrying on his job) to gain and maintain his social prestige, to learn about community activities and problems, to meet civic obligations, to understand world affairs, to have access to and enjoy his literary heritage, and for a host of other reasons.[40]

All peoples and countries need a literate population. Through written (and printed) historical records, they are able to take a long look into the past. Within countries, there is invariably a close correlation between illiteracy and the ignorance, poverty, misery and apathy of the people, or between it and their failure to use competently their resources for increased productivity, their low national and per capita income, their limited scientific, technological, industrial and commercial development and their relative political retardation. On the basis of the experience of the more advanced peoples, the universalizing of literacy among these disadvantaged populations would seem to be one of the prime factors in the elimination of these conditions. Where general literacy prevails, the people can obtain a more comprehensive understanding of inter-people and international relations than they can obtain by other means of mass communication. Thus, they are also enabled to take a long look into the future, and to assume some responsibility for what is passed on to it, as well as to participate in the attempts to build a civilization that is fit for future generations everywhere. Men are beginning to realize that what is written and printed can be a great boon to the future; it can also constitute, however, incriminating evidence of carelessness, profligacy and neglect.

Literacy among the peoples of the world will not of itself promote world peace. But it can be stated with a high degree of certainty that, without the circulation of comprehensive bodies of many different kinds of relevant facts among the citizenry everywhere, without the opportunity for the careful and deliberate consideration of facts, opinions and events that print gives, and without the possibility of the *exchange* of facts, beliefs, values and viewpoints, there is little likelihood of world peace.

The reduction of illiteracy is closely related to educational, social, economic and political progress in single communities, in each of the countries and in the world as a whole. The UNESCO report on illiteracy, just cited, notes that this is not an isolated phenomenon. It is essential to consider it

in all its inter-relationship with other factors of modernization, such as the extension of free and compulsory education, the development of urban industrialization, the utilization of a nation's resources for increased productivity, and the policies towards equitable distribution of a country's material and financial resources for the education of its children and youth.[41]

The ultimate and direct institutional responsibility, however, rests upon adequately organized and supported educational systems. Wherever there has been a high degree of literacy, it has been due to a system of public, free, universal and compulsory education. The Romans were aware of this, although they did not maintain the compulsory feature. Pei points out that, in the later centuries of the Empire, state-endowed *grammatici* were planted in every town and hamlet of Italy and the provinces.[42] These principles are followed in the main in the advanced nations today, and it is certain that wherever a high level of literacy is achieved in the future it will be by similar means.

7. A Note on Modern Storage and Retrieval of Information

The tremendous volume and the ever-accelerating tempo of accumulation of information in modern societies poses problems of storage, since the products of the information explosion promise soon to surpass the capabilities and capacities of classical library systems. The materials must be reduced to the smallest possible compass for storage purposes as compared with the bulk of books and the bound volumes of records, journals and newspapers. The information in storage must also be easily and instantly available. Modern techniques and automated electronic machines are being developed and are increasingly coming to be used both for purposes of condensation and retrieval.

Spoken materials are conserved by means of readily stored perforated tapes and by plastic records. Handscript and type-written materials, and especially the printed books, monographs, research reports, organization records, periodical articles, and other documents, with their accompanying photographs, drawings, tables, charts, and so on, as well as newspapers, can be reduced to microfilm. The newer photo-chronic micro-image process especially produces film on which the printed materials and photographs are greatly reduced in scale, and in multiple quantites, at small cost, and with unrivaled clarity.

The retrieving for use of the stored materials of information involves: (1) selection on the basis of relevancy to the task at hand, (2) identification in storage, (3) indexing, for example, by keywords, (4) coding by abbreviating or assignment of arbitrary symbols such as numbers or letters, and (5) sorting of the materials in storage on the basis of the indexed and coded bibliography. Automated techniques performed with assistance of special machines, including computers, are now employed to expedite each of these processes.[43]

N O T E S

1 "No kind of writing, no matter how crude or primitive, symbolizes ideas divorced from linguistic forms of expression. All writing systems, including the Chinese, symbolize simply linguistic utterances." (Benjamin L. Whorf, *Language, Thought, and Reality: Selected Writings of Benjamin Lee Whorf* (John B. Carroll, ed.; Cambridge: The Technology Press, and New York: John Wiley & Sons, 1956), p. 177.)

2 Mario Pei, *The Story of Language* (Philadelphia: J. B. Lippincott & Co., 1949), p. 86. (Italics added.)

3 Cf. Colin Cherry, *On Human Communication: A Review, A Survey, and A Criticism* (published jointly by Technology Press of M. I. T., Cambridge, Mass., 1957 and John Wiley & Sons, New York, 1957), p. 77.) In the sentence above, reference is to the proportion of the world's languages that do and do not have writing. In terms of world population, the situation is countered to

some extent by the fact that a large number of the speakers of several of the great European-originated "empire" languages—notably English, German and French—can write and read.

4 UNESCO: *World Illiteracy at Mid-Century*, Paris, 1957.

5 *Ibid.*, p. 13.

6 The general definition of literacy recommended by the U. N. Population Commission, and adopted by a considerable number of countries.

7 For greater detail as to continents and regions, *ibid.*, pp. 14–17, and for particular countries, pp. 32–34, 38–44.

8 An interesting aspect of this situation is described in the following: "Distinctive signboards over stores and other places of business, symbolic devices like our cigar-store Indian, and the red and white barber pole were not decorations; they were necessities. Carved Chinese images indicated tea stores, and pictured Beau Brummels directed attention to tailors' establishments in the days of our largely illiterate great-great-grandfathers." Mario Pei, *The Story of English* (Philadelphia: J. B. Lippincott & Co., 1952), p. 337.)

9 U. S. Census, "Educational Attainment: March, 1962," Series P–20, No. 121, Feb. 7, 1963.

10 J. Vendryes, *Language: A Linguistic Introduction to History* (London: Kegan Paul, Trench, Trubner & Co., 1925), pp. 318–320.

11 Note the following comment on early graphic representations as both artistic expression and communication: "The first writers were also the first artists and the walls of their caves were both art gallery and library. Their marvelously lifelike reindeer, bison, and rhinoceros; stick-figure shamans and medicine men; the child's Christmas-tree pattern, repeated over and over again, to denote a fir forest: these were done by brilliant artists for the sheer joy of it, and for another reason as well—the pressing need to shape a message." Michael Girsdansky, *The Adventure of Language* (Englewood Cliffs, N. J.: Prentice-Hall, 1963), p. 143.

12 It should be noted that, in different languages, "to write" is literally "to incise," "to carve," "to inscribe," "to paint."

13 Max Weber, *The Religion of China,* trans. Hans Gerth (New York: Oxford University Press, 1951), pp. 13, 16.

14 Leonard Bloomfield, *Language* (New York: Henry Holt & Sons, 1933), p. 285. The term "word-syllabic writing" is also used. (For a comprehensive treatment of the great writing systems of mankind using these terms, see Ignace J. Gelb, *A Study of Writing* (Chicago: University of Chicago Press, 1954), pp. 60–165.)

15 John Lear, "Communist China: What Science Wants to Know About It," *Saturday Review,* 47 (March 7, 1964), 43–46 (44).

16 Vendryes, pp. 321–323.

17 Roger Brown, *Words and Things* (Glencoe, Ill.: Free Press, 1958), p. 61.

18 Alfred L. Kroeber, *Anthropology* (New York: Harcourt, Brace & Co., 1948), p. 313.

19 *Ibid.*, p. 372.

20 Cf. *ibid.*, p. 313.

21 Says Kroeber, "The history of the alphabet . . . illustrates at one point or another the principles of basic invention, supplementary invention, diffusion, acceptance, refusal, modification, survival, loss, patterning, and function—and the interweaving of all these." (*Ibid.*, p. 509.)

22 Note the following: "We can get an idea of the enormous number of printed or written words that could be formed by different combinations of letters by envisaging the fact that from an alphabet of 23 letters we could construct 8^{23} (8 to the 23rd power), that is, about 50,000 million eight-letter code words." (Michael Polanyi, "Words, Conceptions, and Science," *Twentieth Century,* 158 (Sept., 1955), 256–267 (257).)

23 James H. Breasted, *The Conquest of Civilization* (New York: Harper & Brothers, 1938), p. 61.

24 Thomas Astle, *The Origin and Progress of Writing* (London, 1784, 1803), p. i. (Quoted by Berthold L. Ullman, *Ancient Writing and Its Influence* (New York: Longmans Green & Co., 1932), p. 3.)

25 Two major nineteenth-century anthropologists, Lewis H. Morgan and Edward B. Tylor, cited writing as the boundary line between barbarism and civilization.

26 R. E. L. Faris, "Reflections on the Ability Dimension in Human Society," *American Sociological Review*, 26 (Dec., 1961), 835–843 (838).

27 See particularly Chapter III, Section 9, and Chapter VI, Section 2.

28 Before writing we have no *annals* of a people, only the inexplicated archaeological evidences of their existence (pottery, bricks, buildings, utensils, bones), which require the most expert and cautious interpretation.

29 For Lewis Mumford's graphic and pointed presentation of the "pseudo-environment of paper" in which the inhabitant of the modern metropolis lives—paper in connection with books, newspapers, journals, ledgers, card catalogs, deeds, contracts, mortgages, advertisements, ticker tape and stock quotations, and so on; its connection with creativeness in the theater, literature, music, and scholarship; paper in industry; paper as trash and litter—see "The Paper Dream City," in his *The Culture of Cities* (New York: Harcourt, Brace & Co., 1938), pp. 255–258.

30 Cf. Richard T. La Piere, *Sociology* (New York: McGraw-Hill Book Co., 1946) p. 229; Alfred C. Moorhouse, *The Triumph of the Alphabet: A History of Writing* (New York: Henry Schuman, 1953), p. 196.

31 *Ibid.*, p. 230.

32 Hughes observes that the longer a language has had a recorded literature, the more archaic and the less efficient is its spelling system; thus, for example, the preposterous spelling of both English and French. John P. Hughes, *The Science of Language* (New York: Random House, 1962), p. 141.

33 Most of the material in this paragraph has been taken from Eric Partridge, *The World of Words* (London: George Routledge & Sons, 1938), pp. 179–180. On these points, see also Vendryes, pp. 332–335.

34 Bloomfield, p. 291.

35 La Piere, p. 226. In this connection, Gelb says that "The fact that English has changed relatively little in the last four or five hundred years, in comparison with the strong linguistic changes previous to this time, can be ascribed in some measure to the widespread knowledge of writing in the last few centuries." (*Ibid.*, pp. 223–224.)

36 Charles F. Hockett, *A Course in Modern Linguistics* (New York: Macmillan Co., 1958), p. 545. See also Marjorie S. Zengel, "Literacy as a Factor in Language Change," *American Anthropologist*, 64 (Feb., 1962), 132–139.

37 For a treatment of the present-day counterparts of these and other strategic elites see Suzanne Keller, *Beyond the Ruling Class: Strategic Elites in Modern Society* (New York: Random House, 1963).

38 Cf., Kurt Mayer, *Class and Society* (New York: Doubleday & Co., 1955), p. 13.

39 The definition is that of William S. Gray, *The Teaching of Reading and Writing* (Paris: UNESCO, 1956), p. 24, (cited in UNESCO, *World Illiteracy at Mid-Century*, Paris, 1957, p. 20).

40 These are set forth in detail by Gray, in UNESCO, *op. cit.*

41 *Ibid.*, pp. i–ii.

42 Mario Pei, *The Story of English* (Philadelphia: J. B. Lippincott & Co., 1952), p. 887.

43 Cf. Mortimer Taube and Harold Wooster (eds.), *Symposium on Information Storage and Retrieval* (New York: Columbia University Press, 1958); Martha Boaz, *Modern Trends in Documentation* (New York: Pergamon Press, Ltd., 1959); Joseph N. Bell, "Crisis! How Can We Store Human Knowledge?" *Popular Mechanics*, 118 (Nov., 1962), 104–110, 224; I. Roger Yoshino, Robert W. Heath, and Robert W. Mitchell, "Automated Information Retrieval of Sociological Data," *Sociology and Social Research*, 48 (Oct., 1963), 24–31.

XVIII 🎋 Mass Communication, Language and Modern Society

1. *The Relation of Mass Communication to the Present Study*

It is appropriate to deal with mass communication in our concluding chapter. The sociological treatment of the media and the uses of mass communication should not only throw light upon language in some of its most characteristic and most prevalent forms, but also bring into a new focus some of the most important features of the sociology of language examined up to this point and some of the most important social functions of language.

Mass communication is directly related to social change, especially to the exceedingly dynamic character of modern societies, and to language change itself; it profoundly affects language as a determinant, and has revolutionized the "communications component" of modern societies, especially through increasing the volume, diversification and range of communication; it is an important factor in the uniformation of language (and languages) and of the extension of certain given languages, at the same time as (in some regions, and among certain categories of people of most regions) it encourages and facilitates the knowledge and practice of other languages; it helps to effect the cultural, social and political unification of peoples, plays an important part in socialization and stereotyping on a nationwide and worldwide scale; it is a prime factor in the exercise of social influence, persuasion and power, and in the social control efforts of different types of institutional organizations; it plays an important part in social and ideological conflict, as a highly efficient instrumentality, capable of functioning effectively across ethnic and national boundaries.

In mass communication, we have not only new variations and utilizations of language, but also the unlocking of a set of new social forces of as yet incalculable magnitude and pertinence. As Louis Wirth pointed out more than a decade and a half ago, it is "a gigantic instrument of infinite possibilities for good or evil."[1] In its relatively short career, it has created some new social problems derived from language, and has also aided in resolving others. It has all these and many other effects for all the advanced people, and increasingly for *all* the people of the contemporary world.

A language is, itself, in a very real sense, a mass medium of communication. But the term "mass communication" has special connotations. Mass communication is one of the major combinations of technologies in the modern world, one of the major industries—several industries, in fact. It is a typical product of modern society and absolutely essential to its operation. By means of its different media, it adds new dimensions and increased scope to communication. In its present forms, it involves a vast extension of the spoken and written word, as well as of the other long-used and interrelated auditory and visual means of expression. With mass communication, language has "gone modern."

Mass communication is, as we have said, a *special kind* of communication. It involves: (1) the use of technologically developed, impersonal media, such as printed matter (especially in the form of newspapers, magazines, books, leaflets, and pamphlets), and motion pictures, radio, and television, which are capable of affecting many persons simultaneously (hence, "mass" media); (2) their control and operation by private or public *corporate* organizations; (3) their employment to convey messages simultaneously; (4) their orientation toward a large, scattered, heterogeneous, anonymous and usually unorganized audience ("mass audience").

One fact of crucial importance is their massive effect upon the people of modern societies. Next to old-fashioned, face-to-face, or direct speaker-to-assembly talk, the mass media are the major means whereby people in modern societies (increasingly, throughout the world) receive their linguistic (spoken and written) and most of their other auditory and visual signs and signals.

It is proper that the social sciences, especially sociology, social psychology and political science, have paid so much attention to mass communication. A massive literature exists.[2]

A good deal of this literature reports research, much of which is directed to utilitarian ends, especially how to construct messages, how to have them spread by the most appropriate media, how to make the most effective impact upon the particular type of audience. As Merton and Lazarsfeld have pointed out, mass communications research in the United States has "developed largely in response to market requirements.[3] Students of mass communications, seeking such practical information, have developed quite a battery of statistical measures and other objective testing machinery.

The sociological and social-psychological literature is especially concerned with the following kinds of studies: (1) The content of mass communication messages in terms of themes and plots, and their fitness for particular purposes. (2) Audiences, as to size and composition, the composition studies especially being concerned with income, sex, age and educational level of the members. (3) Audience response, with respect especially to (a) the kinds of appeals and programs and other communications that audiences respond to favorably, resist or are apathetic to, and more significantly to (b) *what* the different population segments just mentioned respond to and *how* they respond, especially in their exercise of selectivity and in their acceptance. (4) The use of different media—newspapers, magazines, leaflets and pamphlets, radio, television—for the achievement of particular desired effects— for example, a radio or television speech, as against a printed pamphlet or purchased printed space. (5) Personal and interpersonal influence: the relative part played by people of different power status, role, personality, reputation—for example, the "influentials," who are the subjects of several studies, in their role as communicators, and the place of *inter*personal influence in the "flow" of mass communications. (6) The relation of mass communication to public opinion: the process of its formation and modification; its content. (7) Some of the effects, favorable and unfavorable, of mass communication: for example, the effect upon juveniles of crime movies and of radio and television programs; the differential effectiveness in influencing voting behavior of radio, television, and newspaper campaigning; effectiveness in the special area of advertising, which is conducted almost entirely by means of mass communication media.

It is not in line with our general objectives in this study to present another summary or digest of these studies (for a number of excellent ones, see the appended bibliography to this study), although the problems with which they are concerned do have vast sociological significance. We will deal very concisely with the emergence of mass communication, its modern societal setting, certain aspects of it as they relate directly to linguistic communication, and to the manner in which the important sociological aspects of language examined in the course of this study are affected by mass communication.

The emergence of mass communication has depended upon both the development of the technical devices (the mass media) *and* the kind of society needing them and capable of using them. Each of these aspects will be briefly examined.

2. *The Development of the Technical Media*

In strict fact, the first mnemonic signs (for example, branches laid certain ways) and the first cut stone tablets, in so far as they conveyed more or less *public* messages, were the first newspapers and books, and the first smoke signals and drumbeats were the first broadcasts. The development of the media was slow, hesitant and limited, however, until very recently.[4]

Printing is an ancient technique, as was mentioned in Chapter XVII. Over the centuries, it has taken advantage of numerous new discoveries and inventions, and has come to be linked with others, thereby increasing its communicative range and effectiveness. The invention of processes for making paper from wood pulp, as against rags, made the paper cheap and its supply abundant. Printing as a process was enhanced by photography and the use of colored representations; the processes of production were vastly speeded up and the output greatly increased by the high-speed power rotary press and the linotype machine; the process of reporting and transmitting of information was hastened by the telegraph, the manual (more recently, the electrical) typewriter, the telephone, and the teletypewriter, and the distribution of the printed media was accelerated and spread by the railways, the auto truck, and the airplane.

The sound film is a twentieth-century development, blending photography, tough and transparent film, electric light and power, and the electronic reproduction of sound. Radio, since the third decade of the present century, and television since World War II, both of them dependent upon the vacuum tube, represent a great triumph of electro-technology and the social utilization of electronic discoveries and inventions.

The greater part of these extraordinary developments in the media of mass communication has come within the lifetime of a man of sixty; what is, in some respects, the most versatile as a medium—namely, television—has appeared and reached its tremendous stature within the lifetime of persons still in their upper teens. Thus, the contemporary upsurge of mass communication has been and is still geared to the recent "technological revolution."

3. The Setting: Mass Society

The societal setting for mass communication is "mass society"—which, in most of its structural forms and operational procedures, is also a very recent development—a product of the successive, interconnected technological and industrial revolutions. In a mass society, the people are assembled in large complexly structured aggregations, often widely dispersed in space. They carry on many diverse but interrelated tasks. Such a society is preponderantly industrialized and urbanized, and a high degree of division of labor and specialization of tasks prevails. The members of the society show great heterogeneity; they come from all walks of life and from all distinguishable social strata, and often demonstrate considerable ethnic variation; they have diversity of standards of living, social values and norms, power, influence and prestige. The people are separated by many forms of horizontal and vertical social distance. Most of the important *social* tasks are conducted by bureaucratic organizations. Related to this is the fact that many of the most important relationships of individuals are of a formal and external nature, focused within secondary as against primary groups, or as members of interdependent secondary groups, though primary groups not only survive but flourish. This increase of secondary relations means less of direct communication, as compared with the amount in the predominantly primary group life of a simpler society, less attachment to other human beings, a high degree of impersonality of relationship and of anonymity as persons, and in most cases a feeling of limited personal involvement in and responsibility for what goes on in the community. The interests that bind people closely to their fellows, other than their own family, are those of special groups; they are such as form the basis of occupational, recreational or religious groups, or the social-class cliques; but these latter interests take up only a limited, and sometimes a conflicting, part of the time, attention and loyalty of the individual. The wider social interests and concerns of people are pursued as members of unorganized or very loosely organized "mass publics," often without any defined leadership or program of action; these do not greatly facilitate concertedness of will and unity of action. In spite of these features, individuals, groups and organizations are more dependent upon each other for all kinds of products and services than was ever the case among the series of more independent self-sufficient groups and localized communities of the older society, with their more tenuous connections.[5]

The mass media of communication and the mass society are inextricably interconnected. The media are a characteristic feature—in considerable degree, one of the major contributory instrumentalities. They are not only essential to communication and consensus in a modern society, they are also the most efficient means yet found of conducting a considerable number of other indispensable social, societal and cultural operations of a functional nature, to be noted below. At the same time the media, in their technological and organizational forms, are an effect of modern sociocultural processes and trends.

4. *What the Mass Media Do to and for Language*

A matter of central importance in the present study is the effects upon language of these recent technological developments. Two aspects present themselves: the communicative effects, and the effects upon language as system.

a / Communicative effects. The different media have utilized the long-standing basic communicative forms of human gesture and speech, and pictography and writing, in ways heretofore unknown and impossible. They constitute the modern technological "extensions" of, and in some instances symbolic "substitutions" for, language. Each of the media creates its own peculiar variants of language; in fact, in a sense, each constitutes a sort of "special" language. Each major medium also has its special types of effects resulting from the forms of representation which it uses, singly or, in several instances, in combination.

Printed matter is based upon writing. As such it maintains all the amplifications, durabilities, and accuracies of writing, as compared with the purely spoken language. It has added to writing as a medium photographs, drawings, colored likenesses, charts, graphs, tables, and other illustrative and emphasis-producing devices, which enhance its expressive and informative power. Printing has also had a standardizing effect on writing, and thus also on the given language, since it created the possibility for—in fact, induced the development of—uniform texts, grammars and lexicons.

Before the advent of printing, communication was by voice and the laboriously produced manuscript (*hand* script). Both of these imposed limitations. At best a speaker could address only a few hundred at a time, and the writer only those to whom a letter or scroll could be circulated. With the mechanization of writing in the form of print came the possibility that communication could be endlessly duplicated.[6] The modern press was, in fact, "the original assembly line."[7] In general, printing gave writing and the copied manuscript a "broadcast" characteristic.

The proper comprehension of the printed text requires the ability to read, and this has historically, and to some extent even today, restricted its social utility. But technology has created illustrations, such as half-tone photographs, colored comics and drawings, which provide a kind of print that requires less reading ability. Seldes has pointed out that the lavish use of illustration not only has given print "a chance to attract people whose eyes would be constantly caught by the visual image," but also, as in the case of such large-circulation magazines as *Life* and *Look,* made it possible to "use visual effects to attract readers to reading matter of a relatively high intellectual order."[8]

Radio, to be sure, is confined to auditory communication, yet, for that very reason, it retains the special reinforcement that emotion and emphasis, expressed through vocal tone, cadence, inflection and style, can give to speech. The radio speaks "to you" and "to me," even if we are literate, more than the printed page does; it can at a given moment speak simultaneously to a billion or more of us, located in every nook and cranny of the world, regardless of whether we are literate or nonliterate.

Radio was the "pivot" on which the revolution in communications turned.[9] For the first time in history it brought news, ideas, entertainment—anything, in fact, that could be expressed by means of sound —to anyone, anywhere, at any time, who could listen by means of a receiving instrument so inexpensive as to be almost universally owned.

The motion picture reproduces the human voice and adds the visual communicative support of facial expression, gesture and posture, attendant upon face-to-face contact. It combines with this all sorts of other sounds and signs, including print, photographic reproduction of setting, persons and actions, and the use of color. Utilizing every basic communicative device, it transmits a fully perceptible, ready-made, auditory–visual message, that requires no imaginative improvisation or translation on the part of the receivers.

Television does much that the motion pictures do—but it does it, not for that rather limited number of people who attend motion picture theaters operating on set time schedules, but for that vast proportion of the population, each of whom has access during every waking moment to one of the millions upon millions of receiving sets. Television, in certain respects, synthesizes the other means of mass communication; it uses the recording of sound, the exact pictorial and graphic reproduction, and captures motion in film form. These it welds together.

Writing, as noted in the preceding chapter, added several important new dimensions and efficacies to speech as a means of social communication. Print greatly increased the range and power of writing. But the mass media developed during the present century have increased and extended the potencies of language in almost geometric ratio. They have stupendously augmented its social scope and range, and the versatility and forcefulness of its influence. All of this gives much greater auditory or visual impressionistic power. Printing, while a tremendous boon, rendered inaccessible the voices and faces of men. Radio, as already noted, restored the personal-voice element; by means of it, vocal communication has come to be almost unrestricted spatially. The movie and television have helped to recover gesture and facial awareness for mass communication. As combinations of auditory and visual media, they coordinate the auditory and visual senses as a team. Furthermore, radio, movie and TV do not need the discursive interruptions essential to print, nor do they require the sharper marshaling of attention upon the messages, as is the case for most people with respect to print. All three potentially give almost universal range to the personalism, the spontaneity and the freedom of the spoken idiom. Film and TV, with their use of visible representations and of color, take language beyond the limitations of "word pictures" and "word sketches"; by means of them, we obtain both an acoustical and a visual image. All the new media have each in their own way greatly increased the psychological and social potentialities and effects of language.

b / Linguistic effects. We have very little information about the effects of mass communication, especially radio and TV, upon the systemic components of language itself. It would seem that the mass media do not change phonology in general to any degree; but do they affect the phonation and articulation of certain portions of the population—for example, children or foreigners? Are there morphological and syntactic effects other than those that flow from the imitation of dialects or speech corruptions (by comics, those playing criminal and illiterate roles, and so on) in TV and radio programs, or those due to the personal grammatical eccentricities of popular broadcasters? There does not appear to be any noticeable departure from standard grammar in newscasting, information programs or public addresses. The news media do not in themselves seem to add to the lexicon, though mass communications have created many new words to identify and describe their mechanisms, techniques, personnel, the content and forms of messages, effects on audiences, and so on.[10] What are their effects, not only upon the persistence of dialects, but upon their very structural makeup? We do not have adequate scientific information on these points.

5. *Crucial Sociological Features of Mass Communication*

The structure of mass communication agencies, and certain inherent features of their operation are of great sociological significance in so far as these affect the nature of the messages, the processes of production and transmission, and the members of the mass society as recipients of the communications.

a / Conducted by profit-making social organizations for unorganized audiences. The sender of a mass communication, whether in a free or totalitarian society, is an organization, usually a large one. In our society the senders are a corporation publishing books or magazines, a press association, the local (regional) newspaper publishing company, a broadcasting network and hundreds of stations utilizing its services and sending forth its news collections, advertising, entertainment and other programs, as well as issuing such materials of local origin, a corporation producing motion pictures and distributing them and local theatres presenting the pictures.

Mass communication *has* to be conducted by an organization with huge capital resources in order to be able to marshal the large, highly diversified, specialized and often far-flung personnel, to provide and operate the expensive, extensive and complicated physical facilities and technological instruments and techniques. This organization is necessary to produce and market the product.

As business concerns, the mass media corporations survive by making a profit; they do this by selling services. The publishers of books must sell their products at a price that produces a profit, or they must go out of business. The movies charge admission. The daily and periodical press depend upon subscriptions and advertising—primarily the latter—for their income and profit. All "commercial" radio and television, as against radio and television programs sponsored and subsidized by institutions, particularly colleges and universities, depends entirely upon advertising. Hence, periodicals, radio and TV must serve their advertisers as well as serving the public, and the demands of business sometimes conflict with the demands of public service.

While the producers are organizations, the receivers or "targets" of the messages are individual persons, unknown to each other, separated from each other physically and socially. Of particular moment is the fact that in contrast to the senders, they are unorganized. Collectively, they constitute a conglomerate mass of heterogeneous elements.

b / A single similar message from a single source for immediate reception. The mass medium sends out a single, and always similar communication: a book, a monograph, a newspaper, a magazine, a motion picture, a radio or television feature or program. It is issued from a single organized source at a given time. It is not addressed to any one in particular, but to the public. Thus one, or a very few persons, participating as senders, speak or write directly—and in some instances incessantly—to many people, often amounting to millions. Their message is meant to reach this large audience in a relatively short time, perhaps even simultaneously; it is usually intended to be consumed immediately (it is not, that is, for permanent records).

c / Centralization and monopolization in the production of the communications. The organizational nature of the mass communication systems brings about a centralization of communications products, whether news or other information, propaganda, advertising, entertainment or formal educational interests. The reading, listening and viewing public sees and hears only what is offered. The sending agent, in the very nature of the operation, thus has some degree of monopoly over what is issued. Under democratic free-market conditions, the monopoly is in effect an allocation of privilege and permission acquired under competitive conditions; in totalitarian countries and in Britain, the monopoly is that of governmentally operated agents.

d / The ubiquity, incessancy and speed of the communications. Everywhere and everytime a radio or television is turned on, there is some sort of communication. The mass-circulation newspapers are published every day in up to half dozen editions. Every newsstand offers the newspapers, often including those from other towns and cities as well, and most settled residents of almost every community subscribe to and regularly receive their local or regional daily or weekly newspaper. There is a persistent and continuous flow of magazines, of pulps, comics, reprints, pocketbooks, and paperbacks. The media operate with great speed and momentum. They occupy more and more of the time and sometimes the attention of people over longer and longer periods every day, and impinge continuously upon almost every person. Modern men find it impossible to escape from the influence of these "ditto devices."[11] Because of them, "The average modern man is never alone."[12]

e / The huge volume of output and the massive impact. The potential influence of the mass media in the United States can be gleaned in some part from recent quantitative data regarding the production of their communications instrumentalities and their circulation or distribution among the public.[13] As of September 30, 1961 there were 1,761 English daily newspapers with a combined circulation of 59,261,464; 558 Sunday newspapers with a combined circulation of 48,216,499; as of March 30, 1962, 8,178 weekly newspapers with a paid circulation of 22,797,449. The total newspaper circulation amounts to 130,275,412. For 1958 (the last date given by the *Statistical Abstract*), there were 4,455 periodicals of all sorts published in the U.S., with a total circulation of 391,936,000. As of September 30, 1962, the seven leading popular magazines, each with a circulation in excess of six and a half millions, had a combined circulation of over 55 million. As to books, a total of 18,060 titles (not including comics) were published in 1961, which was 3,048 more than were issued in 1960. The number of new books in 1963 is given as 19,057. Of these 2,615 were paperbacks. Approximately one third of a billion paperbacks are sold annually—or nearly a million copies over the counter every business day. Close to a billion books are now being sold each year, twice as many as were sold fifteen years ago. As far back as 1950, some 700 million copies of comic books were printed per year.

In 1953, motion-picture attendance was about 2.1 billion, a decline from 3.3 billion in 1948; the industry has not issued attendance figures in recent years, though a recent estimate indicates a weekly attendance of around 45,000,000. Other data, however, are indicative of the status of the industry. In 1958 there were 12,291 motion picture theatres in the U.S., as compared with 14,716 in 1954. Though the total receipts declined from 2,071,000,000 dollars in 1960 to 1,551,000,000 dollars in 1962, the 1962 figure had been only twice exceeded in motion picture annals. It is also noteworthy that the 1960 receipts of more than two billion dollars by the motion picture industry exceeded the 1,970,-000,000 dollars received for *all other* amusement and recreation services in the U.S.

In 1962, there were one or more radio sets in 56,500,000 homes, as against 12,048,762 homes with radios in 1930. In 1962, the U.S. had a total of 176,600,000 radio sets, including secondary as well as primary sets in homes, sets in business places, institutions and automobiles, in contrast to a total of 13,000,000 such sets in 1930. In 1962, there were 56,300,000 TV sets in the U.S.; 90 per cent of all households had one set or more (92 per cent reported in April, 1964), with 13 per cent having two sets or more. It is reported that most TV sets are on five hours a day in the U.S., and that TV shows are played to 50,000,000 simultaneously. The total of 232,900,000 radio and TV sets in the U.S. can be compared with 198,900,000 sets in all of the rest of the world: Europe has the most with 105,000,000, and Africa the least with 8,500,000. In 1963, the U.S. had a total of 3,770 A. M. and 1,218 F. M. radio stations and 564 TV stations on the air, as compared with 936 radio stations in 1945.

f / Universality as well as diversification of appeal. Under the usual conditions of competition in our society, the mass media, in order to make a profit for their producing organizations, must receive the fullest possible reception for their products (whether these be books, magazines, motion pictures, or radio or TV programs). To gain this reception, they seek to make the widest possible appeal to the "public"—that is, as nearly as possible universal appeals in order to "catch" as many purchasers, subscribers, attenders, listeners, viewers as they can for their different kinds and qualities of products. Nearly all segments of the population are now the "targets" of the mass media, and nearly all of these are potential receivers of messages. Several centuries back the situation was quite different: only a selected aristocratic elite received broadcast messages because relatively few were literate, few could buy books, attend theatres, or travel to urban centers for information or entertainment.[14] Now, however, in advanced countries, the whole population is the consuming public, for nearly all can read, and as a result of their relatively high income status can buy such books as they please, subscribe to or purchase magazines, attend movies, as well as having access to all manner of radio and TV programs by means of their privately owned receiving appliances.

Repeated researches have shown, however, that the notion that the audience is an amorphous mass of disconnected and more or less identical individuals—a notion that was held by some during the early days of mass communications—is wholly erroneous. It is heterogeneous and diversified; it consists of many dissimilar population elements differing in interests, tastes and capacity for reception. More concretely, these elements vary as to sex, age, socioeconomic status, educational level, cultural sophistication, ethnicity, regional residence, political persuasion and other categorical group respects, as well as varying in *individual* attributes such as mental capacity and temperamental characteristics. Hence, the so-called receiving public is, in effect, many, many subpublics, even subcultures.

Actually, therefore, to "catch the greatest number" with their messages the mass communication media have to try to "tailor" something for all the numerous and diverse "everybodies"—for all of the most frequently and widely occurring cross-sections of the public.[15] This they do in considerable measure: there are books for the scholarly and for those seeking entertainment, and comics for the illiterates or those temporarily enjoying illiteracy; among the newspapers there are the *New York Times,* the *Christian Science Monitor,* or the *Wall Street Journal* for certain kinds of readers, and the tabloids for the illiterate or the lazy; among the magazines there is the *Reader's Digest* for one type of magazine public, the *U. S. News and World Report* for another, *Harper's,* the *Atlantic Monthly,* and *Saturday Review* for still another; finally, there is the infinite array of sex, snappy story, outdoors, adventure, and other journals, for all sorts of other categories of readers. Radio and TV provide "Meet the Press" for the more thoughtful, "soap-operas" during the day for the stay-at-home women, special features for children and juveniles around dinner time, programs that appeal to the aged, to investors, to farmers, and so on. Attention need only be called to the different kinds and levels of motion pictures for the various levels of customers.

It should also be noted that, in order to make the maximum appeal to the maximum number, the mass media provide diversity of appeal for given categories of people at different times and occasions. People do not want "meat and potatoes" all the time. The professional man, for example, at different times of his working day can avail himself of the domestic and foreign news, market reports, sports and outdoor information, a wide gamut of entertainment features, and political materials.

In general, the universality of appeal of the mass media consists in the fact that they are trying to make all sorts of appeals, for all sorts of people, reading, listening or looking, under all sorts of circumstances and at different times and occasions.

g / Potentiality of social control by means of the media. In the light of the centrality and monopoly of production, as well as of the ubiquity and universality of communications, the persons, groups or organizations controlling the preparation and transmission of mass communications have great *possibilities* of determining what shall be disseminated via the mass media, and thus of influencing the beliefs, providing ideas and viewpoints, molding the opinions and suggesting and directing the behavior, of the millions exposed to these communications. Potentially, the media are also weapons for all kinds of social "causes" and movements. However, a variety of circumstances affect the reception, and an enormous number of intervening variables affect the exposure and responses of the different kinds of people constituting the public. Hence, control of the mass media creates no guarantee of social control (another notion held by some in the early days of mass communication), but rather, as indicated, a potentiality for it. A continuous bombardment does have some effect.

h / One-way communication and indirect feedback. A final crucial condition has to do with the high degree of non-participation of the recipients, the targets, in mass communication. The issuance of a message by way of mass communications is not an expression of interest or creativeness spontaneously occurring among two or more individuals, nor does its transmission take place by chance or in random fashion. The message is consciously designed and produced for chosen purposes, and is transmitted to the consumer through established, organizationally controlled channels; in fact, it may be said to make a "channeled" impact on the target. The transmitting agent, as we have seen, has a single, centralized or monopolized control of the message; the recipients are members of "mass audiences." Hence, there is little or no interaction or exchange of experience between them; they exist as discrete and depersonalized elements of their respective masses. Insofar as they participate, they do so only as spectators.

Communication by means of the mass media, therefore, is not the two-way, three-way, or many-way interaction of the dyad, triad, or larger group of face-to-face associates; it is largely *one-way*—that is, only *from* the sending organization *to* the separate atoms of the mass.

Face-to-face communication is directly and immediately reciprocal as between receiver and sender. It permits "completely symmetrical"[16] feedback—that is, a free-flow reaction or response or "comeback" from the receiver back to the sender. The feedback indicates to the communicator who is listening and who is understanding the message, how the listener is reacting to it.

The recipients in the mass media situation cannot "talk back" directly and immediately; thus they "have to take it," and perhaps become "bottled up" inside. If displeased with the controversial message, about all that most of them can do is to "turn it off."

If there is any feedback in mass communications, it comes with a time lag and in a more or less roundabout manner. It takes such forms as "letters to the editor," telephone calls to radio or TV stations, groundswell reactions in the way of increase or decrease of newspaper and magazine subscriptions when these have taken a stand on controversial issues, increased or decreased listening to or viewing of programs, the increased or decreased purchase of products produced by firms sponsoring and supporting particular programs by their advertising—or other such evidences of increased utilization or patronage on the one hand, or disuse or avoidance on the other. One might also refer here to acceptance of or failure to respond to propagandist and other persuasive efforts, actions of special interest groups, telephone and other polls of listeners of given radio and TV programs, and especially voting, with regard to some messages and issues.

6. *The General Social Functions Performed by Mass Communication*

The *raison d'être* of mass communications in modern society—the reason why they flourish and expand as they do—is the fact that, as they have developed, they have come to be the primary media through which certain very important functions are carried on. Moreover, they have added certain special features and refinements of communicative performance, as they conduct these functions.[17] The most important ones, very briefly presented, are as follows:

a / The provision of public information. This includes: (1) the collection and presentation of information concerning events in the environment, outside as well as inside the given society (the news reporting function); (2) the selection for special comment, evaluation and interpretation of the news and, in some instances, the prescribing of attitudes and action (the editorial function); (3) the distribution of this selected and interpreted information. Concretely, these functions are conducted in greater or lesser measure by the newspapers, weekly news magazines, newsreels of the movies, as well as by radio and TV newscasters and commentators. There are still, of course, "word of mouth" ways of providing some public information.

The mass media, however, are of great importance in providing the citizenry with a flow and vast range of knowledge regarding the world they live in; in furnishing to the people collectively the materials for the formation of public opinion; and in enabling institutional organizations of all categories, but especially governments, to conduct their affairs.

b / Providing publicity for norm violation. Because of their informational function, the mass media are of key importance in conducting the publicity function, which, in turn, is central in the enforcement of social norms. The mass media, by their reporting and treatment, expose and make publicly known social conditions and persons and groups whose actions are at variance with the values and norms held by the majority. The newspapers, journals, radio and TV bring fairly well-known deviations to public view and, as a rule, this exposure leads to some degree of public action against those diverging from the norms, and some reaffirmation of the norms. Exposure activities of the media may actually result in the organization of a crusade.

c / Assisting industry and commerce. This consists mainly of the advertising function—that is, the use mainly of purchased space of printed media, and purchased radio and television time, by commercial and industrial establishments to inform the public of the merits of their products (materials or services) and to solicit their custom. The pertinence of this function is demonstrated by the way the public diminishes its purchases when advertising is reduced by a newspaper shutdown because of a strike.

d / Providing entertainment, amusement and recreation. This function
is to create relaxation, laughter and respite from duties, to provide
enjoyment and enable people to forget their worries, to fill idle time and
to offer an escape from boredom. The comics, novels and plays, operas,
concerts, "soap operas," "Westerns," sportscasts, and so on, presented
by means of printed matter, motion pictures, radio and TV, fulfill this
function, which doubtless occupies more of the time and attention of a
great proportion of the mass communications audience than any of the
others.

Two other general functions—namely, those involving persuasion,
indoctrination and social control and informal and formal education
have such widespread significance in the contemporary world from
the sociological point of view that they will be examined below in
separate discussions.

These social functions affect the kind of messages constructed, and
the conditions under which, as well as the manner in which, they are
transmitted. These functions have certain sociologically significant
effects, which we shall briefly examine in the paragraphs that
follow.

7. *Some Social and Social-Psychological Effects*

Much that is of importance in the lives of members of modern
societies is obtained *only* through the mass media involved in the "communications revolution"; there is no other source. Much else, that was
formerly derived through other ways and means, is now provided by the
media. Moreover, as noted above, they repeatedly impinge upon almost
every member of society every day, as they provide most of the information, diversion, regulation and propaganda they receive. Hence, the
mass media are bound to have some individual, social and social-
psychological effects. We know that they do, from common observation
and from a considerable amount of research bearing upon the subject.
Some of these effects may be merely minor modifications of the effects
of older communicative devices and techniques; others are likely to be
distinctively new—directly correlated with the peculiar forms of functioning of the new media.

The *specific* nature and the *certain* portent of these effects are, however, a somewhat controversial matter today among the students of
mass communications, in contrast to the patterned conceptions of a

quarter of a century ago. While communications research is achieving a considerable degree of uniformity of conclusions on certain problems, the study of effects is still somewhat inconclusive. This is due, in part, to the multiplicity and complexity of the factors involved in each situation in which effects are to be determined. The messages themselves are different in nature and purpose. The intended targets—the individuals—differ in their attitudes, interests, values and prejudices, and also vary from time to time in their conditions of attention, susceptibility, comprehension, favorable or unfavorable reception and motivation. In our society, we have such a variety of constituent groups —occupational and economic, racial and ethnic, religious, and so on— that the mass media are hard put to it to provide common appeals to the members of very many of them. The particular *social* circumstances under which each given instance of transmission–reception occurs is also a factor of moment. The influence of the media also occurs simultaneously with many other influences acting upon the recipients, such as those of the family, of their social class and of friendship or work groups. Hence, even where effect is fairly certain, the medium (or media) cannot be looked upon as the sole cause of the effect, but only as a contributory agent. All these variables must be assessed in combination.

The situation is also due in part to the difficulties of accurately assessing what we *do* know about the effects. Hence, all of our working knowledge regarding the effects is still somewhat tentative. Therefore we should be wary about stating conclusions. Even where the generalizations rest on rather wide consensus to date, they still await—in fact, invite—further investigation.[18]

In our examination we will treat some of the accepted, sociologically significant effects as positive or negative—that is, as in the main contributing to social efficacy or inefficacy.

a / Positive effects.

[1] *A major factor in socialization.* By socialization is meant the congeries of processes whereby the inhabitants of a societal area are subjected continuously, both deliberately and inadvertently, to a host of social influences, pressures and controls, which impart to them the culture of the society and develop them into associates and participants, capable of functioning tolerably well. The major agents in socialization have been, and probably still are, the family, the school and the peer groups. While these are by no means inoperative in modern societies, their influence has been vastly supplemented by the mass media; in fact,

the very sources of non-media influence are themselves exposed to and affected by the mass media. The actuality of this effect is brought into focus by Klapper's suggestion that we "can perform the mental experiment of imagining the process of socialization occurring in a society in which mass media did not exist." Primitive societies had none.[19]

One need only contemplate, as an example of potential effect, the modern teenager exposed to books, including comic books, teenage magazines, newspaper columns, motion pictures, radio and TV programs —all of which provide him with facts, values, tastes, conventions and traditions, and give him cues with regard to all sorts of personal models.

It is also a matter of significance to note that many of the mass communication messages play upon the recipients at times when they are more or less relaxed. The fact that the recipients are unaware of the media as socializing agents, and that their influence is mainly inadvertent, rather than deliberately and consciously didactic, also may enhance their effectiveness.

The fact that the mass communications media affect socialization is undeniable; they play a weighty and possibly an ever increasing part in giving moderns their social and cultural materials for their action in their world. But we still seek answers to such questions as these: Do the impersonal mass media have different effects, as compared with the long-standing sources of socialization (family, and so on)? What is the qualitative normative effect upon the minds, emotions and actions of those exposed to such influences as comics and comic books, crime and violence movies, radio and TV programs, soap operas, puerile advertisements? Do the mass media have different kinds of degrees of socializing effect upon different social levels, different age groups, different educational levels? Do the mass media reinforce the socializing efforts of family and school, or do they weaken and dilute them?

[2] *The extension of culture contacts of and the presentation of "new worlds" to the average man.* A large part of the "picture of the world" held by most of the people in modern societies has come, and still comes, through mass communications. The printing press, by way of the readily transportable book, the newspaper, the bulletin, the periodical, brought the entire world, past and present, to everyone who could read. Today, the movies, radio and TV provide these culture boons to all who can see and hear. The mass media, as they blanket the entire country with their vast volume and diversity of materials, make possible the extension of the viewpoints, insights, interests and conceptions of the common man to a degree unthinkable a half century ago. They have also increased the volume and lifted the level of in-

formation and opinion available to him and his fellows almost everywhere. In fact, he can hardly avoid an expansion of his social and
cultural horizons and the development of worldwide perspectives.

The movies, radio and TV have not only extended the power of
vocal language in all its forms, but are also presenting in vocal form
materials that first appeared in written form—such as novels, plays,
historical incidents and biographies. These have been brought to millions who were not (and are not now) habitual readers.

In general, this means "the enlargement of the spheres of experience
for the average man; indeed, he has an almost limitless variety of 'worlds'
in which to participate, even if only as an interested wish-fulfilling spectator."[20]

[3] *The uniformation and unification of people.* There is a great
likelihood that the mass communications media have some uniformizing
and unifying effect, and this in spite of the fact that, as we have seen,
mass communications audiences consist largely of isolated individuals
and of many special-interest subaudiences. As the result of the single
and uniform messages received simultaneously by millions of recipients,
there is, unavoidably, a new kind of sharing of experience. These
millions can be stirred by the same newsreel, news report, informational program or political speech or debate; they can listen to the
same jokes; they can have the thrill of listening to the launching of a
nation's astronaut into outer space, or can hear and see the President
as he addresses the nation; on occasion, they can suffer the impact
of a joint disaster or sorrow. All this they do together. This seems
to have the effect of interrelating, even merging, the people, at least in
some situations, or in connection with some issues.

The mass media also provide the isolated and separated individuals
and groups with a means of impersonal communication with each
other, at least to the extent of furnishing them with ready and continuous information about each other. Related to this is the fact that
they are the means whereby these discrete social elements acquire
items for opinion about each other, and a roundabout means of
general consensus among and with each other. There is evidence also
that some of the media—for example, certain "light" ones, such as
comic strips, heart-throb and joke columns—serve certain audience
members by providing a common ground for social discourse.

The mass media aid in passing on the common culture to all—
children and adults—and hence tend to unify the society by giving
its members a broader base of common values, norms and collective
ways of acting. They also seem to have the over-all effect of tending
to standardize tastes, attitudes, feelings and thoughts among the mil-

lions in many situations, and thus contributing to uniformity of action. In summary, they can be thought of as a "means through which the sense of membership in a collectivity is created."[21]

Closely related to uniformation and unification is the fact that the mass media have brought about some restoration of "tribalism."[22] This new tribalism is especially bound up with the electronic media, radio and TV. Printed matter, particularly in the form of books and journal articles, to some extent separates people, and often encourages, even invites, individualistic reactions. Print has been "de-tribalizing" in its effect. To be sure, the newspapers and the mass weeklies have changed this somewhat and, as literacy increases, very many read the same printed matter at the same time. But with radio and TV has come the simultaneous sharing of new information regarding persons and events and of new experiences, by almost the entire population. Everything happens to everyone at the same time; almost everybody knows about it, and therefore, to some extent is part of everything that is happening the minute it happens. The effect of this is somewhat similar to the face-to-face vocal message received in concert by the people of the primitive village. It creates a village or tribal outlook among the recipients–participants, potentially on a global scale.

[4] *Greater and wider cohesiveness.* It is possible that modern mass societies, as a consequence of the binding by mass communications, may have a greater social cohesiveness than older societies. The older society, as Green has pointed out, "was actually a series of localized societies formally held together by a loose political federation and several small overlapping trade areas."[23] Each locality had only tenuous connections with individuals and groups outside a narrow geographic radius. Today, thanks in large part to mass communications, there are no limits to the area of attention, interest and concern, and increasingly of involvement and participation.

b / Negative effects. There is an array of closely interrelated negative effects of the mass media.

[1] *Collectivizing, stereotyping and canalizing of attitudes and conduct.* There seems to be a distinct likelihood that the uniformation upon which unification rests is sometimes of dubious value. The repetitiveness and selfsameness of the messages, and the ubiquity and incessancy of their impact, create the wide uniformation indicated. This uniformation in turn, however, in very many cases among the countless individuals influenced by the media, induces mental and social behavior that is collectivized and stereotyped—in some cases,

even automatized. The process can be referred to as "herd" uniformizing. This militates against the conduct so essential to a progressive society: conduct that is individualistic, imaginative, reflecting personal originality, uniqueness, creativeness and richness—conduct that is socially and culturally beyond that of the human "herd." A good many voices with socially useful messages are silenced.

The highly standardized view of culture that comes about as the result of the repetitiveness and stereotyped nature of messages may also bring about a definite loss of subcultural variety and creativity.

Closely related is the tendency of some of the most massive and widely-received messages to make for a canalizing of pre-existent attitudes. Advertising, which plays such an important part in mass communications as the means of financing them, and is therefore the continual accompaniment of the messages as delivered, is typically directed toward the canalizing of pre-existing behavior patterns and attitudes. It seldom seeks to instill utterly new values or attitudes, or to create markedly different behavior patterns.[24] The recipients would hesitate to bridge a wide gap between the new and that to which they were attuned. Hence, the unavoidable or even the voluntarily embraced next step is only in some (possibly conspicuous, but nevertheless superficial) respects different from the last step: simply a switch from one brand of razor blade or automobile or coffee or bread to another.

In general, since the mass media are supported by great business concerns, which are geared to the current social and economic system, the media contribute to the maintenance of that system. But this maintenance must be flexible and sensitive to timely change. There is a feeling on the part of some that economic interest groups are using the mass media to promote a largely unthinking allegiance to our society just as it is, and to insure public conformity to the social and economic status quo.[25]

[2] *Atomizing of social relationships.* By no means contradictory or inconsistent with the effect just discussed is the atomizing effect, which often occurs concurrently with the feeling of unification. This is the result of the fact that most messages are not received in assemblies, but by single individuals, dyads, triads or very small groupings. If the reception does take place in larger groupings, the relations are usually entirely impersonal, and those so related have a feeling of social space among themselves. The recipients of the mass messages in many instances feel isolated and alone, feel the human void about them and are in some ways socially adrift and psychically anomic.

[3] *Passivity, apathy, inarticulateness and "narcotizing" of many of the recipients.* The average person feels that he has little or no control over the messages he receives. He also fears sometimes that some of the intent of the media is to manipulate him—certainly by means of advertising, and occasionally by some types of agencies with respect to some controversial issues.

Moreover, he receives the messages as a member of huge audiences. As such, he feels his insignificance as a tiny unit in a huge mass, and concludes that any public response he might make would be futile. Finally, the fact that mass communication is largely one-way discourages response, especially the desire to "talk back." These situations lead to the passivity, apathy and inarticulateness of the people, especially the "little people" of modern societies.

It is also contended with some point that the herdlike uniformizing and the stress upon conformity to the status quo weaken the audience's capacity for critical thinking or, at any rate, discourages the exercise of critical and creative thought.

Furthermore, while the outpourings of the media enable the modern person to keep abreast of the world, it is suggested that this vast supply of communication may overwhelm many recipients and elicit only a superficial concern with the problems of the world—a superficiality which may cloak mass apathy. "Exposure to the flood of information may serve to narcotize rather than to energize the average reader or listener."[26]

Even the interested and informed citizen obtains so much of his world of social reality through these secondary contacts, that he is in danger of making his reading, viewing and listening, and his thinking about what he reads, views and hears, a "vicarious performance." In general, "quite apart from intent, increasing dosages of mass communications may be inadvertently transforming the energies of men from active participation into passive knowledge."

[4] *Effect upon the taste, morals and behavior of some population elements.* There is some point to the accusation that some of the media, to make the widest possible appeal, gear some of their productions to the level of taste and comprehension of the "greatest number" of those who might possibly be exposed to that type of production. This applies to the mass circulation journals, to some movies and, in large measure, to those radio and TV programs that are intended to divert and entertain the public or a sizable segment of it. Since this level is not high the practice may conduce to a deterioration of aesthetic tastes and popular cultural standards.

In the opinion of some observers, the mass media tend to reduce the likelihood of achieving certain social ends highly prized by those interested in human well-being and progress. They contend that, instead of using his leisure time constructively, the modern man uses it to "read" comic books, view "Westerns," comedy and variety shows on TV, listen to vapid music on the radio, observe crime and horror movies and TV shows.

8. *The Significance of the Audience in Mass Communication*

The mass media are not ends in themselves. They communicate messages to the public—which consists of audiences and subaudiences. It is important, therefore, to be aware of the significance of the audience structure, of the place and effectiveness of the different kinds of mass communication "languages" among the different subaudiences, and of the differential reception of the different kinds of messages—that is, the selectivity tendencies of subaudiences with respect to the message content.

a / The structural context of the audience members. As pointed out above, the mass communications audience is differentiated demographically as to sex and ages, and ecologically as to urban or rural residence and region; its members belong to many kinds of groups (bureaucratic, religious, occupational, political, and so on), have different social positions and roles, engage in or are related through family to different modes of production (for example, mechanical industry, commerce, agriculture), vary as to power, position, ethnic affiliation, social class, wealth and income level, educational and cultural level, and ideological orientation, to mention only the more obvious.

b / The differential effect of the different kinds of mass communications "languages." Printed matter, of course, appeals only to those who can read, and in our society illiteracy is almost negligible. But there are many different levels of intellectual capacity, comprehension and sophistication among those who have reading ability, and there are corresponding grades of reading matter. Radio, potentially, is for all who are without serious aural defects and who listen irrespective of state of literacy or age. The movies and TV potentially appeal to all who can see and hear; hence those excluded from their influence are very few. Of these various media, TV, because of its versatility, can have the most universal audience; its different characteristics complement each other in producing volume, variety and richness of appeal.

Another aspect of considerable consequence for the form of the messages is the fact that radio, TV and the movies have "spectator" audiences which need only to watch and to listen. The effective consumption of printed matter, on the other hand, requires some cerebration and some "translation" of printed words and phrases into experiential images.

While the nature of the "language" of the medium affects in varying degree the message that is received by the public, the variations in the physiological and physical ability to receive it are rather negligible. Yet there is great differentiation in reception. This must be attributed to the fact that: (1) the public consists of many subaudiences, as already noted, (2) the producers provide a wide variety of content in their messages, corresponding somewhat roughly to the major categories of subaudiences, and (3) the subaudiences exercise selectivity in what they read, listen to and view. A purely physical factor, which affects volume of reception in a major way, and variety to a lesser degree, is the accessibility of the messages of the media to the people—a factor already mentioned in another connection above. People have to go to movies, to libraries or stores for books and journals, but they have radio or TV programs in their homes as well as other places (hotel lobbies, taverns, and so on) where they commonly assemble. Hence the effort necessarily exerted by readers of print focuses their selectivity; radio and TV receivers "take it or leave it" on the spot.

c / The differential interests of the subaudiences. A more or less complete inventory of subaudience interests and preferences would require a corresponding inventory of the numerous subaudiences and sub-subaudiences; this has not yet been done. We do have some information, however, with regard to somewhat typical interests of the more common subaudiences. Several samples follow. As the level of formal education declines, so does the quality of what is read. College-educated people read the more serious and intellectually and culturally sophisticated books and journals, and the more "solid" newspapers. The farther down one goes on the educational ladder, the more innocuous becomes what is read or (in the case of comics and some tabloids) "viewed."[27] People at the lower income and educational levels also seem to be unwilling to listen to serious radio and TV broadcasts.

More movie fans are found among the young people and single

people. In general, with increasing age, moviegoing becomes more and more an effort. Single folks are less likely to have "homes" as compared with married folks, and married folks are more likely to have books, magazines, radio and TV programs come into the home. However, the subject matter and culture level of the film is also of great importance in attracting different categories of patrons.

The sexes differ in some interests and respond differently to given kinds of programs or messages. This is true of their reading as well as their listening and viewing habits. Men, in the main, are more interested in current events, public affairs, sports and fiction tales of adventure; women prefer love stories, soap operas, society news. In America young people are much less interested in politics than are older people. American farmers seem to be more interested in serious subject matter than industrial workers.

d / The high degree of selectivity exercised by the subaudience. The public's reaction to mass communications is neither automatic nor unquestioningly receptive. It (the public) does not consist of a group of puppets who "swallow it all." The impact of most of the messages is seldom universal, nor are the messages received by all with uniformity of attention, perception, interest, understanding or behavioral response. Because the communications public consists of many different subaudiences, most of the messages are received with a high degree of selectivity. Given individuals, and particular categories of persons, will read or view or listen to what they are interested in and what they agree with, and ignore or avoid what they are not interested in or capable of being interested in, or what is not congenial with their prior attitudes, habits, beliefs and ideas. What they cannot avoid in the incompatible messages, they "let go in one ear and out the other."[28]

9. *The Mass Media and Social Control*

Mass communications, as we have seen, are positive factors in the socialization and unification of peoples. Closely related is the effect mass media have on the persuasion, indoctrination and other forms of social control of people. It is generally accepted as a scientifically established fact that whatever a person receives in a communications transaction has *some* kind and degree of influence upon him. In the case of the mass media, as a result of the ubiquity of their messages and the in-

cessancy of their impact, they are bound to have some sort of effect—
direct or indirect, positive or negative—on the exposed and always more
or less susceptible human recipients. The continuous and widespread use
of them by astute manipulators—personal and organizational—in order
to influence and control people in the name of different kinds of objectives attests to the fact that they do have utility in this regard.

The "control transaction," however, is a many-faceted affair. This,
too, is an area of controversy as to specific and universally applicable
types of effects. It must be recalled that it is not the media that exercise whatever social control takes place; they are merely instruments,
and all instruments are neutral as to effects. The control effects depend
upon: (1) how they are used, by whom, for what purposes, with what
messages, under what conditions, and (2) how the messages are received, by whom, on the bases of what content and purposes and under
what conditions. The circumstances under which the different kinds of
purposive communication exchanges take place are variable as to kind,
combination and complexity. Some of the fears of a quarter of a century ago have been demonstrated to have been without foundation; there
certainly is no mass, non-discriminatory acceptance of the messages,
especially those suspected of being issued for influence or control purposes, and there is no general or automatic pattern of dominance–
submission. Furthermore, while mass communication is one of our
major industries, it is also one of our newer ones, involving in its operations subtle social and psychological processes, with effects still un-
plumbed. Hence there may be a gap between intention and result, with
unanticipated and unwanted consequences flowing from the content *and*
the techniques of the media.

There is also an obverse aspect. In view of the fact that the media,
as used, *do* control people, the effects of that control are important;
hence there is, in turn, some variously originated and executed social
control of the media themselves.

a / The potentialities of social control by the mass media. The potentiality of social control exercised by the mass media depends upon a
variety of conditions, the most important being: (1) the *totalitarian or
democratic organization of the society* in which they operate, which in
turn determines the authoritarian style of state, or democratic style of
private (or semi-public) ownership and operation; (2) under more
democratic conditions, the kind and degree of *organization* developed
by the organizations of the media areas and imposed upon themselves;
(3) the kind and degree of *regulation* exercised over the agencies by

government, by their own controlling monopolistic organizations, and by spontaneously expressed public opinion, as the public reacts to the products of the media.

In a totalitarian society, the state owns and operates all of the media, and the state, or the dictator and his party or clique, have concentrated, direct, planned and uncontested control over all kinds of messages. The values, norms, purposes and "essential" facts expressed are "official," and all "settled" for the people. The messages, regardless of the department of social life to which they apply—economic, political, recreational, aesthetic—are all strained through the same ideological sieve, and issued deliberately for several central purposes—namely, to maintain the single social philosophy deemed conducive to the survival and prosperity of the dictatorship, to promote and enforce the ways of life advocated by the regime, and to denounce or forbid contrary behavior. Access to the media is closed to all those who oppose the official ideology and program. By censorship, the dictators seek to control all ideas and information that might impair their monolithic control over the state and the people.

Where democratic conditions prevail, the ownership and the condition and objectives of operation are different. In our democracy, neither the state nor the semi-public organizations that conduct the mass media have monopolistic control of the organs or messages of mass communication. The organizations operating *within* the area of a medium (newspaper publishers and chains, journals, motion picture theatres and chains, radio and TV stations and chains) compete with each other; the media themselves compete with each other to some extent (for example, newspapers and journals with radio and TV, motion pictures with TV).

Nevertheless, there is a concentration of control of the media. In the field of the newspapers, we have only two major news collecting agencies, the Associated Press and the United Press International; the United Press, and what was formerly the third agency—the International News Service—merged. In recent times, there has also been the tendency toward the formation of newspaper chains, the elimination of all except one daily in many of the smaller and medium-sized cities, and the combination of two papers under one publisher, often appearing as, respectively, morning and evening papers. As a matter of fact, the publishing of two or more competitive papers exists in the main only in the large cities. At present, there are five major motion picture corporations concerned with production and distribution. In 1961, the 4,399 TV stations were combined for most of their functions into three networks, and the 3,654 radio stations into four. It should be noted that three of the networks controlled both radio and television operations (American Broadcasting Corporation, Columbia Broadcasting System, National Broadcasting Corporation, and Mutual Broadcasting System being confined to radio only).

Whether or not this very considerable concentration of organizational control actually results in appreciable control of the audience depends largely upon the *way* the audience reacts to the output.

b / The users and controllers of mass communications. Those who will seek to use the mass media for control purposes are mainly those who are engaged in some sort of promotional activity, the objective of which is the exercise of power—power over people, so that they will think or believe in a certain way—politically, economically, religiously; so that they will buy some things in preference to others, vote a certain way, or commit themselves to and exert themselves in behalf of some enterprise, possibly some social reform. There is no doubt that mass communication is a potential *source* of power for any promotional group, *if* it can utilize the media.

Unlike the totalitarian societies, where, as we have just noted, the state owns and operates the mass media for its own ends, in our society the media are privately owned and operated. Their use for any function, including that for promotional or other control purposes, must be "purchased" from the agencies.

These "purchasers" are vested interests of one sort or another: propagandists for all sorts of causes, political candidates and parties, commercial and industrial organizations advertising their products or attempting favorably to influence the public (for example, the National Association of Manufacturers), religious personalities and groups and other protagonists.

The media, especially newspapers, journals, radio and TV, are able to conduct all of their social functions (noted in Sect. 6 above) by having the printed space or radio or TV time purchased, either by direct payment by the individuals or organizations involved, or, as is the fact in the great majority of the cases in our American system, by having the newspaper or journal as a whole supported mainly by advertising, and having the radio and TV productions sponsored and paid for by advertising conducted on behalf of mainly commercial and industrial organizations, and also, to some extent, by organizations with other objectives. Thus, the predominant situation is that, except for movies and books, it is not the magazine reader, nor the radio listener, nor the TV viewer, nor in large part the purchaser of or subscriber to a newspaper, who financially supports the communications enterprise; it is the advertiser. Thus, in effect, business (usually "big business") finances the operation of the mass media, and the production and distribution of the large proportion of their messages.

The specific promotional aids purchased—the newspaper and magazine advertisements, the radio and TV commercials—promote certain categories of values and goals, social preferences, motives, conformities; they create an "atmosphere" with social-psychological, ethical, aesthetic and social "pressures," in which every individual affected by the media is immersed. However, the manner and degree to which people are affected varies from person to person.

Concern is sometimes expressed with regard to a related potentiality. It is contended that, because of the tendency toward concentration of organization on the part of producers of mass communications, through press asociations, radio and TV networks, or motion picture combines, there is the *possibility* of imbalance on controversial public issues. The possible intentional or unintentional withholding, distortion, over-emphasis, special selection or other manipulation of information, viewpoints and interpretations—especially those of minority or other specific groups—could result in a sort of unofficial censorship. If this were done on behalf of some particular social class, race, ideological group, political party, economic segment or organization, or social movement, it would be a violation of the principles of freedom and fairness of expression of a democratic society. The fact, however, that the media as organizations and industries are not entirely identical in the social philosophies they maintain, and are in competition with each other at all levels, precludes the likelihood of such control existing, to any considerable degree.

c / The "audience factor" in the control effects. Do the potential controllers, however, actually have the extensive and massive control it was thought they had in the early days of mass communications? The one-way nature of the communications transaction, the "space" between sender and receiver, the heterogeneity of the public as audience, the multiplicity of the subaudiences, the very considerable degree of selective choice of types of messages exercised by the diverse recipients, point to the fact that almost no messages, whether issued with control intention or not, receive universal attention or have a general public-control effect. Whether or not the recipients are influenced, persuaded, or motivated, or their reactions otherwise controlled depends upon a number of factors in addition to those already noted above.

[1] *There is first of all the "personal equation" of the recipients.*

The individual recipient does not simply hear and see "what is there," and let it freely permeate his consciousness, to determine his views and values and actions. Because of mental deficiency on the one hand, or exceptional mentality on the other, or because of peculiar emotional dispositions or deep grooving of interests, beliefs and prejudices, the individual may be more or less immune to certain types of messages. Not infrequently there is misunderstanding or misinterpreting of the content and intent of the message, or some portion of it, simply because it does not conform to his knowledge or taste or prejudice or convictions. The recipient may actually reverse the intended meaning, and receive the very opposite impression from the one intended.

For certain people, or even certain categories of people, the very suspicion that the communication is being used to control, limit or direct their beliefs and actions produces in them an antagonistic attitude toward the presumed controllers and their messages; or they may be violently opposed to or prejudiced against some article advertised, idea or ideology advanced, stand to be taken or action proposed, and stubbornly resist and, if possible, reject the appeal. The effect of the resistance and rejection is often to underscore further their existing viewpoints, prejudices, beliefs or convictions. In other cases, the recipient may pay special heed to those messages or parts of messages which seem to reinforce his own point of view, fit in with his likes and dislikes or organize materials already in his mind.

Thus there is much selective perception and interpretation on purely personal grounds, often in ways unanticipated by the advertiser, campaigner, propagandist or official.

[2] *The one-way nature of the mass communications situation directly affects its actual control effect.* The one-way feature is disadvantageous in the sense that it prevents immediate and direct personal or group "comeback" or "feedback"; but in the case of the possible control effects, there is some advantage for the "persons-as-targets." They are anonymous as far as the powerful or authoritative sender is concerned. There is "safe" physical and social-psychological "space" between producer and receiver. The receivers are in a position to "take it" if they so wish, or to derisively comment "Oh, yeah?" and "leave it" or "turn it off" without penalty. Because of this factor, the recipients, even in dictatorships, can exercise selectivity in their acceptance of messages, although they also have to exercise careful restraint in their overt expressions of response, especially if those responses are not in conformity with the intent of the dictator–sender. This "space" makes possible much ignoring of or opposition to "official" messages in totalitarian

states, that is, to the extent the targets think they can "get away with it." In general, whenever the situation permits, persons read certain materials or listen to or view certain broadcasts, and *not* others; they listen to and view what they *want to* hear and see. Republicans will usually turn to Republican speeches and read Republican newspapers, and Democrats show a similar preference for the propaganda output of their own party; people interested in refrigerators will respond to refrigerator advertisements; Catholics are more likely to avoid birth control propaganda than Protestants. Each issue has its own public.

While people select what they want or what is compatible with their existent views and prejudices, they also show no reluctance in the case of most kinds of issues to disagree with the information or propaganda if it contradicts their own opinions or observations.

[3] *The control that is exercised is in the bulk of the cases along already established lines.* In the light of the preceding factors—and supported by the research findings—it seems to be pretty well agreed that the persuasive efforts of the mass communicators do not greatly change most of the prevailing opinions very much. The most typical effect is reinforcement of existing opinions or beliefs, that is, support for the previously established position of the recipients, or at least, a constancy of the line and direction of opinion. The next most common effect is to bring about some minor change, as in the intensity of some opinion. The rarest effect is bringing about a conversion.[29] The evidence seems to point to the fact that the mass media have done very little changing of basic attitudes and values; their main effect in this respect has been a canalization of them, and not a reshaping.

In practice, therefore, the most successful "control" in the case of advertising or political campaigning or social reforming is to urge the people to do what they already want to do, to try to direct into a particular channel action that the people were rather certain to take anyhow in some form or degree.

[4] *The audiences do some controlling of the media.* At any given moment the recipients of mass communications messages have only what is offered and this influences them in one way or another; it conditions them to *some* degree, and contributes in most individual cases to *certain* (often unanticipated) kinds of valuational, attitudinal and behavioral patterns. But the current messages do not have an absolute, sole or final effect. The recipients are products of lifelong sociocultural conditioning, during the course of which the various groups to which they belong and the subcultures they exemplify have played a weighty part. The recipients resolve themselves, as we have seen, into subaudiences with respect to mass communications reception; as such, they exercise a high

degree of selectivity in what they accept from what is offered. This in turn leads to the important fact, well supported by research, that what they get over a period of time is largely what they, the patrons, support; hence, what is offered is largely what they seem to want and will like.[30] None of the media can ignore the expression of attention, interest and choice of the public. The position of the media is thus well expressed in the old saying: "I am your leader, therefore I must follow you."[31]

Thus, the public plays a very important part in determining what the mass media communicate and what it itself is potentially controlled by.[32]

10. *Social Control of the Messages*

The situation with regard to mass communications and social control is, to some extent, anomalous. As we have just seen, the audiences in some measure influence what the mass media offer. At any given moment, however, mass communications indubitably *do* have some not yet fully determined conditioning effects upon the recipients.

The fact that so much of mass communication is entertainment for all ages and social categories of the population, including millions upon millions of impressionable and malleable children, makes the kind and quality of the conditioning a matter of great social moment. Equally— possibly more—important is the fact that almost all of the information regarding current affairs (local, regional, national, global) is obtained by the people through the mass media. Though the full effect of this process is unknown, it is pretty generally agreed that the messages of the mass communications agencies do in greater or lesser degree supply the people with the materials through which they behold and interpret the world and its events, and also determine many of the appraisals and prescriptions and hence, much of the behavior of the individuals and groups.

In a dictatorship, as we have already noted, the authoritarian power controls the organization and operation of the mass media; it exercises supreme and undivided control over everything issued by the media. In a society like our own, however, where the media are privately owned and operated and competition prevails among them, where all but the most essential public regulation is rejected, where the free people display a variety of values, norms, tastes and goals and permit themselves a wide latitude of behavior, yet where these same people make the ultimate public decisions, the matter is very different.

More than a few people are concerned about the possibility of withheld or "loaded" news and slanted commentaries, about the lack of balance between local, national and international news, about crime and violence in the movies and on TV, the "sappiness" of soap operas, trashy "music" on radio and TV, sexy material on the newsstands and in the movies, the inane or even imbecile nature of some advertisements, the possibility of subversive political propaganda or of messages violating constitutional rights, and so on. What sort of regulatory control or influence is exercised?

In our society three groups participate—in effect, share—in this regulation, such as it is. (1) *Government*. Some Americans are loath to let the government have much to do with mass communications content, and stress the constitutional guarantees of "freedom" of expression which apply to all the media: books, newspapers, radio, TV, movies, speech-making in public assemblies. In our country we do have laws regulating the media as business and communications agencies (although this is not supposed to affect the quality of the messages), and laws governing such matters as libel and misleading advertising. There are, however, some government efforts at the state and local level to control the moral quality of productions by means of obscenity and blasphemy ordinances and laws, and movie and book censorship boards.

(2) *The media*. The media, prompted by their own self-interest, are sensitive to the reaction of the public to their output, and do quite a bit of self-disciplining and self-policing. This extends from local agencies to industries as a whole, for example, the motion picture industry. The media have made some progress in professionalizing their personnel, elevating their service standards, adopting codes of performance, and engaging in some self-criticism.

(3) *The public*. The ultimate responsibility for full and unadulterated information and for entertainment that is morally respectable and in good taste rests upon the public. So far it has by its support and non-support indicated in a general way what it likes. The public also is capable of demanding such regulatory legislation as it wishes. Thus far, however, its voice has been indistinct, and its regulatory activity indecisive.

11. *Mass Communication and International Relations*

Increasingly the influence of the mass media is extending to more and more peoples, of all levels of cultural and societal development, at more and more locations, all over the world. Dramatically apparent is the tremendous growth of the role of the mass media in non-Western countries during this last decade, especially in many of the new states in Asia and Africa. As literacy (slowly) improves, more and more people avail themselves of books, newspapers and magazines. More and more people, even in the "backward" areas, have radios especially and television receivers. In areas where there are many illiterates or people without receiving instruments, many of these people receive the messages by word-of-mouth conveyance from those who directly receive the messages, for example, by newspaper or radio.[33] As the sending machinery improves, the greater becomes the radius of influence of particular stations. More and more people are spending more and more time in exposure to their messages.

These developments in world-wide communication greatly enhance the possibilities of either world social progress or regress. In the latter respect they can be used to interfere with the internal life of other peoples; to indoctrinate (propagandize) peoples in ideologies and practices dangerous to their general and longtime social well-being; to confuse and mislead people as to international developments and issues. In short, they can serve as a means of furthering international suspicions and tensions, and of preventing community of thought. In this concluding section of the final chapter of this book, we shall confine ourselves to several positive and constructive potentialities of mass communications in international relations and activities. This discussion in some measure summarizes the recurrent reference throughout this book to the relationship of language to inter-people and international relations, especially the ways in which it is involved in the "modernization" of the underdeveloped peoples and emerging nations.

a / The direct gains in inter-people communication resulting from the nature of the media. With some of the media, the significance for communication of geographic contiguity, of the means of transportation of men and carried messages, and of political boundaries is disappearing. Printed materials, films and tapes have to be transported across geographic space, and can be held up at political borders. But radio and TV programs cannot be stopped at the boundaries; the lines on maps do not affect the airwaves. Broadcasts, unless "jammed" electronically, can have global range and international reception.

With the greater portion of the population of the world still illiterate, the manner in which some of the mass media overcome some of the communicative obstacles of illiteracy is important. With radio, especially, but also with other media that use sound stimuli, illiterates who speak

or understand the same language, however physically scattered or politically separated they may be, can recieve the same messages. While
the mass media have done little to reduce the age-old linguistic barriers
to intercultural communication by reducing the multiplicity of separate
languages in the world, this is quite likely due to the fact that the great
volume of messages are issued in a relatively small number of "Empire"
languages, that the communications media have hastened the uniformation of language by the greater use of these few languages as international languages.[34]

It is also important that the media that provide or add direct visual
messages to that extent overcome the problem of language diversity *and*
of illiteracy. The exact photographic reproduction speaks a universal
language. The visual message, as noted in Section 4, reduces, even
obviates, the problem of translating from one language into another.
The illiterate, upon seeing the thing, event or process, obtains information and viewpoints that the printed page denies him, and he also may
obtain conceptions of procedures that he could get, but with greater
difficulty and less clarity and accuracy, from oral descriptions and instructions. The more visual means are used, the less vocal language
matters. Furthermore, it might be noted that, with the use of visual and
oral means, the importance decreases, of the critical cultural endowment
of literacy. This does not mean the end of writing or the printed word;
it does mean that visual and oral–aural media become the full partners
of various kinds of printed materials in communicating all kinds of messages between people. It also means, linguistically, that pictography and
speech assume renewed importance.

b / The sociocultural gains of ready inter-people communication. Several important, actually demonstrated boons stand out, of which those
of a more practical nature will first be discussed.

The media are available as agents of universal education. The mere
random exposure to their messages does this to some extent. The
products have a way of reaching the great inert masses of the world,
informing them, providing them with new perspectives, making them
restless and often mobilizing them for action. Some of them have great
potentialities among peoples the world over, in conducting formal educational efforts.

The mass media are of great importance in *accelerating the "modernization" of the two-thirds of the world's population that are more or
less "underdeveloped."* First, they are functioning as means of fertilizing
the ancient and, until recently in many instances, the relatively static
cultures of these peoples with new ideas and new ways of life. Closely

related to this is the secularizing effect—that is, the lessening of the hold of sanctified, archaic, local or ethnocentric traditions, ideas, beliefs and practices, and the embracing of those of greater social sophistication, catholicity and cosmopolitanism. Second, since the greater portion of these underdeveloped people are still illiterate, some of the media provide educational utilities.

There is a third "modernizing" use of high practical significance—namely, the employment, especially of motion pictures and TV, in the instruction of illiterates and of people of different language in constructive technological practices in agriculture, industry, home arts, and even in such private areas of life as personal hygiene and birth-control techniques. This is of special significance for those engaged in foreign aid programs or in teaching agricultural practices, for private and public health advisers or specialists in vocational training and guidance, as they work among foreign, underdeveloped peoples. Often the people have many different dialects among themselves, as well as being unable to understand the language of the instructor or demonstrator (who likewise may be having difficulty in mastering the language or languages of the people he is trying to aid). The people being aided usually have very little scientific knowledge and only a very limited acquaintance with the current biological, chemical, physical and social technologies of the Western World. Even if their language can be used by the instructors, their indigenous language often is lacking in necessary terminology. Because of the problem of illiteracy, written instructional aids cannot be widely used; for that reason, *demonstration* comes to be one of the most important instructional procedures. People can see and understand demonstrations. Many things can be put across, in spite of language difficulties and of deficiences in cultural background. The demonstration does not have to argue; often, seeing is believing. By means of the demonstration, the observers directly acquire know-how, see the actions and sequences involved in the procedure, as well as its effects, and are quite likely to acquire experimental interests and convictions favorable to its use. The aiders, however, cannot provide the many necessary teams for on-the-spot demonstrations among millions of scattered people. But audio-visual media, particularly mobile projection units, using silent movie films and TV (possibly with some of the local language "dubbed" in), can be used. This means an economy of both personnel and funds, and a vast increase in the range of contact and instruction among the peoples.

Beyond these rather practical considerations are the more weighty ones of inter-people understanding, international operation and world well-being and peace. Here the mass media present distinct potentialities.

The world-wide operation of the mass media *helps to bring the various peoples out into the One World* (discussed in Chapter VIII) *both as participants in its activities and as sharers of its cultural wealth.* According to a long-standing sociological principle, as the community increases in size, the general intercommunication becomes attenuated and, with this, common feeling and understanding are correspondingly weakened and common action is reduced. But with the great advances in mass communications the effect has been to increase vastly the potentialities of inter-people communication among the remote and scattered and diverse peoples of the entire globe. The world has been wired into one vast intricate circuit. All kinds of news—for that matter, all kinds of culture materials that can be presented by words or other sounds, by print, in photographed or pictorial form—can be exchanged "between India and Indiana" in detail and almost instantaneously. The mass media can be the destroyers of provincialism and parochialism; as someone has put it, they can help produce people who really live in the world and not just in their own hamlet. Of equal importance is the fact that mass communications have the potentiality for enhancing the specific sensitivities of people to the existence, presence, feelings and thoughts of other people. This, in turn, makes possible a general orientation of feeling and understanding, and something in the way of a common consciousness, irrespective of marked sociocultural differences. With understanding, the possibility exists of finding unity in variety.[35]

Mass communications make possible a wider understanding of, and a basis for coping with, international problems. More and more problems—social, scientific, technological, religious—are worldwide, and cannot be solved piecemeal and in isolation. They require ready, accurate and widely and uniformly comprehensible means of communication to deal with them. Most of the media have contributed, although unevenly, to such ends. When the messages from the various countries can be freely sent and freely received, there will be the possibility of the "free winnowing of ideas" on a world scale. Without this, there can be no durable world peace.

The media can potentially provide the essentials for the cultural and social-psychological "climate" of peace: (a) a body of information for all of the people involved, concerning the nature of the problems and their respective views regarding them; (b) opportunities for discussion in print and on the air; (c) the achievement of a sort of flow of consensus as a basis for majority international opinions on the issues.

By way of general conclusion, it can be said that while we have the communications machinery for the mass production and distribution of the cultural materials for world well-being and peace, the world has lagged in international *social* machinery and general will to put the media to such uses. The most important and potent media, capable of the widest transmission of messages, are operated by and in behalf of national private corporations or national governments, and mainly for national audiences.[36] Nevertheless, it is upon these mass media that the human race must depend to an increasing degree to hold it together, since mass communications has progressively been becoming the main framework of modern social life, both regional and worldwide.[37]

Potentially, under favoring circumstances and with the necessary social instrumentalization, the media can do much to provide the means of communication essential for building the inter-people understanding, amity and cooperation which was so grievously impaired by the "confusion of tongues" and separation of men that occurred when men constructed their "Towers of Babel."

N O T E S

1 "Consensus and Mass Communication," *American Sociological Review,* 13 (Feb., 1948), 1–15.
2 Recent treatments which to some extent summarize important sociological and social-psychological findings are: Carl I. Hovland, "Effects of Mass Media of Communication," in Gardner Lindzey, *Handbook of Social Psychology* (Cambridge, Mass.: Addison–Wesley Publishing Co., Inc., 1954), II, 1063–1103, presenting some 145 selected references; John W. Riley, Jr. and Matilda White Riley, "Mass Communication and the Social System" in Robert K. Merton, Leonard Broom, and Leonard S. Cottrell, Jr. (eds.), *Sociology Today: Problems and Prospects* (New York: Basic Books, 1959), pp. 537–578, in which important points are buttressed by means of 95 footnote references to pertinent articles, books, and monographs; an extensive bibliography, amounting to approximately 250 items, in Joseph T. Klapper, *The Effects of Mass Communication* (Glencoe, Ill.: Free Press. 1960), pp. 258–274. There are also the excellent collections of theoretical and research studies such as Lyman Bryson (ed.), *The Communication of Ideas* (New York: Harper & Bros., 1948); Bernard Berelson and Morris Janowitz (eds.), *Reader in Public Opinion and Communication* (enlarged ed.; Glencoe, Ill.: Free Press, 1953); and Wilbur Schramm (ed.), *Mass Communications* (Urbana, Ill.: University of Illinois Press, 1960).
3 Robert K. Merton, *Social Theory and Social Structure* (revised & enlarged ed.; Glencoe, Ill.: Free Press, 1957), p. 451. In contrast to this utilitarian research is the fact that the specialists in linguistics have paid very little attention to the relationship between language and mass communication. One searches in vain in the issues of *Language, Language and Speech,* the *International Journal of American Linguistics, Lingua, American Speech* (with a few exceptions), or the *American Anthropologist* (during the last ten years)—the years of the stupendous impact of radio and television—for evidence of investigations of the effects of the different media of mass communication on, for example, phonology and pronunciation, word structure and syntax, vocabulary, dialects of regional and ethnic groups. While such journals as *Public Opinion Quarterly* and *Journalism Quarterly* pay vast attention to the social impact, on the other hand, they offer no treatments of linguistic effects.

4 Cf. the introduction to the section on "The Development of Mass Communications," in Wilbur Schramm (ed.), *op. cit.,* pp. 3–7.

5 Some of the characteristics of mass society here presented have been suggested by Wirth, *op. cit.* Some of these features also apply to "civilized" societies, mentioned in Chap. XVII, Sect. 3.

6 Cf. Gilbert Seldes, "Communications Revolution," in Edward Carpenter and Marshall McLuhan (eds.), *Explorations in Communication* (Boston: Beacon Press, 1960), pp. 196–199.

7 Carpenter and McLuhan, p. 208.

8 *Ibid.,* p. 197.

9 *Ibid.,* p. 197.

10 A study by R. C. Simonini, Jr. ("Phonemic and Analogic Lapses in Radio and Television Speech," *American Speech,* 31 (Dec., 1956), 252–263), has called attention to lapses or slips of speech in radio and TV broadcasting in the form of Spoonerisms, Malapropisms, illiteracies, indiscreet remarks, double meanings, and innuendos, and the social, technical, physiological and psychological circumstances in which these occur.

11 The happy term used by McLuhan in Carpenter and McLuhan (eds.), p. 2.

12 Paul Meadows, *The Culture of Industrial Man* (Lincoln: University of Nebraska Press, 1950), p. 101.

13 The data here presented are taken mainly from *World Almanac: 1963* (Harry Hansen, ed.) (New York: *New York World-Telegram and The Sun,* 1963), and *Statistical Abstract of the United States: 1963* (Washington: U. S. Govt. Printing Office, 1963), where they appear under readily identifiable headings. For a most comprehensive presentation of quantitative data regarding the production (and distribution) of mass communication media in the United States, see Fritz Machlup, *The Production and Distribution of Knowledge in the United States* (Princeton, N. J.: Princeton University Press, 1962), Ch. VI, "The Media of Communication," pp. 207–294.

14 Cf. Paul F. Lazarsfeld and Robert K. Merton, "Mass Communication, Popular Taste and Organized Social Action," in Lyman Bryson (ed.), *op. cit.,* pp. 95–118.

15 Just as the various differentiated special-interest and special-activity groups of society have their "special" languages, as we have noted in Chapter XIII, so they also—though not altogether consistently—pay attention to certain kinds of special-interest communications from the mass media.

16 This is the term used by Parsons, in Talcott Parsons, *Structure and Process in Modern Societies* (Glencoe, Ill.: Free Press, 1960), p. 270.

17 For brief treatments, see Harold D. Lasswell, "The Structure and Functions of Communication in Society," in Lyman Bryson (ed.), pp. 37–51; Paul F. Lazarsfeld and Robert K. Merton, "Mass Communication, Popular Taste, and Organized Social Action" in Bryson (ed.), pp. 95–118 (100–106); Wilbur Schramm, *Responsibility in Mass Communication* (New York: Harper & Brothers, 1957), pp. 49–57; Charles R. Wright, *Mass Communication: A Sociological Perspective* (New York: Random House, 1959), pp. 16–23.

18 For more extended treatments of effects, with references to various studies, see Wright, *op. cit.,* pp. 90–120; Schramm (ed.), *Mass Communications* (almost the entire work); Klapper, *op. cit.*

19 Klapper, *op. cit.,* p. 255.

20 Meadows, *op. cit.,* p. 99.

21 Ralph H. Turner and Lewis M. Killian, *Collective Behavior* (Englewood Cliffs, N. J.: Prentice-Hall Inc., 1957), p. 116.

22 A term used and developed by Carpenter and McLuhan, pp. ix, xi. This paragraph is largely derived from that source.

23 Arnold W. Green, *Sociology: An Analysis of Life in Modern Society* (New York: McGraw-Hill Book Co., 1956), p. 290.

24 Lazarsfeld and Merton, p. 510.

25 *Ibid.,* pp. 503–504.
26 This point on the narcotizing effect, as well as the following one, is suggested by (and the quotations are from) Lazarsfeld and Merton, pp. 501–502.
27 On differential reading patterns of newspaper subaudiences, see Wilbur Schramm and David M. White, "Age, Education and Economic Status as Factors in Newspaper Reading," in Schramm (ed.), pp. 439–450.
28 A crucial aspect of audience selectivity will be brought out in the discussion below of mass communication and social control.
29 Cf. Klapper, pp. 15, 18.
30 Inasmuch as the media must usually try to reach audiences as large as possible to get adequate support, this situation sometimes makes it difficult for them to program for elite or minority audiences.
31 Quoted by Wirth, *op. cit.,* p. 8.
32 While the relation between mass communications and public opinion is not to be treated here, it might be pointed out in the present connection that, while the mass media provide a vast portion of the materials for forming public opinion, the mass media also, to a considerable extent, are the reflectors of public opinion.
33 A recent study of the mass media in Egypt states: "Egypt, a country of over twenty-five million inhabitants, undergoing a deep social and political revolution, mirrors quite typically the increasing dependence upon the mass media. . . . In that country in 1956 there were some 405,000 radio receivers in use; by 1960 that number had swelled to over a million sets. In 1960, radio transmission in Arabic amounted to forty-eight and a half hours per day, as compared with only twelve hours transmission as recently as 1956. Daily newspaper circulation rose from half a million in 1956 to over 650,000 by the end of 1960." Ibrahim Abu-Lughod, "The Mass Media and Egyptian Village Life," *Social Forces,* 42 (Oct., 1963), 97–104. The writer also points out that while the urban centers were the principal consumers of the mass media in former times, the media today are reaching the rural areas of Egypt as never before. Considerable attention is paid to mass communication and mass media in Daniel Lerner (with collaboration of Lucille W. Pevsner), *The Passing of Traditional Society: Modernizing the Middle East* (Glencoe, Ill.: Free Press, 1958). For data on the media for the different countries of the world see UNESCO, *World Communications: Press, Radio, Film, Television* (Paris, 1956).
34 It should be pointed out that literacy as such does not necessarily reduce the linguistic barriers to intercultural communication by reducing the number of languages used. Most of the literate peoples of the world do their reading of books, journals and newspapers in their own language.
35 These possibilities have recently been magnificently illustrated in the almost instantaneous expression of common, poignant feeling on the part of almost all of the peoples of the world in connection with the tragic death of President John F. Kennedy.
36 On a tendency toward cooperation by members of different nations in the production of motion pictures, see Arthur Mayer, "The New Film Frontier," *Saturday Review,* 46 (Oct. 5, 1963), 20–21, 67. Note, for example: "Pictures are being shot today in every part of the globe. They are the product of the skills, the dedication, and the teamwork of gifted men and women of every race and nationality. They are directed by Englishmen from books by Frenchmen, adapted to the screen by Greeks, costumed by Italians, photographed by Japanese, edited by Swedes, scored by Russians, with Irish company managers and German sound engineers. They are financed jointly by American capitalists and European socialists."
37 Cf. Wilbur Schramm, *Mass Media and National Development: The Role of Information in Developing Countries* (Stanford, Cal.: Stanford University Press, 1964).

Bibliography

II. The Basic Concepts Involved in a Sociology of
Language: A Paradigmatic Treatment

EXPERIENCE

LINTON, RALPH, *The Study of Man* (New York: Appleton–Century Co.,
1936), pp. 466–469.
WERKMEISTER, WILLIAM H., *A Philosophy of Science* (New York: Harper
& Brothers, 1940), pp. 77–99.

MEANING

CHASE, STUART, *The Proper Study of Mankind* (New York: Harper &
Brothers, 1948), pp. 249–260.
———, *The Tyranny of Words* (New York: Harcourt, Brace & Co., 1938),
pp. 73–116.
OGDEN, C. K. and I. A. RICHARDS, *The Meaning of Meaning* (New York:
Harcourt, Brace & Co., 1947).
WALPOLE, HUGH R., *Semantics: The Nature of Words and Their Meaning*
(New York: W. W. Norton Co., 1941).

COMMUNICATION

CARROLL, JOHN B., *The Study of Language: A Survey of Linguistics and
Related Disciplines in America* (Cambridge: Harvard University Press,
1953), pp. 88–93.
CHERRY, COLIN, *On Human Communication: A Review, A Survey, and A
Criticism* (New York: John Wiley & Sons, 1957).
COOLEY, CHARLES H., *Social Organization* (New York: Charles Scribner's
Sons, 1915), pp. 61–103.
HERTZLER, JOYCE O., *Society in Action* (New York: Dryden Press, 1954),
pp. 64–66.

LEWIS, MORRIS M., *Language in Society* (London: Thomas Nelson & Sons, 1947), pp. 94–111.

MILLER, GEORGE A., *Language & Communication* (New York: McGraw-Hill Book Co., 1951), pp. 249–253.

MORRIS, BERTRAM, "Concerning Communication and the Community," *Philosophical Review*, 53 (July, 1944), 391–399.

SAPIR, EDWARD, "Communication," *Encyclopedia of the Social Sciences* (New York: Macmillan Co., 1931), Vol. 4, 78–80.

CONCEPTUALIZATION

CHASE, STUART, *The Tyranny of Words* (New York: Harcourt, Brace & Co., 1938), pp. 117–181.

WERKMEISTER, WILLIAM H., *A Philosophy of Science* (New York: Harper & Brothers, 1940), pp. 99–107, 462–464, 516–518.

THE SYMBOL-SYSTEM: GENERAL

ANGYAL, ANDRAS, *Foundations for a Science of Personality* (New York: Commonwealth Fund, 1941), pp. 78–86.

BOLTON, C. D., "Behavior, Experience, and Relationships: A Symbolic Interactionist's Point of View," *American Journal of Sociology*, 64 (July, 1958), 45–58.

MARITAIN, JACQUES, "Language and the Theory of Sign," in Anshen, Ruth N. (ed.), *Language: An Enquiry into Its Meaning and Function* (New York: Harper & Brothers, 1957), pp. 86–101.

OGDEN, C. K. and I. A. RICHARDS, *The Meaning of Meaning* (New York: Harcourt, Brace & Co., 1947), pp. 9–109.

RAPOPORT, ANATOL, "The Role of Symbols in Human Behavior," *ETC.: A Review of General Semantics*, 12 (Spring, 1955), 180–188.

REIS, L., "Fact and Symbol," in Bryson, L., L. Finkelstein, R. M. McIver, and R. McKeon (eds.), *Symbols and Values: An Initial Study* (New York: Harper & Brothers, 1954), pp. 477–483.

SOLOMON, ALBERT, "Symbols and Images in the Constitution of Society," in Bryson *et al.*, pp. 103–129.

SAPIR, EDWARD, "Symbolism," *Encyclopedia of the Social Sciences* (New York: Macmillan Co., 1934), Vol. 14, 492–495.

WERKMEISTER, WILLIAM H., *A Philosophy of Science* (New York: Harper & Brothers, 1940), pp. 108–115.

WHITE, L. A., "The Symbol: The Origin and Basis of Human Behavior," *Philosophy of Science*, 8 (Oct. 1940), 451–463.

THE SYMBOL-SYSTEM: LANGUAGE

CHERRY, COLIN, *On Human Communication: A Review, A Survey, and A Criticism* (New York: John Wiley & Sons, 1957), pp. 3–65.

DIAMOND, ARTHUR S., *The History and Origin of Language* (New York: Philosophical Library, 1959), pp. 9–14.

HUGHES, JOHN P., *The Science of Language* (New York: Random House, 1962), pp. 4–8.

LA PIERE, RICHARD T. and PAUL R. FARNSWORTH, *Social Psychology* (3rd ed.) (New York: McGraw-Hill Book Co., 1949), pp. 86–118.

LEE, DOROTHY, *Freedom and Culture* (New York: Spectrum Books, 1959), pp. 79–85.

MEAD, GEORGE H., *Mind, Self, and Society* (Chicago: University of Chicago Press, 1934), pp. 13–18, 46–90, 117–125.

MILLS, C. WRIGHT, "Language, Logic, and Culture," *American Sociological Review*, 4 (Oct., 1939), 670–680.

SAPIR, EDWARD, *Language: An Introduction to the Study of Speech* (New York: Harcourt, Brace & Co., 1921), pp. 10–16.

ULLMAN, STEPHEN, *Words and Their Use* (New York: Philosophical Library, 1951), pp. 13–30.

THE LANGUAGE COMMUNITY

BLOOMFIELD, LEONARD, *Language* (New York: Henry Holt & Co., 1933), pp. 42–56, 444–495.

DEUTSCH, KARL W., *Nationalism and Social Communication: An Inquiry into the Foundations of Nationality* (New York: John Wiley & Sons, 1953), pp. 25–30.

JESPERSEN, OTTO, *Mankind, Nation and Individual from a Linguistic Point of View* (Cambridge: Harvard University Press, 1955), pp. 38–140.

LEWIS, MORRIS M., *Language in Society* (London: Thomas Nelson & Sons, 1947), pp. 112–123, 173–198.

PEI, MARIO, *Language for Everybody* (New York: Devin–Adair Co., 1956), pp. 195–205.

VENDRYES, J., *Language: A Linguistic Introduction to History* (London: Kegan Paul, Trench, Trubner & Company, 1925), pp. 260–279.

VOSSLER, KARL, *The Spirit of Language in Civilization*, trans. Oscar Oeser (London: Routledge & Kegan Paul; reprinted 1951), pp. 107–197.

THE CONTEXT OF SITUATIONS

HAYAKAWA, S. I., *Language in Thought and Action* (New York: Harcourt, Brace & Co., 1949), pp. 1–17.

JESPERSEN, OTTO, *Language: Its Nature, Development, and Origin* (New York: Macmillan Co., 1922), pp. 55–58, 429–431.

LEWIS, MORRIS M., *Language in Society* (London: Thomas Nelson & Sons, 1947), pp. 8–11, 45–46.

MALINOWSKI, BRONISLAW, "The Problem of Meaning in Primitive Languages," in Supplement I to C. K. Ogden and I. A. Richards, *The Meaning of Meaning* (New York: Harcourt, Brace & Co., 1947), pp. 296–336.

PIERIS, RALPH, "Speech and Society: A Sociological Approach to Language," *American Sociological Review*, 16 (Aug., 1951), 499–505.

SAPIR, EDWARD, *Language: An Introduction to the Study of Speech* (New York: Harcourt, Brace & Co., 1921), pp. 211–235.

SILVA-FUENZALIDA, ISMAEL, "Ethnolinguistics and the study of Culture," *American Anthropologist*, 151 (July, 1949), 446–456.

WERKMEISTER, WILLIAM H., "Natural Languages as Cultural Indices," *Philosophy of Science*, 6 (July, 1939), 356–366.

III.   The Major General Functions of Language

ANSHEN, RUTH N. (ed.), *Language: An Enquiry into Its Meaning and Function* (New York: Harper & Brothers, 1957), pp. xvi, 3–17, 349.

BUTLER, J. A. V., *Science and Human Life* (New York: Basic Books, 1957), pp. 81–85.

BUTLER, SAMUEL, "Thought and Language," in Max Black (ed.), *The Importance of Language* (Englewood Cliffs, N.J.: Prentice–Hall, 1962), pp. 13–35.

CASSIRER, ERNST, *Language and Myth*, trans. S. K. Langer (New York: Dover Publications, 1946), pp. ix, 1–16, 23–42.

CHANG, TUNG-SUN, "A Chinese Philosopher's Theory of Knowledge," *ETC.: A Review of General Semantics*, 9 (Spring, 1952), 203–226.

CHERRY, COLIN, *On Human Communication: A Review, A Survey, and A Criticism* (New York: John Wiley & Sons, with Technology Press, M. I. T., 1957), pp. 66–77.

CHURCH, JOSEPH, *Language and the Discovery of Reality: a Developmental Psychology of Cognition* (New York: Random House, 1961), pp. 96–97, 107–108, 147–163.

DE LAGUNA, GRACE A., *Speech—Its Function and Development* (New Haven: Yale University Press, 1927), pp. 138–139.

GERE, STANLEY, "Language and Science: the Rational, Functional Language of Science and Technology," *Philosophy of Science*, 9 (Apr., 1942), 146–161.

HUXLEY, ALDOUS, "Words and Their Meanings," in Max Black (ed.), *op. cit*, pp. 1–12.

LANGER, SUZANNE K., "Philosophy: The Growing Center," in Lynn White, Jr. (ed.), *Frontiers of Knowledge* (New York: Harper & Brothers, 1956), pp. 257–286.

LEE, DOROTHY D., *Freedom and Culture* (New York: Spectrum Books, 1959), pp. 79–80.

LEE, IRVING J., *Language Habits in Human Affairs* (New York: Harper & Brothers, 1941), pp. 15–25, 33–37, 57.

LEWIS, MORRIS M., *Language in Society* (London: Thomas Nelson & Sons, 1947), pp. 23–24, 71–93.

LINDESMITH, ALFRED R. and ANSELM L. STRAUSS, *Social Psychology*, revised edition (New York: Holt, Rinehart and Winston, 1956), pp. 63–79.

MEERLOO, JOOST A. M., *Conversation and Communication: A Psychological Inquiry into Language & Human Relations* (New York: International Universities Press, Inc., 1952), pp. 25–57.

MOORE, WILBERT E., *Man, Time, and Society* (New York: John Wiley & Sons, Inc., 1963).

PALMER, LEONARD R., *An Introduction to Modern Linguistics* (London: Macmillan Co., 1936), pp. 172–186.

WAISMANN, F., "Verifiability," in Anthony Flew (ed.), *Essays in Logic and Language* (New York: Philosophical Library, 1951), pp. 117–144.

WERKMEISTER, WILLIAM H., "Natural Languages as Cultural Indices," *Philosophy of Science*, 6 (July, 1939), 356–366.

IV.   Language as a Social Phenomenon and Social Agency

BARKER, GEORGE C., "The Social Functions of Language," *ETC., A Review of General Semantics,* 2 (Summer, 1945), 228–234.
BARNETT, LINCOLN, *The Treasure of Our Tongue* (New York: Alfred A. Knopf, Inc., 1964), pp. 39–78.
BRAM, JOSEPH, *Language and Society* (New York: Random House, Inc., 1955), pp. 1–9, 19–25.
COHEN, MARCEL, *Pour une sociologie du langage* (Paris: Albin Michel, 1956), pp. 35–64.
KLUCKHOHN, CLYDE, "Notes on Some Anthropological Aspects of Communication," *American Anthropologist,* 63 (Oct., 1961), 895–912.
ORR, WILLIAM F. and STEPHEN C. CAPPANNARI, "The Emergence of Language," *American Anthropologist,* 66 (Apr., 1964), 318–324.
STERN, THEODORE, "Drum and Whistle 'Languages': An Analysis of Speech Surrogates," *American Anthropologist,* 59 (June, 1957), 487–506.
THOMAS, WILLIAM I., *Primitive Behavior* (New York: McGraw–Hill Book Co., 1937), pp. 49–97.

V.   Language as a Social Institution

GENERAL

BLOCH, BERNARD and GEORGE L. TRAGER, *Outline of Linguistic Analysis* (Baltimore: Linguistic Society of America, 1942).
BLOOMFIELD, LEONARD, "A Set of Postulates for the Science of Language," *Language,* 2 (1926), 153–164. Also in Martin Joos (ed.), *Readings in Linguistics: The Development of Descriptive Linguistics in America Since 1925* (New York: American Council of Learned Societies), pp. 26–31.
———, *Language* (New York: Henry Holt & Co., 1933), pp. 74–280.
BODMER, FREDERICK, *The Loom of Language* (New York: W. W. Norton Co., 1944), pp. 76–168.
CARROLL, JOHN B., *The Study of Language* (Cambridge: Harvard University Press, 1953), pp. 213–223.
COHEN, MARCEL, *Pour une sociologie du langage* (Paris: Albin Michel, 1956), pp. 65–77.
DE SAUSSURE, FERDINAND, *Course in General Linguistics,* edited by Charles Bally and Albert Sèchehaye, trans. Wade Baskin (New York: Philosophical Library, 1959), pp. 38–190.
ENTWISTLE, WILLIAM J., *Aspects of Language* (London: Faber & Faber, 1953), pp. 145–225.
FRIES, CHARLES C., *The Structure of English: An Introduction to the Con-*

struction of English Sentences (New York: Harcourt, Brace & Co., 1952).

GRAY, LOUIS H., *Foundations of Language* (New York: The Macmillan Co., 1939).

HALL, EDWARD, *The Silent Language* (New York: Doubleday & Co., 1959), pp. 119–126.

HALL, ROBERT A., JR., *Leave Your Language Alone!* (Ithaca, New York: Linguistica, 1950), pp. 53–129.

HARRIS, ZELLIG S., *Methods in Structural Linguistics* (Chicago: University of Chicago Press, 1951).

HERTZLER, JOYCE O., *American Social Institutions: A Sociological Analysis* (Boston: Allyn & Bacon, 1961), Chs. III, IV, VI (185–192).

HOCKETT, CHARLES F., *A Course in Modern Linguistics* (New York: The Macmillan Co., 1958).

HUGHES, JOHN P., *The Science of Language* (New York: Random House, 1962), Part Two.

PARTRIDGE, ERIC, *The World of Words* (London: George Routledge & Sons, 1938), pp. 199–239.

PEI, MARIO, *Language for Everybody* (New York: Devin–Adair, 1956), pp. 84–92.

——, "The Dictionary as Battlefield," *Saturday Review,* 45 (July 21, 1962), pp. 44–47, 55–56.

PIKE, KENNETH L., *Language in Relation to a Unified Theory of the Structure of Human Behavior,* Part I. Preliminary Edition (Glendale, California: Summer Institute of Linguistics, 1954).

POTTER, SIMEON, *Modern Linguistics* (London: Andre Deutsch, 1957), pp. 36–122.

REVESZ, GÉZA, *The Origins & Prehistory of Language* (New York: Philosophical Library, 1956), pp. 24–30.

SAPIR, EDWARD, "Language," *Encyclopedia of Social Sciences* (New York: The Macmillan Co., 1943), Vol. 9, 155–168.

SCHLAUCH, MARGARET, *The Gift of Language* (New York: Dover Press, 1955), pp. 133–140.

TRAGER, GEORGE L. and HENRY L. SMITH, JR., *An Outline of English Structure* (Washington: American Council of Learned Societies, 1956).

VENDRYES, J., *Language: A Linguistic Introduction to History* (London: Kegan Paul, Trench, Trubner & Co., 1925; reprinted by New York: Barnes & Noble, 1951), pp. 17–230.

WHATMOUGH, JOSHUA, *Language: A Modern Synthesis* (New York: St. Martin's Press, 1956), pp. 8–13, 108–126.

STANDARD LANGUAGE

JESPERSEN, OTTO, *Mankind, Nation and Individual from a Linguistic Point of View* (Cambridge: Harvard University Press, 1925), pp. 123–140.

KROEBER, ALFRED L., *Anthropology* (New York: Harcourt, Brace & Co., 1948), pp. 249–251.

PARTRIDGE, ERIC, *The World of Words* (London: George Routledge & Sons, 1938), pp. 171–198.

VENDRYES, J., *Language: A Linguistic Introduction to History* (London: Kegan Paul, Trench, Trubner & Co., 1925), pp. 260–279.

PLACE AND FUNCTIONS OF
LANGUAGE IN THE VARIOUS
INSTITUTIONALIZED SECTORS
OF HUMAN LIFE

GERTH, HANS H. and C. WRIGHT MILLS, *Character and Social Structure: The Philosophy of Social Institutions* (New York: Harcourt, Brace & Co., 1953), pp. 280–286.
LEWIS, MORRIS M., *Language in Society* (London: Thomas Nelson & Sons, Ltd., 1947), pp. 124–169.
PEI, MARIO, *The Story of Language* (Philadelphia: J. B. Lippincott & Co., 1949), pp. 188–284.

VI.   Language as Sociocultural Index, Record and Determinant

LANGUAGE AS SOCIOCULTURAL
INDEX AND REVEALER OF
SOCIOCULTURAL HISTORY

CHURCH, JOSEPH, *Language and the Discovery of Reality* (New York: Random House, 1961), pp. 137–144.
COHEN, MARCEL, *Pour une sociologie du langage* (Paris: Albin Michel, 1956), pp. 87–88, 146–167.
DE SAUSSURE, FERDINAND, *Course in General Linguistics* Charles Baskin and Albert Sèchehaye (eds.), trans. Wade Baskin (New York: Philosophical Library, 1959), pp. 222–228.
DOOB, LEONARD W., *Social Psychology: An Analysis of Human Behavior* (New York: Henry Holt & Co., 1952), pp. 95–109.
GRAY, LOUIS H., *Foundations of Language* (New York: Macmillan Co., 1939), pp. 10–11, 119–120.
PARTRIDGE, ERIC, *The World of Words* (London: George Routledge & Sons, 1938), pp. 260–314.
PEI, MARIO, *Language for Everybody* (New York: Devin–Adair, 1956), pp. 211–218.
SALMON, LUCY M., "Place-Names and Personal Names as Records of History," *American Speech*, 2 (Feb., 1927), 228–231.
SAMORA, JULIAN and WILLIAM N. DEANE, "Language Usage as a Possible Index of Acculturation," *Sociology and Social Research*, 40 (May–June, 1956), 307–311.
SCHLAUCH, MARGARET, *The Gift of Language* (New York: Dover Publications, 1955), 193–226.
TAYLOR, WALTER W., "Archaeology and Language in Western North America," *American Antiquities*, 27 (July, 1961), 71–81.

VOSSLER, KARL, *The Spirit of Language in Civilization*, trans. Oscar Oeser (London: Routledge & Kegan Paul, 1951), pp. 115–118.

N A M E S   A S   C U L T U R E   R E C O R D I N G S

BARKER, HOWARD F., "Our Leading Surnames," *American Speech*, 1 (June, 1926), 470–477.

———, "How We Got Our Surnames," *American Speech*, 4 (Oct., 1928), 48–53.

———, "The Family Names of American Negroes," *American Speech*, 14 (Oct., 1939), 163–174.

BARNES, WILL C., *Arizona Place Names* (Tucson: University of Arizona Press, 1960).

COHEN, MARCEL, *Pour une sociologie du langage* (Paris: Albin Michel, 1956), pp. 234–236.

DOBBIE, ELLIOT V. K., "Pacific Place Names and the History of Democracy," *American Speech*, 36 (Dec., 1961), 258–265.

FEIPEL, LOUIS N., "American Place-Names," *American Speech*, 1 (Nov., 1925), 78–91.

FITZPATRICK, LILLIAN L., *Nebraska Place-Names* (Lincoln: University of Nebraska Press, 1960).

FLUGEL, INGEBORG, "On the Significance of Names," in J. C. Flugel (ed.), *Men and Their Motives* (New York: International Universities Press, 1947), pp. 214–224.

GUDDE, ERWIN G., *California Place-Names* (Berkeley: University of California Press, 1960).

LAMBERT, ELOISE and MARIO PEI, *Our Names: Where They Came From and What They Mean* (New York: Lothrop, Lee & Shepard Co., 1960).

MARCKWARDT, ALBERT H., *American English* (New York: Oxford University Press, 1958), pp. 151–169.

MENCKEN, H. L., *The American Language* (New York: Alfred A. Knopf, 1948), Supplement II, pp. 396–642.

PEI, MARIO, *The Story of Language* (Philadelphia: J. B. Lippincott & Co., 1949), pp. 57–78.

———, *The Story of English* (Philadelphia: J. B. Lippincott & Co., 1952), pp. 126–135.

REANEY, PERCY H., *The Origin of English Place-Names* (London: Routledge & Kegan Paul, 1960).

REINECKE, JOHN E., "Personal Names in Hawaii," *American Speech*, 15 (Dec., 1940), 345–352.

SAGE, EVAN T., "Classical Place-Names in America," *American Speech*, 4 (Apr., 1929), 261–271.

SALMON, LUCY M., "Place-Names and Personal Names as Records of History," *American Speech*, 2 (Feb., 1927), 228–231.

SYLVESTER, A. H., "Place-Naming in the Northwest," *American Speech*, 18 (Dec., 1943), 241–252.

TRAGER, GEORGE L., "Some Spanish Place Names of Colorado," *American Speech*, 10 (Oct., 1935), 203–207.

WEEKLEY, ERNEST, *The Romance of Names* (New York: E. P. Dutton & Co., 1914), pp. 156–170.

METALINGUISTICS AND LANGUAGE AS DETERMINANT

BASILIUS, HAROLD, "Neo-Humboldtian Linguistics," *Word,* 8 (Aug., 1952), 92–105.

BERTALANFFY, L. VON, "An Essay on the Relativity of Categories," *Philosophy of Science,* 22 (Oct., 1955), 243–263.

BLACK, MAX, "Linguistic Relativity: The Views of Benjamin Lee Whorf," *Philosophical Review,* 68 (Apr., 1959), 228–238.

BROWN, DONNA WORRALL, "Does Language Structure Influence Thought? Comments on the Psycho-Linguistic Experiment at Michigan," *ETC.: A Review of General Semantics,* 17 (Spring, 1960), 330–345.

CAPELL, A., "Language and World View in the Northern Kimberley, Western Australia," *Southwestern Journal of Anthropology,* 16 (Spring, 1960), 1–14.

CARROLL, JOHN B., *The Study of Language: A Survey of Linguistics and Related Disciplines in America* (Cambridge: Harvard University Press, 1953), pp. 43–48.

———, and JOSEPH B. CASAGRANDE, "The Function of Language Classifications in Behavior," in Helen Maccoby, Theodore M. Newcomb and Eugene L. Hartley (eds.), *Readings in Social Psychology,* 3rd ed. (New York: Henry Holt & Co., 1958), pp. 18–31.

CASSIRER, ERNST, "The Influence of Language Upon the Development of Scientific Thought," *Journal of Philosophy,* 39 (June, 1942), 309–327.

———, *Language and Myth,* trans. Suzanne K. Langer (New York: Dover Publications, 1946), pp. 1–17, 23–42.

CHASE, STUART, *Power of Words* (New York: Harcourt, Brace & Co., 1953), pp. 100–109.

———, "How Language Shapes Our Thought," *Harper's Magazine,* 208 (Apr., 1954), 76–82.

CHURCH, JOSEPH, *Language and the Discovery of Reality: A Developmental Psychology of Cognition* (New York: Random House, 1961), pp. 132–136.

FEARING, F., "An Examination of the Conceptions of Benjamin Whorf in the Light of Theories of Perception and Cognition," in Harry Hoijer (ed.), *Language in Culture* (Chicago: University of Chicago Press, 1954), pp. 47–81.

FEUER, L. S., "Sociological Aspects of the Relation Between Language and Philosophy," *Philosophy of Science,* 20 (April, 1955), 85–100.

GREEN, ARNOLD W., *Sociology* (New York: McGraw–Hill Book Co., 1952), pp. 71–75.

HAYAKAWA, S. I., "Semantics, General Semantics, and Related Disciplines," in S. I. Hayakawa (ed.), *Language, Meaning & Maturity* (New York: Harper & Brothers, 1954), pp. 19–37.

HOCART, A. M., "The Psychological Interpretation of Language," *British Journal of Sociology,* 5 (Nov., 1912), 267–279.

HOCKETT, CHARLES F., "Chinese versus English: An Exploration of Whorfian Theses," in Harry Hoijer (ed.), *Language in Culture:* (Chicago: University of Chicago Press, 1954), pp. 106–123. This entire volume is pertinent to the examination of metalinguistics.

524   BIBLIOGRAPHY

HOIJER, HARRY, "Cultural Implications of Some Navaho Linguistic Categories," *Language,* 27 (Apr.–June, 1951), 111–120.

———, "The Relation of Language to Culture," in A. L. Kroeber, *Anthropology Today: An Encyclopedic Inventory* (Chicago: University of Chicago Press, 1953), pp. 554–577.

———, "The Sapir-Whorf Hypothesis," in Harry Hoijer (ed.), *Language in Culture* (Chicago: University of Chicago Press, 1954), pp. 92–106.

KLUCKHOHN, CLYDE, *Mirror for Man* (New York: Whittlesey House, 1949), pp. 145–167.

———, "Notes on Some Anthropological Aspects of Communication," *American Anthropologist,* 63 (Oct., 1961), 895–912.

KRECH, DAVID, RICHARD S. CRUTCHFIELD and EGERTON L. BALLACHEY, *Individual in Society: A Textbook of Social Psychology* (New York: McGraw-Hill Book Co., 1962), pp. 294–298.

KORZYBSKI, ALFRED, *Science and Sanity* (New York: International Non-Aristotelian Library, 1948), pp. 55–98.

LEARY, WILLIAM G., "Studies in Language and Culture in the Training of Foreign Service Personnel," *ETC.: A Review of General Semantics,* 9 (Spring, 1953), 192–202.

LEE, DOROTHY D., "Conceptual Implications of an Indian Language," *Philosophy of Science,* 5 (Jan., 1938), 89–102.

———, "A Linguistic Approach to a System of Value," in T. M. Newcomb and E. L. Hartley (eds.), *Readings in Social Psychology* (New York: Henry Holt & Co., 1947), pp. 219–224. (From "A Primitive System of Values," *Philosophy of Science,* 7 (July, 1940), 355–365.)

LINDESMITH, ALFRED R. and ANSELM L. STRAUSS, *Social Psychology* (rev. ed., New York: Holt, Rinehart & Winston, 1956), pp. 224–232.

MALINOWSKI, BRONISLAW, "The Problem of Meaning in Primitive Languages," in C. K. Ogden and I. A. Richards, *The Meaning of Meaning* (New York: Harcourt, Brace & Co., 1947), Supplement I, pp. 296–336.

MANDELBAUM, D. G. (ed.), *Selected Writings in Language, Culture, and Personality* (Berkeley: University of California Press, 1951).

MILLS, C. WRIGHT, "Language, Logic, and Culture," *American Sociological Review,* 4 (Oct., 1939), 670–680 (672–673).

RAPOPORT, ANATOL, "The Role of Symbols in Human Behavior," *ETC.: A Review of General Semantics,* 12 (Spring, 1955), 180–188.

——— and ARNOLD HOROWITZ, "The Sapir-Whorf-Korzybski Hypothesis: A Report and Reply," *ETC.: A Review of General Semantics,* 17 (Spring, 1960), 346–363.

REDFIELD, ROBERT, *The Primitive World and Its Transformations* (Ithaca: Cornell University Press, 1953), pp. 84–110.

SAPIR, EDWARD, "The Status of Linguistics as a Science," *Language,* 5 (1929), 207–214.

SHOUBY, E., "The Influence of the Arabic Language on the Psychology of the Arabs," *Middle East Journal,* 5 (No. 3, 1951), 284–302.

SPIER, LESLIE, A. IRVING HOLLOWELL and STANLEY S. NEWMAN (eds.), *Society, Culture and Personality* (Menasha, Wisconsin: Sapir Memorial Publishing Fund, 1941).

ULLMAN, STEPHEN, *Words and Their Use* (New York: Philosophical Library, 1951), pp. 87–108.

UNDERHILL, RUTH M., "Vocabulary and Style in an Indian Language," *American Speech*, 9 (Dec., 1934), 279–282.

WAISMANN, F., "Verifiability," in Anthony Flew (ed.), *Essays in Logic and Language* (New York: Philosophical Library, 1951), pp. 117–144.

WATERMAN, JOHN T., "Benjamin Lee Whorf and Linguistic Field Theory," *Southwestern Journal of Anthropology*, 13 (Autumn, 1957), 201–211.

WERKMEISTER, WILLIAM H., "Natural Languages as Cultural Indices," *Philosophy of Science*, 6 (July, 1939), 356–366.

———, *A Philosophy of Science* (New York: Harper & Brothers, 1940), pp. 108–139.

WHORF, BENJAMIN LEE, "Science and Linguistics," *Technology Review*, 44 (Apr., 1940), 229–231, 247–288. Reprinted in S. I. Hayakawa, *Language in Action* (New York: Harcourt, Brace & Co., 1941), pp. 302–322; in T. M. Newcomb and E. L. Hartley (eds.), *Readings in Social Psychology* (New York: Henry Holt & Co., 1947), pp. 210–218; Benjamin Lee Whorf, *Four Articles on Metalinguistics* (Washington: Foreign Service Institute, 1950), pp. 25–45; and in John B. Carroll (ed.), *Language, Thought and Reality: Selected Writings of Benjamin Lee Whorf* (Cambridge: Technology Press of M. I. T., and New York: John Wiley & Sons, 1956), pp. 207–219.

———, "Linguistics as An Exact Science," *Technology Review*, 43 (Dec., 1940), 61–63, 80–83. (Also in Carroll (ed.), pp. 220–232.)

———, "The Relation of Habitual Thought and Behavior to Language," in Leslie Spier (ed.), *Language, Culture and Personality* (Menasha, Wisconsin: Sapir Memorial Publishing Fund, 1941), pp. 73–93; also in S. I. Hayakawa (ed.), pp. 225–251, and John B. Carroll (ed.), pp. 134–159.

———, "Language and Logic," *Technology Review*, 43 (April, 1941), 250–252, 266–272.

———, *Four Articles on Metalinguistics* (Washington: Foreign Service Institute, Department of State, 1950).

———, "An American Indian Model of the Universe," *International Journal of American Linguistics*, 16 (1950), 67–72.

———, "Language, Mind and Reality," *ETC.: A Review of General Semantics*, 9 (Spring, 1952), 167–188. Also in John B. Carroll (ed.), pp. 246–270.

——— For a bibliography of Whorf's published writings, a selected list of his unpublished manuscripts, and a selected list of books and articles relating to Whorf's writings, see Carroll (ed.), pp. 271–278. (See also "Bibliography of the Writings of Benjamin Lee Whorf," compiled by Herbert Hackett in *ETC.: A Review of General Semantics*, 9 (Spring, 1952), 189–191, and *American Anthropology*, 55 (Jan., 1953), 153–155. The great bulk of these items are studies of North and South American Indian Languages.)

THE PROBLEM OF TRANSLATION

CASAGRANDE, JOSEPH B., "The Ends of Translation," *International Journal of American Linguistics*, 20 (No. 4, 1954), 335–340.

CIARDI, JOHN, "Translation: The Art of Failure," *Saturday Review*, 44 (Oct 7, 1961), 17–19.

526 BIBLIOGRAPHY

CLEMENTS, ROBERT J., "Literature by Electronics," *Saturday Review*, 43 (July 16, 1960), 13–15, 39–40.
DE MENASCE, JEAN P., "A Philosophy of Translation," in Ruth N. Anshen, (ed.), *Language: An Enquiry into Its Meaning and Function* (New York: Harper & Brothers, 1957), pp. 321–340.
ERVIN, SUSAN and ROBERT T. BOWER, "Translation Problems in International Surveys," *Public Opinion Quarterly*, 16 (Winter, 1953), 595–604.
MALINOWSKI, BRONISLAW, "The Translation of Untranslatable Words," *Coral Gardens and Their Magic* (New York: American Book Co., 1935), II, 11–22.
UNESCO, *Scientific and Technical Translation and Other Aspects of the Language Problem* (Paris, 1957).
VOSSLER, KARL, *The Spirit of Language in Civilization*, trans. Oscar Oeser (London: Routledge and Kegan Paul, 1951), pp. 175–185.

THE SOCIOLOGY OF KNOWLEDGE

In view of the close relationship between language and the sociology of knowledge, as indicated in the text, a small but select bibliography of readily available references is presented.

ADLER, FRANZ, "The Range of Sociology of Knowledge," in Howard Becker and Alvin Boskoff (eds.), *Modern Sociological Theory* (New York: The Dryden Press, 1957), pp. 396–423.
CHALL, LEO P., "The Sociology of Knowledge," in Joseph S. Roucek (ed.), *Contemporary Sociology* (New York: Philosophical Library, 1958), pp. 268–304.
COSER, LEWIS A. and BERNARD ROSENBERG (eds.), *Sociological Theory* (New York: The Macmillan Co., 1957), pp. 557–574.
DAHLKE, H. OTTO, "The Sociology of Knowledge," in Howard Becker and Frances Bennett Becker (eds.), *Contemporary Social Theory* (New York: Appleton–Century Co., 1940), pp. 64–89.
DE GRÉ, GERARD L., *Society and Ideology: An Inquiry into the Sociology of Knowledge* (New York: Columbia University Bookstore, 1943).
HARTUNG, FRANK E., "Problems of the Sociology of Knowledge," *Philosophy of Science*, 19 (Jan., 1952), pp. 17–32.
HOROWITZ, IRVING L., *Philosophy, Science, and the Sociology of Knowledge* (Springfield, Ill.: Charles C. Thomas, 1961).
MACHLUP, FRITZ, *The Production and Distribution of Knowledge in the United States* (Princeton, N.J.: Princeton University Press, 1962).
MANNHEIM, KARL, *Ideology and Utopia: An Introduction to the Sociology of Knowledge*, trans. Louis Wirth and Edward A. Shils (New York: Harcourt, Brace & Co., 1936).
———, in Paul Kecskemeti (ed.), *Essays in the Sociology of Knowledge* (New York: Oxford University Press, 1953).
MERTON, ROBERT K., "The Sociology of Knowledge," in Georges Gurvitch and Wilbert E. Moore (eds.), *Twentieth Century Sociology* (New York: Philosophical Library, 1945), pp. 366–405. Also in Robert K. Merton, *Social Theory and Social Structure* (revised and enlarged ed., Glencoe, Ill.: Free Press, 1957), pp. 456–488.
MILLS, C. WRIGHT, "Language, Logic and Culture," *American Sociological Review*, 4 (Oct., 1939), 670–680.

————, "Situated Actions and Vocabularies of Motives," *American Socio-logical Review*, 5 (Dec., 1940), 904–914.

STARK, WERNER, *The Sociology of Knowledge: An Essay in Aid of a Deeper Understanding of the History of Ideas* (Glencoe, Ill.: Free Press, 1958).

TAYLOR, STANLEY, "Social Factors and the Validation of Thought," *Social Forces*, 41 (Oct., 1962), 76–82.

WIRTH, LOUIS, Preface to Karl Mannheim, *Ideology and Utopia*, pp. xi–xxx. Reprinted in Elizabeth Wirth Marvick and Albert J. Reiss, Jr. (eds.), *Community Life and Social Policy* (Chicago: University of Chicago Press, 1956).

WOLFF, KURT H., "The Sociology of Knowledge: Emphasis on an Empirical Attitude," *Philosophy of Science*, 10 (Apr., 1943), 104–123.

————, "The Sociology of Knowledge and Sociological Theory," in Llewellyn Gross (ed.), *Symposium on Sociological Theory* (Evanston, Ill.: Row, Peterson & Co., 1959), pp. 567–602.

VII. Sociocultural Change and Changing Language

BAUGH, ALBERT C., *A History of the English Language* (New York: Appleton-Century-Crofts, 1957).

BLOOMFIELD, LEONARD, *Language* (New York: Henry Holt & Co., 1933), pp. 425–495.

COHEN, MARCEL, *Pour une sociologie du langage* (Paris: Albin Michel, 1956), pp. 112–167, 291–306.

DE SAUSSURE, FERDINAND, *Course in General Linguistics*, trans. Wade Baskin (New York: Philosophical Library, 1959), pp. 71–78.

DIAMOND, ARTHUR S., *The History and Origin of Language* (New York: Philosophical Library, 1959), pp. 6–8, 39–59, 142–144, 162–185.

ENTWISTLE, WILLIAM J., *Aspects of Language* (London: Faber & Faber, 1953), pp. 245–257.

ESTRICH, ROBERT M. and HANS SPERBER, *Three Keys to Language* (New York: Rinehart, 1952), pp. 11–16, 103–211.

GRAY, LOUIS H., *Foundations of Language* (New York: Macmillan Co., 1939), pp. 249–276.

HAUGEN, EINAR, *The Norwegian Language in America: A Study of Bilingual Behavior* (Philadelphia: University of Pennsylvania Press, 1953), Vol. II, pp. 337–411.

HOIJER, HARRY, "Linguistic and Cultural Change," *Language*, 24 (Oct.–Dec., 1948), pp. 335–345.

————, "The Relation of Language to Culture," in Alfred L. Kroeber (ed.), *Anthropology Today: An Encyclopedic Inventory* (Chicago: University of Chicago Press, 1953), pp. 554–572.

HUPPÉ, BERNARD F. and JACK KAMINSKY, *Logic and Language* (New York: Alfred A. Knopf, 1956), pp. 83–93.

JESPERSEN, OTTO, *Growth and Structure of the English Language* (Leipzig: Teubner, 1905).

————, *Language: Its Nature, Development, and Origin* (New York: Macmillan Co., 1922), pp. 208–211.

JOHNSON, WENDELL, *People in Quandaries: The Semantics of Personal Adjustment* (New York: Harper & Brothers, 1946), pp. 112–127.

KROEBER, ALFRED L., *Anthropology* (New York: Harcourt, Brace & Co., 1948), pp. 220–222, 228–235.

LAIRD, CHARLTON, *The Miracle of Language* (Cleveland: World Publishing Co., 1953), pp. 89–91, 255–257.

MARCKWARDT, ALBERT H., *American English* (New York: Oxford University Press, 1958), pp. 21–109.

MEILLET, ANTOINE, "How Words Change Their Meanings," in Talcott Parsons, Edward Shils, Kasper D. Naegle, and Joseph R. Pitts (eds.), *Theories of Society: Foundations of Modern Sociological Theory* (New York: Free Press of Glencoe, 1961), II, 1013–1018.

MENCKEN, H. L., *The American Language: An Inquiry into the Development of English in the United States* (New York: Alfred A. Knopf, 1945), Supplement I, pp. 169–331.

PALMER, LEONARD R., *An Introduction to Modern Linguistics* (London: The Macmillan Co., 1936), pp. 151–171.

PARTRIDGE, ERIC, *The World of Words* (London: George Routledge & Sons, 1938), pp. 20–98, 142–169.

PEI, MARIO, *The Story of Language* (Philadelphia: J. B. Lippincott Co., 1949), pp. 149–169.

————, *The Story of English* (Philadelphia: J. B. Lippincott & Co., 1952), pp. 1–125.

————, *Language for Everybody* (New York: Devin–Adair, 1956), pp. 136–176.

ROBERTSON, STUART, *The Development of Modern English* (rev. by F. G. Cassidy; Englewood Cliffs, N.J.: Prentice–Hall, 1954).

SCHLAUCH, MARGARET, *The Gift of Language* (New York: Dover Publications, 1955), pp. 193–226.

SHEARD, J. A., *The Words We Use* (London: Andre Deutsch, 1954), pp. 14–34, 129–319.

SMITH, LOGAN P., *Needed Words* (Oxford: Clarendon Press, 1928), pp. 313–329.

SPICER, EDWARD, "Linguistic Aspects of Yaqui Acculturations," *American Anthropologist,* 45 (July–Sept., 1943), 410–426.

STEWART, GEORGE R., *American Ways of Life* (Garden City, New York: Doubleday & Co., 1951), pp. 27–50.

SYKES, CHRISTOPHER, "What U–Future," in Nancy Mitford (ed.), *Noblesse Oblige* (New York: Harper and Brothers, 1956), pp. 139–156.

ULLMAN, STEPHEN, *Words and Their Use* (New York: Philosophical Library, 1951), pp. 57–85.

VAN PATTEN, N., "Organization of Source Material for the Study of American English and American Dialects," *American Speech,* 4 (Aug., 1929), 425–429.

VENDRYES, J., *Language: A Linguistic Introduction to History* (New York: Barnes & Noble reprint, 1951), pp. 270–279, 344–359.

WEEKLEY, ERNEST, *The Romance of Words* (New York: Dover Publications, 1960; originally published, London: John Murray, 1912), pp. 1–190.

WEINREICH, URIEL, *Languages in Contact: Findings and Problems* (New York: Publications of the Linguistic Circle of New York, No. 1, 1953).
WOOLNER, ALFRED C., *Languages in History and Politics* (New York: Oxford University Press, 1938), pp. 10–20.
WRENN, CHARLES L., *The English Language* (London: Methuen & Co., 1952).

VIII.   The Uniformation and Extension of Language: Historical, Contemporary

GENERAL

AIKIN, JANET R., "English as the International Language," *American Speech,* 9 (Apr., 1934), 98–110.
ALDRICH, VIRGIL C., "Speaking the Same Language," *Ethics,* 65 (Apr., 1955), 213–217.
BARNETT, LINCOLN, *The Treasure of Our Tongue: The Story of English from Its Obscure Beginnings to Its Present Eminence as the Most Widely Spoken Language on Earth* (New York: Alfred A. Knopf, Inc., 1964).
BIDWELL, CHARLES E., "Language, Dialect, and Nationality in Jugoslavia," *Human Relations,* 15 (No. 3, 1962), pp. 217–225.
BODMER, FREDERICK, *The Loom of Language* (New York: W. W. Norton Co., 1944), pp. 9–10, 187–518.
COHEN, MARCEL, *Pour une sociologie du langage* (Paris: Albin Michel, 1956), pp. 271–354.
COLE, G. D. H., *Essays in Social Theory* (London: The Macmillan Co., 1950), pp. 219–220.
ENTWISTLE, WILLIAM J., *Aspects of Language* (London: Faber & Faber, 1953), pp. 305–361.
FLUGEL, JOHN C., "Esperanto and the International Language Movement," in *Men and Their Machines* (New York: International Universities Press, 1947), pp. 159–213.
GOAD, HAROLD E., *Language in History* (Baltimore: Penguin Books, 1953), pp. 15–19.
HALL, ROBERT A., JR., "Leave Your Language Alone!," in Charles B. Jennings, Nancy King and Marjorie Stevenson (eds.), *Weigh the Word* (New York: Harper & Brothers, 1957), pp. 152–160.
HUGHES, JOHN P., *The Science of Language* (New York: Random House, 1962), pp. 73–115.
JACOB, H., *A Planned Auxiliary Language* (London: Dennis Dobson, Ltd., 1957).
JESPERSEN, OTTO, *Mankind, Nation and Individual from a Linguistic Point of View* (Cambridge: Harvard University Press, 1925), pp. 38–83, 106.
LAIRD, CHARLTON, *The Miracle of Language* (Cleveland: World Publishing Co., 1953), pp. 283–291.
LEWIS, MORRIS M., *Language in Society* (London: Thomas Nelson & Sons, 1947), pp. 60–69.

PALMER, LEONARD R., *An Introduction to Modern Linguistics* (London: The Macmillan Co., 1936), pp. 141–143.

PEI, MARIO, *The World's Chief Languages* (London: George Allen & Unwin, 1949), pp. 15–58, 580–583.

———, *The Story of Language* (Philadelphia: J. B. Lippincott & Co., 1949), pp. 285–289, 426–464.

———, *The Story of English* (Philadelphia: J. B. Lippincott & Co., 1952), pp. 296–309.

———, *Language for Everybody* (New York: Devin–Adair, 1956), pp. 26–42, 227–243.

———, *One Language for the World* (New York: Devin–Adair, 1958).

———, "Ending the Language Traffic Jam," *Saturday Review*, 44 (Sept. 9, 1961), 14–16, 51.

UNESCO, *Scientific and Technical Translation and Other Aspects of the Language Problem* (Paris, 1957), pp. 173–218.

VENDRYES, J., *Language: A Linguistic Introduction to History* (London: Kegan Paul, Trench, Trubner & Co., 1925), pp. 260–279.

WHATMOUGH, JOSHUA, *Language: A Modern Synthesis* (New York: St. Martin's Press, 1956), pp. 51–65.

WOOLNER, ALFRED C., *Languages in History and Politics* (New York: Oxford University Press, 1938), pp. 9–22, 32–33, 48–167.

THE SPREAD OF PARTICULAR
LANGUAGES AND THE
LINGUISTIC "EMPIRES"

JESPERSEN, OTTO, *Mankind, Nation and Individual from a Linguistic Point of View* (Cambridge: Harvard University Press, 1925), pp. 46–73.

NICHOLS, W. H., "The World's Languages," *National Geographic Magazine*, 84 (Dec., 1943), 689–700.

PEI, MARIO, *The Story of Language* (Philadelphia: J. B. Lippincott & Co., 1949), pp. 136–168.

SHENTON, HERBERT N., *Cosmopolitan Conversation* (New York: Columbia University Press, 1933).

VOSSLER, KARL, *The Spirit of Language in Civilization*, trans. Oscar Oeser (London: Routledge & Kegan Paul; reprinted 1951), pp. 119–123.

IX.   Language as a Centripetal Factor in Human Societies

LANGUAGE AS A SOCIAL UNIFIER

BLOOMFIELD, LEONARD, *Language* (New York: Henry Holt & Co., 1933), pp. 42–56.

COHEN, MARCEL, *Pour une sociologie du langage* (Paris: Albin Michel, 1956), pp. 107–111.

COOLEY, CHARLES H., *Social Organization* (New York: Charles Scribner's Sons, 1915), pp. 80–90.
HAYAKAWA, S. I., *Language in Thought and Action* (New York: Harcourt, Brace & Co., 1949), pp. 69–81.
LEWIS, MORRIS M., *Language in Society* (London: Thomas Nelson & Sons, 1947), pp. 71–73, 94–99, 137–198.
PIERIS, RALPH, "Speech and Society: A Sociological Approach to Language," *American Sociological Review*, 16 (Aug., 1951), 499–505.
SAPIR, EDWARD, "Language," *Encyclopedia of the Social Sciences* (New York: Macmillan Co., 1943), IX, 155–169.
VOSSLER, KARL, *The Spirit of Language in Civilization*, trans. Oscar Oeser (London: Routledge & Kegan Paul; reprinted in 1951), pp. 174–197.
WAGNER, PHILIP L., *The Human Use of the Earth* (Glencoe, Ill.: Free Press, 1960), pp. 39–53.

ASSIMILATION AND LANGUAGE

DEUTSCH, KARL W., *Nationalism and Social Communication: An Inquiry into the Foundations of Nationality* (New York: John Wiley & Sons, and Cambridge, Mass.: Technology Press of M. I. T., 1953), pp. 97–138.
JESPERSON, OTTO, *Mankind, Nation and Individual from a Linguistic Point of View* (Cambridge: Harvard University Press, 1925), pp. 38–83.
NELSON, LOWRY, *Rural Sociology* (New York: American Book, 1948), pp. 189–201.
ROSENQUIST, CARL M., "Linguistic Changes in the Acculturation of the Swedes of Texas," *Sociology and Social Research*, 16 (Jan.–Feb., 1932), 221–231.
SILVA–FUENZALIDA, ISMAEL, "Ethnolinguistics and the Study of Culture," *American Anthropologist*, 51 (July, 1949), 446–456.
TAFT, DONALD R. and RICHARD ROBBINS, *International Migration in the Modern World* (New York: Ronald Press, 1955), pp. 529–532.

LANGUAGE AND NATIONALITY
AND NATION

BOEHM, MAX H., "Nationalism: Theoretical Aspects," *Encyclopedia of the Social Sciences* (New York: Macmillan, 1938), II, 231–240 (232, 235).
COHEN, MARCEL, *Pour une sociologie du langage* (Paris: Albin Michel, 1956), pp. 307–335.
COMMAGER, HENRY S., "Schoolmaster to America," *Saturday Review*, 41 (Oct. 18, 1958), 10–12, 66–67.
DE FRANCIS, JOHN, *Nationalism and Language Reform in China* (Princeton: Princeton University Press, 1950).
DEUTSCH, KARL W., *Nationalism and Social Communication: An Inquiry into the Foundations of Nationality* (Published jointly by The Technology Press of the Mass. Inst. of Tech., Cambridge, Mass., 1953 and John Wiley & Sons, New York, 1953), pp. 3–14.
DOMINIAN, LEON, *The Frontiers of Language and Nationality in Europe* (New York: Henry Holt & Co., 1917), pp. i–xvi, 1–18, 97–98, 314–342.
EMERSON, RUPERT, *From Empire to Nation: The Rise to Self-assertion of Asian and African Peoples* (Cambridge: Harvard University Press,

1960), Chap. V, "The Nature of Nation," and Chap. VI, "People, Territory, and State," pp. 89–131.

GERTH, HANS H. and C. WRIGHT MILLS, *From Max Weber: Essays in Sociology* (New York: Oxford University Press, 1946), pp. 172–173, 177–179.

HAYES, CARLTON J. H., "Nationalism: Historical Development," *Encyclopedia of the Social Sciences* (New York: Macmillan Co., 1938), II, 240–248.

KOHN, HANS, *The Idea of Nationalism: A Study of Its Origin and Background* (New York: Macmillan Co., 1944), pp. 3–10.

————, *Nationalism: Its Meaning and History* (Princeton: D. Van Nostrand Co., 1955).

LOCKWOOD, W. B., "Language and the Rise of Nations," *Science and Society,* 18 (No. 3, 1954), 245–252.

MACIVER, ROBERT M. and CHARLES H. PAGE, *Society: An Introductory Analysis* (New York: Rinehart & Co., 1949), pp. 296–302.

PARK, ROBERT E., *The Immigrant Press and Its Control* (New York: Harper & Brothers, 1922), pp. 5–15, 33–57.

TAFT, DONALD R. and RICHARD ROBBINS, *International Migration* (New York: Ronald Press, 1955), pp. 116–117, 120, 453–454, 529–532.

VOSSLER, KARL, *The Spirit of Language in Civilization,* trans. Oscar Oeser (London: Routledge & Kegan Paul; reprinted 1951), pp. 115–129.

WARE, CAROLINE E., "Ethnic Communities," *Encyclopedia of the Social Sciences* (New York: Macmillan Co., 1931), VI, 607–613.

LANGUAGE PROBLEMS OF CONTEMPORARY MULTILINGUAL PEOPLES TRYING TO ESTABLISH NATIONAL UNITY

DE FRANCIS, JOHN, *Nationalism and Language Reform in China* (Princeton: Princeton University Press, 1950).

EMERSON, RUPERT, *From Empire to Nation: The Rise to Self-assertion of Asian and African Peoples* (Cambridge: Harvard University Press, 1960), Chap. III, "The Rejection of Colonialism," pp. 37–59; Chap. VII, "Language," pp. 132–148.

HARRIS, SELIG S., *The Most Dangerous Decades: An Introduction to the Comparative Study of Language Development in Multi-lingual States* (New York: Columbia University, Language and Communication Center, 1957).

HSIA, TAO-TAI, "The Language Revolution in Communist China," *Far Eastern Survey,* 25 (Oct., 1956), 145–154.

LEWIS, WILLIAM H., "The Ethiopian Empire," *Middle Eastern Journal,* 11 (Summer, 1956), 257–268.

MAYER, KURT, "Cultural Pluralism and Linguistic Equilibrium in Switzerland," *American Sociological Review,* 16 (Apr., 1951), 157–163.

WHITE, JAMES D., "The Language Front in China," *Saturday Review,* 39 (Mar. 17, 1956), 9–10, 44.

WINDMILLER, MARSHALL, "Linguistic Regionalism in India," *Pacific Affairs,* 27 (Dec., 1954), 291–318.

X. Language as a Centrifugal Factor in Human Societies

BOEHM, MAX H., "Nationalism: Theoretical Aspects," *Encyclopedia of the Social Sciences* (New York: Macmillan Co., 1938), II, 231–240.

CAMPA, ARTHUR L., "Language Barriers in Intercultural Relations," *Journal of Communication*, 1 (Nov. 1, 1951), 41–46.

GLENN, E. S., "Semantic Difficulties in International Communication," *ETC.: A Review of General Semantics*, 11 (Spring, 1954), 163–180.

LEWIS, MORRIS M., *Language in Society* (London: Thomas Nelson & Sons, 1947), pp. 199–220.

MANNING, CLARENCE A., "The Menace of Linguistic Nationalism," *South Atlantic Quarterly*, 44 (Jan., 1945), 13–22.

ORNSTEIN, JACOB, "Our Tongue-tied Generation," *Saturday Review*, 43 (Nov. 26, 1960), 15–17, 32–39.

PARK, ROBERT E., *The Immigrant Press and Its Control* (New York: Harper & Brothers, 1922), pp. 18–28, 55–57, 79–88.

PEI, MARIO, *The Story of Language* (Philadelphia: J. B. Lippincott & Co., 1949), pp. 254–264.

PIERIS, RALPH, "Speech and Society: A Sociological Approach to Language," *American Sociological Review*, 16 (Aug., 1951), 499–505.

STURDEVANT, EDGAR H., *An Introduction to Linguistic Science* (New Haven: Yale University Press, 1947), pp. 124–125.

XI. The Language of Social Control and the Social Control of Language

GENERAL

ALBIG, WILLIAM, *Modern Public Opinion* (New York: McGraw–Hill Book Co., 1956), pp. 96–113.

ARNESON, ELIAS, "Language and Semantics," in Joseph S. Roucek (ed.), *Social Control* (New York: D. Van Nostrand Co., 1955), pp. 223–239.

CHASE, STUART, *The Tyranny of Words* (New York: Harcourt, Brace & Co., 1938).

COHEN, MARCEL, *Pour une sociologie du langage* (Paris: Albin Michel, 1956), pp. 227–263.

HAYAKAWA, S. I., "The Language of Social Control," in *Language in Thought and Action* (New York: Harcourt, Brace & Co., 1949), pp. 100–110.

LA PIERE, RICHARD and PAUL K. FARNSWORTH, *Social Psychology* (3rd ed.; New York: McGraw–Hill Book Co., 1949), pp. 101–139.

LOWENTHAL, LEO and NORBERT GUTERMAN, *Prophets of Deceit: A Study of the Techniques of the American Agitator* (New York: Harper & Brothers, 1949).

LUMLEY, FREDERICK E., *Means of Social Control* (New York: Century Co., 1925), pp. 56–99.

MALINOWSKI, BRONISLAW, *Coral Gardens and Their Magic* (New York: American Book Co., 1935), II, 9–10, 52–61, 213–250.

MARSHALL, JOHN, *Swords and Symbols: The Technique of Sovereignty* (New York: Oxford University Press, 1939).

MEERLOO, JOOST A. M., *Conversation and Communication: A Psychological Inquiry into Language and Human Relations* (New York: International Universities Press, Inc., 1952), pp. 78–110, 114–118, 120–157, 170–174.

THE MAGICAL POWER OF WORDS

CASSIRER, ERNEST, *Language and Myth*, trans. Suzanne K. Langer (New York: Dover Publications, 1946), pp. 44–62.

FRAZER, SIR JAMES G., *The Golden Bough: A Study in Magic and Religion.* (Abridged ed.; New York: The Macmillan Co., 1951), pp. 284–305.

JESPERSEN, OTTO, *Mankind, Nation and Individual* (London: George Allen & Unwin, Ltd., 1946), pp. 166–185.

LEE, IRVING J., *Language Habits in Human Affairs* (New York: Harper & Brothers, 1941), pp. 159–160.

MALINOWSKI, BRONISLAW, "The Power of Words in Magic," in *Argonauts of the Western Pacific* (London: George Routledge & Sons, Ltd., 1922), pp. 428–463.

MEERLOO, JOOST A. M., *Conversation and Communication: A Philosophical Inquiry into Language and Human Relations* (New York: International Universities Press, 1952), pp. 72–75.

NAMES AS CONTROLLERS

ADAMIC, LOUIS, *What's Your Name?* (New York: Harper & Brothers, 1942), pp. 6–9.

HUGHES, EVERETT C. and HELEN M. HUGHES, "What's in A Name?" in *Where People Meet* (Glencoe, Ill.: Free Press, 1960), pp. 130–144.

LÉVY-BRUHL, LUCIEN, *How Primitives Think* (London: Allen & Unwin, 1926), pp. 50–54, 347.

LOTZ, JOHN, "Linguistics," in Lynn White, Jr. (ed.), *Frontiers of Knowledge in the Study of Man* (New York: Harper & Brothers, 1956), pp. 230–231.

LUMLEY, FREDERICK E., *Means of Social Control* (New York: The Century Co., 1925), pp. 288–314.

PEI, MARIO, *The Story of Language* (Philadelphia: J. B. Lippincott & Co., 1949), pp. 57–78.

THOMAS, WILLIAM I., *Primitive Behavior* (New York: McGraw–Hill Book Co., 1909), pp. 78, 91, 97.

WERKMEISTER, WILLIAM H., *A Philosophy of Science* (New York: Harper & Brothers, 1940), pp. 112–117.

TABOO WORDS, EUPHEMISMS, METAPHORS, PROFANITY, EXPLETIVES, HUMOROUS USAGES

ESTRICH, ROBERT M. and HANS SPERBER, *Three Keys to Language* (New York: Rinehart & Co., 1952), pp. 1–55, 276–309.

GRAFF, WILLIAM L., *Language and Languages* (New York: Appleton, 1931), pp. 282–283.

HASS, MARY R., "Interlingual Word Taboos," *American Anthropologist*, 53 (July–Sept., 1951), 338–344.

JOHNSON, BURGES, "The Oath Interjectional," in C. B. Jennings, Nancy King and Margaret Stevenson (eds.), *Weigh the Word* (New York: Harper & Brothers, 1957), pp. 133–138.

LEE, IRVING J., *Language Habits in Human Affairs* (New York: Harper & Brothers, 1941), pp. 159–172.

MENCKEN, H. L., "American Profanity," *American Speech*, 19 (Dec., 1944), 241–249.

———, *The American Language: An Inquiry into the Development of English in the United States* (New York: Alfred A. Knopf, 1945), Supplement I, pp. 565–683.

PALMER, LEONARD R., *An Introduction to Modern Linguistics* (London: The Macmillan Co., 1936), pp. 99–100.

PARTRIDGE, ERIC, *Here, There, and Everywhere: Essays Upon Language* (London: Hamish Hamilton, 1950), pp. 39–49.

PEI, MARIO, *The Story of Language* (Philadelphia: J. B. Lippincott & Co., 1949), pp. 248–253.

SAGARIN, EDWARD, *The Anatomy of Dirty Words* (New York: Lyle Stuart, 1962).

SCHLAUCH, MARGARET, *The Gift of Language* (New York: Dover Publications, 1955), pp. 278–279.

URQUHART, W. S., "Profanity," in *Hastings' Encyclopedia of Religion and Ethics* (Edinburgh: Clark, 1918), X, 378–381.

VENDRYES, J., *Language: A Linguistic Introduction to History* (London: Kegan Paul, Trench, Trubner Co., 1925), pp. 218–221, 256.

PROVERBS

ALBIG, WILLIAM, "Proverbs and Social Control," *Sociology & Social Research*, 15 (July–Aug., 1931), 527–535.

HERTZLER, JOYCE O., "The Social Wisdom of the Primitives, with Special Reference to Their Proverbs," *Social Forces*, 11 (Mar., 1933), 313–326. Also in Joyce O. Hertzler, *Social Thought of Ancient Civilizations* (New York: McGraw-Hill Book Co., 1936, or New York: Russell & Russell, 1962), pp. 373–388.

XII.   Social Differentiation and Linguistic Specialization in the Language Community: I. Theoretical Orientation; the Dialects

GENERAL

COHEN, MARCEL, *Pour une sociologie du langage* (Paris: Albin Michel, 1956), pp. 168–213.

GROSS, EDWARD, *Work and Society* (New York: Thomas Y. Crowell & Co., 1958), pp. 235–241.

JESPERSEN, OTTO, *Language: Its Nature, Development, and Origin* (New York: The Macmillan Co., 1922), pp. 237–254.

KURATH, HANS, "The American Languages," *Scientific American,* 182 (Jan., 1950), 48–51.

LA PIERE, RICHARD T., *Sociology* (New York: McGraw–Hill Co., 1946), pp. 218–224.

———, *A Theory of Social Control* (New York: McGraw–Hill Book Co., 1954), pp. 216–217, 261–263.

LEWIS, MORRIS M., *Language, Thought and Personality in Infancy and Childhood* (New York: Basic Books, 1963), pp. 101–117.

MEILLET, ANTOINE, "How Words Change Their Meanings," in Talcott Parsons, Edward Shils, Kasper D. Naegle, and Jesse R. Pitts (eds.), *Theories of Society* (New York: Free Press of Glencoe, 1961), II, 1013–1018.

MENCKEN, H. L., *The American Language: An Inquiry into the Development of English in the United States* (New York: Alfred A. Knopf, 1948), Supplement II, pp. 332–394.

PARTRIDGE, ERIC, *The World of Words* (London: George Routledge & Sons, Ltd., 1938), pp. 191–198.

———, *Here, There, and Everywhere: Essays upon Language* (London: Hamish Hamilton, 1950), pp. 51–52.

PEI, MARIO, *The Story of English* (Philadelphia: J. B. Lippincott & Co., 1952), pp. 178–217.

POTTER, SIMEON, *Modern Linguistics* (London, Andre Deutsch, Ltd., 1957), pp. 123–140.

VENDRYES, J., *Language: A Linguistic Introduction to History* (London: Kegan Paul, Trench, Trubner & Co., 1925), pp. 240–259.

VOSSLER, KARL, *The Spirit of Language in Civilization,* trans. Oscar Oeser (London: Routledge & Kegan Paul; reprinted, 1951), pp. 160–166.

WEINREICH, URIEL, *Languages in Contact* (New York: Publications of the Linguistic Circle of New York: 1953), pp. 89–99.

SLANG

BERREY, LESTER V. and MELVIN VAN DEN BARK, *The American Thesaurus of Slang: A Complete Reference Book of Colloquial Speech* (2nd ed.; New York: Thomas Y. Crowell Co., 1953).

JESPERSEN, OTTO, *Mankind, Nation and Individual from a Linguistic Point of View* (Cambridge: Harvard University Press, 1925), pp. 149–165.

MENCKEN, H. L., *The American Language* (New York: Alfred A. Knopf, 1948), Supplement II, pp. 643–652.

PARTRIDGE, ERIC, *Slang Today and Yesterday, with a Short Historical Sketch and Vocabularies of English, American, and Australian Slang* (3rd ed.; London: Routledge & Kegan Paul, 1950), pp. 1–42.

———, *A Dictionary of Slang and Unconventional English* (4th ed.; London: Routledge and Kegan Paul, 1949).

PEI, MARIO, *The Story of Language* (Philadelphia: J. B. Lippincott & Co., 1949), pp. 168–180.

———, *The Story of English* (Philadelphia: J. B. Lippincott & Co., 1952), pp. 178–192.

ROBACK, ABRAHAM A., "The Psychology of Slang," in his *Destiny and Motivation in Language* (Cambridge, Mass.: Sci-Art Publishers, 1954), pp. 305–330.

WENTWORTH, HAROLD and STUART B. FLEXNER, *Dictionary of American Slang* (New York: Thomas Y. Crowell & Co., 1960).

WESEEN, MAURICE H., *A Dictionary of American Slang* (New York: Thomas Y. Crowell & Co., 1934).

WILLIS, GEORGE, *The Philosophy of Speech* (New York: The Macmillan Co., no date given, about 1923), pp. 193–197.

DIALECTS

BLOOMFIELD, LEONARD, *Language* (New York: Henry Holt & Co., 1933), pp. 321–345.

DE SAUSSURE, FERDINAND, *Course in General Linguistics,* trans. Wade Baskin (New York: Philosophical Library, 1959), pp. 191–211.

DRAKE, J. A., "The Effect of Urbanization on Regional Vocabulary," *American Speech,* 36 (Feb., 1961), 17–33.

GUMPERZ, JOHN J., "Dialect Differences and Social Stratification in a North Indian Village," *American Anthropologist,* 60 (Aug., 1958), 668–682.

HUGHES, JOHN P., *The Science of Language* (New York: Random House, 1962), pp. 23–30.

KURATH, HANS, *A Word Geography of the Eastern United States* (Ann Arbor: University of Michigan Press, 1949).

———, "Linguistic Regionalism," in M. Jensen (ed.), *Regionalism in America* (Madison: University of Wisconsin Press, 1951), pp. 297–310.

MCDAVID, RAVEN I., "Dialect Geography and Social Science Problems," *Social Forces,* 25 (Dec., 1946), 168–172.

MENCKEN, H. L., *The American Language* (New York: Alfred A. Knopf, 1948), Supplement II, pp. 101–269.

PALMER, LEONARD R., "Linguistic Geography," in *An Introduction to Modern Linguistics* (London: Macmillan Co., 1936), pp. 129–150.

ROBACK, ABRAHAM A., *Destiny and Motivation in Language* (Cambridge, Mass.: Sci-Art Publications, 1954), pp. 279–289.

SAPIR, EDWARD, "Dialect," *Encyclopedia of the Social Sciences* (New York: The Macmillan Co., 1931), V, 123–126.

538 BIBLIOGRAPHY

XIII. Social Differentiation and Linguistic Specialization in the
Language Community: II. The Special Group and
Technical Languages

The files of *American Speech* present dozens of specific studies of special languages of the halfworld and underworld, of occupations, industries
and markets, of the military and of soldiers, of the theater, sports, games
and the jazz world, of school teachers and of religious sects. For a most
detailed account of American trade argots, beginning with advertising agents
and proceeding alphabetically to union men in general, with voluminous
examples of each, see H. L. Mencken, *The American Language,* Supplement II (New York: Alfred A. Knopf, 1948), pp. 652–786. For a succinct
general reference on the various special languages, see Marcel Cohen, *Pour
une sociologie du langage* (Paris: Albin Michel, 1956), pp. 112–121, 188–
194, 208–213, 242–269.

THE LANGUAGE OF
SECRET SOCIETIES

GIST, NOEL P., *Secret Societies: A Cultural Study of Fraternalism in the
United States* (Columbia, Mo.: University of Missouri Studies), Vol. XV,
No. 4 (October 1, 1940), 55–58, 65–68, 93.
MARDEN, CHARLES F., "Secret Societies," in Joseph S. Roucek (ed.), *Social
Control,* 2nd ed. (Princeton, N.J.: D. Van Nostrand Co., 1956), pp.
295–314.
PIDDINGTON, RALPH, *An Introduction to Social Anthropology* (New York:
Frederick A. Praeger, 1950), I, pp. 207–213.
ROUCEK, JOSEPH S., "Sociology of Secret Societies," *American Journal of
Economics and Sociology,* 19 (Jan., 1960), 161–168.
SIMMEL, GEORG, "The Sociology of Secret Societies," *American Journal of
Sociology,* 11 (Jan., 1906), 441–498.

THE POLITICAL LANGUAGES

CAIRNS, HUNTINGTON, "Language of Jurisprudence," in Ruth N. Anshen
(ed.), *Language: An Enquiry into Its Meaning and Function* (New
York: Harper & Brothers, 1957), pp. 232–269.
EKVALL, ROBERT B., *Faithful Echo: The Role of Language in World
Diplomacy* (New Haven: College and University Press, 1964).
LASSWELL, HAROLD D., "The Language of Power," in Harold D. Lasswell,
Nathan Leites *et al., Language of Politics* (New York: George W.
Stuart, 1949), pp. 3–19.
———, "The Language of Politics," in Ruth N. Anshen (ed.), *Language:
An Enquiry into Its Meaning and Function* (New York: Harper &
Brothers, 1957), pp. 270–284.
——— and ABRAHAM KAPLAN, *Power and Society: A Framework for*

Political Inquiry (New Haven: Yale University Press, 1950), pp. 103–141.

———, DAVID LERNER and ITHIEL DE S. POOL, *A Comparative Study of Symbols* (Stanford, Calif.: Stanford University Press, 1952), pp. 1–25.

MARSHALL, JOHN, *Swords and Symbols: The Techniques of Sovereignty* (New York: Oxford Univerity Press, 1939).

THE LANGUAGE OF RELIGION

DEMOS, RAPHAEL, "The Meaningfulness of Religious Language," *Journal of Philosophy and Phenomenological Research,* 18 (Sept., 1957), 96–106.

ESTRICH, ROBERT M. and HANS SPERBER, *Three Keys to Language* (New York: Rinehart & Co., 1952), pp. 64–70.

VOSSLER, KARL, *The Spirit of Language in Civilization,* trans. Oscar Oeser (London: Routledge and Kegan Paul, 1951), pp. 22–42.

THE LANGUAGE OF THE ARTS

BARFIELD, OWEN, *"Poetic Diction and Legal Fiction,"* in Max Black (ed.), *The Importance of Language* (Englewood Cliffs, N.J.: Prentice–Hall, 1962), pp. 51–71.

FERGUSSON, FRANCIS, "Language of the Theater," in Ruth N. Anshen (ed.), *Language: An Enquiry into Its Meaning and Function* (New York: Harper & Brothers, 1957), pp. 285–295.

HOFSTADTER, ALBERT, "The Scientific and Literary Uses of Language," in Lyman Bryson, Louis Finkelstein, Helen Hoagland and Robert M. MacIver (eds.), *Symbols and Society: Fourteenth Symposium of the Conference on Science, Philosophy, and Religion* (New York: Harper & Brothers, 1953), pp. 291–335.

NAUMBERG, MARGARET, "Art as Symbolic Speech," in Ruth N. Anshen (ed.), *Language: An Enquiry into Its Meaning and Function* (New York: Harper & Brothers, 1957), pp. 296–320.

SCHLAUCH, MARGARET, *The Gift of Language* (New York: Dover Publications, 1955), pp. 227–259.

VOSSLER, KARL, *The Spirit of Language in Civilization* (London: Routledge and Kegan Paul, 1951), pp. 217–234.

THE LANGUAGE OF
THE JAZZ COMMUNITY

BALLIETT, WHITNEY, "What are the Cats in the Backroom Doing?" *Saturday Review,* 37 (Feb. 27, 1954), 52, 61.

BECKER, HOWARD S., "The Professional Dance Musician and His Audience," *American Journal of Sociology,* 57 (Sept., 1951), 136–144.

CAMERON, WILLIAM B., "Sociological Notes on the Jam Session," *Social Forces,* 33 (Dec., 1954), 177–182.

GOLD, ROBERT S., "The Vernacular of the Jazz-World," *American Speech,* 32 (Dec., 1957), 271–282.

HART, JAMES D., "Jazz Jargon," *American Speech*, 7 (Apr., 1932), 241–254.

MENCKEN, H. L., *The American Language*, Supplement II (New York: Alfred A. Knopf, 1948), pp. 704–710; or in the one-volume abridged edition, Raven I. McDavid (ed.) (New York: Alfred A. Knopf, 1963), pp. 739–744.

MERRIAM, ALAN P. and RAYMOND W. MACK, "The Jazz Community," *Social Forces*, 38 (Mar., 1960), 211–222.

SHAW, ARNOLD, "The Vocabulary of Tin-Pan Alley Explained," *Music Library Association Notes*, 7 (Dec., 1949), 33–53.

THE LANGUAGE OF SCIENCE

ANSHEN, RUTH N., "Language as Communication," in Ruth N. Anshen (ed.), *Language: An Enquiry into Its Meaning and Function* (New York: Harper & Brothers, 1957), pp. 341–355.

BLOOMFIELD, LEONARD, "Linguistic Aspects of Science," *International Encyclopedia of Unified Science* (Chicago: University of Chicago Press, 1939), Vol. I, No. 4, pp. 1–59.

CASSIRER, ERNST, "The Influence of Language upon the Development of Scientific Thought," *Journal of Philosophy*, 39 (June 4, 1942), 309–327.

GERR, STANLEY, "Language and Science: The Rational, Functional Language of Science and Technology," *Philosophy of Science*, 9 (Apr., 1942), 146–161.

HOUGH, J. N., *Scientific Terminology* (New York: Rinehart & Co., 1953).

MADGE, JOHN, *The Tools of Social Science* (New York: Longmans Green & Co., 1953), pp. 38–58.

MISES, RICHARD VON, *Positivism, A Study in Human Understanding* (Cambridge: Harvard University Press, 1951), pp. 51–54.

ROSE, EDWARD, "The English Record of a National Sociology," *American Sociological Review*, 25 (Apr., 1960), 193–208.

SAVORY, THEODORE H., *The Language of Science: Its Growth, Character, and Usage* (London: Andre Deutsch, 1953).

VOSSLER, KARL, *The Spirit of Language in Civilization* (London: Routledge and Kegan Paul, 1951), pp. 198–216.

XIV.   Social Differentiation and Linguistic Specialization in the Language Community: III. The Languages of the Social Classes

BARBER, BERNARD, *Social Stratification* (New York: Harcourt, Brace & Co., 1957), pp. 151–152.

BEADLE, MURIEL, *These Ruins Are Inhabited* (Garden City, New York: Doubleday & Co., 1961), pp. 143, 209–210.

BERNSTEIN, BASIL, "Some Sociological Determinants of Perception: An Enquiry into Sub-Cultural Differences," *British Journal of Sociology*, 9 (June, 1958), 159–174.

———, "Public Language: Some Sociological Implications of a Linguistic Form," *British Journal of Sociology*, 10 (Dec., 1959), 311–326.

———, "Language and Social Class," *British Journal of Sociology*, 11 (Sept., 1960), 271–276.

———, "Social Class, Linguistic Codes and Grammatical Elements," *Language and Speech*, 5 (Oct.–Dec., 1962), 221–240.

BOSSARD, JAMES H. S., "The Bilingual as a Person—Linguistic Identification with Status," *American Sociological Review*, 10 (Dec., 1945), 699–709.

COHEN, MARCEL, *Pour une sociologie du langage* (Paris: Albin Michel, 1956), pp. 175–180, 198–208.

GERTH, HANS H. and C. WRIGHT MILLS, *Character and Social Structure: The Psychology of Social Institutions* (New York: Harcourt, Brace & Co., 1953), pp. 278–280.

GILMAN, ALBERT and ROGER BROWN, "Who Says 'Tu' to Whom," *ETC.: A Review of General Semantics*, 15 (Spring, 1958), 169–174.

GUMPERZ, JOSEPH J., "Dialect Differences and Social Stratification in a North Indian Village," *American Anthropolgist*, 60 (Aug., 1958), 668–682.

HOCKETT, CHARLES F., *A Course in Modern Linguistics* (New York: Macmillan Co., 1958), "Dialect Geography and Social Stratification," pp. 471–484.

HOGGART, RICHARD, *The Uses of Literacy* (London: Chatto & Windus, 1957), pp. 21, 27–29, 74–75.

JESPERSEN, OTTO, *Mankind, Nation and Individual from a Linguistic Point of View* (Cambridge: Harvard University Press, 1925), pp. 141–148.

LA PIERE, RICHARD T., *Sociology* (McGraw–Hill Book Co., 1946), pp. 221–222.

LAWTON, DENIS, "Social Class Differences in Language Development," *Language and Speech*, 6 (July–Sept., 1963), 109–119.

PEI, MARIO, "The Language of Politeness," in *The Story of Language* (Philadelphia: J. B. Lippincott & Co., 1949), pp. 79–85.

———, *Voices of Man: The Meaning and Function of Language* (New York: Harper and Row, 1962), pp. 90–92.

PIERIS, RALPH, "Speech and Society: A Sociological Approach to Language," *American Sociological Review*, 16 (Aug., 1951), 499–505 (502–504).

———, "Bilingualism and Cultural Marginality," *British Journal of Sociology*, 2 (Dec., 1951), 328–339.

ROSS, ALAN S. C., "U and Non–U: An Essay in Sociological Linguistics," in Max Black (ed.), *The Importance of Language* (Englewood Cliffs, N.J.: Prentice–Hall, 1962), pp. 91–106.

SCHATZMAN, LEONARD L. and ANSELM L. STRAUSS, "Social Class and Modes of Communication," *American Journal of Sociology*, 60 (Jan., 1955), 329–338.

STALIN, JOSEPH, *Marxism and Linguistics* (New York: International Press, 1951), pp. 14–22.

THOMAS, WILLIAM I., *Primitive Behavior* (New York: McGraw–Hill Book Co., 1937), pp. 81–89.

VENDRYES, J., *Language: A Linguistic Introduction to History* (London: Kegan Paul, Trench, Trubner & Co., 1925), pp. 224–226, 243.

XV. Language and the Individual

LANGUAGE AND THE SOCIAL DEVELOPMENT OF THE CHILD

BOSSARD, JAMES H. S., *The Sociology of Child Development* (New York: Harper & Brothers, 1948), pp. 176–179.

CHURCH, JOSEPH, *Language and the Discovery of Reality: A Developmental Psychology of Cognition* (New York: Random House, 1961), pp. 56–122.

COOLEY, CHARLES H., *Social Organization* (New York: Charles Scribner's Sons, 1922), pp. 45–50, 52–54, 61–69, 80–86.

DUNCAN, HUGH D., *Communication and Social Order* (New York: Bedminster Press, 1962), pp. 73–81.

ESPER, ERWIN A., "Language," in G. Murchison (ed.), *Handbook of Social Psychology* (Worcester, Mass.: Clark University Press, 1935), pp. 433–443.

LAGUNA, GRACE M. DE, *Speech: Its Function and Development* (New Haven: Yale University Press, 1927).

LEWIS, MORRIS M., *Infant Speech: A Study of the Beginnings of Language* (2nd ed.; New York: Humanities Press, 1951).

———, *How Children Learn to Speak* (New York: Basic Books, 1959).

———, *Language, Thought, and Personality in Infancy and Childhood* (New York: Basic Books, Inc., 1963).

LINDESMITH, ALFRED R. and ANSELM L. STRAUSS, *Social Psychology* (rev. ed.; New York: Holt, Rinehart & Winston, 1956), pp. 159–196.

LUNDBERG, GEORGE A., CLARENCE SCHRAG, and OTTO N. LARSEN, *Sociology* (New York: Harper & Brothers, 1954), pp. 218–222.

McCARTHY, DOROTHEA, "Language Development in Children," in Leonard Carmichael (ed.), *Manual of Child Psychology* (New York: John Wiley & Sons, 1946), pp. 476–581.

MEAD, GEORGE H., *Mind, Self, and Society* (Chicago: University of Chicago Press, 1934), pp. 49–50, 122–123, 135–226.

MILLER, GEORGE A., *Language and Communication* (New York: McGraw–Hill Book Co., 1951), 140–173.

MILLER, NEAL E. and JOHN DOLLARD, *Social Learning and Imitation* (New Haven: Yale University Press, 1947), pp. 80–84.

PIAGET, JEAN, *The Language and Thought of the Child*, trans. M. Warden (London: Kegan Paul, Trench, Trubner, 1926),

———, *Judgment and Reasoning in the Child*, trans. M. Warden (London: Kegan Paul, Trench, Trubner, 1928).

———, *The Child's Conception of the World*, trans. J. and L. Tomlinson (London: Kegan Paul, Trench, Trubner, 1929).

———, *The Psychology of Intelligence* (London: Routledge & Kegan Paul, 1950).

———, *The Origins of Intelligence in Children*, trans. M. Cook (New York: International Universities Press, 1952).

———, *The Construction of Reality in the Child*, trans. M. Cook (New York: Basic Books, 1954).

SCHRECKER, PAUL, "The Family Conveyance of Tradition," in Ruth N.

Anshen (ed.), *The Family: Its Function and Destiny* (New York: Harper & Brothers, 1949), pp. 406–425 (411–420).

SHERIF, MUZAFER and CAROLINE W. SHERIF, *An Outline of Social Psychology* (New York: Harper & Brothers, 1956), pp. 458–465, 469–482.

TEMPLIN, MILDRED C., *Certain Language Skills in Children* (Minneapolis: University of Minnesota Press, 1957).

LANGUAGE AND THE SELF

BENDA, CLEMENS E., "The Linguistic Basis of Consciousness," *ETC.: A Review of General Semantics, 16* (Spring, 1959), 343–355.

DAVIS, KINGSLEY, *Human Society* (New York: The Macmillan Co., 1949), pp. 208–212.

DOOB, LEONARD W., *Social Psychology: An Analysis of Human Behavior* (New York: Henry Holt & Co., 1952), pp. 109–115.

FIRTH, JOHN R., "Personality and Language in Society," *Sociological Review* (British), 42 (1950), 37–53.

JOHNSON, WENDELL, *People in Quandaries: The Semantics of Personal Adjustment* (New York: Harper & Brothers, 1946), pp. 243–267.

LEWIS, MORRIS M., *Language in Society* (London: Thomas Nelson & Sons, 1947), pp. 71–93.

MEAD, GEORGE H., *Mind, Self, and Society* (Chicago: University of Chicago Press, 1934).

———, "Language and the Development of Self," in T. M. Newcomb, and E. L. Hartley (eds.), *Readings in Social Psychology* (New York: Henry Holt & Co., 1947), pp. 179–189.

MEERLOO, JOOST A. M., *Conversation and Communication: A Psychological Inquiry Into Language and Human Relations* (New York: International Universities Press, 1952), pp. 40–41, 58–71.

SANFORD, FILLMORE H., "Speech and Personality," *Psychological Bulletin,* 39 (Dec., 1942), 811–45 (bibliography, pp. 841–845).

SARBIN, THEODORE R., "Role Theory," in Gardner Lindzey (ed.), *Handbook of Social Psychology* (Cambridge: Addison–Wesley Publishing Co., 1954), pp. 223–258 (238–244).

LACK OF LANGUAGE OR IMPAIRMENT OF LANGUAGE FACILITY

DAVIS, KINGSLEY, "Extreme Social Isolation of a Child," *American Journal of Sociology,* 45 (Jan., 1940), 556–565.

———, "Final Note on a Case of Extreme Isolation," *American Journal of Sociology,* 52 (Mar., 1947), 432–437.

GESELL, ARNOLD, *Wolf Child and Human Child* (New York: Harper & Brothers, 1939).

GOLDSTEIN, KURT, *Human Nature in the Light of Psychology* (Cambridge: Harvard University Press, 1940).

———, *Language and Language Disturbances: Aphasic Symptom Complexes and Their Significance for Medicine and Theory of Language* (New York: Grune & Stratton, 1948).

JOHNSON, WENDALL, "Speech and Personality," in Lyman Bryson (ed.),

The Communication of Ideas (New York: Harper & Brothers, 1948), pp. 53–78.

LINDESMITH, ALFRED R. and ANSELM L. STRAUSS, *Social Psychology* (New York: Holt, Rinehart & Winston, 1956), pp. 131–158.

SINGH, J. A. L. and R. M. ZINGG, *Wolf Children and Feral Man* (New York: Harper & Brothers, 1942).

LANGUAGE AS THE INDEX AND REVEALER OF THE INDIVIDUAL

ALLPORT, GORDON W. and P. E. VERNON, *Studies in Expressive Movement* (New York: Macmillan Co., 1930).

BAKER, SIDNEY J., "The Pattern of Language," *Journal of General Psychology*, 42 (Jan., 1950), pp. 25–66.

BODER, DAVID P. "The Adjective–Verb Quotient: A Contribution to the Psychology of Language," *Psychological Record*, 22 (1940), 310–343.

CHURCH, JOSEPH, *Language and the Discovery of Reality: A Developmental Psychology of Cognition* (New York: Random House, 1961), pp. 130, 189–192.

ESTRICH, ROBERT M. and HANS SPERBER, *Three Keys to Language* (New York: Rinehart, 1952), Chap. 13, "Personal Style," pp. 212–235.

HOFSTADTER, ALBERT, "The Linguistic Persona," in Lyman Bryson, Louis Finkelstein, Helen Hoagland, and Robert M. MacIver (eds.), *Symbols and Society Fourteenth Symposium of the Conference on Science, Philosophy, and Religion* (New York: Harper and Brothers, 1958), pp. 327–333.

HUNTLEY, C. W., "Judgments of Self Based Upon Records of Expressive Behavior," *Journal of Abnormal & Social Psychology*, 35 (July, 1940), 398–427.

SAMORA, JULIAN and WILLIAM N. DEANE, "Language Usage as a Possible Index of Acculturation," *Sociology and Social Research*, 40 (May–June, 1956), 307–311.

SANFORD, FILLMORE H., "Speech and Personality: A Comparative Case Study," *Character & Personality*, 10 (Mar., 1942), 169–198.

SAPIR, EDWARD, "Speech as a Personality Trait," *American Journal of Sociology*, 32 (May, 1927), 892–905.

WOLFF, WERNER, *The Expression of Personality* (New York: Harper & Brothers, 1943).

XVI. Plural Lingualism in the Modern World

BARKER, GEORGE C., "Social Functions of Language in a Mexican–American Community," *Acta Americana*, 5 (July–Sept., 1947), 185–202.

———, "Growing Up in a Bilingual Community," *The Kiva*, 17 (Nov.–Dec., 1951), 17–32.

BOSSARD, JAMES H. S., "The Bilingual as a Person—Linguistic Identification with Status," *American Sociological Review*, 10 (Dec., 1945), 699–709.

BRAZEAU, E. JACQUES, "Language Differences and Occupational Experience," *Canadian Journal of Economic and Political Science*, 24 (Nov., 1958), 531–532.

COHEN, MARCEL, *Pour une sociologie du langage* (Paris: Albin Michel, 1956), pp. 80–81, 113–114, 171–175, 179–184, 221–222, 276–277, 329–330, 347, 356.

GUMPERZ, JOHN J., "Speech Variation and the Study of Indian Civilization," *American Anthropologist*, 63 (Oct., 1961), 976–988.

HAAS, MARY R., "Interlingual Word Taboos," *American Anthropologist*, 53 (July–Sept., 1951), 338–344.

HAUGEN, EINAR, *The Norwegian Language in America: A Study of Bilingual Behavior* (Philadelphia: University of Pennsylvania Press, 1953), I, 1–91; II, 361–411.

———, *Bilingualism in the Americas: A Bibliography and Research Guide* (University, Alabama: University of Alabama Press, 1956).

HECHINGER, FRED M., "Foreign Languages Stage a Comeback," *Saturday Review*, 46 (Feb. 16, 1963), 64–66, 89–91.

HERMAN, SIMON N., "Explorations in the Social Psychology of Language Choice," *Human Relations*, 14 (No. 2, 1961), pp. 149–164.

JOHNSON, GRANVILLE B., JR., "The Relationship Existing between Bilingualism and Racial Attitude," *Journal of Educational Psychology*, 42 (Oct., 1951), 357–365.

LEWIS, MORRIS M., *Language in Society* (London: Thomas Nelson & Sons, 1947), pp. 66–67.

PIERIS, RALPH, "Bilingualism and Cultural Marginality," *British Journal of Sociology*, 2 (Dec., 1951), 328–339.

TAFT, DONALD R. and RICHARD ROBBINS, *International Migration: The Immigrant in the Modern World* (New York: Ronald Press, 1955), pp. 529–532.

VILDOMEC, VEROBOJ, *Multilingualism* (Leyden: A. W. Sythoff, 1953).

WARNER, W. LLOYD and LEO SROLE *The Social Systems of American Ethnic Groups* (New Haven: Yale University Press, 1945), pp. 220–238.

WEINREICH, URIEL, *Languages in Contact: Findings and Problems* (New York: Publications of the Linguistic Circle of New York, No. 1, 1953). See also his bibliography (pp. 123–146) of 658 items.

WHYTE, WILLIAM F. and ALLAN R. HOLMBERG, "The Problem of Language Learning," *Human Organization*, 15 (Fall, 1956), pp. 11–15.

XVII.   The Sociology of Writing

GENERAL

BLOOMFIELD, LEONARD, *Language* (New York: Henry Holt & Co., 1933), pp. 281–296.

BODMER, FREDERICK, *The Loom of Language* (New York: W. W. Norton Co., 1944), pp. 33–75.

BROWN, ROGER, *Words and Things* (Glencoe, Ill.: Free Press, 1958), pp. 57–63.

CHILDE, V. GORDON, *Man Makes Himself* (London: Watts & Co., 1937), pp. 202–256.

COHEN, MARCEL, *Pour une sociologie du langage* (Paris: Albin Michel, 1956), pp. 91–96, 186–188, 217–220.

DE SAUSSURE, FERDINAND, *Course of General Linguistics,* trans. Wade Baskin, (New York: Philosophical Library, 1959), pp. 23–32.

DIRINGER, DAVID, *The Alphabet: A Key to the History of Mankind* (New York: Philosophical Library, 1948).

GELB, IGNACE J., *A Study of Writing* (Chicago: University of Chicago Press, 1959).

GIRSDANSKY, MICHAEL, *The Adventure of Language* (Englewood Cliffs, N.J.: Prentice–Hall, 1963), pp. 140–154.

HOOKE, S. H., "Recording and Writing," in Charles Singer, E. J. Holmyard, and A. R. Hall (eds.), *A History of Technology* (Oxford: Clarendon Press, 1954), I, 744–773.

HUGHES, JOHN P., *The Science of Language* (New York: Random House, 1962), pp. 116–143.

LINTON, RALPH, *The Tree of Culture* (New York: Alfred A. Knopf, 1955), pp. 110–113.

MOORHOUSE, ALFRED C., *The Triumph of the Alphabet: A History of Writing* (New York: Henry Schuman, 1953).

RIESMAN, DAVID, *The Oral Tradition, the Written Word, and the Screen Image* (Yellow Springs, Ohio: Antioch Press, 1955).

ROGERS, FRANCES: *Painted Rock to Printed Page* (Philadelphia: J. B. Lippincott & Co., 1960).

ULLMAN, BERTHOLD L., *Ancient Writing and Its Influence* (New York: Longmans Green & Co., 1932).

VENDRYES, J., *Language: A Linguistic Introduction to History* (London: Kegan Paul, Trench, Trubner & Co., 1925), pp. 315–343.

WAPLES, DOUGLAS, BERNARD BERELSON and FRANKLIN R. BRADSHAW, "The Effects of Reading," from *What Reading Does to People* (Chicago: University of Chicago Press, 1940). (Reproduced in Wilbur Schramm [ed.], *Mass Communications,* Urbana, Ill.: University of Illinois Press, 1960, pp. 487–491).

THE HISTORICAL FORMS
OF WRITING

DIRINGER, DAVID, *The Alphabet: A Key to the History of Mankind* (New York: Philosophical Library, 1948), pp. 17–37.

GELB, IGNACE J., *A Study of Writing* (Chicago: University of Chicago Press, 1952), pp. 1–211.

KROEBER, ALFRED L., *Anthropology* (New York: Harcourt, Brace & Co., 1948), pp. 312–316, 371–372, 509–537.

PEI, MARIO, *The Story of Language* (Philadelphia: J. B. Lippincott & Co., 1949), pp. 86–94.

XVIII. Mass Communication, Language and Modern Society

BAUER, RAYMOND A. and ALICE H. BAUER, "America, Mass Society and Mass Media," *Journal of Social Issues*, 16 (No. 3, 1960), 3–66.

BREED, WARREN, "Mass Communication and Socio-cultural Structure," *Social Forces*, 37 (Dec., 1958), 109–116.

CARPENTER, EDMUND and MARSHALL MCLUHAN (eds.), *Explorations in Communication: An Anthology* (Boston: Beacon Press, 1960), pp. ix–xii, 1–3, 125–135, 162–179, 180–183, 196–199.

DEXTER, LEWIS A., and DAVID MANNING WHITE, *People, Society and Mass Communications* (New York: Free Press of Glencoe, 1964).

ELLIOTT, WILLIAM Y. (ed.), *Television's Impact on American Culture* (East Lansing, Mich.: Michigan State University Press, 1956).

KLAPPER, JOSEPH T., *The Effects of Mass Communication* (Glencoe, Ill.: Free Press, 1960). (Extensive bibliography of about 250 items, pp. 258–274).

LAZARSFELD, PAUL F. and GENEVIEVE KNUPFER, "Communications Research and International Cooperation," in Ralph Linton (ed.), *The Science of Man in the World Crisis* (New York: Columbia University Press, 1945), pp. 465–495.

LAZARSFELD, PAUL F. and ROBERT K. MERTON, "Mass Communication, Popular Taste, and Organized Social Action," in Lyman Bryson (ed.), *The Communication of Ideas* (New York: Harper & Brothers, 1948), pp. 95–118. (Also in Wilbur Schramm, (ed.), *Mass Communications* (Urbana, Ill.: University of Illinois Press, 1960), pp. 492–512.

LUNDBERG, GEORGE A., CLARENCE C. SCHRAG, and OTTO N. LARSEN, *Sociology* (3rd ed., New York: Harper & Row, 1963), pp. 227–265.

MACHLUP, FRITZ, *The Production and Distribution of Knowledge in the United States* (Princeton, N.J.: Princeton University Press, 1962). Ch. VI: The Media of Communication," pp. 207–294).

MEAD, MARGARET, "Some Cultural Approaches to Communication Problems," in Lyman Bryson (ed.), *Communication of Ideas* (New York: Harper & Brothers, 1948), pp. 9–26.

MEADOWS, PAUL, "An Age of Mass Communication," in *The Culture of Industrial Man* (Lincoln: University of Nebraska Press, 1950), pp. 96–112.

MERTON, ROBERT K., MARJORIE FISKE and ALBERTA CURTIS, *Mass Persuasion: The Social Psychology of a War Bond Drive* (New York: Harper & Brothers, 1946).

MILLER, GEORGE A., *Language and Communication* (New York: McGraw-Hill Publishing Co., 1950), pp. 260–269.

PARSONS, TALCOTT, *Structure and Process in Modern Societies* (Glencoe, Ill.: Free Press, 1960), pp. 266–275.

ROSE, ARNOLD M., "Reactions Against the Mass Society," *Sociological Quarterly*, 3 (Oct., 1962), 316–330.

SCHRAMM, WILBUR, *Mass Media and National Development: The Role of Information in Developing Countries* (Stanford, Calif.: Stanford University Press, 1964).

———— (ed.), *The Science of Human Communication: Direction and New Findings in Communication Research* (New York: Basic Books, 1963).

STEINBERG, CHARLES S., *The Mass Communicators: Public Relations, Public Opinion, and Mass Media* (New York: Harper & Brothers, 1958).

UNESCO, *World Communications: Press, Radio, Film, Television* (Paris, 1956).

WILENSKY, HAROLD L., "Mass Society and Mass Culture: Interdependence or Independence?" *American Sociological Review*, 29 (Apr., 1964), 173–197.

WIRTH, LOUIS, "Consensus and Mass Communication," *American Sociological Review*, 13 (Feb., 1948), 1–15.

WRIGHT, CHARLES R., *Mass Communication: A Sociological Perspective* (New York: Random House, 1959).

————, "Functional Analysis and Mass Communication," *Public Opinion Quarterly*, 24 (Winter, 1960), 605–620.

Name Index*

Abu-Lughod, Ibrahim, 513 n
Adamic, Louis, 271, 297 n, 389 n
Adler, Mortimer, 134
Aiken, Janet R., 226 n
Albig, William, 297 n, 299 n
Allport, Floyd H., 297 n
Amen-em-apt, 3
Angelino, Henry, 361 n
Angell, Robert C., 56 n
Anshen, Ruth N., 56 n
Arenson, Elias T., 297 n
Arnold, Matthew, 144
Astle, Thomas, 454, 472 n
Atatürk, 156, 174

Bacon, Francis, 134
Bagehot, Walter, 128
Baker, Sidney J., 226 n, 412 n
Balch, Emily G., 246 n
Baldwin, Bird T., 316 n
Bally, Charles, 14
Barber, Bernard, 388 n
Barker, George C., 425–6, 440 n
Barnett, Lincoln, 139 n
Baugh, Albert C., 107, 135 n
Becker, Ernst, 298 n
Bell, Joseph N., 472 n
Benda, Clemens E., 411 n
Berelson, Bernard, 511 n
Berger, Morroe, 363 n
Bernstein, Basil, 314 n, 369–71, 375, 388 n
Berr, Henri, 96
Block, Bernard, 16, 98 n

Bloomfield, Leonard, 16, 81, 91, 97 n, 98 n, 99 n, 164, 177 n, 224 n, 414, 439 n, 471 n
Boardman, F. W., 299 n
Boas, Franz, 15
Boaz, Martha, 472 n
Boccaccio, 155
Boehm, Max H., 246 n
Bossard, James H. S., 105, 135 n, 389 n, 419, 440 n
Bowen-Jones, H., 262 n
Braley, Kenneth W., 299 n
Bram, Joseph, 226 n, 410 n
Brazeau, E. Jacques, 323–4, 361 n
Breasted, James H., 454, 471 n
Bredemeier, Harry C., 52, 57 n
Brogan, Denis W., 373
Brown, Roger, 452, 471 n
Bruyn, Severyn, 364 n
Burke, Kenneth, 36 n

Cairns, Huntington, 363 n
Carr, Llewelyn J., 56 n
Carroll, John B., 18 n, 36 n, 76, 97 n, 105, 135 n, 137 n, 390, 410 n, 412, 439 n
Carroll, Lewis, 262 n
Casagrande, Joseph B., 138 n, 139 n
Cassirer, Ernst, 43, 56 n, 134, 137 n
Cavan, Ruth S., 362 n
Cervantes, 284
Chaffee, Zechariah, 374
Chall, Leo P., 139 n
Chase, Stuart, 137 n, 225 n
Cherry, Colin, 43, 56 n, 138 n, 470 n

* Confined to names in text and footnotes. See also the topically classified and alphabetically arranged Bibliography, pp. 515–48.

Church, Joseph H., 362 *n*, 405–6, 411 *n*, 413 *n*, 440 *n*
Clements, Robert J., 139 *n*
Clodd, Edward, 297 *n*
Coburn, Paul, 346
Cohen, Marcel, 17 *n*, 18 *n*, 96 *n*, 97 *n*, 363 *n*
Cole, G. D. H., 135 *n*
Commager, Henry Steele, 241, 246 *n*
Cooley, Charles H., 56 *n*, 395
Cornford, Francis, 137 *n*
Cottrell, Fred W., 363 *n*
Critchley, Macdonald, 22 *n*

Davis, Kingsley, 225 *n*, 404–5, 412 *n*
Deane, William N., 105–6, 135 *n*, 262 *n*
De Saussure, Ferdinand, 10–11, 12, 13, 18 *n*, 74, 76, 96 *n*, 97 *n*
Deutsch, Karl W., 246 *n*
Devereux, George, 178 *n*
Dewey, John, 26, 36 *n*
Diamond, Arthur S., 37 *n*
Dillon, Miles, 177 *n*
Disraeli, Benjamin, 267
Dominian, Leon, 389 *n*
Dressler, David, 364 *n*
Dubin, Robert, 286–7, 299 *n*, 362 *n*
Duncan, Hugh D., 315 *n*, 363 *n*
Durkheim, Emile, 57 *n*, 59, 67 *n*, 119, 347, 363 *n*

Elkin, Frederick, 345–6, 363 *n*
Emerson, Rupert, 246 *n*
Entwistle, William J., 18 *n*, 76, 97 *n*, 99 *n*, 314 *n*
Esper, Erwin A., 411 *n*
Estrich, Robert M., 298 *n*, 412 *n*

Fadiman, Clifton, 298 *n*
Faris, Robert E. L., 411 *n*, 455, 472 *n*
Firth, John R., 246 *n*, 411 *n*
Fisher, W. B., 262 *n*
Frazer, Sir James G., 319, 361 *n*
Fries, Charles C., 16, 86–8, 97 *n*, 99 *n*
Fuller, John G., 139 *n*

Gautama, 3
Geisert, Harold L., 225 *n*
Gerster, Georg, 135 *n*
Gerth, Hans, 363 *n*
Girdansky, Michael, 98 *n*, 471 *n*
Gist, Noel P., 362 *n*
Goad, Harold E., 215, 226 *n*
Gold, Robert S., 364 *n*

Goldschmidt, Walter R., 412 *n*
Grammont, Maurice, 14
Granet, Marcel, 125, 138 *n*
Gray, Louis H., 16, 98 *n*, 99 *n*, 107–8, 127, 136 *n*, 226 *n*
Green, Arnold W., 412 *n*, 512 *n*
Greenberg, Joseph H., 135 *n*
Gross, Edward, 362 *n*
Gumperz, John J., 314 *n*, 389 *n*
Gumplowicz, Ludwig, 246 *n*

Hall, A. R., 57 *n*
Hambly, Wilfred D., 361 *n*
Hamilton, Herbert, 224 *n*
Harris, Zellig S., 16
Haugen, Einar, 18 *n*, 97 *n*, 173, 178 *n*, 315 *n*, 414, 426, 435, 439 *n*, 440
Hayakawa, S. I., 22 *n*, 281–2, 298 *n*, 299 *n*
Hayes, Carlton J. H., 178 *n*, 246 *n*
Heath, Robert W., 472 *n*
Hechinger, Fred M., 440 *n*
Heraclitus, 120
Herder, John G., 120
Hertzler, Joyce O., 17 *n*, 57 *n*, 96 *n*, 178 *n*, 224 *n*, 226 *n*, 299 *n*
Herzog, George, 135 *n*, 361 *n*
Hjelmslev, Louis, 15
Hocart A. M., 137 *n*
Hockett, Charles F., 16, 97 *n*, 98 *n*, 137 *n*, 224 *n*, 412 *n*, 439, 472 *n*
Hoggart, Richard, 388 *n*
Hoijer, Harry, 137 *n*
Hollingshead, August B., 388 *n*
Holmyard, E. J., 57 *n*
Hovlane, Carl I., 511 *n*
Hughes, Everett C. and Helen M., 178 *n*, 299 *n*, 315 *n*, 378, 389 *n*
Hughes, John P., 18 *n*, 56 *n*, 76, 84, 97 *n*, 98 *n*, 135 *n*, 177 *n*, 472 *n*
Hugo, Victor, 269
Humboldt, Wilhelm von, 21, 22 *n*, 120
Huppé, Bernard F., 262 *n*

Ichheiser, Gustav, 295, 299 *n*

Jacobs, Melville M., 226 *n*
Jakobson, Roman, 14
James, William, 41
Janowitz, Morris, 511 *n*
Jespersen, Otto, 14, 56 *n*, 155–6, 177 *n*, 180, 187, 224 *n*, 361 *n*, 388 *n*
Johnson, Burges, 298 *n*
Jonson, Ben, 407
Joos, Martin, 16, 18 *n*, 97 *n*, 98 *n*

Kaminsky, Jack J., 262 *n*
Katz, Daniel, 128, 138 *n*, 299 *n*
Katz, Elihu, 224 *n*
Keller, Albert G., 67 *n*, 73–4, 96 *n*, 235, 246 *n*, 361 *n*, 389 *n*
Keller, Suzanne, 472 *n*
Kennedy, R., 389 *n*
Killian, Lewis M., 512 *n*
King, C. Wendell, 299 *n*
Klapper, Joseph T., 491, 511 *n*
Klineberg, Otto, 135 *n*
Kluckhohn, Clyde, 136 *n*
Kohn, Hans, 246 *n*, 262 *n*
Korber, George W., 364 *n*
Korzybski, Alfred, 57 *n*, 120–1, 137 *n*
Kroeber, Alfred L., 67 *n*, 136 *n*, 452, 471 *n*
Kurath, Hans, 16, 315 *n*, 316 *n*

Laguna, Grace de, 297 *n*
Laird, Charlton, 163–4, 178 *n*, 226 *n*, 311, 315 *n*
Lambert, Eloise, 136 *n*
Landis, Paul H., 316 *n*
Langer, Suzanne K., 21, 22 *n*, 412 *n*
Lantis, Margaret, 314 *n*
La Piere, Richard T., 136 *n*, 362 *n*, 472 *n*
Lasswell, Harold D., 340, 363 *n*, 512 *n*
Lazarsfeld, Paul F., 513 *n*
Lear, John, 471 *n*
Lee, Dorothy D., 137 *n*
Lee, Irving J., 21, 22 *n*, 57 *n*, 298 *n*
Lerner, Daniel, 513 *n*
Levin, Martin L., 224 *n*
Lewis, Morris M., 56 *n*, 63, 68 *n*, 172, 178 *n*, 226 *n*, 411 *n*
Lewis, Roy, 388 *n*
Lindesmith, Alfred R., 22 *n*, 36 *n*, 125, 138 *n*, 404, 411 *n*
Lippmann, Walter, 41
Locke, A., 298 *n*
Lotz, John, 21, 22 *n*, 138 *n*, 224 *n*, 262 *n*
Lumley, Frederick E., 296, 299 *n*

MacLeod, R. B., 137 *n*
Malinowski, Bronislaw, 56 *n*, 138 *n*, 139 *n*, 281, 297 *n*
Manning, Clarence A., 262 *n*
Marr, N. Y., 15
Maude, Angus, 388 *n*
Mayer, Arthur, 513 *n*
Mayer, Kurt, 246 *n*, 472 *n*
McDavid, Raven I., 316 *n*

McLuhan, Marshall, 512 *n*
Mead, George H., 36 *n*, 296, 411 *n*
Meadows, Paul, 512 *n*
Meerloo, Joost A. M., 293, 295, 297 *n*, 299 *n*, 361 *n*, 363 *n*, 411 *n*
Meillet, Antoine, 14
Mencken, Henry L., 116, 136 *n*, 277, 298 *n*, 299 *n*, 311, 315 *n*, 362 *n*
Merriam, Alan P., 363 *n*, 364 *n*
Merton, Robert K., 36 *n*, 125, 138 *n*, 511 *n*, 512 *n*
Mezzrow, Milton, 364 *n*
Mills, C. Wright, 126, 138 *n*, 363 *n*
Mitchell, Robert W., 472 *n*
Mitford, Nancy, 372–3, 388 *n*
Morgan, Lewis H., 472 *n*
Moore, Wilbert E., 57 *n*, 362 *n*, 363 *n*
Müller, Max, 56 *n*
Mumford, Lewis, 472 *n*
Munck, Peter A., 316 *n*

Nelson, Kay, 363 *n*
Niceforo, M. Alfredo, 315 *n*
Nicolls, W. H., 225 *n*
Nida, E. A., 16

Ogburn, William F., 363 *n*
Opie, Iona and Peter, 321–2, 361 *n*
Ornstein, Jacob, 263 *n*
Owen, Robert, 295

Page, Charles H., 364 *n*
Palmer, Leonard R., 56 *n*
Park, Robert E., 65, 68 *n*, 224 *n*, 239, 246 *n*, 262 *n*
Parmelee, Maurice, 225 *n*, 226 *n*
Parsons, Talcott, 67 *n*, 512 *n*
Partridge, Eric, 96 *n*, 278, 304, 315 *n*, 362 *n*, 472 *n*
Pear, T. H., 388 *n*
Pei, Mario, 18 *n*, 56 *n*, 97 *n*, 138 *n*, 139 *n*, 175, 177 *n*, 178 *n*, 224 *n*, 225 *n*, 226 *n*, 297 *n*, 314 *n*, 387, 389 *n*, 411 *n*, 469, 470 *n*, 471 *n*, 472 *n*
Petrarch, 155
Pieris, Ralph, 177 *n*, 262 *n*, 361 *n*, 388 *n*, 389 *n*, 440 *n*
Pike, Kenneth L., 16, 97 *n*, 98 *n*
Plato, 43
Polyani, Michael, 471 *n*
Potter, Simeon, 97 *n*, 98 *n*, 99 *n*, 299 *n*, 412 *n*
Pound, Louise, 298 *n*

Radcliffe-Brown, Alfred R., 67 n, 96 n
Randolph, Vance, 178 n
Redlich, Frederick C., 388 n
Révész, Geza, 21, 22 n
Riley, John W., Jr. and Matilda W., 511 n
Roback, Abraham A., 136 n, 293, 299 n, 306, 315 n
Roethlisberger, Fritz J., 362 n
Rogers, Carl R., 362 n
Ross, A. S. C., 372
Rousseau, Jean-Jacques, 96 n
Russell, Bertrand, 43, 56 n

Samora, Julian, 105–6, 135 n, 262 n
Sandburg, Carl, 306
Sapir, Edward, 16, 120, 121–2, 134–135 n, 137 n, 177 n, 309, 315 n, 369, 374–5, 388 n, 408, 412 n, 421
Savory, Theodore H., 387, 389 n
Scanlon, John, 139 n
Schlauch, Margaret, 136 n, 177 n
Schneider, Louis, 177 n
Schramm, Wilbur, 511 n, 512 n, 513 n
Schrecker, Paul, 178 n
Sechehaye, Albert, 18 n
Seldes, Gilbert, 512 n
Shakespeare, William, 155
Sheard, J. A., 389 n
Simonini, R. C., Jr., 512 n
Singer, Charles, 57 n
Smith, Henry L., 136 n
Sommerfelt, A., 14
Sperber, Hans, 298 n, 412 n
Spitz, David, 299 n
Spitz, Rene A., 262 n
Stalin, Joseph, 18 n
Stark, Werner, 133, 139 n
Steinbeck, John, 311–12
Stephenson, Richard M., 52, 57 n
Stern, Benjamin J., 226 n
Strauss, Anselm L., 22 n, 36 n, 125, 138 n, 309, 374–5, 388 n, 404, 411 n
Sturdevant, Edgar H., 134–5 n
Sumner, William G., 67 n, 235, 246 n, 315 n, 361 n, 362 n, 389 n
Sutherland, Edwin H., 362 n

Taube, Mortimer, 472 n
Thomas, Dylan, 118
Thomas, N. W., 361 n
Thomas, William I., 318, 319, 324, 361 n, 362 n
Trager, George L., 16, 98 n, 136 n

Troubetzkoy, Nikolai S., 14
Tumin, Melvin M., 362 n
Turner, Ralph H., 512 n
Tyler, E. B., 248, 262 n, 472 n

Ullman, Stephen, 56 n, 120, 136 n, 137 n, 314 n

Vendryes, Joseph, 14, 67 n, 76, 89, 97 n, 98 n, 99 n, 178 n, 320, 361, 451, 471 n
Voegelin, C. F., 225 n
Vossler, Karl, 67 n, 117, 118, 136 n, 138 n, 241, 246 n, 388 n

Wagner, Philip L., 187
Warfel, Harry R., 79, 97 n, 98 n, 99 n
Warner, W. Lloyd, 62, 67 n, 314 n
Waterman, John T., 136 n
Webb, Alvin B., 364 n
Weber, Max, 246 n, 449, 471 n
Webster, Hutton, 361 n
Webster, Noah, 241–2
Weekly, Ernest, 56 n, 136 n
Weinreich, Uriel, 178 n, 224 n, 361 n, 389
Wells, Rullon S., 18 n
Werkmeister, William H., 57 n, 139 n
West, Michael, 226 n
Westley, William A., 331, 362 n
Whatmough, Joshua, 224 n, 226 n
White, David M., 513 n
White, Leslie A., 37 n
Whitman, Walt, 67 n
Whitney, William Dwight, 15–16
Whorf, Benjamin L., 16, 22 n, 122–3, 127, 133, 136 n, 137 n, 470 n
Willis, George, 177 n, 315 n
Wilson, G. P., 178 n
Wirth, Louis, 132, 474, 512 n
Wolfe, Bernard, 364 n
Woodman, Dorothy, 225 n
Wooster, Harold, 472 n
Woytinsky, E. S., 225 n
Wright, Charles R., 512 n

Yoshino, I. Roger, 472 n

Zengel, Marjorie S., 472 n
Zipf, George, 16

Subject Index

Abstract world and language, 55-6
Administration centers, 190-1
Age-group specialisms, 320-2
Alice and ambiguities, 254
Alphabetic writing, 452-4
American language schools, 261
American linguistic provincialism, 260-1
"Americanese," 180
Anglo-English, 222-3
Antagonistic effects, 255-7
Aphasia, 405
Areal linguistics, 308
Art world language, 349-50
Arts and language spread, 204-6
Arts, language of, 349-50, 539
Assimilation, 116, 231-2, 258
Associational components, 92-4

Babel, Curse of, 248, 261-2
Bamboozler words, 293-4
Basic elements of language, 76-7
Biculturalism and plural lingualism, 421, 428-32
Bilingualism, 414-15; see also Plural lingualism and Ch. XVI
Borrowing and acceptance, 146, 183-185
Bureaucracies, language of, 331-6

Catchwords, 296-7
Censorship, 289, 295-6
Change of language, 140-9, 159-65, 180, 473-4, 527-9
Change of name, 273-4

Child and language, 393-5, 404-5, 431-2, 542-3
Cities:
    and specialisms, 312-13;
    as uniformizers, 191-2
Civilization, 103-4, 216, 454-9
Class distinctions in use of language, 267-73
Class structure and language, 310, 375-7
Colloquialisms, 304-5, 313
Colonization and colonialism, 163
Command language, 286-7
Communication, 26-7, 33, 64, 75-6, 369-71, 442-3, 515-16
Communication net, 26
Community, plural lingual, 418-27
Community participation, 62
Complex societies, special languages of, 312
Computers, translation by, 131
Concealment, languages of, 258, 294-295
Conceptualization, language as instrument of, 27, 42-4, 516
Consensus, 61, 63-4
Conservatism of language, aspects and factors of, 168-76, 465-6
Constructed languages, 221, 433
Contacts, cultural, 159-61
Control of words, 274-80
"Correct" language, 60, 83, 92-4, 381-382
Creative activity, 47-8
Creolized language, 219-20
Cultural levels, 166, 173
Cultural marginality, 424
Cultural superiority-inferiority, 422-4

Culture centers, 191
Culture differences, 104–5
Culture elements as factors in borrow-
ing and acceptance, 183–5

Days of the week, 113
"Dead languages," 51, 107
Decoding and encoding of messages
by individuals, 390–1
Destructive verbal devices, 290–3
Developing nations, language situation in, 242–4, 253, 432–3, 506–
511, 532
Diachronic linguistics, 12–13
Dialects:
bibliography, 537;
formation and maintenance, 309;
nature of, 250, 308–9;
sociological significance, 309–12;
tendency to weaken in modern
countries, factors, 311, 314
Dictatorship:
control of mass communication, 505;
language of, 287–9;
use of press, 463–4
Dictionary as "storehouse," 88–9, 102,
107
Differentiation of speech forms, Chs.
XII–XIV
Diffusion processes, 182–3
Dysphemism, 278–9

Economic activity, 202–3
Economic order, special languages of,
338–9
Economic uniformizers, 193–4
Educated classes and language change,
252–3
Education as linguistic uniformizer,
192–3
Elite speech, 378–9
Emigration-immigration, 161
"Empire" languages, 180, 196–206,
434–6
Enculturation, 391, 393–5
Entertainment, language of, 346
Environments, 23–5, 35
Esoteric languages, 383–4
Ethnic groups, 65, 105, 322–4
Ethnocentrism, 250–2
Ethnophaulisms, 293, 299
Euphemisms, 276–9, 298, 535

Facts and language, 44–6
Family language, 346–7

Family names, 114–16, 382
"Fighting words," 292
Force in linguistic change, 167–8
Foreign language instruction in U. S.,
437–8
Foreign travel and tourism, 161–2
Formal directive language, 285–6
Fraternal orders, secret languages of,
326–8
Functional language forms in social
control, 282–9
Functions of language, general, 35–56

Geographic conditions, 249–50
Grammar in thinking, 43
Grammatical structuring, 79–80
Group identification, language func-
tion in, 40
Group survival, 228, 230
Group symbol, 65
Groups, 382–3, 418–19

Hieroglyphic writing, 451
Historical record, language as, 106–9
Honorific name-calling, 290–1
Horizontal special languages, 313
Human memory, language as, 49–50
Humilific name-calling, 291–3
Humor, language in, 280, 535

Ideographies, 31
Ideographs, 449
Idiolect, 406
Ideological groups, language of, 336–
338
Ideologies spread by language, 204–6
Illiteracy, 469
Immigrant language in U. S., weakening of, 426–7
Immutability of language, 74–5
Indicative function, 40
Individual:
and plural linguality, 427–32;
and social position, 372–3;
and special languages, 384–6;
bibliography, 542–4;
impaired language facility, 402–6;
participation, 410;
revealed by language, 406–10, 544;
socialization of, 399–402
Information, storage and retrieval of,
469–70
Institutional languages:
distinguishing features of each,
339–60;

Institutional languages (*continued*)
general features of, 329–38
Institutionalization of language, 72–73
Instructors and indoctrinators, informal and formal, 92
Intermarriage in language uniformation, 187–8
International plural lingualism, need for, 432–3
Inter-people communication, sociocultural gains of, 508–11
Intra-community plural lingualism: factors, aspects, and extent of, 417–418
Invention and language, 47, 144
Isolation, physical and social, and conservation of language, 168–169

Jazz community, language of, 350–1, 539–40

King James Bible, 141, 175
Knowledge, language and the sociology of, 131–4, 526–7
Knowledge sharing and language, 52

Langage, langue, and *parole,* 11
Language:
and context of the situation, 34–6, 517;
and group identity, distinctiveness, and solidarity, 172–3;
and nationality and nationalism, 233–45;
and operation of social institutions, 95–6, 282;
and self, 395–9;
antiquity of, 19;
as social institution, 71–5, 519–20;
assimilative agent, 231–2;
basic institution, 94–6;
conservatism of, 168–76;
constraining effect on innovative thought, 127–8;
definition of, 11–12, 28–30;
determined by the community, 61;
distinguished from speech, 11–12, 30;
distinguishing aspects, 31–2;
ever-changing, 141–2;
"evolutionary universal," 67–8;
general functions, Ch. III, 518;
great divider, 247–8;

Language (*continued*)
guide to thought, 44;
historical record, 106–9;
humorous use, 280;
importance in human existence, 19–21, 32;
in reorganization of institutions, 96;
in social control, 266–8;
index of group characteristics, 35;
integrative factor, 227–31;
logical organization of, 89–92;
paramount medium of communication, 20;
prerequisite to institutions, 95;
revealer of social processes, 35;
significance in the sociology of knowledge, 131–4;
social origin of, 58;
socially determined and determinative, 34–5;
sociocultural boundary marker, 105;
sociocultural index, 102–6, 521–2;
"standard," 34, 92–4, 520–1;
stratum mobility of, 380–1;
system of communication, 30;
system of rules and principles, 11;
systemic organization: associational, 92; lexical, 88–9; morphological, 80–3; semantic, 89–92; syntactical, 83–8; unit sounds, 77–80;
types of change, 142–9;
unities 180–1;
universality of, 19;
use of for separative purposes, 257–258;
what mass media do to and for it, 478–81
Language associations, 92
Language community, nature and extent, 32–4, 62, 517
Language divergence as social barrier, 65–6
Language facility of the individual, impairment of, 402–6, 543–4
Language loyalty, 194–5
Language of concealment and defense, 294–5
Language of the "isms," 336–7
Language revivals and nationalistic movements, 239–40
Language study, 4–5
Language system:
effects of, 35–6;
nature of, 29–32
Languages, leading world, 210–12
Languages, multiplicity of, 207–10

Levels of usage, language forms at, 304–7
Lexical organization, 88–9
Lexicon, change of, 143
Linguistic adjustment to social change, 151–8
Linguistic change, tempo of, 176–7
Linguistic "empires," 196–206
"Linguistic illiteracy" of Americans, 434
Linguistic intolerance, 257
Linguistic proficiency, 398–9
Linguistic reform movements, 156, 289
"Linguistic Revolution," 63
Linguistic stratification, 365–8
Linguistic system reflecting class structure, 375–7
Linguistic uniformation:
    factors, 185–96;
    need for, 212–14
Linguistics:
    geographical, 11;
    major areas, 16–17;
    major distinctions, 10–11;
    relation to sociology of language, 7;
    schools of, 13–16;
    synchronic and diachronic, 12–13
Literacy, 190, 446, 468–9
Literate-illiterate cleavage, 252–3
Literature:
    as a conserving agency, 170–1;
    uniformizing effect, 190
Liturgical language, 175

Magical power of words, 268–70, 534
Major speech communities of the world, 210–12
Manipulation of "bad" and "good" words, 279–80
Manipulation of language for control purposes, 280–9
"Map" of facts, language as, 46, 57
Mass communication:
    audience factor, 481–2, 496–8, 502–505;
    bibliography, 547–8;
    control of messages, 499–501, 504–506;
    crucial sociological features, 481–7;
    functions performed, 487–9;
    inter-people gains, 507–8;
    its different "languages," 496–7;
    linguistic effects, 480–1;
    relation to sociology of language, 473–6;

Mass communication (continued)
    shaping of attitudes, 493–4;
    social and social psychological effects, 490–6;
    uniformation and unification of people, 492–4;
    universality of appeal, 484–5;
    users as controllers, 501–2
Mass media:
    communicative effects of, 486–7, 503–4;
    what do to and for language, 478–81
Mathematics, language of, 55, 356–358
Mead's analysis of relation of language and development of self, 396–7
Meaning, meanings, and meaning system, 25–6, 91, 126, 253–4, 515
Medicine, language of, 358–9
Metalinguistics, 116–28, 523–5;
    defined, 119
Migrations, 161
Military system, language of, 343–6
Military-political factors, 162, 198–202
Minority groups, linguistic behavior in, 237–9, 424–6
Misinformation, language for, 294
Mnemonic signs, 447–8
Mobility, physical and social, as uniformizer, 194
Morphemes, 80–1
Morphological organization, 80–3
Multiplicity of languages, 248–9

Name-calling, good and bad, 290–3
"Name-dropping," 274
Name selection, factors in, 109–16
Names:
    as cultural recordings of places, things, persons, and families, 109–116, 522;
    classification and identification function, 39–41, 270–1;
    control significance, 270–4, 534;
    social space maintenance, 380;
    status devices, 273
Naming, act of, 56, 393–4
Nation and language, 240–5
Nationalism and language, 236–40, 259
Nationalism as hindrance to universal language, 217–18
Nationalistic movements and language, 239–40
Nationality and language, 233–6

Nationality groups and language, 65, 236
Negro slaves, linguistic effects of, 162-3
Nicknames as disguises, 274
Noisemaking, bullying effect of, 295
Novelty in language, 158
Numerical factors, 80, 105, 165-6, 200

Occupational jargon, 330-1
"One World," language of, 206-23
Organization of sentence, 85-8
Organizations, language of, 286

Parole, 11, 143
Patois, 307
Perceptual-conceptual processes, linguistic system as determinant in, 41-2, 116-31
Personal names, selection of, 113-14
Personal relations, language in, 281-282
Personality and language, 397-8, 407-408
Personnel components of language system, 92-4
Pidgins, 202, 219-20
Plural lingual person, 427-32, 435
Plural lingualism:
  and cultural situation, 420-4;
  bibliography, 544-5;
  factors, 419-20;
  for world, 413-14, 433-9;
  in U. S., 416-17;
  intra-community, 416-18;
  use of term, 414-15
"Poison words," 292
Political aspects of language, 173-4, 188-9, 192-202, 258-9, 340-3, 538-9
Preliterates, recording of experience of, 49-50
Primitive secret societies, secret languages of, 325-6
Primitives, languages of, 102-3
Print and printing, 190, 461-4, 478-480
Proverbs, 284, 535

Reality symbolized in language, 45
Recording function of language, 49-50, 459-61
Region, language as source of information about, 109

Religion:
  and spread of language, 203-4;
  language of, 347-9
Rural-urban differentiation of language, 312-14

SAE ("Standard Average European"), 123-4
Sapir-Whorf hypothesis:
  bibliography, 523-5;
  roots of, 120-3;
  sociocultural implications, 125-31;
  supporting evidence, 123-5
Schizophrenia and language performance, 405-6
"Schools of thought," language of, 335-8
Science, language of, 351-8, 540
Sciences and spread of language, 204-206
Scientific-technological knowledge resting upon writing, 457
Scold words, 292
Secret languages, 295, 324-9
Secret societies and their languages, 324-9, 538
Semantic changes, 146-7
Semantic organization of language, 89-92
Separative effects of language, 255-7
Settlement history and language, 160
Sex specialisms of language, 318-20
Slang, nature, sources, reasons for existence, and contributions to standard language, 305-7
Slogans, 296-7
Social action, language in, 280-9
Social assimilation and language, 231-232
Social change and language, Ch. VII
Social context, language in, 4, 150
Social control:
  bibliography, 533;
  language as a medium, 266-8;
  verbal control techniques and tools, 279-97
Social differentiation:
  and linguistic specialization, Chs. XII-XIV
  and writing, 466-7
  bibliography, 536-41
Social distance and majority-minority speakers, 251-2, 377-80
Social institutions and languages, Ch. V, 69-70, 72-3, 282, 329-60, 519-20

Social instrumentality, language as, 62–6
Social isolation, effect of on language of the individual, 404–5
Social mobility and language, 380–2
Social movements, language of, 287–289, 463
Social organization, relation to language of, 63–6
"Social representations," language as, 59
Social roles of individual and language, 400, 409–10
Social status, 166–7, 409–10, 423–4
Social stratification and language, 365–389, 540–1
Social system, language as, 72–4
Social unifier, language as, 227–31
Socialization and language, 391, 399–401, 490–1
Sociocultural aspects and factors, 102–106, 149–76, 418–27, 459–69, 508–11, 527–9
Sociology, the language of, 153–4, 358
Sociology of knowledge, 131–4, 526–527
Sociology of language, status, nature, and content of, 6–8
Soldier language, 345–6
Space and language, 50–5, 104–5
Special languages, 145–6, 149, 252, Chs. XII–XIV
Speech, 11, 30, 73, 77–80, 209, 404
"Splintered" state of spoken languages, 209–10
Sports, language of, 346
Spread of languages, 196–206
Standard language, 83, 92–4, 140–149, 171, 185–7, 195, 310, 386–388, 520–1
Style of a people and their language, 117–18
Subordination, the language of, 286–287
Supernatural, language as means of comprehension of, 55–6
Suppression of language, 237–9, 256–257
Symbol system, 28–9, 516–17
Synchronic linguistics, 12–13
Syntactical organization, 83–8
Systemic organization of language, 75–92

Tabooing of certain words, 275–6, 535

Technical and organizational languages, 329–38
Technological uniformizers, 193
Technology and language, 48–9, 204–206, 216–17
Time and language, 50–5
Tonal quality as control factor, 267–268
Tower of Babel, 300
Trade centers, 190–1
Translation, problems of, 128–31, 218, 525

Underworld language, 328–9
Uniformation of language, 181, 185–189, 464, 529–32
Unit sounds, organization of, 77–80
Unity, 229–30
Universal language, essential linguistic and social features of, 214–19
Upper classes and language, 192, 379–80, 466–7
Usage, 94

Verbal control devices, 290–7
Vernacular speech, 304
Verstehen and language, 42
Vertical special languages, 303
Vocabulary organization, 88–9

Weltanschauung and language, 102, 118, 122, 125, 129, 219, 231
WORD, the, 269–70
"Word grip," 267
"Wordless" languages, 36–7, 56
Words:
    acquisition of new ones, 144–6;
    and actuality, 45;
    classes of, 84–5;
    classifiers, 40–1;
    construction of, 82–3;
    continual change of, 89;
    counters of thought, 81;
    cultural indicators, 102;
    inciters and destroyers, 190–3;
    magical and sacred powers of, 39, 268–70;
    paralyzers, 295–7;
    spoken, 30–1;
    tranquilizers, 293–4
Work groups, features and functions of the languages of, 330–1
World language, a, 220–3, 433, 436–439

World languages, leading, 210–11
Writing:
  as conserving agency, 170;
  as exact and extended recording of
    knowledge, 50;
  bibliography, 545–7;
  Ch. XVII;
  distinguished from speech, 31;

Writing (*continued*)
  importance of written records, 107;
  in maintaining stratification, 377;
  reform of writing systems, 289;
  uniformizing effects, 190

Xenophobia, linguistic, 172